KT-556-372

Blackstone's Guide to the

# COPYRIGHT, DESIGNS AND
# PATENTS ACT 1988

# Blackstone's Guide to the

# COPYRIGHT, DESIGNS AND PATENTS ACT 1988

The Law of Copyright and Related Rights

## Gerald Dworkin LLB, Solicitor

Herchel Smith Professor of Intellectual Property Law,
Centre for Commercial Law Studies, Queen Mary College,
University of London, Consultant to Mishcon de Reya, Solicitors

&

## Richard D. Taylor MA, LLM, Barrister

Principal Lecturer in Law, Lancashire Polytechnic

BLACKSTONE PRESS LIMITED

First published in Great Britain 1989 by Blackstone Press Limited,
Aldine Place, London W12 8AA


© Gerald Dworkin and Richard Taylor, 1989

The rights of Gerald Dworkin and Richard Taylor to be identified as authors of
this work have been asserted in accordance with ss. 77 and 78 of the Copyright,
Designs and Patents Act 1988.

ISBN: 1 85431 023 2

Typeset by Style Photosetting Ltd, Mayfield
Printed by Redwood Burn Ltd, Trowbridge

All rights reserved. No part of this book may be reproduced or transmitted in any
form or by any means, electronic or mechanical, including photocopying,
recording, or any information storage or retrieval system without prior
permission from the publisher.

# Contents

## PART 3   SPECIAL TOPICS

# Preface

The Copyright, Designs and Patents Act 1988 represents the culmination of over a decade of consideration of proposals for the reform and modernisation of the law. In that period, the importance of, and interest in, this area of the law has continued to grow. This book attempts to provide a reasonably detailed, yet readable, coverage of copyright and related rights. Given the size and complexity of the subject we cannot hope to give a definitive or exhaustive account of the law: this will be the task for the new editions of the leading practitioner texts. Rather, this book is intended as a work of first reference which will provide an explanation of the basic principles and rules so that an informed decision can be made as to whether reference to more detailed works (or specialist advice) is necessary.

It is hoped that the book will be of use not only to the legal profession but also to those many and various sectors of industry, commerce and the arts on which the Act will impinge, as well as to the increasing number of students who are choosing to grapple with this area (although space considerations led us to eschew detailed academic references to the periodical literature).

The Act received the Royal Assent on 15 November 1988. A few provisions relating to patents and also those extending the rights in *Peter Pan* came into effect immediately; those relating to licences of right for pharmaceutical patents come into force on 15 January 1989; but the bulk of the Act will come into force later on in 1989 on the day or days appointed by the Secretary of State. References throughout the book to 'commencement' are references to the date of the bringing into force of the particular Part or sections of the Act being discussed. Nevertheless, the book is written as if the Act is in force. References to sections are, unless otherwise indicated, references to the Copyright, Designs and Patents Act 1988.

Transitional provisions will remain important for many years: we have endeavoured to discuss and explain these wherever relevant and to indicate how the new provisions differ from the old law where appropriate.

Whilst each chapter was initially written individually by a single author, we have both contributed to the final form of each and accept joint responsibility for errors and omissions in what is ultimately a work of joint authorship within section 10 of the Act. We have asserted our moral rights to be identified as authors of the work under section 77 (which will take effect upon commencement of the moral right provisions). We also hope that the book will be the subject to fair dealing only at the hands of critics and reviewers so that we will not have cause to be the first to object to derogatory treatment under section 80!

We especially thank our wives, Celia, the 'driving force' behind the chapters dictated on the highways of New England, and Karen, for their patience and understanding in giving up so many anti-social hours in the cause of copyright law; to Suzanne Emmery for her unerring skill in producing literary works from unpromising drafts. We also acknowledge our debt to Clifford Miller, Gerry Kamstra and all those friends and colleagues in discussion with whom we have sharpened our own appreciation of the Act. Last, we would like to express our warm appreciation to the publishers for the friendly and skilful way in which they maintained the delicate balance between patience and exhortation and for their efficiency in turning our typescript into the finished article in such a short period.

*Gerald Dworkin*
*Richard Taylor*
*December 1988*

# Chapter 1 Introduction to Modern Copyright Law

## What is copyright?

Copyright is a property right which authors have in relation to the works which they create. It is a right to stop others copying or exploiting in various other ways authors' works without permission and subsists for a limited number of years, typically the life of the author and 50 years thereafter. It is best to regard copyright as a 'bundle of rights' in relation to works.

The law protects the *economic* interests of authors, giving them the right to exploit their works and to control their unauthorised use; it now also protects their so-called 'moral rights' which enable authors to be identified with their works and to object to certain kinds of derogatory treatment of them.

Today, copyright is an important economic interest, nationally and internationally. A recent survey has demonstrated that the industries which are directly and substantially dependent on copyright for their commercial viability, for example, publishing, music, films, broadcasting and the theatre, represent 2.6% of the UK gross domestic product, and other industries for which copyright has an economic significance, such as architecture, advertising, applied art and computer services would increase this figure even further (J. Phillips, *The Economic Importance of Copyright* (London: Common Law Institute of Intellectual Property, 1985)).

Typically, the layperson associates copyright law with the rights of an author in relation, for example, to the books which he writes. But copyright covers far more than that. It confers rights on 'authors' in the very widest sense: those who create literary, dramatic, musical and artistic works, which are very broadly defined.

In addition to 'authors' in the traditional sense, those who are primarily responsible for creating literary, dramatic, musical and artistic works, copyright may also subsist in business organisations which are associated with authors in the exploitation of their works: for example, publishers of books and producers of sound recordings and films are given copyright interests because it was thought desirable to extend protection against unauthorised copying, a form of unfair competition, to those who invested money and effort in the entrepreneurial activities which enable, in various media of communication, literary, dramatic, musical and artistic works to reach mass audiences. Thus, *independent* copyrights may now also subsist in sound recordings, films, sound and television broadcasts, cable and satellite programmes and also the typographical arrangement of books.

Hence, copyright can be seen to have a very wide coverage over the following nine descriptions of work:

(a)   original *literary, dramatic, musical* or *artistic works,*
(b)   *sound recordings, films, broadcasts* or *cable programmes,* and
(c)   the *typographical arrangement of published editions.*

This list is set out in s. 1 of the Copyright, Designs and Patents Act 1988.

Although many of these categories are very widely defined, it must be emphasised that unless it can be shown that the matter with which a person is concerned comes within one or other of these categories, no copyright can subsist: these categories comprise the entire subject-matter of copyright; there are no further *copyright* interests.

### Copyright and other rights

Copyright rarely stands alone. There are other rights which are closely associated with copyright activity but which are not designated copyright as such. For example, *performers* and those with whom they have exclusive recording contracts have rights against those who record their live performances without permission; *broadcasters* and others have rights against those who dishonestly receive cable and satellite broadcasts; a *director of a film,* who does not ordinarily have any copyright in the film itself, has moral rights in connection with it. Also, interlinked with copyright law are rights, both *registered* and *unregistered,* in *designs.* All these are so closely related to copyright that they must be considered in this book.

Beyond these copyright and copyright-related rights, there are other intellectual property rights which frequently may be involved in the exploitation and enforcement of copyright. For example, counterfeiters of copyright sound recordings may also infringe rights in trade marks, and commit the tort of passing off, by falsely placing such marks on the records or their containers, and, in some cases, they could even infringe patent rights if the manufacture and sale of these articles is protected by patent. Yet another cause of action which is sometimes associated with copyright is that for *breach of confidence.* For example, an employee who copies his employer's confidential documents and then discloses them without authority to somebody else may be both infringing the copyright in the documents and also acting in breach of confidence, for which the employer can also sue. In some cases, the action for breach of confidence may be available even though the employer does not own the copyright in the documents, as might be the case, for example, where he has commissioned a report from outside consultants.

Apart from intellectual property rights, the importance of *contract* cannot be over-emphasised. The exploitation of copyright inevitably involves contractual arrangements, whether an assignment of a copyright work by an author to a publisher, a licence by a copyright owner to a licensee or any of numerous other transactions. The terms of such contracts, both express and implied, obviously may affect the copyright situation: the general rules of copyright law may simply be the starting-point from which variations inevitably develop.

## Justifications for copyright

Many reasons have been advanced for the existence of a copyright system. For example, it is argued that anybody who creates something should be entitled to own it: a person who writes a book should be as much entitled to the ownership of what he has produced as a person who manufactures any marketable object. Associated with this is the argument that an author is entitled to a reward for creative endeavour. Alternatively, another frequently advanced justification for conferring monopoly rights of any kind upon individuals is that this creates the stimulus to innovate: copyright may act as an incentive for authors to create and for others to invest in the exploitation of such creative works.

Whatever the justifications for copyright laws, it will be seen that they confer property rights which, in many respects, are more limited than those normally associated with property. One reason for this can be seen in the dual principles contained in Art. 27 of the Universal Declaration of Human Rights which is as follows:

(1) Everyone has the right freely to participate in the cultural life of the community, to enjoy the arts and to share in scientific advancement and its benefits.

(2) Everyone has the right to the protection of the moral and material interests resulting from any scientific, literary or artistic production of which he is the author.

Whilst the second paragraph of the Article establishes the property claims of authors, the first emphasises the public interest which necessitates rights in copyright works being limited for the benefit of society.

This need for copyright law to balance competing interests is fundamental to its structure. Interests may vary at different times: not only affecting the balance between authors and the *public,* but also between various copyright owners themselves: for example, the interests of music composers and record producers, or of writers and publishers, may at times be in conflict, and it is desirable to ensure that each receives fair treatment under the law; at other times, their interests may coincide and they may unite in resisting unfair practices by members of the public. Sometimes, different areas of related, though competing, industries may be affected by copyright issues: this has been very much the case as between the producers of blank tapes and recording equipment and the producers of sound recordings. A proper balance based upon equity, fair competition and fair access and the public interest is what the law seeks to achieve. However, achieving this is difficult, to say the least. Hence the pressures to modify or change the law are ever present; but unanimity of views on how to change it is not.

## Limitations on copyright ownership

The following factors illustrate how the author of a copyright work does not have the same wide rights of ownership as can be exercised over other types of property.

*Duration of copyright*
The ownership of most property, subject to dealings with it and to inheritance, lasts in perpetuity; copyright endures for a fixed period of time, usually for 50 years from the death of the author or, in many cases, 50 years from the year in which a work is made or published.

*Copyright confers a limited number of exclusive rights*
Most forms of property enable the owner to control most types of use and enjoyment of the subject-matter of the property. Copyright is more restricted in that the owner has only those rights in relation to a work which are specified in the Act. The most common economic rights conferred upon copyright owners are those which give control over the copying or reproduction of the work and its public performance for commercial purposes. Armed with such rights, copyright owners are in a better position to negotiate, singly or collectively, for the exploitation of their works.

*Copyright protects the form in which a work is expressed but does not protect the underlying ideas or information in the work*
This principle, which is commonly referred to as the 'idea-expression dichotomy', and which will be referred to frequently, is regarded by many as fundamental to copyright law, although, as we shall see in more detail later, it is difficult to apply in practice. To ensure that the law does not confer excessive rights upon individuals, the principle that ideas, opinions, information and facts should be freely available for public use means that copyright law simply protects the way in which the author has *expressed* such ideas or information. 'Copyright can only be claimed in the composition or language which is chosen to express the information or the opinion' (*Football League Ltd* v *Littlewoods Pools Ltd* [1959] Ch 637 at 651 per Upjohn J). The United States Copyright Act 1976, s. 102(b), sets out the principle clearly, in spite of the difficulties inherent in it:

> In no case does copyright protection for an original work of authorship extend to any idea, procedure, process, system, method of operation, concept, principle, or discovery, regardless of the form in which it is described, explained, illustrated, or embodied in such work.

Such a principle is not enshrined in any UK statutory copyright provisions but it has been accepted and, in general, applied by the courts throughout the history of copyright.

Too rigid an application of such a principle, however, would mean that an author's rights could easily be circumvented, and so exceptions and modifications exist to ensure that a more appropriate balance between the authors' rights and the public interest is effected. For example, a publisher cannot publish a

French translation of an English work and claim that because practically every word is expressed in a different form, there is no copyright infringement; nor, by using a similar argument, can a musical be based closely upon a play: the rights of copyright owners have been extended to cover various kinds of 'adaptation' of works.

*Permitted acts and defences*
The balancing factor in favour of the public interest is seen in the many ways in which the copyright legislation permits certain types of acts in relation to copyright works. For example, no licence from the copyright owner is required to use or copy most works for the purposes of *fair dealing* for research, private study, criticism, review and news reporting, for certain educational and library purposes and so forth.

This balancing process, as we shall see, has to be adjusted from time to time. Sometimes this may be the result of a judicial decision and sometimes, albeit infrequently, as a result of legislation. Thus, until the Copyright, Designs and Patents Act 1988, there was generally no *copyright* control to prevent further distribution or dealing with a copyright work once it had been placed lawfully on the market. The author of a novel, or the copyright owners of the works included in a sound recording, could prevent purchasers of the book or of the sound recording from copying them (or, indeed from performing these works in public), but if the book or sound recording had been sold there was no way *under copyright law* in which the authors could prohibit the owners of the book or of the sound recording from renting them out to the public. With the significant developments of audio and video rental activity, this was seen to pose a serious threat to the economic interests of copyright owners, and so the 1988 Act has enlarged the rights of copyright owners in certain cases to give them control over rental activity.

## General principles of copyright law

The statute law on copyright is now contained in the Copyright, Designs and Patents Act 1988. All statute references in this book are to the 1988 Act unless otherwise stated. The previous statute, the Copyright Act 1956, will be repealed as the 1988 Act is brought into force.
There are certain considerations which run through the whole of copyright law and which are listed hereunder.

*Copyright works*
Copyright subsists only in the nine categories of work specified in the 1988 Act. (Previously, Part I of the Copyright Act 1956 dealt with copyright 'works', which were original literary, dramatic, musical and artistic works; the remaining copyright interests in Part II of the 1956 Act were referred to as 'other subject-matter'.) Whether something has sufficient substance to constitute a 'work' is a matter which has been little explored but may acquire some importance in the future.

*Fixation*

Copyright does not subsist in a work until it is recorded in some written or other form, for example, on tape (ss. 3 and 178). A person can create a copyright work by committing it to paper, or recording it in some way personally, or through a secretary or some other amanuensis, or by any other person who records it with the author's permission. Even when a work is recorded without permission, such an unauthorised act is now sufficient to confer a copyright on the author (s. 3 (3)). For example, if a politician gives an extempore interview to news reporters, the penning or taping of his spoken words by the reporters confers the copyright in those words upon the speaker. Obviously this gives the speaker potentially greater control over the reporters' powers to publish these remarks than he possessed under earlier law. The work of such reporters is particularly productive because they may also acquire an independent copyright in the report — the same act of recording the words may thus confer two separate copyrights, one in the speaker and one in the reporters who have used skill and effort in its recording, although express or implied permission for them to exploit their works may be required from the speaker since their use of their work might otherwise infringe the copyright conferred upon the speaker! (See further s. 58 page 78.)

*Originality*

No copyright subsists in a literary, dramatic, musical or artistic work unless it satisfies the test of 'originality' and no copyright subsists in sound recordings, films, broadcasts, cable programmes or published editions of works to the extent that they are copied from previous works. Unlike patent law, where 'originality' involves an inventive step (that is, some development in the state of the art), originality in copyright law means simply that some, albeit limited, work or effort has gone into the creation of the work. In *University of London Press Ltd* v *University Tutorial Press Ltd* [1916] 2 Ch 601 it was argued that no copyright could subsist in mathematics examination papers set by university teachers since the questions involved were similar to those which had been used in previous years and no great effort could have been involved in their setting. The response was that, as the questions had been thought out by the examiners and were not simply copies, copyright could subsist in them.

The fact that a work may have been taken from, or inspired by, a previous work does not prevent it from being original. To the extent that it incorporates a considerable amount of the previous work, the owner of the copyright in the new 'original work' may himself be infringing copyright in the earlier work and he will require permission to exploit his new work, but it will be 'original' nonetheless. On the other hand, there is no originality in a slavish copy. In the recent decision of *Interlego AG* v *Tyco Industries Inc.* [1988] 3 WLR 678 the term of copyright in a set of drawings had expired and the question arose whether it was possible to create a new copyright by producing another set of similar drawings. Although making the fresh set of drawings involved time, skill and labour, they were identical to the first set of drawings and incorporated no changes or modifications of significance; therefore, the court refused to accept that they were original. Had there been a 'significant' modification, the originality requirement might have been satisfied. What then of the examination papers which were very close to previous ones or the reporters' copyright in the very words in which the speaker acquires copyright? It may be, as the Privy Council in *Interlego AG* v *Tyco Industries Inc*. accepted, that the test of 'originality' is slightly different for different classes of work.

Whilst most independent creativity satisfies the originality requirement because the qualifying threshold is so low, the courts baulk at conferring copyright on trivia. Thus, whilst a short letter of no great literary quality may qualify as an original literary work, slogans and catch phrases, such as an advertisement stating that 'Beauty is a necessity not a social luxury', have been regarded as too trivial to satisfy even the minimum requirements of originality. It is here that there is an inverse relationship between the twin requirements of 'originality' and 'work': where the independent effort involved and the length of the 'work' are minimal, an element of creativity will be helpful in establishing the originality requirement.

### The idea-expression dichotomy
This has already been referred to and will be discussed in appropriate places in the book.

### Copying and independent creation
A patent confers upon the patentee inventor complete control over the patented invention. He may restrain others from dealing with the invention, even those who may have produced it quite independently, unaware of the patentee's work. Copyright is quite different. It only operates to prevent a person from *copying* the copyright work. In so far as it is possible for a person to create the same, or similar, work independently, there is no copyright infringement.

### No formalities and no registration requirements
One of the attractions of copyright is that it is acquired automatically as soon as a work is recorded. Unlike patents and registered designs, there are no registration requirements and so the expense and delay necessarily involved in these other rights are avoided. No Berne Convention country may have a registration requirement in its copyright law. The USA is one of the few countries which still requires this. However, as the USA has recently passed legislation enabling it to join the Berne Convention, it is likely that the American registration requirement will be removed soon.

*Notices* Although notices on copyright works are not required under UK copyright law, they are usual and desirable for a number of reasons. First, if UK works are to receive protection in the USA and other Universal Copyright Convention countries which have registration requirements, even though such works have not been registered there, it is necessary to place the copyright symbol ©, accompanied by the name of the copyright owner and the year of first publication, on the work, in such manner and location as to give reasonable notice of the owner's claim to copyright; similarly, with regard to sound recordings, the symbol ℗ should be placed on all copies of the published recordings or their containers and also the principal performer ought similarly to be named (or other formalities complied with). Secondly, although the 1988 Act has not continued the compulsory requirement for copyright notices on sound recordings (CA 1956 s.12(6)(b)), it remains important to continue the practice because of the evidentiary presumptions they create. Where a notice is applied to copies of sound recordings, films or computer programs that: (a) the named person was the owner of the copyright at the date of issues of copies to the public, or (b) that it was first published in a specified year or specified country, that label shall be admissible as evidence that the facts stated are presumed to be correct unless the contrary is proved (ss. 104 to 106).

Thirdly, as a practical matter, it is normally desirable to mark products with some indication of copyright and other rights simply to put people on notice.

*Copyright infringement may have both civil and criminal consequences*
Until recently, copyright infringement was primarily a civil matter and the limited criminal penalties which existed in the copyright legislation were rarely used. All that has now changed. National and international piracy of copyright material has burgeoned alarmingly and as a result of industry pressure the criminal provisions and penalties for commercial copyright piracy have been made far more severe.

*Copyright is a property right distinct from the ownership of the material with which the copyright is associated*
Copyright in a work must not be confused with the ownership of a physical object recording or constituting the work. For example, if X sends a letter to Y, then, in the absence of any special factors, the property in the paper on which the letter is written vests in Y, the recipient, whereas the copyright in the literary work (and, in law, all but the most trivial of missives are literary works) remains with X. Y, as owner of the paper, may destroy it or show it to others. He cannot without authorisation, however, reproduce that letter since that would be an interference with X's copyright. Conversely, should X wish to publish his letters, he would not be able to have access to the letter in which he has copyright without Y's consent as owner of the physical material.

The same would also apply to a book: the book itself, namely the pages and cover, is not the copyright work; rather it is the literary work which is fixed on that material which is. Similarly, with a record: a person who buys a record may do various things with it; play it, or destroy it if he wishes; but since he does not have any copyright interest in the sound recording or the underlying musical work (if it is still in copyright) he cannot do anything which interferes with the rights of copyright owners, for example, copy it or perform the work in public.

The situation becomes even more complex when moral rights are taken into account. For example, Albert, an artist, paints a picture and sells it to Ben. Unless Ben has also bought the copyright, for which a written assignment would normally be required, his right of ownership is restricted to the canvas, and Albert retains copyright in the painting as an artistic work. Here, there are two separate property rights. There may be three! Assume that Albert, the artist, sells the painting to Ben and also expressly transfers the copyright in it to him; and then Ben sells the painting to Charles. Now Charles is the owner of the canvas but Ben is the owner of the copyright and can make, for example, postcard reproductions of the painting for sale. However, Albert retains 'moral rights' in the painting which ensure that he is identified with the painting and enable him to object to any derogatory treatment of it. Thus, he may still be able to control some of Ben's or Charles' activities in relation to the painting. Moral rights are dealt with in chapter 8.

### Several copyright interests may coexist

It is frequently assumed, when a book or a record is sold, or a film is shown, that somebody owns 'the' copyright in the work. This overlooks the fact that normally there will be a number of relevant copyright interests existing at the same time. When a book is sold, the author will be the owner of the copyright in the literary work (unless he has assigned it, for example, to the publisher) and the publisher will have a separate copyright in the typographical arrangement of the work, so controlling its facsimile reproduction, for example, by photocopying. When a musical recording is sold, there will be copyright in the musical work and a distinct copyright in any lyrics associated with the music and the record company will also have a copyright in the sound or the video recording itself. Further, the performers of the music, whilst they may not have any copyright in the musical or literary works, will have rights in their performance, which will also have to be taken into acount. A film may also have many copyright interests associated with it. For example, there may be copyright in the novel upon which the film is based, since that is a literary work; there will be a quite separate copyright in the screenplay as a dramatic work; there will be copyright in the musical works which are used in the film; a copyright in the film itself and, apart from the moral rights which may be vested in all the authors of the works just mentioned, the director of the film, regardless of any copyright interests, may have a moral right in the film; and the performers in the film have their rights too. Thus, any analysis of copyright must take into account the variety of separate interests which may coexist.

### Splitting up copyright rights

Another common complication is that each separate copyright interest may itself be subdivided and exploited in different ways. Take a book as a simple illustration. The author and owner of the copyright in the literary work may transfer to separate parties different rights in that book, for example, the right to publish the book in hardback to X and in paperback to Y; or limit the right to certain countries only; and may give others the right to make translations, the right to make films etc. The fact that a company can show that it has acquired a copyright interest from the 'copyright owner' may not be sufficient if it turns out that what the company proposes to do with the work does not tally with the particular copyright interest which it has acquired.

The situation was well expressed by Quilliam J in a New Zealand case (*J. Albert & Sons Pty Ltd* v *Fletcher Construction Co. Ltd* [1976] RPC 615 at p. 620):

> The result is that an author of a work may assign virtually all his rights in all countries or he may assign some only of his rights or he may assign rights of a certain kind in one country to a particular person and rights of the same kind in another country to another person, and so on. The combination of ways in which he may assign his rights is almost endless. Similarly, a person holding a right from an author may himself make further assignments. In these ways

there may be a multiplicity of rights all stemming from the original work but all different and all capable of separate assignment. . . . It thus becomes a matter of some precision to determine which person is for the moment the owner in which country of which particular aspect of the copyright in a certain work. It seems clear, however, that the legislation is designed to set up means by which such a question may be answered and, moreover, to protect the right of the owner of that aspect of the copyright. It is also apparent that each of the rights referred and protected by the Act is a matter of economic value to its owner.

### The accelerating trend towards collective licensing

Theoretically, the owner of a copyright work, or any part of it, has an individual right in that work or part of it, which he alone may license to individual users of the work and also enforce against individual infringers of the work. In practice, this is an impossible task. For example, a composer of music would ordinarily be unable to cope with requests for licences from all those who might want to perform his work, and in any event the cost of individual applications would be out of all proportion to the individual royalties; nor would it be possible to monitor the use of his music so that he could take proceedings against all those who performed it without authorisation. Instead, licensing bodies have been established to deal with these matters in a more satisfactory way. Thus, the Performing Right Society (PRS) administers the collective licensing of the performing right and related matters in musical works on behalf of composers and lyricists, and Phonographic Performance Ltd (PPL) administers the public performing right in sound recordings on behalf of record companies; and they also take proceedings against infringers. What happens is that in these cases virtually all owners of copyright in musical works and in sound recordings transfer the appropriate exclusive rights in their works to the collecting societies, which can then deal with users in a variety of ways, including the granting of blanket licences, thus ensuring that the copyright owners obtain a proper return for the exploitation of their works.

The PRS and PPL have been operating successfully for many years. There are other collecting societies which operate in other areas, but not in all. Increasingly, the creation of such bodies is becoming the only realistic way in which royalties for the use of works can be obtained. The 1988 Act accordingly now provides the framework for such bodies in a number of areas and also provides for the Copyright Tribunal to oversee the proper administration of schemes. These developments are being made in such a way as to effect a profound modification of the structure of copyright law. What was, and still is, an absolute and exclusive right securing to its owner power over a work against all others, securing to him in particular the power to forbid anyone to exploit his work without his authorisation, is in process of becoming a simple claim securing to the owner nothing but what it is customary to call 'equitable remuneration'. Whether or not such changes are consistent with a pure theory of copyright law matters little. This trend will be examined in more detail later.

## International dimensions

The copyright law we are considering is copyright law as it applies to the United Kingdom. Any person who seeks protection in another country must look to the laws of that country for assistance. The economic potential for copyright works today may, in many cases, be world-wide: a song or film first played in one country might be sung or shown in most countries of the world within a very short time. Consideration of the copyright owner's rights in the UK alone could well be totally inadequate. Therefore, without some kind of international cooperation, the exploitation and policing of copyright would be unworkable. The English author used to, and unfortunately still does, find that his works are being exploited to a significant degree in some parts of the world where the copyright laws do not give him any, or adequate, protection.

Because copyright law has such an international flavour, multilateral conventions have been established to promote international cooperation. The Berne Convention, which came into existence in 1886, is the primary international copyright convention, and the other is the Universal Copyright Convention, which was formed in 1952. The States that are parties to the Berne Convention constitute the Berne Union. Most, but not all, countries in the world are parties to one or other of these conventions and many have signed both. These conventions provide guidelines to ensure that States have certain *minimum* provisions in their copyright laws and also provide the same treatment to authors from other States as they accord to their own nationals: an English author is entitled to the same protection for his works in France and America as are French and American authors in their own countries; and, conversely, French and American authors will be given the same treatment in the UK as a UK national.

*Qualifications for copyright protection*
Since most countries in the world have signed a copyright convention, there is today very wide international protection of copyright works. Thus, UK law provides that a work qualifies for protection by reference to: (a) 'the author' or (b) the country in which the work was first published or, in the case of a broadcast or cable programme, the country from which the broadcast was made or the cable programme was sent. Authors of works qualify for protection if they were British citizens, British Dependent Territories citizens, British Nationals (Overseas), British Overseas citizens, British subjects or British protected persons, or domiciled or resident in the UK at the time the work was made or, more important, are domiciled or resident in any other State which is a party to the Berne Convention or the Universal Copyright Convention and which has been designated by Order in Council. Similarly, for those works where the copyright may be vested in companies, protection will be accorded if the companies were incorporated in the UK or in any other country connected as mentioned (ss. 1(3) and 153 to 162).

Even where there is no qualified author for a work, in spite of these very wide provisions, protection will be given to works which are 'first published' in the UK or in any other Convention country. And 'first published' has been given an extended meaning: there is a special rule whereby even where a work is in fact first published (that is, first made available to the public) in a non-Convention country, it still receives UK protection if it is subsequently published within a Convention country within the next 30 days, for it is then regarded as having been 'simultaneously published' in both countries and hence will be entitled to protection in the latter country and in all other Convention countries (ss. 155(3).

'Publication' in this context means 'the issue of copies to the public' (s. 175(1)). This, in turn, has required judicial elucidation. In *Francis, Day & Hunter* v *Feldman & Co.* [1914] 2 Ch 728, the plaintiffs were the owners of the copyright in a song, 'You Made Me Love You (I Didn't Want To Do It)', composed by an American, which had been published in New York (the USA was not a Convention country at the time). A number of copies were sent to London for 'publication' within the time-limits required for simultaneous publication. The case turned on whether placing for sale six copies of the sheet music on the counter of a retail shop in Charing Cross Road, London, was a 'publication' even though no copies were sold within the appropriate time. The court held that there had been a sufficient invitation to the public to acquire copies and so there was publication. However, the next question was whether this publication was disqualified from consideration as being 'merely colourable and not intended to satisfy the reasonable requirements of the public' (see s. 175(5) of the 1988 Act). Even though the song was not advertised, and there was no immediate demand for it, it was held to be sufficient to show that there was the intention to satisfy the reasonable demands of the public and so it was not 'colourable only'. Today, first publication in the USA, a Universal Copyright (and, shortly, a Berne) Convention country, would be sufficient.)

All this is easier to understand by example. In most cases, works of foreign authors will obtain the same protection as that given to UK authors under UK copyright law, since most countries have signed one or other or both conventions. There are, however, countries which have not signed either convention: for example, Malaysia, Singapore, China. If a work is published in China by a Chinese author then, in the absence of any other factors, he will not be entitled to any copyright in the UK. However, if the work of the Chinese author is first published in the UK, it will receive UK protection (and also protection in all other Convention States). If the work is first published in China, but is then published in the UK within 30 days, it will also receive UK copyright protection. And even if the work is first published in China but, within 30 days, is published say in Canada, then it will receive UK copyright protection because it has been 'simultaneously published' in China and in a Convention country.

In the main, therefore, these rules today deny few authors UK copyright protection. The two major difficulties in the international context are, first, with regard to older works, for example, US films, where it is difficult to establish the dates of first publication of relevant works, the state of the law at that date, and the scope of bilateral agreements which operated before a country joined one of the conventions; and, secondly, with the effectiveness of the protection of UK authors in those convention countries where either the copyright law does not rise very much beyond the minimum set under the conventions or, of greater importance, where the copyright laws are framed satisfactorily but the ability to enforce them is limited.

*'Minimum treatment' versus 'reciprocity' of treatment*
Increasing attention is now being paid to international cooperation and to the international conventions. Two trends are developing: one positive, the other negative.

The first is the control and influence of the Berne Convention on the many changes in national copyright laws which are taking place at the present time. Article 9(2) of the Berne Convention, in providing for a proper balance between the copyright owner and the public interest, states that it shall be a matter for the laws of each member State to determine the special cases when the reproduction of a work without consent may be permitted, but then specifies that any such reproduction must not 'conflict with a normal exploitation of the work' nor 'unreasonably prejudice the legitimate interests of the author'. These expressions have been written into some sections of the 1988 Act and Art. 9 has also been an important consideration which has controlled the number and extent of the permitted acts and defences set out in the legislation.

The negative trend has developed as a reaction to the 'minimum treatment' provision of the conventions. Understandably, some countries are not happy at giving 'foreigners' from other contracting States the full copyright protection which they accord to their own authors, for example, where the extent or level of protection in the other States is less generous. A number of new copyright-related rights have been developed which have been placed outside the framework of copyright law, thus attempting to avoid the minimum treatment obligations relating to copyright. Here, protection is given to a State's own nationals and to others who first publish work in that country, but to other foreigners only if their countries have reciprocal arrangements ensuring that the work in question is protected in a similar way. For example, the US Semiconductor Chip Protection Act 1984 conferred rights on US citizens in relation to semiconductor chips, but this is a *sui generis* right which is not part of copyright law and which confers protection upon non-US citizens only where there are reciprocal arrangements. The UK and other countries hastened to enact similar laws to acquire protection in the US for their own citizens, but also on the basis of reciprocity with all countries (see chapter 15). Similar bilateral 'reciprocity' requirements have been applied in the UK in relation to rights in performances and the unregistered design right. A return to a complex network of bilateral agreements between States around the world can only undermine the influence and effectiveness of the multilateral Conventions.

*The Uruguay GATT Round*
A new and powerful force which has emerged on the international scene has been that exerted, primarily by the USA, through the mechanism of the General Agreement on Tariffs and Trade (GATT). The Uruguay Round negotiations, which commenced in September 1986, have focused upon international piracy and the preparedness of some regimes to provide adequate norms for protection and enforcement: intellectual property laws and their enforcement have been brought into the area of international economic and political bargaining and pressure. The international copyright conventions, whilst going some way towards dealing with these problems, themselves have serious shortcomings: they lack effective international dispute settlement provisions to ensure that

nations live up to their obligations; they do not impose obligations on signatories to provide adequate and effective enforcement, either at the border or domestically, of rights granted under national laws; and the minimum levels of substantive protection imposed by the conventions are sometimes inadequate. The GATT discussions are designed to introduce enforcement procedures dealing with dispute settlement, border measures and domestic enforcement. Some countries are being pressured by promises of economic assistance or threats to withdraw economic assistance, to live up to their international obligations, and also, through adherence to the international conventions and revision of their own laws, to have higher levels of copyright protection. A US trade representative recently expressed the situation thus:

> We have made a good start at putting pirates out of business. Good copyright laws, the first necessary step, have been enacted in many countries which previously had no laws. But many countries are yet to act, and many others still need to improve enforcement. We . . . believe the best way to consolidate these gains is to create binding multilateral obligations which will ensure that nations maintain adequate and effective protection. We continue to seek this goal, through GATT, which complements our bilateral efforts and provides an excellent opportunity for us to drive pirates out of business. (Ambassador Michael B. Smith, reported in *Anti-Piracy News and Copyright Review* (Publishers Association), June 1988.)

*The EEC factor*
UK membership of the European Economic Community affects copyright law in several ways. First, the principle of free movement of goods and services between member States operates to curtail some of the ways in which copyright rights may be exercised against those who acquire copyright goods legitimately in one member State and attempt to import them into the UK for sale and distribution, often at lower prices than those intended for the UK market. The second factor relates to anti-competitive conduct, whether as a result of conditions in copyright licensing agreements or because of possible abuse by a large organisation of a dominant position in the EEC market, for example, by copyright collecting societies whose rules may determine who may or may not have licences for the use of copyright material or the terms upon which such licences are granted.

Ideally, as in other areas of intellectual property law, so also in copyright, all member States should move towards harmonised laws. The European Commission, after 10 years of deliberation on copyright law, has recently produced a discussion document concerning the harmonisation of some aspects of copyright law. However, we are probably some years away from any Directives or obligations to change the UK copyright law set out in the 1988 Act.

## Development of UK copyright law

UK copyright law owes its origins to the development of the printing press in the late 15th century. At that time, control over printing was important to the Crown, both because of the perceived need for political censorship and also because of the potential income which it could attract. It is not appropriate here to go into the history of copyright law. Suffice it to say that the courts were prepared to recognise a form of copyright at common law until the statute 8 Ann (1709), c. 21, recognised copyright as a statutory right of property lasting for a limited term only, with the 'author' as the 'fountainhead' of all rights in copyright works.

Over the years, there were many legislative provisions extending copyright beyond books and printed matter to other creative artistic and aesthetic material. Indeed, in many senses, the extension of copyright law to create and cover new types of works, reflected attempts to deal with unfair competition in relation to the exploitation of developing technologies. For example, at the beginning of the 20th century the advent of the gramophone and the ability to copy gramophone recordings, led to the creation of a new copyright interest in sound recordings. The Copyright Act 1911 was a comprehensive code designed to cater for all the copyright-related developments which had taken place at that time and to ensure that appropriate protection was afforded by the legislation. By the time of the Copyright Act 1956, further developments justified new copyright interests being recognised in television and radio broadcasts, in films and in published editions of works.

### Copyright, Designs and Patents Act 1988

The 1988 Act's genesis can be traced back to the Whitford Committee Report on Copyright and Designs Law 1977 (Cmnd 6732). That report, which contained an extensive review of the then state of copyright law, was followed by a number of government discussion documents, particularly a Green Paper in 1981 *(Reform of the Law Relating to Copyright, Designs and Performers' Protection,* Cmnd 8302), and eventually by the 1986 government White Paper, *Intellectual Property and Innovation* (Cmnd 9712), which proposed:

(a)   to restructure copyright law on a more logical and consistent basis;

(b)   to remove unnecessary obstacles to the use of intellectual property and the exercise of rights (by revising the Copyright Act 1956, a very difficult and complex Act to use, in order to make the whole copyright system more user-friendly);

(c)   to bring the law up to date to cope with the latest technological developments, for example, in computing, broadcasting, photocopying and audio-visual recording; and

(d)   to make certain changes, for example, in relation to moral rights, to enable the UK to be in a position to ratify the latest text (the Paris text 1971) of the Berne Convention.

The Bill introduced in October 1987 received very detailed Parliamentary scrutiny and many changes were made to give effect to the numerous, and frequently competing, pressures brought to bear by interest groups representing different rights owners and also different users.

Whether the current legislation deals satisfactorily with all the new technologies and whether it creates the appropriate balance between authors, producers and publishers and the public remains to be seen.

## Transitional provisions

No new copyright law can break completely with the past. Established rights cannot normally be tampered with and cut down simply because the new law comes into force; retrospective interference with established property rights has to be dealt with expressly. The transitional provisions and savings in the 1988 Act are contained in sch. 1 to the Act.

As a general principle the new copyright provisions apply in relation to things existing at the date the Act came into force as they apply in relation to things coming into existence after that date, but all of that is subject to any express provision to the contrary. Thus, for example, copyright subsists in an existing work after commencement only if copyright subsisted in it immediately before commencement (sch. 1, para. 5(1)) and so on. Indeed, there may be certain rights still in existence which are affected by transitional provisions in earlier legislation. So, for example, under the pre-1956 copyright legislation, any assignment by the holder of a copyright work could not confer upon the assignee any rights in the work for the period beginning 25 years *after* the author's death. The copyright for this last 25 years of the copyright term automatically reverted to the estate of the author. Although this reversionary rule was repealed by the Copyright Act 1956, transitional provisions preserved that law in relation to any assignments of copyright which had taken place before June 1957. There are many authors who assigned their copyright works before June 1957 whose estate could still benefit from this old, and long abolished, law.

The more important transitional provisions will be referred to in the appropriate sections throughout this book.

# Chapter 2 Types of Copyright Work

## Introduction

The law has come to recognise various types of 'work' which may be the subject of copyright. There has been a historical progression from the earlier protection of *literary, dramatic, musical* and *artistic* works to the inclusion in 1911 of *sound recordings* and finally in 1956 the addition of *films, published editions* and *broadcasts* (supplemented in 1984 by the inclusion of *cable programmes*). The 1988 Act is thus the first of the three major pieces of copyright legislation this century not to add a new type of copyright work although it does create a number of related rights such as the author's moral rights, rights in performances and the new unregistered design right. The 1988 Act also ends the formal division that was to be found in the 1956 Act between Part I 'works' (literary, dramatic, musical and artistic works, the classical copyrights which Continentals are inclined to call author's rights) and Part II 'subject-matters' (sound recordings, films, broadcasts and published editions, the entrepreneur's rights which the Continental systems would generally tend to regard as neighbouring rights rather than as true author's rights).

All these are now under the label of copyright 'works' as part of the basic approach of the Act to set out general principles applicable to all types of copyright work wherever possible and only to make distinctions between different types of work where really necessary. As will be seen in subsequent chapters, such distinctions can still be discerned in, for example, the rules governing the duration of copyright under which the former Part I works retain their longer period of protection.

## Overlapping of different copyrights

Before looking at the various types of copyright work in a little more detail it is important to stress (once more) the fact that these separate rights may coexist in relation to what might at first sight seem to be a single subject-matter. Some examples may make this clear and at the same time illustrate the nature of the various types of copyright work.

*Illustration 2.1*   Arthur writes a novel. He acquires a copyright in the novel as a *literary work*. Barbara then writes a play based on the novel and becomes the owner of the copyright in the play as a *dramatic work*. (If she does not have Arthur's permission, she will be infringing Arthur's copyright but she still acquires a copyright herself which she could assert, e.g., against an unauthorised performance of her play.) François (with permission) translates the novel into French and acquires the copyright in the *literary work* represented by that translation. The same would apply to any translations into any other languages or indeed to any other independent translations into French. Barbara's play and the translations into different languages are examples of adaptations of Arthur's literary work, the significance of which is that whilst they are independent copyright works in their own right, anyone copying the adaptation would also be infringing Arthur's initial literary work (s. 21(2)).

Ken then makes a film based on the novel and acquires a copyright in the *film* (again, permission will be needed from Arthur or this will be infringement). The BBC broadcasts the film and acquires its own copyright in the *broadcast* (again the BBC needs Ken's consent or it too will be an infringer). The BBC's copyright in the broadcast would not be infringed by someone independently copying a master tape of the film since its copyright is in the broadcast not the film but it would be infringed, e.g., by someone relaying the *broadcast* to a paying audience in a cinema.

To complete our example, Arthur's novel will no doubt have been published and the publisher gets a separate copyright in the typographical arrangement of the *published edition,* i.e., a right to prevent copying of the typographical arrangement — the appearance of the printed page. This would therefore not be infringed by another publisher independently publishing the novel (although it may mean that Arthur has broken an agreement to grant an exclusive licence to the first publisher) unless the second publisher reproduces the typographical arrangement of the first (which would be inevitable if a photocopying or similar process was used). Similarly the publisher of the French translation would acquire a copyright in the typographical arrangement of the French published edition.

*Illustration 2.2*   John and Paul write a song. Unlike their Beatle namesakes, one (John) writes the words and the other (Paul) writes the music. John acquires the copyright in the *literary work,* the words, and Paul acquires the copyright in the *musical work,* the melody and harmonies. Helen (a singer) makes a recording of the song and she (or, more probably, her record company) acquires a copyright in that *sound recording*. Both John's and Paul's permissions are required, otherwise this is an infringement but again this does not affect the fact that a copyright in the sound recording is acquired. Steve makes a separate recording of the same song (a cover version) and acquires a copyright in that *sound recording*. In marketing Helen's record, her recording company will no doubt commission an attractive sleeve which will constitute an *artistic work*. A local radio station plays Helen's record on one of its programmes and thereby acquires the copyright in the *broadcast* which will be infringed by, for example, another radio station re-broadcasting without permission.

So it can be seen that what might appear to the humble television viewer or

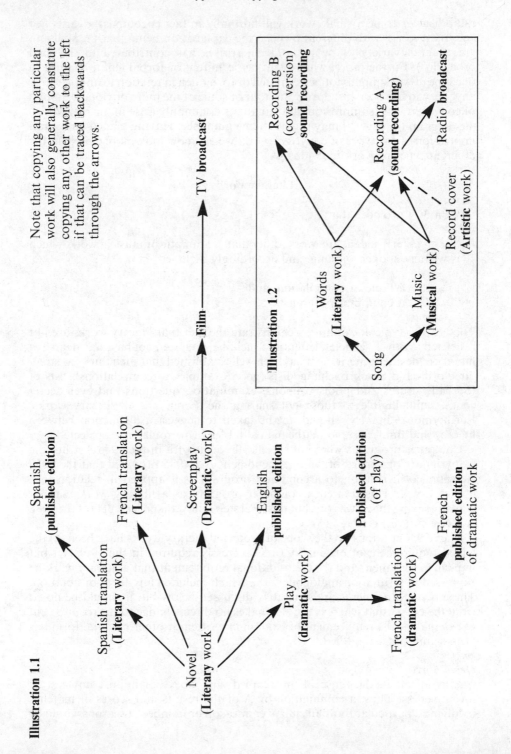

**Illustration 1.1**

Note that copying any particular work will also generally constitute copying any other work to the left if that can be traced backwards through the arrows.

**Illustration 1.2**

radio listener to be a single work will normally in fact encompass a variety of copyright works with different owners (the explanation being that the skill and labour of a variety of people and enterprises has contributed to the final broadcast). Furthermore, what might be permitted or forbidden in relation to one type of work might not be permitted or forbidden in relation to another. For anyone who has been lost during this tour of some of the more obvious examples of copyright works (more complex situations commonly arise in the real world) the diagram on page 19 may provide some guidance. Having gained an overall impression of the types of copyright work, we can now look more closely at the different types of work individually.

### Literary works

Section 3(1) provides that:

> 'literary work' means any work, other than a dramatic or musical work, which is written, spoken or sung, and accordingly includes —
>
> (a)   a table or compilation, and
> (b)   a computer program.

These two (atypical) examples demonstrate the fact that literary works are not restricted to novels, articles, letters and suchlike, and need not have any degree of literary or aesthetic merit. So it has been well established that such things as street directories and Stock Exchange lists (good examples of compilations), lists of football fixtures and pools coupons, examination questions and even secret codes, unintelligible to those not sharing the secret, are all literary works. Furthermore, 'literary' should not be taken to suggest a distinction between literacy and numeracy, so mathematical tables or formulae are protected.

Computer programs were not specifically dealt with in the 1956 Act but the Copyright (Computer Software) Amendment Act 1985 provided that the 1956 Act applied in relation to a computer program as it applied in relation to a literary work. This treated a computer program as a literary work without actually saying that it was one but this final step is now taken by s. 3(1) of the 1988 Act (see further, chapter 15).

The real limitations on the scope of protected literary works have been (a) the added requirement of originality (first expressly required in the 1911 Act but implicit before then) and (b) the traditional requirement that a literary work be expressed in written or analogous form, which included any form of notation. These two requirements are separately discussed below but it should be noted from the outset that whereas the Act makes no direct change to the requirement of originality, the requirement of fixation in written or other material form has been significantly modified.

*Originality*
This is meant in the sense of 'not copied' and does not impose any test of inventiveness. Thus, a compilation by A of the results and scores of matches involving a particular football club over a season or number of seasons would be

an original literary work, even though the information is freely available to anyone who looks up the relevant sources (e.g., newspapers). This would be true even if the same compilation had already been undertaken by B. A and B would both have created identical original literary works since neither had copied from the other. On the other hand, if A took a short cut and did not look up the sources for himself but merely copied B's compilation, A would not have created an original literary work (nor in truth would he have done any compiling) since he has merely copied, and indeed he would be infringing B's copyright.

The requirement of 'not being copied' serves to put an onus on the person claiming copyright to demonstrate the expenditure of his own skill, labour and effort which is the rationale for giving the work protection in the first place. That skill and effort may be purely in selecting and obtaining the information from existing sources (as in most compilations) or partly also in generating the information and ideas in the first place (as in the case of a novel or scientific paper). The more mundane skills involved in compiling rather than generating information may seem less worthy of protection but there is generally no injustice in granting the qualified monopoly represented by copyright since others are free to go to the sources themselves.

Where this is not so, as in *Independent Television Publications Ltd* v *Time Out Ltd* [1984] FSR 64, in which *TV Times* programme listings were held to be an original literary work because of the time and effort spent in devising them, an undesirable monopoly may appear to be created. The result is that no one (without permission) can publish the television schedules as there are no sources other than the copyright work itself to which they can refer. In fact, the monopoly is only so striking because of the relative monopolisation of television broadcasting in this country rather than because of any defect in copyright law. If, as is now beginning to happen, a wider variety of suppliers of television broadcasts were to emerge, the value of the listings of any one such supplier would be correspondingly diminished and indeed a programme provider may be keen to allow his own schedules to be included in a compilation. Ultimately he might be prepared or compelled even to pay for the privilege of having his schedules advertised in this way.

*Titles and names*
Despite the almost reluctant concession of copyright in the *Time Out* case, policy arguments, other than those based on rewarding skill and effort, do sometimes appear to play a role in determining whether a work is original. The cases on titles and names, where the courts seem generally reluctant to grant protection, provide a good example. They can often be superficially explained on the basis of lack of originality, i.e., not *sufficient* skill and effort as in *Rose* v *Information Services Ltd* [1987] FSR 254 (where 'The Lawyer's Diary' was too obvious a name of a diary for lawyers to warrant protection). However, the originality was difficult to deny in *Exxon Corporation* v *Exxon Insurance Consultants International Ltd* [1982] Ch 119, where Standard Oil spent a small fortune in arriving at the invented word 'Exxon' as being the epitome of their corporate identity only to find the defendant insurance agency trading under the same name. Consequently, denial of copyright protection (an injunction was granted on the alternative ground that the defendants were 'passing off' their own business as connected

with that of the plaintiffs) had to be put on the basis that the title was not a literary work since it did not offer 'information, instruction or pleasure in the form of literary enjoyment'. This formulation is not universally accepted as completely satisfactory either in its conception or application to the facts of the case and it is difficult to resist the conclusion that titles are generally denied protection for policy reasons such as the following:

(a) Titles tend to be single words or phrases and to grant copyright protection would effectively monopolise the basic building blocks of language which everyone should be free to use.

(b) Appropriate protection can usually be obtained independently of copyright through the tort of passing off as in the *Exxon* case.

Reason (a) is not particularly compelling because a title would not be infringed by someone who subsequently independently thought of it but the problems of proof inherent in this coupled with reason (b) are sufficient to explain the courts' practice and attitude. Of course, if a name or title is depicted in a particular or special way it may qualify for protecton as an artistic work which was one of the grounds on which an injunction was granted against the use of *The Sun* masthead in a rival's advertising in the recent case of *News Group Newspapers Ltd* v *Mirror Group Newspapers (1986) Ltd* (1988) *The Times,* 27 July 1988.

*Fixation (formerly writing or other material form)*
Opinions differed about whether a literary work had to be in written form under the 1956 Act, the more traditional view being that writing or some other form of notation was essential. Others argued that, for example, a poem or political speech not reduced to writing or otherwise preserved but recorded on a tape recorder would qualify as a literary work just as much as one written down in advance or subsequently.

The 1988 Act now makes it clear (s. 3(2)) that writing is *not* required and that any form of recording will suffice to trigger the creation of a literary, dramatic or musical work. Furthermore, 'It is immaterial . . . whether the work is recorded by or with the permission of the author' (s. 3(3)). Thus the author who works by dictating on to tape for his audio typist is now protected as soon as he records the words on tape and the political speech maker acquires a copyright as soon as his speech is recorded, even if it is done by someone without his consent. If the record is on tape, rather than being a written one, the person making the recording will also acquire a copyright in the sound recording (as a sound recording, not as a literary work so that *this* copyright, as opposed to the speaker's, would not be infringed by someone who took the words from the recording and printed them, e.g., in a newspaper since a sound recording copyright is not infringed in that way).

If, on the other hand, the speech was not recorded on tape but taken down in shorthand by a reporter, as in *Walter* v *Lane* [1900] AC 539 where Lord Rosebery's speeches were taken down by reporters from *The Times,* the speaker would clearly now acquire his copyright in the speech (something not in issue in that case) and the reporter would probably also obtain copyright in his verbatim report (as a literary work) since sufficient skill and effort have been expended in producing it. This latter point was the actual decision in *Walter* v *Lane* where *The Times* was held entitled to restrain the publication of copies of its reports. Although it is sometimes questioned whether the result would be the same now that originality is expressly required, most commentators take the view that if sufficient skill and effort are expended in obtaining the report (contrast a report based on shorthand with the easy option of holding up a tape recorder) then the reporter should be given a copyright which he can assert against competitors seeking to obtain the benefit of his efforts.

It is arguable that even the reporter using a tape recorder should be protected against the copier of his report but if he has any such protection it must be based on his report as an original literary work (based perhaps on his efforts in attending the speech or perhaps in transcribing the tape) rather than on any copyright in his sound recording. The Parliamentary debates reveal that the whole question of the reporter's copyright was deliberately left open in s.3 of the Act in order to allow the courts to develop appropriate principles as they had begun to do in *Walter* v *Lane*.

It is now also clear that a singer, poet or musician who performs an unwritten song, poem or melody which he or she has conceived will acquire a copyright in it as a literary or musical work as appropriate if the performance is recorded on tape. This aspect of the Act, and its relationship with the new rights in performances provided by the Act in addition to copyright, raises some interesting issues which have perhaps not yet been fully thought through. These issues will be further explored in chapter 11 but in the present context one has to address the issue of when an unwritten work is sufficiently conceived for a recording of it to be regarded as a literary (or musical) work.

*The question of the nature of a work*
If someone gives an extempore speech in London on the first of the month which is recorded then the speech may qualify as a literary work (as recorded). The speaker then makes a speech outlining the same ideas but in slightly different language in Preston on the second of the month which is also recorded. Presumably there is a separate copyright in the second speech provided that it is not so similar in language to the first as not to qualify as original. Numerous separate copyrights in various versions of the speech may be created which is a curious if not particularly objectionable result of s. 2(3) (cf. the problem of the constantly updated database, referred to in chapter 15). It is, after all, merely analogous to the situation under the previous law whereby different drafts of the same ultimate book or article could each independently qualify as literary works but the recognition of recordings of oral recitations, which are less time-consuming to execute than written drafts, does tend to multiply the number of possible versions. The result is perhaps even more curious with musical works since extempore musical performances potentially differ so much more from polished musical works committed to writing. The performer may have no precise idea what is to be performed in advance nor any real prospect of being able to perform the same sequence of notes again in the future. Does s. 3(2) give a copyright in the sequence of notes performed if they happen to have been recorded on tape? Or does the notion of a musical work prescribe some more precise conception of the work in the composer's mind prior to its actual

performance? If so, is there a similar requirement in relation to speeches and the like and if there is, how is the existence of the prior mental conception to be proved? The Act seems to have committed itself not only to an increase in the number of literary, dramatic and musical works that will be protected together with a further lowering of the threshold of difficulty of creating them but also to posing some very difficult questions about the nature of a work. These questions appear even more acute when one considers extempore performances by groups of actors or musicians. It may be very difficult to discern accurately the individual words or, more especially, notes from a recording of a complex performance. This consideration suggests that the mere existence of a recording is not of itself sufficient and that something more is required but the difficulty remains of just what this requirement should be and of determining what is sufficient evidence of it. A work is a distinct thing from the performance of it and also from the recording of that performance but if the recording is the only evidence of the existence of the work, these latter two are likely to become confused.

## Dramatic works

Section 3(1) tells us that 'dramatic work' *includes* 'a work of dance or mime' which is commendably shorter than the 1956 Act where the definition included 'a choreographic work or entertainment in dumb show if reduced to writing in the form in which the work or entertainment is to be presented'. Dramatic works are not limited to dance and mime but will also more typically include plays written for the theatre, cinema or television screenplays, or radio plays (thus a sound recording may adequately record certain types of play). Where it is necessary to distinguish a dramatic work from a literary one (which it rarely is), the essence of the distinction would seem to be that a dramatic work is something to be performed by acting or dancing whereas a literary work is merely something to be read or recited (and a musical work something to be played or sung).

The principal change under the new Act, as with literary works, is that reduction to writing is no longer required and any form of recording will suffice. The question again arises as to how far improvised dance routines and mime acts qualify as works and if not all do qualify, what will be the basis of the distinction? That some forms of dramatic performance might not involve the performance of a 'work' may be implicit in s. 180 (2) (dealing with rights in performances) where dramatic performance is not expressly required to be of a dramatic work whereas reading or recitation must be of a literary work. The problem is essentially the same as that already discussed under the nature of a work in relation to literary works.

Some of the older cases on dramatic works may suggest a solution since they were decided prior to the 1956 Act and *actual* reduction to writing was not expressly required. Thus in *Tate* v *Thomas* [1921] 1 Ch 503 and *Tate* v *Fullbrook* [1908] 1 KB 821 such matters as characters, acting style and scenic effects were not protected as dramatic works since they were not *capable* of being printed and published. An improvised (but filmed) dramatic performance could perhaps be protected as a dramatic work *to the extent that* it is possible to write down (whether or not it has been written down) from the film precisely what is being performed. The test would be, in other words, the extent to which precise written instructions could be given to someone not seeing the film to enable them to perform the dramatic work. (The same test could be applied to literary and musical works: the work is made when it is recorded in any form but it is only a work if, or to the extent that, it *could be* recorded in writing.)

Although the statement in the 1956 Act that a dramatic work 'does not include a cinematograph film is omitted from the 1988 Act, the statement is still strictly true. The film is a copyright work in its own right but may also happen to be the vehicle evidencing the creation of a dramatic work, just as a sound recording may now be the vehicle evidencing the creation of a literary or musical work.

## Musical works

These are works 'consisting of music, exclusive of any words or action intended to be sung, spoken or performed with the music'. This tells us very little other than the point already made that the musical copyright for the music in a song is distinct from the literary copyright in the lyric (or the dramatic copyright in any accompanying dance or performance). Most commentators take the view that copyright law has been wise to avoid any attempt to define music in view of the inventiveness and resourcefulness of those who care to style themselves musicians and the present Act continues that cautious and prudent tradition. Notice that adaptations of existing musical works may attract their own copyright in the same way as adaptations (e.g., translations) of literary works. Thus a Vivaldi concerto (originally written for a chamber orchestra) newly arranged for a brass band would attract its own copyright (and might be well worth listening to!). If (unlike the Vivaldi concerto) the original work was still in copyright, permission would have to be obtained or else there would be infringement. Of course, the requirement of originality applies equally to musical works (and to dramatic works) as it does to literary works and so an adaptation will only qualify for its own copyright if sufficient skill and effort have been expended upon it.

It should be stressed again before leaving this topic that a musical work is the composition, not any particular performance or recording of it, and that a sound recording, on the one hand, and the music played in the sound recording, on the other, are quite distinct and separate types of copyright work.

## Artistic works

The extensive definition of 'artistic work' in s. 4 is effectively little different from that in the 1956 Act except that it includes 'collage' and defines photographs rather more helpfully and flexibly (so that the definition is capable of including holograms and, hopefully, any new ways of recording and producing images). Also covered by s. 4(1)(a) are sculptures and 'graphic works', the latter expression including:

(a)   any painting, drawing, diagram, map, chart or plan, and
(b))   any engraving, etching, lithograph, woodcut or similar work.

Section 4(1)(b) makes it clear that a 'work of architecture being a building or model for a building' is covered and s. 4(1)(c) includes 'a work of artistic craftsmanship'.

The key point to note is that the majority of artistic works (those in s. 4(1)(a)) are expressly protected 'irrespective of artistic quality'. As a result, very simple drawings have been held to qualify for copyright protection (although the simpler the drawing, the more exact must be the reproduction to constitute infringement). This has caused immense trouble over the past couple of decades or so in relation to industrial designs since very basic engineering drawings will normally qualify and potentially confer an undesirable monopoly in functional items. This complex issue is discussed further in chapter 12 but for the present the point to be noted is that some rather surprising items can qualify as artistic works, e.g., the frisbee disc found to be an engraving in New Zealand in *Wham-O Manufacturing Co.* v *Lincoln Industries Ltd* [1982] RPC 281 (a decision confirmed by the New Zealand Court of Appeal [1985] RPC 127). See by way of contrast the recent case of *J. & S. Davis (Holdings) Ltd* v *Wright Health Group Ltd* [1988] RPC 403, where a cast for dental impression trays was not regarded as a sculpture since it was not made 'for the purposes of sculpture' (see now s. 4(2)).

Originality is, of course, still a requirement but it is extremely rare for an artistic work to fail on this ground although the House of Lords recently found that slight modifications to an earlier engineering drawing of a Lego brick did not create a new original artistic work in *Interlego AG* v *Tyco Industries Inc.* [1988] 3 WLR 678. The new drawings may have been the result of skill, labour and judgment but that was not sufficient where the skill and judgment lay merely in the process of copying. Whilst this may seem sensible in the context of the facts of the case in question, if a ten-year-old child (or a talented adult) managed to produce a convincing imitation of the *Mona Lisa,* it would seem harsh to conclude that the result is not an original artistic work because the skill, labour and judgment lay merely in copying Da Vinci's work. It would also seem harsh to deny the ten-year-old (or the adult) the right to stop others exploiting his or her version of the *Mona Lisa.* Such a case seems indistinguishable in principle from the shorthand writer's copyright in his report of someone else's speech. It may be that the requirement of originality needs to be interpreted differently for different subspecies of artistic works. Copies of works that can be easily and fairly mechanically produced should not count as original but where the copy requires a good deal of skill or artistic talent, it should perhaps count as an artistic work in its own right.

*Works of artistic craftsmanship*
The wisdom of making artistic quality an irrelevant test for most artistic works can perhaps be seen in the problems that have arisen with this category of work which expressly refers to the quality of being artistic. The House of Lords has indicated that such things as hand-painted tiles, stained-glass windows, wrought-iron gates and certain pieces of furniture might be examples of works of artistic craftsmanship but an acceptable general definition has proved difficult to find. In the leading case of *George Hensher Ltd* v *Restawile Upholstery (Lancs) Ltd* [1976] AC 64 five different Law Lords took five different approaches (altogether nine separate approaches are discernible in the case) but all concurred in the conclusion that a flimsy prototype of a mass-market upholstered chair did

not qualify as a work of *artistic* craftsmanship even if it could be regarded as a work of craftsmanship in the first place, which latter point had, somewhat dubiously in Lord Reid's opinion, been conceded by the defendants. No complete consensus emerged from the case even on such basic points as whether only hand-made items qualify (they certainly have a better chance) or whether the question is one of law or fact. Lord Simon of Glaisdale's judgment contains an erudite (and interesting) discussion of the Arts and Crafts movement and also the following statement:

> I start by re-emphasising that the statutory phrase is not 'artistic work of craftsmanship', but 'work of artistic craftsmanship'. . . .It is therefore misleading to ask, first, is this a work produced by a craftsman, and secondly, is it a work of art? It is more pertinent to ask, is this the work of one who was in this respect an artist-craftsman?

Setting such artistry in wordcraft aside, the factor which seemed to attract the widest range of support as being significant was the intention of the maker and this was the approach applied in *Merlet* v *Mothercare plc* [1986] RPC 115 to deny protection to Madame Merlet's raincosy for her baby which had been unashamedly copied by Mothercare. Walton J took the view that Madame Merlet had designed the raincosy not with any artistic consideration in mind but to protect her baby on a visit to Scotland from 'the assumed rigours of a Highland summer'.

Had Madame Merlet been able to show infringement of her *pattern cuttings* as *drawings,* where, of course, artistic quality is irrelevant, it would have been unnecessary to argue that the finished product was a work of artistic craftsmanship. She is likely to have more success now under the unregistered design right provisions discussed further in chapter 12.

### Sound recordings

This means, you will be surprised to hear, 'a recording of sounds' but more helpfully, 'from which the sounds may be reproduced' (s. 5(1)(a)). Thus it encompasses old 78s, 12-inch singles, cartridges, cassettes, compact discs, digital audio tape and whatever the recording industry comes up with next. To be more accurate, the copyright is not in the actual cassette or disc that you purchase, since s. 5(2) makes it clear that there is no copyright in a recording which merely copies a previous recording, but if you tape the disc you have bought or borrowed you will be *indirectly* copying, and therefore infringing, the original sound recording made by the recording company.

The recording of any sounds, however unoriginal the actual sounds being recorded, will qualify for copyright protection provided that one is not merely recording a previous recording. Of course, there is nothing to prevent anyone else from making an independent recording of similar or identical sounds, e.g., the sounds of Big Ben striking twelve.

Section 5(1)(b) does not limit the definition to a recording of sounds but also includes 'a recording of the whole or any part of a literary, dramatic or musical work, from which sounds reproducing the work or part may be produced'. This is intended to cover such things as piano rolls or the use of a keyboard attached to a device which records the notes on a disc or tape from which the sound can later be reproduced. The point is that no actual sounds are emitted at the time the recording is made and hence it is not a recording of sounds within s. 5(1)(a). Similarly with literary and dramatic works keyed into a computer with a speech synthesiser by means of which the work can later be played back to, for example, a blind person. Note that what is recorded (if not a recording of sounds) must be a literary, dramatic or musical work — see the earlier discussion of the nature of a work.

One change in the definition of sound recordings which should be noted is that the sound-track of a cinema film is now regarded as a sound recording whereas previously it was excluded from the definition of a sound recording and protected as part of the copyright in the film. Thus under the new Act, all films, other than silent films, will give rise to not only a copyright in the film itself but also one in the sound recording (quite apart from other copyrights in the underlying works) although the same person will generally be the owner of both.

Sound recordings are not restricted to music but it is the recording of music which is of the greatest commercial significance and again the distinction between the copyright in the original musical work (the composition) and the copyright in the particular recording of that music should be stressed. These will usually be in separate ownership but both are infringed by home-taping of records, an intractable problem which will be separately discussed in chapter 13.

### Films

These were first given protection in the 1956 Act, previous protection having been possible as a series of photographs (artistic works) or as the embodiment of a dramatic work or even as a sound recording. In granting protection to the film itself, the 1956 Act therefore carefully excluded protection as a dramatic work or photograph, the definitions of both of which expressly excluded cinematograph films (see s. 48 of the 1956 Act). The definition of photograph in the new Act continues to exclude 'part of a film' but there is now no exclusion of films from the definition of dramatic works, no doubt because filming a dramatic performance is one way of 'fixing' a dramatic work so as to bring it into existence and the draftsman wanted to avoid any suggestion that this was not so because the definition of dramatic work excluded films. Thus (as already noted) filming a dramatic performance which has not previously been fixed in writing or otherwise will give rise to two separate copyrights (usually in separate ownerships) — the copyright in the film itself and the copyright in the dramatic work.

The Act now caters much more clearly for magnetic video tape, video discs and any future developments in the technology by defining a film as 'a recording on any medium from which a moving image may by any means be reproduced', the potentially restrictive 'sequence of visual images' in the 1956 Act having been replaced. Unlike the definition of sound recording, which is limited to the recording of sounds etc., there is no limitation on what can be recorded to constitute a film, the emphasis being on what may be produced from the film, i.e., a moving image. Thus a recording of random (or other) sounds on tape which when fed through a special computer produces a series of abstract colourful patterns presumably would constitute a film (as well as a sound recording assuming that the tape can also be used to reproduce the sounds if fed through a different machine).

## Broadcasts and cable programmes

These stand out from the other copyright works in that they are transient and intangible in form even though a permanent recording of the content of the broadcast can be made. Again, it should be stressed that the copyright in the broadcast is quite distinct from any copyright in the content, e.g., if it is a film or play being broadcast, the copyright in the film or dramatic work. Many broadcasts, e.g., of live sporting events, have no copyright *content* at all but there is still a copyright in the broadcast itself which would be infringed, e.g., by recording it for other than private purposes. The copyright in broadcasts and cable programmes is only part of the complex matrix of legal regulation of television and radio and can only be properly understood in that context but some further explanation will be attempted in chapter 16. For the moment, the following basic points should be noted.

*Broadcasts (section 6)*
These are not now limited as they were in the 1956 Act to broadcasts by the BBC or IBA but include all transmissions by *'wireless telegraphy'* which are *'capable of being lawfully received by members of the public'* including *satellite transmissions*. A transmission 'for presentation to members of the public' is also covered, as where a sporting event is beamed live to a stadium hundreds of miles away where it is viewed by the public even though they cannot (lawfully) receive it on their own domestic sets. The removal of the limitation to BBC and IBA broadcasts is necessary given the current policy of deregulation of broadcasting.

The broadcast may be of visual images, sounds (in combination as in television) or just sounds (as in radio) or other matter (e.g., computer programs in electronic form). Encrypted (scrambled) broadcasts are included if the decoding equipment has been made available to the public as will be the case with pay-as-you-view satellite broadcasts. Wireless telegraphy means in lay language (see s. 178 for the technical definition) 'over the airwaves (to be received by aerial or dish) and not piped by cable' but a broadcast remains a broadcast even if a particular recipient receives it by telecommunication system (by cable) linked to a remote aerial or dish, e.g., because the recipient is in a poor reception area (s.6(5)).

Originality is not expressly required but there is no copyright in a broadcast to the extent that it infringes another broadcast or cable programme. Repeat broadcasts (which are not infringements) are only protected for as long as the original broadcast.

*Cable programmes (section 7)*
These were first protected under the Cable and Broadcasting Act 1984. Like broadcasts, the programme may consist of visual images, sounds or other information but these are sent by telecommunications system (i.e., by electronic

means down a wire) rather than being broadcast over the airwaves, and cable programmes are by their nature not required to be as widely receivable as broadcasts. However, certain things are excluded from the definition of a cable programme service (of which a protected cable programme must form part). So, what are essentially two-way private cable systems, e.g., the telephone network, not surprisingly, are not included and closed-circuit systems and suchlike are also excluded. Section 7(2)(a) is intended to exclude private communications, e.g., home banking services, whilst leaving within the definition those forms of cable television which have an interactive facility which *allows* the receiver to respond. So it is intended that in a home shopping service the transmission of the catalogue of goods available would be included and attract a copyright but the response of a customer making a particular order would not be as that is a private matter between the customer and the provider of the service. Given the likely future development of the technology in this area the Act wisely provides a power under s. 7(3) to 'amend subsection (2) so as to add or remove exceptions'.

Since, as we have already seen, a broadcast relayed to a receiver by cable is still a broadcast and has copyright as such, s. 7(6) correspondingly excludes any copyright in the cable programme in such a situation, i.e., where the cable programme is merely the immediate re-transmission of a broadcast. Repeat cable programmes are treated in the same way as repeat broadcasts, i.e., they are only protected for as long as the original was protected. This principle would also appear to apply to broadcasts repeated in a cable programme and vice versa (s. 14(3)). Similarly, a cable programme which infringes a previous broadcast or cable programme (e.g., a repeat without consent) does not acquire any copyright of its own.

### Typographical arrangement of published editions

These were first granted copyright status in the 1956 Act (s. 15) in recognition of the investment of the publisher who will often not own the copyright in the literary or other work being published but whose financial stake in the work as published may be far greater than the actual owner of the literary copyright. Indeed, there may be no literary copyright to protect as in the case of works, such as those of Shakespeare, which have long been in the public domain or in which copyright has now expired (as in the works of D.H. Lawrence). The publisher clearly has an interest in preventing competitors unfairly undercutting him and potential purchasers unfairly by-passing him by photocopying the work as published.

It is only the typographical arrangement which is protected, not, for example, a particular version or translation of a work such as *The Canterbury Tales* although that would be separately protected as a literary work (adaptation). Typographical arrangement is not defined but it is basically the way the printed page is set out (which is inevitably reproduced if it is photocopied).

What is published must be the whole or part of a literary, dramatic or musical work. Hence, published editions of artistic works are not protected as such (the notion of a *typographical* arrangement appears to preclude this anyway although there is no compelling reason why the Act could not have modified the definition to protect a non-typographical arrangement of artistic works). A published

edition of artistic works will, however, normally have some accompanying text
(which will be a literary work) and the typographical arrangement of that text
would be protected. Again, although originality is not expressly required, a
typographical arrangement which reproduces that of a previous published
edition (e.g., a reprint) does not acquire a fresh copyright.

'Published editon' is not specifically defined apart from s. 8 telling us that it
must be of a literary, dramatic or musical work, but 'publication' is defined as the
'issue of copies to the public' and this is stated to include availability 'by means of
an electronic retrieval system' (s. 175(1)). Since 'related expressions' to publication are 'to be construed accordingly' it would appear that electronic publishing
is eligible for the copyright in a published edition.

The term of copyright is dealt with in chapter 3 but it is worth noting that
published editions are only protected for 25 years as opposed to the minimum of
50 (and much longer) for other types of copyright work.

## Typefaces

The protection of typographical arrangements is a separate matter from the legal
protection of typefaces. A typeface does not qualify as an independent type of
copyright work but the design of a typeface may be protected as an artistic work
or as a registered design, giving a right to control *copying* the typeface. However,
s. 54 effectively means that the *use* of a typeface does not infringe any such
copyright nor produce an infringing copy of the typeface although s. 54(2)
preserves liability for persons making or dealing in articles specifically designed
or adapted to produce the typeface. Section 55 also removes any copyright
protection once 25 years have elapsed from the first lawful marketing of such
articles by the copyright owner (which is the latest point by which registered
design protection will also have ceased).

Thus, typefaces themselves, as opposed to their use in a particular typographical arrangement, are not given any special protection, rather their protection as
artistic works is cut down somwhat by the provisions of the Act just mentioned.
This seems a curious way of amending the law to enable the UK to ratify the
Vienna agreement of 1973 for the protection of typefaces, which was expressed to
be the government's intention in the 1986 White Paper. There is nothing in these
provisions to remedy the previously perceived uncertainty about the extent to
which typefaces qualify as artistic works in the first place. In fact the government
acknowledged in the Parliamentary debates that they had realised in preparing
the Bill that the previous doubts about the copyright status of typefaces were
unfounded. All that was needed was some restriction on infringement to protect
printers and other bona fide users of the typeface

## Transitional provisions (schedule 1)

The new definitions of copyright works apply to works created after the
commencement date of Part I of the Act. Works created and qualifying for
copyright before that date continue to have copyright and are deemed to satisfy
Part I of the Act. Thus it is clear enough that a poem written in 1987 was a literary
work under the old law and continues to be one under the new. However, a
sound-track protected as part of a film before commencement will become a

sound recording for copyright purposes after commencement (sch. 1, para. 8).

The question now arises in relation to dance and mime, where writing was previously expressly required, whether an existing recording of an otherwise unfixed dance automatically attracts copyright for the dance as a dramatic work once the Act is in force. Schedule 1, para. 5(1), which states: 'copyright subsists in an existing work after commencement only if copyright subsisted in it immediately before commencement', might be thought to suggest that the answer is no since the dance was not in copyright before commencement. This interpretation, however, is not beyond doubt since it assumes that the unwritten dance is 'an existing work' whereas para. 1(3) states that existing works are works *made* before commencement and under the pre-commencement law this type of dramatic work was only 'made' when reduced to writing (see ss. 48(1) and 49(4) of the 1956 Act). If the dance is not an 'existing work', para. 5(1) is irrelevant. Furthermore, para. 3 states: 'The new copyright provisions apply in relation to things existing at commencement as they apply in relation to things coming into existence after commencement, subject to any express provision to the contrary'. The better view, therefore, would appear to be that the *recording* is an existing *thing* (even though not an existing *work*) and attracts copyright just as much as a recording made after commencement.

The answer to the above question is not as clear as it might be and it is regrettable that the Act does not provide more specifically for a situation where it marks a definite change from the previous law. Furthermore, the problem is not necessarily restricted to dance and mime and is as large as the extent to which s. 3(2) (making recording in writing or *otherwise* sufficient) represents a liberalisation of the previous requirement of fixation in relation to literary and musical works (and dramatic works other than dance or mime).

Most of the other transitional provisions relating to the subsistence of copyright are significant in the context of the duration of copyright and will be discussed in the next chapter.

# Chapter 3 Duration of Copyright

## Introduction

Although copyright is a property right, it does not generally exist in perpetuity and is more in the nature of a long leasehold than a freehold. Different terms of years have been given to different categories of work, sometimes as a matter of policy, sometimes as a historical accident, but one of the aims and effects of the 1988 Act has been to reduce some of the more idiosyncratic differences between the rules applicable to different categories of works and to end those exceptional situations (subject to one remarkable new exception) where copyright could subsist indefinitely or in perpetuity.

To speak of these as 'exceptional situations' is in one sense misleading since common law (i.e., non-statutory) copyright, until its abolition in the Act of 1911, protected *unpublished* works indefinitely but this right would automatically end on publication. Nevertheless, the 1911 and 1956 Acts retained the perpetual protection of copyright for many categories of unpublished works. Although the 1988 Act ends these perpetual copyrights (and also the anomalous university copyrights in certain pre-1911 works which were no longer of any significance) the former rules will remain significant in determining the duration of the copyright in existing works and the transitional rules applicable to these works will, for some time, remain of more significance generally than the rules applicable to new works. The rules for new works, however, are commendably simplified and can be summed up very easily as follows (see also the final column in Table 3.1)

## New works: literary, dramatic, musical and artistic (section 12)

These are protected for the *author's life plus 50 years from the end of the calendar year in which the author dies*. Notice that copyright always expires on 31 December at midnight (end of calendar year) thus minimising any disputes about the precise time and date of the author's death (unless the death occurs at or about midnight of 31 December!). Although this period is far longer than is deserved by some works (such as most compilations) and is regarded as too short by the owners of copyright in more classical works, it is the minimum period specified by the Berne Convention for such works and is the nearest thing to an international norm (although some European countries have longer periods and the minimum under the UCC is life plus 25 years).

To this basic rule of life plus 50 years for literary etc. works, there are a number of exceptions:

(a)   *Works of unknown authorship* (s. 12(2)). Copyright in these expires 50 years after the work is made available to the public, which expression *includes* (apart from obvious things such as publication) public performance or being included in a broadcast or cable programme. If the author does become known after the copyright has expired then the copyright does not revive even if the author is still alive or died less than 50 years previously. However, if the author does become known prior to the 50 years expiring then the usual copyright term of the author's life plus 50 years applies. Curiously, it also appears that copyright in a work of unknown authorship, not made available to the public, subsists indefinitely since there is no provision in the Act for its termination but the practical effect of this is negated by s. 57(1)(b)(ii) which provides that it is not an infringement of copyright in such a situation if it is reasonable to assume that the author (whoever he or she was) died at least 50 years previously.

(b)   *Computer-generated works* (i.e., where there is no human author, see chapter 4) attract a straight period of 50 years from being made since there is no human life in relation to which a copyright term can be measured (s. 12(3)).

(c)   Works of joint authorship are measured in relation to the longest to survive (of those authors whose identity is known — a work is only regarded as of unknown authorship if none of its authors is known) (s. 12(4)). Thus the musical and literary copyrights in the songs of Lennon and McCartney do not expire in the year 2030 (50 years from the death of John Lennon) but will continue for 50 years from the death of Paul McCartney, whenever that should occur.

(d)   *Crown copyright* now lasts for 125 years or 50 years from commercial publication (e.g., by HMSO) whichever is the shorter period (s. 163(3)). The copyright in an Act of Parliament is Crown copyright and lasts for 50 years from the end of the year of royal assent (s. 164(2)).

(e)   *Parliamentary copyright* (a new category of ownership which would formerly have been classed as Crown copyright) only gets a period of 50 years from making (s. 165(3)). Separate provision is made for Parliamentary Bills which attract a very short period — until royal assent or until the Bill is lost (s. 166(5)).

(f)   *International Organisations* (such as Unesco) get a period of 50 years from making (unless a different period is specified by Order in Council) for those rare works that do not attract the normal period of protection by virtue of the status of the author or the country of first publication (s. 168(3)).

### Sound recordings and films (section 13)

Copyright in these lasts for 50 years from the end of the calendar year of making, or if released prior to the expiry of that period, 50 years from the end of the calendar year of release (s. 13(1)). 'Release' is a similar concept to 'first made available to the public' and is defined to mean when 'first published, broadcast or included in a cable programme service' or, in the case of a film or film sound-track, 'when the film is first shown in public' (s. 13(2)). This is much broader than the 'published' criterion of the 1956 Act which meant that r any films, e.g., television films, were not regarded as published even though broadcast and hence could enjoy perpetual copyright even though exploited. Thus the longest period of copyright protection for sound recordings and films is just under 101 years and the shortest period is 50. For example, the copyright in a sound recording made in the early hours of the morning of 1 January 1990 and released any time in 2040 will not expire until midnight on 31 December 2090. If the recording was not released until 2041, however, copyright would already have expired on 31 December 2040.

The above provisions closely follow the Berne Convention (Art. 7(2)) as recommended by the Whitford Committee. Under the previous law, the 50-year period started to run from registration for registrable films which, if the registration were in a year prior to the year of publication (now called release), would mean that the film would receive less protection than the Berne Convention prescribes. In fact, this particular reform was pre-empted by the Films Act 1985 which dismantled the machinery for registration of films and amended the 1956 Act so as to give all films, save those already registered, a period of protection of 50 years from publication.

### Broadcasts and cable programmes (section 14)

The copyright in these lasts until 50 years from the end of the calendar year when the broadcast was *first* made or the cable programme was *first* included in a cable programme service. As mentioned in chapter 2, repeated broadcasts etc. do not get the benefit of a fresh period of 50 years but are protected only so long as is the original broadcast. Repeats after the expiry of the copyright in the original broadcast (i.e., more than 50 years later) do not attract any copyright (in the broadcast as such) at all.

### Published editions (section 15)

Copyright lasts until 25 years from the end of the year in which the edition is *first* published.

### Other rights in copyright works and related rights

The duration of moral rights, rights in performances and design rights is dealt with in the appropriate chapters on those topics.

### Transitional provisions

The new rules obviously apply to works created after the commencement of Part I of the Act. It is also necessary to make provision for the duration of copyright in works already existing at commencement and this is done in para. 12 of sch. 1. These rules are somewhat complex and there is no substitute for a careful reading of sch. 1. What follows is an attempt to outline the basic scheme of the provisions which is as follows:

**Table 3.1    Rules on expiry of copyright**

| Type of work | 1956 Act Rules Does copyright still subsist at commencement of 1988 Act? | |
|---|---|---|
| Literary, dramatic and musical works | Published etc. in author's life. | Author's life + 50 years. |
| | No publication, public performance, issue of records or broadcast in author's life. | 50 years from first publication, performance, record, broadcast etc. [P] |
| Artistic works (generally) | | Author's life + 50 years |
| Artistic works (engravings) | Published in author's life. | Author's life + 50 years. |
| | Not published in author's life. | 50 years from first publication. [P] |
| Artistic works (photographs) | | 50 years from first publication. [P] |
| Sound recordings and unregistered films | | 50 years from first publication. [P] |
| Registered films | | 50 years from registration. |
| Broadcasts and cable programmes | | 50 years from first broadcast or inclusion in cable programme service. |
| Published editions. | | 25 years from first publication. |

[P] Potentially perpetual or indefinite period of copyright.
[T] Termination of potentially perpetual or indefinite period of copyright.

| Transitional rules<br>How long copyright in existing works<br>lasts after commencement of 1988 Act | | 1988 Act<br>Rules for works made<br>after commencement |
|---|---|---|
| | No change. | Author's life + 50 years. |
| Published etc. before commencement. | 50 years from publication etc. | Author's life + 50 years. |
| Unpublished and author dead at commencement. | 50 years from commencement. [T] | |
| Unpublished but author alive at commencement. | Author's life + 50 years. [T] | |
| | No change. | Author's life + 50 years. |
| | No change. | Author's life + 50 years. |
| Published before commencement. | 50 years from publication. | Author's life + 50 years. |
| Unpublished and author dead at commencement. | 50 years from commencement. [T] | |
| Unpublished but author alive at commencement. | Author's life + 50 years. [T] | |
| Unpublished at commencement. | 50 years from commencement. [T] | Author's life + 50 years. |
| Published before commencement. | 50 years from publication. | 50 years from release or 50 years from making if not released within 50 years. |
| Unpublished at commencement. | 50 years from commencement or 50 years from publication if published within 50 years. [T] | |
| Published before commencement. | 50 years from publication. | |
| | 50 years from registration. | Registration system abolished. |
| | No change. | 50 years from first broadcast or inclusion in cable programme service. |
| | No change. | 25 years from first publication. |

For the purposes of this table, sound recordings and photographs made before June 1957 can be treated as published on the date they were made.

(a)   Copyright in existing works where a finite period of time has already begun to run at commencement expires at the end of that finite period (usually 50 years from either publication or the author's death prior to commencement).

(b)   Other copyrights, including formerly potentially perpetual or indefinite copyrights, end 50 years after commencement except:

(i)   for literary, dramatic, musical and artistic works (except photographs) where the author is still alive at commencement, the period is 50 years from his or her death, and

(ii)   in the case of films, sound recordings and anonymous works first published in the 50 years following commencement, copyright does not expire until 50 years from that first publication.

The basic policy of these rules is to curtail any potentially indefinite or perpetual copyright periods, replacing them with the nearest approximation to the period which would apply for new works, but otherwise to let finite periods which have already begun to run continue unchanged. To understand these provisions fully, some knowledge of the provisions on duration of copyright under the 1956 Act is required. These can be summed up as follows:

(a)   Literary, dramatic and musical works. Author's life plus 50 years but if not published or publicly performed etc. (see the proviso to s. 2(3) of the 1956 Act) in the author's lifetime, 50 years from publication, public performance etc. (potentially perpetual).

(b)   Artistic works. Simply author's life plus 50 years but engravings *not published at the author's death* and photographs (whenever published) got 50 years from publication. Engravings were in fact treated identically with literary works except that only publication, and not the wider category of acts specified in s. 2(3) of the 1956 Act, would remove the possibility of perpetual protection. (Note, however, that artistic works of which a corresponding registrable design was applied industrially, effectively lost copyright protection 15 years after the industrial products of the design were first marketed — see chapter 12.)

(c)   Sound recordings. 50 years from publication (potentially perpetual).

(d)   Films. 50 years from registration or publication depending on whether the film was registrable or not.

(e)   Broadcasts and cable programmes. 50 years from first broadcast or cabling.

(f)   Published editions. 25 years from first publication.

Table 3.1 has been devised in order to help guide you through these complex provisions. To use it, locate the type of work with which you are dealing in the first column and then look along to the next main column to decide the first question of whether the work is still in copyright at (i.e., immediately prior to) commencement of the 1988 Act. This involves applying the 1956 Act rules and obviously if copyright has already expired under those rules there can be no question of copyright reviving under the new Act and that is an end of the matter. If, on the other hand, copyright has not expired, one has to look along to the next main column to see for how long after commencement it continues.

To take an example, if A wrote a novel in 1960 which was published in 1961 and A died in 1970, that is a literary work which was published in A's life. According to table 3.1, the work was protected under the 1956 Act for A's life plus 50 years and since A died in 1970 the work continues in copyright until 2020 and so is obviously still in copyright at the commencement of the 1988 Act. Following that line of the table across and looking under the transitional rules for how long copyright in that existing work continues after commencement, we find that the table says 'No change', which means that the work still continues in copyright until 2020 because the new Act does not change the rules for this category of work, even for new works, as can be seen from looking at the final column. However, if A had died in 1960, before the novel was published or publicly performed etc.,that would take us into the next row down in column 2, i.e., a work not published or publicly performed etc. in the author's lifetime. According to table 3.1 the period of protection under the 1956 Act was 50 years from first publication etc. and so the novel is protected for 50 years from 1961, i.e., until 2011, and again is still clearly in copyright at commencement. In the next column, the transitional rules, three alternatives are given and the novel falls into the first of these since it has been published (in 1961) before commencement and the table tells us that the copyright period is still 50 years from publication.

Let us suppose now that A's novel has not yet been published in which case under the 1956 Act the copyright is still potentially perpetual since, if it is never published, copyright will never expire. However, it now falls under the second alternative of the transitional rules, being unpublished and the author dead at commencement. According to table 3.1 the period of protection now is 50 years from commencement and this represents the termination of a formerly potentially perpetual or indefinite copyright. The Act in effect deems the work to be published on commencement. If we now suppose that the work is unpublished but that A did not die in 1960 but is still alive at commencement then we find ourselves in the third alternative under the transitional rules. Since the work is still unpublished, the period of protection under the 1956 Act would still be potentially perpetual but we now find that the transitional rules impose the period of A's life plus 50 years so that the duration of copyright depends on how long after commencement A's death occurs. Notice that the rules under the 1988 Act for literary, dramatic, musical and artistic works made after commencement draw no distinction between published and unpublished works, the period always being the author's life plus 50 years. The appropriate period of protection for other classes of works can be worked out similarly from the table by locating the type of work in column 1 and then following it across the table to find the appropriate rules at each stage. It will be noticed that the transitional rules will remain the most important for quite a long time but that the transitional rules can only be applied if one has first determined that copyright still subsisted under the 1956 Act immediately prior to commencement of the 1988 Act.

## Photographs

Although there were a number of anomalous rules under the 1956 Act, photographs deserve special mention. In contrast to other former Part I works, the author's life was irrelevant and the period was a straight 50 years from publication which although *potentially* perpetual was in practice a much shorter

**Table 3.2    Special rules governing expiry of copyright**

| Type of work | 1956 Act Rules<br>Does copyright still subsist at commencement of 1988 Act? |
| --- | --- |
| Literary, dramatic, musical and artistic works of unknown authorship | 50 years from publication. [P] |
| Crown copyright in literary, dramatic and musical works | 50 years from publication. [P] |
| Crown copyright in engravings and photographs | 50 years from publication. [P] |
| Crown copyright in other artistic works | 50 years from making. |
| Crown copyright in sound recordings and films | 50 years from publication. [P] |

[P] Potentially perpetual or indefinite period of copyright.

| Transitional rules How long copyright in existing works lasts after commencement of 1988 Act | | 1988 Act Rules for works made after commencement |
|---|---|---|
| Published etc. before commencement. | 50 years from publication. | 50 years from being made available to public. [P] But no infringement if reasonable to assume author dead for 50 years. |
| Unpublished at commencement. | 50 years from being made available or 50 years from commencement if not made available within 50 years. [T] | |
| Published etc. before commencement. | 50 years from publication. | 125 years from making or 50 years from commercial publication, whichever period shorter. |
| Unpublished at commencement. | Apply new rules, but if work made more than 75 years before commencement, 50 years from commencement. [T] | |
| Published before commencement. | 50 years from publication. | 125 years from making or 50 years from commercial publication, whichever period shorter. |
| Unpublished at commencement. | 50 years from commencement. [T] | |
| | 50 years from making. | 125 years from making or 50 years from commercial publication, whichever period shorter. |
| Published before commencement. | 50 years from publication. | 50 years from making or 50 years from release if released within 50 years (normal term). |
| Unpublished at commencement. | 50 years from commencement or 50 years from publication if published within 50 years of commencement. [T] | |

[T] Termination of potentially perpetual or indefinite period of copyright.

period than for most other commercially exploited artistic works. The Bill as originally introduced into the House of Lords in October 1987 embodied the White Paper's proposal to further curtail this to a straight 50 years from the taking of the photograph in order to provide what was thought to be a more readily identifiable starting date for the period of protection (and also to remove the potential perpetual copyright). It was argued that this was unfair discrimination against photographers and the rule for photographs was made identical with that for other artistic works. Existing photographs, however, do not get the benefit of the new rules and hence the copyright expires under the transitional provisions 50 years from commencement or 50 years from publication if already published at commencement.

## Crown copyright

Under the 1956 Act, Crown copyright in literary, dramatic and musical works, engravings and photographs was 50 years from publication and if not published was perpetual. For artistic works, other than those just mentioned, the period was 50 years from making with no possibility of perpetual copyright. It was not and is not thought appropriate to tie Crown copyright to the lives of particular Crown servants since this would involve excessive record keeping etc., a problem which of course exists for private sector organisations to whom it might be thought record keeping comes less naturally than to our entrepreneurial Civil Service. However, commercial organisations have not made too much fuss about this, no doubt reasoning that the longer period of protection based on the author's life was worth any inconvenience. The Act now gives the Crown a new period of protection of 125 years from making or 50 years from the commercial publication of the work (e.g., by HMSO), whichever period is the shorter. Given the change, transitional provisions are again required and these are to be found in para. 41 of sch. 1 and their application can be worked out by looking at table 3.2 which works in a similar way to table 3.1. If the Crown has copyright in a literary work published in say 1975 which under the 1956 Act would end in 2025 it will continue to do so under the transitional provisions. However, in the case of a photograph taken in 1975 but not published before commencement the transitional provisions impose a period of 50 years from commencement thus truncating what under the former rules was an indefinite period of protection. For works other than literary, dramatic, musical and artistic ones, there are generally no special Crown copyright rules, the rules being just the same as for other owners of such works. Sound recordings and films are specifically mentioned in para. 40 and they are therefore included in table 3.2 although comparison with table 3.1 will reveal that the provisions are in fact identical. Table 3.2 also details the rules for works of unknown authorship which have already been commented on at page 34 above.

## Parliamentary copyright

The Act draws a novel distinction between Crown copyright and Parliamentary copyright. The distinction seems to have been introduced (at Commons committee stage) partly as an expression of Parliament's independence from the Crown and partly to give Parliament more direct control of reports of its own proceedings in the light of current sound broadcasting and the proposed television experiment. Parliamentary copyright generally only attracts a period of 50 years and does not apply (sch. 1, para. 43(1)) to published works existing at commencement which would fall under the old Crown copyright and would be governed by the transitional provisions of para. 41. Parliamentary copyright applies to works 'made under the direction and control' of either House but it should be stressed that it only applies where there is one of the types of works mentioned in s. 2 of the Act and discussed in chapter 2. In other words, Parliamentary copyright is merely an expression relevant to the ownership and duration of certain copyright works, it is not another type of copyright in the sense that a literary or dramatic work is a type of copyright work. The same is, of course, true of Crown copyright.

Acts of Parliament come under Crown copyright rather than Parliamentary copyright and the copyright subsists from royal assent until 50 years from the end of that calendar year. Parliamentary Bills now, by contrast, fall under Parliamentary copyright which in this exceptional case expires once the Bill has passed into law or on its withdrawal or rejection at the end of a session. This would seem to mean that to the extent that a Bill is enacted without amendment, it could be used to make copies of what has subsequently become the Act provided one is careful to copy the Bill and not the Act! By sch. 1, para. 43(2), public Bills published and introduced into Parliament before commencement (e.g., the Copyright, Designs and Patents Bill) do not come under Parliamentary copyright but would still be treated as Crown copyright and be governed by the transitional provisions for existing Crown copyright works (para. 41).

### *Peter Pan* (section 301 and schedule 6)

By a wonderful irony, amidst the wholesale abolition of perpetual copyrights, the House of Lords accepted an amendment (proposed by Lord Callaghan of Cardiff) which means that the trustees of the Great Ormond Street Hospital for Sick Children have again become entitled to receive royalties relating to *Peter Pan,* notwithstanding that the copyright (which was the subject of a generous gift to them by its author, J. M. Barrie) expired at the end of 1987. The Act does not actually revive the copyright but merely provides for a right to 'a royalty in respect of any public performance, commercial publication, broadcasting or inclusion in a cable programme service of the whole or any substantial part of the work or an adaptation of it' (sch. 6, para. 2(1)). This corresponds to the aspects of the copyright that formerly belonged to the trustees since they did not have the whole of the copyright. For example, they had no rights in respect of the cartoon film made of *Peter Pan* by Walt Disney in 1952. It is now open to anyone to make a fresh film of *Peter Pan,* either as a cartoon or with live actors, but the trustees would be entitled to a royalty in respect of any public performance (or broadcasting) etc. of such a film just as they will clearly be entitled to a royalty on any stage productions or commercially published books.

The right to a royalty differs from copyright in that there is no right in the trustees to *prevent* any future exploitation of *Peter Pan,* just a right to remuneration in return for such exploitation. The Copyright Tribunal (see chapter 7) is given jurisdiction where the amount of the royalty cannot be agreed (para. 5(1)). No royalty is payable for anything which would not be an infringement of copyright because it is a permitted act (see chapter 6) or which is done in pursuance of arrangements made before the passing of the Act (paras 3 and 4). The right to a royalty is one of the few provisions of the Act which (by virtue of s. 305(1)) came into force immediately on royal assent (15 November 1988). It is a provision which can best be regarded as a fairy tale come to life in the House of Lords where it was stressed that it should not be regarded as setting a precedent and that even if it should do so, it was a precedent which could only be followed by one who, like Lord Callaghan, had first become Prime Minister of his country. One cannot do other than conclude by observing (as did Lord Beaverbrook in the House of Lords) the appropriateness of it being *Peter Pan's* copyright which never grows up!

# Chapter 4 Ownership of Copyright

## Introduction

The ownership of copyright in a work at any given time depends on the transactions that have taken place since its initial creation and therefore the Act cannot of itself indicate with certainty the current ownership of any particular copyright. What the Act does is to prescribe who is the *initial* owner of the copyright. This is of fundamental importance since it provides the fixed starting-point for the various, often complex, transactions that may subsequently take place and will also govern entirely the situations where there are no such subsequent dealings.

The basic principle of the Act is simple enough: 'The author of a work is the first owner of any copyright in it' (s. 11(1)). However, there are exceptions for works made by employees in the course of their employment and for Crown and related copyrights which we will look at once we have examined the central concept of authorship.

## Authorship

*Literary, dramatic, musical and artistic works*
The Act simply states that the author in relation to a work 'means the person who creates it' (s. 9(1)). Usually this will be the person whose skill labour and effort it is that warrants copyright protection in the first place. It is normally clear who is the author on this test (note s. 3(2) whereby the author's ownership is not affected by the fact that it is someone else who records or fixes the work) although the matter can be complicated where the supernatural intervenes! In *Cummins* v *Bond* [1927] 1 Ch 167 a medium was held to be the author of a work which she claimed merely to have written down in a seance at the dictation of 'some being no longer inhabiting this world, and who has been out of it for a length of time sufficient to justify the hope that he has no reasons for wishing to return to it'. Eve J was clearly aware of a jurisdictional problem if he were to decide that the real author was the person 'already domiciled on the other side of the inevitable river' but in any case he found that the medium *had exercised sufficient skill, labour and effort to justify being treated as author*. Her activities 'obviously involved a great deal more than mere repetition' and encompassed the 'gift of extremely rapid

writing coupled with a peculiar ability to reproduce in archaic English matter communicated to her in some unknown tongue'. Entertaining as Eve J's judgment is, the principles which he applied remain as valid today as they were back in 1927.

Photographs are again worthy of special mention since under the 1956 Act it was specifically provided that (subject to any agreement to the contrary) the author was the person who, at the time the photograph was taken, owned the material on which it was taken. Many photographers would be using their own film and would therefore be the owners of the copyright in their photographs but equally it would often be the case that the film belonged to someone else who was nowhere near at the time the photograph was taken and who had made no creative contribution to the photograph. The Whitford Committee recommended that the author should be 'the person responsible for the composition of the photograph' which would often but not inevitably be the person who releases the shutter but the White Paper thought that this could lead to uncertainty and preferred the simplicity of making the photographer the author. The Act makes no special provision on this and so photographs are now governed by the general rule that the author is the person who creates a work; although this will generally be the person who is behind the camera, it will not inevitably be so. It should be noted that the photograph is created when the film is exposed (see s. 4, 'recording of light') rather than when it is subsequently developed, so at least the photographer does not have to compete with the developer or printer for authorship. Of course, if the developer subjects the negative to some special process which produces something more than a mere copy of the original negative then the developer may have the copyright in a distinct work just as a translator is the author of his translation as distinct from the work translated.

*Other works*
Section 9(2) specifically directs who is to be taken to be the author/creator of these works but in fact these deeming provisions subtly change the meaning of author from creator to entrepreneur. For *sound recordings and films* it is 'the person by whom the arrangements necessary for the making of the recording or film are undertaken', which represents no change from the previous law for films but does change the position for sound recordings which were formerly governed by a rule similar to that for photographs — the person who owned the record at the time of the recording. This formal change may make little difference in most cases since recording companies will often fulfil the requirements of both the former and the new definition; but it does perhaps make it easier for an independent record producer to acquire copyright in preference to the owner of the tapes on which the recording happens to be made. The first owner of the copyright in a film will continue to be, in most cases, the producer or more likely the production company, rather than the director. Attempts were made in the Parliamentary debates to give the director a joint interest, at least, in the copyright (as in Continental countries which recognise films as being the subject of an author's rather than a neighbouring right) but the view that the artistic contribution of directors was sufficiently protected by the new moral rights was adhered to by the government (see chapter 8).

The author of a *broadcast* is the person who makes it (s. 9(2))b)). This includes the transmitter of a programme if he has responsibility to any extent for its contents and also any person providing the programme who makes with the person transmitting it the arrangements necessary for its transmission (s. 6(3)). The reference to responsibility for its contents is to exclude a mere provider of technical facilities (such as British Telecom in relation to satellite broadcasts). The reference to the provider of the programme is designed to ensure that (as was not the case under the 1956 Act nor under the Bill as initially introduced) ITV companies (Granada, Thames etc.) as well as the IBA would be joint owners of the copyright. The provisions for cable programmes (the person providing the cable programme service: (s. 9(2)(c)) and for published editions (the publisher: (s. 9(2)(d)) appear to be straightforward and require no further comment here.

*Computer-generated works*
Computer-generated works are an interesting hybrid since they are given an entrepreneurial treatment (owned by the person by whom the arrangements necessary for the creation of the work are undertaken) even though the work created is a literary, dramatic, musical or artistic one. However, this does not deprive any creative individual of ownership which should properly be his since computer-generated is a residual category which applies 'in circumstances such that there is no human author' (s. 178). Thus a novel, first fixed by being typed into a word processor, is obviously not computer-generated as it is clear that there is a human author, the novelist. The situation that arose in *Express Newspapers plc* v *Liverpool Daily Post & Echo plc* [1985] FSR 306 is less clear. There, the programmer of a computer was held to be the author of a literary work represented by a series of numbers produced by the computer for a daily newspaper competition. The better view is probably that this would not be a computer-generated work since the computer is being used as a mere tool and it is not difficult to identify an appropriate human author (see chapter 15). Even if such a work is now regarded as computer-generated, the programmer would probably still be regarded as the author (if he is the person making the arrangements) but the difference would be that the term would only be 50 years from creation rather than the author's life plus 50 years.

The computer-generated category is really aimed at more sophisticated devices such as those now beginning to be marketed whereby a computer can produce to order an original piece of music in the style of a known composer. The steps to be taken by the operator of the machine may be so trivial that it is difficult on normal principles to say that he or she is the author. The real creative work is done by those programming the computer in the first place but it would be inconvenient and misleading to treat the programmer as the owner of the copyright in all the music produced by the various machines sold or distributed. The Act therefore *treats* the person who undertakes 'the arrangements necessary for the creation of the work' as the author and that will normally be the operator or the person directing the operation of the machine. Since we are here dealing with deemed rather than genuine authorship the entrepreneurial period of protection of 50 years rather than life plus 50 years is more appropriate.

The recognition of the computer-generated category poses something of a conundrum for existing works since it depends on the assumption that there can be literary, dramatic, musical and artistic works 'in circumstances such that there

is no human author'. Any such works made before commencement would appear
to be works in which copyright subsists and yet there is no author who can be
regarded as the first owner nor any relevant life by which to measure the duration
of copyright!

## Joint authorship

It is often the case that the skill and effort of more than one person is responsible
for the creation of a work and the Act provides for joint authors in such a case.
'Joint' does not ncessarily mean equal (although that division will usually
commend itself on the grounds of simplicity and convenience if not of absolute
accuracy) and the proportionate shares may depend on the quantity and quality
of the different contributions. Nor is a book necessarily a work of joint
authorship merely because there are two or more authors named on the cover.
Each author may have separately contributed particular chapters or sections in
which case the different chapters or sections will be distinct copyright works with
different individual authors. However, if 'the contribution of each author is not
distinct', i.e., they have worked together on the whole book and one cannot point
to specific chapters or sections which are solely the work of one, then it is a work
of joint authorship. The test of being not distinct goes back to the 1911 Act, the
1956 Act having preferred the expression 'not separate'. The House of Lords,
discussing incidentally the example of a book on the present Act, were not happy
with the word 'separate' and prompted the government to resurrect the word
'distinct'. One is tempted to observe that this is a distinction without a difference
but the source of the difficulty is that 'contribution' can refer *either* to the *efforts*
of a contributor or the the *results* of those efforts. It is the latter sense that is
relevant in works of joint authorship (the efforts of individuals are always
separate) and the expression 'not distinct' is probably more apt to suggest this
latter meaning. The intention of the subsection would be more clearly conveyed if
'the contribution of' were to be replaced by or read as 'the part contributed by'.
    Where one of the joint authors does not qualify under s. 154 (i.e., he is a citizen
of a non-Convention country such as Malaysia) and the work *only* qualifies
because of the status of another joint author (i.e., it does not qualify on the
ground of the country of first publication) then the non-qualified author is not a
joint owner and his life is not relevant to the duration of the copyright.

## Employee authors

We have spent some time examining the concept of authorship since s. 11 lays
down a general rule that the author is the first owner. Crown and Parliamentary
copyright apart, the only exception to this now is *a work made by an employee in
the course of his employment* which, subject to any agreement to the contrary,
*belongs to the employer* (s. 11(2)). Under the 1956 Act there were two further
exceptions.

### Removal of the journalists' exception
This exception applied to literary, dramatic and artistic works made by the
employee of a newspaper, magazine etc. for the purpose of publication in the

newspaper, magazine etc. (Copyright Act 1956, s. 4(2)). The employer in this case owned the copyright only in relation to publication in newspapers, magazines etc. and copyright in other respects belonged to the author. This compromise, splitting the copyright between employer and employee, was known as the journalists' exception but, as will be seen, employee journalists are no longer given this favourable treatment.

Both Whitford and the Green Paper had suggested various changes to the rules governing all employee authors along the lines of a generalisation of the journalists' exception: employees should be entitled to the copyright for all purposes not contemplated by the contract of employment. However, these changes were thought to be capable of creating uncertainty and imprecision and of upsetting established understandings and practices. Therefore instead of extending the benefit of the journalists' exception to all other employees, Parliament did away with the split ownership provision altogether! The government yielded to the newspaper publishers who argued that there were no grounds for treating newspaper employers less favourably than others. Thus, they now can compete on equal terms with other employers of journalists, such as broadcasters, and are in a stronger position to exploit their product in other media such as databases. Journalists are of course free to contract for all or part of the copyright despite the loss of the statutory exception but relatively few will be in a good enough bargaining position to do so individually. It should be noted, however, that works of employed journalists *made* before commencement are still subject to the journalists' exception (sch. 1, para. 11(1)).

### In the course of employment

Although the rule giving employers ownership of their employees' works is no longer subject to any specific exceptions, the employer is not entitled to *every* copyright work created by an employee, merely those created 'in the course of his employment'. The meaning of this phrase will depend on the nature of the employment and the scope of what the particular employee is employed to do. The leading case on the issue is *Stephenson Jordan & Harrison Ltd* v *MacDonald & Evans* [1952] RPC 10 where lectures given by an employed accountant (and subsequently incorporated by him in a book) did not belong to the employer even though the employer provided secretarial help and paid the employee's expenses in relation to the lectures. He was employed not to deliver public lectures but to advise clients. Therefore another section of the book based on a report written for a client did belong to the employer. Similarly, in *Byrne* v *Statist Co.* [1914] 1 KB 622 an employee of the *Financial Times* was held to be the owner of the copyright in a translation from Portuguese which he made for his employer in his own time for a separate fee since translations were not part of what he was normally employed to do. The copyright in books and articles written by employed teachers and lecturers generally belongs to the teacher or lecturer since they are usually employed to teach or to lecture rather than to write.

### Commissioned works

The other former exception to the general rule that the author is the first owner of copyright was that copyright in commissioned photographs, portraits, engravings and sound recordings belonged to the commissioner although in all other cases it remained with the author unless the commissioner stipulated for it in the contract (Copyright Act 1956, ss. 4(3) and 12(4)). The commissioner's copyright in photographs etc. has now been removed but the impact of this is partially softened by the creation of a new moral right (see chapter 8) in photographs and films commissioned for private and domestic purposes (s. 85). The result is that the copyright in wedding photographs commissioned by the bride and groom will no longer belong to them but to the photographer (unless they should have the foresight to specifically contract for the copyright) but they will still have protection by means of the new moral right against exploitations which invade their privacy.

The situation before the Act was balanced in a different way: the photographer would normally own the *negative* and could charge for prints etc. in accordance with the contract but the commissioners owned the *copyright* and could prevent any other use of the negative to which they objected. This was very useful to prevent invasions of privacy by publication of the photograph in newspapers as in *Williams* v *Settle* [1960] 1 WLR 1072 where substantial damages were awarded in relation to the use of the wedding photographs of a murder victim (see chapter 10). Similar protection would now only be available under the moral right contained in s. 85. This is of no avail to commercial commissioners who will need to take other steps to protect themselves (see below). However, careful note should be taken of an important transitional provision in sch. 1, para. 11(2). This provides that the copyright in photographs etc. made after commencement still belongs to the commissioner if the work is made in pursuance of a commission made before commencement.

The position for most commissioned works has always been that the author retains the copyright and the assimilation of photographs etc. can be viewed (and was justified in Parliament) as the removal of an anomalous exception. From a conceptual point of view, it is right for the author to be the first owner. However, the rule is not always convenient in practice. The protection of the author in commissioned copyright works contrasts sharply with s. 215(2) which gives first ownership of the design right in a commissioned design to the commissioner and not the designer (and note the similar rule for registered designs). Since the creation of a design will also generally involve the creation of a copyright (artistic) work this contrast is a potential source of friction although there are special provisions to deal with the inter-relationship between copyright and design right which will be discussed in chapter 12.

## Contractual variation of first ownership

*Legal ownership*

The employer's copyright in his employee's works is expressly made subject to contrary agreement. Section 11(1) unequivocally provides in all other cases that the author is the first owner. Thus it would appear that, employer-employee cases apart, any contractual provision cannot affect *first* ownership of copyright which the Act clearly gives to the author; there must be a *transfer* (albeit immediate) of that ownership from the author to the other party. This technicality may perhaps be dismissed as insignificant until one notices that assignments (i.e., transfers) of copyright are required to be in writing and signed by the assignor (ss. 90(3)). Thus commissioners will be well advised to make sure that there is a written agreement, signed by the author, expressed as an assignment of the copyright. The fact that the copyright may not yet have come into existence does not matter, for copyright law has an unusual, but very important provision (s. 91) permitting the assignment of future copyrights. The property right is transferred from the author to the transferee as soon as it comes into existence.

An oral agreement would not be effective to transfer the copyright automatically on creation of the work although it would give a contractual right to call for a subsequent transfer of the copyright. This would be of no avail if the author had sold the copyright (to a bona fide purchaser without notice) in advance of any assignment to the commissioner being executed. The appearance of a third-party transferee seeking to exploit the copyright work would probably be the first occasion upon which the commissioner would realise the need to take a written assignment and by then it would be too late.

The above discussion was applicable even before the 1988 Act to the majority of commissioned works and frequently created practical difficulties in design copyright cases when commissioners of designs and drawings only became aware that they lacked copyright title when they were about to take infringement proceedings. 'Getting in the title' was, and will continue to be, a frustrating and expensive experience and therefore commercial commissioners should ensure that they have something in writing signed by the other party. However, lack of formal title may not always be fatal, as the following section explains.

*Beneficial ownership*
In *Warner* v *Gestetner Ltd* [1988] EIPR D-89, an advertising agency commissioned Warner to produce drawings of cats which were to be used by Gestetner in promoting a new product at a trade fair. Gestetner subsequently used them outside the trade fair in promotional literature and Warner (who was something of an expert in cat drawings) complained that this went beyond the purpose of the agreement and infringed his copyright. There was no formal written contract, the arrangements having been made by telephone. Under the 1956 Act (and also now the 1988 Act) first ownership of the copyright was clearly with Warner, the author. However, Whitford J found that a term could be implied vesting the equitable or beneficial ownership in the commissioner. This at first sight appears to ignore the requirements of notice and signature in ss. 36 and 37 of the 1956 Act (ss. 90 and 91 of the 1988 Act). The case could have been decided more conventionally by finding that Gestetner had an implied licence to use the drawings for the purposes of promoting their business whilst leaving the copyright ownership, and with it the right to object to *other* exploitations, with Warner.

Although the provisions of the Act are capable of producing unsatisfactory results in some situations and a mechanism for avoiding a strict application may sometimes be desirable, there are forceful objections to the approach taken in *Warner* v *Gestetner Ltd*. The clear rules for first ownership established by the Act should not be muddied by the unpredictable discretion of the courts to relocate the equitable ownership. If *Warner* v *Gestetner Ltd* and the earlier cases on equitable ownership (most of which can be explained on other grounds) are correct, then the rules in s. 11 (including the employers' exception) are merely prima facie rules which can be varied by the courts where they feel it to be just (or equitable) to do so on the basis not only of express but also unwritten and implied agreements. Indeed, the House of Lords quite recently in the *Spycatcher* case, *Attorney-General* v *Guardian Newspapers Ltd (No. 2)* [1988] 3 All ER 545, indicated that the copyright in Peter Wright's revelations might well belong in equity to the Crown. If the rationale for this view is simply that the work was produced in breach of a duty of confidence to the Crown, the implications will be considerable.

Thus, whilst the safest course for a commissioner is to get a written, signed assignment of the future copyright, in the absence of this the courts may still be willing in some circumstance to recognise a contractual or equitable right of the commissioner to call for an assignment or otherwise to be treated as beneficial owner.

## Crown copyright

Since 1911 works made or published 'by or under the direction or control' of the Crown or a government department have been owned by the Crown and referred to as Crown copyright. The Whitford Committee criticised the special treatment afforded the Crown and thought that it should be treated in the same way as any other employer of authors or commissioner of works. It was critical of the vagueness of the expression 'by or under the direction or control' and was particularly hostile to the fact that publication by the Crown of a previously unpublished work vested copyright in the Crown and extinguished the original author's copyright.

Some, but not all, of these criticisms were accepted. The Crown no longer acquires copyright simply by virtue of first publication. Of greater significance, perhaps, has been the abandonment of the 'direction or control' formula. A work now only attracts Crown copyright if it is made by an officer or servant of the Crown in the course of his duties (or if it is an Act of Parliament). Commissioned works thus remain with the author and the Whitford approach of treating the Crown in the same way as any other employer as far as ownership is concerned is belatedly adopted.

The result is that many works that would previously have been automatically Crown copyright, either because published by the Crown (as with the Whitford Report itself) or because made under its direction or control, will no longer be so unless the Crown makes specific contractual provision for it. No doubt government departments will be careful to do so and will avoid the problems discussed in the previous section by ensuring that such provision is in writing and signed by the author.

## Parliamentary copyright

The above changes to Crown copyright together with the advent of the broadcasting of Parliament prompted the creation of a new category of copyright — Parliamentary copyright. This ironically retains the 'direction or control' formula but at least explains it as including 'any work made by an officer or employee' of either House 'in the course of his duties' and 'any sound recording, film, live broadcast or live cable programme of the proceedings' of either House (s. 165(4)). The fact that a work is commissioned by either House does not of itself mean that it is made under its direction or control but the circumstances *may* be such that it can be so regarded. A work can be owned by either House individually or, if it is made by or under the direction or control of both Houses, it can be owned by both Houses jointly.

Just as Acts of Parliament are now specifically stated to be Crown copyright (the right to restrain their reproduction was formerly regarded as part of the Crown prerogative), Parliamentary Bills (which would formerly have come under Crown copyright and not the prerogative) are specifically stated to come under Parliamentary copyright. The relatively short life of the copyright in Parliamentary bills has already been noted (see p. 43). Copyright in a public Bill belongs initially to the House into which the Bill is introduced and then, once it has been carried to the other House, to both Houses jointly. Parliamentary copyright does not seem to cover anything that would not previously have been Crown copyright but vesting the rights in Parliament created a need for someone to exercise those rights as the Controller of HMSO does in relation to Crown copyright. Section 167 therefore gives the job to the Speaker (for the Commons) and to the Clerk of the Parliaments (for the Lords) and also treats each House as having the legal capacities of a body corporate (for the purposes of owning copyright).

## Copyright of international organisations

This is specially provided for because of Universal Copyright Convention obligations to protect the publications of the United Nations, its specialised agencies and other similar bodies even if the publication does not qualify under the normal rules relating to the status of the author or the place of first publication. The OECD and the Council of Europe were other examples of international organisations (to be specified by Order in Council) given in the House of Lords. Most publications of international organisations would normally qualify for copyright protection on the grounds of being first published in a Convention country. The rarity of the need for this special provision was highlighted by the example of an international organisation commissioning a work from an Indonesian author which is first published in Saudi Arabia! If protection is only available via s. 168 then the period of protection is 50 years from making rather than the longer period that would ordinarily be available based on the author's life.

## Folklore

Some countries, especially developing ones, are particularly concerned to protect their folklore, i.e., unpublished works believed to come from that country but of which the author is unknown. In order to fulfil our Berne Convention obligations to provide effective means of protection for such works, s. 169 enables bodies set up in the relevant overseas countries to be designated by Order in Council as having authority to exercise the powers of copyright ownership over such works (except the power of assignment). The section only applies to unpublished works because under s. 104(4) the publisher is presumed to be the owner at the time of publication. Note that s. 169 does not apply to British folklore, presumably because we have no Convention obligations in that respect. It is clearly not envisaged that any domestic body should be given the power of protecting British folklore which does not have an identifiable owner under the normal rules.

Section 61 does provide for archival recordings of folksongs to be made by domestic designated bodies without infringing copyright in the music where the words are unpublished and of unknown authorship. This is not, however, a provision assisting enforcement of copyright but rather a provision designed to allow folklore to be preserved without infringing the copyright in the music to which the folksong is put (and also removing the risk of an action by the author of the lyrics if his or her identity should subsequently become known).

# Chapter 5 Exclusive Rights and Infringement

## Introduction

The Copyright, Designs and Patents Act 1988 confers upon the owners of copyright works exclusive rights to do, or to authorise others to do, certain acts in the UK in relation to those works. These acts are set out in s. 16 as being:

    (a)   to copy the work;
    (b)   to issue copies of the work to the public;
    (c)   to perform, show or play the work in public;
    (d)   to broadcast the work or include it in a cable programme service;
    (e)   to make an adaptation of the work or to do any of the above in relation to an adaptation.

Strictly speaking, the Act does not confer a positive right on the copyright owner to do these acts, because he himself may find that his work is derivative and has infringed somebody else's copyright. Rather, it gives the copyright owner the right to stop others infringing his copyright. For example, if Y copies a film in which X has copyright, that does not necessarily mean that X's rights in the film are unassailable. X may have infringed the copyright in Z's play, and so X would be liable to Z for infringement. X's right is merely to stop Y infringing his own copyright.

Copyright infringers are those who do any of the restricted acts, or authorise others to do such acts without authority, or who deal commercially with infringing works when they know or have reason to believe that they are infringing works. Thus, copyright infringement is the other side of the coin to any analysis of exclusive rights and so these two matters will be dealt with together.

Not all categories of copyright works carry the same exclusive rights. For example, it is an infringement of copyright to perform a literary, dramatic or musical work in public, or to play or show in public a sound recording, film or broadcast but not to show an artistic work in public, since there is no public performing right in artistic works. Even within the same category of copyright works, different rights may operate: whilst there is no rental right in relation to literary works generally, there is for one type of literary work, namely computer programs (s. 18(3), see chapter 15). Thus, it is important always to ensure that when an act of infringement is alleged, that act indeed interferes with one at least of the exclusive rights relating to that copyright work.

Infringement involves the doing of any act restricted by the copyright in a work and relates not only to interferences with the whole of a copyright work but also to interferences with any 'substantial part' of such a work. Also, infringement can occur either directly or indirectly (s. 16(3)); and the meaning of infringement is further extended by the notion of *secondary*, in addition to *primary* infringement. Examples will be given in the course of discussing the various exclusive rights.

## Exclusive right to copy a work (section 17)

*Identical copying of the whole*
Any person who makes a 'pirate' copy of a book or of a film clearly copies by reproducing the work in a material form. The simplest example of an identical copy would be reproducing a sound recording by taping it, or a book by photocopying it. The reproduction of literary, dramatic, musical or artistic works can be in 'any material form' (s. 17(2)) and so is not limited to 'carbon copies' of the copyright work in the same medium: copying a printed literary work by hand, or photographing a painting would constitute representations of the work in a material form as would the recording of a musical work.

*Substantial part*
Where only extracts are taken from a copyright work, there will be infringement if they comprise a 'substantial part' of the work. The difficult question then is to determine what proportion of a work constitutes a 'substantial part'. For example, would all or any of the following proportions of a book be a substantial part: 50%, 25%, 10%, 1%? The test is said to be one of *quality* rather than of *quantity*. Whilst the more that is taken increases the likelihood that a substantial part has been taken, quantity is not conclusive and even the copying of a small but nevertheless an important part of a work may be an infringement. It is all a matter of fact and of degree.

*Illustration 5.1* X photocopies one page from a novel of several hundred pages. This is unlikely, in itself, to be a substantial part. However, a photocopy of one page of a major report comprising the recommendations and conclusions almost certainly would be a substantial part.

*Illustration 5.2* X photocopies three chapters of a 20 chapter book. This is very likely to be a substantial part (save in exceptional cases such as *Warwick Films Productions Ltd* v *Eisinger* [1969] 1 Ch 508, discussed on p. 57).

*Illustration 5.3* In *Hawkes & Son (London) Ltd* v *Paramount Film Service Ltd* [1934] 1 Ch 593, the defendant made and distributed a newsreel showing the Prince of Wales at a school opening ceremony. At one stage of the proceedings 'a quota of noise' was contributed for the space of some 20 seconds by the march-past of a boys' band playing the 'Colonel Bogey' march. Was 20 seconds from a march lasting 4 minutes a substantial part of the copyright in the musical work? Slesser LJ said:

Anyone hearing it would know that it was the march called 'Colonel Bogey', and though it may be that it was not very prolonged in its reproduction, it is clearly . . . a substantial, a vital, and an essential part which is there reproduced.

The defendant has a number of available defences in this situation. Because of the problems broadcasters and others have in obtaining copyright clearance for all the copyright material incidentally included in artistic works, sound recordings, films and broadcasts, s. 31 provides that copyright in a work is not infringed by such 'incidental inclusion'. The newsreel is also likely to be fair dealing for the purpose of reporting current events (s. 30(2)). However, the boys' band was, and would still be, liable for performing a work in public, if no licence is obtained.

*Illustration 5.4*   X takes one short scene of less than a minute from a copyright film and uses it in an advertisement without permission. This, too, may comprise a substantial part.

The Act further provides that copying, in relation to a film, television broadcast or cable programme, includes making a photograph of the whole or any substantial part of any image-forming part of the film, broadcast or cable programme (s. 17(4)). Thus, the unauthorised copying of a 'still' frame from a film is automatically an infringement even though the still represents only a fleeting moment or 'image' from the film. The question of 'substantial part' arises only where *part of the frame* is copied *( Spelling Goldberg Productions Inc.* v *BPC Publishing Ltd* [1981] RPC 283). (There is an exception here, though, applicable to photographs of television or cable programmes made for private and domestic use; see s. 71.) When the part reproduced is not an original part of the plaintiff's work, this will not normally constitute a 'substantial' part. Thus, in *Warwick Film Productions Ltd* v *Eisinger* [1969] 1 Ch 508, the author of a copyright work on the trials of Oscar Wilde sued the defendant whose film of the life of Oscar Wilde had taken from the plaintiff's book lengthy extracts from the verbatim proceedings of the trials. However, these transcripts of the trials had, in turn, been copied by the plaintiff from an earlier work: so the court held that whilst, in quantity, the defendant had taken a significant part of the book, in qualitative terms this did not comprise a *substantial* part of the plaintiff's copyright work.

This approach is less likely to be applied where a copyright work is a compilation where greater emphasis is placed on the skill and labour involved in selecting and compiling other material.

## Similarity
More difficult to assess is the situation when a new work is created which is not an *exact* copy but draws heavily upon the whole or a substantial part of an earlier copyright work. A court must be satisfied that, objectively, there is a sufficient degree of similarity between the two works. The fact that the later work may itself attract independent copyright protection does not necessarily mean that there has been no infringement of a substantial part of an earlier work. For example, where a person writes a novel which incorporates many of the same characters and incidents of an earlier work, it may be difficult to decide whether or not a

substantial part of the earlier work has been taken. In a famous American case (*Nichols* v *Universal Pictures Corporation* (1930) 45 F 2d 119) Learned Hand J said at p. 121:

> Upon any work . . . a great number of patterns of increasing generality will fit equally well, as more and more of the incident is left out. The last may perhaps be no more than the most general statement of what the play is about, and at times might consist only of its title; but there is a point in this series of abstractions where they are no longer protected, since otherwise the playwright could prevent the use of his 'ideas', to which, apart from their expression, his property is never extended . . . .
>
> If *Twelfth Night* were copyrighted, it is quite possible that a second comer might so closely imitate Sir Toby Belch or Malvolio as to infringe, but it would not be enough that for one of his characters he cast a riotous knight who kept wassail to the discomfort of the household, or a vain and foppish steward who became amorous of his mistress. These would be no more than Shakespeare's 'ideas' in the play, as little capable of monopoly as Einstein's doctrine of relativity, or Darwin's theory of the origin of species. It follows that the less developed the characters, the less they can be copyrighted; that is the penalty an author must bear for marking them too indistinctly.

In *Ravenscroft* v *Herbert* [1980] RPC 193, however, where this point was acknowledged, the court nevertheless found that the defendant's novel had incorporated large chunks of documented history and other information painstakingly researched by the plaintiff for his novel, and such use went far beyond what was permissible. The court here was prepared to give greater weight to the skill and labour employed by the plaintiff in *compiling* his material than to the claim of the defendant that he was entitled to take historical fact wholesale.

Whether or not a substantial part of sufficient similarity has been taken from an earlier work may well differ depending upon the type of copyright work involved. It will normally be permissible to copy and use factual material from previous works to a greater extent than non-factual: it may be more difficult to establish that the use of considerable material from a historic work is the taking of a substantial part compared with the taking of material from a novel.

Musical infringement actions are often very difficult to decide, and a court may be subjected for days to a range of musical recordings and of musical experts, all 'assisting' the judge to reach his decision. In the well-known case of *Francis Day & Hunter Ltd* v *Bron* [1963] Ch 587, the plaintiffs, who owned the copyright in a once highly popular tune composed in 1926, 'In a Little Spanish Town', alleged that the defendant's song 'Why' which was composed in 1959, infringed that copyright. The only connection between the two pieces of music was in the first eight bars, although one was in 3/4 time and one in 4/4 time. The court accepted that there was similarity in relation to a substantial part, but had it been established that the composer of 'Why' had copied? Surprisingly, the court held that copying need not necessarily be a conscious act; it was possible in law to copy subsconsciously, although the court was not satisfied that this had happened here.

More recently, in *EMI Publishing* v *Papathanasiou* (1987), the composer of the acclaimed theme for the film *Chariots of Fire* was sued for copyright infringement of an earlier similar work. The court decided that, although there was some resemblance between the works, it was in the four notes which were a musical commonplace and so the resemblance was a coincidence: the plaintiff failed either to establish the taking of a 'substantial part' or the causal link essential to conscious or unconscious copying.

### Typographical arrangements

Although the primary protection for typographical arrangements is against those who make facsimile copies of the whole work, the protection will also extend to those who, for example, photocopy substantial parts of a book. Again, it is a matter of fact and degree whether what has been copied constitutes a substantial part. Thus, if a student were to photocopy just a page he might maintain that there was no infringement at all; it might then be arguable that a person could take multiple copies of such a small amount of material. However, in determining whether a substantial part has been taken, the court would interpret the Act in its whole context and, bearing in mind the varying provisions designed to curtail multiple copying, might hold copying in these circumstances to be of a substantial part: anything *worth* multiple copying is likely, qualitatively, to be regarded as substantial.

### Direct and indirect copying

Infringement of copyright may take place either directly or indirectly (s. 16(3)(b)).

*Illustration 5.5*   X has artistic copyright in a painting. Y copies a photograph of the painting and exploits it. Y has, by copying the photograph, indirectly infringed the copyright in the painting.

*Illustration 5.6*   X has copyright in a novel. Y makes a film based on the novel. Z makes a pirate copy of the copyright film. Amongst the copyright infringements which Z commits would be the indirect copying of the novel upon which the film is based.

### Copying in different dimensions

In relation to an *artistic* work, copying includes the making of a copy in three dimensions of a two-dimensional work and the making of a copy in two dimensions of a three-dimensional work (s. 17(3)).

*Illustration 5.7*   In *Bradbury, Agnew & Co v Day* [1916] 32 TLR 349, the plaintiffs owned the copyright in a cartoon in *Punch*, 'Dropping the Pilot'. Actors enacted the cartoon on stage by dressing up and posing to look like the original. This constituted three-dimensional infringement of the two-dimensional cartoon.

*Illustration 5.8*   A owns the artistic copyright in the drawings of a building. B, who has seen the drawings, verbally directs C, who has not, to construct a building in accordance with the drawings. Provided B's verbal description conveys to C the essence of the drawings, C is *indirectly* copying in three dimensions A's copyright drawings.

### Important qualifications

Until 1988, the ability to prevent the three-dimensional copying of two-dimensional artistic works was of major importance in industry: any industrial objects produced from drawings which were copied by competitors could be protected because there would be indirect three-dimensional reproduction of the copyright in the two-dimensional drawings.

*Illustration 5.9*   X makes furniture based upon prior drawings in which copyright still subsists. Y copies the furniture. This constituted indirect three-dimensional reproduction of the drawings and was actionable even though the furniture as opposed to the drawings was not a copyright work (which it would not be unless it qualified as a work of artistic craftsmanship).

However, the situation has now changed. Under the 1988 Act (apart from transitional provisions) it is no longer an infringement of any copyright in a *design document* or *model recording* or *embodying a design* to make an article to that design or to copy an article made to that design (s. 51). However, it may be infringement of the new unregistered design right, which is dealt with in more detail in chapter 12.

### Copying in different dimensions is limited to artistic works

It is not possible to infringe copyright in works other than artistic works by reproducing them in another dimension. For example, X has the literary copyright in a book which incorporates instructions on how to manufacture a product. Y manufactures products in accordance with the instructions. Although Y has indirectly reproduced in three dimensions the two-dimensional literary instructions, this does not constitute copyright infringement (*Brigid Foley Ltd* v *Ellott* [1982] RPC 433). Thus, a woolly jumper could not be an infringing copy of the knitting pattern from which it was made.

## Parody and burlesque

Where a copyright work is subjected to satire, parody or burlesque, it is essential to conjure up or reproduce the work itself, or its essential qualities, otherwise the satire, parody or burlesque fails in its objective. This immediately suggests that such use is likely to involve the taking of a substantial part of the copyright work. If so, does it mean that major constraints can be imposed on parody and satire, possibly threatening freedom to parody or satirise copyright works? Such a possibility has been questioned because it is acknowledged that they are important art-forms and deserving of substantial freedom, both as entertainment and as forms of social and literary criticism, sometimes of more lasting significance than the original works themselves.

Accordingly it has been argued that special rules ought to apply to confer greater freedom on the satirist to make use of copyright works. On occasion the courts have exercised considerable leniency in sanctioning the use of material for purposes of satire. More recently, however, it has been emphasised that there are no special tests which have to be applied: the question remains, does the parody or satire reproduce a substantial part of the copyright work? In assessing this flexible concept a court will consider whether or not such references have been made as are necessary to enable an audience to 'conjure up' the satirised work or whether the so-called satirist or parodist has used far more of the work and, indeed, has gone beyond what is necessary for satire in order to enable him commercially to exploit another's work.

*Illustration 5.10* In *Williamson Music Ltd* v *Pearson Partnership Ltd* [1987] FSR 97, the plaintiff owned the copyright in the words and music of the musical show, *South Pacific*. The defendant produced a lengthy advertisement for a national bus company in which the words of one of the pieces were modified and parodied but the same musical tune used. It was held that this was a taking of a substantial part of the author's work.

*Illustration 5.11* In *Schweppes Ltd* v *Wellingtons Ltd* [1984] FSR 210, the plaintiff claimed that its copyright in the 'Schweppes' Indian tonic water label was infringed by the defendant who used a similar label with the word 'Schlurppes'. The defence that this was a joke in the nature of a caricature cut no ice with the court. Parody was no defence.

It should be noticed that two other factors may be brought into play in balancing the interest of the author of the copyright work and the satirist or parodist. First, the author will be entitled to exercise his moral right of paternity and integrity to restrain certain types of derogatory treatment (see chapter 8). Secondly, however, it may also be possible for the satirist or parodist to rely upon the defence of fair dealing for the purposes of criticism or review. The court often will be able to exercise reasonable judgment in moderating between two important rights.

### Issuing copies to the public

The copyright owner of most works has the exclusive rights to issue copies of the work to the public; and if anybody else first issues the work to the public without authority, he will be an infringer (s. 18(1)).

However, 'issuing to the public' has a limited meaning in that it refers to putting copies of the work into circulation anywhere in the world *for the first time* (s. 18(2)). Where X has already marketed copies of his copyright work and Y subsequently markets pirate copies, Y will not be infringing the exclusive right to issue copies of the work to the public, although, of course, he will be infringing other rights. Thus, infringement of this exclusive right is relatively rare since in most cases the copyright owner will himself have issued, or authorised issues, of copies to the public first.

Thereafter, the copyright owner *normally* has no further rights in connection with the subsequent distribution of these copies.

## Rental rights

An important new extension of this exclusive right of issuing copies to the public has been introduced by the 1988 Act in relation to *sound recordings, films* and *computer programs* so as to include any rental of copies to the public (s. 18(2)). 'Rental' includes any arrangements under which a copy is made available commercially on terms that it will or may be returned (s. 178). This new rental right in the case of sound recordings and films is given to the owners of copyright in those works (normally the producers) but the copyright owners of the underlying rights in the works included in the sound recordings or films do not have a rental right (see chapter 13).

## The performing right

*Performing, showing or playing a work in public (s. 19)*
The performing right is an important source of income for many copyright owners. It applies to public performances of literary, dramatic or musical works and to the playing or showing in public of copyright sound recordings, films, broadcasts and cable programmes.

*Illustration 5.12*   X arranges for the public performance of a copyright play. The licence of the copyright owner is required.

*Illustration 5.12*   X's musical work is performed at a live concert. His consent for such a performance is required.

   The performing rights for the exploitation of music are normally administered by licensing bodies, for example, the PRS. Copyright owners of works normally assign or license the performing and related rights to the licensing body which then grants either blanket licences or specific licences, to businesses and organisations on various terms to reflect the use being made of the relevant works; and copyright owners are reimbursed for the use of their public performing rights (see chapter 7).

*Illustration 5.14*   X has copyright in a painting which is owned by Y. Y places the painting on public exhibition. There is no infringement since the public performing right does not extend to artistic works (but note the possibility of three-dimensional reproduction as in *Bradbury, Agnew & Co* v *Day,* see page 59).

*What is meant by performing in 'public'?*
Whilst there is no statutory definition of the word 'public', the authorities suggest that the performance of the work must be in the presence of persons who are not part of the 'domestic or quasi-domestic' circle. The courts have tended to give the term a wide meaning, taking into account in borderline cases whether or not the performance is one for which the copyright owner deserves to be paid a licence fee.

*Illustration 5.15*   A copyright play is produced by a local Women's Institute for the benefit of the members of that Institute alone. Even though the numbers of persons able to see the play will be limited and access is restricted, this is not a performance to a domestic or quasi-domestic circle and a licence is required (*Jennings* v *Stephens* [1936] Ch 469).

*Illustration 5.16*  Music is played over loudspeakers in a record shop (*Performing Right Society Ltd* v *Harlequin Record Shops Ltd* [1979] FSR 233); or to workers in a factory (*Ernest Turner Electrical Instruments Ltd* v *Performing Right Society Ltd* [1943] Ch 167). These are performances in public. Apart from the nature of the audience, other relevant factors would include the size of the audience and payment.

*Illustration 5.17*  Music is played over the telephone whilst callers are waiting to be connected. Such playing constitutes 'public performance' and a licence for this playing is required.

*Illustration 5.18*  X owns a hotel and provides radio and television sets in public rooms.
   Guests are members of the public. It is here, though, that it becomes important to analyse the various rights involved. The performing rights in underlying works (literary, dramatic and musical, but not artistic, since there is no performance right for artistic works) have to be authorised and hotel licences from, for example, the PRS would be required. What though of all the other copyright interests? Here, the exceptions begin to take effect. Thus, the Copyright Act 1956, s. 40, provided that where a person caused a sound recording or film to be performed in public simply by receiving the broadcast he did not thereby infringe copyright in the sound recording, and as far as the film was concerned, he was treated as if he had been granted a licence by the owner of copyright in the film; and the copyright in the television and sound broadcasts were not infringed by public performance unless they were seen or heard by a paying public. The situation is the same under the 1988 Act (see p. 80-1).

*Illustration 5.19*  X plays records and video films in the lounge of his hotel. Licences in respect of the underlying rights are required. What of the rights in the sound recordings and films? The Copyright Act 1956, s. 12(7), allowed *sound recordings* to be played without the consent of the owner of those rights at premises where persons reside or sleep and where the recordings were played as part of the amenities provided exclusively or mainly for the residents, provided no special admission charge was made. Thus, ordinarily, no licence would be required for the sound recording right, but would be for the film. Under the 1988 Act the exemption relating to the sound recording right in this situation has also been removed, and so licences would be required (see p. 80).

*Illustration 5.20*  X, the hotel owner, transmits video films from a central video cassette recorder to television receivers in guest rooms. Can it be argued that, as each receiver plays to guests in the privacy of their rooms (a domestic or quasi-domestic situation?), there is no performance in public? The better view is that X is providing a service for *all* the guests; that, together, they form a portion of the copyright owner's public and they each see the films as members of sections of the public.

*Illustration 5.21*   X produces a play and Y is a performer in the play, which takes place without consent before an audience in a public theatre. Both X and Y are liable for infringement of the performing right.

*Illustration 5.22*   X produces and records a private performance of a play in which Y is a performer. Z shows the *recording* of the performance in public. Z is liable for infringing, *inter alia,* the performing right in the play (s. 19(2)(b)). Unless X or Y purport to authorise Z to show the recording, they are not themselves liable for infringing the performing right in that case.

## Broadcasting and cable rights

Copyright owners have the exclusive right to broadcast their works or include them in a cable programme service. This right applies to all works except the typographical arrangement of published editions (s. 20). See Chapter 16 for further discussion of broadcasting and cable.

## Adaptations

*Making adaptations*
Should the owner of copyright works have any rights to control modifications of works from one genre to another (for example, making a film from a copyright novel) or alterations of a work within the same genre, for example, changing the arrangements for a musical work? In some cases, though not all, such modifications could involve infringements of moral rights. In addition, however, the copyright in a literary, dramatic or musical work carries an exclusive right 'to make an adaptation of the work' (s. 16(1)(e)).
'Adaptation' is defined very carefully.
In relation to a literary or dramatic work, 'adaptation' is defined by s. 21(3)(a) to mean:

(a)   a translation of the work;
(b)   a version of a dramatic work in which it is converted into a non-dramatic form or vice versa;
(c)   a version of the work in which the story or the action is conveyed wholly or mainly by means of pictures in a form suitable for reproduction in a book, newspaper or journal.

*Illustration 5.23*   Y translates X's English novel into a foreign language without authority. Although every word of the translation may be different, it is nevertheless an adaptation and actionable.
The concept of 'translation' is also applied to the unauthorised use of computer programs when the copyright program is converted into or out of one computer language or code into another. This is dealt with in more detail in chapter 15.

*Illustration 5.24* Y makes a film based upon X's copyright play. Y's film, if substantially similar to the play, infringes the copyright in X's dramatic work.

*Illustration 5.25* Y published in a newspaper without X's authority, a strip-cartoon version of X's copyright book. This is an infringing adaptation.

'Adaptation', in relation to a musical work, means an arrangement or transcription of the work (s. 21(3)(b)). It should be noted here that the owner of a musical work has copyright control over all arrangements or transcriptions of the work and the author (i.e., the composer), whether or not he retains ownership of the copyright, has a moral right of integrity to object to derogatory treatment including an arrangement or transcription of a musical work, provided it involves more than simply a change of key or register (see chapter 8).

*Exclusive right over adaptations (s. 21(2))*
The rights of the owner of copyright in a literary, dramatic or musical work to restrict the making of adaptations of the work also extend to rights over the adaptations themselves. Thus, the copyright owner can exercise any of the exclusive rights appropriate to such adaptations. For example, he can restrain the public performance or broadcasting of an arrangement of his musical composition, whether or not the making of the arrangement was itself an infringement. (In certain cases, though, express or implied licences could affect this position.)

*Adaptations and the idea-expression dichotomy*
The specific types of adaptation which are mentioned in the Act and which have already been examined are such as to enlarge the concept of 'expression' in favour of the copyright owner. Apart from these special cases, the general law of copyright may still enable a court to decide, for example, that a person who uses a sufficient number of ideas, incidents and characters from a protected literary work may be infringing because he is taking a substantial part of the work, notwithstanding the limited amount of copying of the exact wording of the copyright work.

To ensure that the 'adaptation' provisions do not restrict this freedom of the court to determine such matters, there is an enigmatic provision that 'No inference shall be drawn from s. 21 [the section relating to adaptation] as to what does or does not amount to copying a work'! Thus, for example, a *literary work* used in a film does not fall within the scope of 'adaptation' but it could still be 'copying', that is, 'reproducing the work in any material form'.

## Primary and secondary infringement

*Primary infringers* are those who:

(a)    themselves commit an infringing act; or
(b)    authorise another to commit an infringing act (s. 16(2)).

*Secondary infringers* are, broadly speaking, those who do not themselves

infringe or authorise others to infringe but who deal commercially with
infringing copies or articles or premises to be used for infringement (ss. 22-26).

The significance of the distinction between primary and secondary infringers is
that primary infringers are liable even though they are neither aware, nor have
any reason to believe, that they are infringing copyright (although innocent
infringers may be able to avoid paying damages, see chapter 10). Secondary
infringers formerly were only liable if they had *actual* knowledge that the articles
they were dealing with were in fact infringing articles. Under the 1988 Act
secondary infringers are now liable if they know, *or have reason to believe,* that
the article in question is an infringing article, which means that they can be liable,
in effect, for negligence.

Some of these concepts require more detailed examination.

### Primary infringement

Whilst there is usually no difficulty in identifying the person who commits an
infringing act as a primary infringer, there is more difficulty in connection with
the concept of authorisation. For example, is a university library which provides
photocopying equipment for the use of students thereby liable for authorising a
student to commit an infringing act; or is a shop which rents out cassettes or sells
cassette recorders which may, and most likely will, be used for infringing
purposes, liable for authorising such infringements.

The term 'authorised' could be interpreted very broadly and encompass these
actions by providing that a person 'authorises' another to infringe copyright
when he sanctions, approves or countenances the commission of an infringing
act by another, or simply permits another to commit an infringing act. On the
other hand, the courts could take a more restrictive view of the concept of
authorisation and insist, for example, that a person will only be liable for
another's infringing act if he has some form of *control* over the infringer, or if he
grants or purports to grant the infringer the right to commit the act in question.
The courts have adopted the latter approach.

*Illustration 5.26*   X represents the owners of copyright in musical works and
sound recordings. Y manufactures 'tape-to-tape' cassette recorders designed
specifically to enable one cassette to be recorded on to another cassette on the
same machine at high speed. Although it is possible for such machines to be used
to copy non-infringing material, almost inevitably, such machines will be used
for infringing purposes. Can Y be liable for 'authorising' such acts either by
selling the machines or by advertising that such machines can be used for copying
cassettes? Does it matter whether such advertisements contain a simple notice
referring users to the laws of copyright?

In *CBS Songs Ltd* v *Amstrad Consumer Electronics plc* [1988] 2 WLR 1191, the
House of Lords took a very restrictive approach to the concept of authorisation
holding that there was no authorisation simply by supplying another with
equipment which could be used either for infringing or non-infringing purposes,
notwithstanding the fact that most users would be infringing users; nor were the
manufacturers liable for advertising that such machines could be used for
recording 'your favourite cassette'. The fact that there was a small notice,
reminding users that copying some material requires consent, albeit it would in

the main be ignored by users, was an important factor in the decision that no authorisation had taken place. (The topic of audio and video recording will be covered in more detail in chapter 13.)

Thus the concept of authorisation must involve one person purporting to grant to another the right to do an infringing act or requesting him to do that particular act, or when there is some control over that other person failing to take reasonable steps to prevent the infringement by exercising that control. Of the examples given at the start of this section, only that relating to the university library has been held to amount to authorisation and that was in an Australian case (where there was little or no attempt at supervision or control). The difficulty in succeeding on the authorisation issue was one reason why the rental right was introduced (see chapter 13).

### Secondary infringement (ss. 22-26)
Secondary infringers are essentially those who deal commercially with infringing copies or the means to make such copies. It also covers those who provide the premises or apparatus for infringing performances. Thus, where a person possesses infringing copies in the course of a business and/or deals with them in this way, or even when the infringing copies are distributed otherwise than in the course of a business to such an extent as to affect prejudicially the owner of the copyright, or when a person imports infringing copies into the UK otherwise than for private and domestic use, there is liability for secondary infringement. As always with secondary infringement the infringer must know or have reason to believe that the copy is an infringing one.

### Articles specifically designed for making infringing copies
Secondary infringement also occurs when a person makes, or commercially deals with, or imports into the UK, an article 'specifically designed or adapted' for making copies of a work, knowing or having reason to believe that it is to be used to make infringing copies (s. 24(1)).

This provision is intended to be read narrowly and apparently is not aimed at the manufacturer of equipment which can be put to both infringing and non-infringing use. The manufacturers of cassette recorders were not liable as primary infringers in the *Amstrad* case, and will not be liable either as secondary infringers. The section is aimed at articles to be used for infringement on a commercial scale. It seems that the article must be specifically designed for copying *that* particular work, e.g., a mould, and would not include, say, a photocopier. See also, p. 167 on devices designed to circumvent copy protection.

### Permitting the use of premises for infringing performances
Where the copyright in a literary, dramatic or musical work is infringed by a performance at a place of public entertainment, the person who gave permission for that place to be used for the performance is also liable for the infringements unless, when he gave permission, he believed on reasonable grounds that the performance would not infringe copyright (s. 25(1)).

The expression 'place of public entertainment' includes premises which are occupied mainly for other purposes but are from time to time made available for hire for the purposes of public entertainment.

*Illustration 5.27* A school authorises the performance of a copyright play although no consent had been given by the copyright owner. The school authorities are liable for permitting the use of its premises for such a performance.

*Illustration 5.28* A farmer allows his land to be used from time to time for a folk festival. The farmer is under an obligation, if he is to avoid liability for secondary infringement, to ensure that the appropriate licences have been obtained.

### Provision of apparatus for infringing performances

Where copyright in a work is infringed by a public performance of the work, or by the playing or showing of the work in public by means of apparatus for playing sound recordings or showing films, or other similar means, a number of persons connected with this may be liable for secondary infringement; first, the supplier of the apparatus, or a substantial part of it; secondly, the occupier of premises who gave permission for the apparatus to be brought on to it; and thirdly, the person who supplied a copy of a sound recording or film which is put to infringing use, provided, in all cases, that such persons knew, or had reason to believe, that the appropriate infringement would take place (s. 26).

### Parallel imports

In most circumstances, once a copyright owner, or licensee, sells or otherwise parts with an article containing a copyright work, for example, a book or a sound or video recording, the copyright owner cannot thereafter control the further sale or other transfer of that article to other parties. Provided the article is not itself put to further infringing use, for example, by being copied or by being performed in public without permission, the rights of the copyright owner have been 'exhausted'. (That principle has now been modified in relation to sound recordings, films and computer programs by the creation of a rental right, see p. 62.)

The rights of copyright owners, however, are primarily national and the question often arises whether the owners of copyright in this country can exercise any control over the importation of articles containing copyright material from abroad. In so far as such articles contain copyright material which has been produced by persons with no authority to do so, then the copyright owner or licensee in this country has no difficulty in demonstrating that the importers are liable for secondary infringements, provided it can be shown that they knew, or had reason to believe, that the articles were infringing articles.

A more difficult problem, however, arises when the imported articles containing copyright material were made lawfully abroad by, or with the consent of, the UK copyright owner. There may be good reason why the UK copyright owner or licensee would want to resist the importation of articles legitimately produced abroad: for example, price differential, or because the UK owner wants to exploit the copyright work in one medium, for example, by way of cinema distribution, before permitting another method of exploitation, for example, video, to affect his market. Can the UK copyright owner control the entry of such articles if they were made legitimately abroad? The answer may differ depending on whether or not the importation is from a member State of the EEC.

Where the importation is from a non-EEC country, the legislation provides that such imported copies are infringing copies if, *had they been made in the UK,* such a making would have constituted an infringement of the copyright in the work in question, or a breach of an exclusive licence agreement relating to that work (s. 27(3)).

Thus, the legislation has created a 'hypothetical manufacture' test: had the goods not been made abroad, but in the UK, there is liability if such a manufacture in the UK would have constituted infringement. What the legislation does not say is *who* is supposed to be the 'hypothetical manufacturer'. The answer to the hypothetical manufacturer test will clearly differ depending upon whether he is deemed to be the *importer* of the copy into the UK or the *actual manufacturer* of the copy abroad.

English case law so far (see *CBS United Kingdom Ltd* v *Charmdale Record Distributors Ltd* [1981] Ch 91) regards the *actual* manufacturer as the hypothetical manufacturer for these purposes (unlike, for example, Australian law where the legislation specifically states that the hypothetical manufacturer is the importer).

*Illustration 5.29*   O is the owner of the copyright in a book. O sells the book in the UK and also in the USA at different prices. P buys the book in the USA at a low price, imports into the UK and undercuts O's prices for the book in the UK. Here, the actual manufacturer of the book in the USA, O, is also the hypothetical manufacturer in the UK. Had O made the book in the UK, this would not have been an infringement and so there is nothing to stop P from selling the book in this country.

*Illustration 5.30*   O is the owner of the copyright in a sound recording. O grants an exclusive licence to X (UK) to manufacture and distribute the record in the UK and an exclusive licence to Y (USA) to manufacture and distribute the record in the USA. P purchases records from Y in the USA cheaply, imports them into the UK and sells them at a lower price than the UK exclusive licensee, X. In this case the actual manufacturer of the records is Y in the USA; if Y is also deemed to be the hypothetical manufacturer then Y's hypothetical manufacture of the record in the UK would be an infringement of O's and X's rights. Thus, both O and X can sue P for importing these copyright sound recordings into the UK.

*Illustration 5.31*   Assume the same situation as above, save that the exclusive licensee Y is given the licence to manufacture and sell in France, a member State of the EEC, rather than in the USA and P imports into the UK records purchased from Y in France. In this situation once O has agreed to license his rights within the EEC, then his right is exhausted and neither he, nor any licensee, can exercise any copyright rights to prevent the free movement of the copyright articles between member States (s. 27(5); see also chapter 9).

# Chapter 6 Permitted Acts

## Introduction

Chapter 5 outlined the positive side of what constitutes infringement whereas the present chapter examines the permitted acts which operate as qualifications or exceptions to the meaning of infringement. If something is permitted under these provisions then it is not an infringement of copyright, notwithstanding that it would otherwise come within the normal definition of infringement.

The new provisions dealing with permitted acts contain almost as many sections as did the whole of the 1956 Act. This chapter therefore will concentrate on the provisions which are of most general application leaving the provisions aimed specifically at education and libraries and the provisions relating to design right and video and sound recordings to be discussed in more detail in the chapters devoted to those topics.

It should be stressed, as is made clear in s. 28(1), that the defences or immunities given by the various permitted acts are only in relation to infringement of copyright and do not mean that there may not be other legal rights infringed. For example, reproducing a copyright work may not be an infringement of copyright if it is within the fair dealing exception but it might still be a breach of contract or of confidence if access to the work was given in the first place only in return for a promise not to reproduce or disseminate it. The licensing of computer software is a good example of an area where the limitations imposed by the contractual licence may be as important as restrictions imposed by the law of copyright.

Before looking at the various permitted acts set out in the statute it is worth mentioning one former provision which is no longer retained, the statutory recording licence, which, as its name suggests, was more in the nature of a compulsory licence than a permitted act but which demonstrates quite well the interrelationship between permitted acts and licensing provisions. It was formerly provided for in s. 8 of the 1956 Act whereby once the owner of a musical copyright had allowed one recording of the work to be made for retail sale, others were entitled to make their own recordings (cover versions) on payment of a 6.25% royalty. Although the Whitford Committee recommended the retention of the provision, the White Paper found that it had since outlived its usefulness and decided that 'the recording of music would be better left to the operation of the competitive forces in the market'. (The transitional provisions provide that any notice given under s. 8 of the 1956 Act prior to the commencement of the 1988 Act will continue in force for one year.) The result is likely to be a licensing scheme, negotiated between the relevant collecting societies (such as the Mechanical Copyright Protection Society) and the recording companies, to replace the statutory scheme. (There is an international agreement of societies administering rights of recording and mechanical reproduction in Europe, BIEM, and it is likely that this agreement will be extended to cover the UK.) Such licensing schemes are an increasingly important way of enforcing and exploiting copyright and one encouraged by various provisions of the Act. The Copyright Tribunal is given the job of resolving disputes arising in connection with such schemes and the scope of the various permitted acts discussed in this chapter should be considered in conjunction with the availability of these schemes which are further discussed in chapter 7. Such schemes underline the point that whatever is done with the licence of the copyright owner is a permitted act and the following provisions that we will look at are merely those where an act is deemed to be permitted by the statute irrespective of the copyright owner's wishes and without the need for a licence.

One further preliminary point is that the question of infringement can only arise if the whole or a substantial part of the work is taken (see chapter 5), reliance on any of the permitted acts only being necessary once it is shown that this requirement is satisfied.

## Fair dealing

Fair dealing is in practice the most general and perhaps the most important defence or permitted act in relation to copyright. In the 1956 Act, it was only available in relation to Part I works. The provisions of the 1988 Act are no longer quite so restricted but fair dealing is still not indiscriminately available for every type of work.

The first limitation on fair dealing is that it is only available (as under the 1956 Act) for the following three purposes:

(a)  research or private study,
(b)  criticism or review,
(c)  reporting current events.

In respect of the latter two, there must normally be an acknowledgement of the copyright work and of its author.

Attempts were made to provide a generally applicable fair-dealing defence which would be available in respect of any dealing with a work which 'does not conflict with the normal exploitation of the work and does not unreasonably prejudice the copyright owner's legitimate interests' as was recommended in the Whitford Report. However, the government's view was that this would be too wide and imprecise and thus the Act retains only the three allowable purposes set out above, each of which we shall now examine in turn.

*Fair dealing for research or private study (s. 29)*
This exception is the easiest to take advantage of in the sense that no acknowledgement of the copyright or its owner is required and thus it can be done quite informally and without any disclosure at all. The word 'dealing' is to be understood more in the sense of 'use', rather than as requiring any transaction, so that copying a work in the privacy of one's home could count as fair dealing even though no one else is involved. (The government resisted attempts to change the term to 'fair use' to bring it into line with the equivalent defence in the USA, largely on the grounds that the sense of 'fair dealing' in this country was already well established, at least amongst lawyers.)

The exception only applies to literary, dramatic, musical and artistic works (as under the 1956 Act) with the inclusion now of the typographical arrangement of published editions. Thus it still does not apply to sound recordings, films, broadcasts and cable programmes. The significance of this is reduced for broadcasts and cable programmes (and works included in them) by s. 70 which authorises time-shifting for private purposes but the copying of sound recordings and films themselves (other than when included in a broadcast) continues to be unlawful and outside the terms of any fair dealing or other analogous defence. (There are also special provisions relating to educational recording of broadcasts, see chapter 14.) Of course, much home taping might not be regarded as fair anyway but the failure to solve the home-taping problem with a blank tape levy or by any other mechanism means that it is also still unlawful to make a tape of a disc (for which you have paid full price) in order to be able to listen to it in your car (see further chapter 13)

Private study is not defined but case law has established that the private study (or research) must be that of the person claiming the defence. Thus in *Sillitoe* v *McGraw-Hill Book Co. (UK) Ltd* [1983] FSR 545 the publishers of *Study Notes* (on various set texts for school students) which reproduced passages from the original works could not rely on the defence because, *inter alia*, the private study was to be undertaken by the students (who were not the alleged infringers) rather than by the publishers.

What was not entirely clear was whether fair dealing could apply where the copying was done on behalf of or at the specific request of the person doing the research or private study. Section 29(3) now makes it clear that the copying can be done by another person on behalf of the researcher or student so that, for example, a teacher or lecturer, having access to a photocopier, could copy a periodical article on behalf of an individual student. Lest this should tempt the thought that a class set could be provided by all the members of a class separately asking for an individual copy for their own private study, the clause was substantially modified at a late stage to specifically exclude copying from fair dealing if 'the person doing the copying knows or has reason to believe that it will result in copies of substantially the same material being provided to more than one person at substantially the same time and for substantially the same purpose'. This makes it clear that fair dealing for research or private study only covers the production of single and not multiple copies.

It is not possible to be so dogmatic about the quantity of material that can be copied (as opposed to the quantity of copies to be made). Authors and publishers tend to think in terms of low percentages and fixed word limits (10% or 4,000 to

8,000 words depending on the number of extracts, was the essence of their now withdrawn statement of what they would regard as fair dealing) but those seeking to engage in research or private study obviously take a more expansive view. Copying individual journal articles is regarded by some as *capable* of being fair and yet many articles are longer than some books so it is tempting to conclude that it may be permissible in some cases to copy the whole of a book. Publishers would respond that whilst it *may* be fair to copy a single article rather than having to buy a whole issue of a journal, if one wants the whole of a book, the fairest solution is to purchase it.

Fixed proportions or quantities cannot hope to cater for the wide range of situations that can arise and the whole point of the adoption of an open-ended term such as 'fair dealing' is to provide flexibility. Relevant factors will include such matters as whether the copying deprives the copyright owner of a sale which he could otherwise expect to make as well as more obvious matters such as the size or proportion of the extracts copied.

The type of research permissible was a particularly controversial issue in the Parliamentary debates, the Bill initially excluding *commercial* research from fair dealing. Much of British industry, particularly that part which is science or technology based, justifies a great deal of copying, particularly photocopying, of copyright works on the basis that it is fair dealing for the purpose of research. It was argued (successfully) on its behalf that to exclude commercial research would impose additional costs on industry which would decrease its world-wide competitiveness and that any revenue raised would be swallowed up by the administrative costs of collecting it. (It is worth noting that the efficient collection of royalties in other contexts, e.g., performing rights, does not seem to have been too difficult to achieve.) Nevertheless, these arguments, coupled with perceived difficulties for librarians and others having to distinguish between commercial and other research, ultimately won the day and 'research' remains unqualified as it was under the 1956 Act. Those dissatisfied with this conclusion were able to take some solace from the the fact that the express denial that multiple copying can amount to fair dealing in this context means that some of the larger-scale abuses complained of by copyright owners, such as the circulation of multiple copies within large companies, will clearly now be unlawful (unless licensed, e.g., through the CLA; see further, chapter 7).

The meaning of 'fair dealing' for research or private study is also important in determining the scope of some special provisions relating to libraries and archives which are further discussed in chapter 14.

*Fair dealing for the purposes of criticism or review (s. 30(1))*
This exception operates quite differently from the previous type of fair dealing in that typically it will involve not merely the production of a single copy for the researcher or student but the publication of large numbers of copies in a newspaper, journal or book or the dissemination of the work through a film or broadcast. It is clear from s. 30 that the criticism or review may be of the copyright work itself or of another work or even of the performance of a work. For example, one may wish to quote from one author in order to make a (favourable or unfavourable) comparison with or comment about the work actually being criticised or reviewed.

This type of fair dealing applies to *all* categories of work. This is a significant change from the 1956 Act and means that, for example, clips from films could be used on television without infringing copyright and without the owners' permission. However, television reviewers and critics are unlikely to find that they can operate independently of the film producers as far as newly released films are concerned since they need to get hold of legitimate copies of the films in the first place. Nevertheless, films available in the shops in video cassette form (the same would be true of sound recordings) could no doubt be used without consent and be the subject of entertaining (and cheap to produce) review programmes provided the extracts broadcast came within a court's perception of fair dealing.

Again the amount that can be legitimately reproduced is not susceptible to hard-and-fast rules, although it is probably true to say that extracts permissible under this exception will generally tend to be shorter than those permitted under research or private study since the copies are being published rather than being used by one individual. In the *Sillitoe* case above, the extracts in the study aids were sought to be excused under this head too but the extracts (about 5% of the works copied) were held to be unnecessarily long for the amount of comment. Similarly, the defence failed in *Independent Television Publications Ltd* v *Time Out Ltd* [1984] FSR 64 (see page 21), where the purpose was clearly not so much criticism or review but the provision of a (rival) listing service. Competing with the copyright owner usually results in a finding that the dealing is not fair.

On the other hand, in *Hubbard* v *Vosper* [1972] 2 QB 84, Lord Denning MR was prepared to sanction the inclusion in the defendant's book of lengthy extracts from L. Ron Hubbard's writings on scientology as they were included purely for the purposes of criticism. Furthermore, his lordship confirmed the view that criticism of the underlying philosophy of the work could be relied on just as much as criticism of the work itself.

*Hubbard* v *Vosper* is also of interest in connection with the question of whether or not it can be fair to publish part of a previously unpublished work. In *British Oxygen Co. Ltd* v *Liquid Air Ltd* [1925] Ch 383, the defendant circulated to the Stock Exchange, along with its own critical comments, a threatening letter written by the plaintiff to a customer of the defendant. The purpose was to expose and criticise the plaintiff's unsavoury business methods but it was held not to be fair dealing to publish a previously unpublished work. It is doubted whether this case lays down any hard-and-fast rule (or indeed whether the decision would go the same way in today's rather different commercial climate) and the better view seems to be that the fact that a work is previously unpublished will merely make it more difficult to claim fair dealing in relation to it. (This was the view taken by Ungoed-Thomas J in *Beloff* v *Pressdram Ltd* [1973] 1 All ER 241 where nevertheless his lordship found that the publication by *Private Eye* of a confidential memo (from a journalist on the *Observer* to her editor, concerning a leading politician's views about the likely successor to the Prime Minister) was not fair). Although the defence was regarded as being available in *Hubbard* v *Vosper* in relation to bulletins and letters which had not previously been published to the whole world, the material that Vosper had used had in fact already been circulated to a reasonably wide audience consisting of scientologists. Furthermore, the material included a code of 'ethics' which implicitly authorised, *inter alia,* the murder of opponents of scientology who had become 'fair game'. The uncovering of wrongdoing and misdeeds will be the typical sort of situation where disclosure of previously unpublished material may nevertheless be 'fair'.

This links up with the question of the 'public interest' defence which will be discussed later but for the present it is worth noting that the public interest defence has had a lower profile in copyright cases as compared with cases based on breach of confidence precisely because the fair dealing provisions are capable of covering much of the same ground.

Fair dealing for criticism or review can only be relied on if it is accompanied by a sufficient acknowledgement, which identifies the work being copied and its author. It was said in the *Sillitoe* case that this is not satisfied merely by *stating* the author and title but requires some *acknowledgement* in the sense of *recognition* of the 'position and claims' of the author. This interpretation has been subject to some criticism on the grounds that the identity of the person with such claims, the owner (but see now moral rights), may not be known but the Act requires acknowledgement of the author (if known) rather than the owner so that this should not be a problem. Normal practice, at any rate, is merely to state the title and author without any further bowing and scraping.

*Fair dealing for the purpose of reporting current events (s. 30(2))*
This third and final type of fair dealing is similar to the previous one discussed in that it is likely to involve not merely a single copy but the dissemination of a number of copies and it also generally must be accompanied by a sufficient acknowledgement.

However, no acknowledgement is required if the reporting of current events is by means of a sound recording, film, broadcast or cable programme. Notice that this refers to the means of reporting, not the type of work being dealt with. There is therefore no need for an acknowledgement if a literary work is quoted (fairly) on radio or television for the purpose of reporting current events; for example, a critical report on the functioning of a government department quoted in a radio programme discussing the controversy to which the report had given rise.

Again, as with criticism and review, fair dealing for reporting current events is extended to a wider category of works than was hitherto the case. Under the 1956 Act it only applied to literary, dramatic and musical works but not to artistic or to any Part II works. The Bill originally extended it to all types of work but the government yielded to the photographers' lobby which had consistently pressed for the exclusion of photographs. The main use of many photographs is in reporting current events and the fair dealing provision could have been called in aid by those seeking to exploit a 'scoop' photograph without having to pay for it. To burden photographers or their employers with the task of arguing that such unfair competition was not fair dealing was ultimately accepted to be unjustified: there could be few examples of unauthorised yet fair use of photographs in reporting current events.

Table 6.1 summarises the salient characteristics of the three permitted types of fair dealing.

**Table 6.1    Fair dealing**

| For purposes of | Type of work | Restrictions |
|---|---|---|
| Research or private study. | Literary, dramatic,musical and artistic works and published editions. | Single copies only but no acknowledgement necessary. |
| Criticism and review. | All works. | Multiple copies permitted but sufficient acknowledgement required. |
| Reporting current events. | All works except photographs. | Multiple copies permitted. Sufficient acknowledgement required except in reporting done by means of a sound recording, film, broadcast or cable programme. |

In all cases, copying must be 'fair' and in assessing fairness, the amount or proportion of the work copied will be important as will be whether usage competes with copyright owner.

### Incidental inclusion of copyright works (section 31)

This defence echoes, but considerably widens, the defence that was formerly limited to artistic works included in films or television broadcasts by way of background (s. 9(5) of the 1956 Act). Section 31 provides a defence in relation to *any work* incidentally included in an artistic work, sound recording, film, broadcast or cable programme. Thus a television broadcast which happens to include incidental shots of copyright artistic works (which is virtually inevitable) did not and does not infringe copyright and the defence now extends to, e.g., a broadcast of a football match which incidentally includes the sounds of music played over the public address system (contrast *Hawkes & Son (London) Ltd* v *Paramount Film Service Ltd* [1934] 1 Ch 593, discussed in chapter 5). However, s. 31(3) provides that music, lyrics and sound recordings of songs and music are not regarded as incidentally included if they are deliberately included; for example, if the producers of 'Coronation Street' have one of their characters listening to the current No. 1 single (or any other copyright music or sound recording) it would be regarded as deliberately included since the producer has control over the situation and therefore a licence would be required. Conversely, the maker of a documentary does not have the same control and the background music that happened to be picked up would not normally be regarded as deliberately

inc                       s the contrast between deliberate and
inc                    c and lyrics and recordings and broadcasts
of t                  at the omission of other works means that
the                 e deliberately included!

## Defences relating to public administration (sections 45 to 50)

Material to be used in Parliamentary or judicial proceedings or by a royal commission or statutory inquiry can be copied for those purposes without infringing copyright. To take an obvious example, a document required as evidence in a court case may be copied so that in the interests of justice both the parties and the court can have it before them. The exception also applies to reports of such proceedings, so that the document can be reproduced if that is done as part of a bona fide report of the case. However, the Act makes it clear (in s. 45(2)) that this does not excuse the copying, e.g., by one newspaper of another newspaper's report. Similarly, the judgments of the courts can be reported without infringing any copyright that may subsist in them (precisely who such copyright would belong to is not altogether clear) but to copy another's report of a case may still amount to infringement of that other's copyright in the report.

Thus, to benefit from the exception it would seem that the report must be a first-hand one and the reporter (or someone on his behalf) has to go to or attend the source itself, i.e., the sitting of the court or Parliament or the public hearing of a royal commission or statutory inquiry. Taking an extract from someone else's report may be permissible as fair dealing which is a good example of the rule (stated in s. 28(4)) that the fact that an act is not permitted under one section does not mean that it is not permitted under another.

Material which is on a statutory register, or open to public inspection pursuant to a statutory requirement (e.g., planning documents lodged with a local authority) can be copied if the conditions of s. 47 are satisfied. These conditions are such as to exclude anyone wishing to make copies in order to exploit them but are designed to enable persons with genuine reasons for consulting the register to take a copy away in order to examine it later in more detail. The section contains powers to order that such copies be marked in some way to prevent abuse of the exception. Section 49 also provides for copies to be made from public records which are open to public inspection under the Public Records Act 1958, the Public Records (Scotland) Act 1937 or the equivalent Northern Ireland legislation.

The Crown may (under s. 48) copy or publish literary, dramatic, musical or artistic works communicated to it in the course of public business, which expression includes any activity carried on by the Crown. This freedom is limited to 'the purpose for which the work was communicated to it, or any related purpose which could reasonably have been anticipated by the copyright owner' (s. 48(2)). This is designed to ensure that the Crown can, for example, copy and, if necessary, include in the published report memoranda submitted to royal commissions, departmental committees etc. The phrase 'which could reasonably have been anticipated' may seem rather vague and open-ended but it was introduced to cut down what was originally an unrestrictd power to publish for 'any related purpose' and the Crown's powers are subject to contrary agreement.

Those submitting copyright material to the Crown who wish to protect
themselves may wish to consider attempting to obtain some such agreement but
may also find that they lack the requisite bargaining power! At least the Crown
cannot claim this exemption in relation to material which has already been
published and which is therefore already available.

Section 50 provides a defence of statutory authority where a *particular* act is
*specifically* authorised by an Act of Parliament, e.g., (the example given in the
House of Lords) providing a copy of a company's articles of association as
required by s. 19 of the Companies Act 1985 even though the copyright in the
articles may not belong to the company. The words 'particular' and 'specifically'
are designed to exclude arguments along the lines that because there is statutory
authority for the IBA to make broadcasts, it can broadcast copyright music and
sound recordings with impunity. This type of argument fails because this is a
*general* authorisation to broadcast, not the *specific* authorisation of a *particular*
act.

## Notes and recordings of spoken words (section 58)

The recognition of a speaker's copyright in any literary work represented by his
words (see p. 22) posed a potentially serious problem for broadcasters and
journalists who interview politicians and others. Such a speaker could use the
copyright to prevent the publication or dissemination of some ill-chosen remarks
or an embarrassing interview. So s. 58 declares it to be no infringement to use a
record of spoken words for the purpose of reporting current events or of
broadcasting, provided certain conditions are fulfilled. The most important of
these conditions is that neither the making of the record nor its subsequent use
were prohibited by the speaker *in advance*. There is no need to obtain prior
consent as long as the speaker did not positively prohibit the recording or its use.

It is not entirely clear how widely the term 'current events' will be interpreted
(either here or in the context of fair dealing where the phrase also occurs). Would
an interview with a retired politician concerning events which occurred 20 years
ago be protected? It would be easier to say yes if there was current controversy
about those past events. The widest possible interpretation would involve saying
that the interview or spoken words themselves are the 'current events' and
therefore publishing a record of them is 'for the purpose of reporting' them. This
would also avoid imposing a restriction on newspapers and other written media
which did not apply to the broadcasting media (who do not need to be acting for
the purpose of reporting current events). Many interviews reported in newspapers will be eligible for exemption under the fair dealing provisions anyway but
s. 58 avoids the need for an acknowledgement (which is unnecessary anyway for
non-print media). Reporting someone's words usually inevitably involves
acknowledging their authorship. As was remarked in an Australian case
*(Commonwealth of Australia* v *John Fairfax & Sons Ltd* (1980) 147 CLR 39), the
complaint of those seeking to prevent publication of their own embarrassing
words is usually not the lack of, but rather the fact of excessive, acknowledgement! More significantly s. 58 avoids the evaluative question of fairness,
substituting instead the conditions laid down in s. 58(2).

## Reading or recitation of literary or dramatic works in public (section 59)

This is not an infringement provided that only a reasonable extract is taken and it is accompanied by a sufficient acknowledgement. It is really a specialised form of fair dealing which, it should be noted, does not apply to musical works since public performance is more central to the normal mode of exploitation of such works. Permanent records of such recitals in the form of sound recordings and films, and wider dissemination of the public performance, were initially expressly stated not to be authorised in s. 59(2). However,in response to concerns that this would render illegal broadcasts of events such as the National Eisteddfod of Wales the clause was amended, so as to state that broadcasts etc. of recitals exempt under s. 59(1) do not infringe copyright if the broadcast 'consists mainly of material in relation to which it is not necessary to rely on that subsection'. Thus a broadcast is not exempt if it consists predominantly of unlicensed copyright material but if most of the broadcast is of non-copyright material or is licensed by the copyright owner, then the isolated (often unforeseen) recital of copyright material without consent will not cause the broadcast to be an infringing one.

## Abstracts of scientific and technical articles (section 60)

Researchers in science and technology will be familiar with the various abstracting services, such as *Chemical Abstracts,* which classify and publish abstracts of hundreds of thousands of scientific papers published in numerous journals. If such abstracts were written by the abstracters themselves, as they once used to be, there might well be no infringement provided the abstract merely summarised the ideas in the article without copying the form in which the ideas were expressed (see chapter 1). However, generally speaking, the abstract is now written by the original author and published with the paper or article and hence to reproduce the abstract in an abstracting service without permission would clearly be an infringement. No copyright owners appear to have objected in the past to this valuable but potentially unlawful service, consents usually being freely given on the rare occasions on which they were sought. Section 60 places this practice on a somewhat firmer basis for the future but at the same time recognises the ultimate right of the copyright owners to seek some reward. This is done by providing that there is no infringement of copyright in the abstract or article (but this does not cover the typographical arrangement, so the publisher of the abstracting service must reset the abstract) unless there is a licensing scheme in force and certified under s. 143 (see p. 91). Thus abstracting services are not burdened with having to pay or approach various individual copyright holders or publishers, but these latter can organise a licensing scheme if they feel strongly enough about the use of their works. The abstracters would be free to write their own abstracts if they didn't like the terms of any licensing scheme (or alternatively, they could refer the scheme to the Copyright Tribunal, see chapter 7).

One final point is that s. 60 only applies to 'scientific or technical subjects'. There is thus no exemption for abstracts of journals in the humanities. Although it is clear from the debates that technology is the intended context, one looks forward to argument on whether or not subjects such as law can be regarded as technical!

## Exemptions for artistic works

Sections 62 to 65 contain various exemptions concerning artistic works to ensure, for example, that photographing or sketching a publicly exhibited sculpture or a building does not constitute infringement. Neither is it (nor should it be) an infringement of the copyright in the building to reconstruct it and an artist does not infringe copyright in his own work (where the copyright happens to be owned by another) by copying the work 'provided he does not repeat or imitate the main design'.

The essentials of the above exemptions were all to be found formerly in s. 9 of the 1956 Act but s. 63 is new. It deals with the real need for the seller of an artistic work (who is not necessarily the owner of the copyright) to be able to copy (e.g., photograph) it in order to advertise its sale. The exemption is only 'for the purpose of advertising the sale of the work'. Sales catalogues can become collectors' items in themselves and to prevent indirect exploitation of the original artistic work through the trade in such catalogues, s. 63(2) contains the 'dealt with' formula. A copy which is exempt under s. 63 nonetheless becomes an infringing copy once it is 'dealt with' (e.g., sold or offered for sale) for any purpose other than advertising the original work.

## Playing sound recordings for purposes of non-profit-making clubs etc.

Playing a sound recording in public is normally an infringement but s. 67 permits it if it is part of the activities or for the benefit of non-profit-making charitable or social welfare organisations and the proceeds of any charge for admission go solely to the organisation. This exemption was formerly to be found in s. 12(7) of the 1956 Act, which was significantly wider in that it also applied to sound recordings 'provided as part of the amenities . . . for residents or inmates . . . at any premises where persons reside or sleep'. This aspect of the exemption was removed because it was capable of exploitation by commercial enterprises as in the successfully defended action brought against Pontin's holiday camps in *Phonographic Performance Ltd* v *Pontin's Ltd* [1968] Ch 290.

The remaining exemption (for charitable and social welfare organisations) is limited in that it only applies to the sound recording copyright and not to the copyright in the musical work. Thus, although as a result of the section there may be no need to obtain a licence from PPL (which holds the performing rights in sound recordings), there will still be a need for a licence from the Performing Right Society which holds the performing right for the musical work. If the sound recording is of music which has gone out of copyright then no licence will be required even though the sound recording itself is in copyright.

## Free public showing or playing of broadcasts or cable programmes

Some of the distinctions discussed in the previous exception are also relevant to this exception under s. 72 which provides a defence to infringement of copyright in the broadcast itself and of any sound recording or film included in it (as under the 1956 Act). The basic condition to be fulfilled for this exemption is that the audience 'have not paid for admission' and s. 72(3) provides that residents or inmates are not regarded as having so paid. Hence hotels can rely on this exemption, even though they do obviously charge their residents for admission, as can shops, public houses etc. provided they don't so charge. Again there is no exemption from infringement of copyright in any literary, dramatic or musical work included in the broadcast so a licence from the PRS will be necessary. (This requirement may not, however, apply to a hotel which only provided television and radio facilities in guests' bedrooms rather than in, e.g., a television lounge since it is arguable that there would be no public performance to constitute infringement in the first place. Different considerations may apply if the television is used not for receiving broadcasts but for watching an in-house movie channel, see further, chapter 5.)

### Time-shift recording for private and domestic use (section 70)

Recording television and radio broadcasts for private purposes was not an infringement of the broadcaster's copyright under the 1956 Act but it did infringe copyright in any work included in the broadcast such as a sound recording or film or a musical or literary work. Given the high penetration of video recorders in this country in particular and the fact that much video recording was merely to enable the broadcast to be watched once at a later time, after which the tape would be used for another recording, the law made most of us technical infringers for no good reason. Section 70 now brings time-shifters back into respectability and legitimises such recording whether it be from television or radio. The exemption does *not* apply where the recording is made with a view to keeping a permanent copy for repeated viewing or listening but enforcing this limitation is as impracticable as it is with home taping of records, which practice of course also remains unlawful (in the absence of a licence). (See further, chapter 13.)

Section 71 quite separately permits the making, for private and domestic use, of a photograph from a broadcast or cable programme although the exemption is only from infringement of the copyright in the broadcast or cable programme and any film included in it. Such a photograph might still therefore infringe copyright in other types of work included in the broadcast, particularly artistic ones. It is difficult to see why the exemption should be so restricted especially when it is already limited to photographs for private and domestic use.

### Public interest defence

This common law defence is given statutory recognition for the first time in s. 171(3) although its scope remains a matter for the courts. The defence is based on the idea that the public 'need to know' can sometimes override the copyright owner's right to restrict or prevent publication. It more commonly arises in actions for breach of confidence rather than infringement of copyright (as in the recent *Spycatcher* saga ([1988] 3 All ER 545) where the government attempted to use the law on breach of confidence to prevent the publication of the memoirs of Peter Wright, a former employee of the security service) but often a person seeking an injunction to restrain a breach of confidence will also have a right of action in copyright. (In the *Spycatcher* case, the government chose not to rely on any copyright claims it might have.) Not to allow public interest as a defence to infringement of copyright would seriously undermine its utility as a defence to breach of confidence.

Thus, in *Lion Laboratories Ltd* v *Evans* [1985] QB 526, the Court of Appeal lifted injunctions which had been granted to restrain breach of confidence and infringement of copyright which would allegedly be committed by the *Daily Express* publishing a memorandum about the unreliability of intoximeters. In doing so, however, the court stressed the need to differentiate what is interesting to the public (no defence) from what is in the public interest to be made known (defence available). The defence is not available merely to allow the publication of sensational and lurid disclosures but exists 'to protect the community from destruction, damage or harm'. It was also pointed out that in some cases the public interest would require disclosure to the authorities rather than to the public. The precise limits of the defence still await definitive demarcation, a task which Parliament clearly prefers to leave to the courts.

## Other provisions

Infringement of an adaptation automatically involves infringement of the work on which it is based and so s. 76 provides for the corollary that if an act is permitted in relation to an adaptation then it is also permitted in relation to the work from which the adaptation was made. Thus, fair dealing with the translation of a novel is not an infringement of the translation nor of the untranslated novel.

The range of permitted acts set out in the statute also includes a number of quite detailed defences in relation to education, libraries and archives which are more conveniently dealt with in chapter 14. Similarly, specific provisions as to typefaces and design rights are dealt with in chapters 2 and 12 respectively. The Secretary of State's powers to treat the rental of sound recordings, films and computer programs as licensed by the copyright owner is dealt with in chapters 7 and 13 and various provisions as to recordings made by broadcasters etc., are dealt with in chapter 16.

# Chapter 7 Dealings, Licensing
# and the Copyright Tribunal

## Introduction

Being a valuable property right which subsists for a considerable period of time, copyright is often subject to a multitude of complex dealings through which its owner and others seek to obtain remuneration from those wishing to utilise the subject-matter. Three chapters of part I of the Act are principally relevant here:

(a)   Chapter V which lays down the ground rules for the transfer and licensing of copyright.
(b)   Chapter VII which contains the provisions governing licensing schemes and licences administered by collecting societies such as the Performing Right Society.
(c)   Chapter VIII which sets out the constitution, jurisdiction and procedure of the Copyright Tribunal whose function is basically to adjudicate on matters relating to such licensing.

Since the exploitation of copyright is usually effected in a contractual context, it is also necessary to refer to some rules of the common law of contract, such as the law on restraint of trade and undue influence, which have a particular relevance to copyright dealings.

## Ground rules for assignment and licensing (sections 90 to 92)

These have already been touched upon in discussing first ownership of copyright (see chapter 4). The critical points to be aware of are as follows:

(a)   Copyright can be assigned partially, e.g., the owner can assign the right to permit public performance of the work (which will normally be assigned to the PRS) whilst retaining for himself the right to prohibit other types of infringement (e.g., copying). The splitting of the copyright does not have to follow the distinctions between different types of infringement. For example, one may assign the hardback publishing rights to one publisher and the paperback rights to another. Furthermore, the assignment can be limited by time or by geographical area, e.g., the publishing rights in the USA for the next 25 years. As a result, there can be a bewilderingly large number of owners of different parts of the copyright in a single work (see also chapter 1).

(b)    Assignments must be in writing and signed by or on behalf of the assignor (the owner) (s. 90(3)). An oral or unsigned assignment would normally be treated as an agreement to assign which is just as good if it can be specifically enforced but of course it will be of little consolation if the assignor has in the meantime made a valid assignment to a third party. One would be left with merely an action for damages against the assignor.

(c)    Assignments may be of copyrights that have not yet come into existence and such assignments are effective to transfer ownership of the copyright as soon as the work is created (s. 91(1)).

(d)    Licences (which do not transfer any part of the ownership but are merely permissions to do what would otherwise be infringement) are not generally required to be in writing (although it is advisable that they should be especially in the case of exclusive licences, see para (e) below). They do, however, bind subsequent assignees of the copyright except a bona fide purchaser for value who does not know of the licence (ss. 90(4) and 91(3)). Whether the licensee can assign his licence will depend on the terms of his licence or, if no express provision is made, on whether the licence is impliedly personal or assignable. For example, licences to publish are generally regarded as personal.

(e)    Licences may be granted on a non-exclusive basis, i.e., the same permission to copy or perform etc. can be given to other licensees, or it may be an exclusive licence, i.e., one which permits the licensee alone to copy or perform etc. An exclusive licence even excludes the licensor (the owner of the copyright) from doing whatever the licence permits and this puts the licensee in a position almost as though he is the owner. Indeed, s. 101 treats an exclusive licensee as the owner for many purposes connected with remedies but to constitute an exclusive licensee for these purposes the licence has to be in writing and signed by or on behalf of the copyright owner. The distinction between a partial assignment of copyright, e.g., of the French publishing rights, and an exclusive licence, e.g., to publish in France, may be rather a thin one. Although the effects are not dissimilar, an assignment confers better protection on the assignee since ownership provides more protection against inconsistent dealings with third parties than the mere contractual right involved in a licence. Conversely, the original owner will normally be in a stronger position if he has merely granted a licence rather than assigned his copyright. (See *Barker* v *Stickney* [1919] 1 KB 121 where the author had assigned his copyright to a publisher in return for a royalty. The publisher became bankrupt and the defendants purchased the copyright from the publisher. The author had no rights against the defendants but merely had a contractual right to a royalty from the bankrupt publisher. Had the publisher merely been granted a licence, assignable only with the owner's consent, the author would have been protected.)

(f)    Implied licences. Licences to do what would otherwise be an infringement of copyright can often be implied from conduct or out of a contractual relationship. For example, the sending of a letter to a newspaper editor will normally imply a licence for the newspaper to publish it and where a work is commissioned, there will usually be an implied licence for the commissioner to use the work for the purposes for which the commission was made.

The scope of the licence will depend on the purpose of the commission and the size of the fee paid may be relevant. In *Stovin-Bradford* v *Volpoint Properties Ltd* [1971] Ch 1007, only a nominal fee was paid for architects' plans and so it was held that the licence was merely to use them for the purpose of obtaining planning permission, a further fee being anticipated to use them for building if the planning application were to be successful. On the other hand in *Blair* v *Osborne & Tomkins* [1971] 2 QB 78, an architect was paid the full scale fee for plans in advance and therefore the licence extended beyond their use in planning applications and included their use as the basis of the completed buildings. Similarly, the purchase of pattern books may confer the right to reproduce the patterns for domestic purposes (otherwise there would be little point purchasing the patterns) but does not necessarily carry an implied licence to use the patterns for commercial purposes (see *Roberts* v *Candiware Ltd* [1980] FSR 352).

The notion of an implied licence was put forward as a way of authorising the manufacture of spare parts for motor vehicles in *British Leyland Motor Corporation Ltd* v *Armstrong Patents Co. Ltd* [1986] AC 577 but the House of Lords preferred to construct a new limitation on the enforcement of copyright in design drawings, the doctrine of non-derogation of grant. This was seen as being both more appropriate for assertion by third parties (as opposed to the actual purchaser of the vehicle) and also as being incapable of being negated by express provision (see further, chapter 12).

(g)   The permissible terms in assignments and licensing agreements have been significantly affected by Common Market competition policy and the rules on free movement of goods. These are further discussed in chapter 9 but an important principle worth mentioning at this stage is that of exhaustion of rights. In the European context, this means that once an item is lawfully on the market in an EEC country with the consent of the copyright owner (albeit under a licence limited to that country) the licensee or copyright owner in another EEC country cannot object to its importation into that other country. The copyright owner's right is 'exhausted' once the item is lawfully on the market with his consent in the first country. This means that the apparent monopoly given to an exclusive licensee in a particular country is not in fact as great as it might at first appear to be.

(h)   Transmission on death. 'Copyright is transmissible . . . by testamentary disposition. . . as personal or moveable property' (s. 90(1). The distinction between the ownership of the copyright and the ownership of a physical object recording or constituting the work has already been pointed out (above page 8). Section 93, however, provides that a bequest of 'an original document or other material thing' shall also pass the copyrights in any *unpublished* works recorded or embodied in the document etc. 'unless a contrary intention is indicated in the testator's will or a codicil to it' and 'in so far as the testator was the owner of the copyright immediately before his death'.

## Contractual limits on dealings with copyright

Quite apart from the statutory rules on assignments and licences of copyright works, the common law of contract imposes some restrictions. The basic inclination of the courts has, of course, been not to interfere with contracts freely entered into but exceptionally the courts will intervene if there is an unlawful restraint of trade or undue influence.

## Restraint of trade

The leading example here is the case of *A. Schroeder Music Publishing Co. Ltd* v *Macaulay* [1974] 1 WLR 1308 where the plaintiff, a young unknown songwriter, assigned the copyright in all his output of songs for the next five years to the defendant music publisher which was under no obligation to publish any of them. The agreement (in standard form) was renewable for a further five years, the defendant could terminate on one month's notice whereas the plaintiff had no right of termination and the defendant could assign the agreement or any copyright aquired under it without the consent of the plaintiff. The House of Lords held that the contract was unenforceable since it was capable of being enforced so as to sterilise the plaintiff's output rather than to utilise it and was therefore an unreasonable restraint of trade. The finding that the restraint was an unreasonable one was influenced by the House's view that there was a great disparity of bargaining power between the parties, a finding that has been subject to some criticism, but similar conclusions have been drawn in a number of more recent cases concerning songwriters including *O'Sullivan* v *Management Agency & Music Ltd* [1985] QB 428.

## Undue influence

The cases discussed in the previous paragraph treated contracts in restraint of trade as unenforceable rather than void. This view (for which there is not a great deal of other authority) means that copyrights (and royalties) that have already been transferred under the agreement are not recoverable and it is only unperformed obligations which are affected. No such restriction applies to contracts entered into under undue influence where equity can set aside transactions already carried out under the contract. Thus in *O'Sullivan* v *Management Agency & Music Ltd* [1985] QB 428, where there was a relationship of undue influence between the plaintiff and his manager, the Court of Appeal ordered the restitution to the plaintiff of some of his copyrights and also of royalties received by the defendant in respect of them (subject to an allowance for the efforts of the defendant in promoting the plaintiff's success). Property assigned to third parties in good faith and for value could not, however, be recovered.

At one time, Lord Denning attempted to fashion, out of cases including *A. Schroeder Music Publishing Co. Ltd* v *Macaulay* [1974] 1 WLR 1308, a broad principle of relief applicable wherever there was the abuse of inequality of bargaining power *(Lloyds Bank Ltd* v *Bundy* [1975] QB 326). However, the courts have not been receptive to this principle and the House of Lords reiterated the need to bring one's case under the traditional categories in *National Westminster Bank plc* v *Morgan* [1985] AC 686 where it was re-emphasised that for the court to intervene on the basis of undue influence, the bargain must actually be a disadvantageous one from the point of view of the plaintiff who must also be under a sufficient degree of influence by the defendant.

One final point to notice is that whilst the courts now have powers to disallow reliance on unreasonable exemption clauses under the Unfair Contract Terms

Act 1977, sch. 1, para. 1(c), of that Act provides that ss. 2 to 4 of the Act shall not apply to any contract 'so far as it relates to the creation or transfer of a right or interest in . . . copyright . . . or other intellectual property'. Whether this means that the whole contract is outside the scope of ss. 2 to 4 of the 1977 Act or whether (as is more likely) the phrase 'so far as it relates to' means the restriction only applies to those terms creating or transferring a right or interest in copyright, remains to be seen.

### Collective licensing and licensing schemes

*The performing rights experience*
Effective and efficient licensing of copyright works is important, both to the owner, to whom it represents the most obvious way of turning his right to financial advantage, and also to the would-be user, who can only safely use the work if he has a licence (unless his use would not constitute infringement in the first place). In many areas, the negotiation of individual licences for individual users of particular works is not a practical proposition. This has long clearly been so in the case of performing rights where there is little prospect of, e.g., an individual hairdresser, who plays music to his waiting customers, negotiating separate licences with all the various owners of copyright in the music and sound recordings involved. To deal with this kind of problem the Performing Right Society was formed in 1914 (and similar organisations have grown up in other countries) to administer on behalf of the copyright owners the performing (and broadcasting) rights in non-dramatic performances of music and of literary works (lyrics) set to music. It operates by taking an assignment of the performing rights in such works and in return distributing the royalties it collects to its members (over 700,000 of them including members of affiliated overseas societies) in proportion to the usage of their works. It acquires the royalties in return for licensing the users of music, some of whom are required to submit returns showing what music they have used, and it is on the basis of these returns that the society calculates the amounts to which individual members are entitled. The usual type of licence is a blanket one which covers all the works administered by the society including works of members of affiliated organisations overseas. Various schemes or standard tariffs have been negotiated covering different types of user such as hotels and restaurants, retail shops, cinemas, dance-halls, football grounds etc.

A licence is needed whether the performance is a live one in a concert hall, by means of a record in a discothèque or from a radio or television in a shop or restaurant. The rights administered also include the right to broadcast the work and so licences granted to the broadcasting organisations are a significant and highly remunerative part of the society's portfolio. The society does not deal with the performing right in sound recordings (as opposed to the music embodied in such recordings) but these are administered in a similar way by Phonographic Performance Ltd (PPL) and the users of recorded music (in public) will often need a licence from both bodies who, it should be noted, employ inspectors to ensure that there are no premises lacking a licence which ought to have one. The effectiveness and importance of these organisations can be judged from the fact that in 1987 the PRS collected £60 million in UK royalties (of which £36 million was from radio and television broadcasters) and a further £30 million in royalties from overseas. Just over 80% of the total income of £95 million was distributed to members (including about 15% to affiliated foreign societies), the costs of administration being around 18%.

Whilst such societies solve a lot of problems, both for owners and users of copyright material, they also clearly present a potential problem of abuse of monopoly that is not present when the rights are held separately by a large number of individuals. The potential for abuse of this bargaining power was recognised in the 1956 Act by the establishment of the Performing Right Tribunal which was given jurisdiction over disputes arising between licensing bodies (such as PRS) and those requiring licences (or organisations representing such persons). The tribunal could vary the terms of the licence or scheme or declare that the person was entitled to a licence where the licensing body was refusing to grant one. The tribunal had no independent investigative powers but could only act if a dispute was referred to it by one of the parties. Most disputes have been about the charges to be made for licences under particular schemes such as that relating to bingo halls, but equally there have been references by individual licensees, such as Manx Radio who were dissatisfied with the amount of 'needle time' (i.e., the amount of recorded music allowed to be played) being offered by PPL. Manx Radio referred the issue to the Performing Right Tribunal and succeeded in gaining an increase from 25% to 50% of total broadcasting time at the cost of an appropriate increase in the royalties payable. The case illustrates the fact that the monopoly enjoyed by collecting societies, in the absence of any control, could be used not only to extract excessive charges but to pursue other ends such as the encouragement of the employment of live musicians which is behind the needle-time disputes. (PPL has recently been investigated by the Monopolies Commission and, no doubt keen to appear reasonable, has been appearing to adopt a more flexible attitude towards needle-time.)

*The emergence of the wider problem*
The factors that led to the establishment of PRS and PPL have recurred in other contexts since the 1956 Act, largely because of the ever-wider availability of new technology in the form of photocopiers, sound and video recorders etc. which enable a large number of individuals to copy a wide range of works by numerous different authors. It is very difficult for a particular author or publisher to pursue the particular individuals who might be illegally photocopying his work. Conversely, it is very difficult for the individual infringer, who might genuinely be willing to pay an appropriate royalty to legitimise his activities, to deal with all the different owners of the various works that he may wish to copy. The natural solution is therefore the collectivisation of rights in these areas too so that the users of copyright material only need to seek a licence from one, or at least a limited number of, licensors and the owners, through the collecting society, obtain reasonable remuneration for the use of their work. The Copyright Licensing Agency, for example, was formed in 1982 to act on behalf of authors' and publishers' licensing societies and it has negotiated an experimental blanket licence for educational copying in schools and colleges (not including polytechnics) and, more recently, an experimental scheme with a number of universities (see p. 171).

The Act endorses this trend towards collective administration of rights and also follows the Whitford proposal to widen the jurisdiction of the Performing Right Tribunal, rename it the Copyright Tribunal, and increase its membership to take account of the increased workload.

*The provisions of the Act*

As with the 1956 Act, there are two main classes of case over which the Copyright Tribunal is given jurisdiction:

(a)   licensing *schemes* (ss. 117 to 123),
(b)   *licences* granted by *licensing bodies* (ss. 124 to 128).

A licensing *scheme* is not in itself a licence but is something:

'setting out

(a)   the classes of case in which the operator of the scheme . . . is willing to grant copyright licences, and
(b) the terms on which licences would be granted . . .' (s. 116(1)).

The various tariffs operated by the PRS are examples of schemes. Licensing schemes will be the basis on which numerous individual licences (often covering a large number of works) will be granted to individual users. Thus many individual licences are subject to the jurisdiction of the tribunal because the scheme or tariff under which they are granted is itself subject to control but another category of licences, those granted by a licensing body 'otherwise than in pursuance of a licensing scheme' are also controlled under ss. 124 to 128.

None of the above represents a major change of principle from the 1956 Act but the difference comes in the types of licences and schemes that are to be controlled.

### Licensing schemes

As far as schemes are concerned, the tribunal's jurisdiction is extended from performing rights to cover (s. 117):

(a)   literary, dramatic, musical and artistic works and films — schemes operated by a licensing body and covering works of more than one author relating to copying, performing or broadcasting the work (but not publishing it),
(b)   sound recordings, broadcasts, cable programmes and published editions — *all* licensing schemes are covered,
(c)   sound recordings, films and computer programs — licensing schemes relating to the rental of copies to the public are covered.

As far as (c) is concerned, it partly covers (in relation to sound recordings) what is already covered in (b) but the draftsman no doubt thought it better to include licensing schemes for the rental of sound recordings twice rather than risk leaving them out altogether!

Notice that category (a) is, unlike (b) and (c), limited to schemes operated by licensing bodies which means (s. 116) 'a society or other organisation which has as . . . one of its main objects, the negotiation or granting . . . of copyright licences, and whose objects include the granting of licences covering works of more than one author'. This means effectively that only schemes operated collectively rather than by individual authors are caught in relation to literary, dramatic, musical and artistic works and films. This is because these are the works that give rise to what would be regarded in Continental systems as true author's rights and it would probably be a breach of Berne Convention obligations to control the exercise of copyright by individual rights owners. Conversely, para. (b), which is concerned with neighbouring rights, and para. (c), which is concerned with the rental right (which is not guaranteed by the Berne Convention), *would* apply to licensing schemes even though operated by an individual right owner.

Schemes coming within any of the above paras (a) to (c) can be referred to the tribunal:

(a)    in the case of a proposed scheme, by an organisation representing users to whom the scheme would apply (s. 118),

(b)    in the case of a scheme already in operation, by a person requiring a licence or by a representative organisation (s. 119).

In either case, the tribunal can make such order, confirming or varying the scheme, as it determines 'to be reasonable in the circumstances'.

Unlike the situation under the 1956 Act, guidance is provided on the criteria of reasonableness. In particular, s. 129 provides that there should not be unreasonable discrimination between the licensees under the scheme in question and licensees in similar circumstances in similar schemes (as occurred, for example, in a reference to the Performing Right Tribunal (case 9/60) which held that discounts offered by the PRS to the Cinema Exhibitors Association, but not to the smaller but similar Association of Independent Cinemas, were unreasonable). The Act also specifies other relevant factors for particular contexts such as reprographic copying (s. 130), educational recording (s. 131) and others but s. 135 makes it clear that these factors are not exhaustive and that the tribunal should have regard to all relevant considerations. This was the reason given in Parliament for not specifically directing the tribunal to look at royalty rates in other countries which broadcasters regard as much less onerous than those prevalent in this country, since the tribunal would be able to consider such matters anyway if it considered them relevant.

Further references may be made to the tribunal if, for example, its order is causing unfairness or not operating satisfactorily. Such further references, however, must normally not be within 12 months of the first order except with special leave (s. 122).

In addition to *references* of schemes to the tribunal there may be *applications* to the tribunal, either by a person who has been refused a licence falling under a scheme or by one who is seeking a licence for a category of case that is excluded from a scheme (s. 121). A case is regarded as excluded either if it is expressly excluded or is so similar to included categories that it ought to be, but is not, included. If the tribunal finds that the applicant's case is 'well founded', i.e., his case is covered by the scheme or that his exclusion from the scheme is unreasonable or that the terms proposed for a licence covering the excluded case are unreasonable, the tribunal may declare that the applicant is entitled to a licence and may specify the appropriate terms.

### Other licences granted by licensing bodies (sections 124 to 128)

These are one-off licences (which may nevertheless be of very wide application, such as the CLA's licence with local education authorities) granted by a licensing body but which do not come under any of its schemes. The categories of licence covered (s. 124) are the same as the categories of controlled licensing schemes and the tribunal is given very similar powers to that which it possesses in relation to licensing schemes. Since we are here concerned with an individual licensee rather than a scheme applicable to a class of licensees, the initial reference to the tribunal must be by the licensee (s. 126) or proposed licensee (s. 125) and there is no provision for reference by a representative organisation. Note that existing licences can only be referred to the tribunal in the last three months of their life and on the grounds that it is unreasonable that they should expire (s. 126).

Further provisions relating to collective licensing of reprography, both generally and in education, will be considered in chapter 14. The reference of licensing schemes to the tribunal should be distinguished from the certification of a licensing scheme by the Secretary of State under s. 143. Such certification does not relate at all to the reasonableness or otherwise of the scheme but merely guarantees that the scheme clearly identifies the works covered and sets out clearly the payable charges and other terms. It also makes the existence of the scheme a matter of public knowledge and, if a scheme is so certified, it means that an otherwise applicable permitted act is excluded. The relevant permitted acts are conveniently collected together in s. 143(1). For example, the permitted act of copying a scientific journal abstract is not available if there is a certified licensing scheme available covering that particular copying. One must either take out the licence available under the scheme and pay the relevant fee or risk being sued as an infringer. If one considers the scheme to be unreasonable, it can be referred to the Copyright Tribunal, even though certified (as to its clarity) by the Secretary of State.

### Other functions of the Copyright Tribunal

*Compulsory licences*
There are two situations where what amounts to compulsory licences in respect of copyright are made available. The first is where the Secretary of State makes an order under s. 66 treating the rental of sound recordings etc. as licensed by the copyright owner. It was stated in Parliament that this was a power which would probably not need to be exercised but if it does prove necessary, the tribunal will settle the rate of royalty in default of agreement (s. 142). Secondly, where the Monopolies and Mergers Commission finds that conditions in licences (or the refusal to grant licences on reasonable terms) are operating against the public interest, the Minister is now (by virtue of s. 144) given power to provide for licences as of right. (Such powers were noticeably lacking when the Commission

reported on the use by Ford Motors of artistic copyright in spare parts drawings and again in its report on the *TV Times* and *Radio Times* programme listings monopoly (cf. the *Time Out* case discussed in chapter 9), although in the latter case it found that the monopoly was not operating against the public interest.) Again the tribunal is given the task of settling the terms of such a licence in default of agreement (although no criterion, not even reasonableness, for settling the terms is given, the tribunal presumably having to take their lead from the Monopolies and Mergers Commission report). To ensure that there is no conflict with the International Conventions s. 144(3) provides that the Minister 'shall only exercise the powers available by virtue of this section if he is satisfied that to do so does not contravene any Convention relating to copyright to which the United Kingdom is a party'.

The tribunal also has the task of settling (again only in default of agreement) the royalty payable to Great Ormond Street Hospital in relation to *Peter Pan* (sch. 6, para. 5). It also has the function in relation to rights in performances, of giving consent on behalf of performers whose identity or whereabouts cannot be ascertained or who unreasonably withhold consent (s. 190).

## Constitution of the Copyright Tribunal

The Copyright Tribunal will have a chairman and two deputy chairmen, who are to be legally qualified and appointed by the Lord Chancellor, and between two and eight ordinary members appointed by the Secretary of State (s. 145). The government resisted attempts to have nominated representatives from the various sides of industry affected by the tribunal's decisions. The tribunal will sit with the chairman or a deputy chairman and at least two other members, and decisions will be by majority vote (s. 148). Rules will be made prescribing the fees payable (which are not expected to be high and are intended to deter frivolous applications rather than to cover the full running costs), providing for written or oral evidence (it is envisaged that written procedures should be introduced in some cases to save time and running costs) and regulating other matters (s. 150). The tribunal may (under s. 151(1)) make an order for costs against a party but it is envisaged that this power, as with the Performing Right Tribunal, should be sparingly used. There is a right of appeal on a point of law from the tribunal to the High Court (s. 152).

# Chapter 8 Moral Rights

## Introduction: what are moral rights?

'Moral rights' are set out in Article 6 *bis* of the Paris text of the Berne Convention as follows (emphasis added):

(1)  Independently of the author's economic rights, and even after the transfer of the said rights, the author shall have the *right to claim authorship* of the work and to *object to any distortion, mutilation or other modification of, or other derogatory action* in relation to, the said work, which would be *prejudicial to his honour or reputation.*

(2)  The rights granted to the author in accordance with the preceding paragraph shall, after his death, be maintained, at least until the expiry of the economic rights, and shall be exercisable by the persons or institutions authorised by the legislation of the country where protection is claimed. . . .

(3)  The means of redress for safeguarding the rights granted by this Article shall be governed by the legislation of the country where protection is claimed.

The two moral rights provided for in the Berne Convention are commonly described as the right of 'paternity', namely the right to be associated with one's own work aı d the right of 'integrity', namely the right to object to certain types of distortion o  one's work.

## The law before the 1988 Act

Neither of these rights was expressly incorporated into UK copyright legislation prior to the 1988 Act. Instead, it was maintained by many that English law *indirectly* protected such rights by contract and by a combination of common law actions such as passing off or defamation together with a few limited provisions in the Copyright Act 1956.

Thus, s. 43(4) of the 1956 Act (and earlier law) made it actionable *knowingly* to sell an *altered* artistic work, without authority, as the artist's unaltered work. This provision was successfully relied upon, for example, where a fine line drawing made for a newspaper by an artist was published in an altered form on public advertising hoardings throughout the country with the artist author's signature left on the posters. Although the copyright was owned by the defendants, this was an actionable material alteration *(Carlton Illustrators* v *Coleman & Co. Ltd* [1911] 1 KB 771). Another indirect moral right provision existed in the Copyright Act 1956, s. 8(6), in relation to the statutory licence to make sound recordings; which provided that records of adaptations of a musical work could only be made if they did not differ substantially in their treatment of a work, either in respect of style or performers.

In 1977 the Whitford Committee concluded that these indirect methods of protection were inadequate to comply with the Berne Convention. In contrast, leading opinion in the United States, which intends to join the Berne Convention, and in Australia, both with similar common law jurisdictions in this regard, have concluded that similar indirect protection to that in the UK *is* sufficient to satisfy the Berne Convention obligations!

The 1988 Act expressly incorporates the two moral rights contained in Article 6 *bis* and provides for two others as follows:

(a)    the right of paternity (s. 77),
(b)    the right of integrity (s. 80),
(c)    the right to object to false attribution (s. 84),
(d)    the right to privacy of certain photographs and films (s. 85).

Unlike many other countries, the moral rights provisions in UK law have been spelt out in considerable detail, primarily in Chapter IV of Part I of the Act. However, the conditions surrounding them and the many exceptions to their application substantially undermine their real value. Of course, independent rights which were available to aggrieved persons before the 1988 Act, such as for passing off or for defamation, continue to be available.

### General features of moral rights provisions

*Who enjoy the rights?*
The rights of paternity and of integrity are enjoyed by the authors of copyright literary, dramatic, musical or artistic works. Thus, the copyright and moral rights in a work arise together and will generally be in the same ownership initially. Where copyright ownership remains with the author it will still be possible on some occasions indirectly to protect moral rights by the exercise of exclusive copyright rights: for example, to refuse to authorise first publication without appropriate credit, or to license copyright works subject to strict conditions as to alteration to the work. However, part of the value of moral rights to authors is that they can still be exercised even after the copyright ownership has passed to another.

Moral rights are also enjoyed by directors of copyright films, even though most film directors today have no copyright interest in the film: the copyright in the film and the moral right of the director, in the first instance, will be vested in different persons. Why should film directors be given moral rights? Presumably it is in recognition of the artistic contribution which they make to films. Whilst directors, no doubt, would argue that such recognition should entitle them to a joint interest in the copyright in the film, at least they now have moral rights; there are some who contribute to the aesthetic qualities of a work who have neither copyright nor moral rights: for example, performers have neither copyright nor moral rights as such even though some countries do confer moral rights upon them; instead they have a special set of 'copyright-related' rights only (see chapter 11).

The right to object to false attribution of a work is available to *any* person, whether or not such person is an author. The right of privacy in relation to certain photographs and films is enjoyed by the person who commissions the taking of a photograph or the making of a film for private and domestic purposes; that person, in the case of photographs, is no longer, and, in the case of films, never was, given the first ownership of the copyright (see chapter 4).

Where there are works of joint authorship, each joint author is entitled to exercise his rights in the same way as a sole author (s. 88).

## Duration of moral rights
The rights of paternity and integrity and the right of privacy last for the same length as the copyright in the relevant work. The right to object to false attribution continues to subsist for a period of 20 years after a person's death (s. 86).

## Assignment?
Moral rights are, by their very nature, personal to the individual concerned and, accordingly, cannot be assigned (s. 94). However, their exercise can be affected by waiver and consent and they can be transferred on death (see below).

# Right of paternity

The author of a copyright literary, dramatic, musical or artistic work, and the director of a copyright film, has the right to be identified as the author or director of the work (s. 77).

The nature of the right differs slightly depending upon the type of copyright work involved. In most cases the right to be identified operates whenever the work is performed in public, or issued to the public or whenever it is commercially exploited and includes the right to be identified as the author of a work from which any adaptation is made. However, no statutory right to identification applies when musical works are performed in public; the argument being that it would be impractical to require broadcast programmes, for example, to list the composers of all the music which is played in whole or in part on television or radio.

Conversely, the author of an artistic work, who has no exclusive performing right under copyright law (anybody in possession of a painting, in the absence of agreement to the contrary, may show it in public), nevertheless has the right to be identified as the artist should it in fact be shown in public.

The right of paternity can be asserted on each and every copy of the work or, where this is not appropriate, in some other manner likely to bring the author's or director's identity to the notice of a person acquiring a copy. In the case of buildings, the right is to be identified on the constructed building or on the first to

be constructed, by appropriate means visible to persons entering or approaching
the building and, in any case, the identification must be clear and reasonably
prominent (s. 77(7)).

*Assertion*
An important, though controversial, condition precedent to the operation of the
right of paternity is that it must first be 'asserted' by the author (s. 78);
infringements can arise only after assertion.

One justification for the assertion requirement is that it is to protect publishers
and others who deal with copyright material; they need to know exactly what
their responsibilities are. Even so, it cannot but operate on occasions to restrict
further the effectiveness of the right.

Until standard assertions of right are introduced in contracts, the possibility of
overlooking this requirement is likely to be strong. Understandably the author of
a literary work would be surprised to learn that, although his name features
prominently on the work, this is not of itself sufficient to satisfy the requirement
of assertion. Accordingly, authors should assert their rights in contracts with
publishers and also, in order to ensure that others are bound by the right (see s.
78(4)), should have express statements asserting the right of paternity on all
copies of their works. The requirement is relaxed slightly in connection with the
public exhibition of artistic works; usually the name of the author on the original,
or authorised copy, or on the frame to which the artistic work is attached will be
sufficient for assertion purposes (s. 78(3)).

The assertion of the right may be general, or relate to a specified act or
descriptions of act and may be by instrument in writing, or by a statement to that
effect in an assignment of the copyright in the work.

The way in which the right is asserted will affect those who are bound by it. The
provisions are detailed and complex: in most cases third parties will be bound
regardless of whether or not they have notice, but in other cases they will only be
bound provided they have notice that the right has been asserted (s. 78(4)).

**Right to object to derogatory treatment: the right of integrity (section 80)**

*Nature of the right*
Authors of works and film directors may object to certain types of 'treatment' of
their works or films. 'Treatment' means any addition to, deletion from or
alteration to, or adaptation of the relevant work. It does not prevent translations
of literary or dramatic works or any arrangement or transcription of a musical
work involving no more than a change of key or register, since such types of
treatment in most (though not all!) cases preserve the basic integrity of a work (s.
80(2)).

If works are subject to such treatment the right of the author to object arises
only where it is 'derogatory', that is, if it amounts to 'distortion or mutilation of
the work or is otherwise prejudicial to the honour or reputation of the author or
director'.

The words 'or is *otherwise* prejudicial to the honour or reputation of the author
or director' suggest strongly that the treatment complained of must have some
defamatory flavour to it. Thus, changes to the works of authors or directors to

which they object will not be actionable if, whilst they may believe that their artistic integrity has been affected, the evidence shows that there is no damage to honour or, indeed, that a reputation has been enhanced. If this is right, the author's subjective feelings would be overridden by the more objective view of the court.

In some cases, an author's contractual rights may operate in parallel with the right of integrity and either argument will produce the same result. In *Joseph* v *National Magazine Co. Ltd* [1959] Ch 14, the plaintiff author, an expert on jade, had been commissioned to write an article for the defendant's art magazine. The defendant revised the work, changed the title and conclusions and made considerable stylistic and factual alterations. An action for breach of contract was successful, since the contract was for the plaintiff to write in his own way; and damages were awarded for the loss of the plaintiff's chance to enhance his reputation. Now, the plaintiff could rely upon both his contractual and his integrity rights, although if there had been no contractual relationship the right of integrity alone would apply.

Sometimes the contractual and integrity rights will not necessarily coincide. In *Frisby* v *British Broadcasting Corporation* [1967] Ch 932, the plaintiff had been commissioned by the BBC to write a television play and the contract incorporated a provision that 'the BBC shall not without the prior consent of the writer (which consent shall not be unreasonably withheld) make any *structural* alterations as opposed to minor alterations to the . . . script'. The dispute turned on whether the BBC could delete one line relating to sex which the author considered to be of basic importance to his play but which the BBC regarded as a minor alteration. The court first considered whether the contract effected a limited assignment of the copyright to the BBC or a licence, for in the former case the power to make changes is much stronger. It concluded that the contract conferred a licence only and although a licensee has a prima facie right to make even substantial alterations, the court will readily imply a term limiting that right. Here, weight was given to the author's view of the significance of the deleted line and the plaintiff succeeded. The result is unlikely to be different now, for there is nothing to stop the plaintiff using the same *contractual* arguments. Whether he can also successfully rely upon the right of integrity will depend on whether the deletion of the line is a matter prejudicial to honour or reputation. The answer there will turn on whether the court takes an objective view, as suggested above. If it were to hold that the honour or reputation requirement is not satisfied, the contractual protection will have proved to be stronger. Whilst it would not be of importance here, it could adversely affect an author in circumstances where the copyright in the play is *assigned* and the deletions are made by a person not a party to the original contract.

*Inherent limitations to the right of integrity*
Whilst the right of integrity seemingly provides wide protection, the definition itself imposes some inherent limitations. Thus, certain 'derogatory' actions may not come within the expression 'treatment'. To place an artistic work in an inappropriate context may be damaging to the author: for example, placing a 'respectable' artistic work in an exhibition of pornographic material; taking extracts from a literary work or music for inappropriate use in advertising; these

may all be matters to which the author objects but are outside the section. The applicability of the right can be further tested by the interesting case of *Shostakovich* v *Twentieth Century-Fox Film Corporation*. There, several Russian composers complained that the defendants had played *faithful* recordings of their works as background music for a film which was derogatory of the Soviet Union. They objected to the use of their works and names in this context on the ground that it implied their approval of the film's political stance. They failed in the USA, where there are no express moral rights ((1948) 80 NYS 2d 575) but succeeded in France, where there are. The new UK provisions would be of no benefit to the composers: using the music in films in this way would not constitute 'treatment' under s. 80(2)(a).

On the other hand, the controversial practice of colouring classic black and white films appears to come within this definition, although, of course, none of these films would qualify for protection since they were made before the Act came into force (sch. 1, para. 23(2)).

The right of integrity does not extend to, or encompass, the physical relocation of a work (for example, where a sculpture commissioned with a view to being displayed in a town centre meets with the disapproval of the local council, and is relegated to a distant park) or the physical means by which the work is displayed or exhibited and any alteration, destruction or change in the structure containing a work is not actionable.

The right does not extend to preservation of a work; nor is it a right to prevent *destruction*. Graham Sutherland's portrait of Sir Winston Churchill was destroyed by members of Sir Winston's family. Even had all the events occurred after the 1988 Act came into force nothing could have been done by the artist. Nor is any statutory obligation imposed upon persons to ensure that a work is well maintained and does not fall into such a state of disrepair as to 'embarrass' the artist. Should any legitimate restoration or preservation be done to a work, again this will not necessarily be actionable derogatory treatment even though the author may disapprove of what has been done.

## Exceptions to the rights of paternity and integrity

There is a remarkable list of exemptions and qualifications, the most noteworthy of which are as follows:

(a) *Computer programs and computer-generated works.* Neither the right of paternity nor the right of integrity applies to these works.

(b) *Design of typefaces.* The right of paternity does not, but the right of integrity does, apply to typefaces.

(c) *Employees.* Employees (including employee-directors) who produce works in the course of their employment are not entitled to any statutory right to credit for them in relation to any lawful dealings with the works. Nor do they have any right of integrity in relation to such works unless the author or director had at some time been identified with the works; and even here, the extent of an employee's right of integrity is simply to insist that there is a clear and reasonably prominent indication that the work has been subjected to treatment to which the author or director has not consented (ss. 79(3) and 82).

(d) *Reporting current events.* Neither the right of paternity nor the right of integrity applies in relation to any work made for the purpose of reporting current events (ss. 79(5) and 81(3)). The precise ambit of this exception may give rise to difficulty. A work may refer to current events but may not necessarily have been 'made for the purpose of' reporting current events. In such a case, the author's rights of paternity and integrity will still subsist.

(e) *Publications in newspapers, magazines or similar periodicals; and publications in encyclopaedias, dictionaries, year-books or other collective works of reference.* Neither right applies to literary, dramatic, musical or artistic works made for the purposes of such publications or made available with the author's consent for such publication (ss. 79(6) and 81(4)). The press proprietors' lobby was successful in ensuring that moral rights do not apply to works produced either by employed or freelance journalists.

(f) *Crown or Parliamentary copyright or works in which copyright originally vested in an international organisation.* These works are treated, for the purposes of the paternity and integrity rights, in the same way as employee works.

(g) *Copyright exemptions.* A range of permitted acts which do not infringe copyright (see chapter 6), for example, fair dealing for specific purposes, do not infringe the right of paternity (s. 79(4)). The permitted acts do not, however, generally affect the right of integrity.

(h) *Statutory, regulatory and 'good taste' requirements.* The right of integrity does not operate in relation to anything done to a work for the purpose of avoiding the commission of an offence; complying with a statutory duty; or, in the case of the British Broadcasting Corporation, avoiding the inclusion in a programme broadcast by them of anything which offends against good taste or decency or which is likely to encourage or incite to crime or to lead to disorder or to be offensive to public feeling (s. 81(6)) (cf. *Frisby* v *BBC* discussed earlier).

This exemption is designed to permit broadcasters and others to have the freedom to delete or amend material to comply with the law and with appropriate standards of broadcasting. However, where the author has been identified at some time, there must be a sufficient disclaimer: a clear and reasonably prominent indication that the author has not consented to the alteration.

The exemption, though seemingly wide, does have its limits. In *Gilliam* v *American Broadcasting Companies Inc.* (1976) 538 F 2d 14, the authors of the successful television comedy series, 'Monty Python's Flying Circus', entered into licence agreements with the BBC which permitted it to make only minor alterations to the scripts. The BBC licensed Time-Life Films to distribute the 'Monty Python' television programmes in the USA and agreed to a standard clause which permitted Time-Life to edit the programmes 'for insertion of commercials, applicable censorship or governmental . . . rules . . . and National Association of Broadcasters and time segment requirements'. Time-Life, in turn, licensed some of the programmes to ABC and agreed that the programmes could be edited and otherwise be made to conform fully to the policies of ABC's Department of Broadcasting Standards and Practice. Thus, through a chain of apparently standard transactions, the limited editing rights which had been granted by the plaintiffs had developed into very wide powers in the hands of the American Broadcasting Co. It broadcast a 90-minute 'Monty Python' programme and, in accordance with the powers it had negotiated, it deleted 24 minutes of the original material to make advertising space available. The authors successfully sued the defendant in the USA for *copyright* infringement since it had exceeded the terms of the original licence granted to the BBC. On these facts,the right of integrity would now apply, and it is unlikely that reliance could be placed upon the above exemption since the decision to interfere with the programme to facilitate advertising was not in compliance with any statutory duty nor had it been taken under the 'good taste or decency' provisions.

### False attribution of work

Moral rights generally operate to allow a person to be identified with his own work or to object to interference with his own work. The right against false attribution involves the converse situation. The person concerned is complaining that he is not the author of the work, contrary to the assertion made by the defendant (s. 84).

*Illustration 8.1*   In *Moore* v *News of the World Ltd* [1972] 1 QB 441, the *News of the World* published an article, allegedly prepared by the divorced wife of a famous film star, under the headline, 'How my life with the Saint went sour'. As the article was not written by her an action under the Copyright Act 1956, s. 43, succeeded. She would now have an action under s. 84 of the 1988 Act. In many cases, of course, there might also be an action for defamation or passing off.

### Right to privacy in relation to certain photographs and films

A person who for private and domestic purposes commissions the taking of a photograph or the making of a film, where copyright subsists in the resulting work, has certain rights not to have copies of the work issued to the public or the work exhibited or shown in public or broadcast (s. 85). Under the Copyright Act 1956, a right of privacy of a person who commissioned the taking of a portrait, photograph or engraving was recognised by conferring the copyright in such works upon the commissioner subject to any agreement to the contrary. Now, the author of such a work is entitled to the copyright, but the right to privacy is recognised by this power to restrain unauthorised use of the work.

### Consent and waiver of moral rights

In theory, it should not be possible for an author to waive his moral rights. Whilst copyright, which is an economic right, can be transferred, moral rights represent different aspects of copyright which are so personal and important that they should not be capable of surrender and should subsist regardless of other transactions in relation to a work. But theory and practice are far apart. The exceptions and qualifications to moral rights which have already been mentioned are attempts to balance, some would say emasculate, moral rights as against business reality. Further erosions relate to consent and waiver.

   The difficulties which could arise if an author or his personal representatives exercised continuing control over his works, regardless of any agreements expressed in a contract, would create, it was thought, too much uncertainty in connection with the exploitation of copyright works. Accordingly, s. 87 provides that a person may consent to any specific acts which otherwise would constitute infringements of moral rights. Further, it is possible to waive these rights. Although it is provided that any waiver must be in writing, signed by the person giving up the rights, nothing excludes the operation of general contract law or estoppel in relation to informal waiver. So there are a number of ways, formal and informal, in which a person may lose his moral rights either in relation to a specific work or to works generally and, indeed, in relation to existing or future works.

The existence of a power to waive moral rights calls into question the effectiveness of the entire code of moral rights. Presumably, unless a contract can be attacked on the grounds of undue influence or restraint of trade, it will be possible for contracts to contain standard clauses for the waiver of all moral rights. For all save the most successful authors this could indeed be their fate.

What then of the value of the statutory provisions? It has been argued that the code itself will provide an incentive for groups representing authors and publishers to negotiate standard terms with such provisions in mind. For example, whilst the BBC may insist upon a waiver of the statutory moral rights provisions on the grounds that it would otherwise be too difficult for it to work effectively, it may well continue to substitute a code of conduct which in fact gives to the author rights of paternity and of integrity but which are more clearly limited to those occasions when it might be 'reasonable in the circumstances' for the author to assert them.

## Remedies

Section 103(1) provides that infringement of a moral right is actionable as a breach of statutory duty. It is arguable that this should include a power to award additional damages as for infringement of copyright, although it is unfortunate that s. 103(1) did not relate back to s. 96 which deals with copyright remedies generally. Damages will certainly have to encompass non-pecuniary losses as the rights are not economic in nature.

There are a few express matters affecting remedies here. First, in connection with the right of integrity, the court has power, if it thinks it is an adequate remedy in the circumstances, to grant an injunction prohibiting an act unless an approved disclaimer is made dissociating the author or director from the treatment of the work (s. 103(2)). This will be particularly important in circumstances where, perhaps, the cost involved in avoiding the infringement altogether would be excessive compared with the particular harm involved. Secondly, in relation to the right of paternity, the court, when considering remedies, is required to take into account any delay in asserting the right (s. 78(5)). Again, this suggests a kind of estoppel situation where, for example, publishers have invested heavily in preparing for publication a work before the author or director chooses to assert the right. Thirdly, the author of a work of architecture in the form of a building, who is identified on the building, simply has the right to require the identification to be removed if the building has been subjected to derogatory treatment (s. 80(5)).

## Transmission of rights

Although moral rights are not assignable *inter vivos,* s. 95 sets out complex provisions for their transmission on death. The rights of paternity, integrity and of privacy of certain photographs and films can be specifically bequeathed. If there is no such direction in a will, but the copyright in the work in question forms part of the estate, the right passes to the person to whom the copyright passes. However, if neither of these situations applies, then the right is exercisable by the author's personal representatives. (Further complex provisions apply where different rights within a copyright work pass to different persons and the moral rights are split similarly between them.) Any person who acquires moral rights on the death of an author or director is bound by consent or waiver previously given.

These provisions are not only complex in themselves, but can make for considerable difficulty in practice where, as will frequently be the case, the copyright and moral rights are split. For example, an author may have sold different exclusive copyright rights in his novel and may also have made specific provision in his will to different people relating to moral rights. Bearing in mind that these rights also last for 50 years from the death of the author it may become very difficult indeed to identify who can exercise them.

It is highly desirable that any author or director making a will should consider carefully in whom he wishes to entrust his moral rights and that the identity of the guardian of his rights is readily ascertainable by users of the copyright work.

## Transitional provisions (sch. 1, paras 22 to 24)

Nothing *done* before commencement of the 1988 Act is actionable by virtue of any of the moral right provisions.

However, the Copyright Act 1956, s. 43, continues to apply to acts done before commencement. Therefore, the situation in relation to false attribution of authorship continues in more or less the same way. Section 43(4) of the 1956 Act will still be applicable to alterations of artistic works before commencement. Indeed, the test of 'derogatory treatment' under the new right of integrity may be more difficult to satisfy in a case such as *Carlton Illustrators* v *Coleman & Co. Ltd* [1911] 1 KB 771 (see earlier).

The rights of paternity and integrity do not apply in relation to any films made before commencement or to any literary, dramatic, musical or artistic work of an author who died before commencement; nor does the right of privacy (s. 85) apply to films or photographs taken before commencement. Photographs commissioned before commencement but taken afterwards will acquire the right of privacy even though the commissioner is also the first owner (sch. 1, para. 11).

Where the author of a literary, dramatic, musical or artistic work had assigned or licensed it before commencement or where the copyright first vested in a person other than the author, no moral rights can be exercised in relation to anything done by virtue of such assignment or licence.

Lastly, moral rights do not apply to anything done in relation to a record made in pursuance of the Copyright Act 1956, s. 8, which was the (now-abolished) statutory recording licence enabling persons to make sound recordings of musical works.

## Concluding comments

Various criticisms have been made of the way in which the 1988 Act has expressly included moral rights but, through exceptions and qualifications, has severely limited their application.

These were all designed to ensure that the rights should not impose unduly burdensome obstacles to the normal course of copyright business activity. The government was concerned with practicalities, and how exceptions from moral rights could be justified in the light of either British tradition or current practice. Critics, however, were unhappy with this approach: 'There is a real diminution in the value and strength of moral rights, which are crucially weakened . . . [whereby] power is shifted from the author to the proprietor, publisher or other source of economic strength' (M. Fisher MP, HC Deb., 26 May 1988, col. 359).

The question that arises, therefore, is what differences these provisions will make in practice. First, both authors and directors and those who deal with them must consider the rights which now exist and the extent to which they can, or should, be modified by consent or waiver. Contracts dealing with copyright works should now make some provision with regard to moral rights as also should the wills of authors and directors. Organisations which offer standard-term contracts to authors will have to introduce provisions relating to moral rights. In some cases, it may be that these organisations will provide for the waiver of rights and substitute clearer and more acceptable moral rights provisions using the criterion of 'reasonable' conduct on both sides, a specific requirement regrettably absent from the legislation itself. In many cases, therefore, apart from the need to address the issues, little may change, save that the point at which contractual negotiations relating to moral rights issues begin may be rather different. However, with the less well advised, difficulties could arise, particularly in identifying holders of the rights after the author's death.

# Chapter 9
# Copyright, Competition and the EEC Dimension

### Copyright as a qualified monopoly: the problem of monopolies

Copyright is a kind of monopoly. Like any other property right, the owner is
given certain rights to exclude others from access to, or use of, his property, or to
decide whether or not to authorise others to use it and set the conditions for any
such use. As we have seen, there is an important public interest consideration
underlying the entire copyright system: authors and other exploiters of copyright
material are given rights partly to provide an incentive for creativity and the
promotion of the arts, in the broadest sense, for the benefit of society generally.

The creation of exclusive rights, however, represents one side of the coin: the
right to exploit the protected works and to obtain appropriate rewards for their
use. But that may not reflect satisfactorily the other side of the coin: the public
interest may not be satisfied if the copyright owner is not prepared to make his
works available to the public, whether at all, at a reasonable cost, or subject to
reasonable conditions. In certain circumstances, the monopoly rights granted to
copyright owners may clash with the public interest and, in particular, may also
operate in an anti-competitive way.

Copyright, together with the industries and activities associated with the
dissemination of copyright works, ranges through the whole world of information, education and entertainment and touches upon many aspects of our
everyday activities. The economic and social implications of the tensions between
copyright and the public interest — whether it be the interest in ensuring public
access to works upon reasonable terms or the interest in free and fair competition
generally — are of major importance. The critical question is: how can the law
provide a satisfactory reconciliation between copyright as a private property
right and the public interest?

### General methods of reconciling copyright and the public interest

The structure of copyright laws in all countries is designed to effect a reasonable
balance between the public interest in giving authors rights in order to promote
cultural, social and economic progress and the public interest in free access, or
access on reasonable terms, to copyright material. Chapter 6 deals with the very

wide range of acts which are permitted in relation to copyright works, many of which are cases where the private rights of authors in the relevant works have been cut down in response to the perceived greater interest of the public in access to and use of copyright works in specified circumstances. Some of the fundamental concepts in copyright law, for example, the idea-expression dichotomy (see chapter 1) also illustrate this balancing process. All these limitations upon the exclusive rights of copyright owners are matters which are recognised and provided for in the international conventions.

### Collective and compulsory licences

The compulsory licence is a mechanism available to safeguard the public interest in relation to some intellectual property rights, for example, patents and registered and unregistered designs. As opposed to licences that are based upon voluntary agreement between the parties, compulsory licences empower persons in specified circumstances to exploit the intellectual property subject, however, to the payment of compensation (usually a royalty fixed by a public authority) to the owner of the right concerned. In patent law, any person may apply for a compulsory licence (after a certain period) where the patented invention is not being commercially exploited in the UK to the fullest extent that is reasonably practicable or in other related situations (Patents Act 1977, s. 48).

Compulsory licences are rarely popular with rights owners in any areas; and the prospect of compulsory licences has been particularly unpopular with copyright owners. This long-standing hostility is seen in the international conventions, especially the Berne Convention, which in general favour the freedom of the author to exercise his rights as he wishes in preference to the compulsory licence which reduces full property rights to little more than 'equitable rights to remuneration'.

Even so, the Berne Convention permits some compulsory licences: in connection with some aspects of broadcasting (Art. 11 *bis* (2)) and sound recordings (Art. 13(1)) and also in certain limited cases relating to reprographic reproduction; and so also do some of the other international conventions. Under the Copyright Act, 1956, s. 8, there was a compulsory licence provision enabling anybody to make a recording of a musical work (subject to payment of a fixed statutory royalty of 6.25%) once the copyright owner had licensed any person to make and market a recording of the music. (That compulsory licence was abolished by the government because it was felt better to leave such matters to free negotiation and market forces!)

Compulsory licensing, then, is widely regarded as having a weakening effect upon the concept of copyright as a genuine property right. However, *collective* licensing is seen as having a strengthening effect upon the system. The reasons for this have been explained earlier. To work effectively, licensing bodies must have a comprehensive collection of the relevant rights. Therefore, in certain circumstances, the 1988 Act provides reserve powers to grant compulsory licences in relation to specified works (see chapter 7). In these situations, rights owners and collecting societies try to ensure that the remuneration recovered from a system of collective or compulsory licensing, in general to be controlled by the Copyright Tribunal, is not less than would be obtained under voluntary, individual contractual arrangements.

## Copyright and competition

*Under UK law*

Because the scope for granting compulsory licences is still very limited in copyright law, there may still be occasions when the way in which copyright owners deal, or refuse to deal, with their rights may be seen by some as undesirable and, indeed, inconsistent with the competition laws and policies relating to commercial and industrial activities.

Two cases in recent years demonstrate the potential conflict between copyright and competition in English law. The first was where the BBC and ITV successfully relied upon copyright to prevent *Time Out* from copying their weekly programme schedules *(Independent Television Publications Ltd* v *Time Out Ltd* [1984] FSR 64). The defendant argued that if these schedules were protected as compilations under copyright law, this in effect gave the plaintiffs a monopoly over the information itself, which was against the public interest. Why should we all be forced to buy the *Radio Times* and *TV Times* to get full and accurate information about advance programme schedules (apart from the more limited information which newspapers are licensed to give)? Whitford J (in deciding the case) emphasised that these issues went beyond his jurisdiction and, if copyright was to be further circumscribed, it was for Parliament, not for him, to do so. This led the defendant to seek relief through the competition law route.

Under the Competition Act 1980, s. 2, the Office of Fair Trading (OFT) has power to investigate commercial activities to determine whether 'anti-competitive' practices (defined widely by reference to actions which prevent, restrict or distort competition) are being pursued. In this case, the OFT did so determine and this led to the next stage whereby reference has to be made to the Monopolies and Mergers Commission (MMC) for its view on whether such an anti-competitive practice is 'contrary to the public interest'. In the event, the MMC was divided on whether the exercise by the BBC and ITV of their rights in the programme schedules was against the public interest and so the broadcasting companies could not be obliged under competition law to grant a licence.

The second case arose in connection with spare parts for cars. Ford Motor Co., relying upon its then legal right to control its replacement body panels by virtue of its copyright in the underlying drawings, refused to license independent manufacturers to reproduce these spare parts. The OFT and the MMC found that this was an anti-competitive practice within the terms of the Competition Act 1980 and the MMC also declared that Ford's behaviour was contrary to the public interest. Nevertheless, the legislation did not empower it to force Ford to grant licences upon reasonable terms.

Much has happened since then. In *British Leyland Motor Corporation Ltd* v *Armstrong Patents Co. Ltd* [1986] AC 577 (see chapter 7) the House of Lords used the principle of non-derogation of grant to destroy any monopoly in spare parts. Although this was, according to their lordships, based upon the technicalities of copyright law, there is little doubt that the underlying economic and competition implications were responsible for their ruling. Since then, the unregistered design right has been withheld from must-fit spare parts (such as car body panels and replacement exhausts) in any event (see chapter 12).

*The 1988 Act*
Section 144 deals specifically with the situation where a report of the MMC finds
that restrictions in copyright licence agreements or refusals of copyright owners
to grant licences on reasonable terms may be expected to operate, or have
operated, against the public interest. In such cases, the powers of the MMC now
include the power to cancel or modify those conditions and, instead or in
addition, to provide that licences in respect of the copyright shall be available as
of right. (Section 238 introduces similar powers in relation to the design right.)
However, to ensure that the emphasis on a free competition policy does not
override basic copyright law, s. 144(3) provides that the Minister shall only
exercise such powers 'if he is satisfied that to do so does not contravene any
convention relating to copyright to which the United Kingdom is a party'.

At present, however, UK competition law has still had only a relatively limited
impact upon copyright. References may still be made in appropriate cases to the
OFT and, from there, to the MMC, but such references are rare, although further
proposals for strengthening UK competition law are being considered. Of
greater importance, however, are the competition provisions under EEC law.

## EEC competition law

There are two relevant, and fundamentally important, provisions of European
Community law which affect copyright and other intellectual property rights:
first, Arts. 30 to 36 and 59 of the EEC Treaty, which concern the free movement
of goods and services between member States within the Community; secondly,
Arts 85 and 86 relating to agreements which could prevent, restrict or distort
competition within the Common Market, and also to abuses by undertakings
which have a dominant position within the Market.

*Free movement of goods and services*
Articles 30 to 34 of the EEC Treaty provide that quantitative restrictions on
imports and exports, and all measures having equivalent effect, between member
States shall be prohibited. At first sight, there is an obvious conflict between the
nature of all intellectual property rights, whether patents, trade marks, copyright
or designs, which are territorial in nature and the principle of the free movement
of goods and services. The owner of a patent, a trade mark or a copyright in the
UK, as a general proposition, may enforce his rights conferred by English law
only in the UK. Copyright owners, of course, will have separate national
copyrights in most countries which they can exercise and enforce as appropriate.
The rights granted may vary in different countries, and it is possible under UK
*copyright* law for a copyright owner to control or restrict the importation of
certain types of copyright works from other countries. In so far as these copyright
powers are used to prevent copyright works coming into this country from other
member States, this would appear to be contrary to the provisions which are
designed to ensure the free movement of goods between all member States.

These provisions, however, are subject to Art. 36, which provides that the free
movement principle 'shall not preclude . . . the protection of industrial and
commercial property' (which includes copyright) provided that such restrictions
do not 'constitute a means of arbitrary discrimination or a disguised restricton on
trade between member States'.

This does not mean, though, that copyright law is unaffected by the free movement principle. The European Court has tried to effect a compromise between protecting property rights and promoting European policy on the free movement of goods and services by drawing a rather fine distinction. The distinction is between the *'existence'* of a property right, which must be protected and which cannot ordinarily be limited by the principle of free movement of goods and services, and the *'exercise'* of a right, which is not the central aspect of a property right and which is subject to European rules of free movement and competition.

How, then, is this distinction between the 'existence' of a right and the 'exercise' of a right to be made? The answer, according to the European Court of Justice, lies in analysing any property right and separating its essential and fundamental qualities, 'its specific subject-matter', on the one hand, which are to be protected, from the lesser rights, on the other, which can be interfered with. In most cases,the specific subject-matter of a copyright work, as also of other intellectual property rights, comprises the right of the owner to put that work on the market for the first time, either himself or with his consent.

This means that if A is the copyright owner of a novel, he has the right to put that novel on the market or to license somebody else to do so, and he can enforce such a right strictly: he is entitled to some royalty or return either through selling the book or licensing others to do so. Thus, if B publishes the novel in France without A's authority, then regardless of A's rights in France, if B or a purchaser from B attempts to import that copy of the novel into the UK for commercial purposes, A can enforce his UK copyright since the importation is an interference with his specific subject-matter, the *existence* of his copyright, which right is not overridden by Arts 30 and 34. However, if A sells his novel in France or licenses somebody else to sell that novel in France, then, whatever his strict copyright position may be in the UK, he is prevented under the rules of the EEC from using copyright law to restrict the free movement of that copy of the novel, since he has obtained his reward from that transaction once and 'his right has been exhausted'; any additional rights which he may wish to exercise against that work under copyright law are subject to EEC rules, and in particular to those concerning free movement.

This example concerns 'parallel imports': namely, the importation of physical material, such as a book, a record or a film, which embodies copyright works and its marketing alongside identical goods marketed by or with the authority of the UK copyright owner or licensee. The relevant right which has been exhausted is the right to prevent commercial dealings with 'infringing copies' in the UK. Even though they may be infringing copies if imported from countries outside the EEC, they will not be infringing copies if they were marketed by or with the consent of the copyright owner in another member State (s. 27(5) of the 1988 Act) despite the fact that consent was limited to their marketing in that particular State and did not extend to their importation into the UK.

Clearly, though, not all of the rights which comprise the specific subject-matter of copyright will be exhausted by such marketing. The sale of a copyright recording in France, for example, would no more give the purchaser the right to copy it or perform it in public without permission, than it would permit a purchaser of a record in the UK to do this. Those specific rights remain with the copyright owner and they are not exhausted by the sale of the record. Parallel imports were dealt with in chapter 5 but it may be of value to use similar examples again to illustrate the European dimension further.

*Illustration 9.1*   Company A is the owner in the UK and in Portugal of the copyright in the sound recordings of the pop group, the Bee Gees. It had granted an exclusive licence to its UK subsidiary, AUK, and to its Portuguese subsidiary, AP, to manufacture and sell in their respective countries. D obtained records in Portugal made by AP and imported them into the UK. Could AUK sue for copyright infringement? Since this took place *before* Portugal joined the EEC, AUK was entitled to exercise its rights under UK copyright law and sue for infringement. The free movement of goods principle under EEC law did not apply. (*Polydor Ltd* v *Harlequin Record Shops Ltd* [1980] FSR 362, [1982] FSR 358, CA and ECJ.)

*Illustration 9.2*   Were the same facts to take place today, then AUK would be prevented from *exercising* its rights under UK copyright law. The licence granted by A to AP in Portugal had exhausted the rights of the copyright owner or its other licensees in connection with the free movement of records made by AP after they had been sold by AP in Portugal.

*Illustration 9.3*   GEMA is the German copyright society which is concerned with the collection of music royalties on records and cassettes in Germany. In most European countries, including Germany, the royalty rate was 8% of the retail price of the recording. In the UK, under the Copyright Act 1956, s. 8 (which is repealed by the 1988 Act), the statutory royalty under the compulsory licence was only 6.25% of the retail price. The question which arose was whether GEMA, as owner of the relevant copyright interests in Germany, was entitled to stop the importation of records puchased in the UK unless the importers paid the difference between the UK and the German royalty. Under German law, GEMA had a right to prevent the importation of such records without consent. However, the European Court of Justice held that the rights in respect of the reproduction and marketing of those records had been exhausted once they had been placed on the UK market with the consent of the copyright owner; GEMA could not extract the additional royalty in Germany. (*Musik-Vertrieb Membran GmbH* v *GEMA* (cases 55/80 and 57/80) [1981] FSR 433.)

(It should be mentioned, however,that the attitude of the European Court of Justice towards cases where goods have been put on the market in pursuance of a compulsory licence is ambivalent. In *Pharmon BV* v *Hoechst AG* (case 19/84) [1986] FSR 108 the court held that the owner of a patent in one member State could use his rights under patent law to stop the importation of patented products made in another member State by a compulsory licensee since the patent owner had not 'voluntarily' placed the goods upon the market himself or through a licensee of his choice. In the GEMA case, however, it should be noted that the sound recordings were in fact made by or with the consent of the copyright owners: they did not come from a manufacturer who had made use of the compulsory licence provision under the Copyright Act 1956, s. 8)

Although the European law in this area is expressed in terms of *legal* rules and

principles, the economic considerations underlying them are of major importance when the court is considering and developing the law; for example, when
determining which of the rights which make up copyright are part of the specific
subject of the copyright and which are not. Account has to be taken of the fact
that different rights are exploited in different ways and that the same analysis
applied to the free movement of copyright sound recordings, videos or books
after first sale in a member state would not necessarily apply to the performing
right.

*Illustration 9.4*   A owned the copyright in the film *Le Boucher* and granted to B,
a Belgian company, the exclusive right to show the film in Belgian cinemas at any
time but not on Belgian television until 40 months after the first cinema showing.
A also granted a right to G, a German company, to show the film on German
television. The German television broadcast was picked up in Belgium by D, a
Belgian cable company, and relayed to its subscribers in Belgium. When A
brought an action against D for infringement of its Belgian copyright, D argued
that A, having consented to the showing of the film on German television, had
exhausted its performance right with regard thereto and, under Art. 59 (the free
movement of services provision) could not thereafter object to the film being
shown anywhere else within the EEC.

The European Court acknowledged that the problems involved with films
which could be performed repeatedly and indefinitely were not the same as those
governing literary and artistic works made available to the public by means
which were inseparable from the circulation of support material. Different
economic considerations affected the property analysis of the performing right.
The owner of copyright and his licensee have a legitimate interest in controlling
the public showing of the film. The right to insist on royalties for *each* showing
was part of the 'essential function' of copyright for this type of work; the
copyright owner's rights could not be exhausted simply because there had been
one public performance of the work on television.

(*SA Campagnie Générale pour la Diffusion de la Télévision Coditel* v *SA Ciné
Vog Films ( No. 1)* (case 62/79) [1980] ECR 881; see also *Bassett* v *SACEM* [1984]
3 CMLR 233.)

There is a lack of uniformity of copyright law within the EEC; and
harmonisation has not yet taken place. Where there are stronger rights in one
member State in comparison with another, does this entitle a rights owner who
has put goods on the market in one State to use his stronger rights in the other
country to control the importation of those goods; or would that be an
impermissible 'means of arbitrary discrimination or a disguised restriction on
trade between member States'? (Art. 36).

The European Court has recognised that intellectual property laws may differ
between member States and, provided that there is no discrimination based upon
nationality, the consequences of such differences must be accepted. 'In the
present state of Community law and in the absence of Community standardisa-
tion or of a harmonisation of laws, the determination of the conditions and
procedure under which . . . protection is granted is a matter for national rules'
(*Keurkoop BV* v *Nancy Kean Gifts BV* (case 144/81) [1982] ECR 2853; *Thetford* v
*Fiamma* [1988] 3 CMLR 549; *CICRA* v *Renault* (case 53/87, 5 Oct 1988)). It

follows from this that the rights which comprise the specific subject-matter of copyright and which will not ordinarily be interfered with by Community law may differ between member States.

*Illustration 9.5*   A, the owners of the UK copyright in the film, *Never Say Never Again,* assigned the management of the video production rights in Denmark to M. D lawfully purchased a copy of the film in the UK and imported it into Denmark with a view to hiring it out in his video shop in Denmark. At the time of purchase, UK copyright law did not confer any rental right on copyright owners, whereas Danish law did. Thus, UK law allowed the author to control the first sale of a video cassette, not the hiring of it. The question which arose was whether A and M could enforce the rental right against D in Denmark.

D's argument was that as the video cassette had been put on to the UK market by or with the consent of the copyright owner, A, this had exhausted all the relevant UK rights in those video casettes and D was free thereafter to distribute it as he wished. However, the European Court held that the Danish rental right could be enforced against D. Even though the specific subject-matter of the right in the UK did not then include a rental right,this did not prevent the recognition of greater property rights in Denmark.

The Danish legislation was not discriminatory between different nationals. In contrast, the *GEMA* case was, for the extra royalty was claimed on the simple ground of importation from one member State to another.

*(Warner Bros Inc.* v *Christiansen* (1988) case 158/86, *The Times,* 1 June 1988).

The true nature of a rental right had not been considered by the European Court until the *Warner* decision. The court looked at the economic facts: the emergence of a specific market for the rental of video cassettes as distinct from their sale and also the fact that this market affected a wider public than the market for their sale and afforded a major potential source of revenue for the authors of films. A rental right, therefore, was clearly justified on the grounds of protection of industrial and commercial property under Art. 36 and constituted part of its specific subject matter which should not be denied a copyright owner in the name of free movement of goods.

It should be noted that the introduction of a rental right into UK law (1988 Act, s. 18) is unlikely to affect this decision. The sale of the record in the UK without restriction would not, in itself, confer any licence on the purchaser to rent the record and so there would be no exhaustion of *that* specific right anywhere in the EEC.

*Competition policy*
*Article 85* provides that all agreements between undertakings, formal and informal, which may affect trade between member States and which have as their object or effect the prevention, restriction or distortion of competition within the Common Market are void unless given a blanket or individual exemption by the EEC Commission.

In the main, Art. 85 affects the kinds of clauses which can appear in licence agreements. Those which are anti-competitive may fall foul of the law and accordingly it is of the utmost importance for those concerned with licence agreements (other than the very small, which are expressly excluded, and those which have no effect at all upon inter-State trade) to be aware of the general approach adopted by the Commission.

Most of the developments relating to which terms in licences are or are not acceptable have been in other areas of intellectual property, especially patent licensing, rather than in copyright. However, the European Court was called upon to consider some aspects of Art. 85 in relation to copyright in a second application to it in *Coditel SA* v *CinéVog Films SA (No. 2)* (case 262/81) [1982] ECR 3381. Since the court had decided earlier that the free movement of services principle in Art. 59 did not prevent D from protecting its performing right, D then argued that the agreements between the copyright owner and the licensees came within the scope of Art. 85(1) and that their anti-competitive nature had to be considered in the light of both the legal and, more importantly, the economic circumstances. The court agreed that in some situations exclusive licences in relation to films could be anti-competitive. However, the granting of exclusive cinema exhibition licences was simply the means of exploiting one of the fundamental copyright rights, and was not in itself such as to prevent, restrict or distort competition. In particular, the court required those alleging that an exclusive licence of performing rights infringed Art. 85 to bear the onus of proof. It was a task for the national courts to determine whether the agreement was anti-competitive and they would have to investigate in particular:

. . . whether or not the exercise of the exclusive right to exhibit a cinematographic film creates barriers which are artificial and unjustifiable in terms of the needs of the cinematographic industry, or the possibility of charging fees which exceed a fair return on investment, or an exclusivity the duration of which is disproportionate to those requirements, and whether or not, from a general point of view, such exercise within a given geographic area is such as to prevent, restrict or distort competition within the common market.

It can be seen, therefore, that the nature of the exercise in Art. 85 issues is primarily an economic one. Clauses relating to price-fixing, exclusivity, export prohibitions, no-challenge clauses, tying clauses and various other clauses with anti-competitive implications should all be examined with Art. 85 in mind, taking into account that the Commission has established reasonably well-defined rules for clauses in patent and know-how licences (which are not necessarily all applicable to copyright).

*Article 86,* which deals with abuses by undertakings in a dominant position within the Common Market, has a much more direct relevance to copyright matters. It can bite upon any activities of copyright collecting societies, in connection with any of the terms and conditions which they impose in connection with their activities,notwithstanding that they may be national societies since their activities may also affect those in other parts of the Community. These collecting societies have considerable market power not only over their members, since they offer the only practicable means of operating certain types of copyright, but also over those who seek to obtain licences from the societies. Thus, the Commission and the European Court have power to object, for example, to terms in copyright assignments to GEMA which required the assignment of all rights world-wide in respect of present and all future works; whereas a requirement imposed on an author or composer to assign exclusively all his present and future works for a particular category of exploitation may not be an abuse if it can be shown that this is desirable for the efficient exploitation of such rights. (See *Re GEMA* [1971] CMLR D35; *Belgische Radio en Televisie* v *SV SABAM* (case 127/73) [1974] ECR 313; *Greenwich Film Production* v *SACEM* (case 22/79) [1979] ECR 3275).

As in the *Coditel (No. 2) Case* in relation to Art. 85, so, in relation to Art. 86, the European Court of Justice will not ordinarily regard the simple exercise of a copyright, or copyright related, right as an abuse of a dominant position. An additional element must be present. Thus, in *CICRA* v *Renault* (case 53/87, 5 Oct 1988) a car manufacturer, the holder of registered design rights over car body parts, was entitled to exercise these rights against independent manufacturers or wholesalers without falling foul of Art. 86. To have done that, the additional element would have had to comprise, for example, a refusal by the car manufacturers to continue to make spare parts for cars no longer being produced but of which there were still a large number in circulation; or the charging of 'excessive' prices; or the 'arbitrary' refusal to supply spare parts to independent repairers. (See also *Volvo* v *Veng* (case 283/87, 5 Oct 1988)). In this respect, it would appear that the position adopted by the ECJ in recent cases is less intrusive that that adopted earlier in the UK by the MMC in the Ford body panels decision; or, indeed, the underlying competition rationale of the House of Lords in *British Leyland* v *Armstrong Patents* (see Chapter 12).

*The EEC Green Paper*
In June 1988, the EEC Commission adopted the text of a Green Paper, *Copyright and the Challenge of Technology — Copyright Issues Requiring Immediate Action* (COM (88)172). In it, the Commission raised for discussion some of the more urgent copyright issues which are now emerging at Community level as a result of the growing importance of copyright to industry and commerce. Amongst the matters for discussion were piracy; audio-visual home copying; the distribution right, exhaustion and rental right; computer programs; databases; and the role of the Community in bilateral and multilateral external relations. Other matters promised soon include design rights. The progress of Community harmonisation of copyright law has been very slow. It is likely to continue to be so, although there could well be Directives in some areas which will necessitate change to the 1988 legislation.

# Chapter 10 Remedies

## Introduction

Remedies for copyright infringement have to serve the needs of quite different types of copyright owner. At one extreme is the one-off copyright dispute: the author of a book or the composer of a song who is seeking redress against another individual who is alleged to have copied it. At the other extreme is *piracy,* that is, the unauthorised reproduction of copyright and related works for commercial purposes and all subsequent commercial dealings with them. Piracy is a term which also embraces *bootlegging,* that is, the unauthorised commercial recording or dealing with live performances; and *counterfeiting,* which involves the packaging of the infringing copies (often together with the unauthorised use of trade marks) so as to look identical to the genuine products. The scale of piracy in books, sound and video recordings and films has been enormous, both nationally and internationally and, in world-wide terms, runs into billions of pounds.

It is the latter kinds of piracy which cause major economic harm. They have focused attention, in recent years, on the need to make the remedies and procedures available to intellectual property owners more effective. At the international level, the problems are under constant review: for example, within the GATT (General Agreement on Tariffs and Trades) negotiations and by WIPO (World Intellectual Property Organisation); and within the EEC, the European Commission has become a little more active in grappling with these issues. There has also been considerable and increasing activity by trade associations and right-holders' societies both to put pressure on national governments to improve the law and also to assist their own members to enforce their legal rights through the criminal and civil process. For example, the International Federation of Producers of Phonograms and Videograms (IFPI) and the British Phonographic Industry (BPI) have been very active and quite successful in combating piracy in recordings. In 1982, the computer industry formed the Federation Against Software Theft (FAST) out of frustration at the increasing losses caused by piracy. Its initiative led to clarification of the copyright treatment of computer programs and also improvements in the remedies available against infringers.

Another important development has been the reinforcement of civil remedies for copyright and other intellectual property infringements by increasingly severe criminal sanctions. At one time, copyright law was thought of almost exclusively as a civil matter. Now, the range of criminal offences in this area and the penalties for them, have been significantly strengthened.

Procedural matters are also of prime importance in copyright litigation. It can be frustrating for copyright owners with clear legal rights and powerful remedies to find that these are delayed or even neutralised by procedural obstacles placed in their paths. All these issues will emerge more fully as we consider the various remedies in their turn.

### Civil remedies in interlocutory proceedings

*Search and seizure: the Anton Piller order*

The *Anton Piller* order is a judicially created device which enables a plaintiff, in some cases, to take an infringer by surprise and ensure that vital evidence and information required for the enforcement of the plaintiff's rights are not destroyed. The typical situation to be dealt with is one where the defendant has got whiff that proceedings are going to be brought and takes steps immediately to get rid of infringing copyright material and any other incriminating evidence. He can then deny he has ever had any infringing copies. Alternatively where there is some evidence that he has had infringing copies, he might claim that these were inexplicable mavericks amongst the bulk of legitimate material and were unlikely to recur.

In the *Anton Piller* case itself ( *Anton Piller KG* v *Manufacturing Processes Ltd* [1976] Ch 55), the plaintiff sought an *ex parte* order (that is, an order made without notice or warning being given to the defendant, who is not a party to the proceedings) to permit the plaintiff to enter the defendant's premises to inspect and remove relevant documents for safe-keeping. The court, when met with the argument that it had no power to make such an order, something which smacked strongly of being a search warrant in civil proceedings, did not accept the analogy. Lord Denning MR said that it was not like a search warrant because the order only authorised entry and inspection with the permission of the defendant. However, he did go on to say that should the defendant refuse permission, this would be contempt of court and also adverse inferences could be drawn against him!

Whatever the theoretical niceties, this development heralded what was to become a much-used, and sometimes abused, procedure whereby plaintiffs were regularly applying for and obtaining orders which enabled them to clamp down on unlawful trading. Even the decision of the House of Lords in *Rank Film Distributors Ltd* v *Video Information Centre* [1982] AC 380, which held that a defendant could rely on the privilege against self-incrimination to refuse to disclose names and addresses which might implicate him criminally, was reversed by the Supreme Court Act 1981, s. 72, which removed the privilege (although evidence obtained for the civil proceedings may not be used in later criminal proceedings).

In recent years, however, a more even balance has been restored. It has been emphasised that the plaintiff's lawyers have duties of full disclosure to the court when seeking such orders and that the defendant's rights must be safeguarded. Accordingly, *Anton Piller* orders are still granted but the conditions which must be satisfied are that:

(a)   the order is required to enable justice to be done;
(b)   there is grave danger of the defendant destroying, losing or hiding relevant material if the defendant is put on notice;
(c)   the plaintiff has a very strong prima facie case;
(d)   inspection would do no harm to the defendant and his case; and
(e)   potential damage to the plaintiff is likely to be very serious.

The safeguards for the defendant are that:

(a)   the order is served by a solicitor, who is an officer of the court;
(b)   the defendant is given an opportunity to consult his solicitor;
(c)   the defendant is allowed to apply for a discharge of the order; and
(d)   the plaintiff should provide an undertaking in damages, possibly supported by a bond, to ensure that the defendant has an effective remedy should the plaintiff have abused his rights.

In appropriate cases, the scope of an *Anton Piller* order can be very wide indeed hence justifying its description as the civil law's 'nuclear weapon'; it can be used in some circumstances even against innocent infringers; it can require the disclosure and discovery of names and addresses of suppliers and order books (*EMI Ltd* v *Sarwar* [1977] FSR 146; Supreme Court Act 1981, s. 72); it has been granted to plaintiffs against unnamed defendants selling particular categories of infringing articles, for example, against street hawkers (*EMI Records Ltd* v *Kudhail* [1985] FSR 36); it has on occasion been extended to require the defendant not to leave the jurisdiction and to deliver up his passport until the information requested had been obtained (*Bayer AG* v *Winter (No. 1)* [1986] 1 WLR 497). In addition to an *Anton Piller* order, a plaintiff now sometimes also seeks a *'Mareva injunction'* (see Supreme Court Act 1981, s. 37) whereby a defendant is restrained from disposing of assets or removing them from the jurisdiction.

It should be re-emphasised, however, that care must now be taken in preparing an application for an *Anton Piller* order and ensuring that it is sought only in a proper case, lest the plaintiff and his lawyers are penalised. For example, in *Columbia Picture Industries Inc.* v *Robinson* [1987] Ch 38, the court stated that there were five essential criteria which must be observed:

(a)   The order must be drawn so as to extend no further than the minimum extent necessary to achieve its purpose, namely the preservation of documents or articles which might otherwise be destroyed or concealed. Once the plaintiff's solicitors have satisfied themselves what material exists and have had an opportunity to take copies thereof, the material ought to be returned to its owner
(b)   A detailed record of the material taken should always be made by the solicitors who execute the order before material is removed from premises.
(c)   No material should be taken unless clearly covered by the terms of the order.
(d)   Seized material, the ownership of which is in dispute, should be handed over to the defendant's solicitors on their undertaking for its safe custody and production.

(e)   The affidavits in support ought to err on the side of excessive disclosure.

In this case, although the defendants were undoubted video pirates in a big way, the court held that the plaintiffs and their solicitors had been in breach of all five criteria: for example, they had not given sufficient thought to whether material evidence was likely to be destroyed, they had not disclosed all matters to the court (in particular the fact that the defendants had already previously allowed them access to their premises) and their apparent purpose was to use the *Anton Piller* order as a means summarily of closing down the defendants' business. Accordingly, the defendants were awarded £10,000 damages for misuse of the *Anton Piller* remedy. (See also *Jeffrey Rogers Knitwear* v *Vinola* [1985] FRS 184.)

*Interlocutory injunctions*
An interlocutory injunction is an order restraining the defendant from carrying out alleged infringing activities pending the full trial of the action. At one time it was said that it would only be granted where the plaintiff could establish a strong prima facie case. That test was modified by the House of Lords in *American Cyanamid Co.* v *Ethicon Ltd* [1975] AC 396, which placed more emphasis upon the 'balance of convenience' between the two parties rather than the strength of the plaintiff's case.

The principles governing the grant of interlocutory injunctions are:

(a)   the plaintiff must show an 'arguable' case, that is, that there is an issue to be tried;
(b)   damages would not be an adequate remedy (for example, where the defendant's continued sale of infringing articles could do irreparable harm to the plaintiff's business), and
(c)   the balance of convenience lies in favour of granting the injunction.

Where the court finds it difficult to decide one way or another, then the status quo tends to be preserved. It is only in exceptional cases, where the matter is finely balanced, that the court may look at the respective merits of the parties and the strength of the plaintiff's case.

Nevertheless, there are many occasions where the courts tend still to place weight on the strength of the plaintiff's case rather than looking at the balance of convenience. In particular, this is so where the grant or refusal of the injunction will effectively decide the matter. (In many cases, once an *Anton Piller* order has been granted, that effectively terminates the action; and the outcome of the application for an interlocutory injunction often results in the parties not proceeding further.)

Ordinarily, injunctions, especially those at the interlocutory stage, are prohibitory, preventing the defendant continuing to carry on with a particular activity. Mandatory injunctions, those requiring a defendant to take positive action, are less frequent, and are rarely granted at the interlocutory stage. However, a recent example of the grant of a mandatory injunction in interlocutory proceedings occured in *Leisure Data* v *Bell* [1988] FSR 367 where a defendant was obliged to allow the plaintiff to have access to disputed computer program codes for the purpose of maintaining and improving the program pending trial. This was necessary in order to preserve the value of the computer program and no injustice would be done to the defendant.

## Damages

The general principles governing the award of damages in copyright infringement matters are the same as for any other tort action: namely, that damages are compensatory and should, as far as possible, place the plaintiff in the same position as if the infringement had not been committed.

In many cases, a plaintiff's damages may be readily quantified: for example, where there has been clear evidence of lost sales, the loss of profits can be ascertained; where the defendant has infringed copyright when he might have sought an available licence, compensation is likely to be measured in the terms of lost royalties. In some cases, for example, in copyright infringement actions involving books or films, the commercial damage may not be so easily assessable but a fair attempt has to be made.

Copyright is arguably somewhat unusual, however, in that it may be one of those rare actions in civil law where the courts are authorised to award damages which go beyond the principle of compensation and encompass exemplary awards. Section 97(2) permits a court to award such *additional* damages as the justice of the case may require, having regard to all the circumstances, and in particular to the flagrancy of the infringement and any benefit accruing to the defendant by reason thereof. It is not clear whether the term 'additional' is intended to describe aggravated, but still compensatory, damages, or to go beyond compensation and provide extra damages designed to *punish* the defendant for his conduct. Although this matter has not been settled conclusively, the more general approach has been to regard the provision as authorising punitive or exemplary awards.

Under the Copyright Act 1956 a court could only award additional damages if effective relief was not otherwise available to the plaintiff. The 1988 Act has strengthened the courts' powers by removing this limitation. One of the rare cases where additional damages were awarded under the 1956 Act was in *Williams* v *Settle* [1960] 1 WLR 1072, where the owner of copyright in wedding photographs sought damages against the photographer who had sold them to national newspapers for publication following the murder of a member of the plaintiff's family. The court awarded additional damages to reflect the distress suffered both by the plaintiff and his wife for this invasion of privacy. At that time the action was a straightforward case of copyright infringement. No remedy would have been available had the photographer owned the copyright in the photographs. Section 85 of the 1988 Act now provides a person who commissions photographs for private and domestic purposes with a moral right of privacy and the plaintiff in this situation would now be entitled to damages whether or not he owned the copyright in the photographs. Although an infringement of moral rights is actionable as a breach of statutory duty (s. 103), it is arguable that additional damages should be available just as under s. 97(2), since moral rights are a form of copyright within the structure of copyright law. Indeed, there may be more scope for additional damages in moral right cases than in standard copyright situations.

Another example of additional damages being awarded, as also in defamation cases, might be where a newspaper deliberately goes ahead and publishes infringing copyright material believing that any compensation it might have to pay to the plaintiff would be less than the benefits it gains by publication. (cf. *Rookes* v *Barnard* [1964] AC 1129; *Cassell & Co. Ltd* v *Broome* [1972] AC 1027).

Although a person may be liable for primary infringement of copyright without being aware that he was committing an infringing act, damages will not be awarded against him if he can show that he neither knew nor had reason to believe that copyright subsisted in the work (s. 97(1)). This defence is extremely limited and will, for example, fail where the defendant knows that copyright subsists but makes a mistake as to the owner, as in *Byrne* v *Statist* [1914] 1 KB 622. In any case, all the other remedies will be avaiable against the copyright infringer, regardless of knowledge, as s. 97(1) is 'without prejudice to any other remedy'.

### The repealed conversion remedy

The Copyright Act 1956, s. 18, provided a further, notorious 'conversion' remedy: the owner of copyright in a work was deemed to be the *owner* of any infringing copies, or plate used for making infringing copies, and so was entitled to sue for conversion damages as if he were the owner of articles which incorporated the copyright infringement. For example, in *Infabrics Ltd* v *Jaytex Ltd* [1982] AC 1, the defendant had imported thousands of shirts bearing designs which infringed the plaintiff's copyright. Assuming that the plaintiff was entitled to compensatory damages for copyright infringement, the measure would ordinarily be an appropriate royalty for placing the design on a shirt: if the shirt is worth, say, £10 then the royalty for the design might be, say, £1. The measure of damages would be £1 for every infringing copy sold. However, under the conversion remedy, the copyright owner was entitled to regard all those shirts as its own and damages would be the equivalent of £10 for every shirt. This remedy, which was applied widely in industrial design copyright cases was justly described as 'Draconian' and is abolished by the 1988 Act so far as any past or future infringements are concerned (though it continues to exist for *proceedings* begun before commencement sch. 1 para. 31(2)). In the absence of conversion damages, however, the courts may feel freer to award additional damages under s. 97(2) in appropriate cases.

### Delivery up and destruction of infringing articles

Although the owner of copyright is no longer treated as the owner of infringing copies, it is still possible to obtain an order (within six years from their making) that the infringing copies, or articles specifically designed or adapted for making copies, of a particular copyright work be delivered up to him (s. 99). This is normally to enable such items to be ordered to be forfeited or destroyed under s. 114 but no such order would be made if damages for copyright infringement would be an adequate remedy and it is also provided that an application may be made to the court by a defendant showing cause why such infringing copies should not be forfeited or destroyed (s. 114).

## Seizure of infringing copies

The remedy of self-help is not especially favoured in English law: potentially, it is likely to lead to breaches of the peace. However, in the zealous campaign to provide a comprehensive armoury of weapons against all kinds of copyright pirates, a right of self-help has been provided in s. 100. This entitles the owner of a copyright work, or a person authorised by him, to seize and detain any infringing copy which is found exposed or otherwise available for sale or hire, and in respect of which he would be entitled to apply for an order for delivery up under s. 99. Before rights owners dispense with their lawyers and go themselves in search of infringing copies, however, it must be appreciated how narrow this provision really is.

First, before anything can be seized, notice of the time and place of the proposed seizure must be given to a local police station; secondly, although it is possible for a copyright owner to enter premies to which the public have access for the purpose of exercising this remedy, he cannot seize anything in the possession, custody or control of a person at a permanent or regular place of business; and, thirdly, he may not use any force. Thus, it may be that one of the rare cases where this remedy could be available would be against the itinerant street trader, selling pirated goods out of a case, assuming that he is still there when the copyright owner has returned after having given notice to the local police station! Section 114 (orders for forfeiture, destruction. etc.) applies equally to copies seized under s. 100.

## Account of profits

A successful plaintiff has the option to elect for an account of profits rather than damages. An account of profits will entitle him to the profit which the defendant has made from the infringement which, in some cases, may well exceed the damage which the plaintiff has suffered. However, it is an equitable remedy granted within the court's discretion and is rarely sought since usually it is complex and expensive to unravel the profits which the defendant has made as a result of the infringement from the legitimate profits made by him in the normal course of trading.

## Groundless threats of action for copyright infringement

It is always advisable to be circumspect about threatening others for infringement of patents or registered and unregistered designs since the person threatened may have an action for compensation against those who make groundless threats (Patents Act 1977, s. 70; Registered Designs Act 1949, s. 26; Copyright, Designs and Patents Act 1988, s. 253).

No comparable provision exists in copyright law. An attempt to persuade the courts that groundless threats were actionable under general common law was made in *Granby Marketing Services Ltd* v *Interlego AG* [1984] RPC 209. There, the defendant's warning to the plaintiff's customers that the articles they were purchasing infringed copyright led to these customers pulling out of their contracts with the plaintiff. However, it was held that in the absence of malice, the defendant was not liable. Of course, the situation might have been different had there been further evidence of a clear *inducement* by the defendant that the customers should break particular contracts with the plaintiff, in which case there could have been liability for the tort of inducing a breach of contract.

### Equitable jurisdiction of court to refuse remedies

In exceptional cases, it appears that a court has equitable jurisdiction to refuse to allow a particularly undeserving plaintiff to exercise all or any of his copyright rights. This was the approach of some of the Law Lords in the recent *Spycatcher* case *(Attorney-General* v *Guardian Newspapers Ltd (No. 2)* [1988] 3 All ER 545), where an ex-member of the security service had written a book in breach of his obligation of confidence disclosing information prejudicial to the public interest. In so far as the author had copyright in the book (and some members of the court were prepared to say that any copyright belonged to the Crown; see chapter 4), it would not have been enforceable by him. Lord Jauncey of Tullichettle said:

> His action reeked of turpitude. It is in these circumstances inconceivable that a United Kingdom court would afford to him or his publishers any protection in relation to any copyright which either of them may possess in the book. That being so anyone can copy *Spycatcher* in whole or in part without fear of effective restraint by [the author] or those claiming to derive title from him.

This discretion is not limited to matters relating to public security. Its origins were set out, again by Lord Jauncey, as follows:

> The courts of the United Kingdom will not enforce copyright claims in relation to every original . . . work. Equitable relief has been refused where the work contained false statements calculated to deceive the public *(Slingsby* v *Bradford Patent Truck & Trolley Co.* [1905] WN 122; affirmed [1906] WN 51) and where the work was of a grossly immoral tendency *(Glyn* v *Weston Feature Film Co.* [1916] 1 Ch 261). In a passing-off action, *Bile Bean Manufacturing Co.* v *Davidson* [1906] 23 RPC 725, . . . [It was said that]: 'No man is entitled to obtain the aid of the law to protect him in carrying on a fraudulent trade . . . the courts have . . . given effect to the principle which allows nothing to the man who comes before the seat of justice with a *turpis causa'*.

The extent of this discretion is unclear. It is, of course, consistent with principle in relation to equitable remedies, such as an injunction or an account of profits. It is more questionable in relation to established *legal* rights. In any event, it should be emphasised that the plaintiff's hands would have to be very unclean indeed before such property rights would be effectively removed by a court.

### Criminal sanctions

As mentioned earlier, the criminal law provisions in the Copyright Act 1956 were limited, and the penalties low. Even where defendants' acts were clearly dishonest, technical obstacles sometimes enabled them to escape their just deserts. For example, when a cinema projectionist took films away from a cinema overnight for his associates to copy, and then returned them before their absence was noted, it was held that there was no liability for *theft* under the Theft Act 1968, s. 6(1), because there was no intention *permanently* to deprive the owners of the film. That section could only operate if there had been an intention to return the thing in such a changed state that 'it had lost all practical value' *( R* v *Lloyd* [1985] QB 829). Such a case would formerly have been charged as conspiracy to defraud (see *Scott* v *Metropolitan Police Commissioner* [1975] AC 819) but this offence was not available at the time because of the much criticised decision of the House of Lords in *R* v *Ayres* [1984] AC 447. The Criminal Justice Act 1987 has now restored the utility of conspiracy to defraud (for which the maximum penalty is 10 years).

The provisions of the 1956 Act were themselves improved by a number of amending Acts earlier this decade, particularly with regard to sound recordings, films and computer programs, and the Copyright, Designs and Patents Act 1988 strengthens the offences and penalties for certain commercial copyright piracy.

Section 107 sets out a range of offences committed by those who infringe copyright, generally for commercial purposes, when they know *or have reason to believe,* that they are infringing. Penalties include heavy fines, imprisonment (for up to two years) and forfeiture of infringing copies and articles for making them. Search warrants may be issued by magistrates authorising the police to enter and search premises. This latter provision was introduced by the Copyright (Amendment) Act 1983 in respect of films and sound recordings, extended in 1985 to computer programs and widened by the 1988 Act to all categories of copyright works. Where a company has committed a criminal offence with the consent or connivance of a director, manager or other responsible officer, then that person too is guilty of an offence (ss. 107 to 111).

The availability of the criminal law in intellectual property matters is of considerable value. Although prosecutions depend, private prosecutions apart, upon the discretion and priorities of the public prosecuting authorities, the advantages to copyright owners are obvious: penalties are now severe and will act as a major deterrent; the cost is borne by the State rather than by the individual copyright owners; and, in many cases, the copyright owners do not get as personally involved with those concerned with pirate activities. Thus, it is in the interest of copyright owners to band together to form industry organisations which can carry out policing activities on their behalf, including the gathering of information, and, where appropriate, notify the prosecuting authorities with a view to prosecution.

It still remains the case, though, that persons who infringe copyright for their own personal or domestic use will rarely be liable for criminal offences. For example, in *Reid* v *Kennet* [1986] Crim LR 456, a person purchased video cassettes from somebody whom he knew to be in the trade of buying and selling pirate video tapes. It was held that he was not liable for possessing by way of trade an infringing copy under the Copyright Act 1956 (as amended) because 'by way of trade' meant 'in the course of trade'. A person who purchased for his own consumption and not in the course of trade was not guilty of an offence. The situation is no different under s. 107 of the 1988 Act.

## Fraudulent application or use of trade marks

Tucked away at the end of the 1988 Act are important new additions to the Trade Marks Act 1938 (ss. 58A to 58D), which create new criminal offences in relation to the fraudulent application of registered trade marks. It is aimed at counterfeiters and others who are engaged in commercial activities in relation to counterfeit goods. Penalties are higher than those under the Trade Descriptions Act and there are powers of forfeiture (CA 1988 s.300).

Although concerned with trade marks, it is possible that some counterfeiting activity will involve both copyright and trade mark infringements. This section was warmly welcomed by those in industry and commerce affected by counterfeiting, although some reservations were expressed as to whether the criminal law was being invoked a shade too easily in some respects.

## Customs procedures

In theory, cooperation between customs authorities in various countries and rights owners could play a very important part in limiting the international movement of infringing goods and could also be a potent force in preventing the importation of such goods into this country.

Under the Copyright Act 1956, s. 22, it was possible for copyright owners to give notice requiring the customs authorities to treat copies of specified printed material as prohibited goods and prevent their importation, but the right was little used. The 1988 Act, ss. 111 and 112, has now extended the scope of this customs procedure to films and records, but it is necessary for the customs to receive an advance notice from the copyright owner of the time and place of the expected importation of these works. Although this may be an important requirement from the point of view of the customs, it limits the value of the procedure to rights holders.

It may be that more effective customs procedures will have to be developed through international cooperation. Within the EEC, proposals have been made for a computerised administration procedure whereby films and recordings are placed on a register to facilitate customs checks to counteract piracy.

## Trade Descriptions Act 1968

In some cases, the sale of infringing copies, such as records and cassettes, may be an offence under the Trade Descriptions Act 1968, and trading standards officers have been fairly active in following up complaints that traders in their districts have been selling counterfeit material.

## Procedures and presumptions

*Who may sue?*
Copyright infringement actions may be brought by owners of copyright (s. 96) and by exclusive licensees (s. 101). Although English law does not yet provide for 'class actions' as such, it is possible for a single individual or a company to sue *on behalf* of a group of people with common interests. Thus, in *EMI Records Ltd* v

*Riley* [1981] 1 WLR 923, the BPI membership comprised nearly all those who produced sound recordings of music and it sued on behalf of all its members in circumstances where the defendant had admitted that most of the alleged pirate records had been copies of records made by BPI members. Whilst there appears to be no difficulty in such representative bodies obtaining injunctions, it is less clear whether they can obtain damages on behalf of all their members. (See also *CBS/Sony (Hong Kong) Ltd* v *Television Broadcasts Ltd* [1987] FSR 262.)

One of the difficulties in copyright infringement actions is that it is not always easy to establish whether a plaintiff has title to the copyright in question or, indeed, whether copyright subsists in the work. Whilst these requirements are likely to be satisfied in most cases, a defendant can put the plaintiff to proof in an expensive tactical battle.

To some extent, the 1988 Act attempts to assist plaintiffs by applying certain presumptions. Thus, the person named as the author on the copy of a published work is presumed to be the owner of the copyright, unless the contrary is shown, and, where the author of a work is dead or his identity cannot be ascertained, it is presumed, in the absence of evidence to the contrary, that the work is an original work and that the plaintiff's allegations as to the date and place of first publication are correct (s. 104). Other presumptions, both under the Act and under the general rules of civil procedure, deem the plaintiff to be the owner of a copyright work unless the defendant shows good cause why the plaintiff should be put to proof.

It is also difficult, on occasions, for the plaintiff to prove that the defendant has *copied* his work or a substantial part of it. Accordingly, as has already been mentioned, where the plaintiff demonstrates that there is substantial similarity between two works, particularly in the area of musical copyright, and that the defendant has had the opportunity of access to the plaintiff's work, the court may reverse the burden of proof and require the defendant to establish that he has not copied the plaintiff's work *(Francis Day & Hunter Ltd* v *Bron* [1963] Ch 587; *LB (Plastics) Ltd* v *Swish Products Ltd* [1979] FSR 145).

## Moral rights

Section 103 provides that an infringement of any of the moral rights is actionable as a breach of statutory duty owed to the person entitled to the right.

Whilst the remedies available are in the main the same as for other copyright infringements, there are some special provisions which are referred to in chapter 8.

## Rights in performances

Infringement of any of the rights in performances is actionable as a breach of statutory duty. The usual remedies of damages and/or injunction will thus be available to performers and also those with whom they have exclusive recording contracts (see chapter 11). It is not clear, though, whether the omission to refer to any right to obtain additional damages was deliberate. It was suggested earlier that additional damages should be available for infringement of moral rights in spite of failure to mention this expressly; however, since rights in performances are not copyright subject-matter and are dealt with in a separate part of the 1988 Act, the availability of additional damages is less likely.

## Design right

Similar remedies are available for design right infringement as are available for copyright infringement, including the express reference to additional damages (s. 229(3)). Section 253 also provides a remedy for groundless threats of infringement proceedings against alleged secondary infringers but not against alleged primary infringers, namely manufacturers or importers of the article in question (cf. Patents Act 1977, s. 70). Further details are given in chapter 12.

## Transitional provisions

Infringements taking place before commencement of the 1988 Act are in general governed by the pre-1988 law and those after commencement by the new provisions (sch. 1 para. 31). In most cases, apart from those mentioned in this chapter, the situation has not changed significantly. However, conversion damages will not be available for pre-commencement infringements unless *proceedings* are instituted before commencement (see p. 119). Thus anyone currently contemplating an action for copyright infringement would be well advised to institute proceedings before the relevant parts of the Act are brought into force.

# Chapter 11 Rights in Performances

## Introduction and background

Copyright traditionally has concerned itself with creative effort only if translated into a permanent form and, with the exceptions of broadcasts and cable programmes, continues to do so although the method of recording in permanent form has been considerably widened in the 1988 Act (see p. 22). A performance in itself is not something with any degree of permanence and for a long time performers could only exploit their talents through the mechanism of charging for admission to the live performance. The repeated exploitation of a single performance was not possible until the advent of the sound recording and film industries earlier this century. Once it became possible with ease to make an exact and faithful recording of a performance and, perhaps more importantly, there was the means to distribute such a recording on a large scale, performers found that they were in need of protection. Otherwise the demand for, and the marketability of, their live performances would suffer as a consequence of the ready availablity of a substitute in the form of recordings of their own earlier performances.

Parliament initially recognised this by the enactment of the Dramatic and Musical Performers' Protection Act 1925 which was largely re-enacted in 1958. These Acts created summary criminal offences punishable only by relatively light fines although the court did have power to order the destruction of illegal copies of performances in the possession of a convicted person. The Performers' Protection Act 1963 amended and supplemented the 1958 Act in order to give effect to the 1961 Rome Convention for the Protection of Performers, Producers of Phonograms and Broadcasting Organisations. In particular it extended the protection of the 1958 Act from those who perform dramatic and musical works to 'any actors, singers, musicians, dancers or other persons who act, sing, deliver, declaim, play in or otherwise perform literary, dramatic, musical or artistic works'. The Performers' Protection Act 1972 raised the maximum fines for offences under the existing Acts and for the first time made one of them indictable and punishable by imprisonment.

Despite these developments, the protection offered to performers was considered to be defective. Partly this was a matter of the types of performances protected since only those who performed literary, dramatic, musical or artistic works were covered which seemed to leave variety artists such as jugglers and acrobats etc. outside the scope of the Acts. Furthermore, offences under the Acts were required to be committed knowingly which made them difficult to prove against those who dealt with illegal recordings of performances. Much more significant, however, was the fact that the Acts did not expressly confer any civil rights of action.

The past decade has seen a bewildering series of cases where the courts have explored the question of whether an offence under the Performers' Protection Acts can be regarded as giving rise to an action for breach of statutory duty, either to performers themselves or to those, such as recording companies, with whom they have exclusive contracts.

The Court of Appeal ultimately decided in *RCA Corporation* v *Pollard* [1983] Ch 135 that *recording companies* do not have any right of action but it has more recently confirmed that *performers* have a civil right of action in *Rickless* v *United Artists Corporation* [1988] QB 40. This case concerned clips and out-takes (i.e., unused clips of film) from the Pink Panther series of films which featured performances (dramatic rather than musical in this case) by Peter Sellers. These clips were subsequently used to produce a final Pink Panther film *(Trail of the Pink Panther)* after Peter Sellers's death and without either his or his estate's consent. In confirming the trial judge's award of $1,000,000 in damages the Court of Appeal noted its reservations about the fact that the performers' right appears to be a much more absolute one than copyright without any limitation in terms of time and very few limitations in terms of the sort of permitted acts which in copyright law attempt to balance the right owner's interests against the public interest in having reasonable access to the work. (The 1958 Act only exempted records and films etc. made for private and domestic use or for the purpose of reporting current events or where the performance was included only by way of background.)

The position prior to the 1988 Act can therefore be summarised as follows. The majority of, though not all, performers were nominally protected by minor criminal offences which were difficult to enforce and which constituted an insufficient deterrent against 'bootlegging' — the increasingly profitable and widespread unauthorised copying and exploitation of their performances. Performers had belatedly been clearly accorded much more effective civil rights of action but these went almost too far in not being subject to any limit on their duration nor being subject to an appropriate range of exceptions. Record companies and others with exclusive contracts with performers had no civil rights of action even though the competition from bootlegs etc. was likely to damage them as much if not more than the performers themselves. As will be seen, the 1988 Act attempts to improve the situation by providing statutory civil rights of action for both performers and those with whom they have exclusive recording contracts. As with copyright, the new rights are subject to appropriate exceptions and limitations and the Act also takes the opportunity to tighten up the criminal aspects of performers' protection and to bring the law into line with the criminal sanctions available in the copyright area. Since the new rights are not limited just to the performers themselves, they are now generically described as 'rights in performances' rather than 'performers' rights'.

## Basic definitions

*Meaning of 'performance'*
Section 180(2) provides that performance means one of the following categories
of live performance:

(a)    dramatic performance (which includes dance and mime),
(b)    a musical performance,
(c)    a reading or recitation of a literary work, or
(d)    a performance of a variety act or similar presentation.

Category (d) is designed to bring such persons as acrobats and jugglers within
the fold but sportsmen and women will not generally be included although figure
skating and synchronised swimming are examples where the line is perhaps
becoming particularly hard to draw! (Ice dancing, on the other hand, would seem
clearly to qualify under category (a).) Only category (c) retains any reference to a
'work' whereas (a) and (b) merely refer to dramatic and musical 'performance'
respectively without any express requirement that what is performed should
constitute a 'work'. The difference may be solely attributable to the fact that the
expression, 'literary performance', might have appeared clumsy or obscure. It
does mean, however, that improvised musical and dramatic performances
(including dance routines) are protected whether or not they can be said to
constitute a work for copyright purposes (see the discussion at p. 23). Since most
types of infringement of the new rights involve the making of a recording of some
sort, most infringers will also be copyright infringers. Unless the performance is
of a work in which the copyright has already expired (e.g., a Beethoven
symphony) the performer will generally either be performing an existing
copyright work (which will be infringed by the recording of the performance) or
will be performing a previously unfixed work which is 'made' for copyright
purposes as soon as it is recorded and the copyright in which will normally vest in
the performer. For example, a pop group may be performing a new song which
has not previously been recorded (or written down). Even though the first
recording of the work may not be a copyright infringement, any subsequent
exploitation of the work usually will be and so there is a considerable degree of
overlap between copyright protection and the new rights in performances.
Section 180(4) makes it clear that the performance right is independent of any
other right, including copyright, but the new performance right will be of most
importance where the performer is not the owner of any copyright in the work
being performed and where, therefore, the fact that somebody else's copyright is
being infringed is of no practical value to the performer.

*Meaning of 'recording'*
The use of the word 'recording' should not be allowed, by association with the
term 'sound recording', to obscure the fact that films also count as recordings.
Section 180(2) states that:

'recording', in relation to a performance, means a film or sound recording'—

(a)    made directly from the live performance,

(b)    made from a broadcast of, or cable programme including, the performance, or

(c)    made, directly or indirectly, from another recording of the performance.

The Act thus concerns itself not only with the immediate recording of a live performance but also with the subsequent recording of a previously recorded performance. This again means that there may be considerable overlap with copyright.

*Illustration 11.1*  X makes unauthorised copies of a record featuring Y performing his own composition, the record having being published by a recording company (Z) with whom Y had an exclusive recording contract. X is potentially infringing both Y's copyright in his musical work and his performance right since Y's record is a recording of his own performance and X is recording that performance by copying the record. Furthermore X is prima facie infringing Z's sound recording copyright as well as Z's right in the performance of Y.

The value of the performance right, however, is that it is available even where the performer is not the copyright owner or where the work being performed is not in copyright.

*Illustration 11.2*   P is permitted to record Y performing a piece of music by Bach and the recording falls into the hands of X who copies it. Y has a potential action directly against X for infringement of his right in his performance. X will also be infringing P's copyright in his sound recording but this would be of little use to Y. It does not matter that the performance and original recording took place before commencement. Provided X's recording is made after commencement, it can still be an infringement of the performance right in relation to a pre-commencement recording (s. 180(3)).

As has been noted, the Act now confers rights both on performers themselves and on those having recording rights in relation to performances and these two potential right owners will be discussed in turn.

### Rights of performers

*Qualification for protection (section 181)*
A performance qualifies if either it is given by a qualifying individual or takes place in a qualifying country. Under s. 206 a qualifying country means the UK or an EEC member State or a country designated under s. 208 as enjoying reciprocal protection, which will include those non-EEC countries that have signed the Rome Convention or any future convention for the protection of performers. It should be noted that the spread of countries is significantly smaller than under the Berne Convention and the UCC. A qualifying individual is simply a citizen or subject of, or an individual resident in, a qualifying country.

*Illustration 11.3*  Y, a British national, gives a performance in China. Y is a qualifying individual and so the performance qualifies for protection even though China is not a qualifying country.

*Illustration 11.4*  F, a French national, gives a performance in China. Again, the performance is protected against exploitation in the UK since F is a national of an EEC State and is therefore a qualifying individual.

*Illustration 11.5*  C, a Chinese national, gives a performance in Britain. The performance is protected even though C is not a qualifying individual since it is given in a qualifying country. The result would be the same if the performance was given in France (or any other EEC country or one designated under s. 208) but not if the performance was in China.

*Infringement of rights of performers*
Performers' rights can be infringed in three ways:

(a)  by *making* a recording of, *or transmitting live,* a qualifying performance;
(b)  by *exploiting* a recording by using it to show or play in public a qualifying performance or to broadcast or include in a cable programme service such a performance;
(c)  by *importing, possessing or dealing with* an illicit recording of a qualifying performance.

In each case there is only an infringement if the act is done without the performer's consent. This is not expressly required to be in writing but it is obviously prudent to obtain written consent.

*Making recordings and live transmissions (section 182)*
The making of the recording will often be simultaneous with the performance but this will not necessarily be so since 'making a recording' includes making one recording from another (earlier) recording (see the definition of 'recording' above). Making a recording for one's own private and domestic use is not an infringement. Although there is no requirement of knowledge that the recording or broadcasting etc. is without the performer's consent, it is a defence to a claim for damages for the defendant to show that he believed on reasonable grounds that the performer consented. In accordance with general principles, infringement need not be of the whole of the performance; a substantial part will suffice. This will no doubt be interpreted in the same way as in copyright law (see p. 56) so that the quality of what is recorded will be as important as the quantity.

*Illustration 11.6*  X attends a concert by a well-known pop group and records just one of the songs performed (out of a total of 15) in order to exploit the recording commercially. This would constitute a substantial part of the performance. Even if only part of a song was recorded, this might still be a substantial part especially if it was a well-known or easily recognisable part of the group's repertoire (see *Hawkes & Son (London) Ltd* v *Paramount Film Service Ltd* [1934] Ch 593, discussed in chapter 5).

*Illustration 11.7*   The BBC broadcasts the same part of the performance live and without consent. It would also be an infringer.

*Exploiting recordings (section 183)*
This is analogous to the performing and broadcasting rights in copyright. The exploitation of the recording must involve showing or playing the performance in public or broadcasting it or including it in a cable programme service. Notice that for infringement to occur the performer's consent must have been *lacking* on *each* of two occasions:

(a)   when the recording was first made, and
(b)   when the infringing act was done, i.e., at the time of the public playing etc. of the recording.

*Illustration 11.7*   A performance (e.g., of an actor) is recorded *with* his consent. That recording can be shown or played in public or broadcast etc. as many times as the owner of the recording wishes (but not re-recorded, see s. 182) without infringing the performer's right. It may, however, be a breach of the contract under which the consent to the initial recording was given to use the recording without paying a fee on each occasion.

*Illustration 11.8*   The performance is recorded, as in illustration 11.7, with consent but, in order to facilitate it being shown in a number of outlets, copies are made without consent and these are shown in public. The *making* of the copies is an infringement under s. 182 and the showing of *these* copies without consent is an infringement under s. 183 since consent was lacking for both their making and their use.

There is only infringement if the infringer knows or has reason to believe that the recording was *made* without consent, so there is no infringement if X broadcasts a recording supplied to him by Y who provides a forged consent by the performer to the making of the recording: as a result of the forgery, X neither knows nor has reason to believe that the recording was made without consent. The fact that an original recording made without consent was not itself an infringement because it was made for private and domestic use would be no defence if the recording was subsequently shown in public or broadcast without consent since it would then be being put to a use beyond the private and domestic one initially envisaged.

*Importing, possessing and dealing with illicit recordings (section 184)*
By way of contrast with the point just made, a recording is not, and can never become, *illicit* if it is made for private purposes even though made without consent (see s. 197(2)). This is perhaps a little odd when one considers that certain recordings *are* regarded as illicit if they are made for non-infringing purposes (e.g., educational recording) but are subsequently dealt with commercially (s. 197(5)).

Importation is only an infringement if it is otherwise than for the importer's private and domestic use (s. 184(1)(a)). If it is for such use it doesn't seem to matter that the illicit recording was (by definition) not *made* for private purposes; its importation is still not an infringement. This, no doubt, is because the whole thrust of s. 184 is directed at commercial infringers and the remaining types of infringement (under s. 184(1)(b)) of possessing, selling or letting for hire etc. are expressly required to be done in the course of a business.

It is not necessary that the infringer actually knows that the recording is illicit (i.e., made without consent) if he has reason to believe that fact. However, if the recording was initially 'innocently acquired', i.e., without knowing or having reason to believe it was illicit, either by the infringer or a predecessor in title, then the only remedy available in an action for infringement is 'damages not exceeding a reasonable payment in respect of the act complained of' (s. 184(2) and (3)). The value of this limitation is not immediately apparent as it was explained in the debates as only applicable to the remedy in an 'action for infringement'; it was thus said not to preclude an order for delivery up or the right of seizure under ss. 195 and 196 or an order for forfeiture or destruction under s. 204, none of which are strictly remedies in an action for infringement.

### Exclusive recording rights

Before the 1988 Act, the courts had stopped short of giving to recording companies similar remedies to performers against bootleggers. This situation was thought to be unjust, especially considering the investment that a record company might have put into a particular artist or group of artists. Accordingly, ss. 185 to 188 confer 'recording rights' upon a person having an exclusive recording contract with a performer or to whom the benefit of such a contract has been assigned.

An exclusive recording contract does not necessarily give a right to all the performances of a particular performer, it being enough that it gives the exclusive rights to 'one or more of his performances' (s. 185(1)). It does not matter that the performer is not a qualifying individual or that the performance is not given in a qualifying country: the important thing is that the person having recording rights is a qualifying person. The right can be seen to be a purely economic one as the exclusive recording contract must relate to the making of recordings 'with a view to their commercial exploitation'.

As with the rights of performers themselves, the types of infringement fall into three categories

(a)   the making of recordings (s. 186),
(b)   the exploitation of recordings by playing in public etc. (s. 187),
(c)   the importing, possessing etc. of illicit recordings (s. 188).

The main difference in category (a) from rights of performers is that live broadcasting of a performance is not an infringement of the rights of the person having recording rights (since that person does not necessarily have any broadcasting rights). Another difference is that the consent of either the performer or the person having recording rights will suffice to legitimise the recording. If the performer has given consent, that should be, and is, enough for the recorder, and the record company has to look to its contractual rights against the performer if consent has been given improperly.

Similarly with the playing in public etc. of recordings, the consent of *either* the performer *or* the person with the recording rights is good enough to legitimise the exploitation of the recording and, as with rights of performers, one of those consents, either to the making of the recording or to its exploitation, will suffice. (The performer's consent to the making of a record is sufficient under either s. 186 or s. 187 whether or not the performance is a qualifying one but under s. 187 (and s. 188) the performer's consent to the exploitation of the recording is sufficient only if it is a qualifying performance. This is to avoid consent being irresponsibly given by a performer who has no rights of his own to protect. One would have thought that the same considerations would apply equally to consents to making recordings.)

*Illustration 11.9*   P (a performer) has an exclusive recording contract with R in 1990 and R assigns his rights to S in 1991. X makes a recording of one of P's (qualifying) performances in 1990 and Y plays it in public in 1991. If X has the consent of P he will be infringing neither the right of P nor of R. However, if he has the consent of only R, he will still be infringing P's performing right unless R is authorised to give consent on behalf of P. If neither consent to the making of the recording, Y will still not be infringing S's rights if he has the consent of *either* P or S to the playing of the recording in public. To avoid infringement of P's rights, however, he needs P's consent either to the making of the recording or to its being played in public. (If the performance is not a qualifying one, P's consent to the public playing of the recording is no defence to infringement of S's rights but P's consent to the making of the recording would be.)

The broadcasting of a *recording* made without consent is an infringement of the rights of a person having recording rights since it is a further exploitation of a recording which that person had the exclusive right to make in the first place, unlike a *live* transmission, which is not something that a person with a *recording* right can complain about.

The third category of infringement, importing etc., is almost identical with the equivalent provision for infringement of rights of performers except that again the consent (to the importation etc.) of either the performer (in the case of a qualifying performance) or of the person having recording rights will suffice. Note, however, that the definition of 'illicit recording' is slightly different for these purposes (see s. 197(3)) and that a recording is not illicit if it is made either with the performer's consent (irrespective of whether the performance is a qualifying one) or that of the person having recording rights. Thus, again, the consent of either of two people at either of two times (the making of the recording or the importation etc.) will negate infringement.

## Limitations on rights in performances

Part of the reason for the previous hesitancy of the courts in recognising civil rights of action for performers was the fact that such rights would lack the limitations that are normally built into a statutory right (such as copyright) in terms of duration, permitted acts etc. The 1988 Act now imposes such limitations.

*Duration*
Section 191 limits protection to 50 years from the end of the calendar year in which the performance takes place, a similar period to that given to the copyright in sound recordings and films. The period of protection is largely irrelevant to those types of infringement which consist of either contemporaneous recording or broadcasting of a live performance. The 50-year period will, however, apply to the making of a recording of a previous recording (which will therefore be permitted 50 years after the performance) and to the public performance and broadcasting of recordings and to their importation etc.

*Transitional provisions*
Section 180(3) provides that the new rights apply to performances taking place before commencement although nothing done before commencement, or in pursuance of arrangements (e.g., a contract) made before commencement, will count as infringement. Hence, a performance given in 1945 will give rise to rights under the Act which will expire at the end of 1995 and in the meantime it will be an infringement to make a recording without consent from any existing recording (including a recording belonging to the infringer, cf. *Rickless* v *United Artists Corporation* [1988] QB 40). Similarly it would be an infringement to broadcast without consent a recording made without consent.

    Furthermore, anyone in possession in the course of a business of copies of illicit recordings of pre-commencement performances would seem to be liable for infringement and it may not even matter that their possession dates from a time prior to commencement since it is only 'acts' in pursuance of arrangements made prior to commencement that are excluded from infringement and possession is not an act but a state of affairs. Although this appears to be the effect of a literal interpretation of the Act, the courts may well baulk at the imposition of such retrospective liability and find that possession should be interpreted as within the meaning of an 'act' for these purposes so that only possession acquired after the commencement of the Act could give rise to liability. The point ought to have been dealt with more clearly especially since possession is also now made the basis of a criminal offence (s. 198(1)(c)) although for criminal liability the possesion must be 'with a view to committing any act infringing' rights in performances which does at least require an intention to do an act after commencement.

*Permitted acts*
Schedule 2 to the Act sets out a range of permitted acts which are broadly similar to the permitted acts in relation to copyright (see      chapter 6): it would be odd for an act to be immune from copyright infringement but at the same time to be an infringement of the rights of the performers. It is not possible in a work of this nature to go through every permitted act in sch. 2 and reference should be made to the discussion of the equivalent permitted acts in relation to copyright. It should be noted, however, that not every act permitted in relation to copyright appears in sch. 2. For example, there is no equivalent to the time-shifting exception in s. 70 since making a recording of a performance for private and domestic use is not an infringement of the rights in a performance in the first place (see ss. 182(1)(a) and 186(1)) even if the recording is to be kept permanently

and is not made purely for the purposes of time-shifting. Neither is there any equivalent to fair dealing for research or private study (although fair dealing for criticism or review or reporting current events is dealt with in sch. 2, para. 2, which does not impose a requirement for a sufficient acknowledgement).

## Transmission of rights

The Act does not give performers a copyright in their performance but it is not always obvious in what respects the civil rights of action now conferred in respect of performances differ from a true copyright. Part of the answer is in s. 192 which provides in effect that rights in performances are non-assignable and are only transmissible on death, either to the deceased's personal representatives or to a person to whom 'he may be testamentary disposition specifically direct'. Section 192(5) provides that any damages recovered by personal representatives shall devolve as part of the estate as though the right of action had subsisted immediately before the death. (Personal representatives may therefore find themselves having to distribute awards of damages many years after the administration of the estate.)

It should be remembered that although the rights themselves cannot be assigned *inter vivos,* a person may have become a right owner as a result of an assignment of the benefit of an exclusive recording contract (s. 185(2)(b)) or an assignment of the benefit of a licence from a person having an exclusive recording contract (s. 185(3)(b)).

## Power of Copyright Tribunal to give consent (section 190)

This consent can only be given in respect of the making of a recording from a previous recording and is designed to deal with what was characterised in Parliament as the 'tenth spear-carrier' problem. This arises where, for example, broadcasters wish to make such a recording in order to repeat (or market to other broadcasters etc.) an earlier broadcast involving performers whose consent was obtained to the original recording but who were not asked to consent in advance to further recordings in the future. It would be unfortunate if a single (perhaps minor) performer (such as the tenth spear-carrier in a cast of thousands) could prejudice the interests of not only the broadcasters but also of his fellow spear-carriers (who might otherwise be entitled to repeat fees) by unreasonably refusing his consent. The problem is not limited to the tenth spear-carrier who unreasonably withholds consent, as there is, of course, the 'ninth spear-carrier' who can no longer be traced. When Super Channel was launched in 1987, major problems arose because broadcasters' contracts with actors who had taken part in programmes in previous years had not acquired the right to sell those programmes to a satellite-to-cable service of Super Channel's type. 'This meant that fresh consent had to be obtained from every actor in, say, a drama series before it could be made available for showing on the new service. Some actors proved impossible to trace; others refused to consent to this new use. There were cases where only one or two actors withheld consent even though all others in the cast were willing to give it. It was not a happy experience.' (Stephen Edwards, 'The Impact of the CA 1988 on Cable, Satellites and Broadcasting', ESC Conference, November 1988). Thus, now, the tribunal can give consent where either the performer unreasonably withholds consent or his identity or whereabouts cannot be ascertained by reasonable enquiry. The tribunal's jurisdiction still applies even if the original recording was made without consent but this is one of the factors for the tribunal to take into account in exercising its discretion (under s. 190(5)). In default of agreement about payment, the tribunal can 'make such order as it thinks fit' (s. 190(6)).

If the original recording was made with consent, no further consent is required to broadcast *that* recording as it is only the broadcasting of a live performance or of a recording *made without consent* (including a re-recording) that can amount to infringement. In many cases actual consent to future recordings will have been obtained in advance. Section 193 facilitates the giving of consent by performers (and persons having recording rights) by providing that consent may be given not only in relation to individual performances but also in relation to 'a specified description of performances or performances generally, and . . . past or future performances.' Contracts with performers will in future normally take full advantage of these provisions and provide for all foreseeably necessary consents, and the tribunal's powers under s. 190 are principally relevant to re-recordings of pre-commencement performances where the necessity for performers' consents to re-recordings was not appreciated at the time.

## Remedies

In addition to the remedies of damages and injunction, which are available as a consequence of infringement being regarded as a breach of statutory duty, a person having rights in a performance may (under s. 195) seek an order for delivery up of illicit recordings. Furthermore, under s. 196, there is a right of seizure of illicit recordings 'found exposed or otherwise immediately available for sale or hire' but notice of the proposed seizure must be given to the local police station and no force may be used nor should anything be seized which is in the possession etc. of a person at his permanent or regular place of business. A court may (under s. 204) order the destruction or forfeiture of a recording delivered up or seized under the above provisions taking account of the adequacy of the other remedies available for the infringement. These ancillary remedies are similar to those available for infringement of copyright (see chapter 10) and, of course, the courts have all their inherent powers in relation to *Anton Piller* orders, *Mareva* injunctions etc.

### Criminal offences
Section 198 creates a range of offences which are broadly similar to those now applicable in respect of commercial dealing with infringing copies of copyright works. The introduction of criminal liability is nothing new in relation to performers and indeed the provisions of the Performers' Protection Acts were previously confined to the criminal law. The main changes from those previous provisions are that knowledge that the recording is an infringing one is no longer required (reason to believe is now a sufficient alternative), the penalties have been stiffened and brought into line with the penalties for copyright offences, and possession and importation are included for the first time. A further somewhat anomalous difference is that whereas under the old law only broadcasts of *live* performances were criminal it is now only broadcasts of *recordings* that can be.

Section 199 provides for delivery up of illicit recordings found in the possession, custody or control of persons against whom criminal proceedings are brought (whether or not a conviction is obtained) and this may be followed with an order for destruction or forfeiture under s. 204. Section 200 provides for search warrants, s. 201 restates the existing offence of false representation of authority to give consent on behalf of another and s. 202 provides for the liability of company officers where the offence is actually committed by a company.

## Conclusions

The Act certainly improves the position of performers and those with whom they have exclusive recording contracts but at the cost of some complexity. The Act provides protection for the most important economic interests of the performer: the unauthorised recording of live performances. However, it does not provide protection against all types of 'unfair' exploitation of performaces. For example, it does not deal with the misappropriation of the performer's personality. Should a performer have a right to control *all* commercial uses of his or her name, style or personality? Should there be rights for performers, and their estates, to control the unauthorised activities of a modern 'Glenn Miller' band or a modern imitator of the style of Charles Chaplin?

Insofar as the public is not confused or deceived by the defendant's activities, the burden of the complaint would be that the defendant is using the performer's personality to 'reap where he has not sown'. Imitating the style, in contrast to copying the exact material, may raise similar arguments as that involved in the 'idea-expression dichotomy' issue in copyright law. However, sometimes, although the taking of a performer's style may seem more like the appropriation of the idea of a performance rather than its expression, there are many who believe that the law ought to grant to performers protection in some of these situations.

The concept of a right of personality has been recognised in many of the States of the USA either by express statutory provision or through judicial developments. The courts there have had to face the difficulties involved in seeking to protect such 'intangible' interests. Although many of the difficulties have not been finally resolved, attempts have been made to provide a balance between performer's rights and the public interest. Thus, in some of the actions brought by the estate of Elvis Presley against unauthorised productions which imitated his stage performances, the courts have said that if the defendant's primary purpose was to exploit the personality of Elvis Presley, then his estate was entitled to control such activity. However, if the purpose was predominantly to serve a social function, for example, to contribute information to a public debate on political or social issues, or of providing the free expression of creative talent which contributes to societies' cultural enrichment, then the portrayal will generally be immune from liability, In most of the Elvis Presley cases, the shows were primarily for commercial exploitation and the right of publicity was enforceable by the estate.

These issues are not dissimilar to those employed in using copyright works for the purposes of parody, satire or burlesque (see page 60). However, it is likely to be some time before such extensive protection for the personality of performers receives widespread support in English law.

# Chapter 12 Copyright and Designs

## What are designs?

In its broadest sense, the term 'design' refers to all aspects of the arrangement and appearance of an article, and also to any preliminary sketch, drawing or model for it.

Where the design of an article comprises a work of art, pure and simple, such as a sculpture or a painting, there is no problem in accepting that such works should be protected against unlawful copying through copyright law. Thus a sculpture of a ship's anchor, whether elaborate or simple, will be an 'artistic work', for copyright purposes.

In this chapter, the term 'design', for the most part, is focused primarily on the design of *industrial products:* those features of shape or pattern which give them a particular appearance. Designs for mass-produced functional articles, for example, a table lamp in the form of an elaborate anchor, pose difficult problems: should the designer or manufacturer be entitled to stop others from using similar designs, whether independently created or copied? If so, what is the most appropriate form of protection?

The problems are best illustrated by looking at the relationship between aesthetic and functional features stage by stage:

*Functional articles*
The term 'functional' refers primarily to 'useful' as opposed to 'ornamental' and describes those articles whose design is determined to a greater or lesser extent by the job they do, that is, the function they have to perform.

(a)   *Purely, functional, yet inventive, products.* Where a person invents a product, for example, the first ball-point pen, then such a novel and inventive concept and product is patentable and, provided it meets the appropriate conditions under the Patents Act 1977, is entitled to protection for a term of 20 years.

(b)   *Purely functional products with no inventive qualities*
If a pen has no inventive qualities, or if a patent had expired, there is no reason to give those who produce it any particular monopoly rights (although the names of particular businesses dealing in such pens may be protected through trade-mark

law). Accordingly, there may be many businesses selling identical pens and purchasers have no reason to prefer to buy a pen from one business rather than another.

Many solely functional products produce little or no aesthetic reaction from potential purchasers; for example, car engines and other machinery to which no decorative additions have been made. Performance and price are usually the paramount considerations. Many of these functional products may also look attractive to possible purchasers and others, even though the appearance of the article is dictated by its function; for example, the shape of the nose of the Concorde may give that plane a streamlined and attractive appearance of greater aesthetic appeal to some people than the most acclaimed works of art. Nevertheless, its appearance, whether or not attractive, plays no part in its purchase. The plane is bought entirely for its performance. The nose was designed for its aerodynamic qualities, not its attractiveness; any competitor making a similar product would have to produce the same shape.

In these situations, since the manufacturer is making and selling articles which are neither inventive nor have any aesthetically appealing design, it is difficult to justify granting any monopoly rights over such articles.

*Industrial designs*

Today, design is playing an ever-increasing role in industry. Most products are not solely functional but, to a greater or lesser extent, have design features added to them, to make them more attractive to purchasers. In many cases it is the design of an article which is the only way in which a purchaser might be persuaded to buy one article from a range, all of which may be of similar performance and price. In some of these cases, although performance and quality may not always be identical, the design may be the dominant factor in the purchaser's decision. It is not always easy to separate the functional and aesthetic aspects of industrial products, but the kind of articles referred to here are those whose surface pattern, shape or styling undeniably play some part in influencing a purchaser in making a purchase, for example, toy figures, pottery, crockery, cutlery, furniture and similar articles. Here, while the article might not be functionally inventive and so not patentable, considerable effort may have gone into the design aspect, and there is at least a case for saying that the skill, labour and investment put into such designs deserve to be given some form of monopoly protection.

*Artistic designs*

This last category, at the opposite extreme to the purely functional product, comprises articles which are created primarily with artistic and aesthetic intent and are purchased as such, for example, sculptures and engravings. At first sight, there seems no difficulty in accepting that such articles are properly the subject-matter of copyright. However, within this category are also articles which may be created for artistic and aesthetic reasons but which are also exploited industrially, for example, the works of silversmiths, potters, hand-embroiderers etc. When articles such as these are put on to the market in large numbers, it becomes difficult to separate this category from articles which come within the industrial designs category.

There has been controversy over many years and in many countries about the most appropriate ways of protecting these various kinds of articles and designs against copying or other forms of unfair competition. It is necessary now to examine the state of UK law before the 1988 Act, the present law, and also the transitional provisions.

## The law before the 1988 Act

Designs could be protected, directly or indirectly, in the following ways:

*Patents*
If a patent were granted for a new invention, which necessarily incorporated a particular design (for example, a new shape for an aeroplane propellor) then an absolute patent monopoly for up to 20 years would incidentally protect the design. Clearly, however, few designs were protected as such through the patent system.

*Registered trade marks*
Trade marks may be registered in relation to particular classes of goods provided that they are 'distinctive' and distinguish the proprietor's goods from those of his competitor.

   In some cases, it has been possible to register a trade mark for drugs with distinctive *colour* combinations *(Smith Kline & French Laboratories Ltd* v *Sterling-Winthrop Group Ltd* [1975] 1 WLR 914) but attempts to register the distinctive *shape* of goods has been resisted. Thus, in *Re Coca-Cola Co.* [1986] 1 WLR 695, a registered design protecting the shape of the famous Coca-Cola bottle had expired years earlier. The Coca-Cola Co. attempted to register as a trade mark not simply representations of the bottle but the patterning and shape of the bottle itself. The House of Lords held that a trade mark must be something which is applied to the goods rather than being the goods themselves: a bottle was a container for, not a mark applied to, the goods, and so was not registrable. Whilst the rationale of this decision, and its difference from the coloured drugs cases, may be difficult to follow, it is clear that the court objected to the applicant having a perpetual trade mark monopoly over its distinctive shape. It is worth observing, however, that the new European trade-mark system, which will shortly be applicable in the UK, will permit distinctive shapes of goods to be registered.

*Passing off*
The common law action for passing off protects the goodwill of a trader in his business against competitors whose actions may confuse the public into associating their goods with his. This confusion or misrepresentation may occur in connection with the name of the plaintiff or his business, or the quality of his goods and, more importantly here, in connection with the design or get-up of those goods. In most cases, a competitor who closely follows the get-up of the plaintiff's product will usually be able to avoid a passing-off action provided he ensures that there is sufficient information available to a purchaser to avoid possible confusion. Occasionally, however, the courts have enforced a fairly

strong monopoly protection for the long-established get-up of a product, so making it difficult for others to use a similar design in the same market. For example, in *Reckitt & Colman Products Ltd* v *Borden Inc*. [1988] FSR 601, the plaintiff had sold JIF lemon juice for many years in plastic containers resembling a lemon in shape, size and colour. The defendant attempted to introduce lemon-shaped containers to compete with the plaintiff but was prevented from doing so on the ground that these containers had become so distinctive of the plaintiff's product that, even had the defendant marked its containers with its own name and taken various other steps to differentiate the two products, the public would still have been confused or deceived. This was a controversial decision, however, and is under appeal to the House of Lords.

*Registered designs*
Certain industrial designs are registrable under the Registered Designs Act 1949 and receive a monopoly, patent-type, protection for a period which was up to 15 years under the Act as originally enacted but is increased to 25 years by the 1988 Act. These are 'features of shape, configuration, pattern or ornament applied to an article by any industrial process, being features which in the finished article appeal to and are judged by the eye', provided they are novel or original designs. The design may be registered in respect of any specified article of manufacture or set of articles (for example, dinner services) where several articles of the same general character are normally sold together and substantially the same design is applied to all of them. Thus designs may be registered for many articles provided they are applied industrially (that is, if the design was reproduced or intended to be reproduced in more than 50 single articles), for example, designs for children's toys, the shapes of new electronic equipment, furniture, shapes and designs for packaging, the Coca-Cola bottle etc.

However, certain designs are excluded from registration. First, there are those which it is felt more properly come within the copyright system, namely:

(a)   works of sculpture other than casts or models used or intended to be used as models or patterns to be multiplied by any industrial process;
(b)   wall plaques and medals;
(c)   printed matter primarily of a literary or artistic character, including book jackets, calendars, certificates, coupons, dressmaking patterns, greetings cards, leaflets, maps, plans, postcards, stamps, trade advertisements, trade forms, and cards, transfers and the like.

Secondly, it was not the policy of the registered designs system to register solely functional articles, and so s. 1(1) of the Registered Designs Act 1949 excludes:

(a)   a method or principle of construction, or
(b)   features of shape or configuration of an article which—

(i)   are dictated solely by the function which the article has to perform, or
(ii)   are dependent upon the appearance of another article of which the article is intended by the author of the design to form an integral part.

Thus in *Amp Inc.* v *Utilux Pty Ltd* [1972] RPC 103, the House of Lords refused to allow the shape of a 'flag terminal', an electrical terminal for use inside a washing machine, to be registered: the article had been designed with no reference to, or consideration of, 'eye appeal' but rather with its performance. This decision, as we shall see, had important repercussions.

Although a registered designs system is a logical way of protecting novel industrial designs, it may not always satisfy the needs of all sections of industry. For example, the time involved in obtaining registration for designs in fast-moving and fast-changing markets, such as costume jewellery, toys and clothing, may make it inappropriate; as also may be the cost of registration, bearing in mind also the number of designs a trader may have to register. In fact, the system has not been used extensively: the rate of registrations has not exceeded 8,000 a year for most of the past 30 years.

## Copyright
Historically, the copyright system was not concerned with protecting most types of industrially exploited articles with design features. Copyright seemed appropriate protection for only a limited number of designs used in industry. In practice, as will be seen, after 1968, copyright became the most important method of protection for industrial designs.

### Articles embodying designs as copyright works in themselves
A number of designs applied industrially clearly came within the scope of the definition of 'artistic work'; thus, sculptures and engravings were protected as artistic copyright works, irrespective of their artistic quality, and works of architecture, being either buildings or models for buildings, were protected. Had the term 'works of artistic craftsmanship' been given a wide interpretation then many industrially produced articles might also have been given extensive copyright protection. However, as was seen in chapter 2, the House of Lords construed the term very narrowly, and so the prototype of an attractive (at least to a large section of the consuming public, if not the judges) suite of furniture was not regarded as a work of artistic craftsmanship *(George Hensher Ltd* v *Restawile Upholstery (Lancs) Ltd* [1976] AC 64). Nor was a baby's protective waterproof cape, because the designer had no intention of creating a work of art when she made the prototype; it was designed primarily to be a warm, dry, stylish, piece of necessary clothing *(Merlet* v *Mothercare plc* [1986] RPC 115). Thus, relatively few articles attracted copyright protection in their own right.

### Designs reproduced from drawings
Far more important, however, was the development of the law in relation to drawings. In a logical, but unpredictable, way, the past two decades saw a development whereby an increasing number of articles came to be protected under copyright law. The steps in the legal analysis were as follows:

(a)   Drawings were copyright artistic works, irrespective of artistic quality (Copyright Act 1956 s. 3(1)). Any drawing, whether an artist's sketch or an engineering, mechanical or design drawing came within that provision provided it was 'original' and the level of originality here was very low indeed.

(b)   Infringement of copyright takes place by 'reproducing' the drawing.

(c)   Reproduction may occur by copying the drawing itself in two dimensions or by making a three-dimensional copy of the drawing, for example, if a person makes jewellery by copying the design in a drawing or makes a chair from a copyright drawing. The article itself may or may not be a copyright work. (For example, jewellery might well rank as work of artistic craftsmanship but most chairs would not.)

(d)   Reproduction may be either direct or indirect. Accordingly, where X has copyright in an original drawing of an article, infringement may occur either by making an article from the drawing itself or by copying an article made from the drawing. This may happen in many cases even though the person copying another article did not know that there was an underlying drawing.

In this way, copyright began to be used to enable industry to protect its products, most of which were insufficiently novel or original to acquire patent protection, and many not capable of registration under the Registered Designs Act 1949. Take *George Hensher Ltd* v *Restawile Upholstery (Lancs) Ltd,* for example. Had the plaintiff in that case made its furniture from drawings, copyright protection undoubtedly would have subsisted. Thus, increasingly, it became quite unnecessary in most cases to explore further the meaning of 'work of artistic craftsmanship': drawings were all that mattered and so drawings were frequently made solely for the purpose of securing copyright protection.

*Drawings for articles which were registrable under the Registered Designs Act 1949*
Before 1969, if a design was registrable under the Registered Designs Act 1949, it was not possible to exercise any copyright control over its industrial exploitation (Copyright Act 1956, s. 10). However, the Design Copyright Act 1968 amended the law by providing that there could be dual protection. If there was copyright in a registrable design and it was also registered, there would be protection under both Acts. However, to remove the anomaly of having two quite different periods of protection, the copyright protection for works which were also registrable designs was reduced from a period of life plus 50 years to a period of 15 years. For example, if X had a drawing of a new design for a watch, there might be copyright protection based upon the drawing, limited to 15 years, and, if the design was registered, a broadly concurrent 15-year period under the Registered Designs Act 1949.

*Drawings for purely functional articles*
The next development was rather remarkable. The reduction in the period of copyright protection to 15 years was interpreted to apply only to *registrable* designs. Accordingly, if there were a drawing of a solely functional object (for example, the electric flag terminal in *Amp Inc.* v *Utilux Pty Ltd* [1972] RPC 103), the drawing would not be registrable as a registered design and the copyright protection accordingly would not be cut back: there would be full protection of the drawing and articles made directly or indirectly from that drawing for the life of the author plus 50 years. Thus arose, in the view of the Whitford Committee and others, the 'bizarre' situation that 'if a design is unregistrable because it is functional or otherwise unacceptable it could enjoy much longer protection than

a design which is registrable'; whereas, of course, most would regard the more functional designs as deserving of less, not more, protection. The absurdity of the situation was well illustrated in the recent spectacle of Lego arguing in the Privy Council that it should never have been allowed to register the design of its bricks (*Interlego AG* v *Tyco Industries Inc.* [1988] 3 WLR 678)!

### Criticism of the law

These developments in copyright law were highly controversial. The objections most frequently raised were that the term of protection was too long; the right given by copyright effectively resulted in a monopoly with no mechanism for remedying abuses; the protection was uncertain because the right was not registered; and the law was at variance with international practice. A further objection (and one which aroused major criticism in industry) was that the penalties for infringement were too high because 'conversion damages' were available based on the value of infringing copies rather than on the loss of profit. These were frequently out of all proportion to the loss suffered by the copyright owner and to the damages available under other intellectual property laws. (see chapter 10).

Developments came from a number of directions, primarily judicial and legislative.

### Judicial developments: spare parts

The 'spare-parts industries' were major beneficiaries of these copyright design laws. Motor manufacturers, for example, were able to exercise copyright control over spare parts for their vehicles and exclude competition from other spare-part manufacturers. This monopoly was challenged in the House of Lords in *British Leyland Motor Corporation Ltd* v *Armstrong Patents Co. Ltd* [1986] AC 577. British Leyland claimed copyright control, through its drawings, over all the spare parts it manufactured for its vehicles. The case itself involved exhaust pipes. British Leyland had granted licences to a number of competitors, but the defendant was not prepared to pay for a licence and challenged British Leyland's rights. In a controversial analysis, the House of Lords upheld the way in which the law had developed to enable copyright protection in drawings to cover all articles made from those drawings: in the view of the House, reform was a matter for the legislature, not for them. However, the court then struck at copyright over spare parts. It held that manufacturers of products (and others) could not be permitted to exercise copyright control over spare parts required for those articles, since they would be acting in 'derogation of their grant': those who sell a car or other product to a purchaser cannot interfere with a purchaser's right to use that article for the rest of its natural life. Thus, the House of Lords created what was known as a 'spare parts exemption' whereby copyright law could not be used to protect spare parts. (It is interesting to note, however, that protection could exist if those parts were patentable.) How 'spare parts' would be interpreted, and the full scope of the new exemption teased out, were left to conjecture since the 1988 Act introduced a new set of principles relating to the protection of designs and the relationship between the various intellectual property rights.

The second major judicial limitation placed upon the earlier law came in

*Interlego AG* v *Tyco Industries Inc.* [1988] 3 WLR 678. In that case, the manufacturer of the Lego toy building bricks had enjoyed copyright protection, through drawings, over those bricks, but the protection had expired. It sought to rely on new drawings of Lego bricks to extend its copyright protection further. Since the fresh drawings were not *significantly* different from the earlier drawings, the Privy Council refused to accept those drawings as 'original' artistic works (see chapter 1)

*Summary of the law before the 1988 Act*
The most important features were as follows:

(a)   Some novel or original designs were registrable under the Registered Designs Act 1949 and protection would be available for a period of up to 15 years. However, the registered designs system was not extensively used.
(b)   Copyright protection was available, and widely enforced, primarily relying on drawings for industrial or other articles. Copyright protection existed for periods of either 15 years or life plus 50 years; paradoxically, the longer period being reserved for the least deserving articles.
(c)   Copyright protection was not available to prevent competitors manufacturing spare parts.
(d)   The conversion remedy, amongst other matters, compounded the arbitrary and Draconian nature of the law in this area.

## Reform

The government decided to reverse the developments which had taken place under copyright law: in its view, the copyright system was inappropriate for most industrial designs. The only form of intellectual property protection directly available for solely functional products should be the patent, if the product is novel and inventive. However, it also concluded that 'some protection should be available to give the manufacturer who has spent money on design the opportunity to benefit from his investment, thus providing an incentive to further investment'. After considering the possibility of a registration system and also of an 'unfair copying law', it eventually came down in favour of a new *unregistered* design right to coexist with the registered designs provisions. After considerable vacillation over 'spare parts', the decision was taken to remove protection from those spare parts which manufacturers would be obliged to copy if they were to compete.

*The 1988 law*
The new regime is complex and is best analysed right by right, and then illustrated by examples.

## Copyright law

Copyright subsists and will continue to subsist in all *artistic works;* and, in general, the duration will continue to be the life of the author plus 50 years.
    However, there are two major qualifications:

(a)   *Drawings, design documents and models* (s. 51). Industrial design protection based upon copyright drawings alone is no longer possible. Although drawings continue to be artistic works and can be infringed by both two-dimensional and three-dimensional copies, whether direct or indirect, such protection is not available for any *'design document* or model recording or embodying a design' where an article is made to the design (or where an article made to the design is itself copied) *unless that article itself is an artistic work or a typeface.*

'Design' means the design of any aspect of the shape or configuration (whether internal or external) of the whole or part of an article other than surface decoration; and 'design document' means any record of a design, whether in the form of a drawing, a written description, a photograph, data stored in a computer or otherwise.

(b)   *Artistic works which are industrially exploited* (s. 52). Where an artistic work has been industrially exploited, by or with the licence of the copyright owner, the period of copyright protection for such purposes will now be limited to 25 years from the end of the calendar year in which such articles are first marketed. 'Industrial exploitation' means making by an industrial process copies of the artistic work and marketing them in the UK or elsewhere. Section 52(4) provides for the Secretary of State to make orders defining the meaning of 'industrial process'. These will correspond with the earlier copyright and registered designs provisions and will refer to the need to market at least 50 copies of the work before the work can be said to be industrially exploited. Articles of a primarily literary or artistic character will also be excluded.

Thus, any work of 'artistic craftsmanship' or any 'sculpture' industrially exploited in this way will receive 25 years' protection. So it may now become more important, as indicated earlier, to explore further the meaning of 'artistic craftsmanship'. Although the mass-produced suite of furniture with design appeal in *George Hensher Ltd* v *Restawile Upholstery (Lancs) Ltd* came outside this expression, some furniture surely must come within it. For example, furniture made by a present-day Chippendale (possibly chairs designed by the French architect Le Corbusier, which appear now to be very popular) have a stronger case for being regarded as works of artistic craftsmanship. If that is correct, the range of designer furniture between *George Hensher Ltd* v *Restawile Upholstery (Lancs) Ltd* and Le Corbusier may have to be examined, case by case, in the courts!

*Illustration 12.1*   X, an artist, paints a picture of a vase. X has copyright in the artistic work and is protected for a period of his life and 50 years against any person who, without authority, reproduces the painting or reproduces (in three dimensions) the vase represented in the painting, whether for private or industrial purposes. The fact that the vase is capable of being reproduced industrially by X will not limit his full copyright protection, until such time as he takes or authorises such action.

*Illustration 12.2*   X draws a vase as a design for the purposes of industrial exploitation. X cannot rely on the copyright in the drawing of the vase to stop others making a vase from the drawings or from another vase made from those drawings (s. 51). However, if X makes the vase and it is a copyright work in its own right, for example, if it is a 'sculpture' or is a work of artistic craftsmanship, then X can enforce copyright in the vase, although the period of protection will now be limited to 25 years (s. 52). In the latter event, X may also, in addition or alternatively, enforce copyright through the drawings because s. 51 does not come into operation).

*Illustration 12.3*   X produces drawings for a suite of furniture. Y makes the furniture without authority, either by using X's drawings or by copying furniture made to those drawings. If the furniture is not a work of artistic craftsmanship (or a sculpture), then X cannot obtain protection under *copyright* law when Y copies the furniture either from the drawings (because of s. 51) or from furniture which X has made from those drawings (since the furniture itself is not a copyright work).

## Design right (sections 213 to 264)

The 1988 Act excludes the vast majority of industrial designs from copyright protection. In place of that, a new property right has been created for 'original designs'. Like copyright, it attaches automatically to certain designs of articles and provides protection against unauthorised commercial copying of that design, or a substantial part of it, on articles. It is a right which has been created outside the scope of the international copyright conventions and operates on the basis of reciprocity: thus a much narrower class of persons are entitled to the benefit of it.

In an attempt to strike an appropriate balance between the monopoly claim of the designer and the public interest in competition, the design right is limited in several ways: first, the period of protection is restricted to 10 years from marketing (with an overall limit of 15 years from creation); secondly, provision is made for licences of right to be granted after five years; and thirdly, certain 'must-fit' and 'must-match' designs, whose function dictates the design, are excluded from design protection completely.

The nature of this right will be elaborated upon in a little more detail with accompanying illustrations.

*To which articles does design right extend?*
Industrial design is generally understood as meaning the features of the finished article which appeal to and are judged by the eye, and that is how a design is defined for the purposes of the Registered Designs Act 1949. This is not the case for design right. The new design right may subsist in 'any aspect of the shape or configuration (whether internal or external) of the whole or part of an article s. 213(2)). There is no reference to 'eye appeal' in this definition: the right applies both to functional and aesthetic designs. Thus, whilst design right cannot subsist in a method or principle of construction it is possible for it to subsist in the shape of a functional article where there is neither intention nor likelihood that the shape has any eye appeal to the customer.

*Originality*
Design right subsists only in 'original' designs. A design is not original if it is *commonplace* in the design field in question at the time of its creation (s. 213(4)). The threshold for originality for the design right is higher than that required for original copyright works but far lower than the inventive step requirement for originality under patent law. Compared with the former protection of industrial objects under copyright law, this requirement makes the design right much narrower in scope. First, under the law before the commencement of the 1988 Act, it was possible for protection to be given, through drawings, to solely functional objects which had no element of design about them. The new right relates only to 'designs', albeit very widely defined. Secondly, where there is a design, the majority of functional articles may well not satisfy the test of 'originality' for design-right protection. Thirdly, some designs, for example, wrought-iron gates, may well be original under copyright law as works of artistic craftsmanship, but may not necessarily qualify as original designs for design-right purposes since the design of the gate is commonplace.

There is a specific provision which applies design right to articles in 'kit form', that is, a complete or substantially complete set of components intended to be assembled into an article, as it applies in relation to the assembled article. Here, design right may subsist in any aspect of the design of the components of the kit as well as the design of the assembled article (s. 260).

*Who is entitled to design-right protection?*
Broadly, the right is restricted to the designs of articles first marketed in the European Community or designed by a British national or any person habitually resident or domiciled in the UK, elsewhere in the EEC or in a country to which rights have been extended by order because that country protects similar UK designs (the reciprocity principle) (s. 217). Where a country outside the EEC protects the designs of certain functional articles only, then only designs of those articles will be protected in the UK.

*Exceptions to design right*
Design right does not subsist in a method or principle of construction (properly the province of patent law) or to any surface decoration (s. 213(3)).

*'Must-fit' and 'must-match' articles*
As mentioned earlier, the decision in *British Leyland Motor Corporation Ltd* v *Armstrong Patents Co. Ltd* [1986] AC 577 that copyright in drawings for spare parts cannot be used to prevent other manufacturers making and putting such spare parts on the market aroused considerable controversy. At first, the government proposed to include spare parts within design-right protection, although special measures were contemplated to guard against possible abuse by manufacturers of their monopoly to the detriment of the consumer. Finally, however, it was decided that there should be no monopoly protection for those aspects of the design of spare parts and other articles which *necessarily* had to be copied by competitors if they were to compete at all.

Thus, the following are excluded from design right protection:

(a)  *Must-fit*. These are 'features of shape or configuration of an article which enable the article to be connected to, or placed in, around or against, another article so that either article may perform its function' (s. 213(3)). This very companionable definition was directed primarily at those spare parts which were involved in many of the copyright design cases before the 1988 Act, primarily components and spare parts for vehicles but also a wide variety of other articles, for example, vacuum cleaners.

There are a number of difficulties in the drafting of this provision which await judicial resolution. First, it only excludes from design right those features of the shape or configuration of an article which must fit another article in the manner specified. Where such an article also has additional original design features then, presumably, design right will apply to them and competitors will have to design these additional features of 'must-fit' articles differently.

Secondly, the exclusion does not apply to machine components and spare parts alone but also to any article which must fit another article in order to perform its function. The question frequently posed in the Parliamentary debates, to which no authoritative answer was given, concerned Lego toy bricks. Formerly, the copyright in the drawings for Lego bricks enabled copyright protection to extend to the bricks themselves, although the duration of copyright was limited to 15 years because the design was registrable (s. 51 would now remove any copyright protection based upon the drawings). Does design right now apply to the shape or configuration of such designs or are 'original' toy bricks of this kind must-fit articles which suffer the same fate as spare parts? The latter is certainly strongly arguable, even though not intended. Curiously, articles in kit form, would also appear to fall within the exclusion but s. 260 expressly leaves open the question whether design right can subsist in such components.

(b)  *Must-match*. This relates to 'features of shape or configuration of an article which are dependent upon the appearance of another article of which the article is intended by the designer to form an integral part'. An example in mind here was that of car body panels which, of course, must match. Again, however, the scope of this exception is uncertain and questions have been raised as to whether design right can apply, for example, to matching dinner services. There is every economic reason why the design right should apply here, and such was the intention, but it is arguable that the wording of the exclusion ('features of shape or configuration . . . which . . . are dependent upon the appearance of another article of which the article is intended by the designer *to form an integral part'*) catches these too.

### Ownership of design right

The designer is the first owner of design right save where it is created by an employee in the course of employment; and, as with registered designs rather than copyright, the first owner of design right in a commissioned work is the commissioner (s. 215).

### Duration of design right

Design right expires 15 years from the year in which the design was first recorded in a design document, or an article was first made to the design, whichever occurs first. If the article is commercially exploited within the first five years of that period, the duration is 10 years from commercial exploitation. In effect, therefore, the period is normally 10 years from first marketing; which can occur anywhere in the world and by the design owner or with his consent (s. 216).

### Exclusive right of the design-right owner and remedies

The exclusive right of the design-right owner is to reproduce the design for commercial purposes. Any person who copies the design, or a substantial part of it, on articles, whether directly or indirectly, infringes the design right and those who intentionally or negligently commercially deal with articles containing infringing designs are also liable (ss. 226 and 227).

Similar remedies are available to the design-right owner and exclusive licensees as are available to such persons under copyright law, although there are some differences as, for example, the provisions relating to threats (see chapter 10).

### Dealings with design right

Similar rules relate to dealings with design right as to copyright, including power to deal with future design rights (s. 223). Where a registered design is assigned, such assignment carries with it any related design right, unless a contrary intention appears (s. 224).

### Licences of right

An important limitation upon design right, to safeguard competition and the public interest, is the availability of licences of right for any person to manufacture the protected article during the final five years of the term (s. 237). In default of agreement, the terms of the licence of right have to be settled by the Comptroller-General of Patents, Designs and Trade Marks. Also, if any infringement proceedings are taken during the period in respect of which the licence of right is available, the defendant may undertake to take the licence on agreed terms and thus avoid an injunction and forfeiture order being made against him and any damages or account of profits recoverable must not exceed double the amount which would have been payable by him if he had taken a licence on the agreed terms (s. 239).

Although a licence of right is generally available after five years, the Secretary of State has the power to exclude specified designs if it appears necessary in order to comply with any UK international obligation or in order to secure or maintain reciprocal protection for British designs in other countries (s. 245). The obvious example here is that of semiconductor chips where the 10 year period of protection cannot be subjected to a licence of right if protection is to be retained in the USA for British-produced semiconductor chips (see chapter 15).

### Crown rights

The Crown has certain rights to exploit articles, without the licence of the design-right owner, for purposes relating to the services of the Crown, namely, matters relating to national or foreign defence and Health Service purposes subject to compensation as agreed or, in default of agreement, as determined by the court (ss. 240 to 244).

## Registered designs

The registered design system continues in very much the same form as before the 1988 legislation. The changes made to the 1949 Act are relatively minor so as to ensure that there is consistency between the registered system and the unregistered design right (for example, exclusion of must-match designs from registrability) and also to make minor clarifying amendments. For example, the former requirement that registered designs must be 'novel or original', an ambiguous expression to say the least, has been amended so that registered designs now simply have to be 'new'. Similarly, the eye-appeal factor has been revised slightly so that the design will not be registered in respect of an article if the appearance of the article is not material, that is, if aesthetic considerations are not normally taken into account to a material extent by persons acquiring or using articles of that description, and would not be so taken into account if the design were to be applied to the article (s. 265). This provision has been criticised as being a more difficult test to apply.

Certain categories of aesthetic designs, in particular must-match designs, are no longer registrable. This is to ensure consistency with the unregistered design right. What happens then, to such designs which were registered before commencement? A proposal to subject all such registered designs to immediate licences of right was challenged as being retrospective interference with established property rights. Instead, a compromise solution was settled upon which applies only to such (post-commencement unregistrable) designs registered in pursuance of applications made after 12 January 1988: these are entitled to a maximum of 10 years' protection from commencement of the 1988 Act, subject throughout the post-Act period to licences of right (s. 266).

More important, though, is the extension of the period of protection for designs registered after commencement from a maximum of 15 to a maximum of 25 years.

## Interrelationship between rights

Although the scope of copyright protection for industrial designs is now very limited, where it does apply it takes priority over any parallel design right. For example, where an article qualifies as a work of artistic craftsmanship, it is not an infringement of any design right in the design to do anything which is an infringement of the copyright in that work (s. 236). The copyright route must be taken.

Where a design is registrable, it is also possible for the unregistered design right to subsist concurrently with it. Indeed, any application for registration of a design in which a design right subsists cannot be entertained unless made by the person claiming to be the unregistered design right owner (Registered Designs Act 1949, s. 3(2); CA 1988, sch. 4).

Whether there will be a significant increase in the number of registrations of designs to take advantage of the 25-year period of protection as compared with the 10-year provision for design right remains to be seen.

## Transitional provisions

Where a design was recorded or embodied in a design document or model before commencement of the 1988 Act, the exclusion of copyright protection in relation to works made to the design will not apply for 10 years after the commencement of the Act (sch. 1, para. 19).

Thus, all the old law relating to the protection of industrial articles based upon *drawings* will continue to apply. The main difference now, however, will be that the right will not extend beyond 10 years from commencement and will also be subject to a licence of right during the last five years of protection.

Where the period of copyright protection for an artistic work which was also a *registrable* design had been limited before commencement to 15 years (by the Design Copyright Act 1968 and the Copyright Act 1956, s. 10), that period continues to operate (sch. 1, para. 20(1)).

## Summary

The new laws relating to industrial designs are complex and confusing. In order to apply the correct legal provisions to any design articles, a careful analysis will be required. The following summary and illustrations relating to articles and designs created both *before* commencement of the 1988 Act and *after* commencement indicate the approach which will have to be taken in respect of particular articles and designs.

*Rights acquired BEFORE commencement of the 1988 Act*

(a)  *Copyright.*

(i)   If the article in question is a copyright artistic work in its own right, the usual copyright term of life plus 50 years applies prior to commencement. If the work is registrable under the Registered Designs Act 1949, and it is applied industrially, the Copyright Act 1956 s. 10 (as amended), reduced the term of *copyright* protection to 15 years. This limited *copyright* term remains the same under transitional provisions in the 1988 Act (sch. 1, para. 20).

(ii)  If reliance was placed upon copyright in drawings etc. prior to commencement of the 1988 Act then protection under the old law will continue to exist, but only for 10 years from commencement, subject to licences of right in the last five years (as if the unregistered design right law applied). However, the conversion remedy (Copyright Act 1956, s. 18) will not apply in respect of any infringements before or after commencement save for any proceedings *begun* before commencement.

(iii) Nothing affects the operation of any rule of law (for example, the *British Leyland Motor Corporation Ltd* v *Armstrong Patents Co. Ltd* principle of non-derogation from grant) preventing or restricting the enforcement of copyright in relation to a design (sch. 1 para. 19(9)).

(b)  *Registered designs.* If the design was registered under the Registered Designs Act 1949, thus enjoying up to 15 years' registered design protection at commencement, this period continues to run.

(c) *Unregistered design right.* Design right cannot subsist, since it will not apply to a design recorded in a design document, or an article made to the design, before commencement (s. 213(7)).

*Illustration 12.4*   X produces (before commencement) a novel design of a home nuclear fall-out shelter, assembled on site, from pre-cast sections which are bolted together and anchored in concrete foundations.

(a) *Copyright?*

(i)   Arguably, this could be an artistic work ('works of architecture, being either buildings or models for buildings' since a building is defined as 'any structure' (Copyright Act 1956, ss. 3(1)(b) 48; see also Copyright, Designs and Patents Act 1988, s. 4(1)(b) and (2)) and it is an open question whether there is any requirement to show that the work is artistic). If so, the full copyright period of life plus 50 years operates before commencement.

Even if this design is industrially exploited the period of copyright protection for the purpose of industrial exploitation would not be cut down: it is likely to be regarded as solely functional and unregistrable under the Registered Designs Act 1949.

(ii)   If X relies upon drawings for this fall-out shelter, a similar period of copyright protection subsists until commencement. After commencement, however, protection continues for a further 10 years only, subject to a licence of right in the last five years and without the benefit of the conversion remedy.

(b) *Registered design?* No. Solely functional.

(c) *Unregistered design right?* No. Cannot apply to an article made prior to commencement.

*Illustration 12.5*   X manufactures and markets a novel design of a coffee table in the shape of a toadstool.

(a) *Copyright?*

(i)   In some circumstances, this might qualify as an artistic work, either as a work of artistic craftsmanship or as a sculpture (see chapter 2). If so, since the design is capable of registration under the Registered Designs Act 1949, the period of copyright protection was limited to 15 years. After commencement, this copyright period remains the same (Copyright, Designs and Patents Act 1988, s. 52 and sch. 1, para. 20).

It is more likely, however, that the coffee table would not qualify as an artistic work.

(ii)   If X relies upon copyright in the drawings from which the table was made, again the copyright term will be limited to 15 years, since the design is registrable. After commencement, the old law continues to apply, save that the copyright period will last for 10 years from commencement, subject to licences of right etc.

(b)   *Registered design?* If registered prior to commencement, the 15-year period continues to subsist thereafter.

(c)   *Unregistered design right?* Not applicable.

*Illustration 12.6*   X manufactures car exhaust systems and car body panels.

(a)   *Copyright?* The only copyright protection must be based upon drawings. However, the non-derogation from grant principle would probably exclude the exercise of such copyright rights over spare parts.

It is not clear to what extent copyright control could still apply to such articles, if not sold as spare parts or in relation to those aspects of their design which do not come within the must-fit, must-match reasoning in *British Leyland Motor Corporation Ltd* v *Armstrong Patents Co. Ltd.* In so far as copyright subsists and is exercisable, the period of protection is life plus 50 years for the solely functional articles (the exhaust systems) and 15 years for the car body panels in so far as they were registrable designs.

After commencement, any longer copyright period would be restricted to 10 years as above.

(b)   *Registered designs?* It is unlikely that the exhaust systems could be registered. It was possible to register some aspects of the design of the must-match body panels. Any such registration acquires protection for 15 years until commencement and continues thereafter, unless an application for registration for a non-registrable design (after commencement) was made after 12 January 1988, in which case the term is 10 years from commencement subject throughout to licences of right.

*Illustration 12.7*   X is the author of the design of a typeface.

(a)   *Copyright?* Copyright protection will apply to the drawings for individual characters and also for the typeface as a set. In most cases such designs would be registrable and so the copyright period is likely to be cut down to 15 years. After commencement, the period of protection, whatever it may have been, is converted to 25 years *from commencement* (sch. 1, para. 14(5)). The reason for this is not clear.

(b)   *Registered designs?* Individual characters, and possibly the typeface as a set, are registrable, and the period of 15 years remains the same after commencement.

*Rights acquired AFTER commencement of the 1988 Act*

(a)   *Copyright*

(i)   If the article in question is a copyright artistic work in its own right, the usual copyright term of life plus 50 years applies. If the work is exploited industrially, the period of copyright protection is reduced to 25 years from the end of the year of first marketing (s. 52).

(ii)   If there is copyright only in drawings etc. (a design document or model recording or embodying a design) that copyright cannot be used to protect articles made to those drawings etc. (s. 51), unless they are designs of a typeface (s. 55).

(b)  *Registered designs.* If the design is registrable under the amended Registered Designs Act 1949, registered design protection for up to 25 years may be obtained.

(c)  *Unregistered design right.*

(i)  Design right may subsist in an original (not commonplace) design. The period of protection will be normally 10 years from the end of the year of first marketing, subject to a licence of right in the last five years of the term.

(ii)  Design right does not subsist in must-fit or must-match designs.

(iii)  The qualification provisions for design right must be satisfied.

(d)  *Choice of rights.*

(i)  Copyright and registered design may coexist, and infringement actions may be taken in respect of either or both rights.

(ii)  Copyright and design right may coexist in the same article. However, if it is possible to sue for copyright infringement, that route must be taken; an action for design right infringement is not permissible. Section 236 provides that:

> Where copyright subsists in a work which consists of or includes a design in which design right subsists, it is not an infringement of design right in the design to do anything which is an infringement of the copyright in that work.

(iii)  Registered design and design right may coexist and infringement actions may be taken in respect of either or both.

*Illustration 12.8*  X makes a *haute couture* wedding dress from a new design.

(a)  *Copyright?*

(i)  Possibly the dress could be a work of artistic craftsmanship. If so, protection is for life plus 50 years unless exploited industrially (i.e. more than 50 dresses sold), in which case protection is reduced to 25 years.

(ii)  If the dress is a work of artistic craftsmanship it is also possible to rely upon copyright in any drawings relating to the dress should there be any technical or procedural reason for doing so (e.g., if 'originality' is in question).

(b)  *Registered design?* Registered design protection for up to 25 years may be available.

(c)  *Unregistered design right?* This may subsist if it is an original, not commonplace, design. Protection will be for 10 years subject to licence of right for last five years of term.

If an action for copyright infringement is available, a design right action cannot be brought (s. 236).

If X's design had been commissioned by Y, there is an ownership issue: X is the first owner of the copyright in the dress; Y is the first owner of any design right. If both copyright and design right subsist, then, although Y might wish to sue competitors for design right infringement, he cannot do so without X's assistance, since an action is available for copyright infringement (even though it is for X not Y). This could be a potential source of friction unless ownership of copyright and design right are expressly dealt with at the time of commission.

*Illustration 12.9*    X is responsible for making the arrangements for a computer-generated drawing of a novel lampstand for commercial marketing.

(a)    *Copyright?*

(i)    The lampstand is unlikely to be an artistic work in its own right.
(ii)    No reliance can be placed on copyright in the drawings to prevent others marketing copies of the lampstand (s. 51).

(b)    *Registered design?* Protection as a registered design may be available for up to 25 years.
(c)    *Unregistered design right?* This is possible if the design is novel and not commonplace. Protection for 10 years subject to licence of right for last five years of the term.
Note that copyright could exist in the computer-generated drawings of the novel lampstand, but could not be enforced in an industrial copyright context (s. 51). However, design right may not subsist if, though original in the copyright sense, it is not original for unregistered design right purposes (e.g. if the lampstand was novel but commonplace).

*Illustration 12.10*    X produces car exhaust systems.

(a)    *Copyright?* There is no copyright in the exhausts as such; any copyright in drawings will not be enforceable (non-derogation of grant principle; and X also cannot enforce copyright in drawings (s. 51)).
(b)    *Registered design?* Not applicable if the exhausts are solely functional and must fit.
(c)    *Unregistered design right?* Again, not applicable in so far as it is a must-fit exhaust system.

Thus no protection for the car exhausts subsists; unless there are additional features which do not fall within the must-fit, must-match rules.

*Illustration 12.11*    X designs a stick-on shoe sole having an unusual pattern of ribbing which gives a good grip on icy paths.

(a)    *Copyright?* There is no copyright in the article in itself and any drawings cannot be relied upon.
(b)    *Registered design?* This will depend on whether the article is solely functional or whether it has some eye appeal to a purchaser. If the latter, it may be registrable for up to 25 years.

(c) *Unregistered design right?* If an original, and not commonplace, design then protection for 10 years with a licence of right for the last five years of the term.

*Illustration 12.12* X designs a typeface and, with the assistance of sophisticated computer technology, records all relevant design information in a database ready for producing the typeface.

(a) *Copyright?* The preliminary drawings are original artistic works. Section 51 is expressly excluded from operating. Protection extends to any three-dimensional indirect reproduction of the drawings (namely the typeface itself). The period of protection is 25 years from marketing (s. 55).

(b) *Registered design?* Protection as a registered design may be available for up to 25 years.

(c) *Unregistered design right?* This will be inapplicable because of the availability of copyright protection (s. 236).

# Chapter 13 Audio and Visual Recordings

We are all today familiar with, and most of us possess, recording equipment. When this equipment is used to make copies of gramophone records, cassettes or compact discs or to record material from radio or television, whether such material be films or records, the bulk of what is recorded is likely to be material in which copyright interests subsist. Thus, much of that copying, when done without licence, is unlawful and may cause severe economic harm to the record and film industries, composers, performers and others. The three principal areas for concern are first, *commercial piracy*. secondly, *home taping;* and, thirdly, the *renting* or hiring of copyright material, such as videos. These will be dealt with in turn.

## Commercial piracy

Piracy in this context relates to the unauthorised commercial manufacture and subsequent sale, or other distribution, of copies of works protected by copyright and other related rights.

This piracy takes various forms. Some involves counterfeiting whereby, for example, the packaging of a recording is made to look as close to the original as possible, sometimes including the forging of trade marks (in respect of which severer sanctions have been introduced: s. 300). The purchaser here may not realise that he is buying a pirate copy. In other cases the infringers make no attempt to imitate the packaging of the original. The pirated material is packaged with the names and logos of the pirate organisations themselves. There is also a considerable trade in bootleg recordings: tapes recorded from live concerts or radio performances of live concerts for which no permission has been granted by the performers.

In recent years the growth of the pirate recording industries has accelerated, both at home and abroad, as recording equipment has become technically more sophisticated, with the capacity to make fast, cheap and perfect copies. The losses caused by audio and video piracy have reached such proportions as to give serious concern to the recording and film industries and the rights owners.

The law here is usually quite clear. If anybody copies for commercial purposes a record, tape or film without authority, then there is infringement of all the various rights which may exist in the work. For example, in the case of a record, these rights might comprise copyright in the literary and musical works as well as in the sound recording and there may also be infringements of the performers' rights and those with whom they have contracts. If the recording is taken from a broadcast or cable programme, those rights too will be infringed and there may even be infringements of copyright in the designs, written material or photographs on record sleeves or covers. There will also be criminal liability with the prospect of severe penalties. A commercial importer of such material will be liable for secondary infringements if he knows, or has reason to believe, that it is infringing material and, again, there is the possibility of criminal prosecution.

The problems for copyright owners in the UK lie not with the law but with the prospects of enforcement and recent developments have improved these prospects considerably (see chapter 10).

## Home taping

*What happens in practice*
The issues raised by home taping are of quite a different order to those raised by commercial piracy. Most homes today have some recording equipment: whether audio cassette recorders or video cassette recorders or both; and increasingly, of course, personal computers. At one time, the reasonable man was described as the man on the Clapham omnibus, or, in American terms, the man in shirt-sleeves mowing his lawn on a Saturday afternoon. Today, he is as likely to be the man sitting at home in front of a television set using a video cassette recorder or cleaning his car to the sounds of a cassette which has been copied. No matter how law-abiding he may have been in his other activities, much of his home taping was formerly unlawful, although not criminal, even though it was done purely for private and domestic purposes. Lord Templeman recently put the matter in this way:

> From the point of view of society, the present position is lamentable. Millions of breaches of the law must be committed by home copiers every year. Some home copiers may break the law in ignorance, despite extensive publicity and warning notices on records, tapes and films. Some home copiers may break the law because they estimate that the chances of detection are non-existent. Some home copiers may consider that the entertainment and recording industries already exhibit all the characteristics of undesirable monopoly — lavish expenses, extravagant earnings and exorbitant profits — and that the blank tape is the only restraint on further increases in the prices of records. Whatever the reason for home copying, the beat of 'Sergeant Pepper' and the soaring sounds of the *Miserere* from unlawful copies are more powerful than law-abiding instincts or twinges of conscience. (*CBS Songs Ltd* v *Amstrad Consumer Electronics plc* [1988] 2 WLR 1191 at 1209.)

How could this unsatisfactory situation be resolved: should the reasonable man be compelled to comply wih the law; or the law be made to comply with the developing habits of the reasonable man?

### The competing claims

The opposing interest groups have been lined up against each other for several years. Those adversely affected by private copying, namely, the record industry, owners of copyright in films, authors, composers and performers all argue vehemently that home taping, though seemingly harmless, in fact inflicts enormous damage upon creators, performers and producers and causes losses to the UK copyright industry running into millions of pounds. The following, for example, is a typical statement emanating from this side of the fence:

> When people buy blank tapes, they buy the means to copy music. They do not pay for the music. Millions of pounds of investment is put into an industry which produces music that is popular the world over. The majority of blank tapes are imported; most recording equipment is imported. This is a drain on the balance of payments — it is also a drain on a creative British industry. (Statement by the British Phonographic Industry Ltd)

On the other side are the consumers, the tape industry and video and audio cassette manufacturers who maintain that the extent to which the decline in sales in parts of the recording industry is caused by home taping is far from clear. Many factors other than private or home copying are present which account for, or significantly contribute to, the results. Thus, they maintain that home taping:

> is a perfectly reasonable and normal use of copyright material and should be permitted in the UK as in other industrialised countries, without compensation; that, on a proper examination of the nature of home taping, it causes no material economic harm to copyright owners and, indeed, is of benefit to the music industry. ( The Case for Home Taping (Home Taping Rights Campaign Office, 1987).)

### Problems of enforcement

Leaving aside for the present the merits of the arguments, in practice it is almost impossible to enforce compliance with the law in this area. The primary infringers are those who do the recording in their own homes. Even if representatives of rights' owners wish to pursue the copyright infringers into their own homes, which of course they are unlikely to do, their chances of obtaining interlocutory remedies are negligible: in practice, enforcement of the law against the average home taper is a non-starter.

Nor is it possible normally to enforce rights in respect of unlawful home taping against the record or tape manufacturers on the grounds that they *authorise* the infringements. As was seen in the discussion of the *Amstrad* case in chapter 5, they will only be liable for authorisation where they 'grant or purport to grant' authority for copying and, of course, this is not what will be done either when the copying equipment is sold or advertised for sale. As Lord Templeman remarked in the Amstrad case, at pp. 1210–11, those proceedings

> will have served a useful purpose if they remind Parliament of the grievances of the recording companies and other owners of copyright and if at the same

time they draw the attention of Parliament to the fact that home copying cannot be prevented, is widely practised and brings the law into disrepute. . . . A law which is treated with such contempt should be amended or repealed.

*Possible solutions*

Thus, it was incumbent upon the government to seek to provide a fair solution to this problem in the Copyright, Designs and Patents Act 1988. One way, which at least would have acknowledged the reality, could have been the legalisation of home taping for private purposes. However, in so far as this could jeopardise seriously the interests of the owners of rights in the recordings, this would have been incompatible with Art. 9 of the Berne Convention which provides that any exceptions to a copyright owner's reproduction rights 'must not conflict with the normal exploitation of the work nor unreasonably prejudice the legitimate interests of the author'.

Since complete liberty to home tape for private purposes was not possible, a range of other suggested approaches were considered including the followng:

(a)  *Voluntary licences.* In theory a system of voluntary licences could be established whereby home tapers would be required to purchase a licence authorising them to copy at home for private purposes. In fact, this was tried some years ago but predictably very few home tapers made use of it. Therefore, a voluntary licensing system was dismissed as impracticable.

(b)  *A pay-at-source approach.* A variation of voluntary licensing is the possibility of an additional licence fee for private recording being paid at the point of first sale of the legitimate copy of a copyright article. This approach applies in many places in the fields of pay-television, database operation and the marketing of computer software where a rate is charged for the goods or services commensurate with the use which the consumer can be expected to make of them. At present, the music recording industry has objected because it fears that the charge will be seen simply as a price increase to the first purchaser which might further depress markets and exacerbate the home copying problem. This approach, however, has considerable promise for the future (EEC Green Paper, para. 3.7.11).

(c)  *Technical solutions: spoiler systems and anti-copying devices.* The recording industry has for long been developing devices which would be able to block or deter unauthorised recordings. Until recently, such technical solutions have been unsuccessful since counter-devices were developed to neutralise the anti-copying measures. Greater success seemed possible more recently following the introduction of compact disc and digital audio tape (DAT) when the EEC and the US government were considering the mandatory application of a technical anti-copying device known as the CBS Copycode System in all digital recorders to be marketed for private use. No such legislation has been introduced and the recording and hardware industries now appear to favour other technical solutions based on digital recording technology.

However, s. 296 now provides sanctions against those who become commercially involved in cracking anti-copying devices (see p. 167).

(d)   *Payment of a royalty on blank tapes and recording equipment: a blank tape levy*. A widely favoured solution is a compromise whereby, in exchange for home tapers being given the right to record for private and domestic purposes, a levy is imposed either upon blank tapes or upon the recording equipment (which was the method first employed in West Germany) or upon both (which presently operates in West Germany). The revenue thus produced would then be. redistributed to rights owners (not an easy task, incidentally) so honour might be satisfied for both interest groups.

There were various arguments advanced against a levy, particularly the blank tape levy. For example, it was not fair for one industry (tape manufacturers) to subsidise another (the record producers). This was particularly true, said the tape manufacturers, when there really is no home taping problem. A tape levy was too broad and crude in its application, it would provide rough justice that was too rough: why should those who bought and used blank tapes for non-infringing purposes pay a levy: copyright owners would be subsidised at the expense of the public. A levy scheme would be unworkable and unenforceable; the collection and distribution would be prohibitively expensive. It was also objected that the rewards were more likely to go to the record manufacturers than to the composers and other authors and no assistance should be given to enable the 'fat cats to get still fatter'.

Nevertheless, until the very last moment, the UK government had decided that in some areas there was no alternative to the introduction of a compulsory levy on blank recording tape, coupled with a licence for the public to record for private purposes. However, there was then a complete volte-face: it was felt that the levy proposals went too far; that any financial benefit to copyright owners and performers would be outweighed by the adverse effects the levy would have on consumers, especially visually handicapped people. Accordingly, no tape levy was introduced into the 1988 Act.

### The concept of 'time-shifting'
The need to control home taping arises when there is some prejudice to the economic interests of copyright owners. This does not happen in all cases when copyright material is recorded. Surveys have shown that of those who use blank audio tapes in the UK to record from disc or tape, roughly equal proportions copy from originals they own themselves (for use in a car, for example) and from originals borrowed from friends. It is unlikely that those who record from copies they have purchased already would buy second copies in any event. Accordingly, a case could be made out for allowing purchasers to make back-up copies of recordings since normally there is no financial detriment to rights owners. The situation is different, however, when a friend's recording is copied: in many of these cases, though it is not easy to establish what proportion, copying such recordings may be a substitute for purchasing them. Video cassette recorders are also used in different ways: first, they are used for viewing pre-recorded tapes and so no home taping issue arises (although if the pre-recorded tape has been rented, there may be a rental issue; see p. 165); secondly, video cassette recorders are used frequently to record material shown on television to enable the user to view the programme at a more convenient time. Such recording for temporary 'time-shifting' purposes does not unreasonably prejudice the interest of copy-

right owners who have authorised the showing of the material on television in the first place; and, thirdly, some people record material from television for 'librarying' purposes, that is, they build up a collection of material such as films for permanent retention: in this case, there may well be an economic impact upon the rights of copyright owners.

A significant legal difference between time-shifting and librarying was acknowledged by the United States Supreme Court in *Sony Corporation of America* v *Universal City Studies Inc.* [1984] 104 SCt 774 when it decided that recording for time-shifting purposes was justified under American copyright law as a 'fair use'; though recording for librarying was not. Although the much narrower fair-dealing provisions in UK law would not cover time-shifting, s. 70 of the 1988 Act has in effect accepted it as a fair dealing by providing that:

> The making for private and domestic use of a recording of a broadcast or cable programme solely for the purpose of enabling it to be viewed or listened to at a more convenient time does not infringe any copyright in the broadcast or cable programme or in any work included in it.

This section throws up several theoretical problems: for example, may the time-shifting home taper only view or listen to the recording on one occasion; how long is he entitled to keep the recording before he exceeds the permissible limits? (The government had originally suggested that a recording could not be kept for more than 28 days after the relevant broadcast or transmission, but this provision was removed on the grounds of unworkability, having been criticised, *inter alia,* for the concern it would cause to pensioners and others troubled by visions of inspectors searching their homes for recordings kept for more than 28 days.) In practice, of course, it is impossible in most cases for anybody to prevent home tapers from copying for any private domestic purpose. From the point of view of rights owners, therefore, their claims have not been satisfied and in so far as they can demonstrate that Art. 9 of the Berne Convention has been breached, pressure for a change in the law to introduce a blank tape levy or other compensatory mechanism will continue.

In the meantime we can now all sleep more easily in our beds knowing that the video recorder we set to tape the late-night film is not simultaneously making us law-breakers!

*Illustration 13.1*  X buys a pre-recorded cassette and (without any licence) makes a copy of it for use in his car. Prima facie, such copying infringes the reproduction rights of the copyright owners of any literary and musical works and of the sound recording right. There is no infringement of performers' rights as the recording is made for private or domestic use.

*Illustration 13.2*  X borrows a cassette from a friend and copies it. The situation both under the Copyright Act 1956 and the 1988 Act is the same: there is copyright infringement and no defence.

*Illustration 13.3*  X records a live performance of a Beethoven symphony off air (i.e., from radio or television). There is no copyright in the symphony, since it is now in the public domain and so the only copyright interest is in the broadcast. Under the Copyright Act 1956, recording was permissible, since the exclusive rights enjoyed by the copyright owner of the *broadcast* did not cover reproduction for private and domestic use. However, under the 1988 Act the broadcasting right covers all copying, including private and domestic, and so the only available defence now would be if the recording was for private and domestic time-shifting purposes (s. 70).

*Illustration 13.4*   If A had recorded the same Beethoven symphony from the radio but, instead of it being a live performance, it was a recorded performance, then there would be an additional sound recording right involved. Under the Copyright Act 1956, in the absence of a licence, recording for private and domestic use does not infringe the broadcasting right but does infringe the sound recording right and so the recording would have been unlawful. Under the 1988 Act, both the broadcasting and sound recording rights are infringed unless the recording is made for time-shifting purposes (s. 70).

*Illustration 13.5*   A records a film from television for private and domestic purposes. Under the Copyright Act 1956 there would be no infringement of the broadcasting rights but, in the absence of licence, all other copyrights underlying the film, and also copyright in the film itself would be infringed by the home copier. (It should be observed that unravelling the various copyright interests in old, foreign films is particularly complex.) Under the 1988 Act none of these rights would be infringed provided the recording is made for time-shifting purposes.

*Future developments*
The present law can hardly be regarded as satisfactory. All recordings from radio and television of copyright material without permission, even for private purposes, will be unlawful unless done for time-shifting purposes. In addition, any other home taping of audio or visual material will continue to be unlawful (even though widespread) and the law in this area may fall further into disrepute.

The problems have now become more urgent. We are in the midst of rapidly developing changes which, amongst other areas, affects home copying in particular. The traditional analogue recording involves a loss of sound quality every time a copy is made. In practice, therefore, this places a limit on the number of copies which can be made. Analogue recording, though, now looks as if it will shortly be replaced by digital recording, which have no such limits: each copy will be perfect, at least as far as the ordinary listener is concerned, and can serve as a master from which many other generations of copies can be made. A very small number of purchased original recordings could serve to generate many thousands of perfect 'clone' copies. Digital radio receivers are expected to be on the market within two years; digital audio is available now as compact disc and DAT. Digital video will follow within a few years. All leisure, telecommunications and information management technology is moving rapidly into the totally digital domain (EEC Green Paper, para. 3.6.2).

It may be that the solutions which have been discussed and rejected and also the measures introduced into the 1988 Act will have to be reviewed before long.

The EEC Green Paper stated that it was not appropriate to take steps in the member States at this late stage to harmonise existing levy schemes on analogue products: any initiative now would risk being made obsolete by the march of progress within a decade.

### Rental rights and rights of distribution

Until recently once a purchaser bought a copyright work, such as a book or a record, the right of the copyright owner in relation to the further distribution of that work, was exhausted: he could not do anything more. Thus, a library which buys a single copy of a work may, by lending it, enable dozens of other people to read that book, yet the author receives only one royalty from that book. If a person buys a record and lends it to friends, they may enjoy listening to it (provided it is not a public performance) with no obligation to compensate the owners of copyright in that recording. Even where the lending of lawfully made recordings takes place commercially, those involved in the lending will not normally be liable for authorising the infringement even if the borrowers unlawfully copy the recording. Thus, in *CBS Inc.* v *Ames Records & Tapes Ltd* [1982] Ch 91, the owner of a record lending library was held not to be liable for authorising borrowers to infringe copyright even though it was clear that most subscribers borrowed the records in order to copy them. This, of course, is consistent with the *Amstrad* principle (see p. 66).

There are now exceptions to this rule. 'Distribution rights' may now operate, first, in relation to the public lending of books and, secondly, in certain other rental situations.

*Public lending right*
Under the Public Lending Right Act 1979, authors of books living in the UK may register their rights to receive a share, limited to £5,000 per annum from a government fund (£3.5 million in 1988) based upon the number of times that copies of their books were lent out to the public by local libraries. This right, which is outside the copyright system, is at least some recognition that authors should be entitled to receive something in respect of the further distribution of books after they have been sold.

*Rental rights*
Under the law before the 1988 Act the only way that the owner of a copyright interest in a videogram or sound recording could obtain any control over, or reward from, the use of his product in a rental scheme was by contract: he could stipulate, as a condition of the sale of the recording, that it should not be rented out to the public, or he might 'authorise' rental subject to some payment or share of the rental income. Some rights owners, however, were dissatisfied with the inadequate protection provided by such contractual arrangements. There were doubts about the effectiveness of such contractual stipulations and difficulties in tracing and enforcing obligations in the often long chain of transactions between the copyright owners and the rental operators.

*A new rental right*
After considerable hesitation over whether a rental right was needed at all and,

then, when that case was accepted, after further dallying with a limited right for a one or two-year period, the government finally accepted the case for a rental right for the full copyright term:

> We are now persuaded that some genuine objections need to be met. . . . Evidence from Japan suggests that over 90% of rented recordings are copied and this has had a serious effect on the record industry in Japan. If the Japanese experience were repeated here, it would entail lost sales of up to £200 million a year . . . Unless we [provide such a full exclusive right] . . . there will be a serious impact upon the industry. . . . The specific mischief that we seek to put right is that of rental shops which effectively rent for no purpose other than that of making possible illegal copying. These are the overnight-type rental arrangements whereby one rents a compact disc, tapes it and returns it the next day. (Mr Francis Maude MP, 24 May 1988.)

The new rental right has been effected by extending the scope of the exclusive right of copyright owners to 'issue copies to the public' so that in relation to *sound recordings, films and computer programs,* the restricted act of issuing copies to the public also includes 'any rental of copies to the public'. The definition of 'rental' is misleading. Section 178 defines 'rental' in terms of commercial rental but tucked away in sch. 7 are provisions extending the rental right to public libraries. Now, rental of copies of such works without permission infringes copyright and, on the same facts, the defendant in *CBS Inc.* v *Ames Records & Tapes Ltd* would be liable, assuming specific acts of unauthorised rentals could be established (see chapter 5).

It should be noted that the right to control the rental of sound recordings and films is conferred only on *producers* and not on authors (for example, composers) and performers. It was felt by the government that owners of these underlying copyrights are already entitled to prevent recording without consent and that if they also were given the new rental right, this might confer upon them too powerful control over the subsequent exploitation of their works. Thus, it is left for authors and performers to ensure that in their contractual negotiations with record and film producers, the royalty position with regard to rental is taken into account. This approach can be criticised on two scores: first, it is an interesting demonstration of the way in which the entrepreneurial copyright interests have been given greater protection than those of authors in the traditional sense; secondly, it is likely that, in practice, many authors and performers will not have sufficient bargaining strength to ensure that their contracts provide them with any, or a satisfactory, share in the proceeds of rental rights.

*Licences of right (compulsory licences)*
As a corollary to the creation of a rental right the Secretary of State now has power to introduce compulsory licensing of rental (s. 66): *in certain cases* there would be a right for persons to rent to the public copies of certain categories of products subject to the payment of a reasonable royalty (the Copyright Tribunal deciding on that in the case of dispute) and subject also to any licensing scheme that may have been brought into operation. The original government proposal was that this licence of right should arise in relation to all sound recordings, films

and computer programs *after one year*. However, there was strong resistance from various quarters: video, film and sound recording organisations either opposed licences of right entirely or opposed losing their exclusive right after one year; and computer program organisations maintained that the rental of computer programs would lead to massive and undetectable copying which would seriously affect their sales. Accordingly, the Secretary of State has been given very wide discretion to deal with different situations and different areas of the same industry. It is provided that any order 'may make different provision for different cases and may specify cases by reference to any factor relating to the work, the copies rented, the renter or the circumstances of the rental' (s. 66(3)). Government guidance was given in the Parliamentary debates on the way in which rental and compulsory licensing provisions would be expected to operate. Compulsory licensing powers are not likely to be exercised in respect of the ordinary commercial rental of sound recordings, videos and computer programs in their current form. The owners of rights in these products can be expected to stop any rentals that are likely to lead to any loss in sales through copying. The reserve powers would be available only if the rights owners used the rental right in an unacceptable way. Two examples were given of when the compulsory licensing power might be invoked: first, to ensure that public libraries could lend or rent out records and videos in a responsible way, subject to payment of equitable remuneration to rights owners under a licensing scheme; and, secondly, if new products were to be developed which, like the videograms of today, may be best suited for a rental market and the government concluded that the rental right was being used to prevent such a market from developing and that consumers were being forced to buy an expensive product that they would prefer to hire, an order could be made. Thus, in the main, rental rights will be exploited contractually until such time as evidence of abuse in particular situations occurs.

### Copy protection

Reference has already been made to devices designed to circumvent copy protecton. Section 296 applies 'where copies of a copyright work are issued to the public, by or with the licence of the copyright owner, in an electronic form which is copy-protected. 'Copy protection' refers to any device or means intended to prevent copying of a work or to impair the quality of copies made. The person who issues copies of such works to the public can sue, as if for copyright infringement, any person who makes, imports or commercially deals with any apparatus or device designed or adapted to circumvent the form of copy protection employed, or who publishes information intended to enable or to assist persons to circumvent that form of copy protection. Such rights include delivery up or seizure of offending devices. Thus, persons who become involved in assisting people to counter the steps taken by copyright owners or others to prevent unauthorised copying are regarded as the equivalent of copyright infringers.

### Infringing public performances

Where unauthorised public performances of works occur and apparatus for playing sound recordings, showing films, or receiving visual images or sounds conveyed by electronic means is used to facilitate such performances, persons who supply such apparatus knowing, or having reason to believe, that it is to be used to infringe copyright are themselves liable as secondary infringers (s. 26).

## Educational recording of broadcast audio and visual material

Special provisons apply in relation to recording for educational purposes. These are discussed in chapter 14.

# Chapter 14 Reprography, Education and Libraries

## Introduction

A reprographic process is defined in s. 178 as one: (a) for making facsimile copies, or (b) involving the use of an appliance for making multiple copies, but does not include the making of a film or sound recording.

The most common example of reprography is photocopying, a practice that has grown immensely since the passing of the 1956 Act and for which the Act consequently did not adequately provide. Although the problems are not confined to the fields of education and libraries it is in those contexts that most of the developments have occurred and to which the majority of the statutory provisions refer. This chapter therefore looks first at reprography generally before concentrating on the provisions dealing with education and libraries, including in the discussion of these latter subjects related matters which do not strictly amount to reprography such as educational recording.

## Reprography

Reprographic technology has rapidly advanced to the stage whereby virtually every office, and possibly soon every home, is able to afford machines which are relatively cheap to run and are capable of efficiently and speedily producing high-quality copies of any written material. These machines have substantial legitimate and non-infringing uses but, obviously, can also be used to infringe the rights of copyright owners on a huge and often undetectable scale. Their capacity to photocopy for perfectly legitimate purposes makes less attractive any solution to unlawful copying in terms of a levy on either the equipment or the recording medium — the difficulties encountered in trying to impose a levy on blank tapes would be as nothing compared with the opposition that would face any attempt to impose a levy on blank paper! Nor are technical solutions making the printed page impossible or difficult to copy likely to be feasible or desirable.

It is clear that the photocopying of any literary, dramatic, musical or artistic work is prima facie an infringement (provided a substantial part is taken). The most relevant defence here is the fair-dealing exception for research or private study. The amount of photocopying now possible has placed on this exception a weight which it was never designed to bear and has left both copyright owners and those who wish to use their works in an impasse where each side makes exaggerated claims about the extent of its rights but neither side is really sure of its true position. Furthermore, under the 1956 Act, since fair dealing only applied to Part I works, publishers could argue that photocopying any (substantial) part of a published edition was automatically an infringement which could not be saved by the fair dealing defence. As was noted in chapter 6, the new Act extends the defence to published editions but does little else to clarify the amount that can fairly be taken, which inevitably has to remain a flexible concept, although the Act does at least make it clear that the production of multiple copies is not allowed (s. 29(3)).

As a result, as in other areas, attention has switched to a solution based on licensing schemes which are designed to provide users with clearer guidance on what may be copied and which at the same time provide a fair reward for the owners of the copyright in the works being copied. As was discussed in chapter 7, the Copyright Tribunal now exists to resolve disputes where one party to such a licence feels that a fair balance is not being struck. It will be seen in the next section that, under the aegis of the Copyright Licensing Agency (CLA) representing authors and publishers, such schemes had already begun to emerge in the educational field even before the 1988 Act, but licensing schemes for industry and other users are also likely to follow. Quite apart from the specific provisions to be discussed below in relation to education, the Act recognises the likelihood of general licensing schemes for reprographic copying by specifying the factors (detailed on page 172) to be taken into account by the Copyright Tribunal in considering such schemes and also by implying in them an indemnity against infringement of any work within the apparent scope of a licence granted under a scheme or by a licensing body.

## Education

*Background*
Schools, colleges and universities have a particularly healthy appetite for copies of the works of others and it is of course highly desirable that the educational process should expose students and pupils to as wide a range of sources as possible. The problem is that educational users are not always willing or able to pay the price that copyright owners might regard as reasonable. The problem is a complex one because on the one hand there are works (e.g., school textbooks) for which the educational sector is effectively the whole market. Widespread copying of such works might mean they become uneconomic to produce: in the absence of proper controls on, or charges for, photocopying, the supply of such works might dry up and the educational system itself would be the poorer. On the other hand, there are works produced for a completely different market (e.g., a book, written for the mass market, parts of which a teacher wants to make multiple copies of because of its discussion of a topical issue) where, even in the absence of the ability to copy, there would be no question of the teacher buying copies instead. Whilst it is not suggested in this sort of case that unlimited educational use should be completely free of charge, it is at least arguable that the appropriate fee should be considerably less. Until recent years, authors and publishers relied mainly on the tactics of persuasion to encourage educational users to respect copyright and

to seek licences. However, legal proceedings were brought in the early 1980s against a number of local authorities where clear evidence had been obtained of widespread unlawful copying in their schools although these actions were eventually settled.

This more aggressive stance paved the way for a blanket licence between the Copyright Licensing Agency (on behalf of authors and publishers) and local education authorities (on behalf of schools). This licence has been in operation for the three school years 1986/87 to 1988/89 and allows multiple copies of up to 5% of a book published in the UK or the whole of an article in a periodical in return for a total fee over the whole three years of just over £3 million. Certain types of work are excluded, such as printed music, newspapers, maps, workbooks etc., and unauthorised copying outside the terms of the licence and of the Act obviously remains an infringement.

Although a similar agreement has been reached with independent schools, the higher education sector was more reluctant to enter into such a scheme since it claimed that much of what the Copyright Licensing Agency wished to charge a fee for was already permissible either because it did not amount to the taking of a substantial part in the first place or because it constituted fair dealing within the law. However, an experimental scheme was agreed for 1988 between the Committee of Vice Chancellors and Principals (CVCP) and the Copyright Licensing Agency whereby certain universities are operating a 'transactional' licence scheme enabling multiple copies to be made within the same sorts of limits applicable to schools. The difference between this and the schools scheme is that the total licence fee under the university scheme is not fixed in advance but depends on the number of copies actually made, for which a fee of 2.5p per page will be levied. Thus the university scheme requires detailed records to be kept of all copies made under the scheme although it is envisaged that the data acquired under this scheme will enable a collective licence to be negotiated for the future under which (as with the schools scheme) only sample returns from selected institutions will be required.

Another significant difference between the two schemes is that the university scheme expressly preserves, and is without prejudice to, the existing exceptions such as fair dealing. Thus a single copy for research or private study (the CVCP/CLA document misleadingly reverses the order of this phrase to 'private study or research') would be outside the scheme and would not attract a fee. On the other hand, the scheme requires the payment of a fee both for 'systematic' single copying by members of a class instructed by a staff member to obtain such copies and also for each borrowing from a loan collection, for use in a formal class, of a copy made under the scheme. Both schemes have a list of excluded publishers and titles in respect of which copying is not licensed.

*The 1988 Act*
The Act provides positive encouragement to the creation of licensing schemes, not only by giving the Copyright Tribunal the power to arbitrate in disputes arising from such schemes, but also by s. 36. This section operates as a kind of reserve provision. It permits multiple copies of up to 1% of a published literary, dramatic or musical (but not artistic) work to be made in any one quarter of the year by an educational establishment for the purposes of instruction. This

permission is not applicable if 'licences are available authorising the copying in question and the person making the copies knew or ought to have been aware of that fact'. This provides a small, though hardly generous, incentive for those publishers who hitherto may have been reluctant to license any copying to begin to do so since otherwise a limited amount of multiple copying will be permissible free of charge. Any licences offered must not restrict the copying below that which would be permissible in the absence of a licence, although a fee can be charged even for this amount.

If the licence is granted by a licensing body (see chapter 7) then the terms of the licence can be referred to the Copyright Tribunal anyway. In considering the licensing of reprographic copying (whether in the educational sphere or elsewhere), s. 136 requires the Tribunal to have regard to:

(a)   the extent to which published editions of the works in question are otherwise available,

(b)   the proportion of the work to be copied, and

(c)   the nature of the use to which the copies are to be put.

Factor (c), in the present context, obviously directs attention to the fact that the use is educational, which might suggest a lower fee than, say, for commercial use.

In addition to the jurisdiction of the Copyright Tribunal over licences and schemes offered by licensing bodies, the Secretary of State has power under s. 137 to order the inclusion of unreasonably excluded works in licences or schemes for reprographic copying by *educational* establishments for the purposes of instruction. Before making such an order he must give notice to the interested parties and take account of any representations made to him. An order can only be made if adding the works to the scheme 'would not conflict with the normal exploitation of the works or unreasonably prejudice the legitimate interests of the copyright owners', since to do so would not only be unfair but a breach of Art. 9(2) of the Berne Convention from which the wording is taken. The Secretary of State's power only applies to works 'of a description similar to those covered by the scheme or licence' which are 'unreasonably excluded from it' but he can, under s. 140, set up an inquiry as to whether a scheme or general licence should be extended to a new category of works (even though not similar to those already covered). Again, such works should not be included if to do so would conflict with their normal exploitation etc. If a recommendation is made and not implemented within a year, an order may be made granting a statutory royalty-free licence. It should be noted that the powers under ss. 137 to 141 extend to artistic works whereas the 1% per quarter licence under s. 36 only applies to literary, dramatic and musical works.

Thus there are a variety of provisions designed to ensure that licences are available where appropriate to permit copying by educational establishments and to enable a fair balance to be struck between the interests of the copyright owners and the educational users. It remains to be seen precisely what sorts of licences and on what terms emerge against the background of these new provisons.

Reprography apart, there are a number of other provisions in the Act relating to education, i.e., the permitted acts contained in ss. 32 to 35.

*Things done for the purposes of instruction or examination (section 32)*
As far as instruction is concerned, this is a fairly limited provision which only applies to literary, dramatic, musical or artistic works if the copying is *not* done by means of a reprographic process and *is* done by a person giving or receiving instruction. This would exempt a teacher or pupil who writes out the whole of a short literary work (e.g., a poem) on the board or in an exercise book (passages from most longer literary works would not constitute a substantial part in any event). The exception also applies to sound recordings, films, broadcasts and cable programmes if the copy is made in the course of instruction in the making of films or film sound-tracks, a condition which considerably restricts the ambit of this aspect of the exception.

As far as examinations are concerned, *anything* done by way of setting the questions or communicating the questions to candidates or answering the questions is permitted so that the whole or part of a literary work could be included *reprographically* in an examination paper. Although it is not entirely clear how far setting the questions extends, it probably would not permit the photocopying of material to be used in an open-book examination to which the questions would refer or on which examinees would have to base their answers. Reprographic copies of *musical* works are *not* permitted for use by an examination candidate in performing the work but there seems nothing to prohibit reprographic copies for examinations not involving the *performance* but rather the analysis or discussion of the work.

To prevent misuse of any copies legitimately made under s. 32, subsection (5) contains the 'dealt with' formula that occurs frequently in this chapter of the Act. The specific exemptions provided by these provisions cease to apply once such copies are 'sold or let for hire or offered or exposed for sale or hire'.

*Anthologies for educational use (section 33)*
This is someting of an anomaly in that it protects not so much the teacher or pupil but more likely a commercial publisher providing material for use in educational establishments. The exception allows a short passage from a literary or dramatic (but not musical) work to be included in a collection intended for use in educational establishments provided various conditions are complied with including, significantly, that the work taken is not itself intended for use in schools and also that the collection consists mainly of material in which no copyright subsists. Authors and publishers have in the past stated that they would regard the following as short passages: prose extracts of less than 750 words and less than 75 lines from a poem provided in neither case that the extract was more than a third of the original work. Such statements are of as much or as little weight as statements about what is or is not regarded as within fair dealing. That the exception is really a rather specialised form of fair dealing is underlined by the fact that there must be a sufficient acknowledgement.

*Performing, playing or showing a work in educational activities (section 34)*
Performances of literary, dramatic or musical works are not regarded as public

performances (and are therefore not infringements) if they are before an audience consisting of teachers, pupils and others 'directly connected with the activities of the establishment' (e.g., non-teaching staff). The performance must be by a teacher or pupil (as was the case under the 1956 Act) or alternatively now 'by any person for the purposes of instruction'. Thus a visiting drama group or musician would now normally be covered since most such performances could be said to be for the purposes of instruction rather than merely for entertainment. It should be noted that this narrow and ungenerous exception continues to be unavailable in respect of the typical school play or concert performed before parents or relatives because the Act specifically states that a person is not directly connected with the activities of the establishment merely because he is the parent of a pupil. This does not matter too much in the case of musical performances since schools are generally licensed with the PRS through the local education authority for these purposes but as far as performances of literary and dramatic works are concerned, the permission of the copyright owner should be sought. However, some published plays expressly permit non-profit-making performances by educational establishments even if technically in public.

The playing or showing of a sound recording, film, broadcast or cable programme to an audience of teachers and pupils etc. similarly does not count as 'in public' if done for the purposes of instruction.

*Educational recording of broadcasts and cable programmes (section 35)*
Prior to the 1988 Act it was permissible, under various express licences and concessions offered by the BBC and ITV, to record educational and Open University programmes for educational purposes but the vast majority of broadcasts could not be legally recorded. One of the reasons that licences were not available on a wider basis was that, as has been pointed out elsewhere, a broadcast usually encompasses a large number of separate copyright works and the consents of a range of different owners must be obtained before the broadcast can be legally recorded, not to mention the rights of the performers whose consents are similarly required.

Section 35 now provides that recording for educational purposes is no longer an infringement of the broadcast or cable programme *or of any work included in it*. However, this exception does not apply if or to the extent that there is a licensing scheme certified by the Secretary of State under s. 141. This might appear to be an elegant solution to the problem and it is, of course, one adopted in various other contexts such as the copying of scientific abstracts. There is, however, a potential problem in that, as already noted, there will be a variety of copyright owners involved and hence a variety of possible licensing schemes to consider (unless the broadcasting organisations are prepared to take assignments of the various rights involved). Schools and other educational establishments may find that they will need licences from a number of different licensing bodies, once these get themselves geared up to the task, in order to carry out educational recording although licences are likely to be granted more centrally through education authorities rather than individual schools. (Section 131 provides that in considering the charges (if any) for such licences the Copyright Tribunal shall have regard to the extent to which the owners of the copyrights in the works included in the broadcast have already received or are entitled to receive payment in respect of their inclusion). Until such time as a certified licensing scheme is established, the section does provide much greater freedom for educational recording than was previously the case and, unlike the recordings previously permitted by broadcasting authorities, educational recordings can now be kept indefinitely, subject, as usual in this area, to the prohibition on the recording being subsequently dealt with for sale or hire etc.

## Libraries

Libraries are obviously particularly large holders of copyright material and so will often be requested to make copies of such material and be in a position to do so. The Act therefore contains, as did the 1956 Act, a number of special provisions to regulate such copying. Generally speaking, only non-profit-making libraries (such as local authority or educational ones) are given any extra leeway by these provisions and the precise details of the conditions under which such copying is permissible remain to be set out in regulations to be made by the Secretary of State (although guidance can be obtained from the existing regulations, SI 1957 No. 868). In some cases a librarian will have to be satisfied, for example, as to the purposes for which a person is requesting a copy and the Act now enables the regulations to provide that the librarian or person acting on his behalf 'may rely on a signed declaration as to that matter by the person requesting the copy, unless he is aware that it is false in any material particular'. This provision (s. 37(2)(a)) recognises the reality (and the practice under the 1956 Act) that ordinarily librarians cannot be expected to look behind signed statements made by library users. If such a declaration is false and results in a person receiving a copy which would be an infringing one if made by him (e.g., it would not be permitted anyway as fair dealing) then that person (but not the librarian) is treated as an infringer and the copy becomes an infringing one.

*Periodical artcles (section 38)*
Not more than one copy of an article in a periodical (nor more than one article from any one issue) may be supplied to a person satisfying the librarian that he requires it for research or private study and who is required to pay for the cost of producing the copy including a contribution to the general expenses of the library. If the above conditions are complied with (and any others prescribed by regulations) then the copy does not infringe 'any copyright in the text, in any illustrations accompanying the text or in the typographical arrangement'. It can be seen therefore that artistic works are only included in the exemption to the extent that they accompany text and cannot be copied independently. This does not matter greatly since artistic works may be copied for research or private study under s. 29, whether the copy is made by the researcher or student himself or by a person (including a librarian) acting on his behalf. The advantage of relying on the special provision for librarians is that it avoids any dispute about whether the taking of the whole of the article is 'fair' and, furthermore, the librarian at least knows that he is in the clear if he obtains the required signed declarations.

*Parts of published works (section 39)*
Librarians can make copies of parts of published works (other than periodicals

covered by the previous exception) for persons requiring them for research or private study provided no one is supplied with more than one copy nor with more than a reasonable proportion of any work. A payment along the same lines as in the previous exception is required and the exception applies to the same classes of work (not artistic ones unless accompanying text).

The equivalent exception in s. 7(3) of the Copyright Act 1956 was not available if the librarian knew of or could by reasonable enquiry ascertain the name of the person entitled to authorise the copying, but this limitation, which was neither widely known nor adhered to, was thought to be too restrictive and has been removed. Even with this limitation removed it is difficult to believe that the exception is of much importance since it does not appear to cover anything which would not be clearly covered by the normal fair-dealing provision in s. 29. Again, its principal value probably lies in the assurance that it gives to a librarian that he is acting lawfully if the prescribed conditions are complied with irrespective of whether the person to whom he supplies the copy genuinely wants it for research or private study.

*Restrictions on multiple copies (section 40)*
Both the previous exceptions for periodicals and parts of other works are further clarified by a new provision that deals with a former perceived abuse whereby a person could approach a librarian armed with numerous signed requests by different persons for copies of the same material. The regulations must now require the librarian to be satisfied that one person's requirement is not related to any similar requirement of another person. The regulations may (but do not necessarily have to although they almost certainly will) provide that a requirement is related to a similar requirement if it is for 'substantially the same material at substantially the same time and substantially the same purpose' *and* the persons requiring it 'receive instruction to which the material is relevant at the same time and place'. This is clearly designed to prevent the obtaining of 'class sets' of photocopies under these exceptions and s. 29(3) has a more general provision aimed at preventing the fair-dealing exception being used in the same sort of way. These finicky provisions do make for some absurdities. Thus, if students in a group are recommended to read an extract from a work, each student may individually photocopy amounts within the scope of fair dealing for research or private study, but neither the teacher nor librarian nor a designated student may make sufficient copies for and on behalf of the group. The net result is that queues at library photocopiers are likely to increase unnecessarily.

*Supply of copies to other libraries (section 41)*
A librarian may supply a copy to the librarian of another prescribed library in accordance with conditions to be laid down in regulations. The copy may be of a periodical article or of the *whole or part of* a published edition of a literary, dramatic or musical work and is thus wider than the s. 39 exception which is limited to 'a reasonable proportion of' works other than periodical articles. Such a copy again does not infringe any copyright in the text, the accompanying illustrations or the typographical arrangement but the exception is not available (other than for periodical articles) if the librarian knows or could by reasonable

inquiry ascertain the name of a person entitled to authorise the making of the copy (s. 41(2)).

This represents a severe limitation on the utility of the exception since the publisher's name will almost invariably appear on the work and provide the basis at least of such reasonable inquiry. Although it was a restriction that applied to the equivalent provision in the 1956 Act, it does not appear to have been widely appreciated but its re-enactment will no doubt give it wider publicity for the future.

### Preservation or replacement copies (section 42)

Librarians or archivists may copy any item in the *permanent collection* of the library or archive for the purpose of replacement or preservation. The copy may be placed in the permanent collection as a replacement or as an additional copy (in the latter case to prevent unnecessary wear and tear on a valuable original). Such a copy does not infringe any copyright in any literary, dramatic or musical work, or accompanying illustrations nor, in the case of a published edition, in the typographical arrangement. A copy may also be made to *replace* an item in another library's permanent collection which has been lost, destroyed or damaged. The regulations governing this exception are to include a limitation to 'cases where it is not reasonably practicable to purchase a copy of the item'. It is also proposed to restrict, by means of the same regulations, the applicability of the exception to non-lending libraries.

### Unpublished works (section 43)

A single copy of a literary, dramatic or musical work unpublished before being deposited in a library or archive may be supplied to a person requiring it for research or private study provided the copyright owner has not prohibited copying the work.

### Articles of cultural or historical importance (section 44)

Some such articles cannot be exported unless a copy is made and deposited in an appropriate library or archive. This exception provides that there is no infringement of copyright in making that copy. (The owner of the physical embodiment of the work being exported is not necessarily the owner of the copyright(s) in it.)

### Other provisions relating to libraries

Apart from the special provisions in ss. 37 to 44 already discussed it should be remembered that the introduction of a rental right (see p. 165) for sound recordings, films and computer programs will affect public libraries which provide a lending service for such items. If one were to look only at the definition of rental in s. 178, it would appear that only libraries which make a charge would be affected. However, it is here that one learns the importance of reading the whole of an Act, even one as long as this one, for tucked away in sch. 7, paras 6, 8 and 34 are provisions amending various Acts relating to public libraries. These provisions state that the new rental right applies to the lending by such libraries of sound recordings, films or computer programs whether or not a charge is made by the library. This is a substantial provision which should surely not be hidden away in a schedule headed 'Consequential amendments' and which ought to be at least referred to in the s. 178 definition of 'rental'.

It is envisaged that any royalty paid to the copyright owner should be passed on as a charge to the user and the free borrowing of recorded matter from local authority libraries will probably become a thing of the past (many libraries, of course, already make a charge). The Secretary of State has powers (see chapter 13) to grant compulsory licences if the copyright owners exploit the rental right unreasonably.

Libraries ought also to continue to take reasonable steps to avoid their user-operated photocopying facilities being used for copyright infringement. The onus is primarily on the individual library user and the courts would not lightly find that a library was authorising infringement (contrast the result of the Australian case of *Moorhouse* v *University of NSW* 1976 RPC 151 and see chapter 5) but the absence of any attempts to prevent misuse of the facilities (e.g., by the prominent display of clear warning notices) could still give rise to liability.

# Chapter 15 Computer Technology

## Introduction

American law defines a computer program as 'a set of statements or instructions to be used directly or indirectly in a computer in order to bring about a certain result'. More recently, the European Commission has simply described it as 'a set of instructions the purpose of which is to cause an information processing device to perform its functions'. Those instructions, of course, enable the computer to do a variety of things. For example, computer *operating* programs generally manage the internal functions of the computer, act as a brain, and enable the computer to carry out the various required functions. Computer *application* programs are those that usually perform a specific task for the computer user, whether it be word processing or playing chess.

Whatever function the computer program performs, the question which has exercised the computer industry and law-making bodies around the world has been how best to provide reasonable protection to those who invest time, skill and money in devising programs with commercial potential. For quite some time, it was possible to rely upon the law of contract and also, to some extent, on trade secrecy laws, to enable those who created computer programs to establish and enforce those rights against purchasers. This was easier some years ago, when computer programs tended to be used mainly in business situations where there was a direct contractual relationship between program developers and clients. Today, however, computer programs are handled by everybody, whether in business or at home, and the direct contractual link between the author of a computer program and users is less common. That is not to deny the importance of contract, even today, in setting out the terms and conditions subject to which the programs are marketed. But the attempts to establish contractual links with third parties still remain a matter of some uncertainty. For example, the software which is sold to the vast personal computer market usually attempts to incorporate what is known as a 'shrink-wrap' licence whereby the person who opens the package which contains terms as to the use of the computer program arguably contractually accepts them. The terms cover, for example, matters such as that the product is licensed and not sold and that title remains with the manufacturer; that limited back-up copying is permitted; that copying, modifying or transferring the program is restricted or prohibited and that various warranty terms and remedies are disclaimed or limited.

Whether or not contract law is satisfactory, it is necessary to determine what intellectual property rights could or should protect computer software. Whilst it is possible for some novel and inventive computer programs which produce a technical effect to be the subject-matter of patents, by and large the conditons for patentability and the delays and costs involved in registering around the world make patent law an unattractive proposition for all save important and specialised types of program.

Accordingly, the fundamental issue which had to be resolved was whether computer programs were properly the subject-matter of copyright or, indeed, whether this industry was so important that it might be preferable for entirely separate, *sui generis*, laws to be introduced to provide tailor-made protection. Today, the general feeling around the world is that the advantages of copyright protection outweigh the various disadvantages which can be put forward both on conceptual and practical grounds. One of the most important considerations in favour of bringing computer programs within the copyright umbrella is the fact that protection arises automatically and the international conventions ensure that roughly similar protection is likely to be conferred upon authors in all States party to them.

Ten years ago, the 'first generation' of cases began to be heard in countries around the world: they were all concerned with the question whether or not existing copyright laws did confer protection upon computer programs. Those cases were decided in most countries in favour of that proposition and have more recently been overtaken by legislative clarification. The 'second generation' wave of litigation, which is beginning, particularly in the USA, is seeking to establish the scope of protection for computer programs.

### The law before the 1988 Act

The Copyright Act 1956, naturally, made no reference to computer programs. Consequently, if copyright protection was to be available, the computer program, or at least some part of it, would have to be fitted within one of the existing categories of copyright work or copyright subject-matter. In order to do this, it became necessary to examine how computer programs are produced.

Very roughly, the procedure is this. First, a programmer might start with notes or documentation, flow charts or plans, in order to produce what is known as a *source code*. Source codes are written in specially designed 'high-level' languages, such as Fortran, codes which can easily be read and understood by the computer programmer. The source code is then converted, often by some kind of assembler program, into an *object code,* which provides the magnetic signals that drive the machine. The object code is in a 'low-level' language, a string of 0s and 1s, which at one time was said to be unreadable by programmers, although now it is clear that some programmers can read that language.

The above description, brief and general though it may be, was necessary because those who were looking for some copyright interest, had to examine and analyse these stages of the production of the computer program. Clearly, there might be some copyright works in the design material, the written notes being literary works and graphic representations and flow charts being artistic works. More debatable, though, was whether the source code could be a literary work.

General principles of copyright law should not really have posed any problem here. Just as it had been held that the Morse code constituted a literary work (*D.P. Anderson & Co Ltd* v *The Lieber Code Co.* [1917] 2 KB 469), so, too, could a source code which was fixed and provided information to at least some people. English courts were beginning to accept that reasoning. Thus, a number of courts proceeded upon the basis that literary copyright was capable of subsisting in a computer program (*Sega Enterprises Ltd* v *Richards [1983] FSR 73; Thrustcode Ltd* v *W.W. Computing Ltd* [1983] FSR 502).

However, this was only the first part of the problem solved. Those who copied computer programs did not copy the source documents or the source code; they copied the object code. Could it be said that by copying the object code they had reproduced the copyright source code or design documents? This involved an analysis of whether the program which the defendant had copied from the object code, could be said to be a 'reproduction' of the source code. Various arguments were employed against that view: there was no objective similarity between the object code embodied in, for example, ROM (read-only memory) chips and the source code; the defendant has not 'reproduced' the source code but simply manufactured its ROMs in accordance with written or fixed instructions; and the idea-expression dichotomy was also brought into play since the object code embodied the ideas and logical structure of the source code but did not reproduce the expression of the idea. Further, the object code was not an 'adaptation' of the source code, since an adaptation normally had to be a 'work' which the object code *arguably* was not; nor was the object code a 'translation' (a form of adaptation) of the source code, since the object code was not another language, even a computer language, but electrical impulses.

Those who were impatient with these legal niceties, readily accepted that the object code was a reproduction, whether by translation or otherwise, of the source code (see, for example, the US and Canadian decisions, such as *Apple Computer Inc.* v *Mackintosh Computers Ltd* [1986] 28 DLR (4th) 178); indeed, some were even prepared to say that there was a separate literary copyright in the object code itself. Other more conservative courts, such as the High Court of Australia (*Computer Edge Pty Ltd* v *Apple Computer Inc.* [1986] FSR 537), were not prepared to hold that a person who copied an object code was committing an infringing act.

In the UK, the general view was that the courts would accept the broader approach and allow copyright proceedings against those who copied object codes. Before the matter could be authoritatively resolved by the courts, however, the computer industry was successful in its campaign for legislation and the Copyright (Computer Software) Amendment Act 1985 made it quite clear that computer programs would be treated as enforceable copyright works.

The Copyright, Designs and Patents Act 1988 confirms this and also specifically addresses a number of other issues.

### Computer programs as copyright subject-matter

Unlike legislation in most other countries, neither the Copyright (Computer Software) Amendment Act 1985 nor the Copyright, Designs and Patents Act 1988 defines 'computer' or 'computer program'. Presumably, this omission was to ensure that considerable scope would be left to the courts for flexible interpretation in a rapidly developing technology. The 1985 Act provided that copyright law should apply in relation to a computer program 'as it applies' in relation to a literary work and the wording led to some ingenious speculation as to why it was not treated as a literary work as such. The 1988 Act brings computer programs clearly within the fold: literary works 'include' computer programs (s. 3(1)).

As literary works, computer programs must satisfy the usual requirements for protection. First, originality: there would ordinarily be no problem of satisfying the minimal originality requirement here, although it raises a nice point in connection with computer-generated works, which is discussed later. Secondly, copyright will not subsist in a literary work unless 'it is recorded in writing or otherwise'. Again, the requirement for writing is covered, since 'writing' is defined to include 'any form of notation or code, whether by hand or otherwise and regardless of the method by which, or medium in or on which, it is recorded'. This is a very broad definition and will be so construed. The only slight doubt relates to the fact that there is no definition of the term 'recorded': whilst it is clear, when a computer program is printed out in some way, that it is 'recorded', questions may be raised about programs which are stored only in a volatile computer memory.

*Copying, storage and use of computer programs*
The standard definition of copying in relation to a literary work, namely the reproduction of the work in any material form, was not sufficiently wide for the computer industry. The fear is that the courts may say that running a computer program does not amount to performing the restricted act of copying the program, since any copying that takes place occurs within the bowels of the computer, is only momentary, and is purely secondary to the use of the program. Similar considerations might lead the court to say that viewing a stored work on VDU does not fall within the restricted acts. The industry was in favour of a broader set of exclusive copyright rights to cover all unfair uses of computer programs.

The relevant definitions have been framed to meet these objectives. For example, copying in relation to a literary, dramatic, musical or artistic work is expressly stated to include 'storing the work in any medium by electronic means' (s. 17(2)) and copying in relation to any description of work 'includes the making of copies which are transient or are incidental to some other use of the work' (s. 17(6)).

This effectively extends the exclusive rights of copyright owners to control over the *use* of a work, and incidentally has brought about slight distortions to general copyright concepts.

The need to obtain permission for transient or incidental copying applies to all works, not simply to literary, dramatic, musical and artistic works: the development of technology is likely to mean, for example, that commercial sound recordings will be played through computers and so will involve incidental copying (John Butcher MP, HC Deb., 17 May 1988, col. 127).

The exclusive right goes beyond simply copying the computer program in any material form. As before, the exclusive right in connection with 'adaptations' includes 'translations' and 'In relation to a computer program a "translation" includes a version of the program in which it is converted into or out of a computer language or code, otherwise than incidentally in the course of running the program' (s. 21(4)).

Thus, all the problems relating to analysing the relationship between source and object codes have gone. Any slavish copy of a copyright computer program is clearly an infringement and a range of adaptations will also be unlawful.

### 'Non-literal' copying

The question which remains to be solved, however, relates to the extent of the protection which copyright owners now enjoy. The issue has been put in these terms: the courts, in applying the copyright laws to computer programs 'face a dilemma: either they limit copyright protection to literal copying [as extended by the adaptation provisions above], thus giving plagiarists the chance to easily escape liability, or they extend protection to the logic, design and structure of the program thus giving copyright owners monopoly rights over ideas and methods originally reserved to patents' (G. Schumann, (1988) 4 Computer Law and Practice 109).

This is the problem which is exercising courts in the USA in particular. The leading US case, *Whelan Associates Inc.* v *Jaslow Dental Laboratory Inc.* [1987] FSR 1, illustrates the difficulty. The plaintiff was the owner of the copyright in a computer program, Dentalab, which was designed to facilitate the administration of dental laboratories. The defendant (who had been closely associated with, and had written Dentalab for the plaintiff) produced a functionally identical program, Dentcom: it was not a direct translation and it was in a distinct programming language. Could this rank as taking the *expression* of Dentalab or was it simply an independent program for administering dental laboratories, the *idea* for which had been inspired by the plaintiff's program? There were similarities between the two programs: for example, the file structures and screen outputs for each program were virtually identical and various important subroutines within each program, relating to invoicing, accounts, end-of-day and end-of-month procedures etc. were the same. However, many of these similarities were of the kind which would be expected of any program for this purpose.

The court rejected the argument that the defendant had simply copied the idea of the plaintiff's computer program. The idea, it said, would be limited to 'the purpose or function of a utilitárian work . . . and everything that is not necessary to that purpose or function would be part of the expression of the idea'. In this case, the 'structure, sequence and organisation' of the two programs and the 'look and feel' were sufficiently similar to constitute infringement. Where there are various means of achieving the desired purpose, the particular means chosen is not necessary to the purpose, and hence constitutes expression, not idea. Had there been only one set of steps which could have been employed, copying that would have been permissible (in the absence of a patent) since it would have been part of the purpose, function or idea.

The debate in the USA is how to separate the unprotectible concept from protectible expression. Because the idea in *Whelan Associates Inc.* v *Jaslow Dental Laboratory Inc.* was stated so narrowly, simply to run a dental laboratory in an efficient way, much of the structure of the program inevitably became protectible as part of its expression. Concern has been expressed that, whilst it may be a major conceptual breakthrough in the fight against software piracy, there is a danger that such strong protection could preclude the common practices of reverse engineering which occur in the software industry. Computer experts decompile, that is disassemble, the object code and construct different but equivalent source codes to produce similar results. It may be that protection against competition from competitors in the software cloning industry may be desirable for them, but it is arguable that such protection could inhibit software innovators and limit desirable developments and competition. There is a lack of clear policy objectives relating to reverse engineering; as can be seen also in relation to semiconductor chips (see p. 190).

How relevant is this to UK law? As yet, the courts have not had much opportunity of exploring this area. First, of course, the scope of the 'translation' provision in s. 21(4) of the 1988 Act will have to be ascertained. Thereafter, in relation to alleged copying which falls outside the meaning of 'translation', many of the basic approaches in American law could be applicable in the UK. If, as in *Whelan Associates Inc.* v *Jaslow Dental Laboratory Inc.* the parties have formerly been working together (whether in an employer-employee relationship or otherwise), a court may apply the same test in both countries, namely that where there is substantial similarity between the two works, together with the opportunity of access to the plaintiff's work, the burden of disproving copying may shift to the defendant. In *M.S. Associates Ltd* v *Power* [1988] FSR 242, a copyright infringement action was brought against the defendant, an ex-employee of the plaintiff, when he wrote a computer program which was a significant commercial improvement on the plaintiff's program, although there was no discussion on whether that improvement was to the idea or the expression. The defendant did considerable work in devising the new program and there were only about 43 line similarities in a total of 9,000 lines which had been inspected. Nevertheless, bearing in mind the overall structure of the program, together with errors appearing in both programs, the court held that there was at least an arguable case that the second program had taken a substantial part of the first. In essence, this exercise may be similar to infringement actions relating to music or books, but how far English courts will travel along the *Whelan Associates Inc.* v *Jaslow Dental Laboratory Inc.* route remains to be seen.

## Rental right

Section 18(2) of the 1988 Act now confers a rental right in relation, *inter alia,* to computer programs, coupled with a reserve power for the Secretary of State to make orders providing for licences of right (s. 66). This is discussed in chapter 13.

## Back-up copies

Unlike legislation in some other jurisdictions, for example, the USA and Australia, the 1988 Act does not confer any express statutory right upon purchasers to make additional back-up copies, even though this is standard, sensible and 'recommended' procedure. The recent EEC Green Paper on copyright law suggests that any Directive, whilst containing a provision excluding private copying of computer programs in general, should permit the production of a back-up copy or copies by a legitimate user, provided these are destroyed when the right to use the program expires.

Amongst the reasons advanced for not having an express statutory right are, first, the fact that in appropriate cases express licences are always given and secondly, that to confer a general right would make it increasingly difficult to stop unauthorised copying.

Notwithstanding the lack of an express statutory right, s. 56 provides for the typical case where a purchaser does have an express or implied licence, or is otherwise entitled (for example, possibly by praying in aid the non-derogation from grant principle in *British Leyland Motor Corporation Ltd* v *Armstrong Patents Co. Ltd* [1986] AC 577, see chapter 12) to copy a computer program or other work in electronic form. If he transfers the work to a third party, anything which the purchaser was allowed to do may also be done by a transferee. However, any retained copy will become an infringing copy. Back-up copies must be linked to the main copy only. All this is subject to any express terms to the contrary.

## Computer-aided and computer-generated works

In *Express Newspapers plc* v *Liverpool Daily Post & Echo plc* [1985] FSR 306, the plaintiff newspaper publisher ran a 'Millionaire of the Month' competition: cards carrying a five-letter code were distributed at random and the newspaper printed daily a grid containing 25 letters and two separate rows of five letters, which any members of the public could check to see if they qualified for a prize. An action was brought against the defendant which had copied the grids and sequence of letters in its paper. One argument advanced by the defendant was that since the grids of letters were produced with the aid of a computer, they were not authored by the programmer who wrote the relevant software. This was rejected by Whitford J who said that:

> The computer was no more than the tool by which the varying grids of five-letter sequences were produed to the instructions, via the computer programs, of [the programmer]. It is as unrealistic [to suggest that the programmer was not the author] as it would be to suggest that, if you write your work with a pen, it is the pen which is the author of the work rather than the person who drives the pen.

There is now a crucial distinction between a *computer-aided* work, as in the above case, and a *computer-generated* work. The latter work is one which is created without expenditure of significant human skill and effort in the completed work. For example, the compilation of new crossword puzzles, moves generated by computer chess programs or computer-generated original pieces of music in the style of a known composer. The steps to be taken by the operator of the machine may be so trivial that it is difficult on normal principles to say that he or she is the author. The real creative work is done by the person who devises the original computer program, but it would be inconvenient and misleading to treat that programmer in all cases as the owner of the copyright in the new works which his program produces, for example, in all the new music produced by the various programs which are sold to the public. Thus, s. 178 of the 1988 Act defines 'computer-generated' in relation to a work as a work 'generated by computer in circumstances such that there is no human author of the work'. It then becomes necessary to deal with ownership of such works, and s. 9(3) provides that the 'author shall be taken to be the person by whom the arrangements necessary for the creation of the work are undertaken'. (see chapter 4).

This interesting development raises a number of questions. First, can it be said that such works are 'original'? Since the Act accepts that there is no human author, there seems to be little question that if the new work is indeed not copied from an earlier work, the requirement of originality is more than satisfied. Secondly, the line between computer-aided works and computer-generated works may become increasingly difficult to draw and this could be important in connection with authorship and ownership issues. Thirdly, the guidance provided by the Act as to ownership of a computer-generated work is ambiguous: who is the 'person by whom the arrangements necessary for the creation of the work are undertaken'? It would seem not to be the person who devised the instructions and originated the data used to control and condition the computer to produce the particular result; nor would it necessarily be the person running the data through the programmed computer to create the new work. More likely, as with films and sound recordings, the 'producer' will be regarded as the first owner.

## Duration of copyright in computer programs

Although the general rules relating to duration apply to copyright computer programs, there is a special provision for computer-generated works, whereby copyright expires at the end of the period of 50 years from the end of the calendar year in which the work was made (s. 12(3)).

## Computer program notices

Computer program litigation is similar to other intellectual property litigation in that it can often be fraught with difficulties because of the various matters which a plaintiff has to prove. As with other works, various presumptions in favour of plaintiffs operate (see chapter 10) and s. 105(3) provides that:

where copies of [a program in respect of which proceedings are brought] are issued to the public in electronic form bearing a statement —

(a)    that a named person was the owner of copyright in the program at the date of issue of the copies, or
(b)    that the program was first published in a specified country or that copies of it were first issued to the public in electronic form in a specified year,

the statement shall be admissible as evidence of the facts stated and shall be presumed to be correct until the contrary is proved.

## Moral rights

Originally, the moral rights provisions in the 1988 Act were to apply to computer programs in the same way as to other literary works. However, it was thought to be particularly difficult to cope with moral rights in the computer industry and so now neither the right to be identified as author of a work nor the right to object to derogatory treatment of a work applies to computer programs or to any computer-generated work (ss. 79(2) and 81(2)).

## Devices designed to circumvent copy protection

It has been mentioned in chapter 13 that s. 296 contains new laws to combat those who are commercially engaged in circumventing electronic measures in copyright articles designed to prevent unauthorised copying. This section applies to computer programs as to other areas and so the person who produces a computer program or information designed to defeat technical copy-protection devices will be liable to those who put the copy-protected articles on the market.

## Databases

A database is an accumulation of information stored in such a way that it can be systematically searched and retrieved by computer. Databases now come in all shapes and sizes: they can be collections of full-text material, such as encyclopaedias or text books, so providing some kind of general or specialised library; they can be compilations of extracts of copyright works; or collections of material in the public domain, such as lists of names, addresses, prices etc.; or any combination of these. Some databases may hold information that changes infrequently; others may hold constantly changing information, such as hotel or airline reservations; sometimes there is no input from the user, and at other times there may be an interaction between the user and the database. The number of databases in existence for use by the public is growing at an enormous pace: one estimate is that there were about 400 in 1980, rising to 2,900 in 1986 (see EEC Green Paper on copyright law).

In so far as computer programs control the mechanism for operating a database, the general copyright rules apply. Particular problems, however, arise in connection with the compilation and use of the databases themselves.

*Copyright problems in compiling a database*
Clearly, where a database incorporates a copyright work, authorisation to include it is required from the copyright owner. The use and storage rights relating to computer programs are highly relevant: storage of a work in a computer is an infringement (s. 17(2)).

Where *extracts* from copyright material are taken, the need for authorisation will turn on whether a substantial part of a copyright work is being used. Sometimes the *quantity* of material taken from copyright works may be minimal, but the value to the database compiler, and the loss of economic potential to the copyright owner may suggest that a court should have regard to protecting copyright owners against those who seek to copy small extracts for commercial gain. 'What is worth copying is prima facie worth protecting' (*University of London Ltd* v *University Tutorial Press Ltd* [1916] 2 Ch 601, per Petersen J).

English courts have not yet had occasion to grapple with this issue, but other countries have not found it easy. For example, in France, the courts vacillated considerably before finally deciding that a newspaper was unable to stop the defendants from compiling an index of articles in the newspaper with brief quotations to indicate their nature (*Société Microfor* v *Sàrl 'Le Monde'* [1988] FSR 519). However, in the USA, a law publishing company was held to be entitled to protect the page numbering of its report which had been taken by Lexis and used in its database of transcripts of cases, because the page numbering was 'the product of labour, talent or judgment'. In truth, the protection for the page numbers was not sought for its own sake but in order to prevent the defendants taking the benefit of what the publishers had invested in time, skill and money in compiling these reports (*West Publishing Co.* v *Mead Data Central Inc.* [1986] 799 F 2d 1219).

The 1988 Act does not make any special provision on this matter, save that s. 60 provides that, in the absence of a certified licensing scheme, it is not an infringement of copyright to publish in a periodical the abstract which appears with an article on a scientific or technical subject.

*Copyright protection for databases*
There is no doubt that most databases will initially rank as compilations of information qualifying as original literary works. But, how far should copyright protection extend to such works? Many databases hold the equivalent of tens of thousands of pages of material, or more. Can it be said that when an unauthorised user obtains access to the database and uses it without authority, albeit briefly, this is copyright infringement? What constitutes fair dealing with a database? Where a database is being constantly changed and up-dated, does the copyright lie only in the first complete database or are there new copyright works being created regularly, assuming that there is sufficient originality in the constant compilation of new material?

Again, no clear answers are yet provided in English law to deal specifically with these situations. Such problems as arise will be analysed in accordance with the general principle which have been discussed. Perhaps it would have been premature to have dealt specifically with databases in the 1988 Act. Indeed, there are many associated issues which may be better dealt with outside copyright law. The application of the criminal law to computer hacking is but one of the related issues which is currently under consideration (cf. *R* v *Gold* [1988] 2 WLR 984 and the Law Commission working paper No. 110, *Computer Misuse* 1988). Meanwhile, the databases multiply and copyright litigation is to be anticipated.

**Semiconductor chip protection: the topography right**

In general terms, semiconductor chips are articles consisting of two or more layers of semiconductor material which provide the electronic circuitry along which, for example, the signals produced by computer programs run. The complex three-dimensional arrangement of the paths carrying these signals is the topography or design.

In more technical terms, by reg. 2(1) of the Semiconductor Products (Protection of Topography) Regulations 1987 (SI 1987 No. 1497):

'semiconductor product' means an article the purpose, or one of the purposes, of which is the performance of an electronic function and which consists of two or more layers, at least one of which is composed of semiconducting material and in or upon one or more of which is fixed a pattern appertaining to that or another function;

'topography' means the design, however expressed, of any of the following:

(a)   the pattern fixed, or intended to be fixed, in or upon a layer of a semiconductor product;

(b)   the pattern fixed, or intended to be fixed, in or upon a layer of material in the course of, and for the purpose of, the manufacture of a semiconductor product;

(c)   the arrangement of the layers of a semiconductor product in relation to one another.

Thus, semiconductor chips are not computer programs themselves, but the means which facilitate their functioning. The development of new families of semiconductor chips can take many years' work and involve very high cost; on the other hand, copying such chips can be swift and relatively cheap.

It was not clear in many countries whether their copyright or other intellectual property laws afforded any or sufficient protection to semiconductor chip manufacturers against unfair competition. Concern about this was expressed in the US Senate: 'Unless changes in the law occur, conferring some protection upon semiconductor chip products, the industrial leadership enjoyed in the past by the American semiconductor chip industry may vanish'.

Accordingly, the USA enacted the Semiconductor Chip Protection Act 1984 and provided a new *sui generis* right for semiconductor chip products, the law being drawn extensively from patent and copyright principles. In general, protection was conferred upon original 'mask' works for a period of 10 years and this provided the blueprint for the unregistered design right which has been enacted in UK law in the Copyright, Designs and Patents Act 1988 (see chapter 12). The most important aspect of this new law was the aggressive way in which the Americans brandished the banner of reciprocity: unless other countries could satisfy the American authorities that their laws afforded equivalent protection for semiconductor chips, their industries would not be protected in the USA.

There followed a race by other countries with semiconductor chip industries either to persuade the USA that their existing laws provided equivalent protection or that they were proposing to enact such laws. In the UK, a breathing space was negotiated on the basis that industrial design copyright law protected semiconductor chips: the three-dimensional chip products were reproductions of the underlying copyright drawings. This, to say the least, was debatable, since the

Copyright Act 1956, s. 9(8), defence, namely that protection could only be conferred if the non-expert looking at the semiconductor chip could see that it was a reproduction of the underlying drawings, almost certainly operated.

In December 1986, the EEC issued a Directive requiring member States to provide semiconductor chip protection and, as a consequence, the Semiconductor Products (Protection of Topography) Regulations 1987 (SI 1987 No. 1497, made under the European Communities Act 1972) were introduced whereby American-style protection for these products was established.

The basic features of this new 'topography right' are that it arises automatically upon creation in respect of 'original' topographies, namely those that are the result of the 'creator's own intellectual effort (or of the combined intellectual efforts of the creators if there are more than one)' and which are 'not commonplace among creators of topographies or manufacturers of semiconductor products'. The topography right gives exclusive rights to commercial reproduction, exploitation and importation of the product. There are no registration requirements in the UK; the term is for 10 years from the end of the year of first commercial exploitation (or 15 years from creation); and, as with the US law, the right subsists on the basis of reciprocity, being available to citizens or residents of member States of the EEC or of other countries in which there is equivalent protection.

Although this right closely parallels the new unregistered design right, there are important differences. First, there is no licence of right provision for the last five years of the term. Secondly, there is an unusual provision concerning 'reverse engineering'. Regulation 4(2)(b) permits the making of 'any reproduction for the purpose of analysing or evaluating the topography or analysing, evaluating or teaching the concepts, processes, systems or techniques embodied in it' and reg. 6(2) then provides that the topography right 'in one original topography is not infringed by creating another original topography as a result of an analysis or evaluation falling within regulation 4(2)(b)'. Thus, unlike copyright, patents, and designs generally, a person who makes a *derivative* original topography will not be liable to the person whose topography has been used. It is difficult to see the justification for this. If it is to encourage innovation in the semiconductor chip industry, the same argument would apply to patent and copyright law, but similar principles do not exist.

# Chapter 16 Cable and Satellite Broadcasting

## Introduction

Broadcasters are concerned with practically all aspects of copyright law. For example, they are affected significantly by the new copyright position relating to the spoken word and also by the new code of moral rights. Many of these matters have already been discussed in other chapters. This chapter will be concerned primarily with those aspects of copyright law which specifically relate to cable, satellite and other forms of broadcasting.

Many of the day-to-day copyright issues affecting broadcasters are concerned with the contractual arrangements for the use of copyright works. Usually, the licensor is expected to have obtained consents or clearances in respect of all rights relating to material to be contained in programmes other than those from the PRS (for music), Phonographic or Video Performance Ltd (for sound or video recordings) and MCPS (for dubbing). Copyright clearance often involves complex issues of title which require to be settled very quickly. For example, whilst the organisations which administer and grant licences for the use of copyright works on behalf of rights owners may be prepared to licence 'satellite television rights', it may well be that the original grant of a licence for 'television rights' had not envisaged this wider use of a copyright work. Copyright clearance will have to be obtained both from those representing owners of copyright works and also from performers. Hence, issues such as the 'tenth spear-carrier' problem (see chapter 11). In many instances, broadcasters and those acquiring broadcast programmes will not be able to ensure that *all* the relevant rights are traced and consents obtained; and consideration will have to be given to what risks are being assumed and what protection may be appropriate to cover such risks. The media industries and rights owners are concerned, nationally and internationally, with the need to produce voluntarily mutually satisfactory copyright clearance arrangements.

Copyright legislation relating to broadcasting and cable and satellite has been concerned, amongst other matters, with the precise definition of a 'broadcast', for if an organisation makes use of copyright works by transmitting them in circumstances which do not come within the definition of a 'broadcast', there may be no *legal* requirement to obtain, and pay for, the consent of rights owners unless some other exclusive rights of theirs are infringed.

Where broadcasters have consent to transmit copyright works, the legislation must also provide for the circumstances in which cable operators receive and re-transmit such broadcasts. Should they be required to obtain the consent of the original rights owners and of the broadcasting organisation which has a broadcasting right, or should the consent of the broadcasting authority alone be sufficient? In any event, rights owners whose works are used both in the broadcast and in the cable re-transmission should be entitled to adequate compensation for such additional use, but not overcompensation by being paid twice over for the same contemplated use. This has raised yet another issue: should rights owners have absolute rights to prevent broadcasting and cable transmission, in accordance with fundamental copyright law, or should such rights be limited in certain circumstances to an entitlement to adequate remuneration only by way of a compulsory licence?

A further important step, which was taken in the Cable and Broadcasting Act 1984, was the creation of rights in respect of cable programmes.

Some of these matters will be discussed in this chapter. First, however, it is appropriate to mention briefly some of the current revolutionary developments which are taking place both in the technical means of delivering television, radio and other informational services to the public and also in developing governmental policy (influenced by regional and international broadcasting organisations) which is in the course of creating an amost entirely new broadcasting regime.

### Cable and satellite in the modern world

Satellites are playing an ever-increasing part in intercontinental telecommunications. . . . Far-reaching changes are taking place in the distribution of pictures and sounds; technology is gradually bringing about a revolution in the transmission of ideas, whether of a political, informative, cultural, scientific or artistic nature. The use of communication satellites for programme transmission and exchange is changing the accepted approach to sound and television broadcasting and is giving rise to legal problems whose complexity is commensurate with the new possibilities for the conquest of space that have become available to mankind. ('Protection of signals carrying radio and television programmes transmitted by communication satellites'.)

When Claude Masouye made these remarks in 1971 even he was unlikely to have appreciated what technical developments would have occurred in the following two decades.

First, though, a short explanation of the key developments may be in order for those of us unfamiliar with the technology at the frontiers of change.

*The development of broadcasting*
In the early days, when radio was still known as 'the wireless', that word graphically indicated that radio signals were conveyed through the air and not through any wire or other material substance. This was in contrast to a cable system whereby the signals would pass through a material linked, directly or indirectly, between the organisation sending out the signal and the recipient at home.

That fundamental distinction still exists today. Thus, a 'broadcast' refers to a transmission by 'wireless telegraphy' of visual images, sounds or other information; and 'wireless telegraphy' means 'the sending of electromagnetic energy over paths not provided by a material substance constructed or arranged for that purpose' (s. 178). At one time, broadcasts were always 'terrestial', the strength of the signal determining how far around the earth it might go. The development of celestial broadcasting, by way of satellite technology, has opened up new ways of delivering television and radio services to the home. Transmissions of signals to satellites which are then bounced back to earth can cover a very large area.

Such satellite transmissions can reach the ultimate recipient in two ways. First, by a fixed satellite service (FSS). This is a radio-communication service via satellite between earth stations at specified fixed points. The programme-carrying signals are transmitted to the satellite and bounced back to an earth station and then, normally, distributed by a cable distributor to the recipient at home. Secondly, there is direct broadcasting by satellite (DBS). Here the signal is powerful enough to be transmitted by the sender, via the satellite, directly for reception in individual homes without any intervening earth station, provided the recipient is in possession of the equipment to receive the signal.

The International Telecommunications Convention made a clear distinction between DBS and FSS which was carried through into copyright law but this distinction is becoming very difficult to sustain. FSS services can be captured by members of the public with appropriate equipment and, indeed, the direct reception of certain FSS services was licensed in 1985.

There is now a potential mass market in direct-to-home satellite television. DBS can be used to deliver separate sound and data services as well as for broadcasting television channels. Thus, data can be transmitted from a single source to a large number of different points (so-called 'point-to-multi-point links'). An example would be the distribution of pricing information by a retailer from its headquarters to each of many retail outlets. Such data are generally intended for reception by only a restricted group of recipients; indeed, the data may be encrypted to prevent unauthorised persons gaining access. Such services addressed to closed user groups are not considered to be broadcasting for general telecommunications purposes since they are not intended for general reception. Likewise, they would not ordinarily be regarded as broadcasts for copyright purposes, subject to the considerations mentioned below.

Major developments are currently taking place as a result of the launching of high and medium-power satellites offering multi-channel television receivable by small-size dishes. In 1989 it is proposed that there will be several new television channels broadcast on satellites such as Astra (which covers much of Western Europe and has a capacity for 16 television channels), Eutelsat II and British Satellite Broadasting (BSB (UK)) with increasing opportunities for direct payment for television programme services through subscription, whether on a pay-per-channel or pay-per-programme basis. These services are the beginnings of a major new era of satellite television. Franchises will also be granted for local cable and radio services.

*The development of cable*
In the early days, cable was used as a radio and television delivery system to

provide services to parts of the country where off-air reception was poor. The cable systems built in this period were so-called 'narrow-band' systems, capable of carrying only the terrestrial television channels, perhaps together with one or two sound channels. They were thus simply an adjunct to the terrestrial transmission system. Several of these older systems are still operating, together with more recent satellite master antenna television (SMATV) systems in which programme material is received from satellite and delivered to a limited number of users by cable.

Advances in cable technology, however, have enabled it to play a more significant, independent, role in the broadcasting environment. The development of coaxial and fibre optics cable and sophisticated electronic switches has given the new 'broad-band' systems the capacity to carry a large number of television and sound channels, as well as other text and data services. Instead of radio waves being freely transmitted over the air, signals are sent along 'wide-band' cables direct to individual receivers. With this transmission technique, signals retain their high quality, even over long distances. Equally important, they can carry 'return' signals from the home. This opens up the possibility of interactive services, such as home shopping and home banking.

To meet some of the social and other challenges presented by cable, the Cable and Broadcasting Act 1984 provided a regulatory framework for cable and established a Cable Authority which was charged both with promoting the development of broad-band cable, and of supervising the content of programme services carried on cable systems.

Although the growth of new cable systems has been slow, it may well develop more significantly in the future.

### Encryption

Many of the broadcasting and cable programme providers may need to encrypt their signals if they are to maintain effective control over their programmes. There are many advantages in encryption. For example, although a satellite footprint may cover several countries, a programme provider can target a channel with precision at one or more specific countries. This may be desirable for many reasons: some countries may prohibit certain kinds of advertising; live broadcasting of some events, for example, sporting events, may be prohibited within a certain range of the area where they are taking place; rates of subscription may vary between different places and different countries; and access will be provided only to those who pay for the service.

### Relationship between satellite and cable broadcasting

As has been shown, satellite and cable transmissions are complementary and mutually advantageous.

## Broadcasting and cable: problems of definition

### Broadcasting

For copyright purposes, the act of broadcasting should be roughly equivalent to public performance. Consent to the use of works in transmissions ought ordinarily to be required when there is reception by the general public.

However, the concept of broadcasting in copyright law has had an uneasy history. The Copyright Act 1956 simply defined broadcasting by reference to the Wireless Telegraphy Act 1949 which did not indicate clearly that transmissions should be capable of being received by the public. The earlier definition focused to some extent on a subjective test of whether there was an intention for the transmission to be for general reception. Section 6 of the 1988 Act now emphasises the objective facts: a transmission by wireless telegraphy is a broadcast if it is *capable* of being *lawfully* received by members of the public. Thus any transmission by wireless telegraphy will be a broadcast for copyright purposes if the public may lawfully receive it, whether it is primarily aimed at general reception by the public or not. The rationale is that if a transmission is lawfully receivable, copyright owners should be able to control whether their material is included in the transmission, and those responsible for the transmission should have the right to control exploitation by others.

In recent years difficulties have arisen in connection with DBS and FSS transmissions. There was a body of opinion which argued that a DBS transmission from within the UK to a place outside would not be subject to copyright law since there was not a broadcast within the UK: the 'up leg' to the satellite was not a broadcast; the 'down leg' was, but that took place beyond the jurisdiction. This argument was disposed of in the Cable and Broadcasting Act 1984 which enlarged the definition of 'television broadcast' to include broadcasts by DBS.

However, nothing was done about FSS transmissions, which were regarded as being outside the scope of broadcasting or a communication to the public since they were neither intended for direct reception by the public nor, until 1985, permitted under wireless telegraphy law to be so received. This probably left the newly created FSS television programmes, such as Music Box, Sky Channel and Screen Sport outside the sphere of broadcasting, and providers of FSS programme services were under no *legal* obligation to obtain consent or pay licence fees for inclusion of copyright material in their transmissions, although in most cases they agreed to do so. The legal (and thus formal) responsibility for obtaining copyright clearance was that of the cable operators receiving the services at their earth stations and re-transmitting them to their subscribers.

To avoid doubt, s. 6(4) ensures that FSS transmissions are broadcasts for copyright purposes and that the place from which the broadcast is made is the place from which the signals carrying the broadcast are transmitted to the satellite (the up leg). Thus, copyright owners and performers (s. 211) have rights in any FSS service which may *lawfully* be received directly by the public, either in the country of transmission or elsewhere.

Section 6(1)(b) provides for transmissions that are not available to the public generally but are presented to public audiences at particular venues, for example, relays of sporting events or concerts to a stadium or theatre where at least part of the chain of transmissions is by wireless telegraphy. Those transmissions may also disseminate copyright material on a large scale, so it was thought right that copyright controls should apply to them and also that transmissions should be protected against exploitation by others.

### Encrypted transmissions
DBS pay-television transmissions amount to broadcasting, even if encrypted. Similarly, an encrypted FSS transmission will amount to broadcasting provided equipment needed to decode it is generally available to the public, for example, on payment of a standard charge for a pay-television service.

Services for which decoding equipment is not made generally available to the public, such as those encrypted purely to preserve privacy, remain outside the copyright definition of broadcasting (s. 6(2)).

### The broadcaster
Identifying the broadcaster is, amongst other matters, important for the purposes of establishing authorship and ownership of the broadcast.

Section 6(3) provides that the term 'broadcaster' refers both to the person transmitting the programme, if he has responsibility to any extent for its contents, and also to any person providing the programme who makes with the person transmitting it the arrangements necessary for its transmission. This joint arrangement is designed, for example, to meet the position in ITV where the contractor provides the programmes, but the IBA transmits them and has the ultimate legal responsibility.

It would not be appropriate in all circumstances, however, for the person making the transmission to be regarded as the person making the broadcast and thus its author. British Telecom, for example, provides common carrier services for several broadcasters by transmitting services to satellites, without being in any way responsible for, or necessarily even aware of, the contents of the programme. Thus, the requirement that the person transmitting the broadcast is the 'broadcaster' only if he is responsible to some extent for the contents, is to ensure that common carriers such as British Telecom are excluded.

### Cable
The term 'cable programme service' means a service which consists wholly or mainly in sending visual images, sounds or other information by means of a telecommunications system, *otherwise than by wireless telegraphy* (s. 7(1)). A 'telecommunications system' is a system for conveying visual images, sounds or other information by *electronic means,* namely something actuated by electric, magnetic, electro magnetic, electro chemical or electro mechanical energy (s. 178).

Thus, the general effect of s. 7 is to bring within the scope of copyright all cable diffusion services which are receivable by the public: cable systems providing general entertainment will normally be included, and so will databases whose material is available to the general public.

However, it was important in defining 'cable programme service' to ensure that certain interactive and other communications of an essentially private kind, such as ordinary telephone conversations, telebanking or video conferencing services, were excluded.

What should not come within s. 7 are those elements of a service which are genuinely interactive, in the sense that input from the user modifies what is contained in or sent through the system. Thus, the definition of cable programme service is not intended to cover teleshopping through Prestel, or the input into a medical diagnostic service, where data supplied by the user modify the output to subsequent users. These are private communications between a single user of the service and the provider of it; even though the input may become part of the database subsequently included in the cable programme service.

Where there is a mixed service with elements which are genuinely interactive, these are excluded but not those parts which are just concerned to convey images, sounds or other information to the user without any modifiction by him. (John Butcher MP.)

Thus, to take the example of teleshopping, the sending of the catalogue pages to subscribers will be a cable programme service, even though each subscriber may then order goods and receive confirmation of the order; it is only the latter aspect which is taken out of the definition.

*Cable re-transmission*

Cable re-transmission is one of the most important economic forms of cable distribution. Any cable operator who re-transmits a broadcast must consider the copyright interests in the works contained in the broadcast and also the copyright in the broadcast itself. There is a tendency in a number of countries to regard the simultaneous, unaltered and complete re-transmission within the 'service area' as part of the original broadcast, thus weakening the position of owners of rights in the content of the broadcast.

In the UK, too, in certain cases, cable operators do not need consent:

(a)   Where the cable programme service re-transmits a broadcast in pursuance of a 'must-carry' duty there is no infringement of the copyright in the broadcast or of any work included in it. (Legislation requires every licensed diffusion service (which includes wide-band cable services) to carry all BBC and IBA programmes which are provided for reception in the area in which the diffusion service is provided, subject to certain exceptions.)

(b)   Where the broadcast is made for reception in the area in which the cable service is provided and is neither a satellite transmission nor an encrypted teletext transmission, there is no infringement of the copyright in the underlying works, but the consent of the broadcaster is required (s. 73(2)). (Care may be required to ensure that the 'intended reception area' is defined clearly.)

The ground for this exemption is that the communication to the public is the broadcast itself and cable re-transmission does not really constitute a new or separate communication justifying extra remuneration to the *owners of rights in programme content,* who will have been paid by the broadcaster.

The broadcaster (but not, it is argued, the owners of rights in programme content) needs to retain the right to control cable re-transmission, as the basis for recovering from cable operators the charge appropriate to the number of subscribers receiving services via cable rather than off-air. (The claim of the owners of rights in programme content would continue to be against the broadcaster.)

Even though, in the case of FSS programme services, it is less likely that in-area cable transmissions will duplicate the direct reception audience, the government thought that to leave the owners of rights in the programme content the right (along with the broadcaster) to control re-transmissions would be too strong. Therefore, it was decided to limit right owners in the same way as under the Copyright Act 1956, s. 40(3) (1988 Act, s. 73). It should be observed, however, that if the making of the broadcast was an infringement of the copyright in any works, the fact that it was re-transmitted as a programme in a cable programme service will be taken into account in assessing the damages for that infringement (s. 73(3)).

It will often be important, in any event, for the broadcaster to obtain consent for re-transmission. For example, outside the UK, cable operators in many countries within the footprints of satellites will need a licence from the owners of rights in the programme content. It will therefore be necessary for programme providers who intend their programmes to be received in other countries as well as in the UK to ensure that the rights they have obtained include not only the broadcasting right but also the cable diffusion right for the agreed areas.

The failure to allow authors to exercise exclusive rights over their copyright works contained in the re-transmitted programmes has been a matter of some controversy, especially in Europe. It has been argued, for example, that such an approach is inconsistent with the Berne Convention, Art. 11 *bis* (1)(ii) whereby the author has the exclusive right to authorise each and every act of communication to the public. It has been alleged that the 'service-area' theory is unjustifiable and is used to prefer the cable industry over the rights of authors. (This *in-area* exemption is one reason why the UK has made reservations from the European Television Agreement. See later.)

### Specific matters relating to broadcasting and cable

A number of legislative provisions affecting cable and broadcasting have already been covered sufficiently in earlier chapters. For example, the term of copyright for broadcasting and cable programmes (s. 14, see chapter 3); the incidental inclusion of copyright material in, *inter alia,* broadcasts or cable programmes (s. 31, see chapter 6); the recording of broadcasts and cable programmes by or on behalf of educational establishments (s. 35, see chapter 14); recording for the purposes of time-shifting (s. 70, see chapters 6 and 13); the free public showing or playing of broadcasts or cable programmes (s. 72, see chapter 6); the inclusion of an exclusive right to control the making of a photograph of the whole or part of a broadcast or cable programme (s. 17(4)) and the permitted act of making photographs of television broadcasts or cable programmes for private and domestic purposes (s. 71).

Additional matters are noted in the following paragraphs.

*Other permitted acts*
Other permitted acts include provision of copies, by designated bodies, subtitled or otherwise modified for those who are deaf, hard of hearing, or physically or mentally handicapped (s. 74); and also recordings of broadcasts or cable programmes for archival purposes maintained by a designated body (s. 75).

*Subsistence of copyright*
Whilst copyright subsists in broadcasts and cable-originated programmes, there is no copyright in a cable programme if it is included in a cable programme service by reception and immediate re-transmission.

Nor does copyright subsist in any broadcast or cable programme which infringes, or to the extent that it infringes, the copyright in another broadcast or cable programme (ss. 6(6) and 7(6)). This applies also in respect of other copyright works and simply reflects a general point that copyright should not apply to copied material. Presumably, where there is a compilation of recorded material transmitted, for example, in a cable programme, there will be copyright in the compilation (cable programme) but not in the individual parts.

*Public performance right*
Although copyright infringement can take place in certain circumstances by performing broadcasts or cable programmes in public, neither the broadcasters nor cable service providers nor performers are thereby regarded as responsible for infringement (s. 4).

*Ephemeral recording right*
The Copyright Act 1956, s. 6(7), provided that if a person had been authorised to broadcast but not, in express terms, to record the broadcast, that person might nonetheless make a recording for the purpose only of broadcasting the work recorded. Such a recording could not be used for any other purpose, and had to be destroyed within 28 days of first use.

Today, of course, the majority of broadcasts are recorded. Suggestions were made to replace this exception by a statutory licence providing for equitable remuneration but the Whitford Committee recommended that, provided the record made for a broadcast is only used for the purpose originally agreed, there was no harm in the retention of this provision and there was no absolute need to provide for destruction.

The 1988 Act, s. 68, has extended this right to make ephemeral recordings from literary, dramatic and musical works to artistic works, sound recordings and films, and in respect of rights in performances (sch. 2, para. 16); and also to enable the principal broadcaster to authorise others to exercise this right. This was thought not to be in contravention of the provisions of the Berne Convention and was introduced to reflect present-day realities in which it is quite common for those preparing broadcasts to contract out all their production work. However, the requirement that the work be destroyed within 28 days has been retained.

Thus, the exception is still very narrow, and in most cases contractual arrangements should avoid the necessity of attempting to rely upon it.

*Recording for the purposes of supervision or control*
Broadcasting authorities are not liable for copyright infringement when making or using recordings of programmes broadcast by them for the purposes of maintaining supervision and control (s. 69).

*Cable programme services in hotels*
The Copyright Act 1956, s. 48(3B) as amended, allowed free and unrestricted

distribution of all cable programme services as an incidental service in hotels, flats or other premises where persons reside or sleep.

The long-standing criticism of this exemption was reinforced following the DTI decision in 1985 to license satellite master antenna television (SMATV). This enables programme providers to distribute entertainment and other programmes via communication satellites: programme-carrying signals are received by an appropriate dish and then distributed through closed-circuit cable systems in flats, hotels, offices, housing estates, holiday camps, pubs, clubs and rural communities.

The Whitford Committee recommended that this exemption be repealed. Accordingly, there is no exemption in the 1988 Act. Any operator of a cable programme service to such premises will need the licence of the respective rights owners unless he is re-transmitting certain broadcasts.

### Qualification for broadcasters' rights
One of the reservations made by the United Kingdom to the European Television Agreement (ETA) was to enable it to require that to be eligible for protection a foreign broadcasting organisation much be *both* constituted in the territory and under the laws of a country party to the ETA *and* transmitting from that country (under ETA *either* of these criteria is sufficient). This reservation will now be withdrawn. Broadcasters in other States party to the ETA were given the right to control cable diffusion in the UK under the Cable and Broadcasting Act 1984 and all making FSS transmissions classed as broadcasting from the UK are entitled to broadcasters' copyright. Section 156 provides that a broadcast qualifies for copyright protection if it is made from, and a cable programme qualifies for protection if it is sent from, a place in the UK or another country to which the Act extends. (Previously copyright was only accorded to the BBC, IBA and those foreign broadcasting organisations which had been specifically mentioned in the Copyright (International Conventions) Order 1979 (SI 1979 No. 1715).

### Right to control fraudulent reception of transmissions
Copyright does not confer any exclusive right to control *reception* as such. Thus, it was not possible for providers of a pay-television service delivered by FSS satellite to rely on copyright law as a basis on which to recover payment from those who, without authorisation, succeeded in receiving such a service directly but did not re-transmit it to others.

The Cable and Broadcasting Act 1984, ss. 53 and 54, provided a different solution. The dishonest reception of cable programmes, BBC and IBA Television or sound broadcasts, or certain services provided in connection therewith, with intent to avoid payment of any charge applicable to reception, became unlawful. This has been continued, and widened slightly to ensure that it also protects FSS programme providers (ss. 297 to 299).

In addition to the creation of criminal offences, any person who makes charges for the reception of programmes included in a service is entitled to the same remedies as a copyright owner. Thus s. 298(2) provides that the rights conferred by the section are infringed by the manufacture, importation, sale or letting on hire of any apparatus or device which is designed or calculated, or the publication of any information which is calculated, to enable or assist persons to receive the programmes without payment.

*Disputes over FSS and other programme licences*
As with the BBC and IBA, all other broadcasting organisations with broadcasting copyright come within the ambit of the Copyright Tribunal for arbitration over licences.

Section 134 provides guidance for licences in respect of works included in cable re-transmissions. Special attention is addressed to the need to avoid double remuneration. Thus when considering what charges should be made for licences for in-area re-transmission, the Copyright Tribunal must have regard to the extent to which the copyright owner has already received, or is entitled to receive, payment for the other transmission which adequately remunerates him in respect of transmissions to that area. Where the re-transmission goes beyond the area to which the first transmission was made, the tribunal will normally be required to leave the further transmission out of account in considering any charges which should be paid for licences for the first transmission.

## International developments

The accommodation of satellite and cable broadcasting is one of the major challenges which the international protection of copyright has to face today. These matters, at the European level, are being considered at present by two separate bodies.

First, a European Convention on Broadcasting is being prepared by the Council of Europe. Its purpose will be to facilitate the trans-frontier transmission and re-transmission of television programme services which comply with certain prescribed minimum standards covering both minimum programme content and advertising and will also consider copyright issues. Work on the preparation of the convention is not yet complete.

Secondly, and at the same time, the European Community is working on a draft Directive on broadcasting which is intended to provide a limited harmonisation of member States' laws on copyright in the broadcasting field, amongst other matters, to break down the existing barriers to the free movement of broadcasting services throughout the Community. The Green Paper, *Television without Frontiers,* concluded that the present territorial scope of national copyright laws is likely to impede the development of cross-frontier broadcasting, particularly the re-transmission, by cable or otherwise, in one member State of broadcasts received from another. The Commission tentatively proposed that the exclusive right of copyright owners to authorise or prohibit the re-transmission by cable in one member State of broadcasts containing their work and transmitted from another member State should be abolished and replaced by a right to equitable remuneration enforceable only through collecting societies.

Some of the proposals relating to free movement are controversial in the copyright field, and it is not yet clear whether the final recommendations of the Council of Europe and the European Commission will be compatible. It may well be, however, that some changes to the present copyright laws relating to broadcasting and cable transmission will have to move to accord with these developments.

With regard to the European Television Agreement (ETA), the UK has withdrawn some, but not all, of its reservations. It still withholds protection from television broadcasts where the public performance of a broadcast is not to a paying audience (s. 72).

However, broadcasters in other member States of the Council of Europe do now enjoy a right to control cable diffusion of their broadcasts in the UK and one important objective of the ETA in regard to cable diffusion has been satisfied. The UK also withholds from television broadcasters the right to authorise or prohibit cable diffusion of their broadcasts to the public (s. 73). Any changes relating to these reservations may well occur in the more general reviews mentioned above.

# Chapter 17 Patent Aspects of the Act

The Patents Act 1977 remains the principal source of the law relating to UK patents but the 1988 Act makes a number of amendments to the law and practice in this area. Some of these modifications are traceable back to a 1983 Green Paper, *Intellectual Property Rights and Innovation* (Cmnd 9117), and were further discussed in the White Paper of 1986 (Cmnd 9712). An important policy objective of those Papers was to make the patent system more accessible and user-friendly in order to encourage the exploitation of creative ideas. The 1983 Green Paper made recommendations relating to the effects on competition of restrictions in the profession of patent agents and, following a Report of the Office of Fair Trading, 'Review of Restrictions on the Patents Agents' Profession' (September 1986) the Act ends the effective monopoly of patent agents (ss. 274 to 281). In addition to examining professional restrictions, concern was also expressed about the cost of litigation which was an effective barrier to many small and medium-sized businesses. Following the Report of the Oulton Committee on 'Patent Litigation' (November 1987) there is now a new special jurisdiction for a Patents County Court (ss. 287 to 292) which is designed to provide a cheaper and more flexible forum for some patent matters. In addition, the Act deals with the problem of licences of right in respect of the last four years of patents for pharmaceutical inventions patented prior to the 1977 Act (ss. 293 and 294). There are also a large number of miscellaneous amendments in sch. 5 of the Act.

## Ending of the patent agents' monopoly

Under the Patents Act 1977 only a registered patent agent could 'practise, describe himself or hold himself out as a patent agent' and only registered patent agents and solicitors could act for gain on behalf of inventors or others in applying for or obtaining patents (PA 1977, s. 114). The Chartered Institute of Patent Agents maintains the register and seeks to ensure appropriate standards by means of qualifying examinations, professional ethics etc. This system does provide high professional standards but also, as the White Paper put it, 'at the cost of correspondingly "professional" fees'. Following the report of the Director General of Fair Trading, the government decided to expose the profession to wider competition and consequently s. 274 now allows 'Any individual partnership or body corporate' to 'carry on the business of acting as agent for others for the purpose of . . . applying for or obtaining patents . . . or . . . conducting proceedings before the comptroller'.

Having provided the consumer with a wider choice, the Act then attempts to ensure that it is an informed choice by providing that an individual who is not a registered patent agent may not carry on business under a name or other description containing the words 'patent agent' or 'patent attorney' (s. 276(1), contravention of which is a summary offence punishable by fine). Similar restrictions also apply to partnerships and bodies corporate of whom not all the partners or directors are registered patent agents (s. 276(2) and (3)). However, s. 279 provides for rules to be made permitting other partnerships and bodies corporate to be described as patent agents in certain circumstances. This is to enable mixed partnerships of qualified and unqualified persons to develop so that, for example, a person might go to one place where advice on patenting and also on other matters such as development finance might be available. The rules under s. 279 may provide for the number or proportion of partners or directors to be qualified persons and for the identification in advertisements and letters etc. of the qualified and unqualified partners and directors. The regulations may also impose requirements as to the degree of control to be exercised by the qualified over the unqualified persons.

Notwithstanding the above restrictions, solicitors may use the title 'patent attorney' without contravening s. 276 and registered patent agents may use the title patent attorney without contravening s. 21 of the Solicitors Act 1974 or the equivalent provisions for Northern Ireland and Scotland (s. 278). Furthermore, anyone entitled to use the expressions 'European patent agent' or 'European patent attorney' (titles controlled by the European Patent Office) may also do so without contravening s. 276 or the Solicitors Act etc. (ss. 277 and 278).

The result of the above provisions is that an unqualified and unregistered individual may carry on the business of acting as a patent agent, provided that he does not use the title 'patent agent' or 'patent attorney' and that he does not use any 'other expressions . . . which are likely to be understood as indicating that he is entitled to be described as a "patent agent" or "patent attorney" '. An example of such 'other expressions' would be to describe one's business as a 'patent agency' as this would naturally suggest that one was a patent agent, but the use of terms such as 'patent adviser' or 'patent consultant' would be permissible. The Act is designed to allow unregistered patent advisers to provide a service (which it is assumed will generally be at lower cost) to clients whose cases do not require or justify the expertise or expense of a registered patent agent. Whether the small inventor or others will be able to make the right judgment as to the level of expertise that their case requires and whether or not they will appreciate the significance of the presence or absence of the title patent agent, remains to be seen. Although rules may be made (under s. 281) authorising the comptroller of patents *to refuse to deal with, inter alia,* persons who, had they been registered patent agents, would have been liable to be struck off on the ground of misconduct, there is no sanction in the Act available against a person who does not use one of the reserved titles and who merely provides consistently bad *advice* on patent matters. Remedies against such 'consultants', whose reputations have not already put them out of business, must be sought by individual clients in actions for negligence in the civil courts.

Although the Act takes away the patent agents' monopoly, it widens the circumstances in which communications with patent agents (who, of course, must be registered) are privileged from disclosure in legal proceedings. Under s. 104 of the 1977 Act the privilege only applied to 'any communication made for the purpose of any pending or contemplated patent proceedings' whereas s. 280 of the 1988 Act extends it to 'communications as to any matter relating to the protection of any invention, design, technical information, trademark or service mark, or as to any matter involving passing off'. There is thus no longer any requirement that there should be any proceedings contemplated or pending and the communication may relate to rights other than patent rights. Copyright is not specifically mentioned but a communication relating to copyright (or any other right) would be covered if it was itself related to the protection of, say, a label as a trade mark. However, communications relating to copyright which had no bearing on any of the rights mentioned in s. 268 would not be protected; advice on pure copyright matters is not regarded as part of the normal business of patent agents. The privilege is not restricted to advice about the client's own invention, trademark etc.; the words '*any* invention' etc. are intended to make it clear that the communication may be about the scope of someone else's right and, for example, whether it is likely to be infringed.

## Trade mark agents

Unlike the patent profession, there was no previous monopoly relating to acting on behalf of others in trade mark matters and no existing register of trade mark agents. As one might expect, the Act does not create a new monopoly but does provide for the establishment of a register of trade mark agents under rules to be made under s. 282. Persons on the register will not have any monopoly in acting for others in trade mark matters but they will be the only persons who can legally carry on business as a 'registered trade mark agent' or in the course of a business describe or hold themselves out as such (s. 283).

The reservation of the title 'registered trade mark agent' is very similar to the reservation of the titles patent agent and patent attorney. However, it should be noted that s. 283 only reserves the title '*registered* trade mark agent' and so any one can use the title 'trade mark agent'. Contrast the position with patent agents where the title is reserved with or without the prefix 'registered'. The dual function of the word 'registered' in s. 283 as referring both to the trade mark itself and to the agent is perhaps unfortunate. It would be permissible, presumably, for an unregistered person to describe himself as a 'trade mark agent for registered trade marks'!

What is clear is that registered trade mark agents attract the same privilege from disclosure in legal proceedings as do patent agents except that the privilege only applies to 'communications as to any matter relating to the protection of any design, trade mark or service mark, or as to any matter involving passing off' (s. 284(1)). Hence, unlike patent agents, the privilege does not apply to communications relating to the protection of inventions or technical information *per se* (except in so far as such matters themselves relate to the protection of any design etc.).

### Patents county courts

Section 287 empowers the Lord Chancellor to:

> designate any county court as a patents county court and confer on it
> jurisdiction (its 'special jurisdiction') . . .
>
> (a)  relating to patents or designs, or
> (b)  ancillary to, or arising out of the same subject-matter as, proceedings
> relating to patents or designs.

The jurisdiction of the patents county court will not be a local one and indeed it
is not envisaged that there should be more than one initially for the whole
country. The objective is to provide a cheaper and speedier forum for disputes
that do not justify the full panoply and expense of the High Court.

Section 288 provides for financial limits to be set by Order in Council in
relation to the special jurisdiction of the court (£60,000 was mentioned by the
Lord Chancellor during the debates) but the parties may agree by signed
memorandum that the court shall have jurisdiction notwithstanding any such
limit. Section 289 further encourages the use of the patents county court by
providing that no order shall be made under the County Courts Act 1984, s. 41,
transferring the proceedings from the patents county court to the High Court.
Furthermore, in considering whether to make a transfer to or from the High
Court under ss. 40 or 42 of the 1984 Act, the court 'shall have regard to the
financial position of the parties' and the case need not be heard in the High Court
'notwithstanding that the proceedings are likely to raise an important question of
fact or law'. All this, of course, is in furtherance of the objective of making the
patent system accessible to the individual or firm with limited resources.

Section 290 limits the costs recoverable in a High Court case where a pecuniary
remedy is claimed if the amount recovered is less than an amount to be prescribed
by Order in Council. The costs will be limited to those that would have been
recoverable had the action been brought in the county court.

Section 291 provides for the appointment of the patents judge for the patents
county court and for such judge (rather than the registrar) to deal with ('so far as
is practicable and appropriate') any proceedings in the court, including
interlocutory matters. The appointment of a person with the necessary
experience and expertise will be fundamental to the success or otherwise of the
court. Provision is made in s. 292 for registered patent agents to conduct
proceedings etc. in the patents county court as though they were solicitors and for
their undertakings to be binding as though they were solicitors.

These enabling provisions provide little more than a framework for a new
patent court. How flexible and innovative it will turn out to be will depend to a
large extent upon the detailed procedural rules which have yet to be made and the
manner in which they will be operated by the judge. It is to be hoped that the
patents county court, a professionally agreed solution to a highly controversial
issue between the various professions, will show that it is possible to obtain
speedy, just and less expensive litigation without the need to embark upon the
weightier and more expensive patent litigation voyages in the High Court and
beyond.

## Pharmaceutical patents

The pharmaceutical industry is one which attaches particular importance to patent protection. Successful drugs are the result of years of expensive research, development and safety trials and yet they can relatively easily be copied by 'generic' manufacturers who have not had to incur these heavy expenses. It is therefore important for the research-based companies to have a reasonable period free from competition during which they can recoup their expenses and make the level of profits which will encourage and enable them to continue to invest in further research and development. The current 20-year patent term would at first sight appear ample for this purpose but the actual effective period of monopoly is considerably shorter than this because the 20-year period runs from the filing of the patent application rather than the commercial marketing of the drug. This is true with all inventions but the number of years lost with drugs is greater because of the need to satisfy increasingly stringent safety controls. For example, it is claimed on behalf of the pharmaceutical companies that the average development time has increased from three to four years in the 1960s to 10 to 12 years in the 1980s thus severely denting the effective period of monopoly.

The problem is slightly offset by the fact that the 1977 Act, as part of the move towards harmonisation with other European patent systems, increased the patent term from 16 to 20 years. The dispute that has arisen has been in relation to patents granted or applied for prior to the coming into force of the 1977 Act (1 June 1978). Schedule 1 of the 1977 Act divided these into two categories: 'new existing patents' and 'old existing patents'. Old existing patents were those which were already more than 11 years old in June 1978 and these were not given the benefit of the new 20-year term although it remained possible to apply for their extension by up to a maximum of four extra years on the grounds of 'inadequate remuneration'. New existing patents, by contrast (those less than 11 years old at the commencement of the 1977 Act), were given the benefit of the new period of 20 years, although there was no possibility of any further extension. This 'windfall' of an extra four years was not, however, totally unqualified as the patent was made subject to licences of right (compulsory licences) in the extra period of four years. The generic companies have taken full advantage of this by making advance preparations (e.g., by applying for a product licence from the Department of Health) to enter the market as soon as the patent 'goes licence of right' in its 17th year. The research-based companies have tried to combat this, generally unsuccessfully, by alleging that such preparations themselves amount to infringement of the patent (see *The Upjohn Co* v *T. Kerfoot & Co. Ltd* [1988] FSR 1) or by claiming that the licensing authority cannot make use of the research company's confidential information supplied for the purpose of obtaining the original product licence for the drug (see *R* v *Licensing Authority Established under Medicines Act 1968 (ex parte Smith Kline & French Laboratories Ltd)* [1988] 3 WLR 896).

Despite their lack of success in the courts, the pharmaceutical companies succeeded in persuading the government that their average effective patent term had decreased to such an extent that it was endangering their incentive and ability to invest for the future. The government therefore, in 1986, announced its intention to remove the licence of right provision for pharmaceutical patents. An attempt was made to implement this in 1977 through a private member's Bill which was lost through lack of Parliamentary time but s. 293 of the 1988 Act now remedies the situation. It does so by inserting a new para. 4A in sch. 1 to the 1977 Act whereby licences of right in the last four years of new existing patents shall not extend to pharmaceutical use if the proprietor of the patent files an appropriate declaration with the Patent Office. The pharmaceutical companies were keen that this provision should come into force immediately but s. 305(2) provides that it will come into force two months after royal assent which will be on 15 January 1989 and which will provide the necessary time to make the rules providing for the form of the declarations etc. No declaration under s. 293 can be filed if the patent has passed the end of its 15th year on 15 January 1989 (para. 4A(6)(a)). Thus s. 293 has come far too late to save (amongst others) cimetidine (better known as Tagamet), the drug at the centre of the *ex parte Smith Kline & French Laboratories Ltd* case (above), said to be the second largest-selling drug in the world, which went licence of right in June 1988. (This was a drug, however, which had been developed and approved quite quickly and had already had 11 years of effective patent protection.) Furthermore, there can be no declaration if there is already a licence for pharmaceutical use which will be effective after the 16th year of the patent or if there is an outstanding application for the comptroller to settle the terms of such a licence. However, under s. 294, which inserts a new para. 4B into the 1977 Act, such an application to settle the terms of a licence is ineffective if it is made before the beginning of the 16th year of the patent.

The net result is that the new provisions will not benefit drugs which have been patented for 15 (rather than 16) years prior to 15 January 1989. The government was unwilling to interfere with existing applicants for the settlement of a licence as it felt it would be vulnerable to a claim that this amounted to a deprivation of property under the European Convention on Human Rights. The force of this argument might be thought to be slightly weakened by the fact that the Act certainly does invalidate existing applications made *before* the patent has passed the end of its 15th year (para. 4B(2)).

The licence of right provisions continue to apply outside the pharmaceutical sphere although they will eventually disappear in 1998 when the last of the new existing patents finally expire. Para. 4A(3) enables the Secretary of State to exempt other uses from the licence of right provisions. The agrochemicals (pesticides) industry mounted a campaign during the passage of the Bill to exempt their products from licences of right on the basis of similar arguments about loss of effective patent term because of the need to satisfy stringent safety standards. Given the failure of this campaign, it is perhaps unlikely that the Secretary of State will be persuaded to exercise his powers in the remaining few years that licences of right will remain significant. (Licences of right are provided for by the 1977 Act in other contexts, e.g., where the patent is voluntarily endorsed licence of right by the patentee under s. 46 and these will continue despite s. 293 of the 1988 Act.)

**Miscellaneous patent amendments**

Section 295 provides that the 1949 and 1977 Patent Acts are amended in accordance with sch. 5 which contains a total of 30 paragraphs and so only a few of the more interesting ones are mentioned here.

Paragraph 6 liberalises the rules for restoration of lapsed patents under s. 28 of the 1977 Act. The requirement that the proprietor's failure to pay the renewal fee be 'because of circumstances beyond his control' (which in *Textron Inc.'s Patent* [1988] RPC 177 precluded restoration where there was a mistake by a junior employee) is removed and the restriction that the application for restoration had to be made within one year of the lapse of the patent is relaxed. The new period within which applications are to be made is to be prescribed by rules so that the period can be altered again if necessary but the period may well turn out to be the one of 15 months that initially appeared in the Bill.

Paragraph 11 deals with an anomaly caused by the fact that whereas copyright in works produced in the course of employment will normally belong to the employer, that is not of itself sufficient for any associated patent to belong to the employer under s. 39 of the 1977 Act (which imposes additional requirements, for example, that an invention be reasonably expected to result). A new subsection (3) is inserted into s. 39 to protect the employee (or those claiming under him) entitled to a patent under s. 39 from liability for infringement of design right or copyright belonging to the employer 'in any model or document relating to the invention'. Otherwise, an employer could use his copyright or design rights to prevent an employee fully exploiting a patent which it is the policy of s. 39 to leave with the employee.

Paragraph 12 amends s. 46 of the 1977 Act to take account of the European Court of Justice's decision in *Allen & Hanburys Ltd* v *Generics (UK) Ltd* (case 434/85) [1988] FSR 312. Allen & Hanburys' drug salbutamol had been endorsed 'licence of right' but it had still tried to prevent its importation from Italy by Generics pending the decision of the comptroller on Generics' request for a licence. Section 46(3)(c) provides that in such circumstances no injunction should be granted 'in proceedings for infringement of the patent (otherwise than by the importation of any article)'. Since the infringement would be by importation in this case, the statute would appear to allow an injunction but the European Court held that that would constitute arbitrary discrimination between member States of the EEC since an injunction would not be available against a UK manufacturer. The court therefore held that UK courts were precluded from issuing an injunction in such circumstances and s. 46 is now amended so as to be compatible with this decision. Section 46(3)(c) now only preserves the power to grant an injunction (against infringers undertaking to take a licence) where the importation is 'from a country which is not a member State of the European Economic Community' and thus where there is no conflict with the Treaty of Rome.

Paragraph 19 deals with the situation where a person has obtained two patents for the same invention, a European patent (UK) and a domestic UK patent. In pursuance of the general principle that one cannot have two patents for the same invention, s. 73(2) of the 1977 Act provided for the domestic patent, rather than the European one, to be revoked. This could cause difficulties for those who might ultimately decide that they would prefer a domestic UK patent to a European UK-designated patent (e.g., because the domestic patent might also be recognised in British dependencies). Paragraph 19 amends s. 73 so as to enable the patentee to avoid double patenting by choosing to surrender his European patent (UK) rather than his domestic one.

Paragraph 27 amends s. 102 of the Patents Act 1977 (right of audience in patent proceedings) to render it consistent with the abolition of the patent agents' monopoly (discussed earlier in this chapter). It also inserts a new s. 102A to replace the former s. 102(3) dealing with the rights of audience of patent agents, solicitors and non-practising barristers in appeals from the comptroller to the Patents Court and empowers the Lord Chancellor to make regulations governing patent agents and non-practising barristers exercising such rights.

Finally, para. 30 provides for rules to be made concerning the disclosure of an invention 'which requires for its performance the use of a micro-organism'. These will replace the rules currently made under s. 14(4) and (8) of the 1977 Act whereby the micro-organism is made available to the public (including potential competitors) before there is any guarantee that patent protection will actually be secured. The most significant feature of the new rule-making power (enshrined in a new s. 125A of the 1977 Act) is the power to provide that 'samples need only be made available to such persons or descriptions of persons as may be prescribed'. This will enable the UK to adopt the solution (already adopted in the European Patent Office) of restricted availability (until grant) to independent experts who can test on behalf of others without the danger of competitors making illegitimate use of the micro-organism. This should reduce any incentive currently operating which might cause innovators to try to protect micro-organisms as trade secrets rather than disclosing them in return for patent protection.

# Copyright, Designs and Patents Act 1988

**Chapter 48**

**Arrangement of Sections**

**Part I Copyright**

*Chapter I Subsistence, ownership and duration of copyright*

*Introductory*

*Chapter II Rights of copyright owner*

## Part IV Registered designs

*Amendments of the Registered Designs Act 1949*

*Supplementary*

## Part V Patent agents and trade mark agents

*Patent agents*

*Trade mark agents*

*Supplementary*

# Part VI Patents

*Patents county courts*

# Part VII Miscellaneous and general

*Devices designed to circumvent copy-protection*

# Schedules

1988 Chapter 48. An Act to restate the law of copyright, with amendments; to make fresh provision as to the rights of performers and others in performances; to confer a design right in original designs; to amend the Registered Designs Act 1949; to make provision with respect to patent agents and trade mark agents; to confer patents and designs jurisdiction on certain county courts; to amend the law of patents; to make provision with respect to devices designed to circumvent copy-protection of works in electronic form; to make fresh provision penalising the fraudulent reception of transmissions; to make the fraudulent application or use of a trade mark an offence; to make provision for the benefit of the Hospital for Sick Children, Great Ormond Street, London; to enable financial assistance to be given to certain international bodies; and for connected purposes. [Royal assent 15 November 1988]

Be it enacted by the Queen's most Excellent Majesty, by and with the advice and consent of the Lords Spiritual and Temporal, and Commons, in this present Parliament assembled, and by the authority of the same, as follows:—

## Part I Copyright

*Chapter I Subsistence, ownership and duration of copyright*

*Introductory*

*Copyright and copyright works*
**1.**—(1)   Copyright is a property right which subsists in accordance with this Part in the following descriptions of work—

    (a)   original literary, dramatic, musical or artistic works,
    (b)   sound recordings, films, broadcasts or cable programmes, and
    (c)   the typographical arrangement of published editions.

    (2)   In this Part 'copyright work' means a work of any of those descriptions in which copyright subsists.
    (3)   Copyright does not subsist in a work unless the requirements of this Part with respect to qualification for copyright protection are met (see section 153 and the provisions referred to there).

*Rights subsisting in copyright works*
**2.**—(1)   The owner of the copyright in a work of any description has the exclusive right to do the acts specified in Chapter II as the acts restricted by the copyright in a work of that description.
    (2)   In relation to certain descriptions of copyright work the following rights conferred by Chapter IV (moral rights) subsist in favour of the author, director or commissioner of the work, whether or not he is the owner of the copyright—

    (a)   section 77 (right to be identified as author or director),
    (b)   section 80 (right to object to derogatory treatment of work), and
    (c)   section 85 (right to privacy of certain photographs and films).

*Descriptions of work and related provisions*

*Literary, dramatic and musical works*
**3.**—(1)  In this Part—

'literary work' means any work, other than a dramatic or musical work, which is written, spoken or sung, and accordingly includes—

    (a)  a table or compilation, and
    (b)  a computer program;

'dramatic work' includes a work of dance or mime; and
'musical work' means a work consisting of music, exclusive of any words or action intended to be sung, spoken or performed with the music.

(2)  Copyright does not subsist in a literary, dramatic or musical work unless and until it is recorded, in writing or otherwise; and references in this Part to the time at which such a work is made are to the time at which it is so recorded.

(3)  It is immaterial for the purposes of subsection (2) whether the work is recorded by or with the permission of the author; and where it is not recorded by the author, nothing in that subsection affects the question whether copyright subsists in the record as distinct from the work recorded.

*Artistic works*
**4.**—(1)  In this Part 'artistic work' means—

    (a)  a graphic work, photograph, sculpture or collage, irrespective of artistic quality,
    (b)  a work of architecture being a building or a model for a building, or
    (c)  a work of artistic craftsmanship.

(2)  In this Part—

'building' includes any fixed structure, and a part of a building or fixed structure;
'graphic work' includes—

    (a)  any painting, drawing, diagram, map, chart or plan, and
    (b)  any engraving, etching, lithograph, woodcut or similar work;

'photograph' means a recording of light or other radiation on any medium on which an image is produced or from which an image may by any means be produced, and which is not part of a film;
'sculpture' includes a cast or model made for purposes of sculpture.

*Sound recordings and films*
**5.**—(1) In this Part—

'sound recording' means—

    (a)  a recording of sounds, from which the sounds may be reproduced, or
    (b)  a recording of the whole or any part of a literary, dramatic or musical work, from which sounds reproducing the work or part may be produced,

regardless of the medium on which the recording is made or the method by which the sounds are reproduced or produced; and

'film' means a recording on any medium from which a moving image may by any means be produced.

(2)   Copyright does not subsist in a sound recording or film which is, or to the extent that it is, a copy taken from a previous sound recording or film.

*Broadcasts*
**6.**—(1)   In this Part a 'broadcast' means a transmission by wireless telegraphy of visual images, sounds or other information which—

(a)   is capable of being lawfully received by members of the public, or
(b)   is transmitted for presentation to members of the public;

and references to broadcasting shall be construed accordingly.

(2)   An encrypted transmission shall be regarded as capable of being lawfully received by members of the public only if decoding equipment has been made available to members of the public by or with the authority of the person making the transmission or the person providing the contents of the transmission.

(3)   References in this Part to the person making a broadcast, broadcasting a work, or including a work in a broadcast are—

(a)   to the person transmitting the programme, if he has responsibility to any extent for its contents, and
(b)   to any person providing the programme who makes with the person transmitting it the arrangements necessary for its transmission;

and references in this Part to a programme, in the context of broadcasting, are to any item included in a broadcast.

(4)   For the purposes of this Part the place from which a broadcast is made is, in the case of a satellite transmission, the place from which the signals carrying the broadcast are transmitted to the satellite.

(5)   References in this Part to the reception of a broadcast include reception of a broadcast relayed by means of a telecommunications system.

(6)   Copyright does not subsist in a broadcast which infringes, or to the extent that it infringes, the copyright in another broadcast or in a cable programme.

*Cable programmes*
**7.**—(1) In this Part—

'cable programme' means any item included in a cable programme service; and

'cable programme service' means a service which consists wholly or mainly in sending visual images, sounds or other information by means of a telecommunications system, otherwise than by wireless telegraphy, for reception—

(a)   at two or more places (whether for simultaneous reception or at different times in response to requests by different users), or
(b)   for presentation to members of the public,

and which is not, or so far as it is not, excepted by or under the following provisions of this section.

(2)   The following are excepted from the definition of 'cable programme service'—

(a)   a service or part of a service of which it is an essential feature that while visual images, sounds or other information are being conveyed by the person providing the service there will or may be sent from each place of reception, by means of the same system or (as the case may be) the same part of it, information (other than signals sent for the operation or control of the service) for reception by the person providing the service or other persons receiving it;

(b)   a service run for the purposes of a business where—

(i)   no person except the person carrying on the business is concerned in the control of the apparatus comprised in the system,

(ii)   the visual images, sounds or other information are conveyed by the system solely for purposes internal to the running of the business and not by way of rendering a service or providing amenities to others, and

(iii)   the system is not connected to any other telecommunications system;

(c)   a service run by a single individual where—

(i)   all the apparatus comprised in the system is under his control,

(ii)   the visual images, sounds or other information conveyed by the system are conveyed solely for domestic purposes of his, and

(iii)   the system is not connected to any other telecommunications system;

(d)   services where—

(i)   all the apparatus comprised in the system is situated in, or connects, premises which are in single occupation, and

(ii)   the system is not connected to any other telecommunications system,

other than services operated as part of the amenities provided for residents or inmates of premises run as a business;

(e)   services which are, or to the extent that they are, run for persons providing broadcasting or cable programme services or providing programmes for such services.

(3)   The Secretary of State may by order amend subsection (2) so as to add or remove exceptions, subject to such transitional provision as appears to him to be appropriate.

(4)   An order shall be made by statutory instrument; and no order shall be made unless a draft of it has been laid before and approved by resolution of each House of Parliament.

(5)   References in this Part to the inclusion of a cable programme or work in a cable programme service are to its transmission as part of the service; and references to the person including it are to the person providing the service.

(6)   Copyright does not subsist in a cable programme—

(a)   if it is included in a cable programme service by reception and immediate re-transmission of a broadcast, or

(b)   if it infringes, or to the extent that it infringes, the copyright in another cable programme or in a broadcast.

*Published editions*
**8.**—(1)   In this Part 'published edition', in the context of copyright in the typographical arrangement of a published edition, means a published edition of the whole or any part of one or more literary, dramatic or musical works.

(2)   Copyright does not subsist in the typographical arrangement of a published edition if, or to the extent that, it reproduces the typographical arrangement of a previous edition.

## Authorship and ownership of copyright

*Authorship of work*
**9.**—(1)   In this Part 'author', in relation to a work, means the person who creates it.

(2)   That person shall be taken to be—

(a)   in the case of a sound recording or film, the person by whom the arrangements necessary for the making of the recording or film are undertaken;

(b)   in the case of a broadcast, the person making the broadcast (see section 6(3)) or, in the case of a broadcast which relays another broadcast by reception and immediate re-transmission, the person making that other broadcast;

(c)   in the case of a cable programme, the person providing the cable programme service in which the programme is included;

(d)   in the case of the typographical arrangement of a published edition, the publisher.

(3)   In the case of a literary, dramatic, musical or artistic work which is computer-generated, the author shall be taken to be the person by whom the arrangements necessary for the creation of the work are undertaken.

(4)   For the purposes of this Part a work is of 'unknown authorship' if the identity of the author is unknown or, in the case of a work of joint authorship, if the identity of none of the authors is known.

(5)   For the purposes of this Part the identity of an author shall be regarded as unknown if it is not possible for a person to ascertain his identity by reasonable inquiry; but if his identity is once known it shall not subsequently be regarded as unknown.

*Works of joint authorship*
**10.**—(1)   In this Part a 'work of joint authorship' means a work produced by the collaboration of two or more authors in which the contribution of each author is not distinct from that of the other author or authors.

(2)   A broadcast shall be treated as a work of joint authorship in any case where more than one person is to be taken as making the broadcast (see section 6(3)).

(3)   References in this Part to the author of a work shall, except as otherwise provided, be construed in relation to a work of joint authorship as references to all the authors of the work.

*First ownership of copyright*

**11.**—(1)   The author of a work is the first owner of any copyright in it, subject to the following provisions.

(2)   Where a literary, dramatic, musical or artistic work is made by an employee in the course of his employment, his employer is the first owner of any copyright in the work subject to any agreement to the contrary.

(3)   This section does not apply to Crown copyright or Parliamentary copyright (see sections 163 and 165) or to copyright which subsists by virtue of section 168 (copyright of certain international organisations).

## Duration of copyright

*Duration of copyright in literary, dramatic, musical or artistic works*

**12.**—(1)   Copyright in a literary, dramatic, musical or artistic work expires at the end of the period of 50 years from the end of the calendar year in which the author dies, subject to the following provisions of this section.

(2)   If the work is of unknown authorship, copyright expires at the end of the period of 50 years from the end of the calendar year in which it is first made available to the public; and subsection (1) does not apply if the identity of the author becomes known after the end of that period.

For this purpose making available to the public includes—

(a)   in the case of a literary, dramatic or musical work—

(i)   performance in public, or
(ii)   being broadcast or included in a cable programme service;

(b)   in the case of an artistic work—

(i)   exhibition in public,
(ii)   a film including the work being shown in public, or
(iii)   being included in a broadcast or cable programme service;

but in determining generally for the purposes of this subsection whether a work has been made available to the public no account shall be taken of any unauthorised act.

(3)   If the work is computer-generated, neither of the above provisions applies and copyright expires at the end of the period of 50 years from the end of the calendar year in which the work was made.

(4)   In relation to a work of joint authorship—

(a)   the reference is subsection (1) to the death of the author shall be construed—

(i)   if the identity of all the authors is known, as a reference to the death of the last of them to die, and
(ii)   if the identity of one or more of the authors is known and the identity of one or more others is not, as a reference to the death of the last of the authors whose identity is known; and

(b)   the reference in subsection (2) to the identity of the author becoming known shall be construed as a reference to the identity of any of the authors becoming known.

(5)   This section does not apply to Crown copyright or Parliamentary copryright (see sections 163 to 166) or to copyright which subsists by virtue of section 168 (copyright of certain international organisations).

*Duration of copyright in sound recordings and films*
**13.**—(1)   Copyright in a sound recording or film expires—

   (a)   at the end of the period of 50 years from the end of the calendar year in which it is made, or
   (b)   if it is relesed before the end of that period, 50 years from the end of the calendar year in which it is released.

(2)   A sound recording or film is 'released' when—

   (a)   it is first published, broadcast or included in a cable programme service, or
   (b)   in the case of a film or film sound-track, the film is first shown in public;

but in determining whether a work has been released no account shall be taken of any unauthorised act.

*Duration of copyright in broadcasts and cable programmes*
**14.**—(1)   Copyright in a broadcast or cable programme expires at the end of the period of 50 years from the end of the calendar year in which the broadcast was made or the programme was included in a cable programme service.

(2)   Copyright in a repeat broadcast or cable programme expires at the same time as the copyright in the original broadcast or cable programme; and accordingly no copyright arises in respect of a repeat broadcast or cable programme which is broadcast or included in a cable programme service after the expiry of the copyright in the original broadcast or cable programme.

(3)   A repeat broadcast or cable programme means one which is a repeat either of a broadcast previously made or of a cable programme previously included in a cable programme service.

*Duration of copyright in typographical arrangement of published editions*
**15.**   Copyright in the typographical arrangement of a published edition expires at the end of the period of 25 years from the end of the calendar year in which the edition was first published.

## Chapter II Rights of copyright owner

### The acts restricted by copyright

*The acts restricted by copyright in a work*
**16.**—(1)   The owner of the copyright in a work has, in accordance with the following provisions of this Chapter, the exclusive right to do the following acts in the United Kingdom—

   (a)   to copy the work (see section 17);
   (b)   to issue copies of the work to the public (see section 18);
   (c)   to perform, show or play the work in public (see section 19);
   (d)   to broadcast the work or include it in a cable programme service (see section 20);

(e)   to make an adaptation of the work or do any of the above in relation to an adaptation (see section 21);

and those acts are referred to in this Part as the 'acts restricted by the copyright'.

(2)   Copyright in a work is infringed by a person who without the licence of the copyright owner does, or authorises another to do, any of the acts restricted by the copyright.

(3)   References in this Part to the doing of an act restricted by the copyright in a work are to the doing of it—

(a)   in relation to the work as a whole or any substantial part of it, and
(b)   either directly or indirectly;

and it is immaterial whether any intervening acts themselves infringe copyright.

(4)   This Chapter has effect subject to—

(a)   the provisions of Chapter III (acts permitted in relation to copyright works), and
(b)   the provisions of Chapter VII (provisions with respect to copyright licensing).

*Infringement of copyright by copying*
**17.**—(1)   The copying of the work is an act restricted by the copyright in every description of copyright work; and references in this Part to copying and copies shall be construed as follows.

(2)   Copying in relation to a literary, dramatic, musical or artistic work means reproducing the work in any material form. This includes storing the work in any medium by electronic means.

(3)   In relation to an artistic work copying includes the making of a copy in three dimensions of a two-dimensional work and the making of a copy in two dimensions of a three-dimensional work.

(4)   Copying in relation to a film, television broadcast or cable programme includes making a photograph of the whole or any substantial part of any image forming part of the film, broadcast or cable programme.

(5)   Copying in relation to the typographical arrangement of a published edition means making a facsimile copy of the arrangement.

(6)   Copying in relation to any description of work includes the making of copies which are transient or are incidental to some other use of the work.

*Infringement by issue of copies to the public*
**18.**—(1)   The issue to the public of copies of the work is an act restricted by the copyright in every description of copyright work.

(2)   References in this Part to the issue to the public of copies of a work are to the act of putting into circulation copies not previously put into circulation, in the United Kingdom or elsewhere, and not to—

(a)   any subsequent distribution, sale, hiring or loan of those copies, or
(b)   any subsequent importation of those copies into the United Kingdom;

except that in relation to sound recordings, films and computer programs, the restricted act of issuing copies to the public includes any rental of copies to the public.

*Infringement by performance, showing or playing of work in public*
**19.**—(1)   The performance of the work in public is an act restricted by the copyright in a literary, dramatic or musical work.
   (2)   In this Part 'performance', in relation to a work—

   (a)   includes delivery in the case of lectures, addresses, speeches and sermons, and
   (b)   in general, includes any mode of visual or acoustic presentation, including presentation by means of a sound recording, film, broadcast or cable programme of the work.

   (3)   The playing or showing of the work in public is an act restricted by the copyright in a sound recording, film, broadcast or cable programme.
   (4)   Where copyright in a work is infringed by its being performed, played or shown in public by means of apparatus for receiving visual images or sounds conveyed by electronic means, the person by whom the visual images or sounds are sent, and in the case of a performance the performers, shall not be regarded as responsible for the infringement.

*Infringement by broadcasting or inclusion in a cable programme service*
**20.**   The broadcasting of the work or its inclusion in a cable programme service is an act restricted by the copyright in—

   (a)   a literary, dramatic, musical or artistic work,
   (b)   a sound recording or film, or
   (c)   a broadcast or cable programme.

*Infringement by making adaptation or act done in relation to adaptation*
**21.**—(1)   The making of an adaptation of the work is an act restricted by the copyright in a literary, dramatic or musical work.
   For this purpose an adaptation is made when it is recorded, in writing or otherwise.
   (2)   The doing of any of the acts specified in sections 17 to 20, or subsection (1) above, in relation to an adaptation of the work is also an act restricted by the copyright in a literary, dramatic or musical work.
   For this purpose it is immaterial whether the adaptation has been recorded, in writing or otherwise, at the time the act is done.
   (3)   In this Part 'adaptation'—

   (a)   in relation to a literary or dramatic work, means—

   (i)   a translation of the work:
   (ii)   a version of a dramatic work in which it is converted into a non-dramatic work or, as the case may be, of a non-dramatic work in which it is converted into a dramatic work;
   (iii)   a version of the work in which the story or action is conveyed wholly or mainly by means of pictures in a form suitable for reproduction in a book, or in a newspaper, magazine or similar periodical;

   (b)   in relation to a musical work, means an arrangement or transcription of the work.

(4)   In relation to a computer program a 'translation' includes a version of the program in which it is converted into or out of a computer language or code or into a different computer language or code, otherwise than incidentally in the course of running the program.

(5)   No inference shall be drawn from this section as to what does or does not amount to copying a work.  ·

*Secondary infringement of copyright*

*Secondary infringement: importing infringing copy*
**22.**   The copyright in a work is infringed by a person who, without the licence of the copyright owner, imports into the United Kingdom, otherwise than for his private and domestic use, an article which is, and which he knows or has reason to believe is, an infringing copy of the work.

*Secondary infringement: possessing or dealing with infringing copy*
**23.**   The copyright in a work is infringed by a person who, without the licence of the copyright owner—

(a)   possesses in the course of a business,
(b)   sells or lets for hire, or offers or exposes for sale or hire,
(c)   in the course of a business exhibits in public or distributes, or
(d)   distributes otherwise than in the course of a business to such an extent

as to affect prejudicially the owner of the copyright,

an article which is, and which he knows or has reason to believe is, an infringing copy of the work.

*Secondary infringement: providing means for making infringing copies*
**24.**—(1)   Copyright in a work is infringed by a person who, without the licence of the copyright owner—

(a)   makes,
(b)   imports into the United Kingdom,
(c)   possesses in the course of a business, or
(d)   sells or lets for hire, or offers or exposes for sale or hire,

an article specifically designed or adapted for making copies of that work, knowing or having reason to believe that it is to be used to make infringing copies.

(2)   Copyright in a work is infringed by a person who without the licence of the copyright owner transmits the work by means of a telecommunications system (otherwise than by broadcasting or inclusion in a cable programme service), knowing or having reason to believe that infringing copies of the work will be made by means of the reception of the transmission in the United Kingdom or elsewhere.

*Secondary infringement: permitting use of premises for infringing performance*
**25.**—(1)   Where the copyright in a literary, dramatic or musical work is infringed by a performance at a place of public entertainment, any person who gave permission for that place to be used for the performance is also liable for the infringement unless when he gave permission he believed on reasonable grounds that the performance would not infringe copyright.

(2)   In this section 'place of public entertainment' includes premises which are occupied mainly for other purposes but are from time to time made available for hire for the purposes of public entertainment.

*Secondary infringement: provision of apparatus for infringing performance etc.*
**26.**—(1)   Where copyright in a work is infringed by a public performance of the work, or by the playing or showing of the work in public, by means of apparatus for—

  (a)   playing sound recordings,
  (b)   showing films, or
  (c)   receiving visual images or sounds conveyed by electronic means,

the following persons are also liable for the infringement.

(2)   A person who supplied the apparatus, or any substantial part of it, is liable for the infringement if when he supplied the apparatus or part—

  (a)   he knew or had reason to believe that the apparatus was likely to be so used as to infringe copyright, or
  (b)   in the case of apparatus whose normal use involves a public performance, playing or showing, he did not believe on reasonable grounds that it would not be so used as to infringe copyright.

(3)   An occupier of premises who gave permission for the apparatus to be brought on to the premises is liable for the infringement if when he gave permission he knew or had reason to believe that the apparatus was likely to be so used as to infringe copyright.

(4)   A person who supplied a copy of a sound recording or film used to infringe copyright is liable for the infringement if when he supplied it he knew or had reason to believe that what he supplied, or a copy made directly or indirectly from it, was likely to be so used as to infringe copyright.

*Infringing copies*

*Meaning of 'infringing copy'*
**27.**—(1)   In this Part 'infringing copy', in relation to a copyright work, shall be construed in accordance with this section.

(2)   An article is an infringing copy if its making constituted an infringement of the copyright in the work in question.

(3)   An article is also an infringing copy if—

  (a)   it has been or is proposed to be imported into the United Kingdom, and
  (b)   its making in the United Kingdom would have constituted an infringement of the copyright in the work in question, or a breach of an exclusive licence agreement relating to that work.

(4)   Where in any proceedings the question arises whether an article is an infringing copy and it is shown—

  (a)   that the article is a copy of the work, and
  (b)   that copyright subsists in the work or has subsisted at any time,

it shall be presumed until the contrary is proved that the article was made at a time when copyright subsisted in the work.

(5)   Nothing in subsection (3) shall be construed as applying to an article which may lawfully be imported into the United Kingdom by virtue of any enforceable Community right within the meaning of section 2(1) of the European Communities Act 1972.

(6)   In this Part 'infringing copy' includes a copy falling to be treated as an infringing copy by virtue of any of the following provisions—

section 32(5) (copies made for purposes of instruction or examination),

section 35(3) (recordings made by educational establishments for educational purposes),

section 36(5) (reprographic copying by educational establishments for purposes of instruction),

section 37(3)(b) (copies made by librarian or archivist in reliance on false declaration),

section 56(2) (further copies, adaptations etc. of work in electronic form retained on transfer of principal copy),

section 63(2) (copies made for purpose of advertising artistic work for sale),

section 68(4) (copies made for purpose of broadcast or cable programme), or

any provision of an order under section 141 (statutory licence for certain reprographic copying by educational establishments).

*Chapter III Acts permitted in relation to copyright works*

*Introductory*

*Introductory provisions*
**28.**—(1)   The provisions of this Chapter specify acts which may be done in relation to copyright works notwithstanding the subsistence of copyright; they relate only to the question of infringement of copyright and do not affect any other right or obligation restricting the doing of any of the specified acts.

(2)   Where it is provided by this Chapter that an act does not infringe copyright, or may be done without infringing copyright, and no particular description of copyright work is mentioned, the act in question does not infringe the copyright in a work of any description.

(3)   No inference shall be drawn from the description of any act which may by virtue of this Chapter be done without infringing copyright as to the scope of the acts restricted by the copyright in any description of work.

(4)   The provisions of this Chapter are to be construed independently of each other, so that the fact that an act does not fall within one provision does not mean that it is not covered by another provision.

*General*

*Research and private study*
**29.**—(1)   Fair dealing with a literary, dramatic, musical or artistic work for the purposes of research or private study does not infringe any copyright in the work or, in the case of a published edition, in the typographical arrangement.

(2)   Fair dealing with the typographical arrangement of a published edition for the purposes mentioned in subsection (1) does not infringe any copyright in the arrangement.

(3)   Copying by a person other than the researcher or student himself is not fair dealing if—

(a)   in the case of a librarian, or a person acting on behalf of a librarian, he does anything which regulations under section 40 would not permit to be done under section 38 or 39 (articles or parts of published works: restriction on multiple copies of same material), or

(b)   in any other case, the person doing the copying knows or has reason to believe that it will result in copies of substantially the same material being provided to more than one person at substantially the same time and for substantially the same purpose.

*Criticism, review and news reporting*

**30.**—(1)   Fair dealing with a work for the purpose of criticism or review, of that or another work or of a performance of a work, does not infringe any copyright in the work provided that it is accompanied by a sufficient acknowledgement.

(2)   Fair dealing with a work (other than a photograph) for the purpose of reporting current events does not infringe any copyright in the work provided that (subject to subsection (3)) it is accompanied by a sufficient acknowledgement.

(3)   No acknowledgement is required in connection with the reporting of current events by means of a sound recording, film, broadcast or cable programme.

*Incidental inclusion of copyright material*

**31.**—(1)   Copyright in a work is not infringed by its incidental inclusion in an artistic work, sound recording, film, broadcast or cable programme.

(2)   Nor is the copyright infringed by the issue to the public of copies, or the playing, showing, broadcasting or inclusion in a cable programme service, of anything whose making was, by virtue of subsection (1), not an infringement of the copyright.

(3)   A musical work, words spoken or sung with music, or so much of a sound recording, broadcast or cable programme as includes a musical work or such words, shall not be regarded as incidentally included in another work if it is deliberately included.

*Education*

*Things done for purposes of instruction or examination*

**32.**—(1)   Copyright in a literary, dramatic, musical or artistic work is not infringed by its being copied in the course of instruction or of preparation for instruction, provided the copying—

(a)   is done by a person giving or receiving instruction, and
(b)   is not by means of a reprographic process.

(2)   Copyright in a sound recording, film, broadcast or cable programme is not infringed by its being copied by making a film or film sound-track in the

course of instruction, or of preparation for instruction, in the making of films or film sound-tracks, provided the copying is done by a person giving or receiving instruction.

(3)   Copyright is not infringed by anything done for the purposes of an examination by way of setting the questions, communicating the questions to the candidates or answering the questions.

(4)   Subsection (3) does not extend to the making of a reprographic copy of a musical work for use by an examination candidate in performing the work.

(5)   Where a copy which would otherwise be an infringing copy is made in accordance with this section but is subsequently dealt with, it shall be treated as an infringing copy for the purposes of that dealing, and if that dealing infringes copyright for all subsequent purposes.

For this purpose 'dealt with' means sold or let for hire, or offered or exposed for sale or hire.

*Anthologies for educational use*
**33.**—(1)   The inclusion of a short passage from a published literary or dramatic work in a collection which—

(a)   is intended for use in educational establishments and is so described in its title, and in any advertisements issued by or on behalf of the publisher, and

(b)   consists mainly of material in which no copyright subsists,

does not infringe the copyright in the work if the work itself is not intended for use in such establishments and the inclusion is accompanied by a sufficient acknowledgement.

(2)   Subsection (1) does not authorise the inclusion of more than two excerpts from copyright works by the same author in collections published by the same publisher over any period of five years.

(3)   In relation to any given passage the reference in subsection (2) to excerpts from works by the same author—

(a)   shall be taken to include excerpts from works by him in collaboration with another, and

(b)   if the passage in question is from such a work, shall be taken to include excerpts from works by any of the authors, whether alone or in collaboration with another.

(4)   References in this section to the use of a work in an educational establishment are to any use for the educational purposes of such an establishment.

*Performing, playing or showing work in course of activities of educational establishment*
**34.**—(1)   The performance of a literary, dramatic or musical work before an audience consisting of teachers and pupils at an educational establishment and other persons directly connected with the activities of the establishment—

(a)   by a teacher or pupil in the course of the activities of the establishment, or

(b)   at the establishment by any person for the purposes of instruction, is not a public performance for the purposes of infringement of copyright.

(2)   The playing or showing of a sound recording, film, broadcast or cable programme before such an audience at an educational establishment for the purposes of instruction is not a playing or showing of the work in public for the purposes of infringement of copyright.

(3)   A person is not for this purpose directly connected with the activities of the educational establishment simply because he is the parent of a pupil at the establishment.

*Recording by educational establishments of broadcasts and cable programmes*
**35.**—(1)   A recording of a broadcast or cable programme, or a copy of such a recording, may be made by or on behalf of an educational establishment for the educational purposes of that establishment without thereby infringing the copyright in the broadcast or cable programme, or in any work included in it.

(2)   This section does not apply if or to the extent that there is a licensing scheme certified for the purposes of this section under section 143 providing for the grant of licences.

(3)   Where a copy which would otherwise be an infringing copy is made in accordance with this section but is subsequently dealt with, it shall be treated as an infringing copy for the purposes of that dealing, and if that dealing infringes copyright for all subsequent purposes.

For this purpose 'dealt with' means sold or let for hire, or offered or exposed for sale or hire.

*Reprographic copying by educational establishments of passages from published works*
**36.**—(1)   Reprographic copies of passages from published literary, dramatic or musical works may, to the extent permitted by this section, be made by or on behalf of an educational establishment for the purposes of instruction without infringing any copyright in the work, or in the typographical arrangement.

(2)   Not more than one per cent of any work may by copied by or on behalf of an establishment by virtue of this section in any quarter, that is, in any period 1 January to 31 March, 1 April to 30 June, 1 July to 30 September or 1 October to 31 December.

(3)   Copying is not authorised by this section if, or to the extent that, licences are available authorising the copying in question and the person making the copies knew or ought to have been aware of that fact.

(4)   The terms of a licence granted to an educational establishment authorising the reprographic copying for the purposes of instruction of passages from published literary, dramatic or musical works are of no effect so far as they purport to restrict the proportion of a work which may be copied (whether on payment or free of charge) to less than that which would be permitted under this section.

(5)   Where a copy which would otherwise be an infringing copy is made in accordance with this section but is subsequently dealt with, it shall be treated as an infringing copy for the purposes of that dealing, and if that dealing infringes copyright for all subsequent purposes.

For this purpose 'dealt with' means sold or let for hire, or offered or exposed for sale or hire.

*Libraries and archives*

*Libraries and archives: introductory*
**37.**—(1)   In sections 38 to 43 (copying by librarians and archivists)—

(a)   references in any provision to a prescribed library or archive are to a library or archive of a description prescribed for the purposes of that provision by regulations made by the Secretary of State; and

(b)   references in any provision to the prescribed conditions are to the conditions so prescribed.

(2)   The regulations may provide that, where a librarian or archivist is required to be satisfied as to any matter before making or supplying a copy of a work—

(a)   he may rely on a signed declaration as to that matter by the person requesting the copy, unless he is aware that it is false in a material particular, and

(b)   in such cases as may be prescribed, he shall not make or supply a copy in the absence of a signed declaration in such form as may be prescribed.

(3)   Where a person requesting a copy makes a declaration which is false in a material particular and is supplied with a copy which would have been an infringing copy if made by him—

(a)   he is liable for infringement of copyright as if he had made the copy himself, and

(b)   the copy shall be treated as an infringing copy.

(4)   The regulations may make different provision for different descriptions of libraries or archives and for different purposes.

(5)   Regulations shall be made by statutory instrument which shall be subject to annulment in pursuance of a resolution of either House of Parliament.

(6)   References in this section, and in sections 38 to 43, to the librarian or archivist include a person acting on his behalf.

*Copying by librarians: articles in periodicals*
**38.**—(1)   The librarian of a prescribed library may, if the prescribed conditions are complied with, make and supply a copy of an article in a periodical without infringing any copyright in the text, in any illustrations accompanying the text or in the typographical arrangement.

(2)   The prescribed conditions shall include the following—

(a)   that copies are supplied only to persons satisfying the librarian that they require them for purposes of research or private study, and will not use them for any other purpose;

(b)   that no person is furnished with more than one copy of the same article or with copies of more than one article contained in the same issue of a periodical; and

(c)   that persons to whom copies are supplied are required to pay for them a sum not less than the cost (including a contribution to the general expenses of the library) attributable to their production.

*Copying by librarians: parts of published works*
**39.**—(1)   The librarian of a prescribed library may, if the prescribed conditions are complied with, make and supply from a published edition a copy of part of a literary, dramatic or musical work (other than an article in a periodical) without infringing any copyright in the work, in any illustrations accompanying the work or in the typographical arrangement.

(2)   The prescribed conditions shall include the following—

(a)   that copies are supplied only to persons satisfying the librarian that they require them for purposes of research or private study, and will not use them for any other purpose;

(b)   that no person is furnished with more than one copy of the same material or with a copy of more than a reasonable proportion of any work; and

(c)   that persons to whom copies are supplied are required to pay for them a sum not less than the cost (including a contribution to the general expenses of the library) attributable to their production.

*Restriction on production of multiple copies of the same material*
**40.**—(1)   Regulations for the purposes of sections 38 and 39 (copying by librarian of article or part of published work) shall contain provision to the effect that a copy shall be supplied only to a person satisfying the librarian that his requirement is not related to any similar requirement of another person.

(2)   The regulations may provide—

(a)   that requirements shall be regarded as similar if the requirements are for copies of substantially the same material at substantially the same time and for substantially the same purpose; and

(b)   that requirements of persons shall be regarded as related if those persons receive instruction to which the material is relevant at the same time and place.

*Copying by librarians: supply of copies to other libraries*
**41.**—(1)   The librarian of a prescribed library may, if the prescribed conditions are complied with, make and supply to another prescribed library a copy of—

(a)   an article in a periodical, or

(b)   the whole or part of a published edition of a literary, dramatic or musical work,

without infringing any copyright in the text of the article or, as the case may be, in the work, in any illustrations accompanying it or in the typographical arrangement.

(2)   Subsection (1)(b) does not apply if at the time the copy is made the librarian making it knows, or could by reasonable inquiry ascertain, the name and address of a person entitled to authorise the making of the copy.

*Copying by librarians or archivists: replacement copies of works*
**42.**—(1)   The librarian or archivist of a prescribed library or archive may, if the prescribed conditions are complied with, make a copy from any item in the permanent collection of the library or archive—

(a)   in order to preserve or replace that item by placing the copy in its permanent collection in addition to or in place of it, or

(b)   in order to replace in the permanent collection of another prescribed library or archive an item which has been lost, destroyed or damaged,

without infringing the copyright in any literary, dramatic or musical work, in any illustrations accompanying such a work or, in the case of a published edition, in the typographical arrangement.

(2)   The prescribed conditions shall include provision for restricting the making of copies to cases where it is not reasonably practicable to purchase a copy of the item in question to fulfil that purpose.

*Copying by librarians or archivists: certain unpublished works*
**43.**—(1)   The librarian or archivist of a prescribed library or archive may, if the prescribed conditions are complied with, make and supply a copy of the whole or part of a literary, dramatic or musical work from a document in the library or archive without infringing any copyright in the work or any illustrations accompanying it.

(2)   This section does not apply if—

(a)   the work had been published before the document was deposited in the library or archive, or

(b)   the copyright owner has prohibited copying of the work,

and at the time the copy is made the librarian or archivist making it is, or ought to be, aware of that fact.

(3)   The prescribed conditions shall include the following—

(a)   that copies are supplied only to persons satisfying the librarian or archivist that they require them for purposes of research or private study and will not use them for any other purpose;

(b)   that no person is furnished with more than one copy of the same material; and

(c)   that persons to whom copies are supplied are required to pay for them a sum not less than the cost (including a contribution to the general expenses of the library or archive) attributable to their production.

*Copy of work required to be made as condition of export*
**44.**   If an article of cultural or historical importance or interest cannot lawfully be exported from the United Kingdom unless a copy of it is made and deposited in an appropriate library or archive, it is not an infringement of copyright to make that copy.

### Public administration

*Parliamentary and judicial proceedings*
**45.**—(1)   Copyright is not infringed by anything done for the purposes of parliamentary or judicial proceedings.

(2)   Copyright is not infringed by anything done for the purposes of reporting such proceedings; but this shall not be construed as authorising the copying of a work which is itself a published report of the proceedings.

*Royal commissions and statutory inquiries*
**46.**—(1)   Copyright is not infringed by anything done for the purposes of the proceedings of a royal commission or statutory inquiry.

(2)   Copyright is not infringed by anything done for the purpose of reporting any such proceedings held in public; but this shall not be construed as authorising the copying of a work which is itself a published report of the proceedings.

(3)   Copyright in a work is not infringed by the issue to the public of copies of the report of a royal commission or statutory inquiry containing the work or material from it.

(4)   In this section—

'Royal commission' includes a commission appointed for Northern Ireland by the Secretary of State in pursuance of the prerogative powers of Her Majesty delegated to him under section 7(2) of the Northern Ireland Constitution Act 1973; and

'statutory inquiry' means an inquiry held or investigation conducted in pursuance of a duty imposed or power conferrred by or under an enactment.

*Material open to public inspection or on official register*
**47.**—(1)   Where material is open to public inspection pursuant to a statutory requirement, or is on a statutory register, any copyright in the material as a literary work is not infringed by the copying of so much of the material as contains factual information of any description, by or with the authority of the appropriate person, for a purpose which does not involve the issuing of copies to the public.

(2)   Where material is open to public inspection pursuant to a statutory requirement, copyright is not infringed by the copying or issuing to the public of copies of the material, by or with the authority of the appropriate person, for the purpose of enabling the material to be inspected at a more convenient time or place or otherwise facilitating the exercise of any right for the purpose of which the requirement is imposed.

(3)   Where material which is open to public inspection pursuant to a statutory requirement, or which is on a statutory register, contains information about matters of general scientific, technical, commercial or economic interest, copyright is not infringed by the copying or issuing to the public of copies of the material, by or with the authority of the appropriate person, for the purpose of disseminating that information.

(4)   The Secretary of State may by order provide that subsection (1), (2) or (3) shall, in such cases as may be specified in the order, apply only to copies marked in such manner as may be so specified.

(5)   The Secretary of State may by order provide that subsections (1) to (3) apply, to such extent and with such modifications as may be specified in the order—

(a)   to material made open to public inspection by—

(i)   an international organisation specified in the order, or
(ii)   a person so specified who has functions in the United Kingdom under an international agreement to which the United Kingdom is party, or

(b)   to a register maintained by an international organisation specified in the order, as they apply in relation to material open to public inspection pursuant to a statutory requirement or to a statutory register.

(6)   In this section—

'appropriate person' means the person required to make the material open to public inspection or, as the case may be, the person maintaining the register;

'statutory register' means a register maintained in pursuance of a statutory requirement; and

'statutory requirement' means a requirement imposed by provision made by or under an enactment.

(7)   An order under this section shall be made by statutory instrument which shall be subject to annulment in pursuance of a resolution of either House of Parliament.

*Material communicated to the Crown in the course of public business*
**48.**—(1)   This section applies where a literary, dramatic, musical or artistic work has in the course of public business been communicated to the Crown for any purpose by or with the licence of the copyright owner and a document or other material thing recording or embodying the work is owned by or in the custody or control of the Crown.

(2)   The Crown may, for the purpose for which the work was communicated to it, or any related purpose which could reasonably have been anticipated by the copyright owner, copy the work and issue copies of the work to the public without infringing any copyright in the work.

(3)   The Crown may not copy a work, or issue copies of a work to the public, by virtue of this section if the work has previously been published otherwise than by virtue of this section.

(4)   In subsection (1) 'public business' includes any activity carried on by the Crown.

(5)   This section has effect subject to any agreement to the contrary between the Crown and the copyright owner.

*Public records*
**49.**   Material which is comprised in public records within the meaning of the Public Records Act 1958, the Public Records (Scotland) Act 1937 or the Public Records Act (Northern Ireland) 1923 which are open to public inspection in pursuance of that Act, may be copied, and a copy may be supplied to any person, by or with the authority of any officer appointed under that Act, without infringement of copyright.

*Acts done under statutory authority*
**50.**—(1)   Where the doing of a particular act is specifically authorised by an Act of Parliament, whenever passed, then, unless the Act provides otherwise, the doing of that act does not infringe copyright.

(2)   Subsection (1) applies in relation to an enactment contained in Northern Ireland legislation as it applies in relation to an Act of Parliament.

(3)   Nothing in this section shall be construed as excluding any defence of statutory authority otherwise available under or by virtue of any enactment.

*Designs*

## Design documents and models

**51.**—(1)   It is not an infringement of any copyright in a design document or model recording or embodying a design for anything other than an artistic work or a typeface to make an article to the design or to copy an article made to the design.

(2)   Nor is it an infringement of the copyright to issue to the public, or include in a film, broadcast or cable programme service, anything the making of which was, by virtue of subsection (1), not an infringement of that copyright.

(3)   In this section—

'design' means the design of any aspect of the shape or configuration (whether internal or external) of the whole or part of an article other than surface decoration; and

'design document' means any record of a design, whether in the form of a drawing, a written description, a photograph, data stored in a computer or otherwise.

## Effect of exploitation of design derived from artistic work

**52.**—(1)   This section applies where an artistic work has been exploited, by or with the licence of the copyright owner, by—

(a)   making by an industrial process articles falling to be treated for the purposes of this Part as copies of the work, and

(b)   marketing such articles, in the United Kingdom or elsewhere.

(2)   After the end of the period of 25 years from the end of the calendar year in which such articles are first marketed, the work may be copied by making articles of any description, or doing anything for the purpose of making articles of any description, and anything may be done in relation to articles so made, without infringing copyright in the work.

(3)   Where only part of an artistic work is exploited as mentioned in subsection (1), subsection (2) applies only in relation to that part.

(4)   The Secretary of State may by order make provision—

(a)   as to the circumstances in which an article, or any description of article, is to be regarded for the purposes of this section as made by an industrial process.

(b)   excluding from the operation of this section such articles of a primarily literary or artistic character as he thinks fit.

(5)   An order shall be made by statutory instrument which shall be subject to annulment in pursuance of a resolution of either House of Parliament.

(6)   In this section—

(a)   references to articles do not include films; and

(b)   references to the marketing of an article are to its being sold or let for hire or offered or exposed for sale or hire.

## Things done in reliance on registration of design

**53.**—(1)   The copyright in an artistic work is not infringed by anything done—

(a)   in pursuance of an assignment or licence made or granted by a person registered under the Registered Designs Act 1949 as the proprietor of a corresponding design, and

(b)   in good faith in reliance on the registration and without notice of any proceedings for the cancellation of the registration or for rectifying the relevant entry in the register of designs;

and this is so notwithstanding that the person registered as the proprietor was not the proprietor of the design for the purposes of the 1949 Act.

(2)   In subsection (1) a 'corresponding design', in relation to an artistic work, means a design within the meaning of the 1949 Act which if applied to an article would produce something which would be treated for the purposes of this Part as a copy of the artistic work.

### Typefaces

#### Use of typeface in ordinary course of printing

**54.**—(1)   It is not an infringement of copyright in an artistic work consisting of the design of a typeface—

(a)   to use the typeface in the ordinary course of typing, composing text, typesetting or printing,

(b)   to possess an article for the purpose of such use, or

(c)   to do anything in relation to material produced by such use;

and this is so notwithstanding that an article is used which is an infringing copy of the work.

(2)   However, the following provisions of this Part apply in relation to persons making, importing or dealing with articles specifically designed or adapted for producing material in a particular typeface, or possessing such articles for the purpose of dealing with them, as if the production of material as mentioned in subsection (1) did infringe copyright in the artistic work consisting of the design of the typeface—

section 24 (secondary infringement: making, importing, possessing or dealing with article for making infringing copy),

sections 99 and 100 (order for delivery up and right of seizure),

section 107(2) (offence of making or possessing such an article), and

section 108 (order for delivery up in criminal proceedings).

(3)   The references in subsection (2) to 'dealing with' an article are to selling, letting for hire, or offering or exposing for sale or hire, exhibiting in public, or distributing.

#### Articles for producing material in particular typeface

**55.**—(1)   This section applies to the copyright in an artistic work consisting of the design of a typeface where articles specifically designed or adapted for producing material in that typeface have been marketed by or with the licence of the copyright owner.

(2)   After the period of 25 years from the end of the calendar year in which the first such articles are marketed, the work may be copied by making further such articles, or doing anything for the purpose of making such articles, and anything

may be done in relation to articles so made, without infringing copyright in the work.

(3)   In subsection (1) 'marketed' means sold, let for hire or offered or exposed for sale or hire, in the United Kingdom or elsewhere.

### Works in electronic form

#### Transfers of copies of works in electronic form
**56.**—(1)   This section applies where a copy of a work in electronic form has been purchased on terms which, expressly or impliedly or by virtue of any rule of law, allow the purchaser to copy the work, or to adapt it or make copies of an adaptation, in connection with his use of it.

(2)   If there are no express terms—

(a)   prohibiting the transfer of the copy by the purchaser, imposing obligations which continue after a transfer, prohibiting the assignment of any licence or terminating any licence on a transfer, or

(b)   providing for the terms on which a transferee may do the things which the purchaser was permitted to do,

anything which the purchaser was allowed to do may also be done without infringement of copyright by a transferee; but any copy, adaptation or copy of an adaptation made by the purchaser which is not also transferred shall be treated as an infringing copy for all purposes after the transfer.

(3)   The same applies where the original purchased copy is no longer usable and what is transferred is a further copy used in its place.

(4)   The above provisions also apply on a subsequent transfer, with the substitution for references in subsection (2) to the purchaser of references to the subsequent transferor.

### Miscellaneous: literary, dramatic, musical and artistic works

#### Anonymous or pseudonymous works: acts permitted on assumptions as to expiry of copyright or death of author
**57.**—(1)   Copyright in a literary, dramatic, musical or artistic work is not infringed by an act done at a time when, or in pursuance of arrangements made at a time when—

(a)   it is not possible by reasonable inquiry to ascertain the identity of the author, and

(b)   it is reasonable to assume—

(i)   that copyright has expired, or

(ii)   that the author died 50 years or more before the beginning of the calendar year in which the act is done or the arrangements are made.

(3)   In relation to a work of joint authorship—

(a)   the reference in subsection (1) to its being possible to ascertain the identity of the author shall be construed as a reference to its being possible to ascertain the identity of any of the authors, and

(b)   the reference in subsection (1)(b)(ii) to the author having died shall be construed as a reference to all the authors having died.

*Use of notes or recordings of spoken words in certain cases*
**58.**—(1)   Where a record of spoken words is made, in writing or otherwise, for the purpose—

(a)   of reporting current events, or
(b)   of broadcasting or including in a cable programme service the whole or part of the work,

it is not an infringement of any copyright in the words as a literary work to use the record or material taken from it (or to copy the record, or any such material, and use the copy) for that purpose, provided the following conditions are met.

(2)   The conditions are that—

(a)   the record is a direct record of the spoken words and is not taken from a previous record or from a broadcast or cable programme;
(b)   the making of the record was not prohibited by the speaker and, where copyright already subsisted in the work, did not infringe copyright;
(c)   the use made of the record or material taken from it is not of a kind prohibited by or on behalf of the speaker or copyright owner before the record was made; and
(d)   the use is by or with the authority of a person who is lawfully in possession of the record.

*Public reading or recitation*
**59.**—(1)   The reading or recitation in public by one person of a reasonable extract from a published literary or dramatic work does not infringe any copyright in the work if it is accompanied by a sufficient acknowledgement.

(2)   Copyright in a work is not infringed by the making of a sound recording, or the broadcasting or inclusion in a cable programme service, of a reading or recitation which by virtue of subsection (1) does not infringe copyright in the work, provided that the recording, broadcast or cable programme consists mainly of material in relation to which it is not necessary to rely on that subsection.

*Abstracts of scientific or technical articles*
**60.**—(1)   Where an article on a scientific or technical subject is published in a periodical accompanied by an abstract indicating the contents of the article, it is not an infringement of copyright in the abstract, or in the article, to copy the abstract or issue copies of it to the public.

(2)   This section does not apply if or to the extent that there is a licensing scheme certified for the purposes of this section under section 143 providing for the grant of licences.

*Recordings of folksongs*
**61.**—(1)   A sound recording of a performance of a song may be made, for the purpose of including it in an archive maintained by a designated body, without infringing any copyright in the words as a literary work or in the accompanying musical work, provided the conditions in subsection (2) below are met.

(2)   The conditions are that—

(a)   the words are unpublished and of unknown authorship at the time the recording is made,

(b)   the making of the recording does not infringe any other copyright, and

(c)   its making is not prohibited by any performer.

(3)   Copies of a sound recording made in reliance on subsection (1) and included in an archive maintained by a designated body may, if the prescribed conditions are met, be made and supplied by the archivist without infringing copyright in the recording or the works included in it.

(4)   The prescribed conditions shall include the following—

(a)   that copies are only supplied to persons satisfying the archivist that they require them for purposes of research or private study and will not use them for any other purpose, and

(b)   that no person is furnished with more than one copy of the same recording.

(5)   In this section—

(a)   'designated' means designated for the purposes of this section by order of the Secretary of State, who shall not designate a body unless satisfied that it is not established or conducted for profit,

(b)   'prescribed' means prescribed for the purposes of this section by order of the Secretary of State, and

(c)   references to the archivist include a person acting on his behalf.

(6)   An order under this section shall be made by statutory instrument which shall be subject to annulment in pursuance of a resolution of either House of Parliament.

*Representation of certain artistic works on public display*
**62.**—(1)   This section applies to—

(a)   buildings, and

(b)   sculptures, models for buildings and works of artistic craftsmanship, if permanently situated in a public place or in premises open to the public.

(2)   The copyright in such a work is not infringed by—

(a)   making a graphic work representing it,

(b)   making a photograph or film of it, or

(c)   broadcasting or including in a cable programme service a visual image of it.

(3)   Nor is the copyright infringed by the issue to the public of copies, or the broadcasting or inclusion in a cable programme service, of anything whose making was, by virtue of this section, not an infringement of the copyright.

*Advertisement of sale of artistic work*
**63.**—(1)   It is not an infringement of copyright in an artistic work to copy it, or to issue copies to the public, for the purpose of advertising the sale of the work.

(2)   Where a copy which would otherwise be an infringing copy is made in accordance with this section but is subsequently dealt with for any other purpose, it shall be treated as an infringing copy for the purposes of that dealing, and if that dealing infringes copyright for all subsequent purposes.

For this purpose 'dealt with' means sold or let for hire, offered or exposed for sale or hire, exhibited in public or distributed.

*Making of subsequent works by same artist*
**64.**   Where the author of an artistic work is not the copyright owner, he does not infringe the copyright by copying the work in making another artistic work, provided he does not repeat or imitate the main design of the earlier work.

*Reconstruction of buildings*
**65.**   Anything done for the purposes of reconstructing a building does not infringe any copyright—

(a)   in the building, or
(b)   in any drawings or plans in accordance with which the building was, by or with the licence of the copyright owner, constructed.

*Miscellaneous: sound recordings, films and computer programs*

*Rental of sound recordings, films and computer programs*
**66.**—(1)   The Secretary of State may by order provide that in such cases as may be specified in the order the rental to the public of copies of sound recordings, films or computer programs shall be treated as licensed by the copyright owner subject only to the payment of such reasonable royalty or other payment as may be agreed or determined in default of agreement by the Copyright Tribunal.

(2)   No such order shall apply if, or to the extent that, there is a licensing scheme certified for the purposes of this section under section 143 providing for the grant of licences.

(3)   An order may make different provision for different cases and may specify cases by reference to any factor relating to the work, the copies rented, the renter or the circumstaces of the rental.

(4)   An order shall be made by statutory instrument; and no order shall be made unless a draft of it has been laid before and approved by a resolution of each House of Parliament.

(5)   Copyright in a computer program is not infringed by the rental of copies to the public after the end of the period of 50 years from the end of the calendar year in which copies of it were first issued to the public in electronic form.

(6)   Nothing in this section affects any liability under section 23 (secondary infringement) in respect of the rental of infringing copies.

*Playing of sound recordings for purposes of club, society etc.*
**67.**—(1)   It is not an infringement of the copyright in a sound recording to play it as part of the activities of, or for the benefit of, a club, society or other organisation if the following conditions are met.

(2)   The conditions are—

(a)   that the organisation is not established or conducted for profit and its main objects are charitable or are otherwise concerned with the advancement of religion, education or social welfare, and

(b)   that the proceeds of any charge for admission to the place where the recording is to be heard are applied solely for the purposes of the organisation.

*Miscellaneous: broadcasts and cable programmes*

*Incidental recording for purposes of broadcast or cable programme*
**68.**—(1)   This section applies where by virtue of a licence or assignment of copyright a person is authorised to broadcast or include in a cable programme service—

    (a)   a literary, dramatic or musical work, or an adaptation of such a work,
    (b)   an artistic work, or
    (c)   a sound recording or film.

    (2)   He shall by virtue of this section be treated as licensed by the owner of the copyright in the work to do or authorise any of the following for the purposes of the broadcast or cable programme—

    (a)   in the case of a literary, dramatic or musical work, or an adaptation of such a work, to make a sound recording or film of the work or adaptation;
    (b)   in the case of an artistic work, to take a photograph or make a film of the work;
    (c)   in the case of a sound recording or film, to make a copy of it.

    (3)   That licence is subject to the condition that the recording, film, photograph or copy in question—

    (a)   shall not be used for any other purpose, and
    (b)   shall be destroyed within 28 days of being first used for broadcasting the work or, as the case may be, including it in a cable programme service.

    (4)   A recording, film, photograph or copy made in accordance with this section shall be treated as an infringing copy—

    (a)   for the purposes of any use in breach of the condition mentioned in subsection (3)(a), and
    (b)   for all purposes after that condition or the condition mentioned in subsection (3)(b) is broken.

*Recording for purposes of supervision and control of broadcasts and cable programmes*
**69.**—(1)   Copyright is not infringed by the making or use by the British Broadcasting Corporation, for the purpose of maintaining supervision and control over programmes broadcast by them, of recordings of those programmes.
    (2)   Copyright is not infringed by—

    (a)   the making or use of recordings by the Independent Broadcasting Authority for the purposes mentioned in section 4(7) of the Broadcasting Act 1981 (maintenance of supervision and control over programmes and advertisements); or
    (b)   anything done under or in pursuance of provision included in a contract between a programme contractor and the Authority in accordance with section 21 of that Act.

    (3)   Copyright is not infringed by—

(a)   the making by or with the authority of the Cable Authority, or the use by that Authority, for the purpose of maintaining supervision and control over programmes included in services licensed under Part I of the Cable and Broadcasting Act 1984, of recordings of those programmes; or

(b)   a notice or direction given under section 16 of the Cable and Broadcasting Act 1984 (power of Cable Authority to require production of recordings); or

(c)   a condition included in a licence by virtue of section 35 of that Act (duty of Authority to secure that recordings are available for certain purposes).

### Recording for purposes of time-shifting

**70.**   The making for private and domestic use of a recording of a broadcast or cable programme solely for the purpose of enabling it to be viewed or listened to at a more convenient time does not infringe any copyright in the broadcast or cable programme or in any work included in it.

### Photographs of television broadcasts or cable programmes

**71.**   The making for private and domestic use of a photograph of the whole or any part of an image forming part of a television broadcast or cable programme, or a copy of such a photograph, does not infringe any copyright in the broadcast or cable programme or in any film included in it.

### Free public showing or playing of broadcast or cable programme

**72.**—(1)   The showing or playing in public of a broadcast or cable programme to an audience who have not paid for admission to the place where the broadcast or programme is to be seen or heard does not infringe any copyright in—

(a)   the broadcast or cable programme, or

(b)   any sound recording or film included in it.

(2)   The audience shall be treated as having paid for admission to a place—

(a)   if they have paid for admission to a place of which that place forms part; or

(b)   if goods or services are supplied at that place (or a place of which it forms part)—

(i)   at prices which are substantially attributable to the facilities afforded for seeing or hearing the broadcast or programme, or

(ii)   at prices exceeding those usually charged there and which are partly attributable to those facilities.

(3)   The following shall not be regarded as having paid for admission to a place—

(a)   persons admitted as residents or inmates of the place;

(b)   persons admitted as members of a club or society where the payment is only for membership of the club or society and the provision of facilities for seeing or hearing broadcasts or programmes is only incidental to the main purposes of the club or society.

(4)   Where the making of the broadcast or inclusion of the programme in a cable programme service was an infringement of the copyright in a sound

recording or film, the fact that it was heard or seen in public by the reception of the broadcast or programme shall be taken into account in assessing the damages for that infringement.

*Reception and re-transmission of broadcast in cable programme service*
**73.**—(1)    This section applies where a broadcast made from a place in the United Kingdom is, by reception and immediate re-transmission, included in a cable programme service.

(2)    The copyright in the broadcast is not infringed—

(a)    if the inclusion is in pursuance of a requirement imposed under section 13(1) of the Cable and Broadcasting Act 1984 (duty of Cable Authority to secure inclusion in cable service of certain programmes), or

(b)    if and to the extent that the broadcast is made for reception in the area in which the cable programme service is provided and is not a satellite transmission or an encrypted transmission.

(3)    The copyright in any work included in the broadcast is not infringed—

(a)    if the inclusion is in pursuance of a requirement imposed under section 13(1) of the Cable and Broadcasting Act 1984 (duty of Cable Authority to secure inclusion in cable service of certain programmes), or

(b)    if and to the extent that the broadcast is made for reception in the area in which the cable programme service is provided;

but where the making of the broadcast was an infringement of the copyright in the work, the fact that the broadcast was re-transmitted as a programme in a cable programme service shall be taken into account in assessing the damages for that infringement.

*Provision of subtitled copies of brodcast or cable programme*
**74.**—(1)    A designated body may, for the purpose of providing people who are deaf or hard of hearing, or physically or mentally handicapped in other ways, with copies which are subtitled or otherwise modified for their special needs, make copies of television broadcasts or cable programmes and issue copies to the public, without infringing any copyright in the broadcasts or cable programmes or works included in them.

(2)    A 'designated body' means a body designated for the purposes of this section by order of the Secretary of State, who shall not designate a body unless he is satisfied that it is not established or conducted for profit.

(3)    An order under this section shall be made by statutory instrument which shall be subject to annulment in pursuance of a resolution of either House of Parliament.

(4)    This section does not apply if, or to the extent that, there is a licensing scheme certified for the purposes of this section under section 143 providing for the grant of licences.

*Recording for archival purposes*
**75.**—(1)    A recording of a broadcast or cable programme of a designated class, or a copy of such a recording, may be made for the purpose of being placed in an archive maintained by a designated body without thereby infringing any

copyright in the broadcast or cable programme or in any work included in it.

(2)   In subsection (1) 'designated' means designated for the purposes of this section by order of the Secretary of State, who shall not designate a body unless he is satisfied that it is not established or conducted for profit.

(3)   An order under this section shall be made by statutory instrument which shall be subject to annulment in pursuance of a resolution of either House of Parliament.

*Adaptations*

*Adaptations*
**76.**   An act which by virtue of this Chapter may be done without infringing copyright in a literary, dramatic or musical work does not, where that work is an adaptation, infringe any copyright in the work from which the adaptation was made.

*Chapter IV Moral rights*

*Right to be identified as author or director*

*Right to be identified as author or director*
**77.**—(1)   The author of a copyright literary, dramatic, musical or artistic work, and the director of a copyright film, has the right to be identified as the author or director of the work in the circumstances mentioned in this section; but the right is not infringed unless it has been asserted in accordance with section 78.

(2)   The author of a literary work (other than words intended to be sung or spoken with music) or a dramatic work has the right to be identified whenever—

(a)   the work is published commercially, performed in public, broadcast or included in a cable programme service; or
(b)   copies of a film or sound recording including the work are issued to the public;

and that right includes the right to be identified whenever any of those events occur in relation to an adaptation of the work as the author of the work from which the adaptation was made.

(3)   The author of a musical work, or a literary work consisting of words intended to be sung or spoken with music, has the right to be identified whenever—

(a)   the work is published commercially;
(b)   copies of a sound recording of the work are issued to the public; or
(c)   a film of which the sound-track includes the work is shown in public or copies of such a film are issued to the public;

and that right includes the right to be identified whenever any of those events occur in relation to an adaptation of the work as the author of the work from which the adaptation was made.

(4)   The author of an artistic work has the right to be identified whenever—

(a)   the work is published commercially or exhibited in public, or a visual image of it is broadcast or included in a cable programme service;

(b)   a film including a visual image of the work is shown in public or copies of such a film are issued to the public; or

(c)   in the case of a work of architecture in the form of a building or a model for a building, a sculpture or a work of artistic craftsmanship, copies of a graphic work representing it, or of a photograph of it, are issued to the public.

(5)   The author of a work of architecture in the form of a building also has the right to be identified on the building as constructed or, where more than one building is constructed to the design, on the first to be constructed.

(6)   The director of a film has the right to be identified whenever the film is shown in public, broadcast or included in a cable programme service or copies of the film are issued to the public.

(7)   The right of the author or director under this section is—

(a)   in the case of commercial publication or the issue to the public of copies of a film or sound recording, to be identified in or on each copy or, if that is not appropriate, in some other manner likely to bring his identity to the notice of a person acquiring a copy,

(b)   in the case of identification on a building, to be identified by appropriate means visible to persons entering or approaching the building, and

(c)   in any other case, to be identified in a manner likely to bring his identity to the attention of a person seeing or hearing the performance, exhibition, showing, broadcast or cable programme in question;

and the identification must in each case be clear and reasonably prominent.

(8)   If the author or director in asserting his right to be identified specifies a pseudonym, initials or some other particular form of identification, that form shall be used; otherwise any reasonable form of identification may be used.

(9)   This section has effect subject to section 79 (exceptions to right).

*Requirement that right be asserted*
**78.**—(1)   A person does not infringe the right conferred by section 77 (right to be identified as author or director) by doing any of the acts mentioned in that section unless the right has been asserted in accordance with the following provisions so as to bind him in relation to that act.

(2)   The right may be asserted generally, or in relation to any specified act or description of acts—

(a)   on an assignment of copyright in the work, by including in the instrument effecting the assignment a statement that the author or director asserts in relation to that work his right to be identified, or

(b)   by instrument in writing signed by the author or director.

(3)   The right may also be asserted in relation to the public exhibition of an artistic work—

(a)   by securing that when the author or other first owner of copyright parts with possession of the original, or of a copy made by him or under his direction or control, the author is identified on the original or copy, or on a frame, mount or other thing to which it is attached, or

(b)   by including in a licence by which the author or other first owner of copyright authorises the making of copies of the work a statement signed by or on behalf of the person granting the licence that the author asserts his right to be identified in the event of the public exhibition of a copy made in pursuance of the licence.

(4) The persons bound by an assertion of the right under subsection (2) or (3) are—

    (a) in the case of an assertion under subsection (2)(a), the assignee and anyone claiming through him, whether or not he has notice of the assertion;

    (b) in the case of an assertion under subsection (2)(b), anyone to whose notice the assertion is brought;

    (c) in the case of an assertion under subsection (3)(a), anyone into whose hands that original or copy comes, whether or not the identification is still present or visible;

    (d) in the case of an assertion under subsection (3)(b), the licensee and anyone into whose hands a copy made in pursuance of the licence comes, whether or not he has notice of the assertion.

(5) In an action for infringement of the right the court shall, in considering remedies, take into account any delay in asserting the right.

*Exceptions to right*
**79.**—(1) The right conferred by section 77 (right to be identified as author or director) is subject to the following exceptions.

(2) The right does not apply in relation to the following descriptions of work—

    (a) a computer program;

    (b) the design of a typeface;

    (c) any computer-generated work.

(3) The right does not apply to anything done by or with the authority of the copyright owner where copyright in the work originally vested—

    (a) in the author's employer by virtue of section 11(2) (works produced in course of employment), or

    (b) in the director's employer by virtue of section 9(2)(a) (person to be treated as author of film).

(4) The right is not infringed by an act which by virtue of any of the following provisions would not infringe copyright in the work—

    (a) section 30 (fair dealing for certain purposes), so far as it relates to the reporting of current events by means of a sound recording, film, broadcast or cable programme;

    (b) section 31 (incidental inclusion of work in an artistic work, sound recording, film, broadcast or cable programme);

    (c) section 32(3) (examination questions);

    (d) section 45 (parliamentary and judicial proceedings);

    (e) section 46(1) or (2) (royal commissions and statutory inquiries);

    (f) section 51 (use of design documents and models);

(g)   section 52 (effect of exploitation of design derived from artistic work);

(h)   section 57 (anonymous or pseudonymous works: acts permitted on assumptions as to expiry of copyright or death of author).

(5)   The right does not apply in relation to any work made for the purpose of reporting current events.

(6)   The right does not apply in relation to the publication in—

(a)   a newspaper, magazine or similar periodical, or

(b)   an encyclopaedia, dictionary, yearbook or other collective work of reference,

of a literary, dramatic, musical or artistic work made for the purposes of such publication or made available with the consent of the author for the purposes of such publication.

(7)   The right does not apply in relation to—

(a)   a work in which Crown copyright or Parliamentary copyright subsists, or

(b)   a work in which copyright originally vested in an international organisation by virtue of section 168,

unless the author or director has previously been identified as such in or on published copies of the work.

*Right to object to derogatory treatment of work*

*Right to object to derogatory treatment of work*

**80.**—(1)   The author of a copyright literary, dramatic, musical or artistic work, and the director of a copyright film, has the right in the circumstances mentioned in this section not to have his work subjected to derogatory treatment.

(2)   For the purposes of this section—

(a)   'treatment' of a work means any addition to, deletion from or alteration to or adaptation of the work, other than—

(i)   a translation of a literary or dramatic work, or

(ii)   an arrangement or transcription of a musical work involving no more than a change of key or register; and

(b)   the treatment of a work is derogatory if it amounts to distortion or mutilation of the work or is otherwise prejudical to the honour or reputation of the author or director;

and in the following provisions of this section references to a derogatory treatment of a work shall be construed accordingly.

(3)   In the case of a literary, dramatic or musical work the right is infringed by a person who—

(a)   publishes commercially, performs in public, broadcasts or includes in a cable programme service a derogatory treatment of the work; or

(b)   issues to the public copies of a film or sound recording of, or including, a derogatory treatment of the work.

(4)   In the case of an artistic work the right is infringed by a person who—

(a)   publishes commercially or exhibits in public a derogatory treatment of the work, or broadcasts or includes in a cable programme service a visual image of a derogatory treatment of the work,

(b)   shows in public a film including a visual image of a derogatory treatment of the work or issues to the public copies of such a film, or

(c)   in the case of

(i)   a work of architecture in the form of a model for a building,
(ii)   a sculpture, or
(iii)   a work of artistic craftsmanship,

issues to the public copies of a graphic work representing, or of a photograph of, a derogatory treatment of the work.

(5)   Subsection (4) does not apply to a work of architecture in the form of a building; but where the author of such a work is identified on the building and it is the subject of derogatory treatment he has the right to require the identification to be removed.

(6)   In the case of a film, the right is infringed by a person who—

(a)   shows in public, broadcasts or includes in a cable programme service a derogatory treatment of the film; or

(b)   issues to the public copies of a derogatory treatment of the film,

or who, along with the film, plays in public, broadcasts or includes in a cable programme service, or issues to the public copies of, a derogatory treatment of the film sound-track.

(7)   The right conferred by this section extends to the treatment of parts of a work resulting from a previous treatment by a person other than the author or director, if those parts are attributed to, or are likely to be regarded as the work of, the author or director.

(8)   This section has effect subject to sections 81 and 82 (exceptions to and qualifications of right).

*Exceptions to right*
**81.**—(1)   The right conferred by section 80 (right to object to derogatory treatment of work) is subject to the following exceptions.

(2)   The right does not apply to a computer program or to any computer-generated work.

(3)   The right does not apply in relation to any work made for the purpose of reporting current events.

(4)   The right does not apply in relation to the publication in—

(a)   a newspaper, magazine or similar periodical, or

(b)   an encyclopaedia, dictionary, yearbook or other collective work of reference,

of a literary, dramatic, musical or artistic work made for the purposes of such publication or made available with the consent of the author for the purposes of such publication.

Nor does the right apply in relation to any subsequent exploitation elsewhere of such a work without any modification of the published version.

(5) The right is not infringed by an act which by virtue of section 57 (anonymous or pseudonymous works: acts permitted on assumptions as to expiry of copyright or death of author) would not infringe copyright.

(6) The right is not infringed by anything done for the purpose of—

(a) avoiding the commission of an offence,

(b) complying with a duty imposed by or under an enactment, or

(c) in the case of the British Broadcasting Corporation, avoiding the inclusion in a programme broadcast by them of anything which offends against good taste or decency or which is likely to encourage or incite to crime or to lead to disorder or to be offensive to public feeling,

provided, where the author or director is identified at the time of the relevant act or has previously been identified in or on published copies of the work, that there is a sufficient disclaimer.

*Qualification of right in certain cases*
**82.**—(1) This section applies to—

(a) works in which copyright originally vested in the author's employer by virtue of section 11(2) (works produced in course of employment) or in the director's employer by virtue of section 9(2)(a) (person to be treated as author of film),

(b) works in which Crown copyright or Parliamentary copyright subsists, and

(c) works in which copyright originally vested in an international organisation by virtue of section 168.

(2) The right conferred by section 80 (right to object to derogatory treatment of work) does not apply to anything done in relation to such a work by or with the authority of the copyright owner unless the author or director—

(a) is identified at the time of the relevant act, or

(b) has previously been identified in or on published copies of the work;

and where in such a case the right does apply, it is not infringed if there is a sufficient disclaimer.

*Infringement of right by possessing or dealing with infringing article*
**83.**—(1) The right conferrred by section 80 (right to object to derogatory treatment of work) is also infringed by a person who—

(a) possesses in the course of a business, or

(b) sells or lets for hire, or offers or exposes for sale or hire, or

(c) in the course of a business exhibits in public or distributes, or

(d) distributes otherwise than in the course of a business so as to affect prejudicially the honour or reputation of the author or director,

an article which is, and which he knows or has reason to believe is, an infringing article.

(2) An 'infringing article' means a work or a copy of a work which—

(a)   has been subjected to derogatory treatment within the meaning of section 80, and

(b)   has been or is likely to be the subject of any of the acts mentioned in that section in circumstances infringing that right.

*False attribution of work*

*False attribution of work*
**84.**—(1)   A person has the right in the circumstances mentioned in this section—

(a)   not to have a literary, dramatic, musical or artistic work falsely attributed to him as author, and

(b)   not to have a film falsely attributed to him as director;

and in this section an 'attribution', in relation to such a work, means a statement (express or implied) as to who is the author or director.

(2)   The right is infringed by a person who—

(a)   issues to the public copies of a work of any of those descriptions in or on which there is a false attribution, or

(b)   exhibits in public an artistic work, or a copy of an artistic work, in or on which there is a false attribution.

(3)   The right is also infringed by a person who—

(a)   in the case of a literary, dramatic or musical work, performs the work in public, broadcasts it or includes it in a cable programme service as being the work of a person, or

(b)   in the case of a film, shows it in public, broadcasts it or includes it in a cable programme service as being directed by a person,

knowing or having reason to believe that the attribution is false.

(4)   The right is also infringed by the issue to the public or public display of material containing a false attribution in connection with any of the acts mentioned in subsection (2) and (3).

(5)   The right is also infringed by a person who in the course of a business—

(a)   possesses or deals with a copy of a work of any of the descriptions mentioned in subsection (1) in or on which there is a false attribution, or

(b)   in the case of an artistic work, possesses or deals with the work itself when there is a false attribution in or on it,

knowing or having reason to believe that there is such an attribution and that it is false.

(6)   In the case of an artistic work the right is also infringed by a person who in the course of a business—

(a)   deals with a work which has been altered after the author parted with possession of it as being the unaltered work of the author, or

(b)   deals with a copy of such a work as being a copy of the unaltered work of the author,

knowing or having reason to believe that that is not the case.

(7)　References in this section to dealing are to selling or letting for hire, offering or exposing for sale or hire, exhibiting in public, or distributing.

(8)　This section applies where, contrary to the fact—

(a)　a literary, dramatic or musical work is falsely represented as being an adaptation of the work of a person, or

(b)　a copy of an artistic work is falsely represented as being a copy made by the author of the artistic work,

as it applies where the work is falsely attributed to a person as author.

*Right to privacy of certain photographs and films*

### Right to privacy of certain photographs and films

**85.**—(1)　A person who for private and domestic purposes commissions the taking of a photograph or the making of a film has, where copyright subsists in the resulting work, the right not to have—

(a)　copies of the work issued to the public,

(b)　the work exhibited or shown in public, or

(c)　the work broadcast or included in a cable programme service;

and, except as mentioned in subsection (2), a person who does or authorises the doing of any of those acts infringes that right.

(2)　The right is not infringed by an act which by virtue of any of the following provisions would not infringe copyright in the work—

(a)　section 31 (incidental inclusion of work in an artistic work, film, broadcast or cable programme);

(b)　section 45 (parliamentary and judicial proceedings);

(c)　section 46 (royal commissions and statutory inquiries);

(d)　section 50 (acts done under statutory authority);

(e)　section 57 (anonymous or pseudonymous works: acts permitted on assumptions as to expiry of copyright or death of author).

*Supplementary*

### Duration of rights

**86.**—(1)　The rights conferred by section 77 (right to be identified as author or director), section 80 (right to object to derogatory treatment of work) and section 85 (right to privacy of certain photographs and films) continue to subsist so long as copyright subsists in the work.

(2)　The right conferred by section 84 (false attribution) continues to subsist until 20 years after a person's death.

### Consent and waiver of rights

**87.**—(1)　It is not an infringement of any of the rights conferred by this Chapter to do any act to which the person entitled to the right has consented.

(2)　Any of those rights may be waived by instrument in writing signed by the person giving up the right.

(3)　A waiver—

(a)　may relate to a specific work, to works of a specified description or to works generally, and may relate to existing or future works, and

(b) may be conditional or unconditional and may be expressed to be subject to revocation;

and if made in favour of the owner or prospective owner of the copyright in the work or works to which it relates, it shall be presumed to extend to his licensees and successors in title unless a contrary intention is expressed.

(4) Nothing in this Chapter shall be construed as excluding the operation of the general law of contract or estoppel in relation to an informal waiver or other transaction in relation to any of the rights mentioned in subsection (1).

*Application of provisions to joint works*
**88.**—(1) The right conferred by section 77 (right to be identified as author or director) is, in the case of a work of joint authorship, a right of each joint author to be identified as a joint author and must be asserted in accordance with section 78 by each joint author in relation to himself.

(2) The right conferred by section 80 (right to object to derogatory treatment of work) is, in the case of a work of joint authorship, a right of each joint author and his right is satisfied if he consents to the treatment in question.

(3) A waiver under section 87 of those rights by one joint author does not affect the rights of the other joint authors.

(4) The right conferred by section 84 (false attribution) is infringed, in the circumstances mentioned in that section—

(a) by any false statement as to the authorship of a work of joint authorship, and

(b) by the false attribution of joint authorship in relation to a work of sole authorship;

and such a false attribution infringes the right of every person to whom authorship of any description is, whether rightly or wrongly, attributed.

(5) The above provisions also apply (with any necessary adaptations) in relation to a film which was, or is alleged to have been, jointly directed, as they apply to a work which is, or is alleged to be, a work of joint authorship.

A film is 'jointly directed' if it is made by the collaboration of two or more directors and the contribution of each director is not distinct from that of the other director or directors.

(6) The right conferred by section 85 (right to privacy of certain photographs and films) is, in the case of a work made in pursuance of a joint commission, a right of each person who commissioned the making of the work, so that—

(a) the right of each is satisfied if he consents to the act in question, and

(b) a waiver under section 87 by one of them does not affect the rights of the others.

*Application of provisions to parts of works*
**89.**—(1) The rights conferred by section 77 (right to be identified as author or director) and section 85 (right to privacy of certain photographs and films) apply in relation to the whole or any substantial part of a work.

(2) The rights conferred by section 80 (right to object to derogatory

treatment of work) and section 84 (false attribution) apply in relation to the whole or any part of a work.

### Chapter V Dealings with rights in copyright works

### Copyright

#### Assignment and licences

**90.**—(1)   Copyright is transmissible by assignment, by testamentary disposition or by operation of law, as personal or movable property.

(2)   An assignment or other transmission of copyright may be partial, that is, limited so as to apply—

(a)   to one or more, but not all, of the things the copyright owner has the exclusive right to do;

(b)   to part, but not the whole, of the period for which the copyright is to subsist.

(3)   An assignment of copyright is not effective unless it is in writing signed by or on behalf of the assignor.

(4)   A licence granted by a copyright owner is binding on every successor in title to his interest in the copyright, except—

(a)   a purchaser in good faith for valuable consideration and without notice (actual or constructive) of the licence, or

(b)   a person deriving title from such a purchaser;

and references in this Part to doing anything with, or without, the licence of the copyright owner shall be construed accordingly.

#### Prospective ownership of copyright

**91.**—(1)   Where by an agreement made in relation to future copyright, and signed by or on behalf of the prospective owner of the copyright, the prospective owner purports to assign the future copyright (wholly or partially) to another person, then if, on the copyright coming into existence, the assignee or another person claiming under him would be entitled as against all other persons to require the copyright to be vested in him, the copyright shall vest in the assignee or his successor in title by virtue of this subsection.

(2)   In this Part—

'future copyright' means copyright which will or may come into existence in respect of a future work or class of works or on the occurrence of a future event; and

'prospective owner' shall be construed accordingly, and includes a person who is prospectively entitled to copyright by virtue of such an agreement as is mentioned in subsection (1).

(3)   A licence granted by a prospective owner of copyright is binding on every successor in title to his interest (or prospective interest) in the right, except a purchaser in good faith for valuable consideration and without notice (actual or constructive) of the licence or a person deriving title from such a purchaser; and

references in this Part to doing anything with, or without, the licence of the copyright owner shall be construed accordingly.

*Exclusive licences*
**92.**—(1)  In this Part an 'exclusive licence' means a licence in writing signed by or on behalf of the copyright owner authorising the licensee to the exclusion of all other persons, including the person granting the licence, to exercise a right which would otherwise be exercisable exclusively by the copyright owner.

(2)  The licensee under an exclusive licence has the same rights against a successor in title who is bound by the licence as he has against the person granting the licence.

*Copyright to pass under will with unpublished work*
**93.**  Where under a bequest (whether specific or general) a person is entitled, beneficially or otherwise, to

(a)  an original document or other material thing recording or embodying a literary, dramatic, musical or artistic work which was not published before the death of the testator, or

(b)  an original material thing containing a sound recording or film which was not published before the death of the testator,

the bequest shall, unless a contrary intention is indicated in the testator's will or a codicil to it, be construed as including the copyright in the work in so far as the testator was the owner of the copyright immediately before his death.

### Moral rights

*Moral rights not assignable*
**94.**  The rights conferred by Chapter IV (moral rights) are not assignable.

*Transmission of moral rights on death*
**95.**—(1)  On the death of a person entitled to the right conferred by section 77 (right to identification of author or director), section 80 (right to object to derogatory treatment of work) or section 85 (right to privacy of certain photographs and films)—

(a)  the right passes to such person as he may by testamentary disposition specifically direct,

(b)  if there is no such direction but the copyright in the work in question forms part of his estate, the right passes to the person to whom the copyright passes, and

(c)  if or to the extent that the right does not pass under paragraph (a) or (b) it is exercisable by his personal representatives.

(2)  Where copyright forming part of a person's estate passes in part to one person and in part to another, as for example, where a bequest is limited so as to apply—

(a)  to one or more, but not all, of the things the copyright owner has the exclusive right to do or authorise, or

(b)  to part, but not the whole, of the period for which the copyright is to subsist, any right which passes with the copyright by virtue of subsection (1) is correspondingly divided.

(3) Where by virtue of subsection (1)(a) or (b) a right becomes exercisable by more than one person—

(a) it may, in the case of the right conferred by section 77 (right to identification of author or director), be asserted by any of them;

(b) it is, in the case of the right conferred by section 80 (right to object to derogatory treatment of work) or section 85 (right to privacy of certain photographs and films), a right exercisable by each of them and is satisfied in relation to any of them if he consents to the treatment or act in question; and

(c) any waiver of the right in accordance with section 87 by one of them does not affect the rights of the others.

(4) A consent or waiver previously given or made binds any person to whom a right passes by virtue of subsection (1).

(5) Any infringement after a person's death of the right conferred by section 84 (false attribution) is actionable by his personal representatives.

(6) Any damages recovered by personal representatives by virtue of this section in respect of an infringement after a person's death shall devolve as part of his estate as if the right of action had subsisted and been vested in him immediately before his death.

### Chapter VI Remedies for infringement

#### Rights and remedies of copyright owner

*Infringement actionable by copyright owner*
**96.**—(1) An infringement of copyright is actionable by the copyright owner.

(2) In an action for infringement of copyright all such relief by way of damages, injunctions, accounts or otherwise is available to the plaintiff as is available in respect of the infringement of any other property right.

(3) This section has effect subject to the following provisions of this Chapter.

*Provisions as to damages in infringement action*
**97.**—(1) Where in an action for infringement of copyright it is shown that at the time of the infringement the defendant did not know, and had no reason to believe, that copyright subsisted in the work to which the action relates, the plaintiff is not entitled to damages against him, but without prejudice to any other remedy.

(2) The court may in an action for infringement of copyright having regard to all the circumstances, and in particular to—

(a) the flagrancy of the infringement, and

(b) any benefit accruing to the defendant by reason of the infringement,

award such additional damages as the justice of the case may require.

*Undertaking to take licence of right in infringement proceedings*
**98.**—(1) If in proceedings for infringement of copyright in respect of which a licence is available as of right under section 144 (powers exercisable in

consequence of report of Monopolies and Mergers Commission) the defendant undertakes to take a licence on such terms as may be agreed or, in default of agreement, settled by the Copyright Tribunal under that section—

(a)   no injunction shall be granted against him,

(b)   no order for delivery up shall be made under section 94, and

(c)   the amount recoverable against him by way of damages or on an account of profits shall not exceed double the amount which would have been payable by him as licensee if such a licence on those terms had been granted before the earliest infringement.

(2)   An undertaking may be given at any time before final order in the proceedings, without any admission of liability.

(3)   Nothing in this section affects the remedies available in respect of an infringement committed before licences of right were available.

*Order for delivery up*
**99.**—(1)   Where a person—

(a)   has an infringing copy of a work in his possession, custody or control in the course of a business, or

(b)   has in his possession, custody or control an article specifically designed or adapted for making copies of a particular copyright work, knowing or having reason to believe that it has been or is to be used to make infringing copies,

the owner of the copyright in the work may apply to the court for an order that the infringing copy or article be delivered up to him or such other person as the court may direct.

(2)   An application shall not be made after the end of the period specified in section 113 (period after which remedy of delivery up not available); and no order shall be made unless the court also makes, or it appears to the court that there are grounds for making, an order under section 114 (order as to disposal of infringing copy or other article).

(3)   A person to whom an infringing copy or other article is delivered up in pursuance of an order under this section shall, if an order under section 114 is not made, retain it pending the making of an order, or the decision not to make an order, under that section.

(4)   Nothing in this section affects any other power of the court.

*Right to seize infringing copies and other articles*
**100.**—(1)   An infringing copy of a work which is found exposed or otherwise immediately available for sale or hire, and in respect of which the copyright owner would be entitled to apply for an order under section 99, may be seized and detained by him or a person authorised by him.

The right to seize and detain is exercisable subject to the following conditions and is subject to any decision of the court under section 114.

(2)   Before anything is seized under this section notice of the time and place of the proposed seizure must be given to a local police station.

(3)   A person may for the purpose of exercising the right conferred by this section enter premises to which the public have access but may not seize anything in the possession, custody or control of a person at a permanent or regular place

of business of his, and may not use any force.

(4)   At the time when anything is seized under this section there shall be left at the place where it was seized a notice in the prescribed form containing the prescribed particulars as to the person by whom or on whose authority the seizure is made and the grounds on which it is made.

(5)   In this section—

'premises' includes land, buildings, movable structures, vehicles, vessels, aircraft and hovercraft; and

'prescribed' means prescribed by order of the Secretary of State.

(7)   An order of the Secretary of State under this section shall be made by statutory instrument which shall be subject to annulment in pursuance of a resolution of either House of Parliament.

### Rights and remedies of exclusive licensee

*Rights and remedies of exclusive licensee*

**101.**—(1)   An exclusive licensee has, except against the copyright owner, the same rights and remedies in respect of matters occurring after the grant of the licence as if the licence had been an assignment.

(2)   His rights and remedies are concurrent with those of the copyright owner; and references in the relevant provisions of this Part to the copyright owner shall be construed accordingly.

(3)   In an action brought by an exclusive licensee by virtue of this section a defendant may avail himself of any defence which would have been available to him if the action had been brought by the copyright owner.

*Exercise of concurrent rights*

**102.**—(1)   Where an action for infringement of copyright brought by the copyright owner or an exclusive licensee relates (wholly or partly) to an infringement in respect of which they have concurrent rights of action, the copyright owner or, as the case may be, the exclusive licensee may not, without the leave of the court, proceed with the action unless the other is either joined as a plaintiff or added as a defendant.

(2)   A copyright owner or exclusive licensee who is added as a defendant in pursuance of subsection (1) is not liable for any costs in the action unless he takes part in the proceedings.

(3)   The above provisions do not affect the granting of interlocutory relief on an application by a copyright owner or exclusive licensee alone.

(4)   Where an action for infringement of copyright is brought which relates (wholly or partly) to an infringement in respect of which the copyright owner and an exclusive licensee have or had concurrent rights of action—

(a)   the court shall in assessing damages take into account—

(i)   the terms of the licence, and
(ii)   any pecuniary remedy already awarded or available to either of them in respect of the infringement;

(b)   no account of profits shall be directed if an award of damages has been made, or an account of profits has been directed, in favour of the other of them in respect of the infringement; and

(c)   the court shall if an account of profits is directed apportion the profits between them as the court considers just, subject to any agreement between them;

and these provisions apply whether or not the copyright owner and the exclusive licensee are both parties to the action.

(5)   The copyright owner shall notify any exclusive licensee having concurrent rights before applying for an order under section 99 (order for delivery up) or exercising the right conferred by section 100 (right of seizure); and the court may on the application of the licensee make such order under section 99 or, as the case may be, prohibiting or permitting the exercise by the copyright owner of the right conferred by section 100, as it thinks fit having regard to the terms of the licence.

## *Remedies for infringement of moral rights*

### *Remedies for infringement of moral rights*

**103.**—(1)   An infringement of a right conferred by Chapter IV (moral rights) is actionable as a breach of statutory duty owed to the person entitled to the right.

(2)   In proceedings for infringement of the right conferred by section 80 (right to object to derogatory treatment of work) the court may, if it thinks it is an adequate remedy in the circumstances, grant an injunction on terms prohibiting the doing of any act unless a disclaimer is made, in such terms and in such manner as may be approved by the court, dissociating the author or director from the treatment of the work.

## *Presumptions*

### *Presumptions relevant to literary, dramatic, musical and artistic works*

**104.**—(1)   The following presumptions apply in proceedings brought by virtue of this Chapter with respect to a literary, dramatic, musical or artistic work.

(2)   Where a name purporting to be that of the author appeared on copies of the work as published or on the work when it was made, the person whose name appeared shall be presumed, until the contrary is proved—

(a)   to be the author of the work;

(b)   to have made it in circumstances not falling within section 11(2), 163, 165 or 168 (works produced in course of employment, Crown copyright, Parliamentary copyright or copyright of certain international organisations).

(3)   In the case of a work alleged to be a work of joint authorship, subsection (2) applies in relation to each person alleged to be one of the authors.

(4)   Where no name purporting to be that of the author appeared as mentioned in subsection (2) but—

(a)   the work qualifies for copyright protection by virtue of section 155 (qualification by reference to country of first publication), and

(b)   a name purporting to be that of the publisher appeared on copies of the work as first published,

the person whose name appeared shall be presumed, until the contrary is proved, to have been the owner of the copyright at the time of publication.

(5)  If the author of the work is dead or the identity of the author cannot be ascertained by reasonable inquiry, it shall be presumed, in the absence of evidence to the contrary—

    (a)  that the work is an original work, and
    (b)  that the plaintiff's allegations as to what was the first publication of the work and as to the country of first publication are correct.

*Presumptions relevant to sound recordings and films*
**105.**—(1)  In proceedings brought by virtue of this Chapter with respect to a sound recording, where copies of the recording as issued to the public bear a label or other mark stating—

    (a)  that a named person was the owner of copyright in the recording at the date of issue of the copies, or
    (b)  that the recording was first published in a specified year or in a specified country,

the label or mark shall be admissible as evidence of the facts stated and shall be presumed to be correct until the contrary is proved.

(2)  In proceedings brought by virtue of this Chapter with respect to a film, where copies of the film as issued to the public bear a statement—

    (a)  that a named person was the author or director of the film,
    (b)  that a named person was the owner of copyright in the film at the date of issue of the copies, or
    (c)  that the film was first published in a specified year or in a specified country,

the statement shall be admissible as evidence of the facts stated and shall be presumed to be correct until the contrary is proved.

(3)  In proceedings brought by virtue of this Chapter with respect to a computer program, where copies of the program are issued to the public in electronic form bearing a statement—

    (a)  that a named person was the owner of copyright in the program at the date of issue of the copies, or
    (b)  that the program was first published in a specified country or that copies of it were first issued to the public in electronic form in a specified year,

the statement shall be admissible as evidence of the facts stated and shall be presumed to be correct until the contrary is proved.

(4)  The above presumptions apply equally in proceedings relating to an infringement alleged to have occurred before the date on which the copies were issued to the public.

(5)  In proceedings brought by virtue of this Chapter with respect to a film, where the film as shown in public, broadcast or included in a cable programme service bears a statement—

    (a)  that a named person was the author or director of the film, or
    (b)  that a named person was the owner of copyright in the film immediately after it was made,

the statement shall be admissible as evidence of the facts stated and shall be presumed to be correct until the contrary is proved.

This presumption applies equally in proceedings relating to an infringement alleged to have occurred before the date on which the film was shown in public, broadcast or included in a cable programme service.

*Presumptions relevant to works subject to Crown copyright*
**106.**   In proceedings brought by virtue of this Chapter with respect to a literary, dramatic or musical work in which Crown copyright subsists, where there appears on printed copies of the work a statement of the year in which the work was first published commercially, that statement shall be admissible as evidence of the fact stated and shall be presumed to be correct in the absence of evidence to the contrary.

## *Offences*

*Criminal liability for making or dealing with infringing articles etc.*
**107.**—(1)   A person commits an offence who, without the licence of the copyright owner—

  (a)   makes for sale or hire, or
  (b)   imports into the United Kingdom otherwise than for his private and domestic use, or
  (c)   possesses in the course of a business with a view to committing any act infringing the copyright, or
  (d)   in the course of a business—

     (i)   sells or lets for hire, or
     (ii)   offers or exposes for sale or hire, or
     (iii)   exhibits in public, or
     (iv)   distributes, or

  (e)   distributes otherwise than in the course of a business to such an extent as to affect prejudicially the owner of the copyright,

an article which is, and which he knows or has reason to believe is, an infringing copy of a copyright work.

  (2)   A person commits an offence who—

  (a)   makes an article specifically designed or adapted for making copies of a particular copyright work, or
  (b)   has such an article in his possession,

knowing or having reason to believe that it is to be used to make infringing copies for sale or hire or for use in the course of a business.

  (3)   Where copyright is infringed (otherwise than by reception of a broadcast or cable programme)—

  (a)   by the public performance of a literary, dramatic or musical work, or
  (b)   by the playing or showing in public of a sound recording or film,

any person who caused the work to be so performed, played or shown is guilty of an offence if he knew or had reason to believe that copyright would be infringed.

(4)   A person guilty of an offence under subsection (1)(a), (b), (d)(iv) or (e) is liable—

(a)   on summary conviction to imprisonment for a term not exceeding six months or a fine not exceeding the statutory maximum, or both;
(b)   on conviction on indictment to a fine or imprisonment for a term not exceeding two years, or both.

(5)   A person guilty of any other offence under this section is liable on summary conviction to imprisonment for a term not exceeding six months or a fine not exceeding level 5 on the standard scale, or both.

(6)   Sections 104 to 106 (presumptions as to various matters connected with copyright) do not apply to proceedings for an offence under this section; but without prejudice to their application in proceedings for an order under section 108 below.

*Order for delivery up in criminal proceedings*
**108.**—(1)   The court before which proceedings are brought against a person for an offence under section 107 may, if satisfied that at the time of his arrest or charge—

(a)   he had in his possession, custody or control in the course of a business an infringing copy of a copyright work, or
(b)   he had in his possession, custody or control an article specifically designed or adapted for making copies of a particular copyright work, knowing or having reason to believe that it had been or was to be used to make infringing copies,

order that the infringing copy or article be delivered up to the copyright owner or to such other person as the court may direct.

(2)   For this purpose a person shall be treated as charged with an offence—

(a)   in England, Wales and Northern Ireland, when he is orally charged or is served with a summons or indictment;
(b)   in Scotland, when he is cautioned, charged or served with a complaint or indictment.

(3)   An order may be made by the court of its own motion or on the application of the prosecutor (or, in Scotland, the Lord Advocate or procurator-fiscal), and may be made whether or not the person is convicted of the offence, but shall not be made—

(a)   after the end of the period specified in section 113 (period after which remedy of delivery up not available), or
(b)   if it appears to the court unlikely that any order will be made under section 114 (order as to disposal of infringing copy or other article).

(4)   An appeal lies from an order made under this section by a magistrates' court—

(a)   in England and Wales, to the Crown Court, and
(b)   in Northern Ireland, to the county court;

and in Scotland, where an order has been made under this section, the person from whose possession, custody or control the infringing copy or article has been removed may, without prejudice to any other form of appeal under any rule of law, appeal against that order in the same manner as against sentence.

(5)  A person to whom an infringing copy or other article is delivered up in pursuance of an order under this section shall retain it pending the making of an order, or the decision not to make an order, under section 114.

(6)  Nothing in this section affects the powers of the court under section 43 of the Powers of Criminal Courts Act 1973, section 223 or 436 of the Criminal Procedure (Scotland) Act 1975 or Article 7 of the Criminal Justice (Northern Ireland) Order 1980 (general provisions as to forfeiture in criminal proceedings).

*Search warrants*

**109.**—(1)  Where a justice of the peace (in Scotland, a sheriff or justice of the peace) is satisfied by information on oath given by a constable (in Scotland, by evidence on oath) that there are reasonable grounds for believing—

(a)  that an offence under section 107(1)(a), (b), (d)(iv) or (e) has been or is about to be committed in any premises, and

(b)  that evidence that such an offence has been or is about to be committed is in those premises,

he may issue a warrant authorising a constable to enter and search the premises, using such reasonable force as is necessary.

(2)  The power conferred by subsection (1) does not, in England and Wales, extend to authorising a search for material of the kinds mentioned in section 9(2) of the Police and Criminal Evidence Act 1984 (certain classes of personal or confidential material).

(3)  A warrant under this section—

(a)  may authorise persons to accompany any constable executing the warrant, and

(b)  remains in force for 28 days from the date of its issue.

(4)  In executing a warrant issued under this section a constable may seize an article if he reasonably believes that it is evidence that any offence under section 107(1) has been or is about to be committed.

(5)  In this section 'premises' includes land, buildings, moveable structures, vehicles, vessels, aircraft and hovercraft.

*Offence by body corporate: liability of officers*

**110.**—(1)  Where an offence under section 107 committed by a body corporate is proved to have been committed with the consent or connivance of a director, manager, secretary or other similar officer of the body, or a person purporting to act in any such capacity, he as well as the body corporate is guilty of the offence and liable to be proceeded against and punished accordingly.

(2)  In relation to a body corporate whose affairs are managed by its members 'director' means a member of the body corporate.

*Provision for preventing importation of infringing copies*

*Infringing copies may be treated as prohibited goods*

**111.**—(1)  The owner of the copyright in a published literary, dramatic or musical work may give notice in writing to the Commissioners of Customs and Excise—

(a)    that he is the owner of the copyright in the work, and

(b)    that he requests the Commissioners, for a period specified in the notice, to treat as prohibited goods printed copies of the work which are infringing copies.

(2)    The period specified in a notice under subsection (1) shall not exceed five years and shall not extend beyond the period for which copyright is to subsist.

(3)    The owner of the copyright in a sound recording or film may give notice in writing to the Commissioners of Customs and Excise—

(a)    that he is the owner of the copyright in the work,

(b)    that infringing copies of the work are expected to arrive in the United Kingdom at a time and a place specified in the notice, and

(c)    that he requests the Commissioners to treat the copies as prohibited goods.

(4)    When a notice is in force under this section the importation of goods to which the notice relates, otherwise than by a person for his private and domestic use, is prohibited; but a person is not by reason of the prohibition liable to any penalty other than forfeiture of the goods.

*Power of Commissioners of Customs and Excise to make regulations*

**112.**—(1)    The Commissioners of Customs and Excise may make regulations prescribing the form in which notice is to be given under section 111 and requiring a person giving notice—

(a)    to furnish the Commissioners with such evidence as may be specified in the regulations, either on giving notice or when the goods are imported, or at both those times, and

(b)    to comply with such other conditions as may be specified in the regulations.

(2)    The regulations may, in particular, require a person giving such a notice—

(a)    to pay such fees in respect of the notice as may be specified by the regulations;

(b)    to give such security as may be so specified in respect of any liability or expense which the Commissioners may incur in consequence of the notice by reason of the detention of any article or anything done to an article detained;

(c)    to indemnify the Commissioners against any such liability or expense, whether security has been given or not.

(3)    The regulations may make different provision as respects different classes of case to which they apply and may include such incidental and supplementary provisions as the Commissioners consider expedient.

(4)    Regulations under this section shall be made by statutory instrument which shall be subject to annulment in pursuance of a resolution of either House of Parliament.

(5)   Section 17 of the Customs and Excise Management Act 1979 (general provisions as to Commissioners' receipts) applies to fees paid in pursuance of regulations under this section as to receipts under the enactments relating to customs and excise.

*Supplementary*

*Period after which remedy of delivery up not available*
**113.**—(1)   An application for an order under section 99 (order for delivery up in civil proceedings) may not be made after the end of the period of six years from the date on which the infringing copy or article in question was made, subject to the following provisions.
(2)   If during the whole or any part of that period the copyright owner—

(a)   is under a disability, or
(b)   is prevented by fraud or concealment from discovering the facts entitling him to apply for an order,

an application may be made at any time before the end of the period of six years from the date on which he ceased to be under a disability or, as the case may be, could with reasonable diligence have discovered those facts.
(3)   In subsection (2) 'disability'—

(a)   in England and Wales, has the same meaning as in the Limitation Act 1980;
(b)   in Scotland, means legal disability within the meaning of the Prescription and Limitation (Scotland) Act 1973;
(c)   in Northern Ireland, has the same meaning as in the Statute of Limitations (Northern Ireland) 1958.

(4)   An order under section 108 (order for delivery up in criminal proceedings) shall not, in any case, be made after the end of the period of six years from the date on which the infringing copy or article in question was made.

*Order as to disposal of infringing copy or other article*
**114.**—(1)   An application may be made to the court for an order that an infringing copy or other article delivered up in pursuance of an order under section 99 or 108, or seized and detained in pursuance of the right conferred by section 100, shall be)—

(a)   forfeited to the copyright owner, or
(b)   destroyed or otherwise dealt with as the court may think fit,

or for a decision that no such order should be made.
(2)   In considering what order (if any) should be made, the court shall consider whether other remedies available in an action for infringement of copyright would be adequate to compensate the copyright owner and to protect his interests.
(3)   Provision shall be made by rules of court as to the service of notice on

persons having an interest in the copy or other article, and any such person is entitled—

    (a)  to appear in proceedings for an order under this section, whether or not he was served with notice, and

    (b)  to appeal against any order made, whether or not he appeared;

and an order shall not take effect until the end of the period within which notice of an appeal may be given or, if before the end of that period notice of appeal is duly given, until the final determination or abandonment of the proceedings on the appeal.

    (4)  Where there is more than one person interested in a copy or other article, the court shall make such order as it thinks just and may (in particular) direct that the article be sold, or otherwise dealt with, and the proceeds divided.

    (5)  If the court decides that no order should be made under this section, the person in whose possession, custody or control the copy or other article was before being delivered up or seized is entitled to its return.

    (6)  References in this section to a person having an interest in a copy or other article include any person in whose favour an order could be made in respect of it under this section or under section 204 or 231 of this Act or section 58C of the Trade Marks Act 1938 (which make similar provision in relation to infringement of rights in performances, design right and trade marks).

*Jurisdiction of county court and sheriff court*
**115.**—(1)  In England, Wales and Northern Ireland a county court may entertain proceedings under—

    section 99 (order for delivery up of infringing copy or other article),

    section 102(5) (order as to exercise of rights by copyright owner where exclusive licensee has concurrent rights), or

    section 114 (order as to disposal of infringing copy or other article),

where the value of the infringing copies and other articles in question does not exceed the county court limit for actions in tort.

    (2)  In Scotland proceedings for an order under any of those provisions may be brought in the sheriff court.

    (3)  Nothing in this section shall be construed as affecting the jurisdiction of the High Court or, in Scotland, the Court of Session.

## Chapter VII Copyright licensing

### Licensing schemes and licensing bodies

*Licensing schemes and licensing bodies*
**116.**—(1)  In this Part a 'licensing scheme' means a scheme setting out—

    (a)  the classes of case in which the operator of the scheme, or the person on whose behalf he acts, is willing to grant copyright licences, and

    (b)  the terms on which licences would be granted in those classes of case;

and for this purpose a 'scheme' includes anything in the nature of a scheme, whether described as a scheme or as a tariff or by any other name.

(2)   In this Chapter a 'licensing body' means a society or other organisation which has as its main object, or one of its main objects, the negotiation or granting, either as owner or prospective owner of copyright or as agent for him, of copyright licences, and whose objects include the granting of licences covering works of more than one author.

(3)   In this section 'copyright licences' means licences to do, or authorise the doing of, any of the acts restricted by copyright.

(4)   References in this Chapter to licences or licensing schemes covering works of more than one author do not include licences or schemes covering only—

(a)   a single collective work or collective works of which the authors are the same, or

(b)   works made by, or by employees of, or commissioned by, a single individual, firm, company or group of companies.

For this purpose a group of companies means a holding company and its subsidiaries, within the meaning of section 736 of the Companies Act 1985.

*References and applications with respect to licensing schemes*

*Licensing schemes to which ss. 118 to 123 apply*

**117.**   Sections 118 to 123 (references and applications with respect to licensing schemes) apply to—

(a)   licensing schemes operated by licensing bodies in relation to the copyright in literary, dramatic, musical or artistic works or films (or film sound-tracks when accompanying a film) which cover works of more than one author, so far as they relate to licences for—

(i)   copying the work,

(ii)   performing, playing or showing the work in public, or

(iii)   broadcasting the work or including it in a cable programme service;

(b)   all licensing schemes in relation to the copyright in sound recordings (other than film sound-tracks when accompanying a film), broadcasts or cable programmes, or the typographical arrangement of published editions; and

(c)   all licensing schemes in relation to the copyright in sound recordings, films or computer programs so far as they relate to licences for the rental of copies to the public;

and in those sections 'licensing scheme' means a licensing scheme of any of those descriptions.

*Reference of proposed licensing scheme to tribunal*

**118.**—(1)   The terms of a licensing scheme proposed to be operated by a licensing body may be referred to the Copyright Tribunal by an organisation claiming to be representative of persons claiming that they require licences in cases of a description to which the scheme would apply, either generally or in relation to any description of case.

(2)   The Tribunal shall first decide whether to entertain the reference, and may decline to do so on the ground that the reference is premature.

(3)   If the Tribunal decides to entertain the reference it shall consider the matter referred and make such order, either confirming or varying the proposed scheme, either generally or so far as it relates to cases of the description to which the reference relates, as the Tribunal may determine to be reasonable in the circumstances.

(4)   The order may be made so as to be in force indefinitely or for such period as the Tribunal may determine.

*Reference of licensing scheme to tribunal*

**119.**—(1)   If while a licensing scheme is in operation a dispute arises between the operator of the scheme and—

(a)   a person claiming that he requires a licence in a case of a description to which the scheme applies, or

(b)   an organisation claiming to be representative of such persons,

that person or organisation may refer the scheme to the Copyright Tribunal in so far as it relates to cases of that description.

(2)   A scheme which has been referred to the Tribunal under this section shall remain in operation until proceedings on the reference are concluded.

(3)   The Tribunal shall consider the matter in dispute and make such order, either confirming or varying the scheme so far as it relates to cases of the description to which the reference relates, as the Tribunal may determine to be reasonable in the circumstances.

(4)   The order may be made so as to be in force indefinitely or for such period as the Tribunal may determine.

*Further reference of scheme to tribunal*

**120.**—(1)   Where the Copyright Tribunal has on a previous reference of a licensing scheme under section 118 or 119, or under this section, made an order with respect to the scheme, then, while the order remains in force—

(a)   the operator of the scheme,

(b)   a person claiming that he requires a licence in a case of the description to which the order applies, or

(c)   an organisation claiming to be representative of such persons,

may refer the scheme again to the Tribunal so far as it relates to cases of that description.

(2)   A licensing scheme shall not, except with the special leave of the Tribunal, be referred again to the Tribunal in respect of the same description of cases—

(a)   within 12 months from the date of the order on the previous reference, or

(b)   if the order was made so as to be in force for 15 months or less, until the last three months before the expiry of the order.

(3)   A scheme which has been referred to the Tribunal under this section shall remain in operation until proceedings on the reference are concluded.

(4)   The Tribunal shall consider the matter in dispute and make such order, either confirming, varying or further varying the scheme so far as it relates to

cases of the description to which the reference relates, as the Tribunal may determine to be reasonable in the circumstances.

(5)   The order may be made so as to be in force indefinitely or for such period as the Tribunal may determine.

*Application for grant of licence in connection with licensing scheme*
**121.**—(1)   A person who claims, in a case covered by a licensing scheme, that the operator of the scheme has refused to grant him or procure the grant to him of a licence in accordance with the scheme, or has failed to do so within a reasonable time after being asked, may apply to the Copyright Tribunal.

(2)   A person who claims, in a case excluded from a licensing scheme, that the operator of the scheme either—

(a)   has refused to grant him a licence or procure the grant to him of a licence, or has failed to do so within a reasonable time of being asked, and that in the circumstances it is unreasonable that a licence should not be granted, or
(b)   proposes terms for a licence which are unreasonable,

may apply to the Copyright Tribunal.

(3)   A case shall be regarded as excluded from a licensing scheme for the purposes of subsection (2) if—

(a)   the scheme provides for the grant of licences subject to terms excepting matters from the licence and the case falls within such an exception, or
(b)   the case is so similar to those in which licences are granted under the scheme that it is unreasonble that it should not be dealt with in the same way.

(4)   If the Tribunal is satisfied that the claim is well-founded, it shall make an order declaring that, in respect of the matters specified in the order, the applicant is entitled to a licence on such terms as the Tribunal may determine to be applicable in accordance with the scheme or, as the case may be, to be reasonable in the circumstances.

(5)   The order may be made so as to be in force indefinitely or for such period as the Tribunal may determine.

*Application for review of order as to entitlement to licence*
**122.**—(1)   Where the Copyright Tribunal has made an order under section 115 that a person is entitled to a licence under a licensing scheme, the operator of the scheme or the original applicant may apply to the Tribunal to review its order.

(2)   An application shall not be made, except with the special leave of the Tribunal—

(a)   within 12 months from the date of the order or of the decision on a previous application under this section, or
(b)   if the order was made so as to be in force for 15 months or less, or as a result of the decision on a previous application under this section is due to expire within 15 months of that decision, until the last three months before the expiry date.

(3)   The Tribunal shall on an application for review confirm or vary its order as the Tribunal may determine to be reasonable having regard to the terms

applicable in accordance with the licensing scheme or, as the case may be, the circumstances of the case.

*Effect of order of tribunal as to licensing scheme*

**123.**—(1) A licensing scheme which has been confirmed or varied by the Copyright Tribunal—

(a)   under section 118 (reference of terms of proposed scheme), or

(b)   under section 119 or 120 (reference of existing scheme to Tribunal),

shall be in force or, as the case may be, remain in operation, so far as it relates to the description of case in respect of which the order was made, so long as the order remains in force.

(2)   While the order is in force a person who in a case of a class to which the order applies—

(a)   pays to the operator of the scheme any charges payable under the scheme in respect of a licence covering the case in question or, if the amount cannot be ascertained, gives an undertaking to the operator to pay them when ascertained, and

(b)   complies with the other terms applicable to such a licence under the scheme,

shall be in the same position as regards infringement of copyright as if he had at all material times been the holder of a licence granted by the owner of the copyright in question in accordance with the scheme.

(3)   The Tribunal may direct that the order, so far as it varies the amount of charges payable, has effect from a date before that on which it is made, but not earlier than the date on which the reference was made or, if later, on which the scheme came into operation.

If such a direction is made—

(a)   any necessary repayments, or further payments, shall be made in respect of charges already paid, and

(b)   the reference in subsection (2)(a) to the charges payable under the scheme shall be construed as a reference to the charges so payable by virtue of the order.

No such direction may be made where subsection (4) below applies.

(4)   An order of the Tribunal under section 119 or 120 made with respect to a scheme which is certified for any purpose under section 143 has effect, so far as it varies the scheme by reducing the charges payable for licences, from the date on which the reference was made to the Tribunal.

(5)   Where the Tribunal has made an order under section 121 (order as to entitlement to licence under licensing scheme) and the order remains in force, the person in whose favour the order is made shall if he—

(a)   pays to the operator of the scheme any charges payable in accordance with the order or, if the amount cannot be ascertained, gives an undertaking to pay the charges when ascertained, and

(b)   complies with the other terms specified in the order,

be in the same position as regards infringement of copyright as if he had at all material times been the holder of a licence granted by the owner of the copyright in question on the terms specified in the order.

*References and applications with respect to licensing by licensing bodies*

*Licences to which ss. 125 to 128 apply*
**124.**   Sections 125 to 128 (references and applications with respect to licensing by licensing bodies) apply to the following descriptions of licence granted by a licensing body otherwise than in pursuance of a licensing scheme—

(a)   licences relating to the copyright in literary, dramatic, musical or artistic works or films (or film sound-tracks when accompanying a film) which cover works of more than one author, so far as they authorise—

(i)   copying the work,
(ii)   performing, playing or showing the work in public, or
(iii)   broadcasting the work or including it in a cable programme service;

(b)   any licence relating to the copyright in a sound recording (other than a film sound-track when accompanying a film), broadcast or cable programme, or the typographical arrangement of a published edition; and
(c)   all licences in relation to the copyright in sound recordings, films or computer programs so far as they relate to the rental of copies to the public;

and in those sections a 'licence' means a licence of any of those descriptions.

*Reference to tribunal of proposed licence*
**125.**—(1)   The terms on which a licensing body proposes to grant a licence may be referred to the Copyright Tribunal by the prospective licensee.
(2)   The Tribunal shall first decide whether to entertain the reference, and may decline to do so on the ground that the reference is premature.
(3)   If the Tribunal decides to entertain the reference it shall consider the terms of the proposed licence and make such order, either confirming or varying the terms, as it may determine to be reasonable in the circumstances.
(4)   The order may be made so as to be in force indefinitely or for such period as the Tribunal may determine.

*Reference to tribunal of expiring licence*
**126.**—(1)   A licensee under a licence which is due to expire, by effluxion of time or as a result of notice given by the licensing body, may apply to the Copyright Tribunal on the ground that it is unreasonable in the circumstances that the licence should cease to be in force.
(2)   Such an application may not be made until the last three months before the licence is due to expire.
(3)   A licence in respect of which a reference has been made to the Tribunal shall remain in operation until proceedings on the reference are concluded.
(4)   If the Tribunal finds the application well-founded, it shall make an order declaring that the licensee shall continue to be entitled to the benefit of the licence on such terms as the Tribunal may determine to be reasonable in the circumstances.
(5)   An order of the Tribunal under this section may be made so as to be in force indefinitely or for such period as the Tribunal may determine.

*Application for review of order as to licence*
**127.**—(1)   Where the Copyright Tribunal has made an order under section 125 or 126, the licensing body or the person entitled to the benefit of the order may apply to the Tribunal to review its order.

(2)   An application shall not be made, except with the special leave of the Tribunal—

(a)   within 12 months from the date of the order or of the decision on a previous application under this section, or

(b)   if the order was made so as to be in force for 15 months or less, or as a result of the decision on a previous application under this section is due to expire within 15 months of that decision, until the last three months before the expiry date.

(3)   The Tribunal shall on an application for review confirm or vary its order as the Tribunal may determine to be reasonable in the circumstances.

*Effect of order of tribunal as to licence*
**128.**—(1)   Where the Copyright Tribunal has made an order under section 125 or 126 and the order remains in force, the person entitled to the benefit of the order shall if he—

(a)   pays to the licensing body any charges payable in accordance with the order or, if the amount cannot be ascertained, gives an undertaking to pay the charges when ascertained, and

(b)   complies with the other terms specified in the order,

be in the same position as regards infringement of copyright as if he had at all material times been the holder of a licence granted by the owner of the copyright in question on the terms specified in the order.

(2)   The benefit of the order may be assigned—

(a)   in the case of an order under section 125, if assignment is not prohibited under the terms of the Tribunal's order; and

(b)   in the case of an order under section 126, if assignment was not prohibited under the terms of the original licence.

(3)   The Tribunal may direct that an order under section 125 or 126, or an order under section 127 varying such an order, so far as it varies the amount of charges payable, has effect from a date before that on which it is made, but not earlier than the date on which the reference or application was made or, if later, on which the licence was granted or, as the case may be, was due to expire.

If such a direction is made—

(a)   any necessary repayments, or further payments, shall be made in respect of charges already paid, and

(b)   the reference in subsection (1)(a) to the charges payable in accordance with the order shall be construed, where the order is varied by a later order, as a reference to the charges so payable by virtue of the later order.

*Factors to be taken into account in certain classes of case*

*General considerations: unreasonable discrimination*
**129.**   In determining what is reasonable on a reference or application under this

Chapter relating to a licensing scheme or licence, the Copyright Tribunal shall have regard to—

(a)   the availability of other schemes, or the granting of other licences, to other persons in similar circumstances, and

(b)   the terms of those schemes or licences,

and shall exercise its powers so as to secure that there is no unreasonable discrimination between licensees, or prospective licensees, under the scheme or licence to which the reference or application relates and licensees under other schemes operated by, or other licences granted by, the same person.

*Licences for reprographic copying*
**130.**   Where a reference or application is made to the Copyright Tribunal under this Chapter relating to the licensing of reprographic copying of published literary, dramatic, musical or artistic works, or the typographical arrangement of published editions, the Tribunal shall have regard to—

(a)   the extent to which published editions of the works in question are otherwise available,

(b)   the proportion of the work to be copied, and

(c)   the nature of the use to which the copies are likely to be put.

*Licences for educational establishments in respect of works included in broadcasts or cable programmes*
**131.**—(1)   This section applies to references or applications under this Chapter relating to licences for the recording by or on behalf of educational establishments of broadcasts or cable programmes which include copyright works, or the making of copies of such recordings, for educational purposes.

(2)   The Copyright Tribunal shall, in considering what charges (if any) should be paid for a licence, have regard to the extent to which the owners of copyright in the works included in the broadcast or cable programme have already received, or are entitled to receive, payment in respect of their inclusion.

*Licences to reflect conditions imposed by promoters of events*
**132.**—(1)   This section applies to references or applications under this Chapter in respect of licences relating to sound recordings, films, broadcasts or cable programmes which include, or are to include, any entertainment or other event.

(2)   The Copyright Tribunal shall have regard to any conditions imposed by the promoters of the entertainment or other event; and, in particular, the Tribunal shall not hold a refusal or failure to grant a licence to be unreasonable if it could not have been granted consistently with those conditions.

(3)   Nothing in this section shall require the Tribunal to have regard to any such conditions in so far as they—

(a)   purport to regulate the charges to be imposed in respect of the grant of licences, or

(b)   relate to payments to be made to the promoters of any event in consideration of the grant of facilities for making the recording, film, broadcast · or cable programme.

*Licences to reflect payments in respect of underlying rights*
**133.**—(1)  In considering what charges should be paid for a licence—

(a)   on a reference or application under this Chapter relating to licences for rental to the public of copies of sound recordings, films or computer programs, or

(b)   on an application under section 142 (settlement of royalty or other sum payable for deemed licence),

the Copyright Tribunal shall take into account any reasonable payments which the owner of the copyright in the sound recording, film or computer program is liable to make in consequence of the granting of the licence, or of the acts authorised by the licence, to owners of copyright in works included in that work.

(2)   On any reference or application under this Chapter relating to licensing in respect of the copyright in sound recordings, films, broadcasts or cable programmes, the Copyright Tribunal shall take into account, in considering what charges should be paid for a licence, any reasonable payments which the copyright owner is liable to make in consequence of the granting of the licence, or of the acts authorised by the licence, in respect of any performance included in the recording, film, broadcast or cable programme.

*Licences in respect of works included in re-transmissions*
**134.**—(1)   This section applies to references or applications under this Chapter relating to licences to include in a broadcast or cable programme service—

(a)   literary, dramatic, musical or artistic works, or,

(b)   sound recordings or films,

where one broadcast or cable programme ('the first transmission') is, by reception and immediate re-transmission, to be further broadcast or included in a cable programme service ('the further transmission').

(2)   So far as the further transmission is to the same area as the first transmission, the Copyright Tribunal shall, in considering what charges (if any) should be paid for licences for either transmission, have regard to the extent to which the copyright owner has already received, or is entitled to receive, payment for the other transmission which adequately remunerates him in respect of transmissions to that area.

(3)   So far as the further transmission is to an area outside that to which the first transmission was made, the Tribunal shall (except where subsection (4) applies) leave the further transmission out of account in considering what charges (if any) should be paid for licences for the first transmission.

(4)   If the Tribunal is satisfied that requirements imposed under section 13(1) of the Cable and Broadcasting Act 1984 (duty of Cable Authority to secure inclusion of certain broadcasts in cable programme services) will result in the further transmission being to areas part of which fall outside the area to which the first transmission is made, the Tribunal shall exercise its powers so as to secure that the charges payable for licences for the first transmission adequately reflect that fact.

*Mention of specific matters not to exclude other relevant considerations*
**135.**   The mention in sections 129 to 134 of specific matters to which the Copyright Tribunal is to have regard in certain classes of case does not affect the

Tribunal's general obligation in any case to have regard to all relevant considerations.

*Implied indemnity in schemes or licences for reprographic copying*

*Implied indemnity in certain schemes and licences for reprographic copying*
**136.**—(1)   This section applies to—

(a)   schemes for licensing reprographic copying of published literary, dramatic, musical or artistic works, or the typographical arrangement of published editions, and
(b)   licences granted by licensing bodies for such copying,

where the scheme or licence does not specify the works to which it applies with such particularity as to enable licensees to determine whether a work falls within the scheme or licence by inspection of the scheme or licence and the work.

(2)   There is implied—

(a)   in every scheme to which this section applies an undertaking by the operator of the scheme to indemnify a person granted a licence under the scheme, and
(b)   in every licence to which this section applies an undertaking by the licensing body to indemnify the licensee,

against any liability incurred by him by reason of his having infringed copyright by making or authorising the making of reprographic copies of a work in circumstances within the apparent scope of his licence.

(3)   The circumstances of a case are within the apparent scope of a licence if—

(a)   it is not apparent from inspection of the licence and the work that it does not fall within the description of works to which the licence applies; and
(b)   the licence does not expressly provide that it does not extend to copyright of the description infringed.

(4)   In this section 'liability' includes liability to pay costs; and this section applies in relation to costs reasonably incurred by a licensee in connection with actual or contemplated proceedings against him for infringement of copyright as it applies to sums which he is liable to pay in respect of such infringement.

(5)   A scheme or licence to which this section applies may contain reasonable provision—

(a)   with respect to the manner in which, and time within which, claims under the undertaking implied by this section are to be made;
(b)   enabling the operator of the scheme or, as the case may be, the licensing body to take over the conduct of any proceedings affecting the amount of his liability to indemnify.

*Reprographic copying by educational establishments*

*Power to extend coverage of scheme or licence*
**137.**—(1)   This section applies to—

(a)   a licensing scheme to which sections 118 to 123 apply (see section 117) and which is operated by a licensing body, or

(b)   a licence to which sections 125 to 128 apply (see section 124),

so far as it provides for the grant of licences, or is a licence, authorising the making by or on behalf of educational establishments for the purposes of instruction of reprographic copies of published literary, dramatic, musical or artistic works, or of the typographical arrangement of published editions.

(2)   If it appears to the Secretary of State with respect to a scheme or licence to which this section applies that—

(a)   works of a description similar to those covered by the scheme or licence are unreasonably excluded from it, and

(b)   making them subject to the scheme or licence would not conflict with the normal exploitation of the works or unreasonably prejudice the legitimate interests of the copyright owners,

he may by order provide that the scheme or licence shall extend to those works.

(3)   Where he proposes to make such an order, the Secretary of State shall give notice of the proposal to—

(a)   the copyright owners,

(b)   the licensing body in question, and

(c)   such persons or organisations representative of educational establishments, and such other persons or organisations, as the Secretary of State thinks fit.

(4)   The notice shall inform those persons of their right to make written or oral representations to the Secretary of State about the proposal within six months from the date of the notice; and if any of them wishes to make oral representations, the Secretary of State shall appoint a person to hear the representations and report to him.

(5)   In considering whether to make an order the Secretary of State shall take into account any representations made to him in accordance with subsection (4), and such other matters as appear to him to be relevant.

*Variation or discharge of order extending scheme or licence*
**138.**—(1)   The owner of the copyright in a work in respect of which an order is in force under section 137 may apply to the Secretary of State for the variation or discharge of the order, stating his reasons for making the application.

(2)   The Secretary of State shall not entertain an application made within two years of the making of the original order, or of the making of an order on a previous application under this section, unless it appears to him that the circumstances are exceptional.

(3)   On considering the reasons for the application the Secretary of State may confirm the order forthwith; if he does not do so, he shall give notice of the application to—

(a)   the licensing body in question, and

(b)   such persons or organisations representative of educational establishments, and such other persons or organisations, as he thinks fit.

(4)   The notice shall inform those persons of their right to make written or oral representations to the Secretary of State about the application within the

period of two months from the date of the notice; and if any of them wishes to make oral representations, the Secretary of State shall appoint a person to hear the representations and report to him.

(5)   In considering the application the Secretary of State shall take into account the reasons for the application, any representations made to him in accordance with subsection (4), and such other matters as appear to him to be relevant.

(6)   The Secretary of State may make such order as he thinks fit confirming or discharging the order (or, as the case may be, the order as previously varied), or varying (or further varying) it so as to exclude works from it.

*Appeals against orders*
**139.**—(1)   The owner of the copyright in a work which is the subject of an order under section 137 (order extending coverage of scheme or licence) may appeal to the Copyright Tribunal which may confirm or discharge the order, or vary it so as to exclude works from it, as it thinks fit having regard to the considerations mentioned in subsection (2) of that section.

(2)   Where the Secretary of State has made an order under section 138 (order confirming, varying or discharging order extending coverage of scheme or licence)—

(a)   the person who applied for the order, or

(b)   any person or organisation representative of educational establishments who was given notice of the application for the order and made representations in accordance with subsection (4) of that section,

may appeal to the Tribunal which may confirm or discharge the order or make any other order which the Secretary of State might have made.

(3)   An appeal under this section shall be brought within six weeks of the making of the order or such further period as the Tribunal may allow.

(4)   An order under section 137 or 138 shall not come into effect until the end of the period of six weeks from the making of the order or, if an appeal is brought before the end of that period, until the appeal proceedings are disposed of or withdrawn.

(5)   If an appeal is brought after the end of that period, any decision of the Tribunal on the appeal does not affect the validity of anything done in reliance on the order appealed against before that decision takes effect.

*Inquiry whether new scheme or general licence required*
**140.**—(1)   The Secretary of State may appoint a person to inquire into the question whether new provision is required (whether by way of a licensing scheme or general licence) to authorise the making by or on behalf of educational establishments for the purposes of instruction of reprographic copies of—

(a)   published literary, dramatic, musical or artistic works, or

(b)   the typographical arrangement of published editions,

of a description which appears to the Secretary of State not to be covered by an existing licensing scheme or general licence and not to fall within the power conferred by section 137 (power to extend existing schemes and licences to similar works).

(2)   The procedure to be followed in relation to an inquiry shall be such as may be prescribed by regulations made by the Secretary of State.

(3)   The regulations shall, in particular, provide for notice to be given to—

(a)   persons or organisations appearing to the Secretary of State to represent the owners of copyright in works of that description, and

(b)   persons or organisations appearing to the Secretary of State to represent educational establishments,

and for the making of written or oral representations by such persons; but without prejudice to the giving of notice to, and the making of representations by, other persons and organisations.

(4)   The person appointed to hold the inquiry shall not recommend the making of new provision unless he is satisfied—

(a)   that it would be of advantage to educational establishments to be authorised to make reprographic copies of the works in question, and

(b)   that making those works subject to a licensing scheme or general licence would not conflict with the normal exploitation of the works or unreasonably prejudice the legitimate interests of the copyright owners.

(5)   If he does recommend the making of new provision he shall specify any terms, other than terms as to charges payable, on which authorisation under the new provision should be available.

(6)   Regulations under this section shall be made by statutory instrument which shall be subject to annulment in pursuance of a resolution of either House of Parliament.

(7)   In this section (and section 141) a 'general licence' means a licence granted by a licensing body which covers all works of the description to which it applies.

*Statutory licence where recommendation not implemented*
**141.**—(1)   The Secretary of State may, within one year of the making of a recommendation under section 140 by order provide that if, or to the extent that, provision has not been made in accordance with the recommendation; the making by or on behalf of an educational establishment, for the purposes of instruction, of reprographic copies of the works to which the recommendation relates shall be treated as licensed by the owners of the copyright in the works.

(2)   For that purpose provision shall be regarded as having been made in accordance with the recommendation if—

(a)   a certified licensing scheme has been established under which a licence is available to the establishment in question, or

(b)   a general licence has been—

(i)   granted to or for the benefit of that establishment, or

(ii)   referred by or on behalf of that establishment to the Copyright Tribunal under section 125 (reference of terms of proposed licence), or

(iii)   offered to or for the benefit of that establishment and refused without such a reference,

and the terms of the scheme or licence accord with the recommendation.

(3)   The order shall also provide t                    uthorising the making of such copies (not being a lic                   tified licensing scheme or a general licence) shall cease                    that it is more restricted or more onerous than the lic                   order.

(4)   The order shall provide for the li                   but, as respects other matters, subject to any terms spec                  n and to such other terms as the Secretary of State m

(5)   The order may provide that whe                   herwise be an infringing copy is made in accordance w                   by the order but is subsequently dealt with, it shall be treated as an infringing copy for the purposes of that dealing, and if that dealing infringes copyright for all subsequent purposes.

In this subsection 'dealt with' means sold or let for hire, offered or exposed for sale or hire or exhibited in public.

(6)   The order shall not come into force until at least six months after it is made.

(7)   An order may be varied from time to time, but not so as to include works other than those to which the recommendation relates or remove any terms specified in the recommendation, and may be revoked.

(8)   An order under this section shall be made by statutory instrument which shall be subject to annulment in pursuance of a resolution of either House of Parliament.

(9)   In this section a 'certified licensing scheme' means a licensing scheme certified for the purposes of this section under section 143.

*Royalty or other sum payable for rental of certain works*

*Royalty or other sum payable for rental of sound recording, film or computer program*
**142.**—(1)   An application to settle the royalty or other sum payable in pursuance of section 66 (rental of sound recordings, films and computer programs) may be made to the Copyright Tribunal by the copyright owner or the person claiming to be treated as licensed by him.

(2)   The Tribunal shall consider the matter and make such order as it may determine to be reasonable in the circumstances.

(3)   Either party may subsequently apply to the Tribunal to vary the order, and the Tribunal shall consider the matter and make such order confirming or varying the original order as it may determine to be reasonable in the circumstances.

(4)   An application under subsection (3) shall not, except with the special leave of the Tribunal, be made within twelve months from the date of the original order on a previous application under that subsection.

(5)   An order under subsection (3) has effect from the date on which it is made or such later date as may be specified by the Tribunal.

*Certification of licensing schemes*

*Certification of licensing schemes*
**143.**—(1)   A person operating or proposing to operate a licensing scheme may apply to the Secretary of State to certify the scheme for the purposes of—

    (a)   section 35 (educational recording of broadcasts or cable programmes),
    (b)   section 60 (abstracts of scientific or technical articles),
    (c)   section 66 (rental of sound recordings, films and computer programs),
    (d)   section 74 (subtitled copies of broadcasts or cable programmes for people who are deaf or hard of hearing), or
    (e)   section 141 (reprographic copying of published works by educational establishments).

(2)   The Secretary of State shall by order made by statutory instrument certify the scheme if he is satisfied that it—

    (a)   enables the works to which it relates to be identified with sufficient certainty by persons likely to require licences, and
    (b)   sets out clearly the charges (if any) payable and the other terms on which licences will be granted.

(3)   The scheme shall be scheduled to the order and the certification shall come into operation for the purposes of section 35, 60, 66, 74 or 141, as the case may be—

    (a)   on such date, not less than eight weeks after the order is made, as may be specified in the order, or
    (b)   if the scheme is the subject of a reference under section 118 (reference of proposed scheme), any later date on which the order of the Copyright Tribunal under that section comes into force or the reference is withdrawn.

(4)   A variation of the scheme is not effective unless a corresponding amendment of the order is made; and the Secretary of State shall make such an amendment in the case of a variation ordered by the Copyright Tribunal on a reference under section 118, 119 or 120, and may do so in any other case if he thinks fit.

(5)   The order shall be revoked if the scheme ceases to be operated and may be revoked if it appears to the Secretary of State that it is no longer being operated according to its terms.

*Powers exercisable in consequence of competition report*

*Powers exercisable in consequence of report of Monopolies and Mergers Commission*
**144.**—(1)  Where the matters specified in a report of the Monopolies and Mergers Commission as being those which in the Commission's opinion operate, may be expected to operate or have operated against the public interest include—

    (a)   conditions in licences granted by the owner of copyright in a work restricting the use of the work by the licensee or the right of the copyright owner to grant other licences, or
    (b)   a refusal of a copyright owner to grant licences on reasonable terms,

the powers conferred by Part I of Schedule 8 to the Fair Trading Act 1973 (powers exercisable for purpose of remedying or preventing adverse effects specified in report of Commission) include power to cancel or modify those conditions and, instead or in addition, to provide that licences in respect of the copyright shall be available as of right.

(2)   The references in section 56(2) and 73(2) of that Act, and sections 10(2)(b) and 12(5) of the Competition Act 1980, to the powers specified in that Part of that Schedule shall be construed accordingly.

(3)   A Minister shall only exercise the powers available by virtue of this section if he is satisfied that to do so does not contravene any Convention relating to copyright to which the United Kingdom is a party.

(4)   The terms of a licence available by virtue of this section shall, in default of agreement, be settled by the Copyright Tribunal on an application by the person requiring the licence; and terms so settled shall authorise the licensee to do everything in respect of which a licence is so available.

(5)   Where the terms of a licence are settled by the Tribunal, the licence has effect from the date on which the application to the Tribunal was made.

## Chapter VIII The Copyright Tribunal

### The Tribunal

**The Copyright Tribunal**

**145.**—(1)   The Tribunal established under section 23 of the Copyright Act 1956 is renamed the Copyright Tribunal.

(2)   The Tribunal shall consist of a chairman and two deputy chairmen appointed by the Lord Chancellor, after consultation with the Lord Advocate, and not less than two or more than eight ordinary members appointed by the Secretary of State.

(3)   A person is not eligible for appointment as chairman or deputy chairman unless he is a barrister, advocate or solicitor of not less than seven years' standing or has held judicial office.

**Membership of the Tribunal**

**146.**—(1)   The members of the Copyright Tribunal shall hold and vacate office in accordance with their terms of appointment, subject to the following provisions.

(2)   A member of the Tribunal may resign his office by notice in writing to the Secretary of State or, in the case of the chairman or a deputy chairman, to the Lord Chancellor.

(3)   The Secretary of State or, in the case of the chairman or a deputy chairman, the Lord Chancellor may by notice in writing to the member concerned remove him from office if—

(a)   he has become bankrupt or made an arrangement with his creditors or, in Scotland, his estate has been sequestrated or he has executed a trust deed for his creditors or entered into a composition contract, or

(b)   he is incapacitated by physical or mental illness,

or if he is in the opinion of the Secretary of State or, as the case may be, the Lord Chancellor otherwise unable or unfit to perform his duties as member.

(4)   If a member of the Tribunal is by reason of illness, absence or other reasonable cause for the time being unable to perform the duties of his office, either generally or in relation to particular proceedings, a person may be

appointed to discharge his duties for a period not exceeding six months at one time or, as the case may be, in relation to those proceedings.

(5)  The appointment shall be made—

(a)  in the case of the chairman or deputy chairman, by the Lord Chancellor, who shall appoint a person who would be eligible for appointment to that office, and

(b)  in the case of an ordinary member, by the Secretary of State;

and a person so appointed shall have during the period of his appointment, or in relation to the proceedings in question, the same powers as the person in whose place he is appointed.

(6)  The Lord Chancellor shall consult the Lord Advocate before exercising his powers under this section.

*Financial provisions*
**147.**—(1)  There shall be paid to the members of the Copyright Tribunal such remuneration (whether by way of salaries or fees), and such allowances, as the Secretary of State with the approval of the Treasury may determine.

(2)  The Secretary of State may appoint such staff for the Tribunal as, with the approval of the Treasury as to numbers and remuneration, he may determine.

(3)  The remuneration and allowances of members of the Tribunal, the remuneration of any staff and such other expenses of the Tribunal as the Secretary of State with the approval of the Treasury may determine shall be paid out of money provided by Parliament.

*Constitution for purposes of proceedings*
**148.**—(1)  For the purposes of any proceedings the Copyright Tribunal shall consist of—

(a)  a chairman, who shall be either the chairman or a deputy chairman of the 8Tribunal, and

(b)  two or more ordinary members.

(2)  If the members of the Tribunal dealing with any matter are not unanimous, the decision shall be taken by majority vote; and if, in such a case, the votes are equal the chairman shall have a further, casting vote.

(3)  Where part of any proceedings before the Tribunal has been heard and one or more members of the Tribunal are unable to continue, the Tribunal shall remain duly constituted for the purpose of those proceedings so long as the number of members is not reduced to less than three.

(4)  If the chairman is unable to continue, the chairman of the Tribunal shall—

(a)  appoint one of the remaining members to act as chairman, and

(b)  appoint a suitably qualified person to attend the proceedings and advise the members on any questions of law arising.

(5)  A person is 'suitably qualified' for the purposes of subsection (4)(b) if he is, or is eligible for appointment as, a deputy chairman of the Tribunal.

*Jurisdiction and procedure*

*Jurisdiction of the Tribunal*

**149.** The function of the Copyright Tribunal is to hear and determine proceedings under—

(a)   section 118, 119 or 120 (reference of licensing scheme),

(b)   section 121 or 122 (application with respect to entitlement to licence under licensing scheme),

(c)   section 125, 126 or 127 (reference or application with respect to licensing by licensing body),

(d)   section 139 (appeal against order as to coverage of licensing scheme or licence),

(e)   section 142 (application to settle royalty or other sum payable for rental of sound recording, film or computer program),

(f)   section 144(4) (application to settle terms of copyright licence available as of right),

(g)   section 190 (application to give consent for purposes of Part II on behalf of performer),

(h)   paragraph 5 of Schedule 6 (determination of royalty or other remuneration to be paid to trustees for the Hospital for Sick Children).

*General power to make rules*

**150.**—(1)   The Lord Chancellor may, after consultation with the Lord Advocate, make rules for regulating proceedings before the Copyright Tribunal and, subject to the approval of the Treasury, as to the fees chargeable in respect of such proceedings.

(2)   The rules may apply in relation to the Tribunal—

(a)   as respects proceedings in England and Wales, any of the provisions of the Arbitration Act 1950;

(b)   as respects proceedings in Northern Ireland, any of the provisions of the Arbitration Act (Northern Ireland) 1937; and any provisions so applied shall be set out in or scheduled to the rules.

(3)   Provision shall be made by the rules—

(a)   prohibiting the Tribunal from entertaining a reference under section 118, 119 or 120 by a representative organisation unless the Tribunal is satisfied that the organisation is reasonably representative of the class of persons which it claims to represent;

(b)   specifying the parties to any proceedings and enabling the Tribunal to make a party to the proceedings any person or organisation satisfying the Tribunal that they have a substantial interest in the matter; and

(c)   requiring the Tribunal to give the parties to proceedings an opportunity to state their case, in writing or orally as the rules may provide.

(4)   The rules may make provision for regulating or prescribing any matters incidental to or consequential upon any appeal from the Tribunal under section 152 (appeal to the court on point of law).

(5)   Rules under this section shall be made by statutory instrument which

shall be subject to annulment in pursuance of a resolution of either House of Parliament.

*Costs, proof of orders etc.*

**151.**—(1)   The Copyright Tribunal may order that the costs of a party to proceedings before it shall be paid by such other party as the Tribunal may direct; and the Tribunal may tax or settle the amount of the costs, or direct in what manner they are to be taxed.

(2)   A document purporting to be a copy of an order of the Tribunal and to be certified by the chairman to be a true copy shall, in any proceedings, be sufficient evidence of the order unless the contrary is proved.

(3)   As respect proceedings in Scotland, the Tribunal has the like powers for securing the attendance of witnesses and the production of documents, and with regard to the examination of witnesses on oath, as an arbiter under a submission.

### Appeals

*Appeal to the court on point of law*

**152.**—(1)   An appeal lies on any point of law arising from a decision of the Copyright Tribunal to the High Court or, in the case of proceedings of the Tribunal in Scotland, to the Court of Session.

(2)   Provision shall be made by rules under section 150 limiting the time within which an appeal may be brought.

(3)   Provision may be made by rules under that section—

(a)   for suspending, or authorising or requiring the Tribunal to suspend, the operation of orders of the Tribunal in cases where its decision is appealed against;

(b)   for modifying in relation to an order of the Tribunal whose operation is suspended the operation of any provision of this Act as to the effect of the order;

(c)   for the publication of notices or the taking of other steps for securing that persons affected by the suspension of an order of the Tribunal will be informed of its suspension.

### Chapter IX Qualification for and extent of copyright protection

### Qualification for copyright protection

*Qualification for copyright protection*

**153.**—(1)   Copyright does not subsist in a work unless the qualification requirements of this Chapter are satisfied as regards—

(a)   the author (see section 154), or
(b)   the country in which the work was first published (see section 155), or
(c)   in the case of a broadcast or cable programme, the country from which the broadcast was made or the cable programme was sent (see section 156).

(2)   Subsection (1) does not apply in relation to Crown copyright or Parliamentary copyright (see sections 163 to 166), or to copyright subsisting by virtue of section 168 (copyright of certain international organisations).

(3)   If the qualification requirements of this Chapter, or section 163, 165 or 168 are once satisfied in respect of a work, copyright does not cease to subsist by reason of any subsequent event.

*Qualification by reference to author*
**154.**—(1)  A work qualifies for copyright protection if the author was at the material time a qualifying person, that is—

    (a)  a British citizen, a British Dependent Territories citizen, a British National (Overseas), a British Overseas citizen, a British subject or a British protected person within the meaning of the British Nationality Act 1981, or
    (b)  an individual domiciled or resident in the United Kingdom or another country to which the relevant provisions of this Part extend, or
    (c)  a body incorporated under the law of a part of the United Kingdom or of another country to which the relevant provisions of this Part extend.

    (2)  Where, or so far as, provision is made by Order under section 159 (application of this Part to countries to which it does not extend), a work also qualifies for copyright protection if at the material time the author was a citizen or subject of, an individual domiciled or resident in, or a body incorporated under the law of, a country to which the Order relates.

    (3)  A work of joint authorship qualifies for copyright protection if at the material time any of the authors satisfies the requirements of subsection (1) or (2); but where a work qualifies for copyright protection only under this section, only those authors who satisfy those requirements shall be taken into account for the purposes of—

    section 11(1) and (2) (first ownership of copyright; entitlement of author or author's employer),
    section 12(1) and (2) (duration of copyright; dependent on life of author unless work of unknown authorship), and section 9(4) (meaning of 'unknown authorship') so far as it applies for the purposes of section 12(2), and
    section 57 (anonymous or pseudonymous works: acts permitted on assumptions as to expiry of copyright or death of author).

    (4)  The material time in relation to a literary, dramatic, musical or artistic work is—

    (a)  in the case of an unpublished work, when the work was made or, if the making of the work extended over a period, a substantial part of that period;
    (b)  in the case of a published work, when the work was first published or, if the author had died before that time, immediately before his death.

    (5)  The material time in relation to other descriptions of work is as follows—

    (a)  in the case of a sound recording or film, when it was made;
    (b)  in the case of a broadcast, when the broadcast was made;
    (c)  in the case of a cable programme, when the programme was included in a cable programme service;
    (d)  in the case of the typographical arrangement of a published edition, when the edition was first published.

*Qualification by reference to country of first publication*
**155.**—(1)  A literary, dramatic, musical or artistic work, a sound recording or film, or the typographical arrangement of a published edition, qualifies for copyright protection if it is first published—

(a)   in the United Kingdom, or

(b)   in another country to which the relevant provisions of this Part extend.

(2)   Where, or so far as, provision is made by Order under section 159 (application of this Part to countries to which it does not extend), such a work also qualifies for copyright protection if it is first published in a country to which the Order relates.

(3)   For the purposes of this section, publication in one country shall not be regarded as other than the first publication by reason of simultaneous publication elsewhere; and for this purpose publication elsewhere within the previous 30 days shall be treated as simultaneous.

*Qualification by reference to place of transmission*
**156.**—(1)   A broadcast qualifies for copyright protection if it is made from, and a cable programme qualifies for copyright protection if it is sent from, a place in—

(a)   the United Kingdom, or

(b)   another country to which the relevant provisions of this Part extend.

(2)   Where, or so far as, provision is made by Order under section 159 (application of this Part to countries to which it does not extend), a broadcast or cable programme also qualifies for copyright protection if it is made from or, as the case may be, sent from a place in a country to which the Order relates.

### *Extent and application of this Part*

*Countries to which this Part extends*
**157.**—(1)   This Part extends to England and Wales, Scotland and Northern Ireland.

(2)   Her Majesty may by Order in Council direct that this Part shall extend, subject to such exceptions and modifications as may be specified in the Order, to—

(a)   any of the Channel Islands,

(b)   the Isle of Man, or

(c)   any colony.

(3)   That power includes power to extend, subject to such exceptions and modifications as may be specified in the Order, any Order in Council made under the following provisions of this Chapter.

(4)   The legislature of a country to which this Part has been extended may modify or add to the provisions of this Part, in their operation as part of the law of that country, as the legislature may consider necessary to adapt the provisions to the circumstances of that country—

(a)   as regards procedure and remedies, or

(b)   as regards works qualifying for copyright protection by virtue of a connection with that country.

(5)   Nothing in this section shall be construed as restricting the extent of paragraph 35 of Schedule 1 (transitional provisions: dependent territories where

the Copyright Act 1956 or the Copyright Act 1911 remains in force) in relation to the law of a dependent territory to which this Part does not extend.

*Countries ceasing to be colonies*
**158.**—(1)   The following provisions apply where a country to which this Part has been extended ceases to be a colony of the United Kingdom.

(2)   As from the date on which it ceases to be a colony it shall cease to be regarded as a country to which this Part extends for the purposes of—

(a)   section 160(2)(a) (denial of copyright protection to citizens of countries not giving adequate protection to British works), and
(b)   sections 163 and 165 (Crown and Parliamentary copyright).

(3)   But it shall continue to be treated as a country to which this Part extends for the purposes of sections 154 to 156 (qualification for copyright protection) until—

(a)   an Order in Council is made in respect of that country under section 159 (application of this Part to countries to which it does not extend), or
(b)   an Order in Council is made declaring that it shall cease to be so treated by reason of the fact that the provisions of this Part as part of the law of that country have been repealed or amended.

(4)   A statutory instrument containing an Order in Council under subsection (3)(b) shall be subject to annulment in pursuance of a resolution of either House of Parliament.

*Application of this Part to countries to which it does not extend*
**159.**—(1)   Her Majesty may by Order in Council make provision for applying in relation to a country to which this Part does not extend any of the provisions of this Part specified in the Order, so as to secure that those provisions—

(a)   apply in relation to persons who are citizens or subjects of that country or are domiciled or resident there, as they apply to persons who are British citizens or are domiciled or resident in the United Kingdom, or
(b)   apply in relation to bodies incorporated under the law of that country as they apply in relation to bodies incorporated under the law of a part of the United Kingdom, or
(c)   apply in relation to works first published in that country as they apply in relation to works first published in the United Kingdom, or
(d)   apply in relation to broadcasts made from or cable programmes sent from that country as they apply in relation to broadcasts made from or cable programmes sent from the United Kingdom.

(2)   An Order may make provision for all or any of the matters mentioned in subsection (1) and may—

(a)   apply any provisions of this Part subject to such exceptions and modifications as are specified in the Order; and
(b)   direct that any provisions of this Part apply either generally or in relation to such classes of works, or other classes of case, as are specified in the Order.

(3)   Except in the case of a Convention country or another member State of the European Economic Community, Her Majesty shall not make an Order in Council under this section in relation to a country unless satisfied that provision has been or will be made under the law of that country, in respect of the class of works to which the Order relates, giving adequate protection to the owners of copyright under this Part.

(4)   In subsection (3) 'Convention country' means a country which is a party to a Convention relating to copyright to which the United Kingdom is also a party.

(5)   A statutory instrument containing an Order in Council under this section shall be subject to annulment in pursuance of a resolution of either House of Parliament.

*Denial of copyright protection to citizens of countries not giving adequate protection to British works*

**160.**—(1)   If it appears to Her Majesty that the law of a country fails to give adequate protection to British works to which this section applies, or to one or more classes of such works, Her Majesty may make provision by Order in Council in accordance with this section restricting the rights conferred by this Part in relation to works of authors connected with that country.

(2)   An Order in Council under this section shall designate the country concerned and provide that, for the purposes specified in the Order, works first published after a date specified in the Order shall not be treated as qualifying for copyright protection by virtue of such publication if at that time the authors are—

(a)   citizens or subjects of that country (not domiciled or resident in the United Kingdom or another country to which the relevant provisions of this Part extend), or

(b)   bodies incorporated under the law of that country;

and the Order may make such provision for all the purposes of this Part or for such purposes as are specified in the Order, and either generally or in relation to such class of cases as are specified in the Order, having regard to the nature and extent of that failure referred to in subsection (1).

(3)   This section applies to literary, dramatic, musical and artistic works, sound recordings and films; and 'British works' means works of which the author was a qualifying person at the material time within the meaning of section 154.

(4)   A statutory instrument containing an Order in Council under this section shall be subject to annulment in pursuance of a resolution of either House of Parliament.

*Supplementary*

*Territorial waters and the continental shelf*

**161.**—(1)   For the purposes of this Part the territorial waters of the United Kingdom shall be treated as part of the United Kingdom.

(2)   This Part applies to things done in the United Kingdom sector of the continental shelf on a structure or vessel which is present there for purposes directly connected with the exploration of the sea bed or subsoil or the

exploitation of their natural resources as it applies to things done in the United Kingdom.

(3) The United Kingdom sector of the continental shelf means the areas designated by order under section 1(7) of the Continental Shelf Act 1964.

*British ships, aircraft and hovercraft*
**162.**—(1) This Part applies to things done on a British ship, aircraft or hovercraft as it applies to things done in the United Kingdom.

(2) In this section—

'British ship' means a ship which is a British ship for the purposes of the Merchant Shipping Acts (see section 2 of the Merchant Shipping Act 1988) otherwise than by virtue of registration in a country outside the United Kingdom; and

'British aircraft' and 'British hovercraft' mean an aircraft or hovercraft registered in the United Kingdom.

## Chapter X Miscellaneous and general

### Crown and Parliamentary copyright

*Crown copyright*
**163.**—(1) Where a work is made by Her Majesty or by an officer or servant of the Crown in the course of his duties—

(a) the work qualifies for copyright protection notwithstanding section 153(1) (ordinary requirement as to qualification for copyright protection), and

(b) Her Majesty is the first owner of any copyright in the work.

(2) Copyright in such a work is referred to in this Part as 'Crown copyright', notwithstanding that it may be, or have been, assigned to another person.

(3) Crown copyright in a literary, dramatic, musical or artistic work continues to subsist—

(a) until the end of the period of 125 years from the end of the calendar year in which the work was made, or

(b) if the work is published commercially before the end of the period of 75 years from the end of the calendar year in which it was made, until the end of the period of 50 years from the end of the calendar year in which it was first so published.

(4) In the case of a work of joint authorship where one or more but not all of the authors are persons falling within subsection (1), this section applies only in relation to those authors and the copyright subsisting by virtue of their contribution to the work.

(5) Except as mentioned above, and subject to any express exclusion elsewhere in this Part, the provisions of this Part apply in relation to Crown copyright as to other copyright.

(6) This section does not apply to a work if, or to the extent that, Parliamentary copyright subsists in the work (see sections 165 and 166).

*Copyright in Acts and Measures*
**164.**—(1)   Her Majesty is entitled to copyright in every Act of Parliament or Measure of the General Synod of the Church of England.

(2)   The copyright subsists from Royal Assent until the end of the period of 50 years from the end of the calendar year in which Royal Assent was given.

(3)   References in this Part to Crown copyright (except in section 163) include copyright under this section; and, except as mentioned above, the provisions of this Part apply in relation to copyright under this section as to other Crown copyright.

(4)   No other copyright, or right in the nature of copyright, subsists in an Act or Measure.

*Parliamentary copyright*
**165.**—(1)   Where a work is made by or under the direction or control of the House of Commons or the House of Lords—

(a)   the work qualifies for copyright protection notwithstanding section 153(1) (ordinary requirement as to qualification for copyright protection), and

(b)   the House by whom, or under whose direction or control, the work is made is the first owner of any copyright in the work, and if the work is made by or under the direction or control of both Houses, the two Houses are joint first owners of copyright.

(2)   Copyright in such a work is referred to in this Part as 'Parliamentary copyright', notwithstanding that it may be, or have been, assigned to another person.

(3)   Parliamentary copyright in a literary, dramatic, musical or artistic work continues to subsist until the end of the period of 50 years from the end of the calendar year in which the work was made.

(4)   For the purposes of this section, works made by or under the direction or control of the House of Commons or the House of Lords include—

(a)   any work made by an officer or employee of that House in the course of his duties, and

(b)   any sound recording, film, live broadcast or live cable programme of the proceedings of that House;

but a work shall not be regarded as made by or under the direction or control of either House by reason only of its being commissioned by or on behalf of that House.

(5)   In the case of a work of joint authorship where one or more but not all of the authors are acting on behalf of, or under the direction or control of, the House of Commons or the House of Lords, this section applies only in relation to those authors and the copyright subsisting by virtue of their contribution to the work.

(6)   Except as mentioned above, and subject to any express exclusion elsewhere in this Part, the provisions of this Part apply in relation to Parliamentary copyright as to other copyright.

(7)   The provisions of this section also apply, subject to any exceptions or modifications specified by Order in Council, to works made by or under the

direction or control of any other legislative body of a country to which this Part extends; and references in this Part to 'Parliamentary copyright' shall be construed accordingly.

(8)    A statutory instrument containing an Order in Council under subsection (7) shall be subject to annulment in pursuance of a resolution of either House of Parliament.

*Copyright in Parliamentary Bills*
**166.**—(1)    Copyright in every Bill introduced into Parliament belongs, in accordance with the following provisions, to one or both of the Houses of Parliament.

(2)    Copyright in a public Bill belongs in the first instance to the House into which the Bill is introduced, and after the Bill has been carried to the second House to both Houses jointly, and subsists from the time when the text of the Bill is handed in to the House in which it is introduced.

(3)    Copyright in a private Bill belongs to both Houses jointly and subsists from the time when a copy of the Bill is first deposited in either House.

(4)    Copyright in a personal Bill belongs in the first instance to the House of Lords, and after the Bill has been carried to the House of Commons to both Houses jointly, and subsists from the time when it is given a First Reading in the House of Lords.

(5)    Copyright under this section ceases—

    (a)    on Royal Assent, or
    (b)    if the Bill does not receive Royal Assent, on the withdrawal or rejection of the Bill or the end of the Session:

Provided that, copyright in a Bill continues to subsist notwithstanding its rejection in any Session by the House of Lords if, by virtue of the Parliament Acts 1911 and 1949, it remains possible for it to be presented for Royal Assent in that Session.

(6)    References in this Part to Parliamentary copyright (except in section 165) include copyright under this section; and, except as mentioned above, the provisions of this Part apply in relation to copyright under this section as to other Parliamentary copyright.

(7)    No other copyright, or right in the nature of copyright, subsists in a Bill after copyright has once subsisted under this section; but without prejudice to the subsequent operation of this section in relation to a Bill which, not having passed in one Session, is reintroduced in a subsequent Session.

*Houses of Parliament: supplementary provisions with respect to copyright*
**167.**—(1)    For the purposes of holding, dealing with and enforcing copyright, and in connection with all legal proceedings relating to copyright, each House of Parliament shall be treated as having the legal capacities of a body corporate, which shall not be affected by a prorogation or dissolution.

(2)    The functions of the House of Commons as owner of copyright shall be exercised by the Speaker on behalf of the House; and if so authorised by the Speaker, or in case of a vacancy in the office of Speaker, those functions may be discharged by the Chairman of Ways and Means or a Deputy Chairman.

(3)    For this purpose a person who on the dissolution of Parliament was

Speaker of the House of Commons, Chairman of Ways and Means or a Deputy Chairman may continue to act until the corresponding appointment is made in the next Session of Parliament.

(4) The functions of the House of Lords as owner of copyright shall be exercised by the Clerk of the Parliaments on behalf of the House; and if so authorised by him, or in case of a vacancy in the office of Clerk of the Parliaments, those functions may be discharged by the Clerk Assistant or the Reading Clerk.

(5) Legal proceedings relating to copyright—

(a) shall be brought by or against the House of Commons in the name of 'The Speaker of the House of Commons'; and

(b) shall be brought by or against the House of Lords in the name of 'The Clerk of the Parliaments'.

### Other miscellaneous provisions

*Copyright vesting in certain international organisations*
**168.**—(1) Where an original literary, dramatic, musical or artistic work—

(a) is made by an officer or employee of, or is published by, an international organisation to which this section applies, and

(b) does not qualify for copyright protection under section 154 (qualification by reference to author) or section 155 (qualification by reference to country of first publication),

copyright nevertheless subsists in the work by virtue of this section and the organisation is first owner of that copyright.

(2) The international organisations to which this section applies are those as to which Her Majesty has by Order in Council declared that it is expedient that this section should apply.

(3) Copyright of which an international organisation is first owner by virtue of this section continues to subsist until the end of the period of 50 years from the end of the calendar year in which the work was made or such longer period as may be specified by Her Majesty by Order in Council for the purpose of complying with the international obligations of the United Kingdom.

(4) An international organisation to which this section applies shall be deemed to have, and to have had at all material times, the legal capacities of a body corporate for the purpose of holding, dealing with and enforcing copyright and in connection with all legal proceedings relating to copyright.

(5) A statutory instrument containing an Order in Council under this section shall be subject to annulment in pursuance of a resolution of either House of Parliament.

*Folklore etc.: anonymous unpublished works*
**169.**—(1) Where in the case of an unpublished literary, dramatic, musical or artistic work of unknown authorship there is evidence that the author (or, in the case of a joint work, any of the authors) was a qualifying individual by connection with a country outside the United Kingdom, it shall be presumed until the contrary is proved that he was such a qualifying individual and that copyright accordingly subsists in the work, subject to the provisions of this Part.

(2)   If under the law of that country a body is appointed to protect and enforce copyright in such works, Her Majesty may by Order in Council designate that body for the purposes of this section.

(3)   A body so designated shall be recognised in the United Kingdom as having authority to do in place of the copyright owner anything, other than assign copyright, which it is empowered to do under the law of that country; and it may, in particular, bring proceedings in its own name.

(4)   A statutory instrument containing an Order in Council under this section shall be subject to annulment in pursuance of a resolution of either House of Parliament.

(5)   In subsection (1) a 'qualifying individual' means an individual who at the material time (within the meaning of section 154) was a person whose works qualified under that section for copyright protection.

(6)   This section does not apply if there has been an assignment of copyright in the work by the author of which notice has been given to the designated body; and nothing in this section affects the validity of an assignment of copyright made, or licence granted, by the author or a person lawfully claiming under him.

*Transitional provisions and savings*

*Transitional provisions and savings*
**170.**   Schedule 1 contains transitional provisions and savings relating to works made, and acts or events occurring, before the commencement of this Part, and otherwise with respect to the operation of the provisions of this Part.

*Rights and privileges under other enactments or the common law*
**171.**—(1)   Nothing in this Part affects —

(a)   any right or privilege of any person under any enactment (except where the enactment is expressly repealed, amended or modified by this Act);

(b)   any right or privilege of the Crown subsisting otherwise than under an enactment;

(c)   any right or privilege of either House of Parliament;

(d)   the right of the Crown or any person deriving title from the Crown to sell, use or otherwise deal with articles forfeited under the laws relating to customs and excise;

(e)   the operation of any rule of equity relating to breaches of trust or confidence.

(2)   Subject to those savings, no copyright or right in the nature of copyright shall subsist otherwise than by virtue of this Part or some other enactment in that behalf.

(3)   Nothing in this Part affects any rule of law preventing or restricting the enforcement of copyright, on grounds of public interest or otherwise.

(4)   Nothing in this Part affects any right of action or other remedy, whether civil or criminal, available otherwise than under this Part in respect of acts infringing any of the rights conferred by Chapter IV (moral rights).

(5)   The savings in subsection (1) have effect subject to section 164(4) and section 166(7) (copyright in Acts, Measures and Bills: exclusion of other rights in the nature of copyright).

*Interpretation*

*General provisions as to construction*

**172.**—(1)   This Part restates and amends the law of copyright, that is, the provisions of the Copyright Act 1956, as amended.

(2)   A provision of this Part which corresponds to a provision of the previous law shall not be construed as departing from the previous law merely because of a change of expression.

(3)   Decisions under the previous law may be referred to for the purpose of establishing whether a provision of this Part departs from the previous law, or otherwise for establishing the true construction of this Part.

*Construction of references to copyright owner*

**173.**—(1)   Where different persons are (whether in consequence of a partial assignment or otherwise) entitled to different aspects of copyright in a work, the copyright owner for any purpose of this Part is the person who is entitled to the aspect of copyright relevant for that purpose.

(2)   Where copyright (or any aspect of copyright) is owned by more than one person jointly, references in this Part to the copyright owner are to all the owners, so that, in particular, any requirement of the licence of the copyright owner requires the licence of all of them.

*Meaning of 'educational establishment' and related expressions*

**174.**—(1)   The expression 'educational establishment' in a provision of this Part means—

(a)   any school, and

(b)   any other description of educational establishment specified for the purposes of this Part, or that provision, by order of the Secretary of State.

(2)   The Secretary of State may by order provide that the provisions of this Part relating to educational establishments shall apply, with such modifications and adaptations as may be specified in the order, in relation to teachers who are employed by a local education authority to give instruction elsewhere to pupils who are unable to attend an educational establishment.

(3)   In subsection (1)(a) 'school'—

(a)   in relation to England and Wales, has the same meaning as in the Education Act 1944;

(b)   in relation to Scotland, has the same meaning as in the Education (Scotland) Act 1962, except that it includes an approved school within the meaning of the Social Work (Scotland) Act 1968; and

(c)   in relation to Northern Ireland, has the same meaning as in the Education and Libraries (Northern Ireland) Order 1986.

(4)   An order under subsection (1)(b) may specify a description of educational establishment by reference to the instruments from time to time in force under any enactment specified in the order.

(5)   In relation to an educational establishment the expressions 'teacher' and 'pupil' in this Part include, respectively, any person who gives and any person who receives instruction.

(6)   References in this Part to anything being done 'on behalf of' an educational establishment are to its being done for the purposes of that establishment by any person.

(7)   An order under this section shall be made by statutory instrument which shall be subject to annulment in pursuance of a resolution of either House of Parliament.

*Meaning of publication and commercial publication*
**175.**—(1)   In this Part 'publication', in relation to a work—

(a)   means the issue of copies to the public, and
(b)   includes, in the case of a literary, dramatic, musical or artistic work, making it available to the public by means of an electronic retrieval system;

and related expressions shall be construed accordingly.

(2)   In this Part 'commercial publication', in relation to a literary, dramatic, musical or artistic work means—

(a)   issuing copies of the work to the public at a time when copies made in advance of the receipt of orders are generally available to the public, or
(b)   making the work available to the public by means of an electronic retrieval system;

and related expressions shall be construed accordingly.

(3)   In the case of a work of architecture in the form of a building, or an artistic work incorporated in a building, construction of the building shall be treated as equivalent to publication of the work.

(4)   The following do not constitute publication for the purposes of this Part and references to commercial publication shall be construed accordingly—

(a)   in the case of a literary, dramatic or musical work—

(i)   the performance of the work, or
(ii)   the broadcasting of the work or its inclusion in a cable programme service (otherwise than for the purposes of an electronic retrieval system);

(b)   in the case of an artistic work—

(i)   the exhibition of the work;
(ii)   the issue to the public of copies of a graphic work representing, or of photographs of, a work of architecture in the form of a building or a model for a building, a sculpture or a work of artistic craftsmanship,
(iii)   the issue to the public of copies of a film including the work, or
(iv)   the broadcasting of the work or its inclusion in a cable programme service (otherwise than for the purposes of an electronic retrieval system);

(c)   in the case of a sound recording or film—

(i)   the work being played or shown in public, or
(ii)   the broadcasting of the work or its inclusion in a cable programme service.

(5)   References in this Part to publication or commercial publication do not

include publication which is merely colourable and not intended to satisfy the reasonable requirements of the public.

(6)   No account shall be taken for the purposes of this section of any unauthorised act.

*Requirement of signature: application in relation to body corporate*
**176.**—(1)   The requirement in the following provisions that an instrument be signed by or on behalf of a person is also satisfied in the case of a body corporate by the affixing of its seal—

section 78(3)(b) (assertion by licensor of right to identification of author in case of public exhibition of copy made in pursuance of the licence),
section 90(3) (assignment of copyright),
section 91(1) (assignment of future copyright),
section 92(1) (grant of exclusive licence).

(2)   The requirement in the following provisions that an instrument be signed by a person is satisfied in the case of a body corporate by signature on behalf of the body or by the affixing of its seal—

section 78(2)(b) (assertion by instrument in writing of right to have author identified),
section 87(2) (waiver of moral rights).

*Adaptation of expressions for Scotland*
**177.**   In the application of this Part to Scotland—

'account of profits' means accounting and payment of profits;
'accounts' means count, reckoning and payment;
'assignment' means assignation;
'costs' means expenses;
'defendant' means defender;
'delivery up' means delivery;
'estoppel' means personal bar;
'injunction' means interdict;
'interlocutory relief' means interim remedy; and
'plaintiff' means pursuer.

*Minor definitions*
**178.**   In this Part—

'article', in the context of an article in a periodical, includes an item of any description;
'business' includes a trade or profession;
'collective work' means—

(a)   a work of joint authorship, or
(b)   a work in which there are distinct contributions by different authors or in which works or parts of works of different authors are incorporated;

'computer-generated', in relation to a work, means that the work is generated by computer in circumstances such that there is no human author of the work;

'country' includes any territory;

'the Crown' includes the Crown in right of Her Majesty's Government in Northern Ireland or in any country outside the United Kingdom to which this Part extends;

'electronic' means actuated by electric, magnetic, electromagnetic, electrochemical or electromechanical energy and 'in electronic form' means in a form usable only by electronic means;

'employed', 'employee', 'employer' and 'employment' refer to employment under a contract of service or of apprenticeship;

'facsimile copy' includes a copy which is reduced or enlarged in scale;

'international organisation' means an organisation the members of which include one or more States;

'judicial proceedings' includes proceedings before any court, tribunal or person having authority to decide any matter affecting a person's legal rights or liabilities;

'parliamentary proceedings' includes proceedings of the Northern Ireland Assembly or of the European Parliament;

'rental' means any arrangement under which a copy of a work is made available—

    (a)   for payment (in money or money's worth), or

    (b)   in the course of a business, as part of services or amenities for which payment is made,

on terms that it will or may be returned;

'reprographic copy' and 'reprographic copying' refer to copying by means of a reprographic process;

'reprographic process' means a process—

    (a)   for making facsimile copies, or

    (b)   involving the use of an appliance for making multiple copies,

and includes, in relation to a work held in electronic form, any copying by electronic means, but does not include the making of a film or sound recording;

'sufficient acknowledgement' means an acknowledgement identifying the work in question by its title or other description, and identifying the author unless—

    (a)   in the case of a published work, it is published anonymously;

    (b)   in the case of an unpublished work, it is not possible for a person to ascertain the identity of the author by reasonable inquiry;

'sufficient disclaimer', in relation to an act capable of infringing the right conferred by section 80 (right to object to derogatory treatment of work), means a clear and reasonably prominent indication—

    (i)   given at the time of the act, and

    (ii)   if the author or director is then identified, appearing along with the identification,

that the work has been subjected to treatment to which the author or director has not consented;

'telecommunications system' means a system for conveying visual images, sounds or other information by electronic means;

'typeface' includes an ornamental motif used in printing;

'unauthorised', as regards anything done in relation to a work, means done otherwise than—

(a) by or with the licence of the copyright owner, or

(b) if copyright does not subsist in the work, by or with the licence of the author or, in a case where section 11(2) would have applied, the author's employer or, in either case, persons lawfully claiming under him, or

(c) in pursuance of section 48 (copying etc. of certain material by the Crown);

'wireless telegraphy' means the sending of electromagnetic energy over paths not provided by a material substance constructed or arranged for that purpose;

'writing' includes any form of notation or code, whether by hand or otherwise and regardless of the method by which, or medium in or on which, it is recorded, and 'written' shall be construed accordingly.

*Index of defined expressions*
**179.** The following Table shows provisions defining or otherwise explaining expressions used in this Part (other than provisions defining or explaining an expression used only in the same section)—

| | |
|---|---|
| account of profits and accounts (in Scotland) | section 177 |
| acts restricted by copyright | section 16(1) |
| adaptation | section 21(3) |
| archivist (in sections 37 to 43) | section 37(6) |
| article (in a periodical) | section 178 |
| artistic work | section 4(1) |
| assignment (in Scotland) | section 177 |
| author | sections 9 and 10(3) |
| broadcast (and related expressions) | section 6 |
| building | section 4(2) |
| business | section 178 |
| cable programme, cable programme service (and related expressions) | section 7 |
| collective work | section 178 |
| commencement (in Schedule 1) | paragraph 1(2) of that Schedule |
| commercial publication | section 175 |
| computer-generated | section 178 |
| copy and copying | section 17 |
| copyright (generally) | section 1 |
| copyright (in Schedule 1) | paragraph 2(2) of that Schedule |
| copyright owner | sections 101(2) and 173 |
| Copyright Tribunal | section 145 |
| copyright work | section 1(2) |
| costs (in Scotland) | section 177 |

| | |
|---|---|
| country | section 178 |
| the Crown | section 178 |
| Crown copyright | sections 163(2) and 164(3) |
| defendant (in Scotland) | section 177 |
| delivery up (in Scotland) | section 177 |
| dramatic work | section 3(1) |
| educational establishment | section 174(1) to (4) |
| electronic and electronic form | section 178 |
| employed, employee, employer and employment | section 178 |
| exclusive licence | section 92(1) |
| existing works (in Schedule 1) | paragraph 1(3) of that Schedule |
| facsimile copy | section 178 |
| film | section 5 |
| future copyright | section 91(2) |
| general licence (in sections 140 and 141) | section 140(7) |
| graphic work | section 4(2) |
| infringing copy | section 27 |
| injunction (in Scotland) | section 177 |
| interlocutory relief (in Scotland) | section 177 |
| international organisation | section 178 |
| issue of copies to the public | section 18(2) |
| joint authorship (work of) | section 10(1) and (2) |
| judicial proceedings | section 178 |
| librarian (in sections 37 to 43) | section 37(6) |
| licence (in sections 125 to 128) | section 124 |
| licence of copyright owner | sections 90(4), 91(3) and 173 |
| licensing body (in Chapter VII) | section 116(2) |
| licensing scheme (generally) | section 116(1) |
| licensing scheme (in sections 118 to 121) | section 117 |
| literary work | section 3(1) |
| made (in relation to a literary, dramatic or musical work) | section 3(2) |
| musical work | section 3(1) |
| the new copyright provisions (in Schedule 1) | paragraph 1(1) of that Schedule |
| the 1911 Act (in Schedule 1) | paragraph 1(1) of that Schedule |
| the 1956 Act (in Schedule 1) | paragraph 1(1) of that Schedule |
| on behalf of (in relation to an educational establishment) | section 174(5) |
| Parliamentary copyright | sections 165(2) and (7) and 166(6) |
| parliamentary proceedings | section 178 |
| performance | section 19(2) |
| photograph | section 4(2) |
| plaintiff (in Scotland) | section 177 |
| prescribed conditions (in sections 38 to 43) | section 37(1)(b) |
| prescribed library or archive (in sections 38 to 43) | section 37(1)(a) |

| | |
|---|---|
| programme (in the context of broadcasting) | section 6(3) |
| prospective owner (of copyright) | section 91(2) |
| publication and related expressions | section 175 |
| published edition (in the context of copyright in the typographical arrangement) | section 8 |
| pupil | section 174(5) |
| rental | section 178 |
| reprographic copies and reprographic copying | section 178 |
| reprographic process | section 178 |
| sculpture | section 4(2) |
| signed | section 176 |
| sound recording | section 5 |
| sufficient acknowledgement | section 178 |
| sufficient disclaimer | section 178 |
| teacher | section 174(5) |
| telecommunications system | section 178 |
| typeface | section 178 |
| unauthorised (as regards things done in relation to a work) | section 178 |
| unknown (in relation to the author of a work) | section 9(5) |
| unknown authorship (work of) | section 9(4) |
| wireless telegraphy | section 178 |
| work (in Schedule 1) | paragraph 2(1) of that Schedule |
| work of more than one author (in Chapter VII) | section 116(4) |
| writing and written | section 178 |

## Part II Rights in performances

### *Introductory*

*Rights conferred on performers and persons having recording rights*
**180.**—(1)  This Part confers rights—

(a)  on a performer, by requiring his consent to the exploitation of his performances (see sections 181 to 184), and

(b)  on a person having recording rights in relation to a performance, in relation to recordings made without his consent or that of the performer (see sections 185 to 188),

and creates offences in relation to dealing with or using illicit recordings and certain other related acts (see sections 198 and 201).

(2)  In this Part—

'performance' means—

(a)  dramatic performance (which includes dance and mime),

(b)  a musical performance,

(c)  a reading or recitation of a literary work, or

      (d)   a performance of a variety act or any similar presentation,

which is, or so far as it is, a live performance given by one or more individuals; and
    'recording', in relation to a performance, means a film or sound recording—

      (a)   made directly from the live performance,
      (b)   made from a broadcast of, or cable programme including, the performance, or
      (c)   made, directly or indirectly, from another recording of the performance.

    (3)   The rights conferred by this Part apply in relation to performances taking place before the commencement of this Part; but no act done before commencement, or in pursuance of arrangements made before commencement, shall be regarded as infringing those rights.
    (4)   The rights conferred by this Part are independent of—

      (a)   any copyright in, or moral rights relating to, any work performed or any film or sound recording of, or broadcast or cable programme including, the performance, and
      (b)   any other right or obligation arising otherwise than under this Part.

*Performers' rights*

*Qualifying performances*
**181.**   A performance is a qualifying performance for the purposes of the provisions of this Part relating to performers' rights if it is given by a qualifying individual (as defined in section 206) or takes place in a qualifying country (as so defined).

*Consent required for recording or live transmission of performance*
**182.**—(1)   A performer's rights are infringed by a person who, without his consent—

      (a)   makes, otherwise than for his private and domestic use, a recording of the whole or any substantial part of a qualifying performance, or
      (b)   broadcasts live, or includes live in a cable programme service, the whole or any substantial part of a qualifying performance.

    (2)   In an action for infringement of a performer's rights brought by virtue of this section damages shall not be awarded against a defendant who shows that at the time of the infringement he believed on reasonable grounds that consent had been given.

*Infringement of performer's rights by use of recording made without consent*
**183.**   A performer's rights are infringed by a person who, without his consent—

      (a)   shows or plays in public the whole or any substantial part of a qualifying performance, or
      (b)   broadcasts or includes in a cable programme service the whole or any substantial part of a qualifying performance,

by means of a recording which was, and which that person knows or has reason to believe was, made without the performer's consent.

*Infringement of performer's rights by importing, possessing or dealing with illicit recording*
**184.**—(1)   A performer's rights are infringed by a person who, without his consent—

(a)   imports into the United Kingdom otherwise than for his private and domestic use, or
(b)   in the course of a business possesses, sells or lets for hire, offers or exposes for sale or hire, or distributes,

a recording of a qualifying performance which is, and which that person knows or has reason to believe is, an illicit recording.

(2)   Where in an action for infringement of a performer's rights brought by virtue of this section a defendant shows that the illicit recording was innocently acquired by him or a predecessor in title of his, the only remedy available against him in respect of the infringement is damages not exceeding a reasonable payment in respect of the act complained of.

(3)   In subsection (2) 'innocently acquired' means that the person acquiring the recording did not know and had no reason to believe that it was an illicit reco5cing.

## Rights of person having recording rights

*Exclusive recording contracts and persons having recording rights*
**185.**—(1)   In this Part an 'exclusive recording contract' means a contract between a performer and another person under which that person is entitled to the exclusion of all other persons (including the performer) to make recordings of one or more of his performances with a view to their commercial exploitation.

(2)   References in this Part to a 'person having recording rights', in relation to a performance, are (subject to subsection (3)) to a person—

(a)   who is party to and has the benefit of an exclusive recording contract to which the performance is subject, or
(b)   to whom the benefit of such a contract has been assigned,

and who is a qualifying person.

(3)   If a performance is subject to an exclusive recording contract but the person mentioned in subsection (2) is not a qualifying person, references in this Part to a 'person having recording rights' in relation to the performance are to any person—

(a)   who is licensed by such a person to make recordings of the performance with a view to their commercial exploitation, or
(b)   to whom the benefit of such a licence has been assigned,

and who is a qualifying person.

(4)   In this section 'with a view to commercial exploitation' means with a view to the recordings being sold or let for hire, or shown or played in public.

*Consent required for recording of performance subject to exclusive contract*
**186.**—(1)   A person infringes the rights of a person having recording rights in

relation to a performance who, without his consent or that of the performer, makes a recording of the whole or any substantial part of the performance, otherwise than for his private and domestic use.

(2)   In an action for infringement of those rights brought by virtue of this section damages shall not be awarded against a defendant who shows that at the time of the infringement he believed on reasonable grounds that consent had been given.

*Infringement of recording rights by use of recording made without consent*
**187.**—(1)   A person infringes the rights of a person having recording rights in relation to a performance who, without his consent or, in the case of a qualifying performance, that of the performer—

(a)   shows or plays in public the whole or any substantial part of the performance, or
(b)   broadcasts or includes in a cable programme service the whole or any substantial part of the performance,

by means of a recording which was, and which that person knows or has reason to believe was, made without the appropriate consent.

(2)   The reference in subsection (1) to 'the appropriate consent' is to the consent of—

(a)   the performer, or
(b)   the person who at the time the consent was given had recording rights in relation to the performance (or, if there was more than one such person, of all of them).

*Infringement of recording rights by importing, possessing or dealing with illicit recording*
**188.**—(1)   A person infringes the rights of a person having recording rights in relation to a performance who, without his consent or, in the case of a qualifying performance, that of the performer—

(a)   imports into the United Kingdom otherwise than for his private and domestic use, or
(b)   in the course of a business possesses, sells or lets for hire, offers or exposes for sale or hire, or distributes,

a recording of the performance which is, and which that person knows or has reason to believe is, an illicit recording.

(2)   Where in an action for infringement of those rights brought by virtue of this section a defendant shows that the illicit recording was innocently acquired by him or a predecessor in title of his, the only remedy available against him in respect of the infringement is damages not exceeding a reasonable payment in respect of the act complained of.

(3)   In subsection (2) 'innocently acquired' means that the person acquiring the recording did not know and had no reason to believe that it was an illicit recording.

*Exceptions to rights conferred*

*Acts permitted notwithstanding rights conferred by this Part*

**189.** The provisions of Schedule 2 specify acts which may be done notwithstanding the rights conferred by this Part, being acts which correspond broadly to certain of those specified in Chapter III of Part I (acts permitted notwithstanding copyright).

*Power of Tribunal to give consent on behalf of performer in certain cases*

**190.**—(1) The Copyright Tribunal may, on the application of a person wishing to make a recording from a previous recording of a performance, give consent in a case where—

    (a) the identity or whereabouts of a performer cannot be ascertained by reasonable inquiry, or

    (b) a performer unreasonably withholds his consent.

(2) Consent given by the Tribunal has effect as consent of the performer for the purposes of—

    (a) the provisions of this Part relating to performers' rights, and

    (b) section 198(3)(a) (criminal liability: sufficient consent in relation to qualifying performances),

and may be given subject to any conditions specified in the Tribunal's order.

(3) The Tribunal shall not give consent under subsection (1)(a) except after the service or publication of such notices as may be required by rules made under section 150 (general procedural rules) or as the Tribunal may in any particular case direct.

(4) The Tribunal shall not give consent under subsection (1)(b) unless satisfied that the performer's reasons for withholding consent do not include the protection of any legitimate interest of his; but it shall be for the performer to show what his reasons are for withholding consent, and in default of evidence as to his reasons the Tribunal may draw such inferences as it thinks fit.

(5) In any case the Tribunal shall take into account the following factors—

    (a) whether the original recording was made with the performer's consent and is lawfully in the possession or control of the person proposing to make the further recording;

    (b) whether the making of the further recording is consistent with the obligations of the parties to the arrangements under which, or is otherwise consistent with the purposes for which, the original recording was made.

(6) Where the Tribunal gives consent under this section it shall, in default of agreement between the applicant and the performer, make such order as it thinks fit as to the payment to be made to the performer in consideration of consent being given.

*Duration and transmission of rights; consent*

*Duration of rights*

**191.** The rights conferred by this Part continue to subsist in relation to a performance until the end of the period of 50 years from the end of the calendar year in which the performance takes place.

*Transmission of rights*

**192.**—(1)   The rights conferred by this Part are not assignable or transmissible, except to the extent that performers' rights are transmissible in accordance with the following provisions.

(2)   On the death of a person entitled to performers' rights—

(a)   the rights pass to such person as he may by testamentary disposition specifically direct, and

(b)   if or to the extent that there is no such direction, the rights are exercisable by his personal representatives;

and references in this Part to the performer, in the context of the person having performers' rights, shall be construed as references to the person for the time being entitled to exercise those rights.

(3)   Where by virtue of subsection (2)(a) a right becomes exercisable by more than one person, it is exercisable by each of them independently of the other or others.

(4)   The above provisions do not affect section 185(2)(b) or (3)(b), so far as those provisions confer rights under this Part on a person to whom the benefit of a contract or licence is assigned.

(5)   Any damages recovered by personal representatives by virtue of this section in respect of an infringement after a person's death shall devolve as part of his estate as if the right of action had subsisted and been vested in him immediately before his death.

*Consent*

**193.**—(1)   Consent for the purposes of this Part may be given in relation to a specific performance, a specified description of performances or performances generally, and may relate to past or future performances.

(2)   A person having recording rights in a performance is bound by any consent given by a person through whom he derives his rights under the exclusive recording contract or licence in question, in the same way as if the consent had been given by him.

(3)   Where a right conferred by this Part passes to another person, any consent binding on the person previously entitled binds the person to whom the right passes in the same way as if the consent had been given by him.

### Remedies for infringement

*Infringement actionable as breach of statutory duty*

**194.**   An infringement of any of the rights conferred by this Part is actionable by the person entitled to the right as a breach of statutory duty.

*Order for delivery up*

**195.**—(1)   Where a person has in his possession, custody or control in the course if a business an illicit recording of a performance, a person having performer's rights or recording rights in relation to the performance under this Part may apply to the court for an order that the recording be delivered up to him or to such other person as the court may direct.

(2) An application shall not be made after the end of the period specified in section 203; and no order shall be made unless the court also makes, or it appears to the court that there are grounds for making, an order under section 204 (order as to disposal of illicit recording).

(3) A person to whom a recording is delivered up in pursuance of an order under this section shall, if an order under section 204 is not made, retain it pending the making of an order, or the decision not to make an order, under that section.

(4) Nothing in this section affects any other power of the court.

*Right to seize illicit recordings*
**196.**—(1) An illicit recording of a performance which is found exposed or otherwise immediately available for sale or hire, and in respect of which a person would be entitled to apply for an order under section 195, may be seized and detained by him or a person authorised by him.

The right to seize and detain is exercisable subject to the following conditions and is subject to any decision of the court under section 204 (order as to disposal of illicit recording).

(2) Before anything is seized under this section notice of the time and place of the proposed seizure must be given to a local police station.

(3) A person may for the purpose of exercising the right conferred by this section enter premises to which the public have access but may not seize anything in the possession, custody or control of a person at a permanent or regular place of business of his, and may not use any force.

(4) At the time when anything is seized under this section there shall be left at the place where it was seized a notice in the prescribed form containing the prescribed particulars as to the person by whom or on whose authority the seizure is made and the grounds on which it is made.

(5) In this section—

'premises' includes land, buildings, fixed or movable structures, vehicles, vessels, aircraft and hovercraft; and
'prescribed' means prescribed by order of the Secretary of State.

(6) An order of the Secretary of State under this section shall be made by statutory instrument which shall be subject to annulment in pursuance of a resolution of either House of Parliament.

*Meaning of 'illicit recording'*
**197.**—(1) In this Part 'illicit recording', in relation to a performance, shall be construed in accordance with this section.

(2) For the purposes of a performer's rights, a recording of the whole or any substantial part of a performance of his is an illicit recording if it is made, otherwise than for private purposes, without his consent.

(3) For the purposes of the rights of a person having recording rights, a recording of the whole or any substantial part of a performance subject to the exclusive recording contract is an illicit recording if it is made, otherwise than for private purposes, without his consent or that of the performer.

(4) For the purposes of sections 198 and 199 (offences and orders for delivery up in criminal proceedings), a recording is an illicit recording if it is an illicit

recording for the purposes mentioned in subsection (2) or subsection (3).

(5)   In this Part 'illicit recording' includes a recording falling to be treated as an illicit recording by virtue of any of the following provisions of Schedule 2—

paragraph 4(3) (recordings made for purposes of instruction or examination),

paragraph 6(2) (recordings made by educational establishments for educational purposes),

paragraph 12(2) (recordings of performance in electronic form retained on transfer of principal recording), or

paragraph 16(3) (recordings made for purposes of broadcast or cable programme),

but otherwise does not include a recording made in accordance with any of the provisions of that Schedule.

(6)   It is immaterial for the purposes of this section where the recording was made.

### Offences

*Criminal liability for making, dealing with or using illicit recordings*
**198.**—(1)   A person commits an offence who without sufficient consent—

(a)   makes for sale or hire, or

(b)   imports into the United Kingdom otherwise than for his private and domestic use, or

(c)   possesses in the course of a business with a view to committing any act infringing the rights conferred by this Part, or

(d)   in the course of a business—

(i)    sells or lets for hire, or

(ii)   offers or exposes for sale or hire, or

(iii)  distributes,

a recording which is, and which he knows or has reason to believe is, an illicit recording.

(2)   A person commits an offence who causes a recording of a performance made without sufficient consent to be—

(a)   shown or played in public, or

(b)   broadcast or included in a cable programme service,

thereby infringing any of the rights conferred by this Part, if he knows or has reason to believe that those rights are thereby infringed.

(3)   In subsections (1) and (2) 'sufficient consent' means—

(a)   in the case of a qualifying performance, the consent of the performer, and

(b)   in the case of a non-qualifying performance subject to an exclusive recording contract—

(i)   for the purposes of subsection (1)(a) (making of recording), the consent of the performer or the person having recording rights, and

(ii)   for the purposes of subsection (1)(b), (c) and (d) and subsection (2) (dealing with or using recording), the consent of the person having recording rights.

The references in this subsection to the person having recording rights are to the person having those rights at the time the consent is given or, if there is more than one such person, to all of them.

(4)    No offence is committed under subsection (1) or (2) by the commission of an act which by virtue of any provision of Schedule 2 may be done without infringing the rights conferred by this Part.

(5)    A person guilty of an offence under subsection (1)(a), (b) or (d)(iii) is liable—

(a)   on summary conviction to imprisonment for a term not exceeding six months or a fine not exceeding the statutory maximum, or both;

(b)   on conviction on indictment to a fine or imprisonment for a term not exceeding two years, or both.

(6)    A person guilty of any other offence under this section is liable on summary conviction to a fine not exceeding level 5 on the standard scale or imprisonment for a term not exceeding six months, or both.

*Order for delivery up in criminal proceedings*

**199.**—(1)    The court before which proceedings are brought against a person for an offence under section 198 may, if satisfied that at the time of his arrest or charge he had in his possession, custody or control in the course of a business an illicit recording of a performance, order that it be delivered up to a person having performers' rights or recording rights in relation to the performance or to such other person as the court may direct.

(2)    For this purpose a person shall be treated as charged with an offence—

(a)   in England, Wales and Northern Ireland, when he is orally charged or is served with a summons or indictment;

(b)   in Scotland, when he is cautioned, charged or served with a complaint or indictment.

(3)    An order may be made by the court of its own motion or on the application of the prosecutor (or, in Scotland, the Lord Advocate or procurator-fiscal), and may be made whether or not the person is convicted of the offence, but shall not be made—

(a)   after the end of the period specified in section 203 (period after which remedy of delivery up not available), or

(b)   if it appears to the court unlikely that any order will be made under section 204 (order as to disposal of illicit recording).

(4)    An appeal lies from an order made under this section by a magistrates' court—

(a)   in England and Wales, to the Crown Court, and

(b)   in Northern Ireland, to the county court;

and in Scotland, where an order has been made under this section, the person from whose possession, custody or control the illicit recording has been removed may, without prejudice to any other form of appeal under any rule of law, appeal against that order in the same manner as against sentence.

(5)   A person to whom an illicit recording is delivered up in pursuance of an order under this section shall retain it pending the making of an order, or the decision not to make an order, under section 204.

(6)   Nothing in this section affects the powers of the court under section 43 of the Powers of Criminal Courts Act 1973, section 223 or 436 of the Criminal Procedure (Scotland) Act 1975 or Article 7 of the Criminal Justice (Northern Ireland) Order 1980 (general provisions as to forfeiture in criminal proceedings).

*Search warrants*
**200.**—(1)   Where a justice of the peace (in Scotland, a sheriff or justice of the peace) is satisfied by information on oath given by a constable (in Scotland, by evidence on oath) that there are reasonable grounds for believing—

(a)   that an offence under section 198(1)(a), (b) or (d)(iii) (offences of making, importing or distributing illicit recordings) has been or is about to be committed in any premises, and

(b)   that evidence that such an offence has been or is about to be committed is in those premises,

he may issue a warrant authorisng a constable to enter and search the premises, using such reasonable force as is necessary.

(2)   The power conferred by subsection (1) does not, in England and Wales, extend to authorising a search for material of the kinds mentioned in section 9(2) of the Police and Criminal Evidence Act 1984 (certain classes of personal or confidential material).

(3)   A warrant under subsection (1)—

(a)   may authorise persons to accompany any constable executing the warrant, and

(b)   remains in force for 28 days from the date of its issue.

(4)   In this section 'premises' includes land, buildings, fixed or movable structures, vehicles, vessels, aircraft and hovercraft.

*False representation of authority to give consent*
**201.**—(1)   It is an offence for a person to represent falsely that he is authorised by any person to give consent for the purposes of this Part in relation to a performance, unless he believes on reasonable grounds that he is so authorised.

(2)   A person guilty of an offence under this section is liable on summary conviction to imprisonment for a term not exceeding six months or a fine not exceeding level 5 on the standard scale or both.

*Offence by body corporate: liability of officers*
**202.**—(1)   Where an offence under this Part committed by a body corporate is proved to have been committed with the consent or connivance of a director, manager, secretary or other similar officer of the body, or a person purporting to act in any such capacity, he as well as the body corporate is guilty of the offence

and liable to be proceeded against and punished accordingly.

(2)   In relation to a body corporate whose affairs are managed by its members 'director' means a member of the body corporate.

*Supplementary provisions with respect to delivery up and seizure*

*Period after which remedy of delivery up not available*
**203.**—(1)   An application may be made to the court for an order that an illicit recording of a performance delivered up in pursuance of an order under section 195 or 199, or seized and detained in pursuance of the right conferred by section 196, shall be—

(a)   forfeited to such person having performer's rights or recording rights in relation to the performance as the court may direct, or

(b)   destroyed or otherwise dealt with as the court may think fit,

or for a decision that no such order should be made.

(2)   If during the whole or any part of that period a person entitled to apply for an order—

(a)   is under a disability, or

(b)   is prevented by fraud or concealment from discovering the facts entitling him to apply,

an application may be made by him at any time before the end of the period of six years from the date on which he ceased to be under a disability or, as the case may be, could with reasonable diligence have discovered those facts.

(3)   In subsection (2) 'disability'—

(a)   in England and Wales, has the same meaning as in the Limitation Act 1980;

(b)   in Scotland, means legal disability within the meaning of the Prescription and Limitation (Scotland) Act 1973;

(c)   in Northern Ireland, has the same meaning as in the Statute of Limitations (Northern Ireland) 1958.

(4)   An order under section 199 (order for delivery up in criminal proceedings) shall not, in any case, be made after the end of the period of six years from the date on which the illicit recording in question was made.

*Order as to disposal of illicit recording*
**204.**—(1)   Where an illicit recording of a performance has been delivered up in pursuance of an order under section 195 or 199 or has been seized and detained in pursuance of the right conferred by section 196, an application may be made to the court—

(a)   for an order that it shall be forfeited to such person having performers' rights or recording rights in relation to the performance as the court may direct, or shall be destroyed or otherwise dealt with as the court may think fit, or

(b)   for a decision that no such order should be made.

(2)   In considering what order (if any) should be made, the court shall consider whether other remedies available in an action for infringement of the

rights conferred by this Part would be adequate to compensate the person or persons entitled to the rights and to protect their interests.

(3)   Provision shall be made by rules of court as to the service of notice on persons having an interest in the recording, and any such person is entitled—

(a)   to appear in proceedings for an order under this section, whether or not he was served with notice, and
(b)   to appeal against any order made, whether or not he appeared;

and an order shall not take effect until the end of the period within which notice of an appeal may be given or, if before the end of that period notice of appeal is duly given, until the final determination or abandonment of the proceedings on the appeal.

(4)   Where there is more than one person interested in a recording, the court shall make such order as it thinks just and may (in particular) direct that the recording be sold, or otherwise dealt with, and the proceeds divided.

(5)   If the court decides that no order should be made under this section, the person in whose possession, custody or control the recording was before being delivered up or seized is entitled to its return.

(6)   References in this section to a person having an interest in a recording include any person in whose favour an order could be made in respect of the recording under this section or under section 114 or 231 of this Act or section 58C of the Trade Marks Act 1938 (which make similar provision in relation to infringement of copyright, design right and trade marks).

*Jurisdiction of county court and sheriff court*
**205.**—(1)   In England, Wales and Northern Ireland a county court may entertain proceedings under—

section 195 (order for delivery up of illicit recording), or
section 204 (order as to disposal of illicit recording),

where the value of the illicit recordings in question does not exceed the county court limit for actions in tort.

(2)   In Scotland proceedings for an order under either of those provisions may be brought in the sheriff court.

(3)   Nothing in this section shall be construed as affecting the jurisdiction of the High Court or, in Scotland, the Court of Session.

*Qualification for protection and extent*

*Qualifying countries, individuals and persons*
**206.**—(1)   In this Part—

'qualifying country' means—

(a)   the United Kingdom,
(b)   another member State of the European Economic Community, or
(c)   to the extent that an Order under section 208 so provides, a country designated under that section as enjoying reciprocal protection;

'qualifying individual' means a citizen or subject of, or an individual resident in, a qualifying country; and 'qualifying person' means a qualifying individual or a body corporate or other body having legal personality which—

(a)   is formed under the law of a part of the United Kingdom or another qualifying country, and
(b)   has in any qualifying country a place of business at which substantial business activity is carried on.

(2)   The reference in the definition of 'qualifying individual' to a person's being a citizen or subject of a qualifying country shall be construed—

(a)   in relation to the United Kingdom, as a reference to his being a British citizen, and
(b)   in relation to a colony of the United Kingdom, as a reference to his being a British Dependent Territories' citizen by connection with that colony.

(3)   In determining for the purpose of the definition of 'qualifying person' whether substantial business activity is carried on at a place of business in any country, no account shall be taken of dealings in goods which are at all material times outside that country.

*Countries to which this Part extends*
**207.**   This Part extends to England and Wales, Scotland and Northern Ireland.

*Countries enjoying reciprocal protection*
**208.**—(1)   Her Majesty may by Order in Council designate as enjoying reciprocal protection under this Part—

(a)   a Convention country, or
(b)   a country as to which Her Majesty is satisfied that provision has been or will be made under its law giving adequate protection for British performances.

(2)   A 'Convention country' means a country which is a party to a Convention relating to performers' rights to which the United Kingdom is also a Party.
(3)   A 'British performance' means a performance—

(a)   given by an individual who is a British citizen or resident in the United Kingdom, or
(b)   taking place in the United Kingdom.

(4)   If the law of that country provides adequate protection only for certain descriptions of performance, an Order under subsection (1)(b) designating that country shall contain provision limiting to a corresponding extent the protection afforded by this Part in relation to performances connected with that country.
(5)   The power conferred by subsection (1)(b) is exercisable in relation to any of the Channel Islands, the Isle of Man or any colony of the United Kingdom, as in relation to a foreign country.
(6)   A statutory instrument containing an Order in Council under this section shall be subject to annulment in pursuance of a resolution of either House of Parliament.

*Territorial waters and the continental shelf*
**209.**—(1)   For the purposes of this Part the territorial waters of the United Kingdom shall be treated as part of the United Kingdom.

(2)   This Part applies to things done in the United Kingdom sector of the continental shelf on a structure or vessel which is present there for purposes directly connected with the exploration of the sea bed or subsoil or the exploitation of their natural resources as it applies to things done in the United Kingdom.

(3)   The United Kingdom sector of the continental shelf means the areas designated by order under section 1(7) of the Continental Shelf Act 1964.

*British ships, aircraft and hovercraft*
**210.**—(1)   This Part applies to things done on a British ship, aircraft or hovercraft as it applies to things done in the United Kingdom.

(2)   In this section—

'British ship' means a ship which is a British ship for the purposes of the Merchant Shipping Acts (see section 2 of the Merchant Shipping Act 1988) otherwise than by virtue of registration in a country outside the United Kingdom; and
'British aircraft' and 'British hovercraft' mean an aircraft or hovercraft registered in the United Kingdom.

*Interpretation*

*Expressions having same meaning as in copyright provisions*
**211.**—(1)   The following expressions have the same meaning in this Part as in Part I (copyright)—

broadcast,
business,
cable programme,
cable programme service,
country,
defendant (in Scotland),
delivery up (in Scotland),
film,
literary work,
published, and
sound recording.

(2)   The provisions of section 6(3) to (5), section 7(5) and 19(4) (supplementary provisions relating to broadcasting and cable programme services) apply for the purposes of this Part, and in relation to an infringement of the rights conferred by this Part, as they apply for the purposes of Part I and in relation to an infringement of copyright.

*Index of defined expressions*
**212.**   The following Table shows provisions defining or otherwise explaining expressions used in this Part (other than provisions defining or explaining an expression used only in the same section)—

| | |
|---|---|
| broadcast (and related expressions) | section 211 (and section 6) |
| business | section 211(1) (and section 178) |
| cable programme, cable programme service (and related expressions) | section 211 (and section 7) |
| country | section 211(1) (and section 178) |
| defendant (in Scotland) | section 211(1) (and section 177) |
| delivery up (in Scotland) | section 211(1) (and section 177) |
| exclusive recording contract | section 185(1) |
| film | section 211(1) (and section 5) |
| illicit recording | section 197 |
| literary work | section 211(1) (and section 3(1)) |
| performance | section 180(2) |
| published | section 211(1) (and section 175) |
| qualifying country | section 206(1) |
| qualifying individual | section 206(1) and (2) |
| qualifying performance | section 181 |
| qualifying person | section 206(1) and (3) |
| recording (of a performance) | section 180(2) |
| recording rights (person having) | section 185(2) and (3) |
| sound recording | section 211(1) (and section 5) |

## Part III Design right

*Chapter I Design right in original designs*

*Introductory*

*Design right*

**213.**—(1)   Design right is a property right which subsists in accordance with this Part in an original design.

(2)   In this Part 'design' means the design of any aspect of the shape or configuration (whether internal or external) of the whole or part of an article.

(3)   Design right does not subsist in—

(a)   a method or principle of construction,

(b)   features of shape or configuration of an article which—

(i)   enable the article to be connected to, or placed in, around or against another article so that either article may perform its function, or

(ii)   are dependent upon the appearance of another article of which the article is intended by the designer to form an integral part, or

(c)   surface decoration.

(4)   A design is not 'original' for the purposes of this Part if it is commonplace in the design field in question at the time of its creation.

(5)   Design right subsists in a design only if the design qualifies for design right protection by reference to—

(a)   the designer or the person by whom the design was commissioned or the designer employed (see sections 218 and 219), or

(b)   the person by whom and country in which articles made to the design were first marketed (see section 220),

or in accordance with any Order under section 221 (power to make further provision with respect to qualification).

(6)   Design right does not subsist unless and until the design has been recorded in a design document or an article has been made to the design.

(7)   Design right does not subsist in a design which was so recorded, or to which an article was made, before the commencement of this Part.

*The designer*

**214.**—(1)   In this Part the 'designer', in relation to a design, means the person who creates it.

(2)   In the case of a computer-generated design the person by whom the arrangements necessary for the creation of the design are undertaken shall be taken to be the designer.

*Ownership of design right*

**215.**—(1)   The designer is the first owner of any design right in a design which is not created in pursuance of a commission or in the course of employment.

(2)   Where a design is created in pursuance of a commission, the person commissioning the design is the first owner of any design right in it.

(3)   Where, in a case not falling within subsection (2) a design is created by an employee in the course of his employment, his employer is the first owner of any design right in the design.

(4)   If a design qualifies for design right protection by virtue of section 220 (qualification by reference to first marketing of articles made to the design), the above rules do not apply and the person by whom the articles in question are marketed is the first owner of the design right.

*Duration of design right*

**216.**—(1)   Design right expires—

(a)   15 years from the end of the calendar year in which the design was first recorded in a design document or an article was first made to the design, whichever first occurred, or

(b)   if articles made to the design are made available for sale or hire within five years from the end of that calendar year, 10 years from the end of the calendar year in which that first occurred.

(2)   The reference in subsection (1) to articles being made available for sale or hire is to their being made so available anywhere in the world by or with the licence of the design right owner.

### Qualification for design right protection

*Qualifying individuals and qualifying persons*

**217.**—(1)   In this Part—

'qualifying individual' means a citizen or subject of, or an individual habitually resident in, a qualifying country; and

'qualifying person' means a qualifying individual or a body corporate or other body having legal personality which—

(a)   is formed under the law of a part of the United Kingdom or another qualifying country, and

(b)   has in any qualifying country a place of business at which substantial business activity is carried on.

(2)   References in this Part to a qualifying person include the Crown and the government of any other qualifying country.

(3)   In this section 'qualifying country' means—

(a)   the United Kingdom,

(b)   a country to which this Part extends by virtue of an Order under section 255,

(c)   another member State of the European Economic Community, or

(d)   to the extent that an Order under section 256 so provides, a country designated under that section as enjoying reciprocal protection.

(4)   The reference in the definition of 'qualifying individual' to a person's being a citizen or subject of a qualifying country shall be construed—

(a)   in relation to the United Kingdom, as a reference to his being a British citizen, and

(b)   in relation to a colony of the United Kingdom, as a reference to his being a British Dependent Territories' citizen by connection with that colony.

(5)   In determining for the purpose of the definition of 'qualifying person' whether substantial business activity is carried on at a place of business in any country, no account shall be taken of dealings in goods which are at all material times outside that country.

*Qualification by reference to designer*
**218.**—(1)   This section applies to a design which is not created in pursuance of a commission or in the course of employment.

(2)   A design to which this section applies qualifies for design right protection if the designer is a qualifying individual or, in the case of a computer-generated design, a qualifying person.

(3)   A joint design to which this section applies qualifies for design right protection if any of the designers is a qualifying individual or, as the case may be, a qualifying person.

(4)   Where a joint design qualifies for design right protection under this section, only those designers who are qualifying individuals or qualifying persons are entitled to design right under section 215(1) (first ownership of design right: entitlement of designer).

*Qualification by reference to commissioner or employer*
**219.**—(1)   A design qualifies for design right protection if it is created in pursuance of a commission from, or in the course of employment with, a qualifying person.

(2)   In the case of a joint commission or joint employment a design qualifies for design right protection if any of the commissioners or employers is a qualifying person.

(3)   Where a design which is jointly commissioned or created in the course of

joint employment qualifies for design right protection under this section, only those commissioners or employers who are qualifying persons are entitled to design right under section 215(2) or (3) (first ownership of design right: entitlement of commissioner of employer).

*Qualification by reference to first marketing*
**220.**—(1)   A design which does not qualify for design right protection under section 218 or 219 (qualification by reference to designer, commissioner or employer) qualifies for design right protection if the first marketing of articles made to the design—

(a)   is by a qualifying person who is exclusively authorised to put such articles on the market in the United Kingdom, and
(b)   takes place in the United Kingdom, another country to which this Part extends by virtue of an Order under section 255, or another member State of the European Economic Community.

(2)   If the first marketing of articles made to the design is done jointly by two or more persons, the design qualifies for design right protection if any of those persons meets the requirements specified in subsection (1)(a).
(3)   In such a case only the persons who meet those requirements are entitled to design right under section 215(4) (first ownership of design right: entitlement of first marketer of articles made to the design).
(4)   In subsection (1)(a) 'exclusively authorised' refers—

(a)   to authorisation by the person who would have been first owner of design right as designer, commissioner of the design or employer of the designer if he had been a qualifying person, or by a person lawfully claiming under such a person, and
(b)   to exclusivity capable of being enforced by legal proceedings in the United Kingdom.

*Power to make further provision as to qualification*
**221.**—(1)   Her Majesty may, with a view to fulfilling an international obligation of the United Kingdom, by Order in Council provide that a design qualifies for design right protection if such requirements as are specified in the Order are met.
(2)   An Order may make different provision for different descriptions of design or article; and may make such consequential modifications of the operation of sections 215 (ownership of design right) and sections 218 to 220 (other means of qualification) as appear to Her Majesty to be appropriate.
(3)   A statutory instrument containing an Order in Council under this section shall be subject to annulment in pursuance of a resolution of either House of Parliament.

*Dealings with design right*

*Assignment and licences*
**222.**—(1)   Design right is transmissible by assignment, by testamentary disposition or by operation of law, as personal or movable property.
(2)   An assignment or other transmission of design right may be partial, that is limited so as to apply—

(a)   to one or more, but not all, of the things the design right owner has the exclusive right to do;

(b)   to part, but not the whole, of the period for which the right is to subsist.

(3)   An assignment of design right is not effective unless it is in writing signed by or on behalf of the assignor.

(4)   A licence granted by the owner of design right is binding on every successor in title to his interest in the right, except a purchaser in good faith for valuable consideration and without notice (actual or constructive) of the licence or a person deriving title from such a purchaser; and references in this Part to doing anything with, or without, the licence of the design right owner shall be construed accordingly.

*Prospective ownership of design right*
**223.**—(1)   Where by an agreement made in relation to future design right, and signed by or on behalf of the prospective owner of the design right, the prospective owner purports to assign the future design right (wholly or partially) to another person, then if, on the right coming into existence, the assignee or another person claiming under him would be entitled as against all other persons to require the right to be vested in him, the right shall vest in him by virtue of this section.

(2)   In this section—

'future design right' means design right which will or may come into existence in respect of a future design or class of designs or on the occurrence of a future event; and

'prospective owner' shall be construed accordingly, and includes a person who is prospectively entitled to design right by virtue of such an agreement as is mentioned in subsection (1).

(3)   A licence granted by a prospective owner of design right is binding on every successor in title to his interest (or prospective interest) in the right, except a purchaser in good faith for valuable consideration and without notice (actual or constructive) of the licence or a person deriving title from such a purchaser; and references in this Part to doing anything with, or without, the licence of the design right owner shall be construed accordingly.

*Assignment of right in registered design presumed to carry with it design right*
**224.**   Where a design consisting of a design in which design right subsists is registered under the Registered Designs Act 1949 and the proprietor of the registered design is also the design right owner, an assignment of the right in the registered design shall be taken to be also an assignment of the design right, unless a contrary intention appears.

*Exclusive licences*
**225.**—(1)   In this Part an 'exclusive licence' means a licence in writing signed by or on behalf of the design right owner authorising the licensee to the exclusion of all other persons, including the person granting the licence, to exercise a right which would otherwise be exercisable exclusively by the design right owner.

(2)   The licensee under an exclusive licence has the same rights against any

successor in title who is bound by the licence as he has against the person granting the licence.

## Chapter II Rights of design right owner and remedies

### Infringement of design right

*Primary infringement of design right*
**226.**—(1)   The owner of design right in a design has the exclusive right to reproduce the design for commercial purposes—

(a)   by making articles to that design, or
(b)   by making a design document recording the design for the purpose of enabling such articles to be made.

(2)   Reproduction of a design by making articles to the design means copying the design so as to produce articles exactly or substantially to that design, and references in this Part to making articles to a design shall be construed accordingly.
(3)   Design right is infringed by a person who without the licence of the design right owner does, or authorises another to do, anything which by virtue of this section is the exclusive right of the design right owner.
(4)   For the purposes of this section reproduction may be direct or indirect, and it is immaterial whether any intervening acts themselves infringe the design right.
(5)   This section has effect subject to the provisions of Chapter III (exceptions to rights of design right owner).

*Secondary infringement: importing or dealing with infringing article*
**227.**—(1)   Design right is infringed by a person who, without the licence of the design right owner—

(a)   imports into the United Kingdom for commercial purposes, or
(b)   has in his possession for commercial purposes, or
(c)   sells, lets for hire, or offers or exposes for sale or hire, in the course of a business,

an article which is, and which he knows or has reason to believe is, an infringing article.
(2)   This section has effect subject to the provisions of Chapter III (exceptions to rights of design right owner).

*Meaning of 'infringing article'*
**228.**—(1)   In this Part 'infringing article', in relation to a design, shall be construed in accordance with this section.
(2)   An article is an infringing article if its making to that design was an infringement of design right in the design.
(3)   An article is also an infringing article if—

(a)   it has been or is proposed to be imported into the United Kingdom, and

(b)    its making to that design in the United Kingdom would have been an infringement of design right in the design or a breach of an exclusive licence agreement relating to the design.

(4)    Where it is shown that an article is made to a design in which design right subsists or has subsisted at any time, it shall be presumed until the contrary is proved that the article was made at a time when design right subsisted.

(5)    Nothing in subsection (3) shall be construed as applying to an article which may lawfully be imported into the United Kingdom by virtue of any enforceable Community right within the meaning of section 2(1) of the European Communities Act 1972.

(6)    The expression 'infringing article' does not include a design document, notwithstanding that its making was or would have been an infringement of design right.

## Remedies for infringement

### Rights and remedies of design right owner
**229.**—(1)    An infringement of design right is actionable by the design right owner.

(2)    In an action for infringement of design right all such relief by way of damages, injunctions, accounts or otherwise is available to the plaintiff as is available in respect of the infringement of any other property right.

(3)    The court may in an action for infringement of design right, having regard to all the circumstances and in particular to—

(a)    the flagrancy of the infringement, and
(b)    any benefit accruing to the defendant by reason of the infringement,

award such additional damages as the justice of the case may require.

(4)    This section has effect subject to section 233 (innocent infringement).

### Order for delivery up
**230.**—(1)    Where a person—

(a)    has in his possession, custody or control for commercial purposes an infringing article, or
(b)    has in his possession, custody or control anything specifically designed or adapted for making articles to a particular design, knowing or having reason to believe that it has been or is to be used to make an infringing article,

the owner of the design right in the design in question may apply to the court for an order that the infringing article or other thing be delivered up to him or to such other person as the court may direct.

(2)    An application shall not be made after the end of the period specified in the following provisions of this section; and no order shall be made unless the court also makes, or it appears to the court that there are grounds for making, an order under section 231 (order as to disposal of infringing article etc.).

(3)    An application for an order under this section may not be made after the end of the period of six years from the date on which the article or thing in question was made, subject to subsection (4).

(4)    If during the whole or any part of that period the design right owner—

(a)   is under a disability, or

(b)   is prevented by fraud or concealment from discovering the facts entitling him to apply for an order,

an application may be made at any time before the end of the period of six years from the date on which he ceased to be under a disability or, as the case may be, could with reasonable diligence have discovered those facts.

(5)   In subsection (4) 'disability'—

(a)   in England and Wales, has the same meaning as in the Limitation Act 1980;

(b)   in Scotland, means legal disability within the meaning of the Prescription and Limitation (Scotland) Act 1973;

(c)   in Northern Ireland, has the same meaning as in the Statute of Limitations (Northern Ireland) 1958.

(6)   A person to whom an infringing article or other thing is delivered up in pursuance of an order under this section shall, if an order under section 231 is not made, retain it pending the making of an order, or the decision not to make an order, under that section.

(7)   Nothing in this section affects any other power of the court.

*Order as to disposal of infringing articles etc.*
**231.**—(1)   An application may be made to the court for an order that an infringing article or other thing delivered up in pursuance of an order under section 230 shall be—

(a)   forfeited to the design right owner, or

(b)   destroyed or otherwise dealt with as the court may think fit,

or for a decision that no such order should be made.

(2)   In considering what order (if any) should be made, the court shall consider whether other remedies available in an action for infringement of design right would be adequate to compensate the design right owner and to protect his interests.

(3)   Provision shall be made by rules of court as to the service of notice on persons having an interest in the article or other thing, and any such person is entitled—

(a)   to appear in proceedings for an order under this section, whether or not he was served with notice, and

(b)   to appeal against any order made, whether or not he appeared;

and an order shall not take effect until the end of the period within which notice of an appeal may be given or, if before the end of that period notice of appeal is duly given, until the final determination or abandonment of the proceedings on the appeal.

(4)   Where there is more than one person interested in an article or other thing, the court shall make such order as it thinks just and may (in particular) direct that the thing be sold, or otherwise dealt with, and the proceeds divided.

(5)   If the court decides that no order should be made under this section, the person in whose possession, custody or control the article or other thing was

before being delivered up or seized is entitled to its return.

(6)   References in this section to a person having an interest in an article or other thing include any person in whose favour an order could be made in respect of it under this section or under section 114 or 204 of this Act or section 58C of the Trade Marks Act 1938 (which make similar provision in relation to infringement of copyright, rights in performances and trade marks).

*Jurisdiction of county court and sheriff court*
**232.**—(1)   In England, Wales and Northern Ireland a county court may entertain proceedings under—

section 230 (order for delivery up of infringing article etc.),
section 231 (order as to disposal of infringing article etc.), or
section 235(5) (application by exclusive licensee having concurrent rights),

where the value of the infringing articles and other things in question does not exceed the county court limit for actions in tort.

(2)   In Scotland proceedings for an order under any of those provisions may be brought in the sheriff court.

(3)   Nothing in this section shall be construed as affecting the jurisdiction of the High Court or, in Scotland, the Court of Session.

*Innocent infringement*
**233.**—(1)   Where in an action for infringement of design right brought by virtue of section 226 (primary infringement) it is shown that at the time of the infringement the defendant did not know, and had no reason to believe, that design right subsisted in the design to which the action relates, the plaintiff is not entitled to damages against him, but without prejudice to any other remedy.

(2)   Where in an action for infringement of design right brought by virtue of section 227 (secondary infringement) a defendant shows that the infringing article was innocently acquired by him or a predecessor in title of his, the only remedy available against him in respect of the infringement is damages not exceeding a reasonable royalty in respect of the act complained of.

(3)   In subsection (2) 'innocently acquired' means that the person acquiring the article did not know and had no reason to believe that it was an infringing article.

*Rights and remedies of exclusive licensee*
**234.**—(1)   An exclusive licensee has, except against the design right owner, the same rights and remedies in respect of matters occurring after the grant of the licence as if the licence had been an assignment.

(2)   His rights and remedies are concurrent with those of the design right owner; and references in the relevant provisions of this Part to the design right owner shall be construed accordingly.

(3)   In an action brought by an exclusive licensee by virtue of this section a defendant may avail himself of any defence which would have been available to him if the action had been brought by the design right owner.

*Exercise of concurrent rights*
**235.**—(1)   Where an action for infringement of design right brought by the design right owner or an exclusive licensee relates (wholly or partly) to an

infringement in respect of which they have concurrent rights of action, the design right owner or, as the case may be, the exclusive licensee may not, without the leave of the court, proceed with the action unless the other is either joined as a plaintiff or added as a defendant.

(2)   A design right owner or exclusive licensee who is added as a defendant in pursuance of subsection (1) is not liable for any costs in the action unless he takes part in the proceedings.

(3)   The above provisions do not affect the granting of interlocutory relief on the application of the design right owner or an exclusive licensee.

(4)   Where an action for infringement of design right is brought which relates (wholly or partly) to an infringement in respect of which the design right owner and an exclusive licensee have concurrent rights of action—

(a)   the court shall, in assessing damages, take into account—

(i)   the terms of the licence, and

(ii)   any pecuniary remedy already awarded or available to either of them in respect of the infringement;

(b)   no account of profits shall be directed if an award of damages has been made, or an account of profits has been directed, in favour of the other of them in respect of the infringement; and

(c)   the court shall if an account of profits is directed apportion the profits between them as the court considers just, subject to any agreement between them;

and these provisions apply whether or not the design right owner and the exclusive licensee are both parties to the action.

(5)   The design right owner shall notify any exclusive licensee having concurrent rights before applying for an order under section 230 (order for delivery up of infringing article etc.); and the court may on the application of the licensee make such order under that section as it thinks fit having regard to the terms of the licence.

### Chapter III Exceptions to rights of design right owners

#### Infringement of copyright

*Infringement of copyright*
**236.**   Where copyright subsists in a work which consists of or includes a design in which design right subsists, it is not an infringement of design right in the design to do anything which is an infringement of the copyright in that work.

#### Availability of licences of right

*Licences available in last five years of design right*
**237.**—(1)   Any person is entitled as of right to a licence to do in the last five years of the design right term anything which would otherwise infringe the design right.

(2)   The terms of the licence shall, in default of agreement, be settled by the comptroller.

(3)   The Secretary of State may if it appears to him necessary in order to—

(a)   comply with an international obligation of the United Kingdom, or

(b)   secure or maintain reciprocal protection for British designs in other countries,

by order exclude from the operation of subsection (1) designs of a description specified in the order or designs applied to articles of a description so specified.

(4)   An order shall be made by statutory instrument; and no order shall be made unless a draft of it has been laid before and approved by a resolution of each House of Parliament.

*Powers exercisable for protection of the public interest*
**238.**—(1)   Where the matters specified in a report of the Monopolies and Mergers Commission as being those which in the Commission's opinion operate, may be expected to operate or have operated against the public interest include—

(a)   conditions in licences granted by a design right owner restricting the use of the design by the licensee or the right of the design right owner to grant other licences, or

(b)   a refusal of a design right owner to grant licences on reasonable terms, the powers conferred by Part I of Schedule 8 to the Fair Trading Act 1973 (powers exercisable for purpose of remedying or preventing adverse effects specified in report of Commission) include power to cancel or modify those conditions and, instead or in addition, to provide that licences in respect of the design right shall be available as of right.

(2)   The references in sections 56(2) and 73(2) of that Act, and sections 10(2)(b) and 12(5) of the Competition Act 1980, to the powers specified in that Part of that Schedule shall be construed accordingly.

(3)   The terms of a licence available by virtue of this section shall, in default of agreement, be settled by the comptroller.

*Undertaking to take licence of right in infringement proceedings*
**239.**—(1)   If in proceedings for infringement of design right in a design in respect of which a licence is available as of right under section 237 or 238 the defendant undertakes to take a licence on such terms as may be agreed or, in default of agreement, settled by the comptroller under that section—

(a)   no injunction shall be granted against him,

(b)   no order for delivery up shall be made under section 230, and

(c)   the amount recoverable against him by way of damages or on an account of profits, shall not exceed double the amount which would have been payable by him as licensee if such a licence on those terms had been granted before the earliest infringement.

(2)   An undertaking may be given at any time before final order in the proceedings, without any admission of liability.

(3)   Nothing in this section affects the remedies available in respect of an infringement committed before licences of right were available.

*Crown use of designs*

*Crown use of designs*
**240.**—(1)   A government department, or a person authorised in writing by a government department, may without the licence of the design right owner—

(a)   do anything for the purpose of supplying articles for the services of the Crown, or

(b)   dispose of articles no longer required for the services of the Crown;

and nothing done by virtue of this section infringes the design right.

(2)   References in this Part to 'the services of the Crown' are to—

(a)   the defence of the realm,
(b)   foreign defence purposes, and
(c)   health service purposes.

(3)   The reference to the supply of articles for 'foreign defence purposes' is to their supply—

(a)   for the defence of a country outside the realm, in pursuance of an agreement or arrangement to which the government of that country and Her Majesty's Government in the United Kingdom are parties; or

(b)   for use by armed forces operating in pursuance of a resolution of the United Nations or one of its organs.

(4)   The reference to the supply of articles for 'health service purposes' are to their supply for the purpose of providing—

(a)   pharmaceutical services,
(b)   general medical services, or
(c)   general dental services,

that is, services of those kinds under Part II of the National Health Service Act 1977, Part II of the National Health Service (Scotland) Act 1978 or the corresponding provisions of the law in force in Northern Ireland.

(5)   In this Part—

'Crown use', in relation to a design, means the doing of anything by virtue of this section which would otherwise be an infringement of design right in the design; and

'the government department concerned', in relation to such use, means the government department by whom or on whose authority the act was done.

(6)   The authority of a government department in respect of Crown use of a design may be given to a person either before or after the use and whether or not he is authorised, directly or indirectly, by the design right owner to do anything in relation to the design.

(7)   A person acquiring anything sold in the exercise of powers conferred by this section, and any person claiming under him, may deal with it in the same manner as if the design right were held on behalf of the Crown.

*Settlement of terms for Crown use*
**241.**—(1)   Where Crown use is made of a design, the government department concerned shall—

(a)   notify the design right owner as soon as practicable, and
(b)   give him such information as to the extent of the use as he may from time to time require,

unless it appears to the department that it would be contrary to the public interest to do so or the identity of the design right owner cannot be ascertained on reasonable inquiry.

(2)   Crown use of a design shall be on such terms as, either before or after the use, are agreed between the government department concerned and the design right owner with the approval of the Treasury or, in default of agreement, are determined by the court.

In the application of this subsection to Northern Ireland the reference to the Treasury shall, where the government department referred to in that subsection is a Northern Ireland department, be construed as a reference to the Department of Finance and Personnel.

(3)   Where the identity of the design right owner cannot be ascertained on reasonable inquiry, the government department concerned may apply to the court who may order that no royalty or other sum shall be payable in respect of Crown use of the design until the owner agrees terms with the department or refers the matter to the court for determination.

*Rights of third parties in case of Crown use*
**242.**—(1)   The provisions of any licence, assignment or agreement made between the design right owner (or anyone deriving title from him or from whom he derives title) and any person other than a government department are of no effect in relation to Crown use of a design, or any act incidental to Crown use, so far as they—

(a)   restrict or regulate anything done in relation to the design, or the use of any model, document or other information relating to it, or

(b)   provide for the making of payments in respect of, or calculated by reference to such use;

and the copying or issuing to the public of copies of any such model or document in connection with the thing done, or any such use, shall be deemed not to be an infringement of any copyright in the model or document.

(2)   Subsection (1) shall not be construed as authorising the disclosure of any such model, document or information in contravention of the licence, assignment or agreement.

(3)   Where an exclusive licence is in force in respect of the design—

(a)   if the licence was granted for royalties—

(i)   any agreement between the design right owner and a government department under section 241 (settlement of terms for Crown use) requires the consent of the licensee, and

(ii)   the licensee is entitled to recover from the design right owner such part of the payment for Crown use as may be agreed between them or, in default of agreement, determined by the court;

(b)   if the licence was granted otherwise than for royalties—

(i)   section 241 applies in relation to anything done which but for section 240 (Crown use) and subsection (1) above would be an infringement of the rights of the licensee with the substitution for references to the design right owner of references to the licensee, and

(ii)   section 241 does not apply in relation to anything done by the licensee by virtue of an authority given under section 240.

(4)   Where the design right has been assigned to the design right owner in consideration of royalties—

(a)   section 241 applies in relation to Crown use of the design as if the references to the design right owner included the assignor, and any payment for Crown use shall be divided between them in such proportion as may be agreed or, in default of agreement, determined by the court; and

(b)   section 241 applies in relation to any act incidental to Crown use as it applies in relation to Crown use of the design.

(5)   Where any model, document or other information relating to a design is used in connection with Crown use of the design, or any act incidental to Crown use, section 241 applies to the use of the model, document or other information with the substitution for the references to the design right owner of references to the person entitled to the benefit of any provision of an agreement rendered inoperative by subsection (1) above.

(6)   In this section—

'act incidental to Crown use' means anything done for the services of the Crown to the order of a government department by the design right owner in respect of a design;

'payment for Crown use' means such amount as is payable by the government department concerned by virtue of section 241; and

'royalties' includes any benefit determined by reference to the use of the design.

*Crown use: compensation for loss of profit*

**243.**—(1)   Where Crown use is made of a design, the government department concerned shall pay—

(a)   to the design right owner, or

(b)   if there is an exclusive licence in force in respect of the design, to the exclusive licensee,

compensation for any loss resulting from his not being awarded a contract to supply the articles made to the design.

(2)   Compensation is payable only to the extent that such a contract could have been fulfilled from his existing manufacturing capacity; but is payable notwithstanding the existence of circumstances rendering him ineligible for the award of such a contract.

(3)   In determining the loss, regard shall be had to the profit which would have been made on such a contract and to the extent to which any manufacturing capacity was under-used.

(4)   No compensation is payable in respect of any failure to secure contracts for the supply of articles made to the design otherwise than for the services of the Crown.

(5)   The amount payable shall, if not agreed between the design right owner or licensee and the government department concerned with the approval of the

Treasury, be determined by the court on a reference under section 252, and it is in addition to any amount payable under section 241 or 242.

(6)   In the application of this section to Northern Ireland, the reference in subsection (5) to the Treasury shall, where the government department concerned is a Northern Ireland department, be construed as a reference to the Department of Finance and Personnel.

*Special provision for Crown use during emergency*

**244.**—(1)   During a period of emergency the powers exercisable in relation to a design by virtue of section 240 (Crown use) include power to do any act which would otherwise be an infringement of design right for any purpose which appears to the government department concerned necessary or expedient—

(a)   for the efficient prosecution of any war in which Her Majesty may be engaged;

(b)   for the maintenance of supplies and services essential to the life of the community;

(c)   for securing a sufficiency of supplies and services essential to the well-being of the community;

(d)   for promoting the productivity of industry, commerce and agriculture;

(e)   for fostering and directing exports and reducing imports, or imports of any classes, from all or any countries and for redressing the balance of trade;

(f)   generally for ensuring that the whole resources of the community are available for use, and are used, in a manner best calculated to serve the interests of the community; or

(g)   for assisting the relief of suffering and the restoration and distribution of essential supplies and services in any country outside the United Kingdom which is in grave distress as the result of war.

(2)   References in this Part to the services of the Crown include, as respects a period of emergency, those purposes; and references to 'Crown use' include any act which would apart from this section be an infringement of design right.

(3)   In this section 'period of emergency' means a period beginning with such date as may be declared by Order in Council to be the beginning, and ending with such date as may be so declared to be the end, of a period of emergency for the purposes of this section.

(4)   No Order in Council under this section shall be submitted to Her Majesty unless a draft of it has been laid before and approved by a resolution of each House of Parliament.

*General*

*Power to provide for further exceptions*

**245.**—(1)   The Secretary of State may if it appears to him necessary in order to—

(a)   comply with an international obligation of the United Kingdom, or

(b)   secure or maintain reciprocal protection for British designs in other countries,

by order provide that acts of a description specified in the order do not infringe design right.

(2) An order may make different provision for different descriptions of design or article.

(3) An order shall be made by statutory instrument and no order shall be made unless a draft of it has been laid before and approved by a resolution of each House of Parliament.

### Chapter IV Jurisdiction of the comptroller and the court

### Jurisdiction of the comptroller

*Jurisdiction to decide matters relating to design right*

**246.**—(1) A party to a dispute as to any of the following matters may refer the dispute to the comptroller for his decision—

    (a)  the subsistence of design right,

    (b)  the term of design right, or

    (c)  the identity of the person in whom design right first vested;

and the comptroller's decision on the reference is binding on the parties to the dispute.

(2) No other court or tribunal shall decide any such matter except—

    (a)  on a reference or appeal from the comptroller,

    (b)  in infringement or other proceedings in which the issue arises incidentally, or

    (c)  in proceedings brought with the agreement of the parties or the leave of the comptroller.

(3) The comptroller has jurisdiction to decide any incidental question of fact or law arising in the course of a reference under this section.

*Application to settle terms of licence of right*

**247.**—(1) A person requiring a licence which is available as of right by virtue of—

    (a)  section 237 (licences available in last five years of design right), or

    (b)  an order under section 238 (licences made available in the public interest),

may apply to the comptroller to settle the terms of the licence.

(2) No application for the settlement of the terms of a licence available by virtue of section 237 may be made earlier than one year before the earliest date on which the licence may take effect under that section.

(3) The terms of a licence settled by the comptroller shall authorise the licensee to do—

    (a)  in the case of a licence available by virtue of section 237, everything which would be an infringement of the design right in the absence of a licence;

    (b)  in the case of a licence available by virtue of section 238, everything in respect of which a licence is so available.

(4) In settling the terms of a licence the comptroller shall have regard to such factors as may be prescribed by the Secretary of State by order made by statutory instrument.

(5)   No such order shall be made unless a draft of it has been laid before and approved by a resolution of each House of Parliament.

(6)   Where the terms of a licence are settled by the comptroller, the licence has effect—

(a)   in the case of an application in respect of a licence available by virtue of section 237 made before the earliest date on which the licence may take effect under that section, from that date;

(b)   in any other case, from the date on which the application to the comptroller was made.

*Settlement of terms where design right owner unknown*
**248.**—(1)   This section applies where a person making an application under section 247 (settlement of terms of licence of right) is unable on reasonable inquiry to discover the identity of the design right owner.

(2)   The comptroller may in settling the terms of the licence order that the licence shall be free of any obligation as to royalties or other payments.

(3)   If such an order is made the design right owner may apply to the comptroller to vary the terms of the licence with effect from the date on which his application is made.

(4)   If the terms of a licence are settled by the comptroller and it is subsequently established that a licence was not available as of right, the licensee shall not be liable in damages for, or for an account of profits in respect of, anything done before he was aware of any claim by the design right owner that a licence was not available.

*Appeals as to terms of licence of right*
**249.**—(1)   An appeal lies from any decision of the comptroller under section 247 or 248 (settlement of terms of licence of right) to the Appeal Tribunal constituted under section 28 of the Registered Designs Act 1949.

(2)   Section 28 of that Act applies to appeals from the comptroller under this section as it applies to appeals from the registrar under that Act; but rules made under that section may make different provision for appeals under this section.

*Rules*
**250.**—(1)   The Secretary of State may make rules for regulating the procedure to be followed in connection with any proceeding before the comptroller under this Part.

(2)   Rules may, in particular, make provision—

(a)   prescribing forms;
(b)   requiring fees to be paid;
(c)   authorising the rectification of irregularities of procedure;
(d)   regulating the mode of giving evidence and empowering the comptroller to compel the attendance of witnesses and the discovery of and production of documents;
(e)   providing for the appointment of advisers to assist the comptroller in proceedings before him;
(f)   prescribing time limits for doing anything required to be done (and providing for the alteration of any such limit); and

(g)   empowering the comptroller to award costs and to direct how, to what party and from what parties, costs are to be paid.

(3)   Rules prescribing fees require the consent of the Treasury.

(4)   The remuneration of an adviser appointed to assist the comptroller shall be determined by the Secretary of State with the consent of the Treasury and shall be defrayed out of money provided by Parliament.

(5)   Rules shall be made by statutory instrument which shall be subject to annulment in pursuance of a resolution of either House of Parliament.

### *Jurisdiction of the court*

*References and appeals on design right matters*
**251.**—(1)   In any proceedings before him under section 246 (reference of matter relating to design right) the comptroller may at any time order the whole proceedings or any question or issue (whether of fact or law) to be referred, on such terms as he may direct, to the High Court or, in Scotland, the Court of Session.

(2)   The comptroller shall make such an order if the parties to the proceedings agree that he should do so.

(3)   On a reference under this section the court may exercise any power available to the comptroller by virtue of this Part as respects the matter referred to it and, following its determination, may refer any matter back to the comptroller.

(4)   An appeal lies from any decision of the comptroller in proceedings before him under section 246 (decisions on matters relating to design right) to the High Court or, in Scotland, the Court of Session.

*Reference of disputes relating to Crown use*
**252.**—(1)   A dispute as to any matter which falls to be determined by the court in default of agreement under—

(a)   section 241 (settlement of terms for Crown use),
(b)   section 242 (rights of third parties in case of Crown use),
(c)   section 243 (Crown use: compensation for loss of profit),

may be referred to the court by any party to the dispute.

(2)   In determining a dispute between a government department and any person as to the terms for Crown use of a design the court shall have regard to—

(a)   any sums which that person or a person from whom he derives title has received or is entitled to receive, directly or indirectly, from any government department in respect of the design; and
(b)   whether that person or a person from whom he derives title has in the court's opinion without reasonable cause failed to comply with a request of the department for the use of the design on reasonable terms.

(3)   One of two or more joint owners of design right may, without the concurrence of the others, refer a dispute to the court under this section, but shall not do so unless the others are made parties; and none of those others is liable for any costs unless he takes part in the proceedings.

(4)   Where the consent of an exclusive licensee is required by section

242(3)(a)(i) to the settlement by agreement of the terms for Crown use of a design, a determination by the court of the amount of any payment to be made for such use is of no effect unless the licensee has been notified of the reference and given an opportunity to be heard.

(5)   On the reference of a dispute as to the amount recoverable as mentioned in section 242(3)(a)(ii) (right of exclusive licensee to recover part of amount payable to design right owner) the court shall determine what is just having regard to any expenditure incurred by the licensee—

(a)   in developing the design, or
(b)   in making payments to the design right owner in consideration of the licence (other than royalties or other payments determined by reference to the use of the design).

(6)   In this section 'the court' means—

(a)   in England and Wales, the High Court or any patents county court having jurisdiction by virtue of an order under section 287 of this Act,
(b)   in Scotland, the Court of Session, and
(c)   in Northern Ireland, the High Court.

### Chapter V Miscellaneous and general

#### Miscellaneous

*Remedy for groundless threats of infringement proceedings*
**253.**—(1)   Where a person threatens another person with proceedings for infringement of design right, a person aggrieved by the threats may bring an action against him claiming—

(a)   a declaration to the effect that the threats are unjustifiable;
(b)   an injunction against the continuance of the threats;
(c)   damages in respect of any loss which he has sustained by the threats.

(2)   If the plaintiff proves that the threats were made and that he is a person aggrieved by them, he is entitled to the relief claimed unless the defendant shows that the acts in respect of which proceedings were threatened did constitute, or if done would have constituted, an infringement of the design right concerned.

(3)   Proceedings may not be brought under this section in respect of a threat to bring proceedings for an infringement alleged to consist of making or importing anything.

(4)   Mere notification that a design is protected by design right does not constitute a threat of proceedings for the purposes of this section.

*Licensee under licence of right not to claim connection with design right owner*
**254.**—(1)   A person who has a licence in respect of a design by virtue of section 237 or 238 (licences of right) shall not, without the consent of the design right owner—

(a)   apply to goods which he is marketing, or proposes to market, in reliance on that licence a trade description indicating that he is the licensee of the design right owner, or

(b)    use any such trade description in an advertisement in relation to such goods.

(2)    A contravention of subsection (1) is actionable by the design right owner.

(3)    In this section 'trade description', the reference to applying a trade description to goods and 'advertisement' have the same meaning as in the Trade Descriptions Act 1968.

### Extent of operation of this Part

*Countries to which this Part extends*

**255.**—(1)    This Part extends to England and Wales, Scotland and Northern Ireland.

(2)    Her Majesty may by Order in Council direct that this Part shall extend, subject to such exceptions and modifications as may be specified in the Order, to—

(a)    any of the Channel Islands,

(b)    the Isle of Man, or

(c)    any colony.

(3)    That power includes power to extend, subject to such exceptions and modifications as may be specified in the Order, any Order in Council made under section 221 (further provision as to qualification for design right protection) or section 256 (countries enjoying reciprocal protection).

(4)    The legislature of a country to which this Part has been extended may modify or add to the provisions of this Part, in their operation as part of the law of that country, as the legislature may consider necessary to adapt the provisions to the circumstances of that country; but not so as to deny design right protection in a case where it would otherwise exist.

(5)    Where a country to which this Part extends ceases to be a colony of the United Kingdom, it shall continue to be treated as such a country for the purposes of this Part until—

(a)    an Order in Council is made under section 256 designating it as a country enjoying reciprocal protection, or

(b)    an Order in Council is made declaring that it shall cease to be so treated by reason of the fact that the provisions of this Part as part of the law of that country have been amended or repealed.

(6)    A statutory instrument containing an Order in Council under subsection (5)(b) shall be subject to annulment in pursuance of a resolution of either House of Parliament.

*Countries enjoying reciprocal protection*

**256.**—(1)    Her Majesty may, if it appears to Her that the law of a country provides adequate protection for British designs, by Order in Council designate that country as one enjoying reciprocal protection under this Part.

(2)    If the law of a country provides adequate protection only for certain classes of British design, or only for designs applied to certain classes of article, any Order designating that country shall contain provision limiting, to a

corresponding extent, the protection afforded by this Part in relation to designs connected with that country.

(3)   An Order under this section shall be subject to annulment in pursuance of a resolution of either House of Parliament.

*Territorial waters and the continental shelf*
**257.**—(1)   For the purposes of this Part the territorial waters of the United Kingdom shall be treated as part of the United Kingdom.

(2)   This Part applies to things done in the United Kingdom sector of the continental shelf on a structure or vessel which is present there for purposes directly connected with the exploration of the sea bed or subsoil or the exploitation of their natural resources as it applies to things done in the United Kingdom.

(3)   The United Kingdom sector of the continental shelf means the areas designated by order under section 1(7) of the Continental Shelf Act 1964.

### Interpretation

*Construction of references to design right owner*
**258.**—(1)   Where different persons are (whether in consequence of a partial assignment or otherwise) entitled to different aspects of design right in a work, the design right owner for any purpose of this Part is the person who is entitled to the right in the respect relevant for that purpose.

(2)   Where design right (or any aspect of design right) is owned by more than one person jointly, references in this Part to the design right owner are to all the owners, so that, in particular, any requirement of the licence of the design right owner requires the licence of all of them.

*Joint designs*
**259.**—(1)   In this Part a 'joint design' means a design produced by the collaboration of two or more designers in which the contribution of each is not distinct from that of the other or others.

(2)   References in this Part to the designer of a design shall, except as otherwise provided, be construed in relation to a joint design as references to all the designers of the design.

*Application of provisions to articles in kit form*
**260.**—(1)   The provisions of this Part apply in relation to a kit, that is, a complete or substantially complete set of components intended to be assembled into an article, as they apply in relation to the assembled article.

(2)   Subsection (1) does not affect the question whether design right subsists in any aspect of the design of the components of a kit as opposed to the design of the asembled article.

*Requirement of signature: application in relation to body corporate*
**261.**   The requirement in the following provisions that an instrument be signed by or on behalf of a person is also satisfied in the case of a body corporate by the affixing of its seal—

section 222(3) (assignment of design right),
section 223(1) (assignment of future design right),
section 225(1) (grant of exclusive licence).

*Adaptation of expressions in relation to Scotland*
**262.** In the application of this Part to Scotland—

'account of profits' means accounting and payment of profits;
'accounts' means count, reckoning and payment;
'assignment' means assignation;
'costs' means expenses;
'defendant' means defender;
'delivery up' means delivery;
'injunction' means interdict;
'interlocutory relief' means interim remedy; and
'plaintiff' means pursuer.

*Minor definitions*
**263.**—(1)   In this Part—

'British design' means a design which qualifies for design right protection by reason of a connection with the United Kingdom of the designer or the person by whom the design is commissioned or the designer is employed;
'business' includes a trade or profession;
'commission' means a commission for money or money's worth;
'the comptroller' means the Comptroller General of Patents, Designs and Trade Marks;
'computer-generated', in relation to a design, means that the design is generated by computer in circumstances such that there is no human designer,
'country' includes any territory;
'the Crown' includes the Crown in right of Her Majesty's Government in Northern Ireland;
'design document' means any record of a design, whether in the form of a drawing, a written description, a photograph, data stored in a computer or otherwise;
'employee', 'employment' and 'employer' refer to employment under a contract of service or of apprenticeship;
'government department' includes a Northern Ireland department.

(2)   References in this Part to 'marketing', in relation to an article, are to its being sold or let for hire, or offered or exposed for sale or hire, in the course of a business, and related expressions shall be construed accordingly; but no account shall be taken for the purposes of this Part of marketing which is merely colourable and not intended to satisfy the reasonable requirements of the public.

(3)   References in this Part to an act being done in relation to an article for 'commercial purposes' are to its being done with a view to the article in question being sold or hired in the course of a business.

*Index of defined expressions*
**264.**   The following Table shows provisions defining or otherwise explaining expressions used in this Part (other than provisions defining or explaining an expression used only in the same section)—

account of profits and accounts (in Scotland)     section 262
assignment (in Scotland)                          section 262

| | |
|---|---|
| British designs | section 263(1) |
| business | section 263(1) |
| commercial purposes | section 263(3) |
| commission | section 263(1) |
| the comptroller | section 263(1) |
| computer-generated | section 263(1) |
| costs (in Scotland) | section 262 |
| country | section 263(1) |
| the Crown | section 263(1) |
| Crown use | sections 240(5) and 244(2) |
| defendant (in Scotland) | section 262 |
| delivery up (in Scotland) | section 262 |
| design | section 213(2) |
| design document | section 263(1) |
| designer | sections 214 and 259(2) |
| design right | section 213(1) |
| design right owner | sections 234(2) and 258 |
| employee, employment and employer | section 263(1) |
| exclusive licence | section 225(1) |
| government department | section 263(1) |
| government department concerned (in relation to Crown use) | section 240(5) |
| infringing article | section 228 |
| injunction (in Scotland) | section 262 |
| interlocutory relief (in Scotland) | section 262 |
| joint design | section 259(1) |
| licence (of the design right owner) | sections 222(4), 223(3) and 258 |
| making articles to a design | section 226(2) |
| marketing (and related expressions) | section 263(2) |
| original | section 213(2) |
| plaintiff (in Scotland) | section 262 |
| qualifying individual | section 217(1) |
| qualifying person | section 217(1) and (2) |
| signed | section 261 |

## Part IV Registered designs

### Amendments of the Registered Designs Act 1949

*Registrable designs*
**265.**—(1)   For section 1 of the Registered Designs Act 1949 (designs registrable under that Act) substitute— [see sch. 4 for the substituted s. 1].

(2)   The above amendment does not apply in relation to applications for registration made before the commencement of this Part; but the provisions of section 266 apply with respect to the right in certain designs registered in pursuance of such an application.

*Provisions with respect to certain designs registered in pursuance of application made before commencement*
**266.**—(1)   Where a design is registered under the Registered Designs Act 1949 in

pursuance of an application made after 12 January 1988 and before the commencement of this Part which could not have been registered under section 1 of that Act as substituted by section 265 above—

(a)   the right in the registered design expires 10 years after the commencement of this Part, if it does not expire earlier in accordance with the 1949 Act, and

(b)   any person is, after the commencement of this Part, entitled as of right to a licence to do anything which would otherwise infringe the right in the registered design.

(2)   The terms of a licence available by virtue of this section shall, in default of agreement, be settled by the registrar on an application by the person requiring the licence; and the terms so settled shall authorise the licensee to do everything which would be an infringement of the right in the registered design in the absence of a licence.

(3)   In settling the terms of a licence the registrar shall have regard to such factors as may be prescribed by the Secretary of State by order made by statutory instrument.

No such order shall be made unless a draft of it has been laid before and approved by a resolution of each House of Parliament.

(4)   Where the terms of a licence are settled by the registrar, the licence has effect from the date on which the application to the registrar was made.

(5)   Section 11B of the 1949 Act (undertaking to take licence of right in infringement proceedings), as inserted by section 270 below, applies where a licence is available as of right under this section, as it applies where a licence is available as of right under section 11A of that Act.

(6)   Where a licence is available as of right under this section, a person to whom a licence was granted before the commencement of this Part may apply to the registrar for an order adjusting the terms of that licence.

(7)   An appeal lies from any decision of the registrar under this section.

(8)   This section shall be construed as one with the Registered Designs Act 1949.

*Authorship and first ownership of designs*
**267.**—(1)   Section 2 of the Registered Designs Act 1949 (proprietorship of designs) is amended as follows,

(2)   For subsection (1) substitute— [see sch. 4 for the substituted s. 2(1), (1A) and (1B)].

(3)   After subsection (2) insert — [see sch. 4 for the inserted s. 1(3) and (4)].

(4)   The amendments made by this section do not apply in relation to an application for registration made before the commencement of this Part.

*Right given by registration of design*
**268.**—(1)   For section 7 of the Registered Designs Act 1949 (right given by registration) substitute— [see sch. 4 for the substituted s. 7].

(2)   The above amendment does not apply in relation to a design registered in pursuance of an application made before the commencement of this Part.

*Duration of right in registered design*
**269.**—(1)   For section 8 of the Registered Designs Act 1949 (period of right) substitute— [see sch. 4 for the substituted ss. 8, 8A and 8B].

(2)   The above amendment does not apply in relation to the right in a design registered in pursuance of an application made before the commencement of this Part.

*Powers exercisable for protection of the public interest*
**270.**   In the Registered Designs Act 1949 after section 11 insert— [see sch. 4 for the inserted ss. 11A and 11B].

*Crown use: compensation for loss of profit*
**271.**—(1)   In Schedule 1 to the Registered Designs Act 1949 (Crown use), after paragraph 2 insert— [see sch. 4 for the inserted para. 2A].

(2)   In paragraph 3 of that Schedule (reference of disputes as to Crown use), for subparagraph (1) substitute— [see sch. 4 for the substituted para. 3(1)].

(3)   The above amendments apply in relation to any Crown use of a registered design after the commencement of this section, even if the terms for such use were settled before commencement.

*Minor and consequential amendments*
**272.**   The Registered Designs Act 1949 is further amended in accordance with Schedule 3 which contains minor amendments and amendments consequential upon the provisions of this Act.

*Supplementary*

*Text of Registered Designs Act 1949 as amended*
**273.**   Schedule 4 contains the text of the Registered Designs Act 1949 as amended.

*Part V Patent agents and trade mark agents*

*Patent agents*

*Persons permitted to carry on business of a patent agent*
**274.**—(1)   Any individual, partnership or body corporate may, subject to the following provisions of this Part, carry on the business of acting as agent for others for the purpose of—

   (a)   applying for or obtaining patents, in the United Kingdom or elsewhere, or
   (b)   conducting proceedings before the comptroller relating to applications for, or otherwise in connection with, patents.

(2)   This does not affect any restriction under the European Patent Convention as to who may act on behalf of another for any purpose relating to European patents.

*The register of patent agents*
**275.**—(1)   The Secretary of State may make rules requiring the keeping of a register of persons who act as agent for others for the purposes of applying for or obtaining patents; and in this Part a 'registered patent agent' means a person whose name is entered in the register kept under this section.

(2)   The rules may contain such provision as the Secretary of State thinks fit regulating the registration of such persons, and may in particular—

(a)   require the payment of such fees as may be prescribed, and
(b)   authorise in prescribed cases the erasure from the register of the name of any person registered in it, or the suspension of a person's registration.

(3)   The rules may delegate the keeping of the register to another person, and may confer on that person—

(a)   power to make regulations—

(i)   with respect to the payment of fees, in the cases and subject to the limits prescribed by rules, and
(ii)   with respect to any other matter which could be regulated by rules, and

(b)   such other functions, including disciplinary functions, as may be prescribed by rules.

(4)   Rules under this section shall be made by statutory instrument which shall be subject to annulment in pursuance of a resolution of either House of Parliament.

*Persons entitled to describe themselves as patent agents*
**276.**—(1)   An individual who is not a registered patent agent shall not—

(a)   carry on a business (otherwise than in partnership) under any name or other description which contains the words 'patent agent' or 'patent attorney'; or
(b)   in the course of a business otherwise describe himself, or permit himself to be described, as a 'patent agent' or 'patent attorneys'.

(2)   A partnership shall not—

(a)   carry on a business under any name or other description which contains the words 'patent agent' or 'patent attorney'; or
(b)   in the course of a business otherwise describe itself, or permit itself to be described as, a firm of 'patent agents' or 'patent attorneys',

unless all the partners are registered patent agents or the partnership satisfies such conditions as may be prescribed for the purposes of this section.
(3)   A body corporate shall not—

(a)   carry on a business (otherwise than in partnership) under any name or other description which contains the words 'patent agent' or 'patent attorney'; or
(b)   in the course of a business otherwise describe itself, or permit itself to be described as, a 'patent agent' or 'patent attorney',

unless all the directors of the body corporate are registered patent agents or the body satisfies such conditions as may be prescribed for the purposes of this section.
(4)   Subsection (3) does not apply to a company which began to carry on business as a patent agent before 17 November 1917 if the name of a director or the manager of the company who is a registered patent agent is mentioned as being so registered in all professional advertisements, circulars or letters issued by or with the company's consent on which its name appears.

(5)   Where this section would be contravened by the use of the words 'patent agent' or 'patent attorney' in reference to an individual, partnership or body corporate, it is equally contravened by the use of other expressions in reference to that person, or his business or place of business, which are likely to be understood as indicating that he is entitled to be described as a 'patent agent' or 'patent attorney'.

(6)   A person who contravenes this section commits an offence and is liable on summary conviction to a fine not exceeding level 5 on the standard scale; and proceedings for such an offence may be begun at any time within a year from the date of the offence.

(7)   This section has effect subject to—

(a)   section 277 (persons entitled to describe themselves as European patent attorneys etc.), and

(b)   section 278(1) (use of term 'patent attorney' in reference to solicitors).

*Persons entitled to describe themselves as European patent attorneys etc.*
**277.**—(1)   The term 'European patent attorney' or 'European patent agent' may be used in the following cases without any contravention of section 276.

(2)   An individual who is on the European list may—

(a)   carry on business under a name or other description which contains the words 'European patent attorneys' or 'European patent agent', or

(b)   otherwise describe himself, or permit himself to be described, as a 'European patent attorney' or 'European patent agent'.

(3)   A partnership of which not less than the prescribed number or proportion of partners is on the European list may—

(a)   carry on a business under a name or other description which contains the words 'European patent attorneys' or 'European patent agents', or

(b)   otherwise describe itself, or permit itself to be described, as a firm which carries on the business of a 'European patent attorney' or 'European patent agent'.

(4)   A body corporate of which not less than the prescribed number or proportion of directors is on the European list may—

(a)   carry on a business under a name or other description which contains the words 'European patent attorney' or 'European patent agent', or

(b)   otherwise describe itself, or permit itself to be described as, a company which carries on the business of a 'European patent attorney' or 'European patent agent'.

(5)   Where the term 'European patent attorney' or 'European patent agent' may, in accordance with this section, be used in reference to an individual, partnership or body corporate, it is equally permissible to use other expressions in reference to that person, or to his business or place of business, which are likely to be understood as indicating that he is entitled to be described as a 'European patent attorney' or 'European patent agent'.

*Use of the term 'patent attorney': supplementary provisions*
**278.**—(1)   The term 'patent attorney' may be used in reference to a solicitor, and

a firm of solicitors may be described as a firm of 'patent attorneys', without any contravention of section 276.

(2) No offence is committed under the enactments restricting the use of certain expressions in reference to persons not qualified to act as solicitors—

(a) by the use of the term 'patent attorney' in reference to a registered patent agent, or

(b) by the use of the term 'European patent attorney' in reference to a person on the European list.

(3) The enactments referred to in subsection (2) are section 21 of the Solicitors Act 1974, section 31 of the Solicitors (Scotland) Act 1980 and Article 22 of the Solicitors (Northern Ireland) Order 1976.

*Power to prescribe conditions etc. for mixed partnerships and bodies corporate*
**279.**– (1) The Secretary of State may make rules—

(a) prescribing the conditions to be satisfied for the purposes of section 276 (persons entitled to describe themselves as patent agents) in relation to a partnership where not all the partners are qualified persons or a body corporate where not all the directors are qualified persons, and

(b) imposing requirements to be complied with by such partnerships and bodies corporate.

(2) The rules may, in particular—

(a) prescribe conditions as to the number or proportion of partners or directors who must be qualified persons;

(b) impose requirements as to—

(i) the identification of qualified and unqualified persons in professional advertisements, circulars or letters issued by or with the consent of the partnership or body corporate and which relate to it or to its business; and

(ii) the manner in which a partnership or body corporate is to organise its affairs so as to secure that qualified persons exercise a sufficient degree of control over the activities of unqualified persons.

(3) Contravention of a requirement imposed by the rules is an offence for which a person is liable on summary conviction to a fine not exceeding level 5 on the standard scale.

(4) The Secretary of State may make rules prescribing for the purposes of section 277 the number or proportion of partners of a partnership or directors of a body corporate who must be qualified persons in order for the partnership or body to take advantage of that section.

(5) In this section 'qualified person'—

(a) in subsections (1) and (2), means a person who is a registered patent agent, and

(b) in subsection (4), means a person who is on the European list.

(6) Rules under this section shall be made by statutory instrument which shall be subject to annulment in pursuance of a resolution of either House of Parliament.

*Privilege for communications with patent agents*
**280.**—(1)   This section applies to communications as to any matter relating to the protection of any invention, design, technical information, trade mark or service mark, or as to any matter involving passing off.

(2)   Any such communication—

(a)   between a person and his patent agent, or

(b)   for the purpose of obtaining, or in response to a request for, information which a person is seeking for the purpose of instructing his patent agent,

is privileged from disclosure in legal proceedings in England, Wales or Northern Ireland in the same way as a communication between a person and his solicitor or, as the case may be, a communication for the purpose of obtaining, or in response to a request for, information which a person seeks for the purpose of instructing his solicitor.

(3)   In subsection (1) 'patent agent' means—

(a)   a registered patent agent or a person who is on the European list,

(b)   a partnership entitled to describe itself a firm of patent agents or as a firm carrying on the business of a European patent attorney, or

(c)   a body corporate entitled to describe itself as a patent agent or as a company carrying on the business of a European patent attorney.

(4)   It is hereby declared that in Scotland the rules of law which confer privilege from disclosure in legal proceedings in respect of communications extend to such communications as are mentioned in this section.

*Power of comptroller to refuse to deal with certain agents*
**281.**—(1)   This section applies to business under the Patents Act 1949, the Registered Designs Act 1949 or the Patents Act 1977.

(2)   The Secretary of State may make rules authorising the comptroller to refuse to recognise as agent in respect of any business to which this section applies—

(a)   a person who has been convicted of an offence under section 88 of the Patents Act 1949, section 114 of the Patents Act 1977 or section 276 of this Act;

(b)   an individual whose name has been erased from and not restored to, or who is suspended from, the register of patent agents on the ground of misconduct;

(c)   a person who is found by the Secretary of State to have been guilty of such conduct as would, in the case of an individual registered in the register of patent agents, render him liable to have his name erased from the register on the ground of misconduct;

(d)   a partnership or body corporate of which one of the partners or directors is a person whom the comptroller could refuse to recognise under paragraph (a), (b) or (c) above.

(3)   The rules may contain such incidental and supplementary provisions as appear to the Secretary of State to be appropriate and may, in particular, prescribe circumstances in which a person is or is not to be taken to have been guilty of misconduct.

(4)   Rules made under this section shall be made by statutory instrument which shall be subject to annulment in pursuance of a resolution of either House of Parliament.

(5)   The comptroller shall refuse to recognise as agent in respect of any business to which this section applies a person who neither resides nor has a place of business in the United Kingdom, the Isle of Man or another member State of the European Economic Community.

*Trade mark agents*

*The register of trade mark agents*

**282.**—(1)   The Secretary of State may make rules requiring the keeping of a register of persons who act as agent for others for the purpose of applying for or obtaining the registration of trade marks; and in this Part a 'registered trade mark agent' means a person whose name is entered in the register kept under this section.

(2)   The rules may contain such provision as the Secretary of State thinks fit regulating the registration of persons, and may in particular—

(a)   require the payment of such fees as may be prescribed, and,

(b)   authorise in prescribed cases the erasure from the register of the name of any person registered in it, or the suspension of a person's registration.

(3)   The rules may delegate the keeping of the register to another person, and may confer on that person—

(a)   power to make regulations—

(i)   with respect to the payment of fees, in the cases and subject to the limits prescribed by rules, and

(ii)   with respect to any other matter which could be regulated by rules, and

(b)   such other functions, including disciplinary functions, as may be prescribed by rules.

(4)   Rules under this section shall be made by statutory instrument which shall be subject to annulment in pursuance of a resolution of either House of Parliament.

*Unregistered persons not to be described as registered trade mark agents*

**283.**—(1)   An individual who is not a registered trade mark agent shall not—

(a)   carry on a business (otherwise than in partnership) under any name or other description which contains the words 'registered trade mark agent'; or

(b)   in the course of a business otherwise describe or hold himself out, or permit himself to be described or held out, as a registered trade mark agent.

(2)   A partnership shall not—

(a)   carry on a business under any name or other description which contains the words 'registered trade mark agent'; or

(b)   in the course of a business otherwise describe or hold itself out, or permit itself to be described or held out, as a firm of registered trade mark agents, unless all the partners are registered trade mark agents or the partnership satisfies such conditions as may be prescribed for the purposes of this section.

(3)   A body corporate shall not—

(a)   carry on a business (otherwise than in partnership) under any name or other description which contains the words 'registered trade mark agent'; or

(b)   in the course of a business otherwise describe or hold itself out, or permit itself to be described or held out, as a registered trade mark agent,

unless all the directors of the body corporate are registered trade mark agents or the body satisfies such conditions as may be prescribed for the purposes of this section.

(4)   The Secretary of State may make rules prescribing the conditions to be satisfied for the purposes of this section in relation to a partnership where not all the partners are registered trade mark agents or a body corporate where not all the directors are registered trade mark agents; and the rules may, in particular, prescribe conditions as to the number or proportion of partners or directors who must be registered trade mark agents.

(5)   Rules under this section shall be made by statutory instrument which shall be subject to annulment in pursuance of a resolution of either House of Parliament.

(6)   A person who contravenes this section commits an offence and is liable on summary conviction to a fine not exceeding level 5 on the standard scale; and proceedings for such an offence may be begun at any time within a year from the date of the offence.

*Privilege for communications with registered trade mark agents*
**284.**—(1)   This section applies to communications as to any matter relating to the protection of any design, trade mark or service mark, or as to any matter involving passing off.

(2)   Any such communication—

(a)   between a person and his trade mark agent, or

(b)   for the purpose of obtaining, or in response to a request for, information which a person is seeking for the purpose of instructing his trade mark agent,

is privileged from disclosure in legal proceedings in England, Wales or Northern Ireland in the same way as a communication between a person and his solicitor or, as the case may be, a communication for the purpose of obtaining, or in response to a request for, information which a person seeks for the purpose of instructing his solicitor.

(3)   In subsection (1) 'trade mark agent' means—

(a)   a registered trade mark agent, or

(b)   a partnership entitled to describe itself as a firm of registered trade mark agents, or

(c)   a body corporate entitled to describe itself as a registered trade mark agent.

(4)   It is hereby declared that in Scotland the rules of law which confer

privilege from disclosure in legal proceedings in respect of communications extend to such communications as are mentioned in subsection (1).

## *Supplementary*

### *Offences committed by partnerships and bodies corporate*

**285.**—(1)  Proceedings for an offence under this Part alleged to have been committed by a partnership shall be brought in the name of the partnership and not in that of the partners; but without prejudice to any liability of theirs under subsection (4) below.

(2)  The following provisions apply for the purposes of such proceedings as in relation to a body corporate—

   (a)  any rules of court relating to the service of documents;
   (b)  in England, Wales or Northern Ireland, Schedule 3 to the Magistrates' Courts Act 1980 or Schedule 4 to the Magistrates' Courts (Northern Ireland) Order 1981 (procedure on charge of offence).

(3)  A fine imposed on a partnership on its conviction in such proceedings shall be paid out of the partnership assets.

(4)  Where a partnership is guilty of an offence under this Part, every partner, other than a partner who is proved to have been ignorant of or to have attempted to prevent the commission of the offence, is also guilty of the offence and liable to be proceeded against and punished accordingly.

(5)  Where an offence under this Part committed by a body corporate is proved to have been committed with the consent or connivance of a director, manager, secretary or other similar officer of the body, or a person purporting to act in any such capacity, he as well as the body corporate is guilty of the offence and liable to be proceeded against and punished accordingly.

### *Interpretation*

**286.**  In this Part—

   'the comptroller' means the Comptroller-General of Patents, Designs and Trade Marks;
   'director', in relation to a body corporate whose affairs are managed by its members, means any member of the body corporate;
   'the European list' means the list of professional representatives maintained by the European Patent Office in pursuance of the European Patent Convention;
   'registered patent agent' has the meaning given by section 275(1);
   'registered trade mark agent' has the meaning given by section 282(1).

## Part VI Patents

### *Patents county courts*

#### *Patents county courts: special jurisdiction*

**287.**—(1)  The Lord Chancellor may by order made by statutory instrument designate any county court as a patents county court and confer on it jurisdiction (its 'special jurisdiction') to hear and determine such descriptions of proceedings—

(a)    relating to patents or designs, or

(b)    ancillary to, or arising out of the same subject-matter as, proceedings relating to patents or designs,

as may be specified in the order.

(2)    The special jurisdiction of a patents county court is exercisable throughout England and Wales, but rules of court may provide for a matter pending in one such court to be heard and determined in another or partly in that and partly in another.

(3)    A patents county court may entertain proceedings within its special jurisdiction notwithstanding that no pecuniary remedy is sought.

(4)    An order under this section providing for the discontinuance of any of the special jurisdiction of a patents county court may make provision as to proceedings pending in the court when the order comes into operation.

(5)    Nothing in this section shall be construed as affecting the ordinary jurisdiction of a county court.

*Financial limits in relation to proceedings within special jurisdiction of patents county court*

**288.**—(1)    Her Majesty may by Order in Council provide for limits of amount or value in relation to any description of proceedings within the special jurisdiction of a patents county court.

(2)    If a limit is imposed on the amount of a claim of any description and the plaintiff has a cause of action for more than that amount, he may abandon the excess; in which case a patents county court shall have jurisdiction to hear and determine the action, but the plaintiff may not recover more than that amount.

(3)    Where the court has jurisdiction to hear and determine an action by virtue of subsection (2), the judgment of the court in the action is in full discharge of all demands in respect of the cause of action, and entry of the judgment shall be made accordingly.

(4)    If the parties agree, by a memorandum signed by them or by their respective solicitors or other agents, that a patents county court shall have jurisdiction in any proceedings, that court shall have jurisdiction to hear and determine the proceedings notwithstanding any limit imposed under this section.

(5)    No recommendation shall be made to Her Majesty to make an Order under this section unless a draft of the Order has been laid before and approved by a resolution of each House of Parliament.

*Transfer of proceedings between High Court and patents county court*

**289.**—(1)    No order shall be made under section 41 of the County Courts Act 1984 (power of High Court to order proceedings to be transferred from the county court) in respect of proceedings within the special jurisdiction of a patents county court.

(2)    In considering in relation to proceedings within the special jurisdiction of a patents county court whether an order should be made under section 40 or 42 of the County Courts Act 1984 (transfer of proceedings from or to the High Court), the court shall have regard to the financial position of the parties and may order the transfer of the proceedings to a patents county court or, as the case may be, refrain from ordering their transfer to the High Court notwithstanding that the proceedings are likely to raise an important question of fact or law.

*Limitation of costs where pecuniary claim could have been brought in patents county court*

**290.**—(1)   Where an action is commenced in the High Court which could have been commenced in a patents county court and in which a claim for a pecuniary remedy is made, then, subject to the provisions of this section, if the plaintiff recovers less than the prescribed amount, he is not entitled to recover any more costs than those to which he would have been entitled if the action had been brought in the county court.

(2)   For this purpose a plaintiff shall be treated as recovering the full amount recoverable in respect of his claim without regard to any deduction made in respect of matters not falling to be taken into account in determining whether the action could have been commenced in a patents county court.

(3)   This section does not affect any question as to costs if it appears to the High Court that there was reasonable ground for supposing the amount recoverable in respect of the plaintiff's claim to be in excess of the prescribed amount.

(4)   The High Court, if satisfied that there was sufficient reason for bringing the action in the High Court, may make an order allowing the costs or any part of the costs on the High Court scale or on such one of the county court scales as it may direct.

(5)   This section does not apply to proceedings brought by the Crown.

(6)   In this section 'the prescribed amount' means such amount as may be prescribed by Her Majesty for the purposes of this section by Order in Council.

(7)   No recommendation shall be made to Her Majesty to make an Order under this section unless a draft of the Order has been laid before and approved by a resolution of each House of Parliament.

*Proceedings in patents county court*

**291.**—(1)   Where a county court is designated a patents county court, the Lord Chancellor shall nominate a person entitled to sit as a judge of that court as the patents judge.

(2)   County court rules shall make provision for securing that, so far as is practicable and appropriate—

(a)   proceedings within the special jurisdiction of a patents county court are dealt with by the patents judge, and

(b)   the judge, rather than a registrar or other officer of the court, deals with interlocutory matters in the proceedings.

(3)   County court rules shall make provision empowering a patents county court in proceedings within its special jurisdiction, on or without the application of any party—

(a)   to appoint scientific advisers or assessors to assist the court, or

(b)   to order the Patent Office to inquire into and report on any question of fact or opinion.

(4)   Where the court exercises either of those powers on the application of a party, the remuneration or fees payable to the Patent Office shall be at such rate as may be determined in accordance with county court rules and shall be costs of the proceedings unless otherwise ordered by the judge.

(5)   Where the court exercises either of those powers of its own motion, the remuneration or fees payable to the Patent Office shall be at such rate as may be determined by the Lord Chancellor with the approval of the Treasury and shall be paid out of money provided by Parliament.

*Rights and duties of registered patent agents in relation to proceedings in patents county court*

**292.**—(1)   A registered patent agent may do, in or in connection with proceedings in a patents county court which are within the special jurisdiction of that court, anything which a solicitor of the Supreme Court might do, other than prepare a deed.

(2)   The Lord Chancellor may by regulations provide that the right conferred by subsection (1) shall be subject to such conditions and restrictions as appear to the Lord Chancellor to be necessary or expedient; and different provision may be made for different descriptions of proceedings.

(3)   A patents county court has the same power to enforce an undertaking given by a registered patent agent acting in pursuance of this section as it has, by virtue of section 142 of the County Courts Act 1984, in relation to a solicitor.

(4)   Nothing in section 143 of the County Courts Act 1984 (prohibition on persons other than solicitors receiving remuneration) applies to a registered patent agent acting in pursuance of this section.

(5)   The provisions of county court rules prescribing scales of costs to be paid to solicitors apply in relation to registered patent agents acting in pursuance of this section.

(6)   Regulations under this section shall be made by statutory instrument which shall be subject to annulment in pursuance of a resolution of either House of Parliament.

*Licences of right in respect of certain patents*

*Restriction of acts authorised by certain licences*

**293.**   In paragraph 4(2)(c) of Schedule 1 to the Patents Act 1977 (licences to be available as of right where term of existing patent extended), at the end insert ',but subject to paragraph 4A below', and after that paragraph insert—

'4A.—(1)   If the proprietor of a patent for an invention which is a product files a declaration with the Patent Office in accordance with this paragraph, the licences to which persons are entitled by virtue of paragraph 4(2)(c) above shall not extend to a use of the product which is excepted by or under this paragraph.

(2)   Pharmaceutical use is excepted, that is—

(a)   use as a medicinal product within the meaning of the Medicines Act 1968, and

(b)   the doing of any other act mentioned in section 60(1)(a) above with a view to such use.

(3)   The Secretary of State may by order except such other uses as he thinks fit; and an order may—

(a)   specify as an excepted use any act mentioned in section 60(1)(a) above, and

(b)   make different provision with respect to acts done in different circumstances or for different purposes.

(4)   For the purposes of this paragraph the question what uses are excepted, so far as that depends on—

(a)   orders under section 130 of the Medicines Act 1968 (meaning of 'medicinal product'), or

(b)   orders under sub-paragraph (3) above,

shall be determined in relation to a patent at the beginning of the sixteenth year of the patent.

(5)   A declaration under this paragraph shall be in the prescribed form and shall be filed in the prescribed manner and within the prescribed time-limits.

(6)   A declaration may not be filed—

(a)   in respect of a patent which has at the commencement of section 293 of the Copyright, Designs and Patents Act 1988 passed the end of its fifteenth year; or

(b)   if at the date of filing there is—

(i)   an existing licence for any description of excepted use of the product, or

(ii)   an outstanding application under section 46(3)(a) or (b) above for the settlement by the comptroller of the terms of a licence for any description of excepted use of the product,

and, in either case, the licence took or is to take effect at or after the end of the sixteenth year of the patent.

(7)   Where a declaration has been filed under this paragraph in respect of a patent—

(a)   section 46(3)(c) above (restriction of remedies for infringement where licences available as of right) does not apply to an infringement of the patent in so far as it consists of the excepted use of the product after the filing of the declaration; and

(b)   section 46(3)(d) above (abatement of renewal fee if licences available as of right) does not apply to the patent.'.

*When application may be made for settlement of terms of licence*
**294.**   In Schedule 1 to the Patents Act 1977, after the paragraph inserted by section 293 above, insert—

'4B.—(1)   An application under section 46(3)(a) or (b) above for the settlement by the comptroller of the terms on which a person is entitled to a licence by virtue of paragraph 4(2)(c) above is ineffective if made before the beginning of the sixteenth year of the patent.

(2)   This paragraph applies to applications made after the commencement of section 294 of the Copyright, Designs and Patents Act 1988 and to any application made before the commencement of that section in respect of a patent which has not at the commencement of that section passed the end of its fifteenth year.'.

*Patents: miscellaneous amendments*

*Patents: miscellaneous amendments*

**295.**   The Patents Act 1949 and the Patents Act 1977 are amended in accordance with Schedule 5.

## Part VII Miscellaneous and General

*Devices designed to circumvent copy-protection*

*Devices designed to circumvent copy-protection*

**296.**—(1)   This section applies where copies of a copyright work are issued to the public, by or with the licence of the copyright owner, in an electronic form which is copy-protected.

(2)   The person issuing the copies to the public has the same rights against a person who, knowing or having reason to believe that it will be used to make infringing copies—

(a)   makes, imports, sells or lets for hire, offers or exposes for sale or hire, or advertises for sale or hire, any device or means specifically designed or adapted to circumvent the form of copy-protection employed, or

(b)   publishes information intended to enable or assist persons to circumvent that form of copy-protection,

as a copyright owner has in respect of an infringement of copyright.

(3)   Further he has the same rights under section 99 or 100 (delivery up or seizure of certain articles) in relation to any such device or means which a person has in his possession, custody or control with the intention that it should be used to make infringing copies of copyright works, as a copyright owner has in relation to an infringing copy.

(4)   References in this section to copy-protection include any device or means intended to prevent or restrict copying of a work or to impair the quality of copies made.

(5)   Expressions used in this section which are defined for the purposes of Part I of this Act (copyright) have the same meaning as in that Part.

(6)   The following provisions apply in relation to proceedings under this section as in relation to proceedings under Part I (copyright)—

(a)   sections 104 to 106 of this Act (presumptions as to certain matters relating to copyright), and

(b)   section 72 of the Supreme Court Act 1981, section 15 of the Law Reform (Miscellaneous Provisions) (Scotland) Act 1985 and section 94A of the Judicature (Northern Ireland) Act 1978 (withdrawal of privilege against self-incrimination in certain proceedings relating to intellectual property);

and section 114 of this Act applies, with the necessary modifications, in relation to the disposal of anything delivered up or seized by virtue of subsection (3) above.

*Fraudulent reception of transmissions*

*Offence of fraudulently receiving programmes*

**297.**—(1)   A person who dishonestly receives a programme included in a broadcasting or cable programme service provided from a place in the United Kingdom with intent to avoid payment of any charge applicable to the reception of the programme commits an offence and is liable on summary conviction to a fine not exceeding level 5 on the standard scale.

(2)   Where an offence under this section committed by a body corporate is proved to have been committed with the consent or connivance of a director, manager, secretary or other similar officer of the body, or a person purporting to act in any such capacity, he as well as the body corporate is guilty of the offence and liable to be proceeded against and punished accordingly.

In relation to a body corporate whose affairs are managed by its members 'director' means a member of the body corporate.

*Rights and remedies in respect of apparatus etc. for unauthorised reception of transmissions*

**298.**—(1)   A person who—

(a)   makes charges for the reception of programmes included in a broadcasting or cable programme service provided from a place in the United Kingdom, or

(b)   sends encrypted transmissions of any other description from a place in the United Kingdom,

is entitled to the following rights and remedies.

(2)   He has the same rights and remedies against a person who—

(a)   makes, imports or sells or lets for hire any apparatus or device designed or adapted to enable or assist persons to receive the programmes or other transmissions when they are not entitled to do so, or

(b)   publishes any information which is calculated to enable or assist persons to receive the programmes or other transmissions when they are not entitled to do so,

as a copyright owner has in respect of an infringement of copyright.

(3)   Further, he has the same rights under section 99 or 100 (delivery up or seizure of certain articles) in relation to any such apparatus or device as a copyright owner has in relation to an infringing copy.

(4)   Section 72 of the Supreme Court Act 1981, section 15 of the Law Reform (Miscellaneous Provisions) (Scotland) Act 1985 and section 94A of the Judicature (Northern Ireland) Act 1978 (withdrawal of privilege against self-incrimination in certain proceedings relating to intellectual property) apply to proceedings under this section as to proceedings under Part I of this Act (copyright).

(5)   In section 97(1) (innocent infringement of copyright) as it applies to proceedings for infringement of the rights conferred by this section, the reference to the defendant not knowing or having reason to believe that copyright subsisted in the work shall be construed as a reference to his not knowing or having reason to believe that his acts infringed the rights conferred by this section.

(6)   Section 114 of this Act applies, with the necessary modifications, in relation to the disposal of anything delivered up or seized by virtue of subsection (3) above.

*Supplementary provisions as to fraudulent reception*
**299.**—(1)   Her Majesty may by Order in Council—

    (a)   provide that section 297 applies in relation to programmes included in services provided from a country or territory outside the United Kingdom, and
    (b)   provide that section 298 applies in relation to such programmes and to encrypted transmissions sent from such a country or territory.

(2)   No such order shall be made unless it appears to Her Majesty that provision has been or will be made under the laws of that country or territory giving adequate protection to persons making charges for programmes included in broadcasting or cable programme services provided from the United Kingdom or, as the case may be, for encrypted transmissions sent from the United Kingdom.

(3)   A statutory instrument containing an Order in Council under subsection (1) shall be subject to annulment in pursuance of a resolution of either House of Parliament.

(4)   Where sections 297 and 298 apply in relation to a broadcasting or cable programme service, they also apply to any service run for the person providing that service, or a person providing programmes for that service, which consists wholly or mainly in the sending by means of a telecommunications system of sounds or visual images, or both.

(5)   In sections 297 and 298, and this section, 'programme', 'broadcasting' and 'cable programme service', and related expressions, have the same meaning as in Part I (copyright).

*Fraudulent application or use of trade mark*

*Fraudulent application or use of trade mark an offence*
**300.**   In the Trade Marks Act 1938 the following sections are inserted before section 59, after the heading *'Offences and restraint of use of Royal Arms'*—

    *'Fraudulent application or use of trade mark an offence*
    **58A.**—(1)   It is an offence, subject to subsection (3) below, for a person—

        (a)   to apply a mark identical to or nearly resembling a registered trade mark to goods, or to material used or intended to be used for labelling, packaging or advertising goods, or
        (b)   to sell, let for hire, or offer or expose for sale or hire, or distribute—

            (i)   goods bearing such a mark, or
            (ii)   material bearing such a mark which is used or intended to be used for labelling, packaging or advertising goods, or

        (c)   to use material bearing such a mark in the course of a business for labelling, packaging or advertising goods, or
        (d)   to possess in the course of a business goods or material bearing such a mark with a view to doing any of the things mentioned in paragraphs (a) to (c),

    when he is not entitled to use the mark in relation to the goods in question and the goods are not connected in the course of trade with a person who is so entitled.

(2)   It is also an offence, subject to subsection (3) below, for a person to possess in the course of a business goods or material bearing a mark identical to or nearly resembling a registered trade mark with a view to enabling or assisting another person to do any of the things mentioned in subsection (1)(a) to (c), knowing or having reason to believe that the other person is not entitled to use the mark in relation to the goods in question and that the goods are not connected in the course of trade with a person who is so entitled.

(3)   A person commits an offence under subsection (1) or (2) only if—

(a)   he acts with a view to gain for himself or another, or with intent to cause loss to another, and

(b)   he intends that the goods in question should be accepted as connected in the course of trade with a person entitled to use the mark in question;

and it is a defence for a person charged with an offence under subsection (1) to show that he believed on reasonable grounds that he was entitled to use the mark in relation to the goods in question.

(4)   A person guilty of an offence under this section is liable—

(a)   on summary conviction to imprisonment for a term not exceeding six months or a fine not exceeding the statutory maximum, or both;

(b)   on conviction on indictment to a fine or imprisonment for a term not exceeding 10 years, or both.

(5)   Where an offence under this section committed by a body corporate is proved to have been committed with the consent or connivance of a director, manager, secretary or other similar officer of the body, or a person purporting to act in any such capacity, he as well as the body corporate is guilty of the offence and liable to be proceeded against and punished accordingly.

In relation to a body corporate whose affairs are managed by its members "director" means a member of the body corporate.

(6)   In this section "business" includes a trade or profession.

*Delivery up of offending goods and material*
**58B.**—(1)   The court by which a person is convicted of an offence under section 58A may, if satisfied that at the time of his arrest or charge he had in his possession, custody or control—

(a)   goods or material in respect of which the offence was committed, or

(b)   goods of the same description as those in respect of which the offence was committed, or material similar to that in respect of which the offence was committed, bearing a mark identical to or nearly resembling that in relation to which the offence was committed,

order that the goods or material be delivered up to such person as the court may direct.

(2)   For this purpose a person shall be treated as charged with an offence—

(a)   in England, Wales and Northern Ireland, when he is orally charged or is served with a summons or indictment;

(b)   in Scotland, when he is cautioned, charged or served with a complaint or indictment.

(3)   An order be made by the court of its own motion or on the application of the prosecutor (or, in Scotland, the Lord Advocate or procurator-fiscal), but shall not be made if it appears to the court unlikely that any order will be made under section 58C (order as to disposal of offending goods or material).

(4)   An appeal lies from an order made under this section by a magistrates' court—

(a)   in England and Wales, to the Crown Court, and

(b)   in Northern Ireland, to the county court.

and in Scotland, where an order has been made under this section, the person from whose possession, custody or control the goods or material have been removed may, without prejudice to any other form of appeal under any rule of law, appeal against that order in the same manner as against sentence.

(5)   A person to whom goods or material are delivered up in pursuance of an order under this section shall retain it pending the making of an order under section 58C.

(6)   Nothing in this section affects the powers of the court under section 43 of the Powers of Criminal Courts Act 1973, section 223 or 436 of the Criminal Procedure (Scotland) Act 1975 or Article 7 of the Criminal Justice (Northern Ireland) Order 1980 (general provisions as to forfeiture in criminal proceedings).

*Order as to disposal of offending goods or material*
**58C.**—(1)   Where goods or material have been delivered up in pursuance of an order under section 58B, an application may be made to the court for an order that they be destroyed or forfeited to such person as the court may think fit.

(2)   Provision shall be made by rules of court as to the service of notice on persons having an interest in the goods or material, and any such person is entitled—

(a)   to appear in proceedings for an order under this section, whether or not he was served with notice, and

(b)   to appeal against any order made, whether or not he appeared;

and an order shall not take effect until the end of the period within which notice of an appeal may be given or, if before the end of that period notice of appeal is duly given, until the final determination or abandonment of the proceedings on the appeal.

(3)   Where there is more than one person interested in goods or material, the court shall make such order as it thinks just.

(4)   References in this section to a person having an interest in goods or material include any person in whose favour an order could be made under this section or under section 114, 204 or 231 of the Copyright, Designs and Patents Act 1988 (which make similar provision in relation to infringement of copyright, rights in performances and design right).

(5)   Proceedings for an order under this section may be brought—

(a)   in a county court in England, Wales and Northern Ireland, provided the value of the goods or material in question does not exceed the county court limit for actions in tort, and

(b)   in a sheriff court in Scotland;

but this shall not be construed as affecting the jurisdiction of the High Court or, in Scotland, the Court of Session.

*Enforcement of section 58A*

**58D.**—(1)   The functions of a local weights and measures authority include the enforcement in their area of section 58A.

(2)   The following provisions of the Trade Descriptions Act 1968 apply in relation to the enforcement of that section as in relation to the enforcement of that Act—

section 27 (power to make test purchases),

section 28 (power to enter premises and inspect and seize goods and documents),

section 29 (obstruction of authorised officers), and

section 33 (compensation for loss, etc. of goods seized under s. 28).

(3)   Subsection (1) above does not apply in relation to the enforcement of section 58A in Northern Ireland, but the functions of the Department of Economic Development include the enforcement of that section in Northern Ireland.

For that purpose the provisions of the Trade Descriptions Act 1968 specified in subsection (2) apply as if for the references to a local weights and measures authority and any officer of such an authority there were substituted references to that Department and any of its officers.

(4)   Any enactment which authorises the disclosure of information for the purpose of facilitating the enforcement of the Trade Descriptions Act 1968 shall apply as if section 58A above were contained in that Act and as if the functions of any person in relation to the enforcement of that section were functions under that Act.'.

*Provisions for the benefit of the Hospital for Sick Children*

*Provisions for the benefit of the Hospital for Sick Children*

**301.**   The provisions of Schedule 6 have effect for conferring on trustees for the benefit of the Hospital for Sick Children, Great Ormond Street, London, a right to a royalty in respect of the public performance, commercial publication, broadcasting or inclusion in a cable programme service of the play *Peter Pan* by Sir James Matthew Barrie, or of any adaptation of that work, notwithstanding that copyright in the work expired on 31 December 1987.

*Financial assistance for certain international bodies*

### Financial assistance for certain international bodies

**302.**—(1) The Secretary of State may give financial assistance, in the form of grants, loans or guarantees to—

(a) any international organisation having functions relating to trade marks or other intellectual property, or

(b) any Community institution or other body established under any of the Community Treaties having any such functions,

with a view to the establishment or maintenance by that organisation, institution or body of premises in the United Kingdom.

(2) Any expenditure of the Secretary of State under this section shall be defrayed out of money provided by Parliament; and any sums received by the Secretary of State in consequence of this section shall be paid into the Consolidated Fund.

*General*

### Consequential amendments and repeals

**303.**—(1) The enactments specified in Schedule 7 are amended in accordance with that Schedule, the amendments being consequential on the provisions of this Act.

(2) The enactments specified in Schedule 8 are repealed to the extent specified.

### Extent

**304.**—(1) Provision as to the extent of Part I (copyright), Part II (rights in performances) and Part III (design right) is to be found in sections 157, 207 and 255 respectively; the extent of the other provisions of this Act is as follows.

(2) Part IV to VII extend to England and Wales, Scotland and Northern Ireland, except that—

(a) sections 287 to 292 (patents county courts) extend to England and Wales only,

(b) the proper law of the trust created by Schedule 6 (provisions for the benefit of the Hospital for Sick Children) is the law of England and Wales, and

(c) the amendments and repeals in Schedules 7 and 8 have the same extent as the enactments amended or repealed.

(3) The following provisions extend to the Isle of Man subject to any modifications contained in an Order made by Her Majesty in Council—

(a) sections 293 and 294 (patents: licences of right), and

(b) paragraphs 24 and 29 of Schedule 5 (patents: effect of filing international application for patent and power to extend time limits).

(4) Her Majesty may by Order in Council direct that the following provisions extend to the Isle of Man, with such exceptions and modifications as may be specified in the Order—

(a) Part IV (registered designs),

(b) Part V (patent agents),

(c)   the provisions of Schedule 5 (patents: miscellaneous amendments) not mentioned in subsection (3) above, '

(d)   sections 297 to 299 (fraudulent reception of transmissions), and

(e)   section 300 (fraudulent application or use of trade mark).

(5)   Her Majesty may by Order in Council direct that sections 297 to 299 (fraudulent reception of transmissions) extend to any of the Channel Islands, with such exceptions and modifications as may be specified in the Order.

(6)   Any power conferred by this Act to make provision by Order in Council for or in connection with the extent of provisions of this Act to a country outside the United Kingdom includes power to extend to that country, subject to any modifications specified in the Order, any provision of this Act which amends or repeals an enactment extending to that country.

*Commencement*

**305.**—(1)   The following provisions of this Act come into force on Royal Assent—

paragraphs 24 and 29 of Schedule 5 (patents: effect of filing international application for patent and power to extend time-limits);

section 301 and Schedule 6 (provisions for the benefit of the Hospital for Sick Children).

(2)   Sections 293 and 294 (licences of right) come into force at the end of the period of two months beginning with the passing of this Act.

(3)   The other provisions of this Act come into force on such day as the Secretary of State may appoint by order made by statutory instrument, and different days may be appointed for different provisions and different purposes.

*Short title*

**306.**   This Act may be cited as the Copyright, Designs and Patents Act 1988.

### Schedule 1 Copyright: transitional provisions and savings

*Introductory*

**1.**—(1)   In this Schedule—

'the 1911 Act' means the Copyright Act 1911,

'the 1956 Act' means the Copyright Act 1956, and

'the new copyright provisions' means the provisions of this Act relating to copyright, that is, Part I (including this Schedule) and Schedules 3, 7 and 8 so far as they make amendments or repeals consequential on the provisions of Part I.

(2)   References in this Schedule to 'commencement', without more, are to the date on which the new copyright provisions come into force.

(3)   References in this Schedule to 'existing works' are to works made before commencement; and for this purpose a work of which the making extended over a period shall be taken to have been made when its making was completed.

**2.**—(1)   In relation to the 1956 Act, references in this Schedule to a work include any work or other subject-matter within the meaning of that Act.

(2)   In relation to the 1911 Act—

(a)   references in this Schedule to copyright include the right conferred by section 24 of that Act in substitution for a right subsisting immediately before the commencement of that Act;

(b)   references in this Schedule to copyright in a sound recording are to the copyright under that Act in records embodying the recording; and

(c)   references in this Schedule to copyright in a film are to any copyright under that Act in the film (so far as it constituted a dramatic work for the purposes of that Act) or in photographs forming part of the film.

### General principles: continuity of the law

**3.**   The new copyright provisions apply in relation to things existing at commencement as they apply in relation to things coming into existence after commencement, subject to any express provision to the contrary.

**4.**—(1)   The provisions of this paragraph have effect for securing the continuity of the law so far as the new copyright provisions re-enact (with or without modification) earlier provisions.

(2)   A reference in an enactment, instrument or other document to copyright, or to a work or other subject-matter in which copyright subsists, which apart from this Act would be construed as referring to copyright under the 1956 Act shall be construed, so far as may be required for continuing its effect, as being, or as the case may require, including, a reference to copyright under this Act or to works in which copyright subsists under this Act.

(3)   Anything done (including subordinate legislation made), or having effect as done, under or for the purposes of a provision repealed by this Act has effect as if done under or for the purposes of the corresponding provision of the new copyright provisions.

(4)   References (expressed or implied) in this Act or any other enactment, instrument or document to any of the new copyright provisions shall, so far as the context permits, be construed as including, in relation to times, circumstances and purposes before commencement, a reference to corresponding earlier provisions.

(5)   A reference (express or implied) in an enactment, instrument or other document to a provision repealed by this Act shall be construed, so far as may be required for continuing its effect, as a reference to the corresponding provision of this Act.

(6)   The provisions of this paragraph have effect subject to any specific transitional provision or saving and to any express amendment made by this Act.

### Subsistence of copyright

**5.**—(1)   Copyright subsists in an existing work after commencement only if copyright subsisted in it immediately before commencement.

(2)   Subparagraph (1) does not prevent an existing work qualifying for copyright protection after commencement—

(a)   under section 155 (qualification by virtue of first publication), or

(b)   by virtue of an Order under section 159 (application of Part I to countries to which it does not extend).

**6.**—(1)   Copyright shall not subsist by virtue of this Act in an artistic work made before 1 June 1957 which at the time when the work was made constituted a design capable of registration under the Registered Designs Act 1949 or under the enactments repealed by that Act, and was used, or intended to be used, as a model or pattern to be multiplied by an industrial process.

(2)   For this purpose a design shall be deemed to be used as a model or pattern to be multiplied by any industrial process—

(a)   when the design is reproduced or is intended to be reproduced on more than 50 single articles, unless all the articles in which the design is reproduced or is intended to be reproduced together form only a single set of articles as defined in section 44(1) of the Registered Designs Act 1949, or

(b)   when the design is to be applied to—

(i)   printed paper hangings,

(ii)   carpets, floor cloths or oil cloths, manufactured or sold in lengths or pieces,

(iii)   textile piece goods, or textile goods manufactured or sold in lengths or pieces, or

(iv)   lace, not made by hand.

**7.**—(1)   No copyright subsists in a film, as such, made before 1 June 1957.

(2)   Where a film made before that date was an original dramatic work within the meaning of the 1911 Act, the new copyright provisions have effect in relation to the film as if it was an original dramatic work within the meaning of Part I.

(3)   The new copyright provisions have effect in relation to photographs forming part of a film made before 1 June 1957 as they have effect in relation to photographs not forming part of a film.

**8.**—(1)   A film sound-track to which section 13(9) of the 1956 Act applied before commencement (film to be taken to include sounds in associated sound-track) shall be treated for the purposes of the new copyright provisions not as part of the film, but as a sound recording.

(2)   However—

(a)   copyright subsists in the sound recording only if copyright subsisted in the film immediately before commencement, and it continues to subsist until copyright in the film expires;

(b)   the author and first owner of copyright in the film shall be treated as having been author and first owner of the copyright in the sound recording; and

(c)   anything done before commencement under or in relation to the copyright in the film continues to have effect in relation to the sound recording as in relation to the film.

**9.**   No copyright subsists in—

(a)   a broadcast made before 1 June 1957, or

(b)   a cable programme included in a cable programme service before 1 January 1985;

and any such broadcast or cable programme shall be disregarded for the purposes of section 14(2) (duration of copyright in repeats).

*Authorship of work*

**10.**   The question who was the author of an existing work shall be determined in accordance with the new copyright provisions for the purposes of the rights conferred by Chapter IV of Part I (moral rights), and for all other purposes shall be determined in accordance with the law in force at the time the work was made.

*First ownership of copyright*

**11.**—(1)   The question who was first owner of copyright in an existing work shall be determined in accordance with the law in force at the time the work was made.

(2)   Where before commencement a person commissioned the making of a work in circumstances falling within—

(a)   section 4(3) of the 1956 Act or paragraph (a) of the proviso to section 5(1) of the 1911 Act (photographs, portraits and engravings), or
(b)   the proviso to section 12(4) of the 1956 Act (sound recordings),

those provisions apply to determine first ownership of copyright in any work made in pursuance of the commission after commencement.

*Duration of copyright in existing works*

**12.**—(1)   The following provisions have effect with respect to the duration of copyright in existing works.

The question which provision applies to a work shall be determined by reference to the facts immediately before commencement; and expressions used in this paragraph which were defined for the purposes of the 1956 Act have the same meaning as in that Act.

(2)   Copyright in the following descriptions of work continues to subsist until the date on which it would have expired under the 1956 Act—

(a)   literary, dramatic or musical works in relation to which the period of 50 years mentioned in the proviso to section 2(3) of the 1956 Act (duration of copyright in works made available to the public after the death of the author) has begun to run;
(b)   engravings in relation to which the period of 50 years mentioned in the proviso to section 3(4) of the 1956 Act (duration of copyright in works published after the death of the author) has begun to run;
(c)   published photographs and photographs taken before 1 June 1957;
(d)   published sound recordings and sound recordings made before 1 June 1957;
(e)   published films and films falling within section 13(3)(a) of the 1956 Act (films registered under former enactments relating to registration of films).

(3)   Copyright in anonymous or pseudonymous literary, dramatic, musical or artistic works (other than photographs) continues to subsist—

(a)   if the work is published, until the date on which it would have expired in accordance with the 1956 Act, and
(b)   if the work is unpublished, until the end of the period of 50 years from the end of the calendar year in which the new copyright provisions come into

force or, if during that period the work is first made available to the public within the meaning of section 12(2) (duration of copyright in works of unknown authorship), the date on which copyright expires in accordance with that provision;

unless, in any case, the identity of the author becomes known before that date,in which case section 12(1) applies (general rule: life of the author plus 50 years).

(4)  Copyright in the following descriptions of work continues to subsist until the end of the period of 50 years from the end of the calendar year in which the new copyright provisions come into force—

(a)  literary, dramatic and musical works of which the author has died and in relation to which none of the acts mentioned in paragraphs (a) to (e) of the proviso to section 2(3) of the 1956 Act has been done;

(b)  unpublished engravings of which the author has died;

(c)  unpublished photographs taken on or after 1 June 1957.

(5)  Copyright in the following descriptions of work continues to subsist until the end of the period of 50 years from the end of the calendar year in which the new copyright provisions come into force—

(a)  unpublished sound recordings made on or after 1 June 1957;

(b)  films not falling within subparagraph 2(e) above,

unless the recording or film is published before the end of that period in which case copyright in it shall continue until the end of the period of 50 years from the end of the calendar year in which the recording or film is published.

(6)  Copyright in any other description of existing work continues to subsist until the date on which copyright in that description of work expires in accordance with sections 12 to 15 of this Act.

(7)  The above provisions do not apply to works subject to Crown or Parliamentary copyright (see paragraph 41, 42 and 43 below).

### Perpetual copyright under the Copyright Act 1775

**13.**—(1)  The rights conferred on universities and colleges by the Copyright Act 1775 shall continue to subsist until the end of the period of 50 years from the end of the calendar year in which the new copyright provisions come into force and shall then expire.

(2)  The provisions of the following Chapters of Part I—

Chapter III (acts permitted in relation to copyright works),
Chapter VI (remedies for infringement),
Chapter VII (provisions with respect to copyright licensing),
Chapter VIII (the Copyright Tribunal),

apply in relation to those rights as they apply in relation to copyright under this Act.

### Acts infringing copyright

**14.**—(1)  The provisions of Chapters II and III of Part I as to the acts constituting an infringement of copyright apply only in relation to acts done after commencement; the provisions of the 1956 Act continue to apply in relation to acts done before commencement.

(2)   So much of section 18(2) as extends the restricted act of issuing copies to the public to include rental to the public of copies of sound recordings, films or computer programs does not apply in relation to a copy of a sound recording, film or computer program acquired by any person before commencement for the purpose of renting it to the public.

(3)   For the purposes of section 27 (meaning of 'infringing copy') the question whether the making of an article constituted an infringement of copyright, or would have done if the article had been made in the United Kingdom, shall be determined—

(a)   in relation to an article made on or after 1 June 1957 and before commencement, by reference to the 1956 Act, and

(b)   in relation to an article made before 1 June 1957, by reference to the 1911 Act.

(4)   For the purposes of the application of sections 31(2), 51(2) and 62(3) (subsequent exploitation of things whose making was, by virtue of an earlier provision of the section, not an infringement of copyright) to things made before commencement, it shall be assumed that the new copyright provisions were in force at all material times.

(5)   Section 55 (articles for producing material in a particular typeface) applies where articles have been marketed as mentioned in subsection (1) before commencement with the substitution for the period mentioned in subsection (3) of the period of 25 years from the end of the calendar year in which the new copyright provisions come into force.

(6)   Section 56 (transfer of copies, adaptations etc. of work in electronic form) does not apply in relation to a copy purchased before commencement.

(7)   In section 65 (reconstruction of buildings) the reference to the owner of the copyright in the drawings or plans is, in relation to buildings constructed before commencement, to the person who at the time of the construction was the owner of the copyright in the drawings or plans under the 1956 Act, the 1911 Act or any enactment repealed by the 1911 Act.

**15.**—(1)   Section 57 (anonymous or pseudonymous works; acts permitted on assumptions as to expiry of copyright or death of author) has effect in relation to existing works subject to the following provisions.

(2)   Subsection (1)(b)(i) (assumption as to expiry of copyright) does not apply in relation to—

(a)   photographs, or

(b)   the rights mentioned in paragraph 13 above (rights conferred by the Copyright Act 1775).

(3)   Subsection (1)(b)(ii) (assumption as to death of author) applies only—

(a)   where paragraph 12(3)(b) above applies (unpublished anonymous or pseudonymous works), after the end of the period of 50 years from the end of the calendar year in which the new copyright provisions come into force, or

(b)   where paragraph 12(6) above applies (cases in which the duration of copyright is the same under the new copyright provisions as under the previous law).

**16.**   The following provisions of section 7 of the 1956 Act continue to apply in relation to existing works—

(a)   subsection (6) (copying of unpublished works from manuscript or copy in library, museum or other institution);

(b)   subsection (7) (publication of work containing material to which subsection (6) applies), except paragraph (a) (duty to give notice of intended publication);

(c)   subsection (8) (subsequent broadcasting, performance etc. of material published in accordance with subsection (7));

and subsection (9)(d) (illustrations) continues to apply for the purposes of those provisions.

**17.**   Where in the case of a dramatic or musical work made before 1 July 1912, the right conferred by the 1911 Act did not include the sole right to perform the work in public, the acts restricted by the copyright shall be treated as not including—

(a)   performing the work in public,

(b)   broadcasting the work or including it in a cable programme service, or

(c)   doing any of the above in relation to an adaptation of the work;

and where the right conferred by the 1911 Act consisted only of the sole right to perform the work in public, the acts restricted by the copyright shall be treated as consisting only of those acts.

**18.**   Where a work made before 1 July 1912 consists of an essay, article or portion forming part of and first published in a review, magazine or other periodical or work of a like nature, the copyright is subject to any right of publishing the essay, article, or portion in a separate form to which the author was entitled at the commencement of the 1911 Act, or would if that Act had not been passed, have become entitled under section 18 of the Copyright Act 1842.

*Designs*

**19.**—(1)   Section 51 (exclusion of copyright protection in relation to works recorded or embodied in design document or models) does not apply for 10 years after commencement in relation to a design recorded or embodied in a design document or model before commencement.

(2)   During those 10 years the following provisions of Part III (design right) apply to any relevant copyright as in relation to design right—

(a)   sections 237 to 239 (availability of licences of right), and

(b)   sections 247 and 248 (application to comptroller to settle terms of licence of right).

(3)   In section 237 as it applies by virtue of this paragraph, for the reference in subsection (1) to the last five years of the design right term there shall be substituted a reference to the last five years of the period of 10 years referred to in

subparagraph (1) above, or to so much of those last five years during which copyright subsists.

(4)    In section 239 as it applies by virtue of this paragraph, for the reference in subsection (1)(b) to section 230 there shall be substituted a reference to section 99.

(5)    Where a licence of right is available by virtue of this paragraph, a person to whom a licence was granted before commencement may apply to the comptroller for an order adjusting the terms of that licence.

(6)    The provisions of sections 249 and 250 apply in relation to proceedings brought under or by virtue of this paragraph as to proceedings under Part III.

(7)    A licence granted by virtue of this paragraph shall relate only to acts which would be permitted by section 51 if the design document or model had been made after commencement.

(8)    Section 100 (right to seize infringing copies etc.) does not apply during the period of 10 years referred to in subparagraph (1) in relation to anything to which it would not apply if the design in question had been first recorded or embodied in a design document or model after commencement.

(9)    Nothing in this paragraph affects the operation of any rule of law preventing or restricting the enforcement of copyright in relation to a design.

**20.**—(1)    Where section 10 of the 1956 Act (effect of industrial application of design corresponding to artistic work) applied in relation to an artistic work at any time before commencement, section 52(2) of this Act applies with the substitution for the period of 25 years mentioned there of the relevant period of 15 years as defined in section 10(3) of the 1956 Act.

(2)    Except as provided in subparagraph (1), section 52 applies only where articles are marketed as mentioned in subsection (1)(b) after commencement.

### Abolition of statutory recording licence

**21.**    Section 8 of the 1956 Act (statutory licence to copy records sold by retail) continues to apply where notice under subsection (1)(b) of that section was given before the repeal of that section by this Act, but only in respect of the making of records—

(a)    within one year of the repeal coming into force, and
(b)    up to the number stated in the notice as intended to be sold.

### Moral rights

**22.**—(1)    No act done before commencement is actionable by virtue of any provision of Chapter IV of Part I (moral rights).

(2)    Section 43 of the 1956 Act (false attribution of authorship) continues to apply in relation to acts done before commencement.

**23.**—(1)    The following provisions have effect with respect to the rights conferred by—

(a)    section 77 (right to be identified as author or director), and
(b)    section 80 (right to object to derogatory treatment of work).

(2)    The rights do not apply—

(a)   in relation to a literary, dramatic, musical and artistic work of which the author died before commencement; or

(b)   in relation to a film made before commencement.

(3)   The rights in relation to an existing literary, dramatic, musical or artistic work do not apply—

(a)   where copyright first vested in the author, to anything which by virtue of an assignment of copyright made or licence granted before commencement may be done without infringing copyright;

(b)   where copyright first vested in a person other than the author, to anything done by or with the licence of the copyright owner.

(4)   The rights do not apply to anything done in relation to a record made in pursuance of section 8 of the 1956 Act (statutory recording licence).

**24.**   The right conferred by section 85 (right to privacy of certain photographs and films) does not apply to photographs taken or films made before commencement.

*Assignments and licences*

**25.**—(1)   Any document made or event occurring before commencement which had any operation—

(a)   affecting the ownership of the copyright in an existing work, or

(b)   creating, transferring or terminating an interest, right or licence in respect of the copyright in an existing work,

has the corresponding operation in relation to copyright in the work under this Act.

(2)   Expressions used in such a document shall be construed in accordance with their effect immediately before commencement.

**26.**—(1)   Section 91(1) of this Act (assignment of future copyright: statutory vesting of legal interest on copyright coming into existence) does not apply in relation to an agreement made before 1 June 1957.

(2)   The repeal by this Act of section 37(2) of the 1956 Act (assignment of future copyright: devolution of right where assignee dies before copyright comes into existence) does not affect the operation of that provision in relation to an agreement made before commencement.

**27.**—(1)   Where the author of a literary, dramatic, musical or artistic work was the first owner of the copyright in it, no assignment of the copyright and no grant of any interest in it, made by him (otherwise than by will) after the passing of the 1911 Act and before 1 June 1957, shall be operative to vest in the assignee or grantee any rights with respect to the copyright in the work beyond the expiration of 25 years from the death of the author.

(2)   The reversionary interest in the copyright expectant on the termination of that period may after commencement be assigned by the author during his life but in the absence of any assignment shall, on his death, devolve on his legal personal representatives as part of his estate.

(3)   Nothing in this paragraph affects—

(a) an assignment of the reversionary interest by a person to whom it has been assigned,

(b) an assignment of the reversionary interest after the death of the author by his personal representatives or any person becoming entitled to it, or

(c) any assignment of the copyright after the reversionary interest has fallen in.

(4) Nothing in this paragraph applies to the assignment of the copyright in a collective work or a licence to publish a work or part of a work as part of a collective work.

(5) In subparagraph (4) 'collective work' means—

(a) any encyclopaedia, dictionary, yearbook, or similar work;

(b) a newspaper, review, magazine, or similar periodical; and

(c) any work written in distinct parts by different authors, or in which works or parts of works of different authors are incorporated.

**28.**—(1) This paragraph applies where copyright subsists in a literary, dramatic, musical or artistic work made before 1 July 1912 in relation to which the author, before the commencement of the 1911 Act, made such an assignment or grant as was mentioned in paragraph (a) of the proviso to section 24(1) of that Act (assignment or grant of copyright or performing right for full term of the right under the previous law).

(2) If before commencement any event has occurred or notice has been given which by virtue of paragraph 38 of Schedule 7 to the 1956 Act had any operation in relation to copyright in the work under that Act, the event or notice has the corresponding operation in relation to copyright under this Act.

(3) Any right which immediately before commencement would by virtue of paragraph 38(3) of that Schedule have been exercisable in relation to the work, or copyright in it, is exercisable in relation to the work or copyright in it under this Act.

(4) If in accordance with paragraph 38(4) of that Schedule copyright would, on a date after the commencement of the 1956 Act, have reverted to the author or his personal representatives and that date falls after the commencement of the new copyright provisions—

(a) the copyright in the work shall revert to the author or his personal representatives, as the case may be, and

(b) any interest of any other person in the copyright which subsists on that date by virtue of any document made before the commencement of the 1911 Act shall thereupon determine.

**29.** Section 92(2) of this Act (rights of exclusive licensee against successors in title of person granting licence) does not apply in relation to an exclusive licence granted before commencement.

*Bequests*

**30.**—(1) Section 93 of this Act (copyright to pass under will with original document or other material thing embodying unpublished work)—

(a) does not apply where the testator died before 1 June 1957, and

(b)   where the testator died on or after that date and before commencement, applies only in relation to an original document embodying a work.

(2)   In the case of an author who died before 1 June 1957, the ownership after his death of a manuscript of his, where such ownership has been acquired under a testamentary disposition made by him and the manuscript is of a work which has not been published or performed in public, is prima facie proof of the copyright being with the owner of the manuscript.

### Remedies for infringement

**31.**—(1)   Sections 96 and 97 of this Act (remedies for infringement) apply only in relation to an infringement of copyright committed after commencement; section 17 of the 1956 Act continues to apply in relation to infringements committed before commencement.

(2)   Sections 99 and 100 of this Act (delivery up or seizure of infringing copies etc.) apply to infringing copies and other articles made before or after commencement; section 18 of the 1956 Act, and section 7 of the 1911 Act, (conversion damages etc.), do not apply after commencement except for the purposes of proceedings begun before commencement.

(3)   Sections 101 and 102 of this Act (rights and remedies of exclusive licensee) apply where sections 96 to 100 of this Act apply; section 19 of the 1956 Act continues to apply where section 17 or 18 of that Act applies.

(4)   Sections 104 to 106 of this Act (presumptions) apply only in proceedings brought by virtue of this Act; section 20 of the 1956 Act continues to apply in proceedings brought by virtue of that Act.

**32.**   Sections 101 and 102 of this Act (rights and remedies of exclusive licensee) do not apply to a licence granted before 1 June 1957.

**33.**—(1)   The provisions of section 107 of this Act (criminal liability for making or dealing with infringing articles etc.) apply only in relation to acts done after commencement; section 21 of the 1956 Act (penalties and summary proceedings in respect of dealings which infringe copyright) continues to apply in relation to acts done before commencement.

(2)   Section 109 of this Act (search warrants) applies in relation to offences committed before commencement in relation to which section 21A or 21B of the 1956 Act applied; sections 21A and 21B continue to apply in relation to warrants issued before commencement.

### Copyright Tribunal: proceedings pending on commencement

**34.**—(1)   The Lord Chancellor may, after consultation with the Lord Advocate, by rules make such provision as he considers necessary or expedient with respect to proceedings pending under Part IV of the 1956 Act immediately before commencement.

(2)   Rules under this paragraph shall be made by statutory instrument which shall be subject to annulment in pursuance of a resolution of either House of Parliament.

### Qualification for copyright protection

**35.**   Every work in which copyright subsisted under the 1956 Act immediately before commencement shall be deemed to satisfy the requirements of Part I of this Act as to qualification for copyright protection.

## Dependent territories

**36.**—(1) The 1911 Act shall remain in force as part of the law of any dependent territory in which it was in force immediately before commencement until—

    (a) the new copyright provisions come into force in that territory by virtue of an Order under section 157 of this Act (power to extend new copyright provisions), or

    (b) in the case of any of the Channel Islands, the Act is repealed by Order under subparagraph (3) below.

(2) An Order in Council in force immediately before commencement which extends to any dependent territory any provisions of the 1956 Act shall remain in force as part of the law of that territory until—

    (a) the new copyright provisions come into force in that territory by virtue of an Order under section 157 of this Act (power to extend new copyright provisions), or

    (b) in the case of the Isle of Man, the Order is revoked by Order under subparagraph (3) below;

and while it remains in force such an Order may be varied under the provisions of the 1956 Act under which it was made.

(3) If it appears to Her Majesty that provision with respect to copyright has been made in the law of any of the Channel Islands or the Isle of Man otherwise than by extending the provisions of Part I of this Act, Her Majesty may by Order in Council repeal the 1911 Act as it has effect as part of the law of that territory or, as the case may be, revoke the Order extending the 1956 Act there.

(4) A dependent territory in which the 1911 or 1956 Act remains in force shall be treated, in the law of the countries to which Part I extends, as a country to which that Part extends; and those countries shall be treated in the law of such a territory as countries to which the 1911 Act or, as the case may be, the 1956 Act extends.

(5) If a country in which the 1911 or 1956 Act is in force ceases to be a colony of the United Kingdom, section 158 of this Act (consequences of country ceasing to be colony) applies with the substitution for the reference in subsection (3)(b) to the provisions of Part I of this Act of a reference to the provisions of the 1911 or 1956 Act, as the case may be.

(6) In this paragraph 'dependent territory' means any of the Channel Islands, the Isle of Man or any colony.

**37.**—(1) This paragraph applies to a country which immediately before commencement was not a dependent territory within the meaning of paragraph 36 above but—

    (a) was a country to which the 1956 Act extended, or

    (b) was treated as such a country by virtue of paragraph 39(2) of Schedule 7 to that Act (countries to which the 1911 Act extended or was treated as extending);

and Her Majesty may by Order in Council conclusively declare for the purposes of this paragraph whether a country was such a country or was so treated.

(2)   A country to which this paragraph applies shall be treated as a country to which Part I extends for the purposes of sections 154 to 156 (qualification for copyright protection) until—

(a)   an Order in Council is made in respect of that country under section 159 (application of Part I to countries to which it does not extend), or

(b)   an Order in Council is made declaring that it shall cease to be so treated by reason of the fact that the provisions of the 1956 Act or, as the case may be, the 1911 Act, which extended there as part of the law of that country have been repealed or amended.

(3)   A statutory instrument containing an Order in Council under this paragraph shall be subject to annulment in pursuance of a resolution of either House of Parliament.

### Territorial waters and the continental shelf

**38.**   Section 161 of this Act (application of Part I to things done in territorial waters or the United Kingdom sector of the continental shelf) does not apply in relation to anything done before commencement.

### British ships, aircraft and hovercraft

**39.**   Section 162 (British ships, aircraft and hovercraft) does not apply in relation to anything done before commencement.

### Crown copyright

**40.**—(1)   Section 163 of this Act (general provisions as to Crown copyright) applies to an existing work if—

(a)   section 39 of the 1956 Act applied to the work immediately before commencement, and

(b)   the work is not one to which section 164, 165 or 166 applies (copyright in Acts, Measures and Bills and Parliamentary copyright); (see paragraphs 42 and 43 below).

(2)   Section 163(1)(b) (first ownership of copyright) has effect subject to any agreement entered into before commencement under section 39(6) of the 1956 Act.

**41.**—(1)   The following provisions have effect with respect to the duration of copyright in existing works to which section 163 (Crown copyright) applies.

The question which provision applies to a work shall be determined by reference to the facts immediately before commencement; and expressions used in this paragraph which were defined for the purposes of the 1956 Act have the same meaning as in that Act.

(2)   Copyright in the following descriptions of work continues to subsist until the date on which it would have expired in accordance with the 1956 Act—

(a)   published literary, dramatic or musical works;

(b)   artistic works other than engravings or photographs;

(c)    published engravings;

(d)    published photographs and photographs taken before 1 June 1957;

(e)    published sound recordings and sound recordings made before 1 June 1957;

(f)    published films and films falling within section 13(3)(a) of the 1956 Act (films registered under former enactments relating to registration of films).

(3)    Copyright in unpublished literary, dramatic or musical works continues to subsist until—

(a)    the date on which copyright expires in accordance with section 163(3), or

(b)    the end of the period of 50 years from the end of the calendar year in which the new copyright provisions come into force,

whichever is the later.

(4)    Copyright in the following descriptions of work continues to subsist until the end of the period of 50 years from the end of the calendar year in which the new copyright provisions come into force—

(a)    unpublished engravings;

(b)    unpublished photographs taken on or after 1 June 1957.

(5)    Copyright in a film or sound recording not falling within subparagraph (2) above continues to subsist until the end of the period of 50 years from the end of the calendar year in which the new copyright provisions come into force, unless the film or recording is published before the end of that period, in which case copyright expires 50 years from the end of the calendar year in which it is published.

**42.**—(1)    Section 164 (copyright in Acts and Measures) applies to existing Acts of Parliament and Measures of the General Synod of the Church of England.

(2)    References in that section to Measures of the General Synod of the Church of England include Church Assembly Measures.

*Parliamentary copyright*

**43.**—(1)    Section 165 of this Act (general provisions as to Parliamentary copyright) applies to existing unpublished literary, dramatic, musical or artistic works, but does not otherwise apply to existing works.

(2)    Section 166 (copyright in Parliamentary Bills) does not apply—

(a)    to a public Bill which was introduced into Parliament and published before commencement,

(b)    to a private Bill of which a copy was deposited in either House before commencement, or

(c)    to a personal Bill which was given a First Reading in the House of Lords before commencement.

*Copyright vesting in certain international organisations*

**44.**—(1)    Any work in which immediately before commencement copyright subsisted by virtue of section 33 of the 1956 Act shall be deemed to satisfy the requirements of section 168(1); but otherwise section 168 does not apply to works made or, as the case may be, published before commencement.

(2)   Copyright in any such work which is unpublished continues to subsist until the date on which it would have expired in accordance with the 1956 Act, or the end of the period of 50 years from the end of the calendar year in which the new copyright provisions come into force, whichever is the earlier.

*Meaning of 'publication'*

**45.**   Section 175(3) (construction of building treated as equivalent to publication) applies only where the construction of the building began after commencement.

*Meaning of 'unauthorised'*

**46.**   For the purposes of the application of the definition in section 178 (minor definitions) of the expression 'unauthorised' in relation to things done before commencement —

(a)   paragraph (a) applies in relation to things done before 1 June 1957 as if the reference to the licence of the copyright owner were a reference to his consent or acquiescence;

(b)   paragraph (b) applies with the substitution for the words from 'or, in a case' to the end of the words 'or any person lawfully claiming under him'; and

(c)   paragraph (c) shall be disregarded.

### Schedule 2 Rights in performances: permitted acts

*Introductory provisions*

**1.**—(1)   The provisions of this Schedule specify acts which may be done in relation to a performance or recording notwithstanding the rights conferred by Part II; they relate only to the question of infringement of those rights and do not affect any other right or obligation restricting the doing of any of the specified acts.

(2)   No inference shall be drawn from the description of any act which may by virtue of this Schedule be done without infringing the rights conferred by Part II as to the scope of those rights.

(3)   The provisions of this Schedule are to be construed independently of each other, so that the fact that an act does not fall within one provision does not mean that it is not covered by another provision.

*Criticism, reviews and news reporting*

**2.**—(1)   Fair dealing with a performance or recording—

(a)   for the purpose of criticism or review, of that or another performance or recording, or of a work; or

(b)   for the purpose of reporting current events,

does not infringe any of the rights conferred by Part II.

(2)   Expressions used in this paragraph have the same meaning as in section 30.

*Incidental inclusion of performance or recording*

**3.**—(1)   The rights conferred by Part II are not infringed by the incidental inclusion of a performance or recording in a sound recording, film, broadcast or cable programme.

(2)   Nor are those rights infringed by anything done in relation to copies of, or the playing, showing, broadcasting or inclusion in a cable programme service of, anything whose making was, by virtue of subparagraph (1), not an infringement of those rights.

(3)   A performance or recording so far as it consists of music, or words spoken or sung with music, shall not be regarded as incidentally included in a sound recording, broadcast or cable programme if it is deliberately included.

(4)   Expressions used in this paragraph have the same meaning as in section 31.

*Things done for purposes of instruction or examination*

**4.**—(1)   The rights conferred by Part II are not infringed by the copying of a recording of a performance in the course of instruction, or of preparation for instruction, in the making of films or film sound-tracks, provided the copying is done by a person giving or receiving instruction.

(2)   The rights conferred by Part II are not infringed—

(a)   by the copying of a recording of a performance for the purposes of setting or answering the questions in an examination, or

(b)   by anything done for the purposes of an examination by way of communicating the questions to the candidates.

(3)   Where a recording which would otherwise be an illicit recording is made in accordance with this paragraph but is subsequently dealt with, it shall be treated as an illicit recording for the purposes of that dealing, and if that dealing infringes any right conferred by Part II for all subsequent purposes.

For this purpose 'dealt with' means sold or let for hire, or offered or exposed for sale or hire.

(4)   Expressions used in this paragraph have the same meaning as in section 32.

*Playing or showing sound recording, film, broadcast or cable programme at educational establishment*

**5.**—(1)   The playing or showing of a sound recording, film, broadcast or cable programme at an educational establishment for the purposes of instruction before an audience consisting of teachers and pupils at the establishment and other persons directly connected with the activities of the establishment is not a playing or showing of a performance in public for the purposes of infringement of the rights conferred by Part II.

(2)   A person is not for this purpose directly connected with the activities of the educational establishment simply because he is the parent of a pupil at the establishment.

(3)   Expressions used in this paragraph have the same meaning as in section 34 and any provision made under section 174(2) with respect to the application of that section also applies for the purposes of this paragraph.

*Recording of broadcasts and cable programmes by educational establishments*

**6.**—(1)   A recording of a broadcast or cable programme, or a copy of such a recording, may be made by or on behalf of an educational establishment for the educational purposes of that establishment without thereby infringing any of the rights conferred by Part II in relation to any performance or recording included in it.

(2)   Where a recording which would otherwise be an illicit recording is made in accordance with this paragraph but is subsequently dealt with, it shall be treated as an illicit recording for the purposes of that dealing, and if that dealing infringes any right conferred by Part II for all subsequent purposes.

For this purpose 'dealt with' means sold or let for hire, or offered or exposed for sale or hire.

(3)   Expressions used in this paragraph have the same meaning as in section 35 and any provision made under section 174(2) with respect to the application of that section also applies for the purposes of this paragraph.

*Copy of work required to be made as condition of export*

**7.**—(1)   If an article of cultural or historical importance or interest cannot lawfully be exported from the United Kingdom unless a copy of it is made and deposited in an appropriate library or archive, it is not an infringement of any right conferred by Part II to make that copy.

(2)   Expressions used in this paragraph have the same meaning as in section 44.

*Parliamentary and judicial proceedings*

**8.**—(1)   The rights conferred by Part II are not infringed by anything done for the purposes of parliamentary or judicial proceedings or for the purpose of reporting such proceedings.

(2)   Expressions used in this paragraph have the same meaning as in section 45.

*Royal Commissions and statutory inquiries*

**9.**—(1)   The rights conferred by Part II are not infringed by anything done for the purposes of the proceedings of a royal commission or statutory inquiry or for the purpose of reporting any such proceedings held in public.

(2)   Expressions used in this paragraph have the same meaning as in section 46.

*Public records*

**10.**—(1)   Material which is comprised in public records within the meaning of the Public Records Act 1958, the Public Records (Scotland) Act 1937 or the Public Records Act (Northern Ireland) 1923 which are open to public inspection in pursuance of that Act, may be copied, and a copy may be supplied to any person, by or with the authority of any officer appointed under that Act, without infringing any right conferred by Part II.

(2)   Expressions used in this paragraph have the same meaning as in section 49.

*Acts done under statutory authority*

**11.**—(1) Where the doing of a particular act is specifically authorised by an Act of Parliament, whenever passed, then, unless the Act provides otherwise, the doing of that act does not infringe the rights conferred by Part II.

(2) Subparagraph (1) applies in relation to an enactment contained in Northern Ireland legislation as it applies to an Act of Parliament.

(3) Nothing in this paragraph shall be construed as excluding any defence of statutory authority otherwise available under or by virtue of any enactment.

(4) Expressions used in this paragraph have the same meaning as in section 50.

*Transfer of copies of works in electronic form*

**12.**—(1) This paragraph applies where a recording of a performance in electronic form has been purchased on terms which, expressly or impliedly or by virtue of any rule of law, allow the purchaser to make further recordings in connection with his use of the recording.

(2) If there are no express terms—

(a) prohibiting the transfer of the recording by the purchaser, imposing obligations which continue after a transfer, prohibiting the assignment of any consent or terminating any consent on a transfer, or

(b) providing for the terms on which a transferee may do the things which the purchaser was permitted to do,

anything which the purchaser was allowed to do may also be done by a transferee without infringement of the rights conferred by this Part, but any recording made by the purchaser which is not also transferred shall be treated as an illicit recording for all purposes after the transfer.

(3) The same applies where the original purchased recording is no longer usable and what is transferred is a further copy used in its place.

(4) The above provisions also apply on a subsequent transfer, with the substitution for references in subparagraph (2) to the purchaser of references to the subsequent transferor.

(5) This paragraph does not apply in relation to a recording purchased before the commencement of Part II.

(6) Expressions used in this paragraph have the same meaning as in section 56.

*Use of recordings of spoken works in certain cases*

**13.**—(1) Where a recording of the reading or recitation of a literary work is made for the purpose—

(a) of reporting current events, or

(b) of broadcasting or including in a cable programme service the whole or part of the reading or recitation,

it is not an infringement of the rights conferred by Part II to use the recording (or to copy the recording and use the copy) for that purpose, provided the following conditions are met.

(2)   The conditions are that—

(a)   the recording is a direct recording of the reading or recitation and is not taken from a previous recording or from a broadcast or cable programme;

(b)   the making of the recording was not prohibited by or on behalf of the person giving the reading or recitation;

(c)   the use made of the recording is not of a kind prohibited by or on behalf of that person before the recording was made; and

(d)   the use is by or with the authority of a person who is lawfully in possession of the recording.

(3)   Expressions used in this paragraph have the same meaning as in section 58.

### Recordings of folksongs

**14.**—(1)   A recording of a performance of a song may be made for the purpose of including it in an archive maintained by a designated body without infringing any of the rights conferred by Part II, provided the conditions in subparagraph (2) below are met.

(2)   The conditions are that—

(a)   the words are unpublished and of unknown authorship at the time the recording is made,

(b)   the making of the recording does not infringe any copyright, and

(c)   its making is not prohibited by any performer.

(3)   Copies of a recording made in reliance on subparagraph (1) and included in an archive maintained by a designated body may, if the prescribed conditions are met, be made and supplied by the archivist without infringing any of the rights conferred by Part II.

(4)   In this paragraph—

'designated body' means a body designated for the purposes of section 61, and

'the prescribed conditions' means the conditions prescribed for the purposes of subsection (3) of that section;

and other expressions used in this paragraph have the same meaning as in that section.

### Playing of sound recordings for purposes of club, society etc.

**15.**—(1)   It is not an infringement of any right conferred by Part II to play a sound recording as part of the activities of, or for the benefit of, a club, society or other organisation if the following conditions are met.

(2)   The conditions are—

(a)   that the organisation is not established or conducted for profit and its main objects are charitable or are otherwise concerned with the advancement of religion, education or social welfare, and

(b)   that the proceeds of any charge for admission to the place where the recording is to be heard are applied solely for the purposes of the organisation.

(3)   Expressions used in this paragraph have the same meaning as in section 67.

*Incidental recording for purposes of broadcast or cable programme*

**16.**—(1)   A person who proposes to broadcast a recording of a performance, or include a recording of a performance in a cable programme service, in circumstances not infringing the rights conferred by Part II shall be treated as having consent for the purposes of that Part for the making of a further recording for the purposes of the broadcast or cable programme.

(2)   That consent is subject to the condition that the further recording—

(a)   shall not be used for any other purpose, and

(b)   shall be destroyed within 28 days of being first used for broadcasting the performance or including it in a cable programme service.

(3)   A recording made in accordance with this paragraph shall be treated as an illicit recording—

(a)   for the purposes of any use in breach of the condition mentioned in subparagraph (2)(a), and

(b)   for all purposes after that condition or the condition mentioned in subparagraph (2)(b) is broken.

(4)   Expressions used in this paragraph have the same meaning as in section 68.

*Recordings for purposes of supervision and control of*
*broadcasts and cable programmes*

**17.**—(1)   The rights conferred by Part II are not infringed by the making or use by the British Broadcasting Corporation, for the purpose of maintaining supervision and control over programmes broadcast by them, of recordings of those programmes.

(2)   The rights conferred by Part II are not infringed by—

(a)   the making or use of recordings by the Independent Broadcasting Authority for the purposes mentioned in section 4(7) of the Broadcasting Act 1981 (maintenance of supervision and control over programmes and advertisements); or

(b)   anything done under or in pursuance of provision included in a contract between a programme contractor and the Authority in accordance with section 21 of that Act.

(3)   The rights conferred by Part II are not infringed by—

(a)   the making by or with the authority of the Cable Authority, or the use by that Authority, for the purpose of maintaining supervision and control over programmes included in services licensed under Part I of the Cable and Broadcasting Act 1984, of recordings of those programmes; or

(b)   anything done under or in pursuance of—

(i)   a notice or direction given under section 16 of the Cable and Broadcasting Act 1984 (power of Cable Authority to require production of recordings); or

(ii)   a condition included in a licence by virtue of section 35 of that Act (duty of Authority to secure that recordings are available for certain purposes).

(4)   Expressions used in this paragraph have the same meaning as in section 69.

*Free public showing or playing of broadcast or cable programme*

**18.**—(1)   The showing or playing in public of a broadcast or cable programme to an audience who have not paid for admission to the place where the broadcast or programme is to be seen or heard does not infringe any right conferred by Part II in relation to a performance or recording included in—

(a)   the broadcast or cable programme, or
(b)   any sound recording or film which is played or shown in public by reception of the broadcast or cable programme.

(2)   The audience shall be treated as having paid for admission to a place—

(a)   if they have paid for admission to a place of which that place forms part; or
(b)   if goods or services are supplied at that place (or a place of which it forms part)—

(i)   at prices which are substantially attributable to the facilities afforded for seeing or hearing the broadcast or programme, or
(ii)   at prices exceeding those usually charged there and which are partly attributable to those facilities.

(3)   The following shall not be regarded as having paid for admission to a place—

(a)   persons admitted as residents or inmates of the place;
(b)   persons admitted as members of a club or society where the payment is only for membership of the club or society and the provision of facilities for seeing or hearing broadcasts or programmes is only incidental to the main purposes of the club or society.

(4)   Where the making of the broadcast or inclusion of the programme in a cable programme service was an infringement of the rights conferred by Part II in relation to a performance or recording, the fact that it was heard or seen in public by the reception of the broadcast or programme shall be taken into account in assessing the damages for that infringement.

(5)   Expressions used in this paragraph have the same meaning as in section 72.

*Reception and re-transmission of broadcast in cable programme service*

**19.**—(1)   This paragraph applies where a broadcast made from a place in the United Kingdom is, by reception and immediate re-transmission, included in a cable programme service.

(2)   The rights conferred by Part II in relation to a performance or recording included in the broadcast are not infringed—

(a)   if the inclusion of the broadcast in the cable programme service is in pursuance of a requirement imposed under section 13(1) of the Cable and Broadcasting Act 1984 (duty of Cable Authority to secure inclusion in cable service of certain programmes), or

(b)   if and to the extent that the broadcast is made for reception in the area in which the cable programme service is provided;

but where the making of the broadcast was an infringement of those rights, the fact that the broadcast was re-transmitted as a programme in a cable programme service shall be taken into account in assessing the damages for that infringement.

(3)   Expressions used in this paragraph have the same meaning as in section 73.

*Provision of subtitled copies of broadcast or cable programme*

**20.**—(1)   A designated body may, for the purpose of providing people who are deaf or hard of hearing, or physically or mentally handicapped in other ways, with copies which are subtitled or otherwise modified for their special needs, make recordings of television broadcasts or cable programmes without infringing any right conferred by Part II in relation to a performance or recording included in the broadcast or cable programme.

(2)   In this paragraph 'designated body' means a body designated for the purposes of section 74 and other expressions used in this paragraph have the same meaning as in that section.

*Recording of broadcast or cable programme for archival purposes*

**21.**—(1)   A recording of a broadcast or cable programme of a designated class, or a copy of such a recording, may be made for the purpose of being placed in an archive maintained by a designated body without thereby infringing any right conferred by Part II in relation to a performance or recording included in the broadcast or cable programme.

(2)   In this paragraph 'designated class' and 'designated body' means a class or body designated for the purposes of section 75 and other expressions used in this paragraph have the same meaning as in that section.

## Schedule 3 Registered designs:
## minor and consequential amendments of 1949 Act

[Schedule 3 makes minor and consequential amendments to the Registered Designs Act 1949. That Act as amended in accordance with ss. 265 to 272 and sch. 3 is set out in sch. 4. The text of sch. 3 itself is not reproduced here.]

## Schedule 4 The Registered Designs Act 1949 as amended

*Registrable designs and proceedings for registration*

*Designs registrable under Act*
**1.**—(1)   In this Act 'design' means features of shape, configuration, pattern or

ornament applied to an article by any industrial process, being features which in the finished article appeal to and are judged by the eye, but does not include—

    (a)   a method or principle of construction, or

    (b)   features of shape or configuration of an article which—

        (i)   are dictated solely by the function which the article has to perform, or

        (ii)   are dependent upon the appearance of another article of which the article is intended by the author of the design to form an integral part.

(2)   A design which is new may, upon application by the person claiming to be the proprietor, be registered under this Act in respect of any article, or set of articles, specified in the application.

(3)   A design shall not be registered in respect of an article if the appearance of the article is not material, that is, if aesthetic considerations are not normally taken into account to a material extent by persons acquiring or using articles of that description, and would not be so taken into account if the design were to be applied to the article.

(4)   A design shall not be regarded as new for the purposes of this Act if it is the same as a design—

    (a)   registered in respect of the same or any other article in pursuance of a prior application, or

    (b)   published in the United Kingdom in respect of the same or any other article before the date of the application,

or if it differs from such a design only in immaterial details or in features which are variants commonly used in the trade.

This subsection has effect subject to the provisions of sections 4, 6 and 16 of this Act.

(5)   The Secretary of State may by rules provide for excluding from registration under this Act designs for such articles of a primarily literary or artistic character as the Secretary of State thinks fit.

*Proprietorship of designs*

**2.**—(1)   The author of a design shall be treated for the purposes of this Act as the original proprietor of the design, subject to the following provisions.

(1A)   Where a design is created in pursuance of a commission for money or money's worth, the person commissioning the design shall be treated as the original proprietor of the design.

(1B)   Where, in a case not falling within subsection (1A), a design is created by an employee in the course of his employment, his employer shall be treated as the original proprietor of the design.

(2)   Where a design, or the right to apply a design to any article, becomes vested, whether by assignment, transmission or operation of law, in any person other than the original proprietor, either alone or jointly with the original proprietor, that other person, or as the case may be the original proprietor and that other person, shall be treated for the purposes of this Act as the proprietor of the design or as the proprietor of the design in relation to that article.

(3)   In this Act the 'author' of a design means the person who creates it.

(4)   In the case of a design generated by computer in circumstances such that

there is no human author, the person by whom the arrangements necessary for the creation of the design are made shall be taken to be the author.

*Proceedings for registration*
**3.**—(1) An application for the registration of a design shall be made in the prescribed form and shall be filed at the Patent Office in the prescribed manner.

(2) An application for the registration of a design in which design right subsists shall not be entertained unless made by the person claiming to be the design right owner.

(3) For the purpose of deciding whether a design is new, the registrar may make such searches, if any, as he thinks fit.

(4) The registrar may, in such cases as may be prescribed, direct that for the purpose of deciding whether a design is new an application shall be treated as made on a date earlier or later than that on which it was in fact made.

(5) The registrar may refuse an application for the registration of a design or may register the design in pursuance of the application subject to such modifications, if any, as he thinks fit; and a design when registered shall be registered as of the date on which the application was made or is treated as having been made.

(6) An application which, owing to any default or neglect on the part of the applicant, has not been completed so as to enable registration to be effected within such time as may be prescribed shall be deemed to be abandoned.

(7) An appeal lies from any decision of the registrar under this section.

*Registration of same design in respect of other articles etc.*
**4.**—(1) Where the registered proprietor of a design registered in respect of any article makes an application—

(a) for registration in respect of one or more other articles, of the registered design, or

(b) for registration in respect of the same or one or more other articles, of a design consisting of the registered design with modifications or variations not sufficient to alter the character or substantially to affect the identity thereof,

the application shall not be refused and the registration made on that application shall not be invalidated by reason only of the previous registration or publication of the registered design:

Provided that the right in a design registered by virtue of this section shall not extend beyond the end of the period, and any extended period, for which the right subsists in the original registered design.

(2) Where any person makes an application for the registration of a design in respect of any article and either—

(a) that design has been previously registered by another person in respect of some other article; or

(b) the design to which the application relates consists of a design previously registered by another person in respect of the same or some other article with modifications or variations not sufficient to alter the character or substantially to affect the identity thereof,

then, if at any time while the application is pending the applicant becomes the registered proprietor of the design previously registered, the foregoing provisions of this section shall apply as if at the time of making the application the applicant had been the registered proprietor of that design.

*Provisions for secrecy of certain designs*
**5.**—(1)  Where, either before or after the commencement of this Act, an application for the registration of a design has been made, and it appears to the registrar that the design is one of a class notified to him by the Secretary of State as relevant for defence purposes, he may give directions for prohibiting or restricting the publication of information with respect to the design, or the communication of such information to any person or class of persons specified in the directions.

(2)  The Secretary of State shall by rules make provision for securing that where such directions are given—

(a)  the representation or specimen of the design, and

(b)  any evidence filed in support of the applicant's contention that the appearance of an article is material (for the purposes of section 1(3) of this Act),

shall not be open to public inspection at the Patent Office during the continuance in force of the directions.

(3)  Where the registrar gives any such directions as aforesaid, he shall give notice of the application and of the directions to the Secretary of State, and thereupon the following provisions shall have effect, that is to say:—

(a)  the Secretary of State shall, upon receipt of such notice, consider whether the publication of the design would be prejudicial to the defence of the realm and unless a notice under paragraph (c) of this subsection has previously been given by that authority to the registrar, shall reconsider that question before the expiration of nine months from the date of filing of the application for registration of the design and at least once in every subsequent year;

(b)  for the purpose aforesaid, the Secretary of State may, at any time after the design has been registered or, with the consent of the applicant, at any time before the design has been registered, inspect the representation or specimen of the design, or any such evidence as is mentioned in subsection (2)(b) above, filed in pursuance of the application;

(c)  if upon consideration of the design at any time it appears to the Secretary of State that the publication of the design would not, or would no longer, be prejudicial to the defence of the realm, he shall give notice to the registrar to that effect;

(d)  on the receipt of any such notice the registrar shall revoke the directions and may, subject to such conditions, if any, as he thinks fit, extend the time for doing anything required or authorised to be done by or under this Act in connection with the application or registration, whether or not that time has previously expired.

(4)  No person resident in the United Kingdom shall, except under the authority of a written permit granted by or on behalf of the registrar, make or cause to be made any application outside the United Kingdom for the registration of a design of any class prescribed for the purposes of this subsection unless—

(a)   an application for registration of the same design has been made in the United Kingdom not less than six weeks before the application outside the United Kingdom; and

(b)   either no directions have been given under subsection (1) of this section in relation to the application in the United Kingdom or all such directions have been revoked:

Provided that this subsection shall not apply in relation to a design for which an application for protection has first been filed in a country outside the United Kingdom by a person resident outside the United Kingdom.

*Provisions as to confidential disclosure etc.*
**6.**—(1)   An application for the registration of a design shall not be refused, and the registration of a design shall not be invalidated, by reason only of—

(a)   the disclosure of the design by the proprietor to any other person in such circumstances as would make it contrary to good faith for that other person to use or publish the design;

(b)   the disclosure of the design in breach of good faith by any person other than the proprietor of the design; or

(c)   in the case of a new or original textile design intended for registration, the acceptance of a first and confidential order for goods bearing the design.

(2)   An application for the registration of a design shall not be refused and the registration of a design shall not be invalidated by reason only—

(a)   that a representation of the design, or any article to which the design has been applied, has been displayed, with the consent of the proprietor of the design, at an exhibition certified by the Secretary of State for the purposes of this subsection;

(b)   that after any such display as aforesaid, and during the period of the exhibition, a representation of the design or any such article as aforesaid has been displayed by any person without the consent of the proprietor; or

(c)   that a representation of the design has been published in consequence of any such display as is mentioned in paragraph (a) of this subsection,

if the application for registration of the design is made not later than six months after the opening of the exhibition.

(3)   An application for the registration of a design shall not be refused, and the registration of a design shall not be invalidated, by reason only of the communication of the design by the proprietor thereof to a government department or to any person authorised by a government department to consider the merits of the design, or of anything done in consequence of such a communication.

(4)   Where an application is made by or with the consent of the owner of copyright in an artistic work for the registration of a corresponding design, the design shall not be treated for the purposes of this Act as being other than new by reason only of any use previously made of the artistic work, subject to subsection (5).

(5)   Subsection (4) does not apply if the previous use consisted of or included the sale, letting for hire or offer or exposure for sale or hire of articles to which had been applied industrially—

(a)   the design in question, or

(b)   a design differing from it only in immaterial details or in features which are variants commonly used in the trade,

and that previous use was made by or with the consent of the copyright owner.

(6)   The Secretary of State may make provision by rules as to the circumstances in which a design is to be regarded for the purposes of this section as 'applied industrially' to articles, or any description of articles.

## Effect of registration etc.

### Right given by registration

**7.**—(1)   The registration of a design under this Act gives the registered proprietor the exclusive right—

(a)   to make or import—

(i)   for sale or hire, or
(ii)   for use for the purposes of a trade or business, or

(b)   to sell, hire or offer or expose for sale or hire,

an article in respect of which the design is registered and to which that design or a design not substantially different from it has been applied.

(2)   The right in the registered design is infringed by a person who without the licence of the registered proprietor does anything which by virtue of subsection (1) is the exclusive right of the proprietor.

(3)   The right in the registered design is also infringed by a person who, without the licence of the registered proprietor makes anything for enabling any such article to be made, in the United Kingdom or elsewhere, as mentioned in subsection (1).

(4)   The right in the registered design is also infringed by a person who without the licence of the registered proprietor—

(a)   does anything in relation to a kit that would be an infringement if done in relation to the assembled article (see subsection (1)), or

(b)   makes anything for enabling a kit to be made or assembled, in the United Kingdom or elsewhere, if the assembled article would be such an article as is mentioned in subsection (1);

and for this purpose a 'kit' means a complete or substantially complete set of components intended to be assembled into an article.

(5)   No proceedings shall be taken in respect of an infringement committed before the date on which the certificate of registration of the design under this Act is granted.

(6)   The right in a registered design is not infringed by the reproduction of a feature of the design which, by virtue of section 1(1)(b), is left out of account in determining whether the design is registrable.

### Duration of right in registered design

**8.**—(1)   The right in a registered design subsists in the first instance for a period of five years from the date of the registration of the design.

(2)   The period for which the right subsists may be extended for a second,

third, fourth and fifth period of five years, by applying to the registrar for an extension and paying the prescribed renewal fee.

(3) If the first, second, third or fourth period expires without such application and payment being made, the right shall cease to have effect; and the registrar shall, in accordance with rules made by the Secretary of State, notify the proprietor of that fact.

(4) If during the period of six months immediately following the end of that period an application for extension is made and the prescribed renewal fee and any prescribed additional fee is paid, the right shall be treated as if it had never expired, with the result that—

(a) anything done under or in relation to the right during that further period shall be treated as valid,

(b) an act which would have constituted an infringement of the right if it had not expired shall be treated as an infringement, and

(c) an act which would have constituted use of the design for the services of the Crown if the right had not expired shall be treated as such use.

(5) Where it is shown that a registered design—

(a) was at the time it was registered a corresponding design in relation to an artistic work in which copyright subsists, and

(b) by reason of a previous use of that work would not have been registrable but for section 6(4) of this Act (registration despite certain prior applications of design),

the right in the registered design expires when the copyright in that work expires, if that is earlier than the time at which it would otherwise expire, and it may not thereafter be renewed.

(6) The above provisions have effect subject to the proviso to section 4(1) (registration of same design in respect of other articles etc.).

*Restoration of lapsed right in design*
**8A.**—(1) Where the right in a registered design has expired by reason of a failure to extend, in accordance with section 8(2) or (4), the period for which the right subsists, an application for the restoration of the right in the design may be made to the registrar within the prescribed period.

(2) The application may be made by the person who was the registered proprietor of the design or by any other person who would have been entitled to the right in the design if it had not expired; and where the design was held by two or more persons jointly, the application may, with the leave of the registrar, be made by one or more of them without joining the others.

(3) Notice of the application shall be published by the registrar in the prescribed manner.

(4) If the registrar is satisfied that the proprietor took reasonable care to see that the period for which the right subsisted was extended in accordance with section 8(2) or (4), he shall, on payment of any unpaid renewal fee and any prescribed additional fee, order the restoration of the right in the design.

(5) The order may be made subject to such conditions as the registrar thinks fit, and if the proprietor of the design does not comply with any condition the

registrar may revoke the order and give 'such consequential directions as he thinks fit.

(6)   Rules altering the period prescribed for the purposes of subsection (1) may contain such transitional provisions and savings as appear to the Secretary of State to be necessary or expedient.

*Effect of order for restoration of right*
**8B.**—(1)   The effect of an order under section 8A for the restoration of the right in a registered design is as follows.

(2)   Anything done under or in relation to the right during the period between expiry and restoration shall be treated as valid.

(3)   Anything done during that period which would have constituted an infringement if the right had not expired shall be treated as an infringement—

(a)   if done at a time when it was possible for an application for extension to be made under section 8(4); or
(b)   if it was a continuation or repetition of an earlier infringing act.

(4)   If after it was no longer possible for such an application for extension to be made, and before publication of notice of the application for restoration, a person—

(a)   began in good faith to do an act which would have constituted an infringement of the right in the design if it had not expired, or
(b)   made in good faith effective and serious preparations to do such an act,

he has the right to continue to do the act or, as the case may be, to do the act, notwithstanding the restoration of the right in the design; but this does not extend to granting a licence to another person to do the act.

(5)   If the act was done, or the preparations were made, in the course of a business, the person entitled to the right conferred by subsection (4) may—

(a)   authorise the doing of that act by any partners of his for the time being in that business, and
(b)   assign that right, or transmit it on death (or in the case of a body corporate on its dissolution), to any person who acquires that part of the business in the course of which the act was done or the preparations were made.

(6)   Where an article is disposed of to another in exercise of the rights conferred by subsection (4) or subsection (5), that other and any person claiming through him may deal with the article in the same way as if it had been disposed of by the registered proprietor of the design.

(7)   The above provisions apply in relation to the use of a registered design for the services of the Crown as they apply in relation to the infringement of the right in the design.

*Exemption of innocent infringer from liability for damages*
**9.**—(1)   In proceedings for the infringement of the right in a registered design damages shall not be awarded against a defendant who proves that at the date of the infringement he was not aware, and had no reasonable ground for supposing, that the design was registered; and a person shall not be deemed to have been aware or to have had reasonable grounds for supposing as aforesaid by reason

only of the marking of an article with the word 'registered' or any abbreviation thereof, or any word or words expressing or implying that the design applied to the article has been registered, unless the number of the design accompanied the word or words or the abbreviation in question.

(2)   Nothing in this section shall affect the power of the court to grant an injunction in any proceedings for infringement of the right in a registered design.

## Compulsory licence in respect of registered design

**10.**—(1)   At any time after a design has been registered any person interested may apply to the registrar for the grant of a compulsory licence in respect of the design on the ground that the design is not applied in the United Kingdom by any industrial process or means to the article in respect of which it is registered to such an extent as is reasonable in the circumstances of the case; and the registrar may make such order on the application as he thinks fit.

(2)   An order for the grant of a licence shall, without prejudice to any other method of enforcement, have effect as if it were a deed executed by the registered proprietor and all other necessary parties, granting a licence in accordance with the order.

(3)   No order shall be made under this section which would be at variance with any treaty, convention, arrangement or engagement applying to the United Kingdom and any convention country.

(4)   An appeal shall lie from any order of the registrar under this section.

## Cancellation of registration

**11.**—(1)   The registrar may, upon a request made in the prescribed manner by the registered proprietor, cancel the registration of a design.

(2)   At any time after a design has been registered any person interested may apply to the registrar for the cancellation of the registration of the design on the ground that the design was not, at the date of the registration thereof, new . . ., or on any other ground on which the registrar could have refused to register the design; and the registrar may make such order on the application as he thinks fit.

(3)   At any time after a design has been registered, any person interested may apply to the registrar for the cancellation of the registration on the ground that—

(a)   the design was at the time it was registered a corresponding design in relation to an artistic work in which copyright subsisted, and

(b)   the right in the registered design has expired in accordance with section 8(5) of this Act (expiry of right in registered design on expiry of copyright in artistic work);

and the registrar may make such order on the application as he thinks fit.

(4)   A cancellation under this section takes effect—

(a)   in the case of cancellation under subsection (1), from the date of the registrar's decision,

(b)   in the case of cancellation under subsection (2), from the date of registration,

(c)   in the case of cancellation under subsection (3), from the date on which the right in the registered design expired,

or, in any case, from such other date as the registrar may direct.

(5)   An appeal lies from any order of the registrar under this section.

*Powers exercisable for protection of the public interest*
**11A.**—(1)   Where a report of the Monopolies and Mergers Commission has been laid before Parliament containing conclusions to the effect—

   (a)   on a monopoly reference, that a monopoly situation exists and facts found by the Commission operate or may be expected to operate against the public interest,

   (b)   on a merger reference, that a merger situation qualifying for investigation has been created and the creation of the situation, or particular elements in or consequences of it specified in the report, operate or may be expected to operate against the public interest,

   (c)   on a competition reference, that a person was engaged in an anti-competitive practice which operated or may be expected to operate against the public interest, or

   (d)   on a reference under section 11 of the Competition Act 1980 (reference of public bodies and certain other persons), that a person is pursuing a course of conduct which operates against the public interest,

the appropriate Minister or Ministers may apply to the registrar to take action under this section.

(2)   Before making an application the appropriate Minister or Ministers shall publish, in such manner as he or they think appropriate, a notice describing the nature of the proposed application and shall consider any representations which may be made within 30 days of such publication by persons whose interests appear to him or them to be affected.

(3)   If on an application under this section it appears to the registrar that the matters spcified in the Commission's report as being those which in the Commission's opinion operate, or operated or may be expected to operate, against the public interest include—

   (a)   conditions in licences granted in respect of a registered design by its proprietor restricting the use of the design by the licensee or the right of the proprietor to grant other licences, or

   (b)   a refusal by the proprietor of a registered design to grant licences on reasonable terms,

he may by order cancel or modify any such condition or may, instead or in addition, make an entry in the register to the effect that licences in respect of the design are to be available as of right.

(4)   The terms of a licence available by virtue of this section shall, in default of agreement, be settled by the registrar on an application by the person requiring the licence; and terms so settled shall authorise the licensee to do everything which would be an infringement of the right in the registered design in the absence of a licence.

(5)   Where the terms of a licence are settled by the registrar, the licence has effect from the date on which the application to him was made.

(6)   An appeal lies from any order of the registrar under this section.

(7)   In this section 'the appropriate Minister or Ministers' means the Minister

or Ministers to whom the report of the Monopolies and Mergers Commission was made.

*Undertaking to take licence of right in infringement proceedings*
**11B.**—(1)   If in proceedings for infringement of the right in a registered design in respect of which a licence is available as of right under section 11A of this Act the defendant undertakes to take a licence on such terms as may be agreed or, in default of agreement, settled by the registrar under that section—

(a)   no injunction shall be granted against him, and
(b)   the amount recoverable against him by way of damages or on an account of profits shall not exceed double the amount which would have been payable by him as licensee if such a licence on those terms had been granted before the earliest infringement.

(2)   An undertaking may be given at any time before final order in the proceedings, without any admission of liability.

(3)   Nothing in this section affects the remedies available in respect of an infringement committed before licences of right were available.

*Use for services of the Crown*
**12.**   The provisions of the First Schedule to this Act shall have effect with respect to the use of registered designs for the services of the Crown and the rights of third parties in respect of such use.

*International arrangements*

*Orders in Council as to convention countries*
**13.**—(1)   His Majesty may, with a view to the fulfilment of a treaty, convention, arrangement or engagement, by Order in Council declare that any country specified in the Order is a convention country for the purposes of this Act:
   Provided that a declaration may be made as aforesaid for the purposes either of all or of some only of the provisions of this Act, and a country in the case of which a declaration made for the purposes of some only of the provisions of this Act is in force shall be deemed to be a convention country for the purposes of those provisions only.

(2)   His Majesty may by Order in Council direct that any of the Channel Islands, any colony, . . . shall be deemed to be a convention country for the purposes of all or any of the provisions of this Act; and an Order made under this subsection may direct that any such provisions shall have effect, in relation to the territory in question, subject to such conditions or limitations, if any, as may be specified in the Order.

(3)   For the purposes of subsection (1) of this section, every colony, protectorate, territory subject to the authority or under the suzerainty of another country, and territory administered by another country . . . under the trusteeship system of the United Nations, shall be deemed to be a country in the case of which a declaration may be made under that subsection.

*Registration of design where application for protection in convention country has been made*
**14.**—(1)   An application for registration of a design in respect of which protection has been applied for in a convention country may be made in

accordance with the provisions of this Act by the person by whom the application for protection was made or his personal representative or assignee:

Provided that no application shall be made by virtue of this section after the expiration of six months from the date of the application for protection in a convention country or, where more than one such application for protection has been made, from the date of the first application.

(2)   Where an application for registration of a design is made by virtue of this section the application shall be treated, for the purpose of determining whether that or any other design is new, as made on the date of the application for protection in the convention country or, if more than one such application was made, on the date of the first such application.

(3)   Subsection (2) shall not be construed as excluding the power to give directions under section 3(4) of this Act in relation to an application made by virtue of this section.

(4)   Where a person has applied for protection for a design by an application which—

(a)   in accordance with the terms of a treaty subsisting between two or more convention countries, is equivalent to an application duly made in any one of those convention countries; or

(b)   in accordance with the law of any convention country, is equivalent to an application duly made in that convention country,

he shall be deemed for the purposes of this section to have applied in that convention country.

*Extension of time for applications under s.14 in certain cases*
**15.**—(1)   If the Secretary of State is satisfied that provision substantially equivalent to the provision to be made by or under this section has been or will be made under the law of any convention country, he may make rules empowering the registrar to extend the time for making application under subsection (1) of section fourteen of this Act for registration of a design in respect of which protection has been applied for in that country in any case where the period specified in the proviso to that subsection expires during a period prescribed by the rules.

(2)   Rules made under this section—

(a)   may, where any agreement or arrangement has been made between His Majesty's Government in the United Kingdom and the government of the convention country for the supply or mutual exchange of information or articles, provide, either generally or in any class of case specified in the rules, that an extension of time shall not be granted under this section unless the design has been communicated in accordance with the agreement or arrangement;

(b)   may, either generally or in any class of case specified in the rules, fix the maximum extension which may be granted under this section;

(c)   may prescribe or allow any special procedure in connection with applications made by virtue of this section;

(d)   may empower the registrar to extend, in relation to an application made by virtue of this section, the time limited by or under the foregoing provisions of this Act for doing any act, subject to such conditions, if any, as may be imposed by or under the rules;

(e)	may provide for securing that the rights conferred by registration on an application made by virtue of this section shall be subject to such restrictions or conditions as may be specified by or under the rules and in particular to restrictions and conditions for the protection of persons (including persons acting on behalf of His Majesty) who, otherwise than as the result of a communication made in accordance with such an agreement or arrangement as is mentioned in paragraph (a) of this subsection, and before the date of the application in question or such later date as may be allowed by the rules, may have imported or made articles to which the design is applied or may have made any application for registration of the design.

*Protection of designs communicated under international agreements*
**16.**—(1)	Subject to the provisions of this section, the Secretary of State may make rules for securing that, where a design has been communicated in accordance with an agreement or arrangement made between His Majesty's Government in the United Kingdom and the government of any other country for the supply or mutual exchange of information or articles,—

(a)	an application for the registration of the design made by the person from whom the design was communicated or his personal representative or assignee shall not be prejudiced, and the registration of the design in pursuance of such an application shall not be invalidated, by reason only that the design has been communicated as aforesaid or that in consequence thereof—

(i)	the design has been published or applied, or
(ii)	an application for registration of the design has been made by any other person, or the design has been registered on such an application;

(b)	any application for the registration of a design made in consequence of such a communication as aforesaid may be refused and any registration of a design made on such an application may be cancelled.

(2)	Rules made under subsection (1) of this section may provide that the publication or application of a design, or the making of any application for registration thereof shall, in such circumstances and subject to such conditions or exceptions as may be prescribed by the rules, be presumed to have been in consequence of such a communication as is mentioned in that subsection.

(3)	The powers of the Secretary of State under this section, so far as they are exercisable for the benefit of persons from whom designs have been communicated to His Majesty's Government in the United Kingdom by the government of any other country, shall only be exercised if and to the extent that the Secretary of State is satisfied that substantially equivalent provision has been or will be made under the law of that country for the benefit of persons from whom designs have been communicated by His Majesty's Government in the United Kingdom to the government of that country.

(4)	References in the last foregoing subsection to the communication of a design to or by His Majesty's Government or the government of any other country shall be construed as including references to the communication of the design by or to any person authorised in that behalf by the government in question.

*Register of designs etc.*

*Register of designs*

**17.**—(1)   The registrar shall maintain the register of designs, in which shall be entered—

(a)   the names and addresses of proprietors of registered designs;

(b)   notices of assignments and of transmissions of registered designs; and

(c)   such other matters as may be prescribed or as the registrar may think fit.

(2)   No notice of any trust, whether express, implied or constructive, shall be entered in the register of designs, and the registrar shall not be affected by any such notice.

(3)   The register need not be kept in documentary form.

(4)   Subject to the provisions of this Act and to rules made by the Secretary of State under it, the public shall have a right to inspect the register at the Patent Office at all convenient times.

(5)   Any person who applies for a certified copy of an entry in the register or a certified extract from the register shall be entitled to obtain such a copy or extract on payment of a fee prescribed in relation to certified copies and extracts; and rules made by the Secretary of State under this Act may provide that any person who applies for an uncertified copy or extract shall be entitled to such a copy or extract on payment of a fee prescribed in relation to uncertified copies and extracts.

(6)   Applications under subsection (5) above or rules made by virtue of that subsection shall be made in such manner as may be prescribed.

(7)   In relation to any portion of the register kept otherwise than in documentary form—

(a)   the right of inspection conferred by subsection (4) above is a right to inspect the material on the register; and

(b)   the right to a copy or extract conferred by subsection (5) above or rules is a right to a copy or extract in a form in which it can be taken away and in which it is visible and legible.

(8)   Subject to subsection (11) below, the register shall be prima facie evidence of anything required or authorised to be entered in it and in Scotland shall be sufficient evidence of any such thing.

(9)   A certificate purporting to be signed by the registrar and certifying that any entry which he is authorised by or under this Act to make has or has not been made, or that any other thing which he is so authorised to do has or has not been done, shall be prima facie evidence, and in Scotland shall be sufficient evidence, of the matters so certified.

(10)   Each of the following—

(a)   a copy of an entry in the register or an extract from the register which is supplied under subsection (5) above;

(b)   a copy or any representation, specimen or document kept in the Patent Office or an extract from any such document,

which purports to be a certified copy or certified extract shall, subject to subsection (11) below, be admitted in evidence without further proof and without production of any original; and in Scotland such evidence shall be sufficient evidence.

(11)   In the application of this section to England and Wales nothing in it shall be taken as detracting from section 69 or 70 of the Police and Criminal Evidence Act 1984 or any provision made by virtue of either of them.

(12)   In this section 'certified copy' and 'certified extract' means a copy and extract certified by the registrar and sealed with the seal of the Patent Office.

*Certificate of registration*
**18.**—(1)   The registrar shall grant a certificate of registration in the prescribed form to the registered proprietor of a design when the design is registered.

(2)   The registrar may, in a case where he is satisfied that the certificate of registration has been lost or destroyed, or in any other case in which he thinks it expedient, furnish one or more copies of the certificate.

*Registration of assignments etc.*
**19.**—(1)   Where any person becomes entitled by assignment, transmission or operation of law to a registered design or to a share in a registered design, or becomes entitled as mortgagee, licensee or otherwise to any other interest in a registered design, he shall apply to the registrar in the prescribed manner for the registration of his title as proprietor or co-proprietor or, as the case may be, of notice of his interest, in the register of designs.

(2)   Without prejudice to the provisions of the foregoing subsection, an application for the registration of the title of any person becoming entitled by assignment to a registered design or a share in a registered design, or becoming entitled by virtue of a mortgage, licence or other instrument to any other interest in a registered design, may be made in the prescribed manner by the assignor, mortgagor, licensor or other party to that instrument, as the case may be.

(3)   Where application is made under this section for the registration of the title of any person, the registrar shall, upon proof of title to his satisfaction—

(a)   where that person is entitled to a registered design or a share in a registered design, register him in the register of designs as proprietor or co-proprietor of the design, and enter in that register particulars of the instrument or event by which he derives title; or

(b)   where that person is entitled to any other interest in the registered design, enter in that register notice of his interest, with particulars of the instrument (if any) creating it.

(3A)   Where design right subsists in a registered design, the registrar shall not register an interest under subsection (3) unless he is satisfied that the person entitled to that interest is also entitled to a corresponding interest in the design right.

(3B)   Where design right subsists in a registered design and the proprietor of the registered design is also the design right owner, an assignment of the design right shall be taken to be also an assignment of the right in the registered design, unless a contrary intention appears.

(4)   Subject to any rights vested in any other person of which notice is entered in the register of designs, the person or persons registered as proprietor of a registered design shall have power to assign, grant licences under, or otherwise deal with the design, and to give effectual receipts for any consideration for any such assignment, licence or dealing.

Provided that any equities in respect of the design may be enforced in like manner as in respect of any other personal property.

(5)   Except for the purposes of an application to rectify the register under the following provisions of this Act, a document in respect of which no entry has been made in the register of designs under subsection (3) of this section shall not be admitted in any court as evidence of the title of any person to a registered design or share of or interest in a registered design unless the court otherwise directs.

### Rectification of register

**20.**—(1)   The court may, on the application of any person aggrieved, order the register of designs to be rectified by the making of any entry therein or the variation or deletion of any entry therein.

(2)   In proceedings under this section the court may determine any question which it may be necessary or expedient to decide in connection with the rectification of the register.

(3)   Notice of any application to the court under this section shall be given in the prescribed manner to the registrar, who shall be entitled to appear and be heard on the application, and shall appear if so directed by the court.

(4)   Any order made by the court under this section shall direct that notice of the order shall be served on the registrar in the prescribed manner; and the registrar shall, on receipt of the notice, rectify the register accordingly.

(5)   A rectification of the register under this section has effect as follows—

   (a)   an entry made has effect from the date on which it should have been made,

   (b)   an entry varied has effect as if it had originally been made in its varied form, and

   (c)   an entry deleted shall be deemed never to have had effect,

unless, in any case, the court directs otherwise.

### Power to correct clerical errors

**21.**—(1)   The registrar may, in accordance with the provisions of this section, correct any error in an application for the registration or in the representation of a design, or any error in the register of designs.

(2)   A correction may be made in pursuance of this section either upon a request in writing made by any person interested and accompanied by the prescribed fee, or without such a request.

(3)   Where the registrar proposes to make any such correction as aforesaid otherwise than in pursuance of a request made under this section, he shall give notice of the proposal to the registered proprietor or the applicant for registration of the design, as the case may be, and to any other person who

appears to him to be concerned, and shall give them an opportunity to be heard before making the correction.

## Inspection of registered designs

**22.**—(1) Where a design has been registered under this Act, there shall be open to inspection at the Patent Office on and after the day on which the certificate of registration is issued—

(a) the representation or specimen of the design, and

(b) any evidence filed in support of the applicant's contention that the appearance of an article is material (for the purposes of section 1(3) of this Act).

This subsection has effect subject to the following provisions of this section and to any rules made under section 5(2) of this Act.

(2) In the case of a design registered in respect of an article of any class prescribed for the purposes of this subsection, no representation, specimen or evidence filed in pursuance of the application shall, until the expiration of such period after the day on which the certificate of registration is issued as may be prescribed in relation to articles of that class, be open to inspection at the Patent Office except by the registered proprietor, a person authorised in writing by the registered proprietor, or a person authorised by the registrar or by the court:

Provided that where the registrar proposes to refuse an application for the registration of any other design on the ground that it is the same as the first-mentioned design or differs from that design only in immaterial details or in features which are variants commonly used in the trade, the applicant shall be entitled to inspect the representation or specimen of the first-mentioned design filed in pursuance of the application for registration of that design.

(3) In the case of a design registered in respect of an article of any class prescribed for the purposes of the last foregoing subsection, the representation, specimen or evidence shall not, during the period prescribed as aforesaid, be inspected by any person by virtue of this section except in the presence of the registrar or of an officer acting under him; and except in the case of an inspection authorised by the proviso to that subsection, the person making the inspection shall not be entitled to take a copy of the representation, specimen or evidence or any part thereof.

(4) Where an application for the registration of a design has been abandoned or refused, neither the application for registration nor any representation, specimen or evidence filed in pursuance thereof shall at any time be open to inspection at the Patent Office or be published by the registrar.

## Information as to existence of right in registered design

**23.** On the request of a person furnishing such information as may enable the registrar to identify the design, and on payment of the prescribed fee, the registrar shall inform him—

(a) whether the design is registered and, if so, in respect of what articles, and

(b) whether any extension of the period of the right in the registered design has been granted, and shall state the date of registration and the name and address of the registered proprietor.

... ... ... ... ... ... ...

## Legal proceedings and appeals

*Certificate of contested validity of registration*
**25.**—(1)   If in any proceedings before the court the validity of the registration of a design is contested, and it is found by the court that the design is validly registered, the court may certify that the validity of the registration of the design was contested in those proceedings.

(2)   Where any such certificate has been granted, then if in any subsequent proceedings before the court for infringement of the right in the registered design or for cancellation of the registration of the design, a final order or judgment is made or given in favour of the registered proprietor, he shall, unless the court otherwise directs, be entitled to his costs as between solicitor and client:

Provided that this subsection shall not apply to the costs of any appeal in any such proceedings as aforesaid.

*Remedy for groundless threats of infringement proceedings*
**26.**—(1)   Where any person (whether entitled to or interested in a registered design or an application for registration of a design or not) by circulars, advertisements or otherwise threatens any other person with proceedings for infringement of the right in a registered design, any person aggrieved thereby may bring an action against him for any such relief as is mentioned in the next following subsection.

(2)   Unless in any action brought by virtue of this section the defendant proves that the acts in respect of which proceedings were threatened constitute or, if done, would constitute, an infringement of the right in a registered design the registration of which is not shown by the plaintiff to be invalid, the plaintiff shall be entitled to the following relief, that is to say:—

(a)   a declaration to the effect that the threats are unjustifiable;
(b)   an injunction against the continuance of the threats; and
(c)   such damages, if any, as he has sustained thereby.

(2A)   Proceedings may not be brought under this section in respect of a threat to bring proceedings for an infringement alleged to consist of the making or importing of anything.

(3)   For the avoidance of doubt it is hereby declared that a mere notification that a design is registered does not constitute a threat of proceedings within the meaning of this section.

*The court*
**27.**—(1)   In this Act 'the court' means—

(a)   in England and Wales, the High Court or any patents county court having jurisdiction by virtue of an order under section 287 of the Copyright, Designs and Patents Act 1988,
(b)   in Scotland, the Court of Session, and
(c)   in Northern Ireland, the High Court.

(2)   Provision may be made by rules of court with respect to proceedings in the High Court in England and Wales for references and applications under this Act to be dealt with by such judge of that court as the Lord Chancellor may select for the purpose.

*The Appeal Tribunal*
**28.**—(1)   Any appeal from the registrar under this Act shall lie to the Appeal Tribunal.

(2)   The Appeal Tribunal shall consist of

(a)   one or more judges of the High Court nominated by the Lord Chancellor, and

(b)   one judge of the Court of Session nominated by the Lord President of that Court.

(2A)   At any time when it consists of two or more judges, the jurisdiction of the Appeal Tribunal—

(a)   where in the case of any particular appeal the senior of those judges so directs, shall be exercised in relation to that appeal by both of the judges, or (if there are more than two) by two of them, sitting together, and

(b)   in relation to any appeal in respect of which no such direction is given, may be exercised by any one of the judges;

and, in the exercise of that jurisdiction, different appeals may be heard at the same time by different judges.

(3)   The expenses of the Appeal Tribunal shall be defrayed and the fees to be taken therein may be fixed as if the Tribunal were a court of the High Court.

(4)   The Appeal Tribunal may examine witnesses on oath and administer oaths for that purpose.

(5)   Upon any appeal under this Act the Appeal Tribunal may by order award to any party such costs or expenses as the Tribunal may consider reasonable and direct how and by what parties the costs are to be paid; and any such order may be enforced—

(a)   in England and Wales or Northern Ireland, in the same way as an order of the High Court;

(b)   in Scotland, in the same way as a decree for expenses granted by the Court of Session.

... ... ... ... ... ... ...

(7)   Upon any appeal under this Act the Appeal Tribunal may exercise any power which could have been exercised by the registrar in the proceeding from which the appeal is brought.

(8)   Subject to the foregoing provisions of this section the Appeal Tribunal may make rules for regulating all matters relating to proceedings before it under this Act, including right of audience.

(8A)   At any time when the Appeal Tribunal consists of two or more judges, the power to make rules under subsection (8) of this section shall be exercisable by the senior of those judges:

Provided that another of those judges may exercise that power if it appears to him that it is necessary for rules to be made and that the judge (or, if more than one, each of the judges) senior to him is,for the time being prevented by illness, absence or otherwise from making them.

(9) An appeal to the Appeal Tribunal under this Act shall not be deemed to be a proceeding in the High Court.

(10) In this section 'the High Court' means the High Court in England and Wales; and for the purposes of this section the seniority of judges shall be reckoned by reference to the dates on which they were appointed judges of that court or the Court of Session.

*Powers and duties of registrar*

*Exercise of discretionary powers of registrar*
**29.** Without prejudice to any provisions of this Act requiring the registrar to hear any party to proceedings thereunder, or to give to any such party an opportunity to be heard, rules made by the Secretary of State under this Act shall require the registrar to give to any applicant for registration of a design an opportunity to be heard before exercising adversely to the applicant any discretion vested in the registrar by or under this Act.

*Costs and security for costs*
**30.**—(1) Rules made by the Secretary of State under this Act may make provision empowering the registrar, in any proceedings before him under this Act—

    (a) to award any party such costs as he may consider reasonable, and
    (b) to direct how and by what parties they are to be paid.

(2) Any such order of the registrar may be enforced—

    (a) in England and Wales or Northern Ireland, in the same way as an order of the High Court;
    (b) in Scotland, in the same way as a decree for expenses granted by the Court of Session.

(3) Rules made by the Secretary of State under this Act may make provision empowering the registrar to require a person, in such cases as may be prescribed, to give security for the costs of—

    (a) an application for cancellation of the registration of a design,
    (b) an application for the grant of a licence in respect of a registered design, or
    (c) an appeal from any decision of the registrar under this Act,

and enabling the application or appeal to be treated as abandoned in default of such security being given.

*Evidence before registrar*
**31.** Rules made by the Secretary of State under this Act may make provision—

    (a) as to the giving of evidence in proceedings before the registrar under this Act by affidavit or statutory declaration;
    (b) conferring on the registrar the powers of an official referee of the Supreme Court as regards the examination of witnesses on oath and the discovery and production of documents; and

(c)   applying in relation to the attendance of witnesses in proceedings before the registrar the rules applicable to the attendance of witnesses in proceedings before such a referee.

... ... ... ... ... ... ...

## Offences

### Offences under s.5
**33.**—(1)   If any person fails to comply with any direction given under section 5 of this Act or makes or causes to be made an application for the registration of a design in contravention of that section, he shall be guilty of an offence and liable—

(a)   on conviction on indictment to imprisonment for a term not exceeding two years or a fine, or both;

(b)   on summary conviction to imprisonment for a term not exceeding six months or a fine not exceeding the statutory maximum, or both.

... ... ... ... ... ... ...

### Falsification of register etc.
**34.**   If any person makes or causes to be made a false entry in the register of designs, or a writing falsely purporting to be a copy of an entry in that register, or produces or tenders or causes to be produced or tendered in evidence any such writing, knowing the entry or writing to be false, he shall be guilty of an offence and liable—

(a)   on conviction on indictment to imprisonment for a term not exceeding two years or a fine, or both;

(b)   on summary conviction to imprisonment for a term not exceeding six months or a fine not exceeding the statutory maximum, or both.

### Fine for falsely representing a design as registered
**35.**—(1)   If any person falsely represents that a design applied to any article sold by him is registered in respect of that article, he shall be liable on summary conviction to a fine not exceeding level 3 on the standard scale; and for the purposes of this provision a person who sells an article having stamped, engraved or impressed thereon or otherwise applied thereto the word 'registered', or any other word expressing or implying that the design applied to the article is registered, shall be deemed to represent that the design applied to the article is registered in respect of that article.

(2)   If any person, after the right in a registered design has expired, marks any article to which the design has been applied with the word 'registered', or any word or words implying that there is a subsisting right in the design under this Act, or causes any such article to be so marked, he shall be liable on summary conviction to a fine not exceeding level 1 on the standard scale.

### Offence by body corporate: liability of officers
**35A.**—(1)   Where an offence under this Act committed by a body corporate is proved to have been committed with the consent or connivance of a director, manager, secretary or other similar officer of the body, or a person purporting to

act in any such capacity, he as well as the body corporate is guilty of the offence and liable to be proceeded against and punished accordingly.

(2)   In relation to a body corporate whose affairs are managed by its members 'director' means a member of the body corporate.

*Rules etc.*

*General power of Secretary of State to make rules etc.*
**36.**—(1)   Subject to the provisions of this Act, the Secretary of State may make such rules as he thinks expedient for regulating the business of the Patent Office in relation to designs and for regulating all matters by this Act placed under the direction or control of the registrar or the Secretary of State.

(1A)   Rules may, in particular, make provision—

(a)   prescribing the form of applications for registration of designs and of any representations or specimens of designs or other documents which may be filed at the Patent Office, and requiring copies to be furnished of any such representations, specimens or documents;

(b)   regulating the procedure to be followed in connection with any application or request to the registrar or in connection with any proceeding before him, and authorising the rectification of irregularities of procedure;

(c)   providing for the appointment of advisers to assist the registrar in proceedings before him;

(d)   regulating the keeping of the register of designs;

(e)   authorising the publication and sale of copies of representations of designs and other documents in the Patent Office;

(f)   prescribing anything authorised or required by this Act to be prescribed by rules.

(1B)   The remuneration of an adviser appointed to assist the registrar shall be determined by the Secretary of State with the consent of the Treasury and shall be defrayed out of money provided by Parliament.

(2)   Rules made under this section may provide for the establishment of branch offices for designs and may authorise any document or thing required by or under this Act to be filed or done at the Patent Office to be filed or done at the branch office at Manchester or any other branch office established in pursuance of the rules.

*Provisions as to rules and Orders*
**37.**—(1) ... ... ... ... ... ... .

(2)   Any rules made by the Secretary of State in pursuance of section 15 or section 16 of this Act, and any order made, direction given, or other action taken under the rules by the registrar, may be made, given or taken so as to have effect as respects things done or omitted to be done on or after such date, whether before or after the coming into operation of the rules or of this Act, as may be specified in the rules.

(3)   Any power to make rules conferred by this Act on the Secretary of State or on the Appeal Tribunal shall be exercisable by statutory instrument; and the Statutory Instruments Act 1946, shall apply to a statutory instrument containing rules made by the Appeal Tribunal in like manner as if the rules had been made by a Minister of the Crown.

(4)    Any statutory instrument containing rules made by the Secretary of State under this Act shall be subject to annulment in pursuance of a resolution of either House of Parliament.

(5)    Any Order in Council made under this Act may be revoked or varied by a subsequent Order in Council.

... ... ... ... ... ... ...

## Supplemental

### Hours of business and excluded days

**39.**—(1)    Rules made by the Secretary of State under this Act may specify the hour at which the Patent Office shall be deemed to be closed on any day for purposes of the transaction by the public of business under this Act or of any class of such business, and may specify days as excluded days for any such purposes.

(2)    Any business done under this Act on any day after the hour specified as aforesaid in relation to business of that class, or on a day which is an excluded day in relation to business of that class, shall be deemed to have been done on the next following day not being an excluded day; and where the time for doing anything under this Act expires on an excluded day, that time shall be extended to the next following day not being an excluded day.

### Fees

**40.**    There shall be paid in respect of the registration of designs and applications therefor, and in respect of other matters relating to designs arising under this Act, such fees as may be prescribed by rules made by the Secretary of State with the consent of the Treasury.

### Service of notices etc. by post

**41.**    Any notice required or authorised to be given by or under this Act, and any application or other document so authorised or required to be made or filed, may be given, made or filed by post.

### Annual report of registrar

**42.**    The Comptroller-General of Patents, Designs and Trade Marks shall, in his annual report with respect to the execution of the Patents Act 1977, include a report with respect to the execution of this Act as if it formed a part of or was included in that Act.

### Savings

**43.**—(1)    Nothing in this Act shall be construed as authorising or requiring the registrar to register a design the use of which would, in his opinion, be contrary to law or morality.

(2)    Nothing in this Act shall affect the right of the Crown or of any person deriving title directly or indirectly from the Crown to sell or use articles forfeited under the laws relating to customs or excise.

### Interpretation

**44.**—(1)    In this Act, except where the context otherwise requires, the following expressions have the meanings hereby respectively assigned by them, that is to say—

'Appeal Tribunal' means the Appeal Tribunal constituted and acting in accordance with section 28 of this Act as amended by the Administration of Justice Act 1969;

'article' means any article of manufacture and includes any part of an article if that part is made and sold separately;

'artistic work' has the same meaning as in Part I of the Copyright, Designs and Patents Act 1988;

'assignee' includes the personal representative of a deceased assignee, and references to the assignee of any person include references to the assignee of the personal representative or assignee of that person;

'author', in relation to a design, has the meaning given by section 2(3) and (4);

... ... ... ... ... ... ...

'corresponding design', in relation to an artistic work, means a design which if applied to an article would produce something which would be treated for the purposes of Part I of the Copyright, Designs and Patents Act 1988 as a copy of that work;

'the court' shall be construed in accordance with section 27 of this Act;

'design' has the meaning assigned to it by section 1(1) of this Act;

'employee', 'employment' and 'employer' refer to employment under a contract of service or of apprenticeship;

... ... ... ... ... ... ...

'prescribed' means prescribed by rules made by the Secretary of State under this Act;

'proprietor' has the meaning assigned to it by section two of this Act;

'registered proprietor' means the person or persons for the time being entered in the register of designs as proprietor of the design;

'registrar' means the Comptroller-General of Patents Designs and Trade Marks;

'set of articles' means a number of articles of the same general character ordinarily on sale or intended to be used together, to each of which the same design, or the same design with modifications or variations not sufficient to alter the character or substantially to affect the identity thereof, is applied.

(2)   Any reference in this Act to an article in respect of which a design is registered shall, in the case of a design registered in respect of a set of articles, be construed as a reference to any article of that set.

(3)   Any question arising under this Act whether a number of articles constitute a set of articles shall be determined by the registrar; and notwithstanding anything in this Act any determination of the registrar under this subsection shall be final.

(4)   For the purposes of subsection (1) of section 14 and of section 16 of this Act, the expression 'personal representative', in relation to a deceased person, includes the legal representative of the deceased appointed in any country outside the United Kingdom.

*Application to Scotland*
**45.**   In the application of this Act to Scotland—
... ... ... ... ... ... ...

(3)   The expression 'injunction' means 'interdict'; the expression 'arbitrator' means 'arbiter'; the expression 'plaintiff' means 'pursuer'; the expression 'defendant' means 'defender'.

*Application to Northern Ireland*
**46.**   In the application of this Act to Northern Ireland—
... ... ... ... ... ... ...
(3)   References to enactments include enactments comprised in Northern Ireland legislation:
(3A)   References to the Crown include the Crown in right of Her Majesty's Government in Northern Ireland:
(4)   References to a government department shall be construed as including references to a Northern Ireland department, and in relation to a Northern Ireland department references to the Treasury shall be construed as references to the Department of Finance and Personnel;
... ... ... ... ... ... ...

*Application to Isle of Man*
**47.**   This Act extends to the Isle of Man, subject to any modifications contained in an Order made by Her Majesty in Council, and accordingly, subject to any such Order, references in this Act to the United Kingdom shall be construed as including the Isle of Man.

*Territorial waters and the continental shelf*
**47A.**—(1)   For the purposes of this Act the territorial waters of the United Kingdom shall be treated as part of the United Kingdom.
(2)   This Act applies to things done in the United Kingdom sector of the continental shelf on a structure or vessel which is present there for purposes directly connected with the exploration of the sea bed or subsoil or the exploitation of their natural resources as it applies to things done in the United Kingdom.
(3)   The United Kingdom sector of the continental shelf means the areas designated by order under section 1(7) of the Continental Shelf Act 1964.

*Repeals, savings, and transitional provisions*
**48.**—(1)... ... ... ... ... ... ...
(2)   Subject to the provisions of this section, any Order in Council, rule, order, requirement, certificate, notice, decision, direction, authorisation, consent, application, request or thing made, issued, given or done under any enactment repealed by this Act shall, if in force at the commencement of this Act, and so far as it could have been made, issued, given or done under this Act, continue in force and have effect as if made, issued, given or done under the corresponding enactment of this Act.
(3)   Any register kept under the Patents and Designs Act 1907, shall be deemed to form part of the corresponding register under this Act.
(4)   Any design registered before the commencement of this Act shall be deemed to be registered under this Act in respect of articles of the class in which it is registered.
(5)   Where, in relation to any design the time for giving notice to the registrar under section 59 of the Patents and Designs Act 1907, expired before the

commencement of this Act and the notice was not given, subsection (2) of section 6 of this Act shall not apply in relation to that design or any registration of that design.

(6)   Any document referring to any enactment repealed by this Act shall be construed as referring to the corresponding enactment of this Act.

(7)   Nothing in the foregoing provisions of this section shall be taken as prejudicing the operation of section 38 of the Interpretation Act 1889 (which relates to the effect of repeals).

*Short title and commencement*
**49.**—(1)   This Act may be cited as the Registered Designs Act 1949.

(2)   This Act shall come into operation on the first day of January, 1950, immediately after the coming into operation of the Patents and Designs Act 1949.

*First Schedule Provisions as to the use of registered designs for the services of the Crown and as to the rights of third parties in respect of such use*

### Use of registered designs for services of the Crown

1.—(1)   Notwithstanding anything in this Act, any Government department, and any person authorised in writing by a Government department, may use any registered design for the services of the Crown in accordance with the following provisions of this paragraph.

(2)   If and so far as the design has before the date or registration thereof been duly recorded by or applied by or on behalf of a Government department otherwise than in consequence of the communication of the design directly or indirectly by the registered proprietor or any person from whom he derives title, any use of the design by virtue of this paragraph may be made free of any royalty or other payment to the registered proprietor.

(3)   If and so far as the design has not been so recorded or applied as aforesaid, any use of the design made by virtue of this paragraph at any time after the date of registration thereof, or in consequence of any such communication as aforesaid, shall be made upon such terms as may be agreed upon, either before or after the use, between the Government department and the registered proprietor with the approval of the Treasury, or as may in default of agreement be determined by the court on a reference under paragraph 3 of this Schedule.

(4)   The authority of a Government department in respect of a design may be given under this paragraph either before or after the design is registered and either before or after the acts in respect of which the authority is given are done, and may be given to any person whether or not he is authorised directly or indirectly by the registered proprietor to use the design.

(5)   Where any use of a design is made by or with the authority of a Government department under this paragraph, then, unless it appears to the department that it would be contrary to the public interest so to do, the department shall notify the registered proprietor as soon as practicable after the use is begun, and furnish him with such information as to the extent of the use as he may from time to time require.

(6)   For the purposes of this and the next following paragraph 'the services of the Crown' shall be deemed to include—

(a)  the supply to the government of any country outside the United Kingdom, in pursuance of an agreement or arrangement between Her Majesty's Government in the United Kingdom and the government of that country, of articles required—

(i)  for the defence of that country; or

(ii)  for the defence of any other country whose government is party to any agreement or arrangement with Her Majesty's said Government in respect of defence matters;

(b)  the supply to the United Nations, or the government of any country belonging to that organisation, in pursuance of an agreement or arrangement between Her Majesty's Government and that organisation or government, of articles required for any armed forces operating in pursuance of a resolution of that organisation or any organ of that organisation;

and the power of a Government department or a person authorised by a Government department under this paragraph to use a design shall include power to sell to any such government or to the said organisation any articles the supply of which is authorised by this subparagraph, and to sell to any person any articles made in the exercise of the powers conferred by this paragraph which are no longer required for the purpose for which they were made.

(7)   The purchaser of any articles sold in the exercise of powers conferred by this paragraph, and any person claiming through him, shall have power to deal with them in the same manner as if the rights in the registered design were held on behalf of His Majesty.

### Rights of third parties in respect of Crown use

2.—(1)  In relation to any use of a registered design, or a design in respect of which an application for registration is pending, made for the services of the Crown—

(a)  by a Government department or a person authorised by a Government department under the last foregoing paragraph; or

(b)  by the registered proprietor or applicant for registration to the order of a Government department,

the provisions of any licence, assignment or agreement made, whether before or after the commencement of this Act, between the registered proprietor or applicant for registration or any person who derives title from him or from whom he derives title and any person other than a Government department shall be of no effect so far as those provisions restrict or regulate the use of the design, or any model, document or information relating thereto, or provide for the making of payments in respect of any such use, or calculated by reference thereto; and the reproduction or publication of any model or document in connection with the said use shall not be deemed to be an infringement of any copyright or design right subsisting in the model or document.

(2)   Where an exclusive licence granted otherwise than for royalties or other

benefits determined by reference to the use of the design is in force under the registered design then—

(a)   in relation to any use of the design which, but for the provisions of this and the last foregoing paragraph, would constitute an infringement of the rights of the licensee, subparagraph (3) of the last foregoing paragraph shall have effect as if for the reference to the registered proprietor there would substituted a reference to the licensee; and

(b)   in relation to any use of the design by the licensee by virtue of an authority given under the last foregoing paragraph, that paragraph shall have effect as if the said subparagraph (3) were omitted.

(3)   Subject to the provisions of the last foregoing subparagraph, where the registered design or the right to apply for or obtain registration of the design has been assigned to the registered proprietor in consideration of royalties or other benefits determined by reference to the use of the design, then—

(a)   in relation to any use of the design by virtue of paragraph 1 of this Schedule, subparagraph (3) of that paragraph shall have effect as if the reference to the registered proprietor included a reference to the assignor, and any sum payable by virtue of that subparagraph shall be divided between the registered proprietor and the assignor in such proportion as may be agreed upon between them or as may in default of agreement be determined by the court on a reference under the next following paragraph; and

(b)   in relation to any use of the design made for the services of the Crown by the registered proprietor to the order of a Government department, subparagraph (3) of paragraph 1 of this Schedule shall have effect as if that use were made by virtue of an authority given under that paragraph.

(4)   Where, under subparagraph (3) of paragraph 1 of this Schedule, payments are required to be made by a Government department to a registered proprietor in respect of any use of a design, any person being the holder of an exclusive licence under the registered design (not being such a licence as is mentioned in subparagraph (2) of this paragraph) authorising him to make that use of the design shall be entitled to recover from the registered proprietor such part (if any) of those payments as may be agreed upon between that person and the registered proprietor, or as may in default of agreement be determined by the court under the next following paragraph to be just having regard to any expenditure incurred by that person—

(a)   in developing the said design; or

(b)   in making payments to the registered proprietor, other than royalties or other payments determined by reference to the use of the design, in consideration of the licence;

and if, at any time before the amount of any such payment has been agreed upon between the Government department and the registered proprietor, that person gives notice in writing of his interest to the department, any agreement as to the amount of that payment shall be of no effect unless it is made with his consent.

(5)   In this paragraph 'exclusive licence' means a licence from a registered proprietor which confers on the licensee, or on the licensee and persons

authorised by him, to the exclusion of all other persons (including the registered proprietor), any right in respect of the registered design.

*Compensation for loss of profit*

2A.—(1)   Where Crown use is made of a registered design, the government department concerned shall pay—

(a)   to the registered proprietor, or

(b)   if there is an exclusive licence in force in respect of the design, to the exclusive licensee,

compensation for any loss resulting from his not being awarded a contract to supply the articles to which the design is applied.

(2)   Compensation is payable only to the extent that such a contract could have been fulfilled from his existing manufacturing capacity; but is payable notwithstanding the existence of circumstances rendering him ineligible for the award of such a contract.

(3)   In determining the loss, regard shall be had to the profit which would have been made on such a contract and to the extent to which any manufacturing capacity was under-used.

(4)   No compensation is payable in respect of any failure to secure contracts for the supply of articles to which the design is applied otherwise than for the services of the Crown.

(5)   The amount payable under this paragraph shall, if not agreed between the registered proprietor or licensee and the government department concerned with the approval of the Treasury, be determined by the court on a reference under paragraph 3; and it is in addition to any amount payable under paragraph 1 or 2 of this Schedule.

(6)   In this paragraph—

'Crown use', in relation to a design, means the doing of anything by virtue of paragraph 1 which would otherwise be an infringement of the right in the design; and

'the government department concerned', in relation to such use, means the government department by whom or on whose authority the act was done.

*Reference of disputes as to Crown use*

3.—(1)   Any dispute as to—

(a)   the exercise by a Government department, or a person authorised by a Government department, of the powers conferred by paragraph 1 of this Schedule,

(b)   terms for the use of a design for the services of the Crown under that paragraph,

(c)   the right of any person to receive any part of a payment made under paragraph 1(3), or

(d)   the right of any person to receive a payment under paragraph 2A,

may be referred to the court by either party to the dispute.

(2)   In any proceedings under this paragraph to which a Government department are a party, the department may—

(a)   if the registered proprietor is a party to the proceedings, apply for cancellation of the registration of the design upon any ground upon which the registration of a design may be cancelled on an application to the court under section twenty of this Act;

(b)   in any case, put in issue the validity of the registration of the design without applying for its cancellation.

(3)   If in such proceedings as aforesaid in question arises whether a design has been recorded or applied as mentioned in paragraph 1 of this Schedule, and the disclosure of any document recording the design, or of any evidence of the application thereof, would in the opinion of the department be prejudicial to the public interest, the disclosure may be made confidentially to counsel for the other party or to an independent expert mutually agreed upon.

(4)   In determining under this paragraph any dispute between a Government department and any person as to terms for the use of a design for the services of the Crown, the court shall have regard to any benefit or compensation which that person or any person from whom he derives title may have received, or may be entitled to receive, directly or indirectly from any Government department in respect of the design in question.

(5)   In any proceedings under this paragraph the court may at any time order the whole proceedings or any question or issue of fact arising therein to be referred to a special or official referee or an arbitrator on such terms as the court may direct; and references to the court in the foregoing provisions of this paragraph shall be construed accordingly.

### Special provisions as to Crown use during emergency

4.—(1)   During any period of emergency within the meaning of this paragraph, the powers exercisable in relation to a design by a Government department, or a person authorised by a Government department under paragraph 1 of this Schedule shall include power to use the design for any purpose which appears to the department necessary or expedient—

(a)   for the efficient prosecution of any war in which His Majesty may be engaged;

(b)   for the maintenance of supplies and services essential to the life of the community;

(c)   for securing a sufficiency of supplies and services essential to the well-being of the community;

(d)   for promoting the productivity of industry, commerce and agriculture;

(e)   for fostering and directing exports and reducing imports, or imports of any classes, from all or any countries and for redressing the balance of trade;

(f)   generally for ensuring that the whole resources of the community are available for use, and are used, in a manner best calculated to serve the interests of the community; or

(g)   for assisting the relief of suffering and the restoration and distribution of essential supplies and services in any part of His Majesty's dominions or any foreign countries that are in grave distress as the result of war;

and any reference in this Schedule to the services of the Crown shall be construed as including a reference to the purposes aforesaid.

(2)  In this paragraph the expression 'period of emergency' means a period beginning on such date as may be declared by Order in Council to be the commencement, and ending on such date as may be so declared to be the termination, of a period of emergency for the purposes of this paragraph.

(3)  No Order in Council under this paragraph shall be submitted to Her Majesty unless a draft of it has been laid before and approved by a resolution of each House of Parliament.

... ... ... ... ... ... ...

## Schedule 5 Patents: minor amendments

### Withdrawal of application before publication of specification

**1.**  In section 13(2) of the Patents Act 1949 (duty of comptroller to advertise acceptance of and publish complete specification) after the word 'and' in the first place where it occurs, insert "unless the application is withdrawn".

### Correction of clerical errors

**2.**—(1)  In section 15 of the Patents Act 1977 (filing of application), after subsection (3) insert—

'(3A)  Nothing in subsection (2) or (3) above shall be construed as affecting the power of the comptroller under section 117(1) below to correct errors or mistakes with respect to the filing of drawings.'.

(2)  The above amendment applies only in relation to applications filed after the commencement of this paragraph.

### Supplementary searches

**3.**—(1)  Section 17 of the Patents Act 1977 (preliminary examination and search) is amended as follows.

(2)  In subsection (7) (supplementary searches) for 'subsection (4) above)' substitute 'subsections (4) and (5) above' and for 'it applies' substitute 'they apply'.

(3)  After that subsection add—

'(8)  A reference for a supplementary search in consequence of—

(a)  an amendment of the application made by the applicant under section 18(3) or 19(1) below, or
(b)  a correction of the application, or of a document filed in connection with the application, under section 117 below,

shall be made only on payment of the prescribed fee, unless the comptroller directs otherwise.'.

**4.**  In section 18 of the Patents Act 1977 (substantive examination and grant or refusal of patent), after subsection (1) insert—

'(1A)  If the examiner forms the view that a supplementary search under section 17 above is required for which a fee is payable, he shall inform the comptroller, who may decide that the substantive examination should not proceed until the fee is paid; and if he so decides, then unless within such period as he may allow—

    (a)  the fee is paid, or

    (b)  the application is amended so as to render the supplementary search unnecessary,

he may refuse the application'.

**5.**  In section 130(1) of the Patents Act 1977 (interpretation), in the definition of 'search fee', for 'section 17 above' substitute 'section 17(1) above'.

### Application for restoration of lapsed patent

**6.**—(1)  Section 28 of the Patents Act 1977 (restoration of lapsed patents), is amended as follows.

    (2)  For subsection (1) (application for restoration within period of one year) substitute—

    '(1)  Where a patent has ceased to have effect by reason of a failure to pay any renewal fee, an application for the restoration of the patent may be made to the comptroller within the prescribed period.

    (1A)  Rules prescribing that period may contain such transitional provisions and savings as appear to the Secretary of State to be necessary or expedient.'.

    (3)  After subsection (2) insert—

    '(2A)  Notice of the application shall be published by the comptroller in the prescribed manner.'.

    (4)  In subsection (3), omit paragraph (b) (requirement that failure to renew is due to circumstances beyond proprietor's control) and the word 'and' preceding it.

    (5)  This amendment does not apply to a patent which has ceased to have effect in accordance with section 25(3) of the Patents Act 1977 (failure to renew within prescribed period) and in respect of which the period referred to in subsection (4) of that section (six months' period of grace for renewal) has expired before commencement.

    (6)  Omit subsections (5) to (9) (effect of order for restoration).

    (7)  After that section insert—

*'Effect of order for restoration of patent*
**28A.**—(1)  The effect of an order for the restoration of a patent is as follows.

    (2)  Anything done under or in relation to the patent during the period between expiry and restoration shall be treated as valid.

    (3)  Anything done during that period which would have constituted an infringement if the patent had not expired shall be treated as an infringement—

    (a)  if done at a time when it was possible for the patent to be renewed under section 25(4); or

    (b)  if it was a continuation or repetition of an earlier infringing act.

(4)   If after it was no longer possible for the patent to be so renewed, and before publication of notice of the application for restoration, a person—

(a)   began in good faith to do an act which would have constituted an infringement of the patent if it had not expired, or

(b)   made in good faith effective and serious preparations to do such an act,

he has the right to continue to do the act or, as the case may be, to do the act, notwithstanding the restoration of the patent; but this right does not extend to granting a licence to another person to do the act.

(5)   If the act was done, or the preparations were made, in the course of a business, the person entitled to the right conferred by subsection (4) may—

(a)   authorise the doing of that act by any partners of his for the time being in that business, and

(b)   assign that right, or transmit it on death (or in the case of a body corporate on its dissolution), to any person who acquires that part of the business in the course of which the act was done or the preparations were made.

(6)   Where a product is disposed of to another in exercise of the rights conferred by subsection (4) or (5), that other and any person claiming through him may deal with the product in the same way as if it had been disposed of by the registered proprietor of the patent

(7)   The above provisions apply in relation to the use of a patent for the services of the Crown as they apply in relation to infringement of the patent.'.

**8.**   In consequence of the above amendments—

(a)   in section 60(6)(b) of the Patents Act 1977, for 'section 28(6)' substitute 'section 28A(4) or (5)'; and

(b)   in sections 77(5), 78(6) and 80(4) of that Act, for the words from 'section 28(6)' to the end substitute 'section 28A(4) and (5) above, and subsections (6) and (7) of that section shall apply accordingly.'.

*Determination of right to patent after grant*

**9.**—(1)   Section 37 of the Patents Act 1977 (determination of right to patent after grant) is amended as follows.

(2)   For subsection (1) substitute—

'(1)   After a patent has been granted for an invention any person having or claiming a proprietary interest in or under the patent may refer to the comptroller the question—

(a)   who is or are the true proprietor or proprietors of the patent,

(b)   whether the patent should have been granted to the person or persons to whom it was granted, or

(c)   whether any right in or under the patent should be transferred or granted to any other person or persons;

and the comptroller shall determine the question and make such order as he thinks fit to give effect to the determination'.

(3)   Substitute 'this section'—

(a)   in subsections (4) and (7) for 'subsection (1)(a) above' and
(b)   in subsection (8) for 'subsection (1) above'.

**10.**   In section 74(6) (meaning of 'entitlement proceedings'), for 'section 37(1)(a) above' substitute 'section 37(1) above'.

### Employees' inventions

**11.**—(1)   In section 39 of the Patents Act 1977 (right to employees' inventions), after subsection (2) add—

'(3)   Where by virtue of this section an invention belongs, as between him and his employer, to an employee, nothing done—

(a)   by or on behalf of the employee or any person claiming under him for the purposes of pursuing an application for a patent, or
(b)   by any person for the purpose of performing or working the invention,

shall be taken to infringe any copyright or design right to which, as between him and his employer, his employer is entitled in any model or document relating to the invention.'.

(2)   In section 43 of the Patents Act 1977 (supplementary provisions with respect to employees' inventions), in subsection (4) (references to patents to include other forms of protection, whether in UK or elsewhere) for 'in sections 40 to 42' substitute 'in sections 39 to 42.'.

### Undertaking to take licence in infringement proceedings

**12.**—(1)   Section 46 of the Patents Act 1977 (licences of right) is amended as follows.
(2)   In subsection (3)(c) (undertaking to take licence in infringement proceedings) after the words '(otherwise than by the importation of any article' insert 'from a country which is not a member State of the European Economic Community'.
(3)   After subsection (3) insert—

'(3A)   An undertaking under subsection (3)(c) above may be given at any time before final order in the proceedings, without any admission of liability.'.

### Power of comptroller on grant of compulsory licence

**13.**   In section 49 of the Patents Act 1977 (supplementary provisions with respect to compulsory licences), omit subsection (3) (power to order that licence has effect to revoke existing licences and deprive proprietor of power to work invention or grant licences).

### Powers exercisable in consequence of report of Monopolies and Mergers Commission

**14.**   For section 51 of the Patents Act 1977 (licences of right: application by Crown in consequence of report of Monopolies and Mergers Commission) substitute—

*'Powers exercisable in consequence of report of Monopolies and Mergers Commission*

**51.**—(1)   Where a report of the Monopolies and Mergers Commission has been laid before Parliament containing conclusions to the effect—

(a)   on a monopoly reference, that a monopoly situation exists and facts found by the Commission operate or may be expected to operate against the public interest,

(b)   on a merger reference, that a merger situation qualifying for investigation has been created and the creation of the situation, or particular elements in or consequences of it specified in the report, operate or may be expected to operate against the public interest,

(c)   on a competition reference, that a person was engaged in an anti-competitive practice which operated or may be expected to operate against the public interest, or

(d)   on a reference under section 11 of the Competition Act 1980 (reference of public bodies and certain other persons), that a person is pursuing a course of conduct which operates against the public interest,

the appropriate Minister or Ministers may apply to the comptroller to take action under this section.

(2)   Before making an application the appropriate Minister or Ministers shall publish, in such manner as he or they think appropriate, a notice describing the nature of the proposed application and shall consider any representations which may be made within 30 days of such publication by persons whose interests appear to him or them to be affected.

(3)   If on an application under this section it appears to the comptroller that the matters specified in the Commission's report as being those which in the Commission's opinion operate, or operated or may be expected to operate, against the public interest include—

(a)   conditions in licences granted under a patent by its proprietor restricting the use of the invention by the licensee or the right of the proprietor to grant other licences, or

(b)   a refusal by the proprietor of a patent to grant licences on reasonable terms,

he may by order cancel or modify any such condition or may, instead or in addition, make an entry in the register to the effect that licences under the patent are to be available as of right.

(4)   In this section "the appropriate Minister or Ministers" means the Minister or Ministers to whom the report of the Commission was made.'

*Compulsory licensing: reliance on statements in competition report*

**15.**   In section 53(2) of the Patents Act 1977 (compulsory licensing: reliance on statements in reports of Monopolies and Mergers Commission)—

(a)   for 'application made in relation to a patent under sections 48 to 51 above' substitute 'application made under section 48 above in respect of a patent'; and

(b)   after 'Part VII of the Fair Trading Act 1973' insert 'or section 17 of the Competition Act 1980'.

*Crown use: compensation for loss of profit*

**16.**—(1)   In the Patents Act 1977, after section 57 insert—

*'Compensation for loss of profit*
**57A.**—(1)   Where use is made of an invention for the services of the Crown, the government department concerned shall pay—

(a)   to the proprietor of the patent, or
(b)   if there is an exclusive licence in force in respect of the patent, to the exclusive licensee,

compensation for any loss resulting from his not being awarded a contract to supply the patented product or, as the case may be, to perform the patented process or supply a thing made by means of the patented process.

(2)   Compensation is payable only to the extent that such a contract could have been fulfilled from his existing manufacturing or other capacity; but is payable notwithstanding the existence of circumstances rendering him ineligible for the award of such a contract.

(3)   In determining the loss, regard shall be had to the profit which would have been made on such a contract and to the extent to which any manufacturing or other capacity was under-used.

(4)   No compensation is payable in respect of any failure to secure contracts to supply the patented product or, as the case may be, to perform the patented process or supply a thing made by means of the patented process, otherwise than for the services of the Crown.

(5)   The amount payable shall, if not agreed between the proprietor or licensee and the government department concerned with the approval of the Treasury, be determined by the court on a reference under section 58, and is in addition to any amount payable under section 55 or 57.

(6)   In this section "the government department concerned", in relation to any use of an invention for the services of the Crown, means the government department by whom or on whose authority the use was made.

(7)   In the application of this section to Northern Ireland, the reference in subsection (5) above to the Treasury shall, where the government department concerned is a department of the Government of Northern Ireland, be construed as a reference to the Department of Finance and Personnel.'.

(2)   In section 58 of the Patents Act 1977 (reference of disputes as to Crown use), for subsection (1) substitute—

'(1)   Any dispute as to—

(a)   the exercise by a government department, or a person authorised by a government department, of the powers conferred by section 55 above,
(b)   terms for the use of an invention for the services of the Crown under that section,

(c)　the right of any person to receive any part of a payment made in pursuance of subsection (4) of that section, or

(d)　the right of any person to receive a payment under section 57A,

may be referred to the court by either party to the dispute after a patent has been granted for the invention.';

and in subsection (4) for 'under this section' substitute 'under subsection (1)(a), (b) or (c) above'.

(3)　In section 58(11) of the Patents Act 1977 (exclusion of right to compensation for Crown use if relevant transaction, instrument or event not registered), after 'section 57(3) above)' insert ', or to any compensation under section 57A above,'.

(4)　The above amendments apply in relation to any use of an invention for the services of the Crown after the commencement of this section, even if the terms for such use were settled before commencement.

*Right to continue use begun before priority date*

**17.**　For section 64 of the Patents Act 1977 (right to continue use begun before priority date) substitute—

'*Right to continue use begun before priority date*

**64.**—(1)　Where a patent is granted for an invention, a person who in the United Kingdom before the priority date of the invention—

(a)　does in good faith an act which would constitute an infringement of the patent if it were in force, or

(b)　makes in good faith effective and serious preparations to do such an act,

has the right to continue to do the act or, as the case may be, to do the act, notwithstanding the grant of the patent; but this right does not extend to granting a licence to another person to do the act.

(2)　If the act was done, or the preparations were made, in the course of a business, the person entitled to the right conferred by subsection (1) may—

(a)　authorise the doing of that act by any partners of his for the time being in that business, and

(b)　assign that right, or transmit it on death (or in the case of a body corporate on its dissolution), to any person who acquires that part of the business in the course of which the act was done or the preparations were made.

(3)　Where a product is disposed of to another in exercise of the rights conferred by subsection (1) or (2), that other and any person claiming through him may deal with the product in the same way as if it had been disposed of by the registered proprietor of the patent.'.

*Revocation on grounds of grant to wrong person*

**18.**　In section 72(1) of the Patents Act 1977 (grounds for revocation of patent), for paragraph (b) substitute—

'(b)    that the patent was granted to a person who was not entitled to be granted that patent;'.

*Revocation where two patents granted for same invention*

**19.**   In section 73 of the Patents Act 1977 (revocation on initiative of comptroller), for subsections (2) and (3) (revocation of patent where European patent (UK) granted in respect of same invention) substitute—

'(2)   If it appears to the comptroller that a patent under this Act and a European patent (UK) have been granted for the same invention having the same priority date,and that the applications for the patents were filed by the same applicant or his successor in title, he shall give the proprietor of the patent under this Act an opportunity of making observations and of amending the specification of the patent, and if the proprietor fails to satisfy the comptroller that there are not two patents in respect of the same invention, or to amend the specification so as to prevent there being two patents in respect of the same invention, the comptroller shall revoke the patent.

(3)   The comptroller shall not take action under subsection (2) above before—

(a)   the end of the period for filing an opposition to the European patent (UK) under the European Patent Convention, or

(b)   if later, the date on which opposition proceedings are finally disposed of;

and he shall not then take any action if the decision is not to maintain the European patent or if it is amended so that there are not two patents in respect of the same invention.

(4)   The comptroller shall not take action under subsection (2) above if the European patent (UK) has been surrendered under section 29(1) above before the date on which by virtue of section 25(1) above the patent under this Act is to be treated as having been granted or, if proceedings for the surrender of the European patent (UK) have been begun before that date, until those proceedings are finally disposed of; and he shall not then take any action if the decision is to accept the surrender of the European patent.'.

*Applications and amendments not to include additional matter*

**20.**   For section 76 of the Patents Act 1977 (amendments of applications and patents not to include added matter) substitute—

*'Amendments of applications and patents not to include added matter*
**76.**—(1)   An application for a patent which—

(a)   is made in respect of matter disclosed in an earlier application, or in the specification of a patent which has been granted, and

(b)   discloses additional matter, that is, matter extending beyond that disclosed in the earlier application, as filed, or the application for the patent, as filed,

may be filed under section 8(3), 12 or 37(4) above, or as mentioned in section

15(4) above, but shall not be allowed to proceed unless it is amended so as to exclude the additional matter.

(2)   No amendment of an application for a patent shall be allowed under section 17(3), 18(3) or 19(1) if it results in the application disclosing matter extending beyond that disclosed in the application as filed.

(3)   No amendment of the specification of a patent shall be allowed under section 27(1), 73 or 75 if it—

(a)   results in the specification disclosing additional matter, or
(b)   extends the protection conferred by the patent.'.

*Effect of European patent (UK)*

**21.**—(1)   Section 77 of the Patents Act 1977 (effect of European patent (UK)) is amended as follows.

(2)   For subsection (3) (effect of finding of partial validity on pending proceedings) substitute—

'(3)   where in the case of a European patent (UK)—

(a)   proceedings for infringement, or proceedings under section 58 above, have been commenced before the court or the comptroller and have not been finally disposed of, and
(b)   it is established in proceedings before the European Patent Office that the patent is only partially valid,

the provisions of section 63 or, as the case may be of subsections (7) to (9) of section 58 apply as they apply to proceedings in which the validity of a patent is put in issue and in which it is found that the patent is only partially valid.'.

(3)   For subsection (4) (effect of amendment or revocation under European Patent Convention) substitute—

'(4)   Where a European patent (UK) is amended in acordance with the European Patent Convention, the amendment shall have effect for the purposes of Parts I and III of this Act as if the specification of the patent had been amended under this Act; but subject to subsection (6)(b) below.

(4A)   Where a European patent (UK) is revoked in accordance with the European Patent Convention, the patent shall be treated for the purposes of Parts I and III of this Act as having been revoked under this Act.'.

(4)   In subsection (6) (filing of English translation), in paragraph (b) (amendments) for 'a translation of the amendment into English' substitute 'a translation into English of the specification as amended'.

(5)   In subsection (7) (effect of failure to file translation) for the words from 'a translation' to 'above' substitute 'such a translation is not filed'.

*The state of the art: material contained in patent applications*

**22.**   In section 78 of the Patents Act 1977 (effect of filing an application for a European patent (UK)), for subsection (5) (effect of withdrawal of application etc.) substitute—

'(5)   Subsections (1) to (3) above shall cease to apply to an application for a European patent (UK), except as mentioned in subsection (5A) below, if

(a)   the application is refused or withdrawn or deemed to be withdrawn, or
(b)   the designation of the United Kingdom in the application is withdrawn or deemed to be withdrawn,

but shall apply again if the rights of the applicant are re-established under the European Patent Convention, as from their re-establishment.

(5A)   The occurrence of any of the events mentioned in subsection (5)(a) or (b) shall not affect the continued operation of section 2(3) above in relation to matter contained in an application for a European patent (UK) which by virtue of that provision has become part of the state of the art as regards other inventions.'.

*Jurisdiction in certain proceedings*

**23.**   Section 88 of the Patents Act 1977 (jurisdiction in legal proceedings in connection with Community Patent Convention) is repealed.

*Effect of filing international application for patent*

**24.**—(1)   Section 89 of the Patents Act 1977 (effect of filing international application for patent) is amended as follows.
(2)   After subsection (3) insert—

'(3A)   If the relevant conditions are satisfied with respect to an application which is amended in accordance with the Treaty and the relevant conditions are not satisfied with respect to any amendment, that amendment shall be disregarded.'.

(3)   After subsection (4) insert—

'(4A)   In subsection (4)(a) "a copy of the application" includes a copy of the application published in accordance with the Treaty in a language other than that in which it was filed.'.

(4)   For subsection (10) (exclusion of certain applications subject to European Patent Convention) substitute—

'(10)   The foregoing provisions of this section do not apply to an application which falls to be treated as an international application for a patent (UK) by reason only of its containing an indication that the applicant wishes to obtain a European patent (UK); but without prejudice to the application of those provisions to an application which also separately designates the United Kingdom.'.

(5)   The amendments in this paragraph shall be deemed always to have had effect.
(6)   This paragraph shall be repealed by the order bringing the following paragraph into force.

**25.** For section 89 of the Patents Act 1977 (effect of filing international application for patent) substitute—

*'Effect of international application for patent*
**89.**—(1) An international application for a patent (UK) for which a date of filing has been accorded under the Patent Co-operation Treaty shall, subject to—

> section 89A (international and national phases of application), and
> section 89B (adaptation of provisions in relation to international application),

be treated for the purposes of Parts I and III of this Act as an application for a patent under this Act.

(2) If the application, or the designation of the United Kingdom in it, is withdrawn or (except as mentioned in subsection (3)) deemed to be withdrawn under the Treaty, it shall be treated as withdrawn under this Act.

(3) An application shall not be treated as withdrawn under this Act if it, or the designation of the United Kingdom in it, is deemed to be withdrawn under the Treaty—

> (a) because of an error or omission in an institution having functions under the Treaty, or
> (b) because, owing to circumstances outside the applicant's control, a copy of the application was not received by the International Bureau before the end of the time limited for that purpose under the Treaty,

or in such other circumstances as may be prescribed.

(4) For the purposes of the above provisions an application shall not be treated as an international application for a patent (UK) by reason only of its containing an indication that the applicant wishes to obtain a European patent (UK), but an application shall be so treated if it also separately designates the United Kingdom.

(5) If an international application for a patent which designates the United Kingdom is refused a filing date under the Treaty and the comptroller determines that the refusal was caused by an error or omission in an institution having functions under the Treaty, he may direct that the application shall be treated as an application under this Act, having such date of filing as he may direct.

*International and national phases of application*
**89A.**—(1) The provisions of the Patent Co-operation Treaty relating to publication, search, examination and amendment, and not those of this Act, apply to an international application for a patent (UK) during the international phase of the application.

(2) The international phase of the application means the period from the filing of the application in accordance with the Treaty until the national phase of the application begins.

(3) The national phase of the application begins—

> (a) when the prescribed period expires, provided any necessary

translation of the application into English has been filed at the Patent Office and the prescribed fee has been paid by the applicant; or

    (b)   on the applicant expressly requesting the comptroller to proceed earlier with the national phase of the application, filing at the Patent Office—

        (i)   a copy of the application, if none has yet been sent to the Patent Office in accordance with the Treaty, and

        (ii)   any necessary translation of the application into English,

and paying the prescribed fee.

    For this purpose a "copy of the application" includes a copy published in accordance with the Treaty in a language other than that in which it was originally filed.

    (4)   If the prescribed period expires without the conditions mentioned in subsection (3)(a) being satisfied, the application shall be taken to be withdrawn.

    (5)   Where during the international phase the application is amended in accordance with the Treaty, the amendment shall be treated as made under this Act if—

    (a)   when the prescribed period expires, any necessary translation of the amendment into English has been filed at the Patent Office, or

    (b)   where the applicant expressly requests the comptroller to proceed earlier with the national phase of the application, there is then filed at the Patent Office—

        (i)   a copy of the amendment, if none has yet been sent to the Patent Office in accordance with the Treaty, and

        (ii)   any necessary translation of the amendment into English;

otherwise the amendment shall be disregarded.

    (6)   The comptroller shall on payment of the prescribed fee publish any translation filed at the Patent Office under subsection (3) or (5) above.

*Adaptation of provisions in relation to international application*
**89B.**—(1)   Where an international application for a patent (UK) is accorded a filing date under the Patent Co-operation Treaty—

    (a)   that date, or if the application is re-dated under the Treaty to a later date that later date, shall be treated as the date of filing the application under this Act,

    (b)   any declaration of priority made under the Treaty shall be treated as made under section 5(2) above, and where in accordance with the Treaty any extra days are allowed, the period of 12 months specified in section 5(2) shall be treated as altered accordingly, and

    (c)   any statement of the name of the inventor under the Treaty shall be treated as a statement filed under section 13(2) above.

    (2)   If the application, not having been published under this Act, is published in accordance with the Treaty it shall be treated, for purposes other than those mentioned in subsection (3), as published under section 16

above when the conditions mentioned in section 89A(3)(a) are complied with.

(3)   For the purposes of section 55 (use of invention for service of the Crown) and section 69 (infringement of rights conferred by publication) the application, not having been published under this Act, shall be treated as published under section 16 above—

(a)   if it is published in accordance with the Treaty in English, on its being so published; and

(b)   if it is so published in a language other than English—

(i)   on the publication of a translation of the application in accordance with section 89A(6) above, or

(ii)   on the service by the applicant of a translation into English of the specification of the application on the government department concerned or, as the case may be, on the person committing the infringing act.

The reference in paragraph (b)(ii) to the service of a translation on a government department or other person is to its being sent by post or delivered to that department or person.

(4)   During the international phase of the application, section 8 above does not apply (determination of questions of entitlement in relation to application under this Act) and section 12 above (determination of entitlement in relation to foreign and convention patents) applies notwithstanding the application; but after the end of the international phase, section 8 applies and section 12 does not.

(5)   When the national phase begins the comptroller shall refer the application for so much of the examination and search under sections 17 and 18 above as he considers appropriate in view of any examination or search carried out under the Treaty.'.

*Proceedings before the court or the comptroller*

**26.**   In the Patents Act 1977, after section 99 (general powers of the court) insert—

*'Power of Patents Court to order report*
**99A.**—(1)   Rules of court shall make provision empowering the Patents Court in any proceedings before it under this Act, on or without the application of any party, to order the Patent Office to inquire into and report on any question of fact or opinion.

(2)   Where the court makes such an order on the application of a party, the fee payable to the Patent Office shall be at such rate as may be determined in accordance with rules of court and shall be costs of the proceedings unless otherwise ordered by the court.

(3)   Where the court makes such an order of its own motion, the fee payable to the Patent Office shall be at such rate as may be determined by the Lord Chancellor with the approval of the Treasury and shall be paid out of money provided by Parliament.

*Power of Court of Session to order report*
**99B.**—(1)   In any proceedings before the Court of Session under this Act

the court may, either of its own volition or on the application of any party, order the Patent Office to inquire into and report on any question of fact or opinion.

(2)   Where the court makes an order under subsection (1) above of its own volition the fee payable to the Patent Office shall be at such rate as may be determined by the Lord President of the Court of Session with the consent of the Treasury and shall be defrayed out of moneys provided by Parliament.

(3)   Where the court makes an order under subsection (1) above on the application of a party, the fee payable to the Patent Office shall be at such rate as may be provided for in rules of court and shall be treated as expenses in the cause.'.

**27.**   For section 102 of the Patents Act 1977 (right of audience in patent proceedings) substitute—

*'Right of audience etc. in proceedings before comptroller*
**102.**—(1)   A party to proceedings before the comptroller under this Act, or under any treaty or international convention to which the United Kingdom is a party, may appear before the comptroller in person or be represented by any person whom he desires to represent him.

(2)   No offence is committed under the enactments relating to the preparation of documents by persons not legally qualified by reason only of the preparation by any person of a document, other than a deed, for use in such proceedings.

(3)   Subsection (1) has effect subject to rules made under section 281 of the Copyright, Designs and Patents Act 1988 (power of comptroller to refuse to recognise certain agents).

(4)   In its application to proceedings in relation to applications for, or otherwise in connection with, European patents, this section has effect subject to any restrictions imposed by or under the European Patent Convention.

*Right of audience etc. in proceedings on appeal from the comptroller*
**102A.**—(1)   A solicitor of the Supreme Court may appear and be heard on behalf of any party to an appeal under this Act from the comptroller to the Patents Court.

(2)   A registered patent agent or a member of the Bar not in actual practice may do, in or in connection with proceedings on an appeal under this Act from the comptroller to the Patents Court, anything which a solicitor of the Supreme Court might do, other than prepare a deed.

(3)   The Lord Chancellor may by regulations—

(a)   provide that the right conferred by subsection (2) shall be subject to such conditions and restrictions as appear to the Lord Chancellor to be necessary or expedient, and

(b)   apply to persons exercising that right such statutory provisions, rules of court and other rules of law and practice applying to solicitors as may be specified in the regulations;

and different provision may be made for different descriptions of proceedings.

(4) Regulations under this section shall be made by statutory instrument which shall be subject to annulment in pursuance of a resolution of either House of Parliament.

(5) This section is without prejudice to the right of counsel to appear before the High Court.'.

### Provision of information

**28.** In section 118 of the Patents Act 1977 (information about patent applications etc.), in subsection (3) (restriction on disclosure before publication of application: exceptions) for 'section 22(6)(a) above' substitute 'section 22(6) above'.

### Power to extend time-limits

**29.** In section 123 of the Patents Act 1977 (rules), after subsection (3) insert—

'(3A) It is hereby declared that rules—

(a) authorising the rectification of irregularities of procedure, or

(b) providing for the alteration of any period of time,

may authorise the comptroller to extend or further extend any period notwithstanding that the period has already expired.'.

### Availability of samples of micro-organisms

**30.** In the Patents Act 1977 after section 125 insert—

*Disclosure of invention by specification: availability of samples of micro-organisms*
**125A.**—(1) Provision may be made by rules prescribing the circumstances in which the specification of an application for a patent, or of a patent, for an invention which requires for its performance the use of a micro-organism is to be treated as disclosing the invention in a manner which is clear enough and complete enough for the invention to be performed by a person skilled in the art.

(2) The rules may in particular require the applicant or patentee—

(a) to take such steps as may be prescribed for the purposes of making available to the public samples of the micro-organism, and

(b) not to impose or maintain restrictions on the uses to which such samples may be put, except as may be prescribed.

(3) The rules may provide that, in such cases as may be prescribed, samples need be made available to such persons or descriptions of persons as may be prescribed; and the rules may identify a description of persons by reference to whether the comptroller has given his certificate as to any matter.

(4) An application for revocation of the patent under section 72(1)(c) above may be made if any of the requirements of the rules cease to be complied with.'.

## Schedule 6 Provisions for the benefit of the Hospital for Sick Children

### *Interpretation*

**1.**—(1)   In this Schedule—

'the hospital' means The Hospital for Sick Children, Great Ormond Street, London,

'the trustees' means the special trustees appointed for the Hospital under the National Health Service Act 1977; and

'the work' means the play *Peter Pan* by Sir James Matthew Barrie.

(2)   Expressions used in this Schedule which are defined for the purposes of Part I of this Act (copyright) have the same meaning as in that Part.

### *Entitlement to royalty*

**2.**—(1)   The trustees are entitled, subject to the following provisions of this Schedule, to a royalty in respect of any public performance, commercial publication, broadcasting or inclusion in a cable programme service of the whole or any substantial part of the work or an adaptation of it.

(2)   Where the trustees are or would be entitled to a royalty, another form of remuneration may be agreed.

### *Exceptions*

**3.**   No royalty is payable in respect of—

(a)   anything which immediately before copyright in the work expired on 31 December 1987 could lawfully have been done without the licence, or further licence, of the trustees as copyright owners; or

(b)   anything which if copyright still subsisted in the work could, by virtue of any provision of Chapter III of Part I of this Act (acts permitted notwithstanding copyright), be done without infringing copyright.

### *Saving*

**4.**   No royalty is payable in respect of anything done in pursuance of arrangements made before the passing of this Act.

### *Procedure for determining amount payable*

**5.**—(1)   In default of agreement application may be made to the Copyright Tribunal which shall consider the matter and make such order regarding the royalty or other remuneration to be paid as it may determine to be reasonable in the circumstances.

(2)   Application may subsequently be made to the Tribunal to vary its order, and the Tribunal shall consider the matter and make such order confirming or varying the original order as it may determine to be reasonable in the circumstances.

(3)   An application for variation shall not, except with the special leave of the Tribunal, be made within 12 months from the date of the original order or of the order on a previous application for variation.

(4)   A variation order has effect from the date on which it is made or such later date as may be specified by the Tribunal.

*Sums received to be held on trust*

**6.**   The sums received by the trustees by virtue of this Schedule, after deduction of any relevant expenses, shall be held by them on trust for the purposes of the Hospital.

*Right only for the benefit of the Hospital*

**7.**—(1)   The right of the trustees under this Schedule may not be assigned and shall cease if the trustees purport to assign or charge it.

. (2)   The right may not be the subject of an order under section 92 of the National Health Service Act 1977 (transfers of trust property by order of the Secretary of State) and shall cease if the Hospital ceases to have a separate identity or ceases to have purposes which include the care of sick children.

(3)   Any power of Her Majesty, the court (within the meaning of the Charities Act 1960) or any other person to alter the trusts of a charity is not exercisable in relation to the trust created by this Schedule.

## Schedule 7 Consequential amendments: general

*British Mercantile Marine Uniform Act 1919 (c. 62)*

**1.**   For section 2 of the British Mercantile Marine Uniform Act 1919 (copyright in distinctive marks of uniform) substitute—

'*Right in registered design of distinctive marks of uniform*
**2.**   The right of the Secretary of State in any design forming part of the British Mercantile Marine uniform which is registered under the Registered Designs Act 1949 is not limited to the period prescribed by section 8 of that Act but shall continue to subsist so long as the design remains on the register.'.

*Chartered Associations (Protection of Names and Uniforms) Act 1926 (c. 26)*

**2.**   In section 1(5) of the Chartered Associations (Protection of Names and Uniforms) Act 1926 for 'the copyright in respect thereof' substitute 'the right in the registered design'.

*Patents, Designs, Copyright and Trade Marks (Emergency) Act 1939 (c. 107)*

**3.**—(1)   The Patents, Designs, Copyright and Trade Marks (Emergency) Act 1939 is amended as follows.

(2)   In section 1 (effect of licence where owner is enemy or enemy subject)—

(a)   in subsection (1) after 'a copyright' and 'the copyright' insert 'or design right';

(b)   in subsection (2) after 'the copyright' insert 'or design right' and for 'or copyright' substitute, 'copyright or design right'.

(3)   In section 2 (power of comptroller to grant licences)—

(a)   in subsection (1) after 'a copyright', 'the copyright' (twice) and 'the said copyright' insert 'or design right' and for 'or copyright' (twice) substitute, 'copyright or design right';

(b)   in subsections (2) and (3) for 'or copyright' substitute, 'copyright or design right';

(c)   in subsection (4) and in subsection (5) (twice) after 'the copyright' insert 'or design right';

(d)   in subsection (8)(c) for 'or work in which copyright subsists' substitute 'work in which copyright subsists or design in which design right subsists'.

(4)   In section 5 (effect of war on international arrangements)—

(a)   in subsection (1) for 'section twenty-nine of the Copyright Act 1911' substitute 'section 159 or 256 of the Copyright, Designs and Patents Act 1988 (countries enjoying reciprocal copyright or design right protection)';

(b)   in subsection (2) after 'copyright' (four times) insert 'or design right' and for 'the Copyright' Act 1911' (twice) substitute 'Part I or III of the Copyright, Designs and Patents Act 1988'.

(5)   In section 10(1) (interpretation) omit the definition of 'copyright', and for the definitions of 'design', 'invention', 'patent' and 'patentee' substitute—

'"design" has in reference to a registered design the same meaning as in the Registered Designs Act 1949, and in reference to design right the same meaning as in Part III of the Copyright, Designs and Patents Act 1988;

"invention" and "patent" have the same meaning as in the Patents Act 1977.'.

### Crown Proceedings Act 1947 (c. 44)

**4.**—(1)   In the Crown Proceedings Act 1947 for section 3 (provisions as to industrial property) substitute—

*'Infringement of intellectual property rights*
**3.**—(1)   Civil proceedings lie against the Crown for an infringement committed by a servant or agent of the Crown, with the authority of the Crown, of—

(a)   a patent,
(b)   a registered trade mark or registered service mark,
(c)   the right in a registered design,
(d)   design right, or
(e)   copyright;

but save as provided by this subsection no proceedings lie against the Crown by virtue of this Act in respect of an infringement of any of those rights.

(2)   Nothing in this section, or any other provision of this Act, shall be construed as affecting—

(a)   the rights of a government department under section 55 of the Patents Act 1977, Schedule 1 to the Registered Designs Act 1949 or section 240 of the Copyright, Designs and Patents Act 1988 (Crown use of patents and designs), or

(b)   the rights of the Secretary of State under section 22 of the Patents

Act 1977 or section 5 of the Registered Designs Act 1949 (security of information prejudicial to defence or public safety).'.

(2)   In the application of subparagraph (1) to Northern Ireland—

(a)   the reference to the Crown Proceedings Act 1947 is to that Act as it applies to the Crown in right of Her Majesty's Government in Northern Ireland, as well as to the Crown in right of Her Majesty's Government in the United Kingdom, and

(b)   in the substituted section 3 as it applies in relation to the Crown in right of Her Majesty's Government in Northern Ireland, subsection (2)(b) shall be omitted.

*Patents Act 1949 (c. 88)*

**5.**   In section 47 of the Patents Act 1949 (rights of third parties in respect of Crown use of patent), in the closing words of subsection (1) (which relate to the use of models or documents), after 'copyright' insert 'or design right'.

*Public Libraries (Scotland) Act 1955 (c. 27)*

**6.**   In section 4 of the Public Libraries (Scotland) Act 1955 (extension of lending power of public libraries), make the existing provision subsection (1) and after it add—

'(2)   The provisions of Part I of the Copyright, Designs and Patents Act 1988 (copyright) relating to the rental of copies of sound recordings, films and computer programs apply to any lending by a statutory library authority of copies of such works, whether or not a charge is made for that facility.'.

*London County Council (General Powers) Act 1958 (c. xxi)*

**7.**   In section 36 of the London County Council (General Powers) Act 1958 (power as to libraries: provision and repair of things other than books) for subsection (5) substitute—

'(5)   Nothing in this section shall be construed as authorising an infringement of copyright.'.

*Public Libraries and Museums Act 1964 (c. 75)*

**8.**   In section 8 of the Public Libraries and Museums Act 1964 (restrictions on charges for library facilities), after subsection (5) add—

'(6)   The provisions of Part I of the Copyright, Designs and Patents Act 1988 (copyright) relating to the rental of copies of sound recordings, films and computer programs apply to any lending by a library authority of copies of such works, whether or not a charge is made for that facility.'.

*Marine etc. Broadcasting (Offences) Act 1967 (c. 41)*

**9.**   In section 5 of the Marine etc. Broadcasting (Offences) Act 1967 (provision of material for broadcasting by pirate radio stations)—

(a)   in subsection (3)(a) for the words from 'cinematograph film' to 'in the record' substitute 'film or sound recording with intent that a broadcast of it'; and

(b)   in subsection (6) for the words from 'and references' to the end substitute 'and "film", "sound recording", "literary, dramatic or musical work" and "artistic work" have the same meaning as in Part I of the Copyright, Designs and Patents Act 1988 (copyright)'.

### Medicines Act 1968 (c. 67)

**10.**—(1)   Section 92 of the Medicines Act 1968 (scope of provisions restricting promotion of sales of medicinal products) is amended as follows.

(2)   In subsection (1) meaning of 'advertisement') for the words from 'or by the exhibition' to 'service' substitute 'or by means of a photograph, film, sound recording, broadcast or cable programme,'.

(3)   In subsection (2) (exception for the spoken word)—

(a)   in paragraph (a) omit the words from 'or embodied' to 'film'; and

(b)   in paragraph (b) for the words from 'by way of' to the end substitute 'or included in a cable programme service'.

(4)   For subsection (6) substitute—

(6)   In this section "film", "sound recording", "broadcast", "cable programme", "cable programme service", and related expressions, have the same meaning as in Part I of the Copyright, Designs and Patents Act 1988 (copyright).'.

### Post Office Act 1969 (c. 48)

**11.**   In Schedule 10 the the Post Office Act 1969 (special transitional provisions relating to use of patents and registered designs), in the closing words of paragraphs 8(1) and 18(1) (which relate to the use of models and documents), after 'copyright' insert 'or design right'.

### Merchant Shipping Act 1970 (c. 36)

**12.**   In section 87 of the Merchant Shipping Act 1970 (merchant navy uniform), for subsection (4) substitute—

'(4)   Where any design forming part of the merchant navy uniform has been registered under the Registered Designs Act 1949 and the Secretary of State is the proprietor of the design, his right in the design is not limited to the period prescribed by section 8 of that Act but shall continue to subsist so long as the design remains registered.'.

### Taxes Management Act 1970 (c. 9)

**13.**   In section 16 of the Taxes Management Act 1970 (returns to be made in respect of certain payments)—

(a)   in subsection (1)(c), and

(b)   in subsection (2)(b),

for 'or public lending right' substitute, 'public lending right, right in a registered design or design right'.

*Tribunals and Inquiries Act 1971 (c. 62)*

**14.**   In Part I of Schedule 1 to the Tribunals and Inquiries Act 1971 (tribunals under direct supervision of Council on Tribunals) renumber the entry inserted by the Data Protection Act 1984 as '5B' and before it insert—

'Copyright.          5A. The Copyright Tribunal.'

*Fair Trading Act 1973 (c. 41)*

**15.**   In Schedule 4 to the Fair Trading Act 1973 (excluded services), for paragraph 10 (services of patent agents) substitute—

'10.   The services of registered patent agents (within the meaning of Part V of the Copyright, Designs and Patents Act 1988) in their capacity as such.';

and in paragraph 10A (services of European patent attorneys) for 'section 84(7) of the Patents Act 1977' substitute 'Part V of the Copyright, Designs and Patents Act 1988'.

*House of Commons Disqualification Act 1975 (c. 24)*

**16.**   In Part II of Schedule 1 to the House of Commons Disqualificaton Act 1975 (bodies of which all members are disqualified), at the appropriate place insert 'The Copyright Tribunal'.

*Northern Ireland Assembly Disqualification Act 1975 (c. 25)*

**17.**   In Part II of Schedule 1 to the Northern Ireland Assembly Disqualification Act 1975 (bodies of which all members are disqualified), at the appropriate place insert 'The Copyright Tribunal'.

*Restrictive Trade Practices Act 1976 (c. 34)*

**18.**—(1)   The Restrictive Trade Practices Act 1976 is amended as follows.

   (2)   In Schedule 1 (excluded services) for paragraph 10 (services of patent agents) substitute—

'10.   The services of registered patent agents (within the meaning of Part V of the Copyright, Designs and Patents Act 1988) in their capacity as such.';

and in paragraph 10A (services of European patent attorneys) for 'section 84(7) of the Patents Act 1977' substitute 'Part V of the Copyright, Designs and Patents Act 1988'.

   (3)   In Schedule 3 (excepted agreements), after paragraph 5A insert—

*'Design right*

**5B.**—(1)   This Act does not apply to—

   (a)   a licence granted by the owner of a licensee of any design right,
   (b)   an assignment of design right, or
   (c)   an agreement for such a licence or assignment,

if the licence, assignment or agreement is one under which no such restrictions as are described in section 6(1) above are accepted, or no such information provisions as are described in section 7(1) above are made, except in respect of articles made to the design; but subject to the following provisions.

(2)   Subparagraph (1) does not exclude a licence, assignment or agreement which is a design pooling agreement or is granted or made (directly or indirectly) in pursuance of a design pooling agreement.

(3)   In this paragraph a "design pooling agreement" means an agreement—

(a)   to which the parties are or include at least three persons (the "principal parties") each of whom has an interest in one or more design rights, and

(b)   by which each principal party agrees, in respect of design right in which he has, or may during the currency of the agreement acquire, an interest to grant an interest (directly or indirectly) to one or more of the other principal parties, or to one or more of those parties and to other persons.

(4)   In this paragraph—

"assignment", in Scotland, means assignation; and

"interest" means an interest as owner or licensee of design right.

(5)   This paragraph applies to an interest held by or granted to more than one person jointly as if they were one person.

(6)   References in this paragraph to the granting of an interest to a person indirectly are to its being granted to a third person for the purpose of enabling him to make a grant to the person in question.'.

### Resale Prices Act 1976 (c. 53)

**19.**   In section 10(4) of the Resale Prices Act 1976 (patented articles: articles to be treated in same way), in paragraph (a) after 'protected' insert 'by design right or'.

### Patents Act 1977 (c. 37)

**20.**   In section 57 of the Patents Act 1977 (rights of third parties in respect of Crown use of patent), in the closing words of subsection (1) (which relate to the use of models or documents), after 'copyright' insert 'or design right'.

**21.**   In section 105 of the Patents Act 1977 (privilege in Scotland for communications relating to patent proceedings), omit 'within the meaning of section 104 above', made the existing text subsection (1), and after it insert—

'(2)   In this section—

"patent proceedings" means proceedings under this Act or any of the relevant conventions, before the court, the comptroller or the relevant convention court, whether contested or uncontested and including an application for a patent; and

"the relevant conventions" means the European Patent Convention, the Community Patent Convention and the Patent Cooperation Treaty.'.

**22.**   In section 123(7) of the Patents Act 1977 (publication of case reports by the comptroller)—

(a)    for 'and registered designs' substitute 'registered designs or design right',

(b)    for 'and copyright' substitute ',copyright and design right'.

**23.**   In section 130(1) of the Patents Act 1977 (interpretation), in the definition of 'court', for paragraph (a) substitute—

'(a)   as respects England and Wales, the High Court or any patents county court having jurisdiction by virtue of an order under section 287 of the Copyright, Designs and Patents Act 1988);'.

*Unfair Contract Terms Act 1977 (c. 50)*

**24.**   In paragraph 1 of Schedule 1 to the Unfair Contract Terms Act 1977 (scope of main provisions: excluded contracts), in paragraph (c) (contracts relating to grant or transfer of interest in intellectual property) after 'copyright' insert 'or design right'.

*Judicature (Northern Ireland) Act 1978 (c. 23)*

**25.**   In section 94A of the Judicature (Northern Ireland) Act 1978 (withdrawal of privilege against self-incrimination in certain proceedings relating to intellectual property), in subsection (5) (meaning of 'intellectual property') after 'copyright' insert 'or design right'.

*Capital Gains Tax Act 1979 (c. 14)*

**26.**   In section 18(4) of the Capital Gains Tax Act 1979 (situation of certain assets for purposes of Act), for paragraph (h) (intellectual property) substitute—

'(ha)   patents, trade marks, service marks, and registered designs are situated where they are registered, and if registered in more than one register, where each register is situated, and rights or licences to use a patent, trade mark, service mark or registered design are situated in the United Kingdom if they or any right derived from them are exercisable in the United Kingdom,

(hb)   copyright, design right and franchises, and rights or licences to use any copyright work or design in which design right subsists, are situated in the United Kingdom if they or any right derived from them are exercisable in the United Kingdom,'.

*British Telecommunications Act 1981 (c. 38)*

**27.**   In Schedule 5 to the British Telecommunications Act 1981 (special transitional provisions relating to use of patents and registered designs), in the closing words of paragraphs 9(1) and 19(1) (which relate to the use of models and documents), after 'copyright' insert 'or design right'.

*Supreme Court Act 1981 (c. 54)*

**28.**—(1)   The Supreme Court Act 1981 is amended as follows.

(2)   In section 72 (withdrawal of privilege against self-incrimination in certain proceedings relating to intellectual property), in subsection (5) (meaning of 'intellectual property') after 'copyright' insert, 'design right'.

(3)   In Schedule 1 (distribution of business in the High Court), in paragraph 1(i) (business assigned to the Chancery Division: causes and matters relating to certain intellectual property) for 'or copyright' substitute, 'copyright or design right'.

*Broadcasting Act 1981 (c. 68)*

**29.**—(1)   The Broadcasting Act 1981 is amended as follows.

(2)   In section 4 (general duties of IBA as regards programmes) for subsection (7) substitute—

'(7)   For the purpose of maintaining supervision and control over the programmes (including advertisements) broadcast by them the Authority may make and use recordings of those programmes or any part of them.'.

(3)   In section 20(9), omit paragraph (a).

*Cable and Broadcasting Act 1984 (c. 46)*

**30.**—(1)   The Cable and Broadcasting Act 1984 is amended as follows.

(2)   In section 8, omit subsection (8).

(3)   In section 49 (power of Secretary of State to give directions in the public interest), for subsection (7) substitute—

'(7)   For the purposes of this section the place from which a broadcast is made is, in the case of a satellite transmission, the place from which the signals carrying the broadcast are transmitted to the satellite.'.

(4)   In section 56(2) (interpretation) omit the definition of 'the 1956 Act'.

*Companies Act 1985 (c. 6)*

**31.**—(1)   Part XII of the Companies Act 1985 (registration of charges) is amended as follows.

(2)   In section 396 (registration of charges in England and Wales: charges which must be registered), in subsection (1)(j) for the words from 'on a patent' to the end substitute 'or on any intellectual property', and after subsection (3) insert—

'(3A)   The following are "intellectual property" for the purposes of this section—

(a)   any patent, trade mark, service mark, registered design, copyright or design right;

(b)   any licence under or in respect of any such right.'.

(3)   In section 410 (registration of charges in Scotland: charges which must be registered), in subsection (3)(c) (incorporeal moveable property) after subparagraph (vi) insert—

'(vii)   a registered design or a licence in respect of such a design,

(viii)   a design right or a licence under a design right,'.

*Law Reform (Miscellaneous Provisions) (Scotland) Act 1985 (c. 73)*

**32.**   In section 15 of the Law Reform (Miscellaneous Provisions) (Scotland) Act

1985 (withdrawal of privilege against self-incrimination in certain proceedings relating to intellectual property), in subsection (5) (meaning of 'intellectual property') after 'copyright' insert 'or design right'.

### Atomic Energy Authority Act 1986 (c. 3)

**33.** In section 8(2) of the Atomic Energy Authority Act 1986 (powers of Authority as to exploitation of research: meaning of 'intellectual property'), after 'copyrights' insert, 'design rights'.

### Education and Libraries (Northern Ireland) Order 1986 (SI 1986/594 (NI3))

**34.** In Article 77 of the Education and Libraries (Northern Ireland) Order 1986 (charges for library services), after paragraph (2) add—

'(3)  The provisions of Part I of the Copyright, Designs and Patents Act 1988 (copyright) relating to the rental of copies of sound recordings, films and computer programs apply to any lending by a board of copies of such works, whether or not a charge is made for that facility.'.

### Companies (Northern Ireland) Order 1986 (SI 1986/1032 (NI 6))

**35.** In Article 403 of the Companies (Northern Ireland) Order 1986 (registration of charges: charges which must be registered), in paragraph (1)(j) for the words from 'on a patent' to the end substitute 'or on any intellectual property', and after paragraph (3) insert—

'(3A)  The following are "intellectual property" for the purposes of this article—

(a)  any patent, trade mark, service mark, registered design, copyright or design right;
(b)  any licence under or in respect of any such right.'.

### Income and Corporation Taxes Act 1988 (c. 1)

**36.**—(1)  The Income and Corporation Taxes Act 1988 is amended as follows.

(2)  In section 83 (fees and expenses deductible in computing profits and gains of trade) for 'the extension of the period of copyright in a design' substitute 'an extension of the period for which the right in a registered design subsists'.

(3)  In section 103 (charge on receipts after discontinuance of trade, profession or vocation), in subsection (3) (sums to which the section does not apply), after paragraph (b) insert—

'(bb)  a lump sum paid to the personal representatives of the designer of a design in which design right subsists as consideration for the assignment by them, wholly or partially, of that right,'.

(4)  In section 387 (carry forward as losses of certain payments made under deduction of tax), in subsection (3) (payments to which the section does not apply), in paragraph (e) (copyright royalties) after 'applies' insert 'or royalties in respect of a right in a design to which section 537B applies'.

(5)  In section 536 (taxation of copyright royalties where owner abroad), for the definition of 'copyright' in subsection (2) substitute—

'copyright does not include copyright in—

(i)   a cinematograph film or video recording, or
(ii)   the sound-track of such a film or recording, so far as it is not separately exploited; and'.

(6)   In Chapter I of Part XIII (miscellaneous special provisions: intellectual property), after section 537 insert—

'*Designs*

*Relief for payments in respect of designs*
**537A.**—Where the designer of a design in which design right subsists assigns that right, or the author of a registered design assigns the right in the design, wholly or partially, or grants an interest in it by licence, and

(a)   the consideration for the assignment or grant consists, in whole or in part, of a payment to which this section applies, the whole amount of which would otherwise be included in computing the amount of his profits or gains for a single year of assessment, and
(b)   he was engaged in the creation of the design for a period of more than 12 months,

he may, on making a claim, require that effect shall be given to the following provision in connection with that payment.

(2)   If the period for which he was engaged in the creation of the design does not exceed 24 months, then, for all income tax purposes, one-half only of the amount of the payment shall be treated as having become receivable on the date on which it actually became receivable and the remaining half shall be treated as having become receivable 12 months before that date.

(3)   If the period for which he was engaged in the creation of the design exceeds 24 months, then, for all income tax purposes, one-third only of the amount of the payment shall be treated as having become receivable on the date on which it actually became receivable, and one-third shall be treated as having become receivable 12 months, and one-third 24 months, before that date.

(4)   This section applies to—

(a)   a lump sum payment, including an advance on account of royalties which is not returnable, and
(b)   any other payment of or on account of royalties or sums payable periodically which does not only become receivable more than two years after articles made to the design or, as the case may be, articles to which the design is applied are first made available for sale or hire.

(5)   A claim under this section with respect to any payment to which it applies by virtue only of subsection (4)(b) above shall have effect as a claim with respect to all such payments in respect of rights in the design in question which are receivable by the claimant, whether before or after the claim; and such a claim may be made at any time not later than 5th April next following the expiration of eight years after articles made to the design or, as the case

may be, articles to which the design is applied were first made available for sale or hire.

(6)    In this section—

(a)    "designer" includes a joint designer, and

(b)    any reference to articles being made available for sale or hire is to their being so made available anywhere in the world by or with the licence of the design right owner or as the case may be, the proprietor of the registered design.

*Taxation of design royalties where owner abroad*

**537B.**—(1)    Where the usual place of abode of the owner of a right in a design is not within the United Kingdom, section 349(1) shall apply to any payment of or on account of any royalties or sums paid periodically for or in respect of that right as it applies to annual payments not payable out of profits or gains brought into charge to income tax.

(2)    In subsection (1) above—

(a)    "right in a design" means design right or the right in a registered design,

(b)    the reference to the owner of a right includes a person who, notwithstanding that he has assigned the right to some other person, is entitled to receive periodical payments in respect of the right, and

(c)    the reference to royalties or other sums paid periodically for or in respect of a right does not include royalties or sums paid in respect of articles which are shown on a claim to have been exported from the United Kingdom for distribution outside the United Kingdom.

(3)    Where a payment to which subsection (1) above applies is made through an agent resident in the United Kingdom and that agent is entitled as against the owner of the right to deduct any sum by way of commission in respect of services rendered, the amount of the payment shall for the purposes of section 349(1) be taken to be diminished by the sum which the agent is entitled to deduct.

(4)    Where the person by or through whom the payment is made does not know that any such commission is payable or does not know the amount of any such commission, any income tax deducted by or assessed and charged on him shall be computed in the first instance on, and the account to be delivered of the payment shall be an account of, the total amount of the payment without regard being had to any diminution thereof, and in that case, on proof of the facts on a claim, there shall be made to the agent on behalf of the owner of the right such repayment of income tax as is proper in respect of the sum deducted by way of commission.

(5)    The time of the making of a payment to which subsection (1) above applies shall, for all tax purposes, be taken to be the time when it is made by the person by whom it is first made and not the time when it is made by or through any other person.

(6)    Any agreement for the making of any payment to which subsection (1) above applies in full and without deduction of income tax shall be void.'.

(7)   In section 821 (payments made under deduction of tax before passing of Act imposing income tax for that year), in subsection (3) (payments subject to adjustment) after paragraph (a) insert—

> '(aa)   any payment for or in respect of a right in a design to which section 537B applies; and'

(8)   In Schedule 19 (apportionment of income of close companies), in paragraph 10(4) (cessation or liquidation: debts taken into account although creditor is participator or associate), in paragraph (c) (payments for use of certain property) for the words from 'tangible property' to 'extend)' substitute—

> '—
>
> (i)   tangible property,
>
> (ii)   copyright in a literary, dramatic, musical or artistic work within the meaning of Part I of the Copyright, Designs and Patents Act 1988 (or any similar right under the law of a country to which that Part does not extend), or
>
> (iii)   design right,'.

(9)   In Schedule 25 (taxation of United Kingdom-controlled foreign companies: exempt activities), in paragraph 9(1)(a) (investment business: holding of property) for 'patents or copyrights' substitute 'or intellectual property' and after that subparagraph insert—

> '(1A)   In subparagraph (1)(a) above "intellectual property" means patents, registered designs, copyright and design right (or any similar rights under the law of a country outside the United Kingdom).'.

## Schedule 8 Repeals

| Chapter | Short title | Extent of repeal |
|---|---|---|
| 1939 c. 107. | Patents, Designs, Copyright and Trade Marks (Emergency) Act 1939. | In section 10(1), the definition of 'copyright'. |
| 1945 c. 16. | Limitation (Enemies and War Prisoners) Act 1945. | In sections 2(1) and 4(a), the reference to section 10 of the Copyright Act 1911. |
| 1949 c. 88. | Registered Designs Act 1949. | In section 3(2), the words 'or original'. Section 5(5). In section 11(2), the words 'or original'. In section 14(3), the words 'or the Isle of Man'. Section 32. Section 33(2). Section 37(1). |

| Chapter | Short title | Extent of repeal |
|---------|-------------|------------------|
| | | Section 38. |
| | | In section 44(1), the definitions of 'copyright' and 'Journal'. |
| | | In section 45, paragraphs (1) and (2). |
| | | In section 46, paragraphs (1) and (2). |
| | | Section 48(1). |
| | | In Schedule 1, in paragraph 3(1), the words 'in such manner as may be prescribed by rules of court'. |
| | | Schedule 2. |
| 1956 c. 74. | Copyright Act 1956. | The whole Act. |
| 1957 c. 6. | Ghana Independence Act 1957. | In Schedule 2, paragraph 12. |
| 1957 c. 60. | Federation of Malaya Independence Act 1957. | In Schedule 1, paragraphs 14 and 15. |
| 1958 c. 44. | Dramatic and Musical Performers' Protection Act 1958. | The whole Act. |
| 1958 c. 51. | Public Records Act 1958. | Section 11. Schedule 3. |
| 1960 c. 52. | Cyprus Independence Act 1960. | In the Schedule, paragraph 13. |
| 1960 c. 55. | Nigeria Independence Act 1960. | In Schedule 2, paragraphs 12 and 13. |
| 1961 c. 1. | Tanganyika Independence Act 1961. | In Schedule 2, paragraphs 13 and 14. |
| 1961 c. 16. | Sierra Leone Independence Act 1961. | In Schedule 3, paragraphs 13 and 14. |
| 1961 c. 25. | Patents and Designs (Renewals, Extensions and Fees) Act 1961. | The whole Act. |
| 1962 c. 40. | Jamaica Independence Act 1962. | In Schedule 2, paragraph 13. |
| 1962 c. 54. | Trinidad and Tobago Independence Act 1962. | In Schedule 2, paragraph 13. |
| 1963 c. 53. | Performers' Protection Act 1963. | The whole Act. |
| 1964 c. 46. | Malawi Independence Act 1964. | In Schedule 2, paragraph 13. |
| 1964 c. 65. | Zambia Independence Act 1964. | In Schedule 1, paragraph 9. |

| Chapter | Short title | Extent of repeal |
|---------|-------------|------------------|
| 1964 c. 86. | Malta Independence Act 1964. | In Schedule 1, paragraph 11. |
| 1964 c. 93. | Gambia Independence Act 1964. | In Schedule 2, paragraph 12. |
| 1966 c. 24. | Lesotho Independence Act 1966. | In the Schedule, paragraph 9. |
| 1966 c. 37. | Barbados Independence Act 1966. | In Schedule 2, paragraph 12. |
| 1967 c. 80. | Criminal Justice Act 1967. | In Parts I and IV of Schedule 3, the entries relating to the Registered Designs Act 1949. |
| 1968 c. 56. | Swaziland Independence Act 1968. | In the Schedule, paragraph 9. |
| 1968 c. 67. | Medicines Act 1968. | In section 92(2)(a), the words from 'or embodied' to 'film'. Section 98. |
| 1968 c. 68. | Design Copyright Act 1968. | The whole Act. |
| 1971 c. 4. | Copyright (Amendment) Act 1971. | The whole Act. |
| 1971 c. 23. | Courts Act 1971. | In Schedule 9, the entry relating to the Copyright Act 1956. |
| 1971 c. 62. | Tribunals and Inquiries Act 1971. | In Schedule 1, paragraph 24. |
| 1972 c. 32. | Performers' Protection Act 1972. | The whole Act. |
| 1975 c. 24. | House of Commons Disqualification Act 1975. | In Part II of Schedule 1, the entry relating to the Performing Right Tribunal. |
| 1975 c. 25. | Northern Ireland Assembly Disqualification Act 1975. | In Part II of Schedule 1, the entry relating to the Performing Right Tribunal. |
| 1977 c. 37. | Patents Act 1977. | Section 14(4) and (8). In section 28(3), paragraph (b) and the word 'and' preceding it. Section 28(5) to (9). Section 49(3). Section 72(3). Sections 84 and 85. Section 88. Section 104. |

| Chapter | Short title | Extent of repeal |
|---|---|---|
| | | In section 105, the words 'within the meaning of section 104 above'. Sections 114 and 115. Section 123(2)(k). In section 130(1), the definition of 'patent agent'. In section 130(7), the words '88(6) and (7),'. In Schedule 5, paragraphs 1 and 2, in paragraph 3 the words 'and 44(1)' and 'in each case', and paragraphs 7 and 8. |
| 1979 c. 2. | Customs and Excise Management Act 1979. | In Schedule 4, the entry relating to the Copyright Act 1956. |
| 1980 c. 21. | Competition Act 1980. | Section 14. |
| 1981 c. 68. | Broadcasting Act 1981. | Section 20(9)(a). |
| 1982 c. 35. | Copyright Act 1956 (Amendment) Act 1982. | The whole Act. |
| 1983 c. 42. | Copyright (Amendment) Act 1983. | The whole Act. |
| 1984 c. 46. | Cable and Broadcasting Act 1984. | Section 8(8). Section 16(4) and (5). Sections 22 to 24. Section 35(2) and (3). Sections 53 and 54. In section 56(2), the definition of 'the 1956 Act'. In Schedule 5, paragraphs 6, 7, 13 and 23. |
| 1985 c. 21. | Films Act 1985. | Section 7(2). |
| 1985 c. 41. | Copyright (Computer Software) Amendment Act 1985. | The whole Act. |
| 1985 c. 61. | Administration of Justice Act 1985. | Section 60. |
| 1986 c. 39. | Patents, Designs and Marks Act 1986. | In Schedule 2, paragraph 1(2)(a), in paragraph 1(2)(k) the words 'subsection (1)(j) of section 396 and' and in paragraph 1(2)(l) the |

| Chapter | Short title | Extent of repeal |
|---------|-------------|------------------|
| 1988 c. 1. | Income and Corporation Taxes Act 1988. | words 'subsection (2)(i) of section 93'. In Schedule 29, paragraph 5. |

# Index